Date D-

C

Kurzman, Dan.   23382
    Day of the bomb : countdown to Hiroshima / Dan
Kurzman. -- New York ; Toronto : McGraw-Hill,
c1986.
    xiv, 546 p. : ill.

Bibliography: p. 505–532.
02502410   LC: 85013214   ISBN: 0070356831

1. World War, 1939–1945 – Personal narratives.
2. Nuclear warfare – Moral and religious aspects.
3. Hiroshima–shi (Japan) – History – Bombardment,
1945. I. Title.

DAY
OF
THE
BOMB

BOOKS BY DAN KURZMAN

Kishi and Japan: The Search for the Sun
Subversion of the Innocents
Santo Domingo: Revolt of the Damned
Genesis 1948: The First Arab-Israeli War
The Race for Rome
The Bravest Battle: The 28 Days of the Warsaw Ghetto Uprising
Miracle of November: Madrid's Epic Stand, 1936
Ben-Gurion: Prophet of Fire

DAY OF THE BOMB

Countdown to Hiroshima

DAN KURZMAN

McGraw-Hill Book Company

New York St. Louis San Francisco Toronto Hamburg Mexico iv

1 2 3 4 5 6 7 8 9 DOC DOC 8 7 6 5

ISBN 0-07-035683-1

LIBRARY OF CONGRESS CATALOGING IN PUBLICATION DATA

Kurzman, Dan.
  Day of the bomb.
  1. Hiroshima-shi (Japan)—History—Bombardment,
1945. 2. World War, 1939–1945—Biography. 3. Atomic
warfare—Moral and religious aspects. I. Title.
D767.25.H6K865 1985   940.54'25   85-13214
ISBN 0-07-035683-1

BOOK DESIGN BY PATRICE FODERO

For my dear wife, Florence,
whom I shall love eternally—
whether the world survives or not

ACKNOWLEDGMENTS

I am deeply grateful to my wife, Florence, for her vital contribution to this book. She collaborated closely with me, rewriting, researching, editing, offering imaginative suggestions at moments when the mind went as blank as the paper in the typewriter.

I also wish to thank Gladys Justin Carr, editor-in-chief, and Leslie Meredith, editor, of McGraw-Hill for their fine editing and supreme patience; Kaori Sato, Motoharu Saito, and Kei Kurasu for skillfully translating Japanese works into English; Kaori, as well as Yuko Yamaoka and Shijo Kiyamachi, for interpreting at interviews with great sensitivity; Kinji Kawamura, director of the Japan Press Center in Tokyo, and his assistant, Seiichi Soeda, for so graciously helping me to obtain the information I wanted in Japan; my agent, Ned Leavitt of William Morris Agency, for his aid and encouragement; my brother Cal, dean of Learning Resources at the College of Marin, and my brother-in-law Fred L. Knopf for facilitating my research; and Penny Ward for typing the manuscript swiftly and expertly.

Others whom I would like to thank for their help include:

Dean Allard—Navy Historical Center, Washington, D.C.; Dennis Bilger—archivist, Harry S. Truman Library, Indepen-

dence, Missouri; Katherine Bowman—library technician, Navy
Department Library, Washington, D.C.; Robin Burgess—research assistant, Harry S. Truman Library; Richard S. Christian—
army nuclear test program official; Albert B. Christman—naval
historian; Lynda Corey Claassen—head, Special Collections Library, University of California, San Diego; Bernard R. Crystal—
librarian, Rare Book and Manuscript Library, Columbia University, New York; William Dudley—Naval Historical Center; Janet
Fries—photographer; Shoichi Fujii—assistant chief, International
Relations Section, Office of the Mayor, Hiroshima; Jerome Grossman—president, Council for a Livable World, Boston; Lillian Gu-
tierrez—archivist, library, University of California, San Diego;
Kimball Higgs—archivist, library, University of California, San
Diego; James Huffman—history professor, Tokyo University; Neil
Johnson—archivist, Harry S. Truman Library; Virginia John-
son—travel agent in Tokyo; Vincent C. Jones—chief military his-
torian, Department of the Army; Tadahiro Kida—chief, General
Affairs Section, Atomic Bomb Hospital, Hiroshima; Robert L.
Kirschenbaum—president, Pacific Press Service, Tokyo; Robert
B. Klaverkamp—publisher, *Asiaweek*, Tokyo; Erwin Mueller—
archivist, Harry S. Truman Library; Charles Warren Ohrvall—
archivist, Harry S. Truman Library; Tim Pickwell—archivist,
library, University of California, San Diego; Richard L.
Ray—historian, National Atomic Museum, Albuquerque, New
Mexico; Edward Reese—archivist, Modern Military Branch, Na-
tional Archives; Liz Safly—research assistant, Harry S. Truman
Library; Charles and Helen Sutton—directors, World Friendship
Center, Hiroshima; John Taylor—archivist, Modern Military
Branch, National Archives; Tim Troy—librarian, New York
Public Library; Benedict K. Zobrist—director, Harry S. Truman
Library.

The following were among those kind enough to grant me
interviews:

Luis Alvarez—nuclear scientist; Koremasa Anami—son of
General Anami; R. Gordon Arneson—aide to Secretary Stimson
and secretary of the Interim Committee; Admiral William Benson—friend of Admiral Leahy; Hans Bethe—nuclear scientist;
Walter Brown—aide to Secretary Byrnes; McGeorge Bundy—intimate of Secretary Stimson; Martha Burroughs—widow of Captain
William S. Parsons; Rear Admiral Sherman E. Burroughs—friend

of Captain Parsons; Thomas C. Cartwright—American POW in Hiroshima; Clark Clifford—aide to President Truman; William Doering—science professor and associate of Leo Szilard; Bernard Feld—nuclear scientist; Allan Forbes—associate of Szilard; Sue Gentry—hometown friend of President Truman; General Richard H. Groves—son of General Leslie R. Groves; Tomin Harada— plastic surgeon who operated on Seiko Ogawa and many other disfigured Hiroshima victims; Saburo Hayashi—aide to General Anami; Morris R. Jeppson—Captain Parsons' assistant on *Enola Gay*; Hideaki Kase—son of Toshikazu Kase, Foreign Minister Togo's assistant; Koichi Kido—Lord Keeper of the Privy Seal (interviewed in 1958); Takahito Kido—Son of Marquis Koichi Kido; Nobusuke Kishi—Japan's economic czar during war, Prime Minister after war; Arnold Kramish—scientist and expert on Russian atomic bomb; Shinichiro Kurose—survivor of Hiroshima atomic bombing; Ralph E. Lapp—nuclear scientist; William H. Leahy—son of Admiral Leahy; Miyoko Matsubara—survivor of Hiroshima atom bombing, schoolmate of Seiko Ogawa; Matthew Meselson—science professor and associate of Szilard; Motojiro Mori—Japanese journalist and politician; Philip Morrison—nuclear scientist; General Kenneth Nichols—assistant to General Groves; Haruhiko Nishi—associate of Foreign Minister Togo; Yuichiro Nishina—son of Yoshio, the Japanese nuclear scientist; Seiko Ogawa (Ikeda)—survivor of Hiroshima atom bombing; Isidor I. Rabi—nuclear scientist; Francis Racker—sister-in-law of Szilard; Dorothy Rindquist—Admiral Leahy's secretary; Donald Russell—aide to Secretary Byrnes; Charlotte Cramer Sachs—wife of Alexander Sachs; Jiro Sakata—Japanese journalist in Moscow during war; Kojiro Sato—son of Ambassador Sato; Robert Serber—nuclear scientist; Tazu Shibama—survivor of Hiroshima atomic bombing; Takeso Shimoda—diplomat in Moscow during war; Alice Kimball Smith—Cyril's wife and noted author; Cyril Smith—metallurgy expert at Los Alamos; John W. Snyder—Truman's Secretary of the Treasury; Uchigi Sugita—staff officer under General Anami; Hajime Suzuki—son of Prime Minister Suzuki; Eizo Tajima—assistant to nuclear scientist Nishina; Akihiro Takahashi—atomic bombing survivor and head of Hiroshima Peace Culture Foundation; Edward Teller—nuclear physicist; Paul Tibbets—pilot of *Enola Gay*; Ise Togo—daughter of Foreign Minister Togo; Shigehiko Togo—grandson of Foreign Minister

x   Acknowledgments

Togo; John Walker—husband of Louise Leahy Walker; Louise
Leahy Walker—granddaughter of Admiral Leahy; Egon A.
Weiss—brother-in-law of Szilard; Steven Weiss—nephew of Szilard; Victor Weisskopf—nuclear scientist; Eugene P. Wigner—nuclear scientist.

CONTENTS

Contents

PREFACE

D*ay of the Bomb* recounts the events that led to the decision to drop an atomic bomb on Hiroshima—perhaps the most significant decision in recorded history. The story is told through the key characters in that momentous drama, which lies at the root of the nuclear trauma gripping the world today. It probes the minds, motives, and actions of the men involved in the first nuclear holocaust, from the scientist who created the bomb to the engineer who assembled it to the President who used it to the militarist who defied it to the Emperor who bowed to it to the spy who worked on it to the victim who survived it.

Like actors in a Greek tragedy, the characters were caught up in a relentless machine of inevitability that probably no one could have switched off. They were motivated by idealism, chauvinism, egoism, humanitarianism, pragmatism, politics, ideology, ambition, and fear. Each individual had to solve his own personal moral dilemma. Was it right to loose a force that might ultimately devour the world? Would even more people die if the bomb was not dropped? Should one listen to his conscience or to his leaders? They struggled with each other, they struggled with themselves, prisoners of their temperaments, backgrounds, and dreams.

This book is based on hundreds of interviews, thousands of documents, and many unpublished diaries and memoirs, as well as published material, obtained in the United States and Japan over a period of more than three years. Much of the information appears here for the first time, including material from the personal unpublished notes of General Leslie R. Groves and recently opened files of the FBI, the Truman Library, the James F. Byrnes Collection at Clemson University, and the Leo Szilard Collection at the University of California at San Diego. All of the material in this book has been exhaustively checked for accuracy.

Though this work deals with the past, it relates with burning relevance to the present and the future as we ponder with growing alarm how we can survive the nuclear age, how in some new crisis, perhaps the last, it may also be impossible to switch off the machine.

Dan Kurzman
Hiroshima, Japan

DAY OF THE BOMB

PROLOGUE

I

August 6, 1945, day of the bomb: At 3 A.M., Navy Captain William S. Parsons squatted in the cramped bomb bay of the specially built B-29, the *Enola Gay*, and began to tinker with the 10-foot-long atomic bomb hanging from a hook in the ceiling like a helpless whale. As the plane sailed through the clear night under the gaze of a million blinking eyes, he was almost deafened by the roar of the engine mingling with the whine of air that seeped through the crack between the two bomb bay doors. Yet the eerie sense of being trapped in the eye of a tornado was perhaps welcome, for it may have helped to drive from his mind the full meaning of this mission.

While an assistant, First Lieutenant Morris R. Jeppson, squatted beside him and silently passed him tools in the glow of a flashlight, Parsons, the *Enola Gay*'s weaponeer, carefully inserted the explosive detonating charge through the tail of the bomb. His hands were black with graphite lubricant and he cut his fingers on the sharply tooled steel edges.

"Put on your gloves," Jeppson shouted over the thunder.

But Parsons merely shook his head. How could he work if he lost his sense of touch? He had to feel the cold metal, the intricate innards. He handled the gleaming black monster with tenderness, almost as if it were a baby. And in a sense, "Little Boy," as it was nicknamed, was his little boy.

As chief of the Ordnance Division in the atomic bomb project, code-named the "Manhattan Project," Parsons had supervised the design and assembly of the bomb, and was intimately familiar with every bolt, fuse, and wire. He had nursed the bomb, coaxed it, lavished his attention upon it. And now that his magnificent creation was about to be tested, the father, appropriately, was by its side, priming it for its plunge into posterity.

Although Colonel Paul Tibbets was the pilot of the aircraft, Parsons, who was respected as perhaps the finest gunnery engineer in the navy, was in fact the tactical commander and would decide on all matters involving the use or the emergency disposal of the bomb. Brigadier General Leslie R. Groves, head of the Manhattan Project, had complete faith in him, but Parsons knew Groves would explode almost as furiously as the bomb if he were aware that it was being armed in midair.

Two months earlier, Parsons himself, as well as Groves, had vetoed the idea of arming the missile in flight, afraid that something could go wrong. However, Parsons had seen dozens of B-29s crash while taking off from his base on the South Pacific island of Tinian in the Marianas, about 100 miles from Guam, and he now feared that his plane might crash, too—and blow up half the island. Besides, one of the scientists working on the bomb had invented a new "double-plug" safety system that would keep apart the two pieces of uranium 235 within the weapon and thus prevent a premature explosion while the captain worked in flight.

The day before takeoff, Parsons had argued his case with Brigadier General Thomas F. Farrell, who was directing operations on the island, and told him of his fear.

He understood, Farrell said, "But what can we do about it?"

Arm the bomb in midair.

Characteristically, Parsons thought of saving lives. It was better to risk losing the crew than risk losing all the people on the island. But to Farrell this was not military logic, and he knew it wouldn't be to Groves, either. Their main concern was the success of the mission, and there was *less* chance of something going wrong if the bomb was armed on the ground.

"Oh, fine," the general replied. "We lose the crew, the plane, the bomb, and you, but *we* don't blow up. Besides, you've never done such a job. Do you know how?"

"No," Parsons said, "but I've got all day and night to learn."

Farrell gave in, ready to brave Groves' rage. How could he say "no" to someone who so earnestly pleaded not to risk more human life than was necessary?

Now, aboard the plane, Parsons' bleeding fingers worked swiftly, efficiently, having practiced every step in the arming procedure for hours and hours before takeoff. The captain prayed that Groves' anxiety would prove groundless. Still, at this strange moment of communion between man and machine, in the intimacy of a tiny "storm-racked" compartment deep in the heavens, he could not imagine that his baby would throw a tantrum before it was time.

And it didn't. Parsons finished inserting the detonating charge after fifteen minutes and, with Jeppson, climbed out of the bomb bay. Later, Jeppson returned and precariously threaded his way along a catwalk toward the nose of the bomb, removed three green plugs from the side of the missile, and replaced them with the red ones. The electrical circuit was now complete. And so was Parsons' job—one of the most remarkable in engineering history.

Parsons, or "Deak," as he was called, was a handsome man with intelligent eyes and a melancholy smile, though a hairline that had receded to the center of his scalp made him look older than his 44 years. Modest and reticent, he was deemed by many the ideal naval officer, straight-backed, fair-minded, cool-tempered. And though his shyness betrayed a certain insecurity, he was a supreme optimist, even a fatalist in some ways. He had a family and a dangerous job, but he never drew up a will or took out life insurance. Nothing would ever happen to him, he apparently thought—though he carried a pistol with him on this extraordinary flight so he could shoot himself if he was about to be captured. Nor did he have time to think about his personal fate. He was legendary for his infinite dedication to whatever task he undertook, whether building bombs or battering tennis balls. He would analyze, test, reanalyze, retest, until he achieved the desired results.

Parsons had pioneered in the development of radar and the proximity fuse before working on the atomic bomb, then watched from a warship with satisfaction as the fuse for the first time helped gunners shoot down a Japanese plane over the Pacific. Yet Parsons did not seek fame—and would gain little despite his key role in building and arming the bomb. True, he wanted to be an admiral like his father-in-law, Admiral Cluverius, but he was convinced that his job on the bomb would *deprive* him of that rank, since he would not be able to accumulate the required time at sea. So eager was he for sea duty that when his wife gave birth to their last child, the captain of the ship he was about to sail on had to *order* the reluctant father to disembark so he could stay with his family.

Now, even General Groves' decision to put him aboard the plane carrying the first atomic bomb could not, under naval regulations, help his career. But though crushed when he learned that he would not command the cruiser he coveted, Parsons stoically flung himself into his new assignment. He accepted orders without a murmur and, as a colleague put it, would have cleaned latrines or put the bomb together with equal gusto.

Not everyone thought, however, that Parsons was suited to work on the bomb. According to a friend, he loathed the idea of creating an object of mass destruction, of loosing a Frankenstein monster that might one day surge out of control. Deak, says this colleague, was too compassionate a man for the job. It wasn't surprising that after the war Parsons wrote another colleague, referring to the decision to drop the bomb on a city without first warning the enemy:

"The conditions in Japan at the end of July 1945 were ideal for such warning."

But sensitive as he was, Parsons seldom revealed his feelings to anyone, bottling them up within himself. About the only time his wife every saw him weep was when his 4-year-old polio-stricken daughter Hannah died in his arms on the way to the hospital.

Had Hannah lived, she would now, on the day of the bomb, be 13—the same age as Seiko Ogawa.

II

On this historic day, Seiko was awakened by the screech of an air-raid siren at about the time Captain Parsons was arming the atomic bomb. Normally, she and her family, who lived in a suburb of Hiroshima, would rush to an underground shelter; on this morning, however, everyone was too sleepy and by now hopelessly fatalistic. Though a chill of fear surged through her, Seiko was consoled by the thought that except for a few stray bombs, Hiroshima had not been attacked throughout the war.

But even after this warning proved to be just another false alarm—an observer plane had apparently flown over the city—she could not go back to sleep. As on many nights, it was not only the fear of death, but the longing for peace, that kept her up.

Peace would end all the killing and she could go back to school to resume her studies and her drama training. Seiko was one of the prettiest girls in the Hiroshima Girls' Commerce Junior High School, where she was a first-year student. Her short black hair framed a heart-shaped face with a small mouth that curved easily into a smile, and large eyes that sensitively registered her mood. Seiko was also the school's finest actress. Just before the war, she had been selected to play the leading role in a citywide drama festival, where her performance was greeted with thunderous applause. She decided then that she would devote her life to the theater, and even her strict father agreed to let her do so.

But then the storm broke, smashing dreams as well as men. It was hard, however, to kill a dream. Seiko's dream had survived almost every hardship war could impose. In a sense, its durability was as troubling as it was tranquilizing, for her father, whom she loved dearly, was an unbending traditionalist who had taught her that Emperor and country took precedence over every personal need or aspiration. Yet, all she thought of was peace, though peace at this time would mean Japan's defeat. She found solace from this dilemma only in hard work, for then she would be too tired to dream.

Though Seiko's father was a well-to-do food merchant, there was little food available to feed the family and money had small value. At the same time, her school closed down some months earlier when it seemed the city might be bombed. Hiroshima, was, after all, a military center, in fact the nerve center of the defense system for the western half of Japan. Medieval Hiroshima Castle, with its classical Japanese upturned eaves, housed army divisional headquarters for southern Japan. Thousands of troops passed through Hiroshima to be trained and equipped to hurl the enemy back into the sea if it should try to invade the southern Japanese island of Kyushu. In addition, about 40,000 more troops manning some thirty-five major military installations were based in the city. Thousands of people also worked in shipyards and vital war industries and additional thousands manufactured parts for guns, bombs, boats, and planes in their homes. Even hospital patients were put to work—building booby traps. To the people of Hiroshima the mystery was why their city had escaped major bombing until now. It was even rumored that President Truman didn't want to damage Hiroshima because he had a relative living there.

Seiko and her classmates were ordered to dig shelters on nearby Hijiyama hill, and after digging for hours they lugged heavy sacks of discarded dirt to the school grounds in the Tsurumi district, sprawled in the center of the city, where they cultivated sweet potatoes, beans, cucumbers, and onions to guard against the threat of starvation.

On the day of the bomb, the young girls were to be given an even more difficult task. Together with hundreds of other students, they would gather in an area near Seiko's school where scores of wood and paper houses had been dismantled to create a fire lane that, hopefully, would limit conflagration in case of an air raid. The authorities in Hiroshima were well aware of the burning hell Tokyo had become during incendiary attacks and were forcing at least some of Hiroshima's 400,000 inhabitants to move in with friends and relatives in the suburbs or in other towns. Seiko and her schoolmates would now salvage what they could.

People seeking fuel for their homes had already carried off the wood, but the children would collect the roof tiles scattered about and deposit them in dumping areas. They would even pick up the nails, which could be used to make wooden sandals, or *geta*, for persons without footwear. Seiko was almost looking forward to this new job, which would leave her little time for dreaming. . . .

Though Seiko finally managed to fall asleep, the siren again woke her at about 5 A.M. Another false alarm. And soon it was dawn, an orange summer dawn that promised a splendid day. Seiko wearily rose and was soon on the train to midtown Hiroshima where, at 7 A.M., she joined her teacher and classmates near the working area. Two minutes later the siren sounded once more, and everyone scrambled into houses and woods nearby. After a half hour, a signal whined all-clear, and the teacher led her pupils to Tsurumi Bridge, which spanned one of the seven tentacles of the Ota River that twisted through this delta city of six islands and connected the working zone with Hijiyama hill. Seiko and the others began picking up tiles and nails and in four-girl teams carried them in sacks to the dumping area near the river.

The curling waterway sparkled in the sunshine, reflecting the sharp curves of the hill, and Seiko rejoiced in this scene of beauty and peace, which seemed so grotesquely incongruous with the sirens that warned of disaster and the barren fields where people had once lived happily in homes alive with family chatter and children's laughter. Could anyone imagine that death might leap from a sky so blue, turning people into shadows and their dreams into dust?

III

In nearby Hiroshima Castle, on the day of the bomb, about ten captured American airmen sat motionless on a wooden floor. They had been locked up for days in a 24-by-15-foot room in this military stronghold, forbidden to move or talk, feeling as inert as their ill-fated planes at the bottom of the ocean. Most of them were crewmen of a B-24 bomber called the *Lonesome Lady*. With thirty-five other B-24s, it had zoomed out of Okinawa on an important mission a week earlier, on July 28.

The mission was to bomb and sink Japan's last battleship, the *Haruna*, which lay crippled in Kure Harbor, 12 miles southeast of Hiroshima. Second Lieutenant Thomas C. Cartwright, pilot of the *Lonesome Lady*, was thankful that he had a first-class crew; its members had begun training together in California in October 1944 and were like a closely knit family. And he was cheered as well by the symbolic meaning of his mission, which could be instrumental in ending the war. What would the Emperor say when he learned that his last battleship had sunk out of sight?

Even so, while his intellectual reserve gave an impression of calm, the tall, wiry Cartwright was nervous. The youngest member of the crew at 21—having left Clemson University at 18 to volunteer for duty—he had piloted the plane on other missions but never on one like this. No B-24 had ever flown such a long distance before, and extra fuel tanks had to be installed in the bomb bay. This meant that the 50-caliber machine guns the plane usually carried had to be removed to compensate for the extra weight and replaced with "broomsticks"—harmless wooden replicas that supposedly would fool the enemy. Cartwright didn't like games—or guns that wouldn't shoot.

Also, the target was especially difficult, for Kure Harbor resembled an amphitheater, surrounded by land on three sides. And along the banks, antiaircraft guns slanted into the sky like stiff lashes on a huge eye.

At about noon, as the *Lonesome Lady* and its sisters swooped over Kure Harbor, Cartwright wondered if the Emperor might not have a reprieve. For the sky was 80 percent overcast, and it was impossible to see the target clearly. Nevertheless, the bombs had to be dropped, and they were. A strike! The rising spiral of smoke and flame signaled the end of Japan's largest surviving warship.

But perhaps of the *Lonesome Lady* as well. For just as Cartwright and his comrades began to rejoice, the plane lurched crazily. Flak from the *Haruna* or the shore batteries had hit the *Lonesome Lady*'s vital section where the wings were joined to the fuselage. Cartwright, who knew the plane had been struck but not the extent of the damage, called the tail gunner over the intercom. No answer. He had parachuted out.

"Go check the damage!" he ordered his engineer.

A minute later, the engineer came rushing back. "We're on fire!" he cried.

"Quick! Get the fire extinguisher!"

"It won't do any good. We're gonna blow up!"

The hydraulic system ceased to function and Cartwright began losing control of the plane, which was gliding at 10,000 feet. He knew there was no choice.

"Bail out!" he cried, his eyes burning from the smoke.

Somebody kicked out the bomb bay doors, and the crew members jumped, one by one. But, before Cartwright himself could leap out, the plane turned over and started screaming down. Finally, a few hundred feet from the ground, it leveled off, and he managed to hurl himself out, landing hard in a pine forest. He gathered up his parachute and instinctively hid it under a bush. Trembling from the ordeal, he stumbled along a dirt path for hours seeking a village. There was no way for a Westerner to hide in this country without dying of thirst or starvation. He would turn himself in to the Japanese authorities as he had been instructed.

What would they do to him? Torture him? Kill him? He drove these thoughts from his mind and imagined he was back in his native York, South Carolina, on a hike with his postmaster father or on a stroll with his childhood sweetheart.

Suddenly a tremendous thirst seized him as he struggled along under a relentless summer sun. Was there no one he could surrender to? He finally came to a farm and staggered toward a raggedly dressed peasant working in the fields. When the peasant saw him, he gaped as if confronted by a monster from Mars. Cartwright reached for the pistol in his belt and tried to hand it over to him. But the man, expecting to be shot, screamed and begged for mercy—until Cartwright pointed to a path and made him understand that he simply wanted to go to the nearest village.

The peasant led him to one nearby and Cartwright entered the local police station, adding to the sensation created a little earlier when his co-pilot, Second Lieutenant Durden Looper, was brought in. The villagers had never dreamed that the enemy would take note of their little hamlet. Cartwright lay his pistol on a desk. It was the only weapon in the station—aside from pitchforks and clubs.

The two prisoners, forbidden to speak and blindfolded with hands tied behind their back, were then marched to a larger village several miles away. They were forced to squat in the town square while crowds shouted insults and threw sticks at them. But a military truck soon came and drove them to a place that buzzed with the sounds of a city. Later, Cartwright would realize what city it was.

Hiroshima.

IV

Parsons, who would drop the bomb, and Seiko and the American captives who, it seemed, would reap its fury, symbolized the irrationality of nuclear war. Yet rational men had made such war inevitable.

President Harry S Truman was terrified when he entered the White House and inherited the bomb, but Hiroshima would be a magic medicine for his ego if not, as he hoped, for the ills of the world.

Emperor Hirohito, who never considered himself a god, watched helplessly from his palace bunker as hundreds of thousands died in his sacred name believing the lie he was forced to perpetuate.

Klaus Fuchs, the German-born physicist, helped build the bomb so he could hand over its secrets to Russia and, in one of history's great ironies, foiled man's best efforts to erect an impenetrable security barrier.

Leo Szilard, the Hungarian scientist, persuaded American leaders to build the bomb because he feared Hitler would build one first, then realized to his horror that he had planted the seeds of cataclysm he had sought to destroy.

Admiral Kantaro Suzuki, Japan's aging Prime Minister and most honored war hero, vowed after surviving an assassin's bullets to save his country and himself from death—but his priority wasn't clear.

J. Robert Oppenheimer, in charge of building the bomb, felt that Hiroshima would bring him the recognition he craved—and the power he needed to prevent more Hiroshimas, his antidote for a troubled conscience.

Marquis Koichi Kido, the Emperor's chief adviser and childhood playmate, lived to serve, protect, and manipulate his master, appeasing the militarists in the process, but finally turning against them to save the soul of Japan.

Secretary of War Henry L. Stimson wanted Hiroshima to whet Stalin's appetite for atomic secrets, which the United States would dangle before him as a reward for Soviet democratization and decent international behavior.

General Korechika Anami, the war minister, was obligated to the Emperor to make peace and to his fellow militarists to continue the war—a conflict that could have only one painful solution.

General Leslie R. Groves, head of the Manhattan Project, was determined to drop the bomb before the fighting ended and a congressional investigation began—on why he "squandered" $2 billion on an unused bomb.

Foreign Minister Shigenori Togo, who had reluctantly supported the Pearl Harbor attack, tried to salve his conscience and save his country four years later with desperate peace moves that the militarists opposed and the Americans—as they waited for the bomb—ignored.

Secretary of State James F. Byrnes saw the bomb as a club that would intimidate Stalin into abandoning his dreams of aggression and guarantee American dominance in the world.

Yoshio Nishina, the leading Japanese physicist, was ordered to build an atomic bomb during the war, but he used this experience to plan an atomic paradise after the war.

Admiral William Leahy, the knightly presidential chief of staff, urged Truman not to use the "barbarous" weapon; but who would listen to an old sailor with sentimental prejudices against killing women and children in war?

Ambassador to Moscow Naotake Sato pleaded with his government to make peace and with Russia to pave the way, but was derided in Tokyo and double-crossed in Moscow.

All these men were caught in the merciless machine activating the bomb, some reluctantly, others willingly, most unwittingly. None could switch it off.

Chapter 1

THE
INITIATOR

I

Leo Szilard *tried* to switch off the machine—up to the day of the bomb. Normally, Szilard, a rotund 47-year-old physicist with a round, pixyish face, saw humor in life and was tolerant of people's foibles, refusing to let them dilute his unlimited faith in the human spirit. A pair of horn-rimmed spectacles magnified the quizzical glint in his eyes, which mocked anyone cut from a more cynical mold. But in the weeks before the bomb, his humor and tolerance had dissipated.

Szilard felt that the weapon, if dropped, would not only ravage Japanese cities but would set the stage for Armageddon. How long could the world survive once the United States had set a precedent by loosing this monstrous bomb? He collared colleague after colleague and in a clipped Hungarian accent brusquely demanded to know the answer; he called protest meetings in his laboratory at the University of Chicago; he denounced the generals and politicians for ignoring the passionate petitions he had urged his fellow scientists to sign.

These colleagues either blindly followed this "warm, gentle, totally objective" man, agreeing with him that politics was too important to leave to the politicians, or regarded him, for all his brilliance, as a gadfly with megalomaniacal tendencies. Even some who followed him did not deny that he used people. But since he did so only in the service of mankind, they asked, what did it matter? He led not by authority, but by example. Yes, he once said that "Homo sapiens resembles the apes in most respects, [though] Homo sapiens is completely devoid of imagination." But should he be condemned for sneering at mediocrity?

Yet, the example Szilard set was ironic. The man who was insisting that the bomb not be dropped was the same man who was largely responsible for its creation. It had been conceived in his mind and born mainly of his efforts. With the Italian physicist Enrico Fermi, he had discovered at Columbia University that a nuclear chain reaction was possible and that an atomic bomb could therefore be built. If not for his initiative, the bomb might never have been completed during World War II and Russia could have been the first nation to possess it. He hadn't wanted to kill anyone with it; he had simply wanted to keep the enemy from killing anyone. Building the bomb was the only way to make sure Hitler could not terrorize the world with a bomb of his own.

II

Szilard had been obsessed with saving the world ever since the age of 10, when he was overwhelmed by Imre Madách's Hungarian classic, *The Tragedy of Man*. As he would later describe the book:

"The devil shows Adam the history of mankind, with the sun dying down. Only Eskimos are left and they worry chiefly because there are too many Eskimos and too few seals. The thought is that there remains a rather narrow margin of hope."

Szilard's awareness of this narrow margin helped to stir his intense early interest in physics, which he would later feel held the key to whether the margin would disappear altogether. The secrets of the universe could, when revealed, be used either to ravage or to rescue humanity. He would learn the secrets so that he might rescue it.

Further stimulating Szilard was the special environment that pervaded prosperous Budapest in his youthful years. Free of security woes, the educated classes had time to indulge passions, with those studying science forced to think originally since the teaching system in that field was so poor. As a result, Hungary bred a number of enormously talented physicists, mostly Jews, who would one day, together with Szilard, become scientific titans— Edward Teller, Eugene Wigner, John von Neumann, Michael Polanyi.

Only Szilard, however, was equally gifted in several scientific fields—biology and electrical engineering as well as physics. A laboratory dilettante, he would focus on a particular project in one field or another just long enough to assure success, but not long enough to win a Nobel Prize or comparable recognition, leaving the glory to others who would complete his work. Too many truths awaited discovery for him to waste time on any but the most basic questions.

Because one could not make a living as a physicist in Hungary except as a teacher—and Hungarian law excluded most Jews from this profession—Szilard studied electrical engineering. He went first to a school in Budapest and then, after enduring a year in the Hungarian army, to the Institute of Technology in Berlin. There he switched to theoretical physics and became a student of Einstein, who found that the young man sometimes solved problems that stumped even him. Szilard grappled with these problems in his small rented room that was so bare visitors had to be served tea while squatting on the floor. After earning his doctorate in 1922, he made scientific history with a paper on information theory and cybernetics that helped lay the groundwork for the cyclotron. And with Einstein he took out a patent on an electric contrivance for pumping liquid metals.

But Szilard, iconoclast that he was, mixed his physics with prescriptions for saving mankind. He approached Socialist leader H. N. Brailsford once with a scheme for choosing "twelve just men" who, in their wisdom, would keep peace in the world. Brailsford, however, never pursued the idea, perhaps because Einstein told him that Szilard might "exaggerate the significance of reason in human affairs."

Szilard then cooked up another plan for at least saving Germany, persuaded in the mid-1920s that a dictator would ride to power in that country on a wave of political and economic chaos.

He thus tried to set up an elite organization called the Bund, made up of bright, scientifically trained German youth, which would guide public opinion on vital issues and even govern if the parliamentary system collapsed. This system would operate according to his rather original view of democracy, which he once whimsically described in these terms:

"I'm all for the democratic principle that one idiot is as good as one genius, but I draw the line when someone concludes that two idiots are better than one genius."

The Bund effort failed, though Szilard's prediction proved correct in 1933 when Hitler rose to power in an economically prostrate Germany. Szilard watched in horror while foul-mouthed Nazi students spat poison at their teachers and intellectual life grew stagnant. He kept two suitcases packed in his room at the faculty club of the Kaiser Wilhelm Institute and was ready to go "when things got too bad." Endowed with an extraordinary sense of survival to complement his gift of prophecy, he kept his suitcases packed, literally, for much of his life, as he found himself fleeing from one crisis after another, real or imagined, and finally from the monster that he himself would create.

"When Szilard fled," says one acquaintance, "he quivered in every muscle like a thoroughbred horse in the starting stall."

But his inclination toward flight, it seems, stemmed more from cunning than from cowardice. If mankind's fate was to perish, why facilitate the process? Let fate seek him out. And others, too. After the Reichstag (Parliament) fire in February 1933, Szilard rushed to Vienna, where he tried to find jobs outside Germany for fellow anti-Nazi scientists. But fearing that Hitler would soon march into Austria, he raced on to London and set up a committee there to save more people.

Ironically, Szilard himself was so impoverished that Einstein and Wigner, Szilard's colleague from Hungary, had to solicit money from fellow scientists, including some of those rescued, in order to keep the rescuer alive.

III

The monster that would ultimately pursue Szilard was conceived during a moment of inspired reverie on a gloomy London day in September 1933, while Szilard was waiting at a street corner for the light to turn green. He was pondering a newspaper article he had just read in which Lord Ernest Rutherford, the most distinguished British physicist, was quoted as saying that anyone who talked about the liberation of atomic energy on an industrial scale was talking "moonshine." Szilard was not so sure, and he wondered how Rutherford could be.

Some months before this moment of curb-stone reflection, Szilard had been captivated by an H. G. Wells novel, *The World Set Free*. In this 1913 book, the author foresaw the massive release of atomic energy, the development of atomic bombs, and a nuclear world war in which the major cities of the world would be destroyed. Szilard was so impressed by Wells' prophetic fantasy that he would write to a friend that "the forecasts of the writers may prove to be more accurate than the forecasts of the scientists."

Shortly, Szilard met Wells' German publisher, Otto Mandl, who suggested that mankind could save itself only by leaving the earth. Szilard was intrigued by this far-out theory; if he concluded that Mandl was probably right, he replied, he would focus on nuclear physics, because only through the liberation of atomic energy could man obtain the means to leave the earth, or for that matter, the solar system.

Now, as these events sped through Szilard's mind, the traffic light flashed green, and it turned out to be a signal of revelation. Einstein had shown that vast stores of energy were trapped in the atomic nucleus, but no one had yet found a way to release this dormant energy. Szilard now thought of the neutron, which British scientist James Chadwick had discovered only a year earlier, in 1932. Each atom was composed of electrically charged particles—positive (protons), negative (electrons), and neutral (neutrons). All these particles remained firmly in place in most elements, but in radioactive ones they were in constant flux and motion, with the neutrons acting like bullets, capable of piercing other atoms and splitting them apart with tremendous energy. This energy, once liberated, could be harnessed to turn the wheels of civilization—or to exterminate civilization—if a chain reaction could generate enough power. Szilard, apparently, was the first person to see the political implications of the neutron.

At this obscure but key moment in human history, Szilard suddenly perceived a way to make a chain reaction. He had to find an element composed of atoms that, when split, would emit more than one neutron for each neutron absorbed. Then, each neutron released would split another atom in a chain reaction. Should this process be allowed to escalate out of control, a tremendous explosion would occur, just as H. G. Wells had foreseen.

By the time Szilard reached the opposite curb, he was as horrified as he was excited. What if Hitler found the element first? His sense of doom grew, but so did his determination to conquer the threat—especially when, soon afterwards, Frédéric Joliot-Curie and Mme. Joliot-Curie, France's leading nuclear scientists, announced that they had discovered artificial radioactivity. The tools were at hand to explore the possibilities of a chain reaction. Incredibly, H. G. Wells had predicted in his book that artificial radioactivity would be discovered, and in this year of 1933! Would his prediction of world nuclear war also come true?

Faced with this momentous question, Szilard decided that he must channel all his thoughts into finding a way to save the world. Leisure, he was convinced, induced thought and creativity, one reason why he viewed his more leisure-minded European colleagues as superior in many ways to the frantically working American scientists. (Leisure to Szilard did not mean exercise. "When I feel the need [for exercise]," he would say, "I lie down until the urge passes.")

Szilard moved into the Strand Palace Hotel in London, preferring the transient nature of hotel living to the frightening permanence of a home, which he could less easily abandon at a moment's notice. And hardly had he put down his suitcases when he tore off his clothing, ensconced himself in a tub of hot water, and soaked for hours just thinking, interrupted only by a troubled chambermaid who would knock on the door occasionally and ask, "Are you all right, sir?"

Szilard was all right, but he had plenty to think about. Without a steady flow of funds or a laboratory where he could hang up his white coat, how would he track down the mystery element? Beryllium might be it, he suspected, but he would have to systematically test every one of the ninety-two elements. Szilard stayed locked in the hotel room for a week, nibbling on food sent up to him, snatching a few hours of sleep, then returning to the bathtub to continue his silent dialogue with himself. Finally, after exploring, by reason or imagination, every road that could lead to success, Szilard stumbled out of the tub, dressed, and departed, primed for a new campaign to save humanity.

He approached the British War Office for help, the British Admiralty, his own colleagues. Beryllium? A chain reaction? Sheer fantasy! Szilard then tried Chaim Weizmann, the Zionist leader and renowned chemist, feeling that the expression "chain reaction" would at least have a familiar ring to him since chemical mixtures often had them.

"How much money do you need?" asked Weizmann.

Ten thousand dollars would suffice.

Weizmann would see what he could do. But he could do nothing.

Even some laboratory equipment sent to Szilard by a friend in America didn't work.

Yet Szilard was not discouraged. He had so much faith in his chain reaction theory that he tried to take out a patent on it and assign it to the British army so that it could be kept a secret. The army didn't want it. But to Szilard's delight—and surprise—the British Admiralty did, and classified the patent top secret in 1934.

He would later patent other nuclear processes as well, not to make money—he deemed it his fate to earn just enough money to survive—but to be able to control the danger he foresaw. A nonprofit research corporation led by enlightened men would eventually, he hoped, serve as custodian of the secrets and use them for further research to better man's condition.

If Szilard felt depressed or frustrated while seeking help in saving the world, he would often turn for sympathy to a young woman he met in Berlin in 1934, a highly intelligent physics and psychology student, Gertrud Weiss, who would later become a medical doctor. It was the beginning of a relationship that would culminate in marriage seventeen years later. Usually a long-distance relationship, the only kind compatible with his lust for travel and hotel life that symbolized to him the freedom he needed to carry out his mission. Szilard would not allow personal ties to infringe on that freedom—an inflexible rule that would mean heartache and loneliness for Trude until Szilard's last years. Yet Szilard was her mentor and master, who must approve almost everything she did, even from afar. In her devotion to him, Trude was willing to sacrifice her own happiness so that mankind might benefit.

IV

In January 1938, after Hitler swallowed the Rhineland, Szilard once more glanced over his shoulder and grabbed his suitcases. He fled to New York, certain that Europe would soon be flung into war. In a fit of pessimism he abandoned his search for the mystery element and even tried to withdraw his application for a patent on the chain reactor. But after a year in America, the situation suddenly changed.

In early January 1939, while Szilard was at Princeton visiting Eugene Wigner, who was teaching there, his friend gave him sensational news: Niels Bohr, the famous Danish physicist, had just arrived from Denmark after escaping from that Nazi-occupied country in a British Mosquito. He had been given a seat over the bomb bay so that he could be dropped in the sea in case the Germans attacked the plane. They must not learn the atomic secrets locked in his brain. Now he had come to Princeton with the greatest scientific secret of all time. Bubbling with excitement, Bohr revealed that two German scientists, Otto Hahn and Friedrich Strassmann, had induced fission in the nucleus of uranium. They had bombarded this element with neutrons and produced barium.

What did this mean? Even Hahn and Strassmann did not know—until Hahn's former assistant Lise Meitner and her nephew Otto Frisch guessed what had happened and proved their thesis: that the absorption of a neutron by a uranium nucleus had caused the nucleus to split into two nearly equal parts. The mystery element, uranium, had been found; a chain reaction was possible! But Szilard did not bubble. Germans had solved the riddle, even if two of them, Meitner and Frisch, were Jewish.

Bohr's startling message convinced Szilard that a nuclear race would soon begin, if it had not already begun. And he was right. In France, scientists tripped over themselves rushing to the patent office to file five patents covering the use of nuclear energy, including one for the construction of a uranium bomb. In Britain, government leaders speeded up atomic research and dock workers unloaded crates of uranium from the Belgian Congo, where mine operators promised British officials not to sell any to the Germans. And in Germany, scientists at the Kaiser Wilhelm Institute produced fission while others drew up plans to build a "uranium device."

Almost feeling the earth erupt under him in a German nuclear attack, Szilard urgently sought a meeting with another great scientist who had just fled Europe—Enrico Fermi, the Italian physicist. Fermi, a balding, good-natured, quiet-spoken man, had altered basic nuclear matter in 1934 by bombarding sixty different elements with neutrons and producing artificial radiation in forty of them. Unwittingly, he had fractured the atom. Awarded the Nobel Prize in 1938, Fermi went to Stockholm to claim it and never returned to Mussolini's Italy. Szilard first sent Isidor Rabi, another Nobel Prize–winning colleague, to see Fermi and explain to him the need for crash research on a chain reaction, but Rabi returned with a concise message from the Italian: "Nuts!"

"Why did he say, 'Nuts'?" Szilard asked in dismay.

"Well, I don't know," Rabi replied. "But he is in and we can ask him."

Together they went to see Fermi, and Rabi said: "Look, Fermi . . . Szilard wants to know why you said, 'Nuts!' "

Because, explained Fermi, he saw only a "remote possibility" of a chain reaction.

Szilard was exasperated. Was one to shrug off even a "remote possibility" that an answer might be found to human survival? Fermi, who was both a theoretical and experimental physicist, was considered a greater scientist than Szilard, but Szilard had more original solutions to problems than almost anyone. And now, he felt certain, he would solve one of the most important problems in history.

Szilard had his experimental apparatus sent to him from Oxford, corralled a research partner, Walter Zinn, and borrowed $2000 from a friend as security for a gram of radium so he could conduct experiments, a debt he was able to repay only many years later. He worked day and night, almost without sleep. Sleep, he felt, "may well have been the most useful kind of activity during the evolution of man," but it was not very useful now. One day he would have to find a way "to get rid of sleep."

Finally, on March 3, 1939, in a laboratory at Columbia University, where he was given "guest" research privileges (unlike Fermi, he was not offered a permanent appointment, nor did he wish to be tied down with one), he flicked a switch, leaned back in his chair, and, in trepidation, gazed at a cathode-ray screen. Flashes of light suddenly flitted across the screen; about two neutrons were being emitted from every uranium atom undergoing fission.

Szilard had his proof: He knew that a chain reaction could be induced and atomic energy liberated. He continued to stare in fascination at the screen for about ten minutes, then switched off the set and returned to his cluttered room in nearby King's Crown Hotel. He couldn't sleep.

"I knew," he would say, "that the world was headed for sorrow."

And where could he run to now with his suitcases?

V

Meanwhile, Fermi, despite his skepticism, conducted an experiment of his own at Columbia with the assistance of Herbert Anderson and John Dunning and also confirmed that a chain reaction was no longer simply a "remote possibility." Szilard, Fermi, and Wigner then met with George B. Pegram, chairman of the physics department at Columbia. They debated how to deal with this scientific breakthrough that could change the face of the earth.

Awaken the government, Wigner urged, and seek its help for a large-scale experiment. For who could be sure that a chain reaction would be induced in a *large mass* containing uranium? After all, uranium was about 99 percent uranium 238 and less than 1 percent uranium 235. And apparently only U^{235} would undergo fission if it absorbed a neutron. Perhaps U^{238} would compete too strongly with U^{235} for neutrons to permit a chain reaction. And, in any case, there was less than an ounce of metal uranium to be found in the whole United States. It *was* clear to everyone, though, that if America didn't start building an atomic bomb soon, Hitler might get one first.

Fermi, the best known of the group, rushed to Washington for a meeting with Charles Edison, assistant secretary of the navy, whom Pegram knew, to enlighten him on the need for the experiments. But his plea was greeted by Edison and his advisers with almost sneering cynicism. After the conference one of the advisers telephoned a colleague of Fermi and asked:

"Who is this man Fermi? What kind of a man is he? Is he a Fascist or what? What is he?"

Apparently Fermi had spoken in a low-key, supercautious way, playing down, in the academic tradition, the prospects for success. Why, the navy wondered, should the government support experiments that the scientists themselves were not confident would work? Obviously, these foreigners didn't understand that this government, unlike many in Europe, did not finance universities and would only contribute funds to defense projects when preliminary experiments had confirmed that national security required such support. If they wanted money for such experiments, let them get it from private sources. One didn't see *American* scientists banging on doors and barging in with hands outstretched. *They* understood.

Szilard and his alien colleagues did, too; they understood, as witnesses, the terror of the Fascist lash, the absurdity of counting money in the face of such terror, indeed in the face now of mankind's liquidation. And Szilard understood something more: that no savior of mankind could afford to retreat or sulk over his wounds until he had fulfilled his mission.

VI

But fear went hand in hand with fanaticism. Szilard grew obsessed with the thought that Hitler might have the means to doom his mission. Normally, he enjoyed tossing ideas around, sharing them, fondling them, even writing them down and mailing them to himself so that he could document the dates when they occurred and remind himself of arguments he must use in defending them. Ideas, he felt, should never be secret. But now he badgered his colleagues, many of whom valued personal recognition more than he, to keep the momentous discovery a secret lest the Nazi scientists profit from the knowledge.

Never! cried Fermi, who had seen in Fascist Italy how censorship could cripple intellectual activity. And most of the nuclear physicists echoed him, especially after Joliot-Curie in France reported in the scientific journal *Nature* that he, too, had discovered that neutrons were emitted in the fission of uranium. Szilard wrote and then wired Joliot-Curie, urging him to keep all future developments secret.

"In certain circumstances," he urged in his letter, "[a chain reaction] might lead to the construction of bombs which would be extremely dangerous in general and particularly in the hands of certain governments. . . . We all hope there will be no or at least not sufficient neutron emission and therefore nothing to worry about."

Szilard thus indicated he was willing to forgo the glory and satisfaction of succeeding in the most important experiment in history—not to mention the huge benefits that nuclear power would bring to mankind—so that mankind would not be threatened by this power. But Joliot-Curie was clearly not willing to do so. After a long silence, he finally spurned Szilard's plea, arguing that word had leaked out anyway and it was too late to stop the leak. A colleague of Joliot-Curie would later explain, however, that "France's reputation was for women's fashions and the niceties of life. Joliot wanted to change that."

Joliot-Curie was right. It was too late—from the moment his article appeared. The German government, as Szilard feared, immediately set up a research project known as the "Uranium Club" and appealed to the military for an important nuclear program. And among other countries spurred by the article to start bombarding their atoms was the Soviet Union. The "leak" gradually swelled into a flood as information gushed forth from Allied research centers. And even Szilard finally had to end his campaign after Rabi warned him that he might lose his "guest" privileges at Columbia if he did not. The irony was that amid the nuclear machinery grinding in Germany and elsewhere, Washington still scoffed at the "harebrained" idea of an atomic bomb—an idea being pushed by untrustworthy foreigners.

Szilard, however, would not relent. He was determined to find a way to sustain a chain reaction in a large mass. Then Washington would have to listen to him. He teamed up with Fermi and Herbert Anderson at Columbia to explore whether heavy water, an isotope of hydrogen, could be used to slow down neutrons so they would more easily strike uranium nuclei and set off a chain reaction. When the experiment failed, Szilard wanted to substitute graphite for heavy water, but Fermi was cool to the idea, perhaps, in part, because he had grown cool to Szilard.

Szilard was full of ideas but wouldn't share in the work. A man determined to save the world could not get bogged down in routine mechanical detail. In fact, he hired a young physicist to do his laboratory work for him. This irked Fermi, who by contrast would use his hands as well as his head, pursuing an experiment to its conclusion. Szilard attributed Fermi's skepticism toward his graphite proposal to intellectual laziness; it was, after all, easier to compute mixtures of uranium and other elements. He also felt that Fermi, steeped in eternal truths, lacked a sense of urgency. In a hundred or a thousand years, who would understand why people were now fighting each other?

Thus, Szilard, who feared there might be no people around to ponder the problem in a hundred years, decided to launch his graphite experiment with only the help of his laboratory assistant. However, it cost money to borrow a chunk of graphite. He thus appealed to the navy again, this time on his own, but the reply was cogent: No!

Meanwhile the news grew worse. The Nazis invaded Czechoslovakia in spring 1939 and seized control of its uranium mines, ominously forbidding export of the ore. Eventually, Szilard was sure, they would try to take over the richest uranium deposits of all—in the Belgian Congo. He must warn the Belgians not to sell any uranium to Hitler. But why should they listen to him any more than the Americans did? He thought of people who might know important Belgians. Einstein! His old mentor was a friend of the Belgian queen mother, Elizabeth. . . .

VII

In July 1939, Szilard was driven by his Hungarian colleague, Eugene Wigner, to Peconic, Long Island, where Einstein went to sail on vacations. (For all his technical genius, Szilard couldn't drive a car.) The two men searched for Einstein's cabin, finally finding it on Old Grove Road after being led there by a young boy, who could never have guessed that he was playing a role in one of the most important encounters that would ever take place. Einstein, dressed casually in undershirt, rolled-up pants, and slippers, greeted his visitors warmly and led them onto a screened porch, where he lit up his pipe and listened to Szilard's story of the great atomic peril.

Though his formula $E=mc^2$ was the root basis for a chain reaction and this phenomenon was the talk of the scientific world, Einstein had isolated himself so completely in his own little cosmos that he apparently didn't know about it. Szilard, as he spoke, was not very optimistic that his host would help him save mankind. The great scientist would need considerable coaxing to lend his name to a venture that could lead nowhere. Besides, Einstein had been a fervent pacifist until recently and even now deplored the use of force unless absolutely necessary. Would he entangle himself in a campaign to build a weapon that could cause incalculable destruction?

Szilard, however, soon realized that Einstein, unlike other scientists, had too big a name to worry about making a fool of himself, and too logical a mind to cling to dogma when mankind's fate was at stake.

"It will be a hard thing to put this across to the military mind," Einstein declared after Szilard had talked for about twenty minutes.

And though Einstein himself had expressed doubt in the past that atomic energy "will ever be obtainable," Einstein now shared the fears of his guests. With the Germans probably working on the bomb, he dared not gamble that he had been right and risk the destruction of civilization.

He would do anything that needed to be done, he said.

Szilard felt enormous relief. He would now stage manage the drama that would lead to a new age.

Perhaps, he suggested, Einstein could advise the Belgian queen mother to warn her government about the danger of selling Nazi Germany any uranium ore.

Einstein, however, didn't want to exploit his friendship with the queen mother. He would write instead to a Belgian Cabinet minister he knew, and send a copy of the letter to the Belgian ambassador in Washington.

But was it correct, Wigner asked, to approach a foreign government without first consulting the State Department?

It was then decided that Einstein would write the letter and a copy would be sent to the State Department with a note asking that it approve the message. If a reply was not received within two weeks, the message would be mailed to the Belgians. And in refined German, Einstein dictated a draft of the letter while Wigner sat at a table scribbling furiously, with Szilard poised over his shoulder. The visitors then departed in triumph.

VIII

By the time Szilard returned home and began typing out a draft of Einstein's letter, tremors had shaken the triumph. Szilard grew uneasy, for neither he nor Einstein, he realized, knew how to deal with the government. Was the letter, on which man's future might depend, simply to be filed away in some bureaucrat's drawer? He mailed two drafts to Einstein, asking him to choose one, but wondered whether he was doing the right thing. With anxiety, he went to seek advice from an old friend, Gustave Stolper, a former German publisher and member of the Reichstag, who was now living as a refugee in New York. Stolper sent him to see Alexander Sachs.

An intimate of President Roosevelt, the Russian-born Sachs was a self-made, self-assured man who looked like comedian Ed Wynn but saw nothing funny about the future. He was economic adviser to the Lehman Corporation, a Wall Street investment firm, and was known as the "economic Jeremiah" for his gloomy views on the world's destiny. He had predicted the 1929 stock market crash and Hitler's rise to power among other disasters. Swayed by Sachs' foresight, Roosevelt named him his chief economist and organizer of the National Recovery Act (NRA) soon after taking office. Sachs, no longer with the government, was now predicting a new catastrophe—World War II. He had just written a typically verbose memorandum to himself called "Notes on Imminence World War in Perspective Accrued Errors and Cultural Crisis of the Inter-War Decades."

So when Szilard called on him, Sachs immediately grasped the significance of his visitor's mission. Here, perhaps, was the key to victory in the coming war.

A letter to the State Department? That would be like sending a message in a bottle tossed into the sea. Yes, Einstein should write a letter, but *directly* to the President. And Sachs would be willing to deliver it personally.

Szilard was elated. At last he had a channel to the top. No more patronizing assistant secretaries or sneering admirals to block the way. Now the most powerful man in the world would know that he must act soon or possibly leave the distinction to Hitler. In late July 1939, Szilard visited Einstein again, this time chauffeured by dour-faced Edward Teller, another of his Hungarian colleagues, who was now teaching physics at George Washington University and would years later become the "father of the H-bomb."

Einstein agreed; he would write directly to the President, who had once invited him to stay overnight at the White House. They discussed the contents of the new letter over tea, deciding to add a subtly worded proposal that the government help the scientists wangle aid from private sources. In view of past experiences, who could expect the government to do more?

After consulting with Sachs, Szilard sent two drafts to Einstein with some scientific articles and slipped into the envelope his own memorandum for the President. Since American cynicism toward new weapons had stung Szilard sharply, in his memorandum he appealed first to Roosevelt's sense of national pride, stressing that atomic energy could power ships and industry and lift the economic face of the nation. He then stated that the destructive power of an atomic bomb "would go far beyond all military conceptions" and urge that a quantity of uranium be brought to the United States from the Belgian Congo before the Germans invaded Belgium.

Einstein sent back to Szilard a signed draft of his own message, together with a cautionary suggestion that his "manager" and his colleagues curb their "inner resistance" and try not to act "too cleverly" in pursuing their goal. Szilard *was* at times abrasively impetuous. He now read and reread the Einstein letter as if the fate of humanity hinged on the nuance of each word. It said:

> Sir: Some recent work by E. Fermi and L. Szilard, which has been communicated to me in manuscript, leads me to expect that the element uranium may be turned into a new and important source of energy in the immediate future. Certain aspects of the situation seem to call for watchfulness and, if necessary, quick action on the part of the Administration. I believe, therefore, that it is my duty to bring to your attention the following facts and recommendations.

In the course of the last four months it has been made probable—through the work of Joliot in France as well as Fermi and Szilard in America—that it may become possible to set up nuclear chain reactions in a large mass of uranium, by which vast amounts of power and large quantities of new radium-like elements would be generated. Now it appears almost certain that this could be achieved in the immediate future.

This new phenomenon would also lead to the construction of bombs, and it is conceivable—though much less certain—that extremely powerful bombs of a new type may thus be constructed. A single bomb of this type, carried by boat or exploded in a port, might very well destroy the whole port together with some of the surrounding territory. However, such bombs might very well prove to be too heavy for transportation by air.

The letter then stated that good uranium ore was available in Canada, Czechoslovakia, and especially in the Belgian Congo, and it urged the President to appoint someone to serve as a liaison with the scientists, who would keep the government informed on their progress and seek funds and equipment from private sources. The final paragraph warned that Hitler had stopped the export of uranium from Czechoslovakia and that his scientists were probing into the atom.

Who would be the best "middleman" to submit and explain the letter to the President? Though Alexander Sachs had offered to do so, Szilard thought that others might be more suitable, among them Colonel Charles Lindbergh, the famous aviator. Lindbergh was disturbingly tolerant toward Hitler, but on technical matters no man could influence the President more than he. Szilard chose Lindbergh, and wrote the flyer on August 16, 1939, explaining the importance of recent discoveries and requesting a meeting with him to discuss an approach to the President. When there was no reply, he wrote again. Still no reply. Meanwhile, Lindbergh delivered a speech supporting "neutrality" even though Hitler had just invaded Poland, launching World War II. In fury, Szilard wrote Einstein that the aviator "is in fact not our man."

He now decided that Alexander Sachs was. Sachs tried to get in to see Roosevelt, but the President was preoccupied at this tumul-

tuous time with revising the Neutrality Act. And it would be useless, Sachs felt, to send him the material.

But Szilard's impatience grew. On October 3, he wrote Einstein that "Sachs confessed that he is still sitting on the letter" and
"there is a distinct possibility that he will be of no use to us. If this
is the case, we must put the matter in someone else's hands.
Wigner and I have decided to accord Sachs ten days' grace."

In despair, Szilard felt he might have to rely entirely on private
industry to finance and facilitate further experiments on the chain
reaction, though the prospect of getting such aid seemed dim. And
so he met with officials of the Union Carbon and Carbide Company, who were a bit upset when Szilard, rather than the better-
known Fermi, whom they expected, turned up. Who was this
rather odd man who seemed to be asleep while others talked, then
suddenly sprang to life with impetuous demands and aggressive
questions? What did Szilard want?

About $2,000 worth of graphite on loan to measure its absorp-
tion of neutrons.

The company's director of research was skeptical. "You know,"
he said, "I am a gambling man myself, but you are now asking me
to gamble with the stockholders' money, and I am not sure that I
can do that. What would be the practical applications of such a
chain reaction?"

It was really too early to say, Szilard replied. After all, what
could Union Carbide do with an atomic bomb?

And so the meeting failed. Szilard was more depressed than
ever. Would Hitler think twice about gambling with stockholders'
money if he knew the secret of the bomb? Should Sachs fail to
meet the deadline, where could he turn for help?

Sachs, however, now moved quickly, writing Roosevelt directly
that he wished to discuss the new discoveries with him. And the
President agreed.

IX

The visitor was exhilarated as he stepped into the Oval Office
in the White House on October 12, 1939, and saw his old friend
and boss greet him with a smile.

"Alex, what are you up to now?" Roosevelt asked.

With the President pressed for time, Sachs immediately told him and began reading a long statement of his own, hardly pausing for breath between labyrinthine sentences. Noting that the President was growing weary, he switched to Einstein's letter, but to no avail.

It was all very interesting, Roosevelt interrupted, but it seemed a bit premature for the government to involve itself at this stage. Besides, it was time for his next appointment.

Sachs was crushed. Premature? With Hitler on a rampage? Could he at least see the President the next morning for breakfast? Well, all right.

That night Sachs paced the floor of his room at the Carlton Hotel, unable to sleep. Finally he tried to sleep sitting in a chair. No luck. Thus, in the wee hours, he went for a walk in a small park across the street and sat meditating on a bench. How could he win over the President? It seemed hopeless. Suddenly, he had an idea! With a great sense of relief, he returned to the hotel, took a shower, and, shortly afterwards, called again at the White House.

Sitting in his wheelchair at the breakfast table, the President asked him with a teasing grin: "What bright idea have you got now? How much time would you like to explain it?"

Not much, replied Sachs. "All I want to do is to tell you a story. During the Napoleonic wars a young American inventor came to the French Emperor and offered to build a fleet of steamships with the help of which Napoleon could, in spite of the uncertain weather, land in England. Ships without sails? This seemed to the great Corsican so impossible that he sent [Robert] Fulton away. In the opinion of the English historian Lord Acton, this is an example of how England was saved by the shortsightedness of an adversary. Had Napoleon shown more imagination and humility at that time, the history of the nineteenth century would have taken a very different course."

When Sachs had finished, Roosevelt did not immediately reply. He scribbled a note on a sheet of paper and gave it to a servant, who left but soon returned with a package. Unwrapping it, the President removed a bottle of old French brandy from Napoleon's time and filled two glasses. He raised his, nodded to Sachs, and toasted him.

"Alex," Roosevelt finally said, "what you are after is to see that the Nazis don't blow us up."

"Precisely."

Roosevelt then summoned General Edwin M. Watson, his aide, who was known as "Pa."

"Pa," the President said, holding up the documents that Sachs had brought, "this requires action!"

And thus was the decision to build history's first nuclear bomb casually made between sips of French brandy.

X

Szilard was euphoric when Sachs phoned him with the news. The world might yet be saved! He was especially pleased that Roosevelt had, on Sachs' advice, agreed to form a three-man Uranium Committee under Chairman Lyman J. Briggs, director of the National Bureau of Standards and a former soil scientist, to maintain contact between the Administration and the physicists. The committee would meet a few days later, and Szilard, Wigner, and Teller would explain what the physicists needed. Szilard still felt it would be useless to ask the government for money at this point, but a government blessing could lead to foundation grants.

However, when the group met in Washington on October 21, the army representative on the committee, Lieutenant Colonel Keith F. Adamson, startled the scientists by asking: "How much money do you need?"

About $2,000 for pure graphite, Szilard replied, his hopes rising. And perhaps later, another $4,000 for a few experiments.

But his hopes plunged again when Adamson seemed as skeptical as the Union Carbide man had been. Atomic research should be left to the universities, the colonel felt. It was naïve to believe that a new explosive could make a significant contribution to defense. Once, he was outside an ordnance depot when it blew up and "it didn't even knock me down." Anyway, when a new weapon was created, it usually took two wars before one could know whether the weapon was any good or not. In the final analysis, it was not weapons but troop morale that won wars.

Wigner interrupted. If weapons were not very important, he

said in a high-pitched voice, why did the army ask for such a large defense budget? Perhaps it should be cut.

Szilard froze. But Adamson simply replied: "Well, as far as the $2,000 is concerned, you can have it."

Silence prevailed for a moment, as if there were need to adjust to a new era, perhaps a new universe. Who could have dreamed just a few moments earlier that the government would spend money on a phantom bomb out of H. G. Wells? Who could imagine now that the $2,000 would ultimately snowball into $2 billion? Szilard's campaign for human survival had finally borne fruit.

XI

Or so Szilard thought. For several months after the meeting in October 1939, not a word—or cent—trickled out of Washington. Everybody there, it seemed, had lost interest in the project, too concerned with Hitler's imminent invasion of the West European democracies. Fermi began experimenting on cosmic rays, and Sachs could get nowhere. He sent letters signed by Einstein to Watson and Briggs, but the Uranium Committee was not satisfied with the progress reports on the chain reaction.

The committee didn't understand, Szilard's group argued. Money was needed in order to *make* more progress.

But Briggs and his colleagues did understand the Pentagon's argument *against* giving the money. With Hitler threatening to overrun Europe, this was no time to divert war resources to experiments on a fantastic new weapon dreamed up by overimaginative foreign scientists.

In desperation, Szilard decided to force the issue again. He went back to Einstein with a bold new idea: To save the world, they would blackmail the U.S. government. Szilard would write a scientific paper claiming that a graphite-uranium system would chain-react, as he was sure it would, then show it to the government and threaten to publish it if Washington did not contribute the needed funds immediately. After all, if prospects for an atomic bomb were really as poor as the government thought, what harm could be done? It was a question Szilard asked ironically; he apparently had no intention of carrying out his threat. If the threat didn't yield money, it might at least yield an order silencing voices that were so irresponsibly telling the enemy how to build a bomb.

Einstein agreed, as he almost always did to Szilard's suggestions, and the paper was submitted to the navy. At the same time, Einstein wrote to Sachs: Would he please speak once more with Roosevelt?

On March 7, 1940, Sachs visited Einstein, and the scientist dictated a letter addressed to his guest but meant for the eyes of the President.

Since the outbreak of war [he wrote] interest in uranium has intensified in Germany. I have now learned [apparently from Szilard] that research there is being carried out in great secrecy and that it has been extended. . . .

Einstein also repeated Szilard's "blackmail" threat, if in milder form. A paper on the chain reaction would be published—unless, of course, the government banned it from print.

Sachs personally took this letter to the President and suggested that the government provide $100,000 for a large-scale experiment. And once again, Szilard's relentless pounding on doors forced them to creak open. In the summer of 1940, Washington banned publication of nuclear research information. But even before that, Sachs opened a letter from the President proposing that the Uranium Committee meet to get things started again. The committee, with guests Szilard, Fermi, and Sachs present, gathered on April 27, 1940. Shortly afterwards, at long last, $6,000 flowed forth for experiments on a graphite-uranium system.

But then, another hitch. A special advisory group of scientists was formed on Szilard's advice, but at its first meeting in Washington, Briggs made no flowery welcoming speech. Their group, he told members, would be dissolved immediately. Why? If a chain reaction proved impossible, he blandly explained, Congress might investigate. And the government would be embarrassed if the public knew that Washington had financed a project recommended by men who were not "Americans of long standing"—meaning almost all the scientists involved. Szilard and his colleagues were angry and hurt, and Wigner, who had only recently become an American citizen, stood up and made a dramatic announcement: He would refuse to work any longer with uranium. And it appeared that Szilard and other colleagues might follow suit, thus seriously impeding atomic progress.

XII

In May, just as it seemed that plans for an atomic bomb were finally doomed, Hitler came to the rescue by invading Belgium. Would the uranium of the Congo now fall into his hands? Sachs wasted no time. After consulting with Einstein, Szilard, and other scientists, he wrote the President again. The supply of uranium from the Belgian Congo might be cut off, he warned. The government, therefore, should urgently back the atomic research program. Four days later, Sachs advised Gerald Watson that the White House should set up a committee of executives, engineers, and economists who would supervise all technical defense projects.

The White House now responded swiftly. On June 15, 1940, the day Paris fell to Hitler, Roosevelt formed such a committee, to be called the Office of Scientific Research and Development, under Vannevar Bush. A salty New Hampshire farmer and one of the nation's finest mathematicians and electrical engineers, Bush had previously served as president of the Carnegie Institute of Washington and as chairman of the National Advisory Committee for Aeronautics, which was to prepare the United States for air war. The Uranium Committee, renamed the National Defense and Research Committee, became a subunit of Bush's office under his deputy, James B. Conant, president of Harvard University.

Bush, however, was not very optimistic. On July 16, after only a month on the job, he wrote the President: His committee believed the "possibility of a successful outcome [of the atomic project] was very remote" and thus was not "diverting to the work" many top scientists, who were needed for more important projects.

Even so, as a "safety measure," Columbia University was now granted $40,000 to complete research on a chain reaction. Thus, on November 1, 1940, Szilard went on the Columbia payroll for the first time. He was no longer an unpaid "guest" scientist. "But with a view to the possibility that our effort might come to nothing," he would later say, apparently without resentment, "it was deemed advisable to set my salary at a low figure, i.e., $4,000 a year." The man who first discovered the possibilities of a chain reaction, who finally convinced the government that it must act immediately to build an atomic bomb before Hitler could, would earn little more than the average associate professor did.

But at least now he could afford to dine occasionally in expensive restaurants and greedily devour the hors d'oeuvres he craved by the plateful.

Chapter 2

THE
PUPPETEER

I

Had Marquis Koichi Kido, Lord Keeper of the Privy Seal, not been a Japanese leader, he might have sympathized with Szilard. For Kido, Emperor Hirohito's chief adviser, understood how hard it was to get a government to make a bold move—even in the face of potential catastrophe.

Ever since the first glorious months of the war, Kido had been trying to persuade military rulers to negotiate peace before America grew too strong. But they had furiously spurned his pleas. Now, on the day of the bomb, only virtual unconditional surrender, he knew, could save Japan from utter destruction. And it was the militarists who were demanding a negotiated peace. But it was too late.

Too late for Seiko Ogawa to save her dream, and too late for Kido to save his. It was a dream, he now realized, that was doomed from the start, a dream too splendid, too awesome, too bold for a jealous world ever to accept: He had dreamed of a great Japanese Empire stretching all the way to Singapore and perhaps beyond. And now the survival of Japan itself was in doubt.

Kido did not impress one as an empire builder, even a frustrated one. He had the tense, harried air of a business executive constantly flirting with bankruptcy; he looked the part, too, with his slight form wrapped in an elegant vest, his thick, neatly trimmed mustache, his bare fuzz of hair, and his darting eyes that peered searchingly through large round glasses like radar guiding him through a storm. Yet he was shrewd, resourceful, and, when necessary, devious. The perfect politician. He was, in fact, one of the most powerful men in Japan.

As Lord Keeper of the Privy Seal, Kido guarded the Emperor's signature seals, which he stamped on Imperial rescripts and official state documents. But he was far more than a palace clerk. He was the Emperor's eyes, ears, and voice, as well as his chief adviser. For at least one hour a day, he would keep His Imperial Majesty up to date on all important events inside and outside Japan, on the latest court gossip, on exactly how the sands of political power were shifting from minute to minute. He offered advice on all problems and, by turning the key to the throne room solely for those he trusted, made sure nobody else's advice conflicted with his own; only the ministers of war and navy could enter without his nod. He thus decided, with nominal help from the senior statesmen, who would be Prime Minister and what the Emperor should say, especially in situations critical to the life of the nation.

Actually, the Emperor had little direct influence on the government, for tradition dictated that he approve government decisions whether he agreed with them or not. But political leaders were always cautious about defying the known will of the Emperor, and Kido, while pretending to be above politics as his job officially required, would not hesitate to make this will known. However, even the knowledge that the Emperor wished to avoid war had not deterred the militarists governing Japan from launching an attack on the United States. It was unthinkable that they would disobey a direct order from the Emperor; but it was almost as unthinkable that the Emperor would *issue* a direct order. The military thus slyly took advantage of an Imperial tradition that technically protected it from charges of defying the Imperial will.

Kido, whose own will was the Imperial will, had tried to prevent war, preferring to let destiny flow at its own inexorable pace. But once the impetuous military had ruled for war, he pragmatically approved the inevitable. Now, however, almost four years later in the heat of a bloody summer, destiny had run its course. And Japan writhed in agony under the blows of the enemy, its cities a smoldering tribute to the god of war. In devastated Tokyo, the Emperor himself had been forced to flee his trembling palace and seek safety in the Imperial cellar. Was this an omen? Was the Imperial system, the soul of Japan, to be buried under the scorched debris, together with the dream? If so, better for Japan to die.

As realistically as he had accepted war, Kido now struggled behind the scenes for peace—on any terms that would allow Japan to save its soul. He had read the Potsdam Declaration made by America, Britain, and China: Japan would be destroyed if it did not surrender unconditionally at once. What did this mean? The Emperor was not mentioned. Was he to keep his throne? The military had made the most of this ambiguity. The war must go on! Never mind that Japan didn't have the planes, the ships, the oil to fight much longer. If necessary, every Japanese would meet the invader on the shores of the nation with bamboo spear in hand. Suddenly, the peace conspiracy led by Kido began sinking along with the warships.

Yet Kido had hopes of keeping it afloat, even though the Kempei Tai, the dreaded military police, were keeping a sharp eye on him and were ready to arrest, and perhaps torture him—using the techniques prescribed in an official manual—on the mere suspicion that he was *thinking* about peace. Now that the meeting of enemy leaders in Potsdam (Germany) was over, Stalin would be returning to Moscow. And waiting for him at the steps of the Kremlin would be Ambassador Sato with a proposal in hand: Russia would mediate a peace with the Western powers in return for Japanese territorial and trade concessions. Japan's fate now rested with Stalin. Maybe he could still arrange a peace that would keep Japan's soul intact, though no one could be sure the military would agree to *any* deal that meant its own destruction.

II

If Kido himself had once dreamed of conquest, it was not Hitler's kind. His aim was not to enslave people, but to "liberate" them, to help them rise from poverty and flourish under a Japan that the gods had singled out as a "superior" nation, one that therefore had the moral right to dominate them (though he preferred to use the word "guide")—and, incidentally, enjoy access to their oil, rubber, and other resources so scarce at home. Japan would build a hierarchical Greater East Asia Co-Prosperity Sphere, parallel in structure to the internal social order at home, with itself perched at the top.

Within this traditional order, overseen by the godly Emperor, every individual was fixed in his place according to class, occupation, family position, age, and sex. (Today this system is not as tight.) Like tiny springs or screws fitted into a wristwatch, the human parts were held in place by a complicated network of interlocking obligations called *on*. One received his most important *on* from the Emperor, his parents, and his ancestors, with whom close bonds of indebtedness were woven at birth. Repayment for the goodness of the Emperor, called *chu*, and of one's parents, called *ko*, was required throughout life; one owed them absolute obedience and devotion.

In addition, repayment of *giri*, which is less important and thus more troubling, was due in-laws, relatives, teachers, and all acquaintances who had ever bestowed upon one the slightest favor or gift. Further, one owed it to his family name to repay his debts to everybody else and to clear his name when it had been besmirched, however insignificantly, by proving the detractor wrong, by taking revenge on him, or sometimes by committing suicide. One also had to maintain strict self-discipline, never outwardly expressing "human feelings," or *ninjo*, especially in the presence of strangers, though the Japanese are among the most emotional and sentimental people in the world. *Ninjo* was channeled into a separate compartment of life, quite separate from the sphere of obligations, and expressed through poetry, art, and lovemaking with a mistress, prostitute, or occasionally one's wife.

Once an individual acquired an obligation, shirking it would mean loss of face and would bring down upon him the wrath and ridicule of the community. If the violation was important enough, he would be socially ostracized and even disowned by his family; he might even be forced to join the *hinen*, meaning "not men," doomed to the fringe itinerant life of a beggar, prostitute, or wandering musician. The bond of debt was once so tight that proud samurai soldiers did not hesitate to slay their families or themselves if this was the only way to meet their obligations and assuage the anger of their lord. Even in World War II, many Japanese soldiers killed themselves rather than surrender. Capture meant one had reneged on his debt to the Emperor and would thus be savagely cut off from society. (Paradoxically, those who were captured suddenly found themselves free men, released from all social pressures and obligations that had bound them at home. For they had gone beyond the realm in which Japanese moral law ruled. Thus, many of those once fanatical fighters felt no qualms about giving military information to their captors.)

Japan began to apply its domestic rules abroad in the 1930s, only to find that other countries refused to help it organize an Asian community based on Japanese hierarchical principles, even "in their own interest." Japan thus leaped upon them with the same brutal rage that Japanese society directed toward individual members who defied traditional social custom. The rage was far more brutal abroad, of course, because of the lack of environmental controls. There were no rules governing murder or rape by Japanese in foreign lands. Japan understood the rights of neither individuals nor individual nations.

III

Kido, like most intelligent and educated Japanese, did not condone such brutality, although it was his country's system that fostered it. When questioned after the war by Allied officers, he would say, probably in all sincerity:

"Japan's intention was to teach [the Asian nations] and to lead them and then give them self-determination and independence."

Meaning, in the Japanese cultural context, within a Japan-controlled structure of nations.

Now the dream was dead, and Kido, racked by uncertainty, anguished by failure, would peer from the window of his office upon the rubble of destiny. He had failed not only the Emperor but his illustrious ancestors in whose hearts the dream had budded. His grandfather was Koin Kido, one of the bright young samurai leaders of the powerful Choshu clan that inhabited southwestern Honshu, the central and main island of Japan. Koin had helped to overthrow the Tokugawa Shogunate in 1867 and finally restore the long-forgotten Emperor to power after 700 years of rule by dynastic warlords, or shoguns, who had usurped the Emperor's prerogatives, leaving him an obscure figure on a meaningless throne. Koin then helped to create a new Japan out of the old rotting one.

To assure their absolute control, the Tokugawa shoguns, ruling the nation from Edo, as Tokyo was then called, had with cruel thoroughness petrified Japan's social and political structure for 200 years. They suppressed all creative tendencies, frozen all existing institutions, and regulated every phase of life, even prescribing the proper size of children's dolls. They not only retained the ancient feudal caste system but forbade members of each of the four castes—samurai, peasant, artisan, and merchant—to shift from one to another. And they so solidified the concept of *on* that, among the samurai at least, suicide became the natural method of atoning for one's failure or inability to repay a debt.

Koin Kido's Choshu samurai clan had almost alone resisted these stunting regulations, even though the shogun kept Choshu wives hostage part of the year just to make sure their husbands obeyed. Choshu resented most deeply of all the enforced peace. The various clans could no longer fight each other to enhance their power, or even to avenge a misdeed. The samurai were warriors without wars to fight. They had become social parasites, jobless, obsolete figures who could find satisfaction only in dreams of bygone battles fought by their forefathers.

Finally, in 1863, the Choshu samurai decided to defy the rules and fight. And their chosen foe was the horde of American "barbarians," who, under Commodore Matthew C. Perry, was trying to "corrupt" this long-isolated nation with Western goods and ideas. The Choshu leaders schemed to bar Perry's "black ships" and all foreign vessels from sailing through the legendary Gates of Bakan, the Straits of Shimonoseki separating the island of Honshu from that of Kyushu. Mounting ancient muzzle-loading guns and mortars on a string of forts that rimmed the shoreline, the warriors waited for their first unsuspecting victim in what would be a distant forerunner of Pearl Harbor. The clan saw nothing immoral in a surprise attack. The only immorality was to lose, for to lose a battle was to lose face.

The samurai damaged the first ship, but a second one passed

through, its guns blazing, followed later by a European fleet, and the Choshu batteries crumbled. Koin Kido and his fellows had learned their lesson, a lesson that would spark a process fated to culminate in the deadly glow of the atomic bomb. Just as Japan, twelve centuries earlier, had imported Chinese civilization whole- sale, to be woven into the unique Japanese culture, so would the country now absorb Western technology and modernize itself thoroughly. Then, one day, it would crush the "barbarians" with their own weapons.

But first, the Choshu leaders decided, they would have to oust the Tokugawa Shogunate and restore the Emperor, for those who protected this divine symbol controlled Japan. By legend, the Emperor was a direct descendant of the Sun Goddess, but he had always been a tool in the hands of the political leaders in power.

Koin Kido and his clansmen purchased some rifles abroad, replaced armor plating with cloth uniforms, and, rousing the peo- ple with the battle cry "Restore the Emperor and expel the barbari- ans!" attacked the decadent, sword-swinging shogunate army. With the defenders smashed in 1867, the last of the Tokugawa resigned, and on January 3, 1868, young Emperor Meiji, the grandfather of Hirohito, emerged from his "exile" in the old capital of Kyoto. The shogunate, he solemnly announced in Edo (Tokyo), had been abolished and the Imperial House restored to power.

Soon a new modern Japan burgeoned from the feudal isolation of the past as the new leaders inundated the country with "barbar- ian" goods and know-how. These leaders, mainly warriors from Choshu and the rival Satsuma clan, which also helped crush the Tokugawa, did not, in launching the Meiji Restoration, simply strive for an industrial revolution. They wanted a psychological and spiritual one, too. For they needed a powerful glue to bind the long-divided nation together so they could more easily control it.

With Japan, in a sense, now one great clan, the fierce loyalties that the samurai had felt toward their warlords were channeled to the Emperor, who, despite his new symbolic value, remained a pawn of the government. A pawn who was, however, as the public was constantly reminded, no mere warlord but a god and the very soul of Japan.

Meanwhile, the leaders based every reform on military needs, though Koin Kido, the keenest brain among them, tried to restrain the army, as his grandson would do almost seventy-five years later.

Don't attack Korea, he advised the Cabinet. Don't appoint army officers to government posts. Japan must advance gradually, discreetly. No unnecessary gambles. Even so, he called on his colleagues to allot "three-fifths of the [budget] for military purposes." How, after all, could Japan grow strong enough to eventually fight the barbarians without more guns? This was a question that would echo in the mind of Koin Kido's grandson on the eve of Pearl Harbor.

IV

The Imperial House did not forget Koin Kido's role in restoring to the Emperor the powers, however nominal, befitting a descendant of the Sun Goddess. The Imperial family was, after all, just as bound by the Japanese code of obligations as its subjects were. When Hirohito was a boy, Koin's son, Takamasa, was titled a marquis, and Takamasa's son, Koichi, born in 1889, served as an elder brother to the young prince. The two boys played soldier together and rejoiced when the Japanese navy struck without warning in 1905 and knocked out most of the Russian fleet at Port Arthur and Chemulpo. Even Prince Ito, the Japanese Prime Minister, had not expected to win this war with Russia. Before it began, he uttered to a colleague words that Koichi Kido would never forget: "We are bound to fight, even at the price of our very national existence. It is futile to discuss the outcome, success or failure. . . . I say frankly I expect no success."

Yet Japan succeeded, just as it had ten years earlier when the new Japanese army, in its first test, routed Chinese forces in China and Korea to win Formosa, the Pescadores, and a corner of Manchuria. Yes, there was reason to rejoice; Japan's future never seemed so full of promise, nor did Kido's. It wasn't every child who played soldier with the future Emperor.

V

Hardly had Kido been graduated from Kyoto Imperial University in 1916 when he began spiraling through the bureaucratic ranks. From important positions in the Ministries of Agriculture and Commerce, he landed in the palace in 1930 as chief secretary to the Lord Keeper of the Privy Seal, a job that gave him valuable insights into the secrets of Imperial power.

Kido's rise now paralleled that of the militarists. In 1931, fanatical army officers detonated a bomb on the tracks of the South Manchurian Railway near Mukden, Manchuria, which Japanese troops had been occupying since the war with China in 1895, and accused Chinese agents of sabotage. Japanese forces then devoured southern Manchuria. The Mukden Incident was to most Japanese like a spectacular new sunrise. The Sun Goddess was suddenly resurrected. She had almost been forgotten in the 1920s when Japanese leaders, caught up in the peaceful, democratic aftermath of World War I, tended to ignore the militant mission of their forefathers.

Democratic institutions budded and warm relations with China blossomed. But then Chiang Kai-shek, the Chinese leader, unleashed his Nationalist hordes against the warlords and Communists in a drive to unify his country, and many Japanese as well as British and Americans stationed in China were killed or wounded in the crossfire. At the same time, the bitter winds of depression began blowing in from the Western world. Japan's silk market collapsed, laid-off workers roamed the streets, small firms went bankrupt and were greedily consumed by Japan's new huge combines.

But now, in 1931, the Sun Goddess reappeared to save the nation. Military secret societies and fascistic national socialist parties sprouted like poisonous herbs, and assassins plotted coups as intricately structured as the tea ceremony. Kido, as secretary to the Lord Keeper, was horrified to learn a month after the Mukden Incident that army officers, in the Emperor's name, were planning to murder the whole Cabinet, seize power, and kidnap Hirohito, whisking him to a warship "for his own protection" until "the situation was resolved." A return to the Tokugawa era when the Emperor was held virtual prisoner! Kido felt a sense of shame that most army leaders were Choshu clansmen. What would his grandfather have said?

The plot failed, but, Kido feared, the plotters would try again. And they did—in 1933 and 1936. These revolts were also crushed, but the three brushes with calamity would haunt Kido until the day of the bomb, coloring his policies, weakening his nerve. To save a god, he decided, he would deal with the devil. Perhaps the army couldn't be stopped, but it could be appeased. And the government, unwilling to commit suicide, thought so, too. It thus applauded the Manchurian takeover, encouraging the military to grow ever more aggressive. Finally, on July 7, 1937, China erupted in violence again when Japanese troops in the north provoked a battle at the Marco Polo bridge near Wanping and soon gulped down the whole Tientsin-Peking region. The Japanese government, though aghast, took another deep swallow and cried *"Banzai!"*

Kido was among those who cried the loudest. How could he survive in a military snakepit without feeding the snakes? Thus, as minister of education he ordered schools to teach Japanese youth about the "divine mission" so their greatest desire would be to die for the Emperor, and he allowed some liberal professors who questioned government policies to be fired and arrested. Then, as home minister and acting police chief, he did nothing to stop demonstrators from violently protesting against Britain for resisting Japanese expansion in Asia.

At the same time, however, Kido tried to keep the extremists in check by slipping them money donated by Choshu comrades who now controlled some of Japan's most powerful combines. And he helped to build a giant Fascist-styled, but relatively moderate, political party that would gobble up all other moderate parties so that it would be strong enough to stand up to the extremists.

VI

Actually, Kido admired these good patriots, who, however misled, were men with the fire and zeal of his grandfather. But hadn't his grandfather cautioned against moving too swiftly and gambling with destiny? Prince Ito, true, had gambled in 1905 and won. But Russia was at that time a corrupt, crumbling, feudal monarchy that could not field a first-class army. America, which was now demanding that Japanese forces get out of China, was another story. An old story. It had destroyed a few Choshu forts almost a century earlier. This time, if it could conquer its isolationist mood, it could conquer all of Japan.

In 1940, at the height of this crisis, Kido became Lord Keeper of the Privy Seal, and now the two former playmates played together for stakes that might have shaken even Kido's brave grandfather. One of the first things Kido did to help calm his fears was to escort the Emperor on a visit to the shrine of the Sun Goddess, which graced a wooded hill on Ise Peninsula overlooking the sea. As he waited under the trees while Hirohito entered a sacred little white hut to communicate with the deity, he "wept" and "reflected with awe on the importance of [his] new position." He would say: "Before the Imperial shrine of Japan, my mind widened and I felt large and fearless."

But not for long. For with World War II under way, Hitler blitzkrieged through France and the Low Countries, orphaning French Indo-China and the Dutch East Indies, which now hung like ripe fruit ready for the picking. Kido and the Emperor were tempted, longing to fulfil the dream, but were afraid that another tug at America's tail might drag Roosevelt into war. To the militarists, however, now was the moment to strike south, war or no war. And so eager were they that Kido feared they might strike even without the Emperor's approval, as they had done in China. Such a move could not only plunge Japan into an unwinnable war, but possibly detonate a Communist revolution at home.

Wait a little longer, Kido begged the military leaders. America would soon be drawn into war in Europe and would be so preoccupied there that Japan could do as it wished in Asia.

But the militarists wouldn't listen. The way to keep America from attacking in Asia, they claimed, was to join a Tripartite Pact with Germany and Italy. Washington would hesitate to split its forces between Europe and Asia.

Kido disagreed. Such a pact would guarantee an attack on Japan, since America would automatically be at war with Japan if it struck in Europe.

However, at an Imperial Conference on September 19, 1940, the militarists had their way. Before the meeting, Kido warned the Emperor that a pact would be disastrous. But Hirohito, sitting on his ornamental throne in front of a gold screen, helplessly listened in silence as government leaders called for an alliance with Hitler and Mussolini. Kido the peacemaker became Kido the traditionalist. Approve the pact, he now advised: However disagreeable, even catastrophic, a government decision might seem, the Emperor should not veto it. How could Japan survive if it violated tradition? Would the Emperor himself survive? The military might make a coup and keep him prisoner, as it had tried to do in the past. Only later, when the country was in desperate straits, would he ask how Japan could survive if it *didn't* violate tradition.

Confident that America wouldn't dare intervene militarily, the Japanese army thrust into northern Indo-China a few days after the conference. Washington then stopped the flow of all scrap iron and steel to Japan, the life's blood of the nation. War now seemed inevitable. But Kido continued in his own deviously paradoxical way to struggle for peace, intriguing with the Prime Minister, Prince Fumimaro Konoye, and other peace advocates while appearing to agree with military leaders who demanded that Japan fulfil its destiny. He helped to plot the ouster of Foreign Minister Yosuke Matsuoka because Matsuoka wanted to tighten ties with Hitler and to aid him in his attack on Russia by immediately charging through the Siberian snows. Yes, the Japanese would thrust into Siberia, it was decided at an Imperial Conference on July 2, 1941, but only when Hitler was about to topple the Kremlin.

Kido also tried to influence War Minister Hideki Tojo, one of the most war-minded of the warlords, who was determined to strike into southeast Asia. Tojo, a shaven-headed man with a thick black mustache and round glasses, was known as "The Razor" because of his sharp temperament. Beneath his hard, inanimate expression was hidden an almost mystical personality. A cold white nationalistic flame burned within him with as much intensity as any fire—and was not as likely to be whipped up by wind or quenched by water as the kind of passion found in most men. His career had been undistinguished for almost thirty years, until he made a name for himself as chief of the Kempei Tai in Manchuria, where he disposed of soldiers suspected of disloyalty with remarkable efficiency in his dank torture cells. Now, as war minister, he was conservative enough to please the senior officers and aggressive enough to satisfy the young hotheads.

On September 6, 1941, Japan's leaders met secretly in the presence of the Emperor to settle the question of war or peace with the Western democracies once and for all. Fighting for a new diplomatic drive were Prime Minister Konoye and most other members of the Cabinet, backed by Kido behind the scenes. Pushing for war were Tojo and his militarist partners, who felt that since war could no longer be avoided, Japan should launch it under the most advantageous conditions.

The Emperor, now regretting his silence at the meeting on the

Tripartite Pact a year earlier, was determined to speak his mind this time.

No, advised Kido, turning traditionalist again. Say only a few words at the end. Ask simply for "a full measure of cooperation in bringing diplomatic negotiation to an amicable conclusion."

But when it became clear from the debate that the militarists were set on war, Hirohito suddenly rose before the golden screen. The gathering sat transfixed, eyes looking down, fingers extended along the seams of trousers in deference to a god. Most unusual! The Emperor simply didn't speak at Imperial conferences, except to close the meeting with a few words. And it was not time for that. Was he about to embrace the call for war? His Majesty took off his glasses and rubbed a gloved thumb over the lenses to remove the mist caused by the heat, prolonging the bewilderment. Then he spoke.

He had not heard quite enough, he said in a high-pitched voice that cut through the muggy air like the wail of a flute. What should have priority—war or diplomacy? He had no doubt about his own answer. What was it? He drew a slip of paper out of his pocket. Would they please listen while he read aloud a poem that his grandfather, the Emperor Meiji, had once composed:

> The seas surround all quarters of the globe
>   And my heart cries out to the nations of the world.
>   Why then do the winds and waves of strife
>   Disrupt the peace between us?

Then Hirohito commented: He had often read and appreciated this poem, and "kept in my heart the Emperor Meiji's spirit of peace. It has been my wish to perpetuate this spirit."

The Japanese leaders, even the peacemakers, were shocked. His Imperial Majesty suggesting what the political and military chiefs should do? By traditional standards, this oblique plea for peace was virtually an Imperial command. Not at all Japanese! Yet the militarists could not make it appear that they were disobeying him. They agreed to compromise. The United States would have until October 31 to sign an accord with Japan. If the deadline passed without one, Japan would decide definitely on war or peace. Meanwhile, it would step up its preparations for war.

Undaunted, Kido suggested a new plan to Konoye: Delay a Southeast Asian thrust for ten years, but throw everything into a final campaign to subdue China. Maybe America would swallow this solution. The Prime Minister barely listened.

Kido and Konoye had been friends since childhood, and both had been playmates of the Emperor. Leader of the ancient, aristocratic Fujiwara clan that had advised Emperors for 1,300 years, Konoye, a charming, handsome sybarite who captivated the ladies, craved the benevolent authoritarianism of premilitary days when life was less taut and precarious and he could stay in bed nursing a hangover half the day without seeming unpatriotically idle. He had been Prime Minister three times under military patronage while serving as Hirohito's troubleshooter—with Kido's blessing—in many conflicts with the militarists, secret societies, and foreign governments. He had survived because he was so close to the Emperor, because he was extraordinarily flexible, and because he always knew when to quit. And never, he felt, was there a more appropriate time to quit than now.

Who would replace him? Kido made a desperate decision: He placed his last hopes for peace on the leading warlord—Tojo! The general seemed to him the only man who could keep the army under control and possibly prevent a coup by leftist soldiers. He was a necessary compromise between the relatively moderate but less influential senior officers and the fanatical, war-minded juniors who were ready to provoke an international incident that would inevitably lead to war. After all, hadn't Tojo agreed to keep talks with America alive? If America would bend only a little, Kido felt, he would have an excuse to advise the Emperor to break tradition and directly command the military to halt their war plan.

Kido felt he made the right decision even after Tojo visited him on October 16, before he took power, and made his policy clear to him: The general would go to war if America didn't meet Japan's deadline for an accord.

But what if the navy didn't agree with this decision? Kido replied, knowing that some officers on the navy general staff were opposed to war.

Then it would be impossible to wage war, Tojo conceded, knowing that his navy minister, Admiral Shigetaro Shimada, and the navy chief of staff, Admiral Osami Nagano, favored war. But in that case, he growled, "what will happen to Japan?"

"If we let you act as you wish," Kido answered, "Japan will become a fourth-rate power."

But afraid to be charged with treasonous defeatism, he would not dare suggest anything worse might be in store for Japan.

Kido now became bolder. A few days later, after the Emperor had summoned Tojo and Shimada to invest them with power, Kido told them in the waiting room in his usual foggy language: "I am commanded to convey to you the Imperial desire that careful consideration be taken by studying the internal and external situations more comprehensively and more deeply than ever, regardless of the resolution of September 6th."

They would, of course, study these situations.

Kido was relieved, feeling that "war had been averted" after all. And the Emperor agreed. It paid to talk tough.

"There is a saying, isn't there?" he said to Kido. "You cannot obtain a tiger's cub unless you brave the tiger's den."

But the tiger was not that easily tamed, and it bared its teeth with more ferocity than ever. Kido now saw the navy as the only chance. And so did the Emperor. "As the navy is having great trouble reaching unanimity of opinion," Hirohito said to the Lord Keeper, "I feel as if I should avoid a U.S.-Japanese war, if that is at all possible, but just how, realistically, can I manage it?"

"I don't think it is proper, even after long deliberation," Kido replied, "for the throne to take a step if there is still any shadow of doubt in the Imperial mind. This is especially true on the present occasion because the decision is a unique one of great gravity. So I advise Your Majesty to summon at once the navy minister and the navy chief of staff and ascertain the true feeling in the guts of the navy."

The Emperor agreed and summoned Shimada and Nagano.

Did the navy want war? Hirohito asked.

Yes, the navy wanted war!

The last chance was gone—for Japan, and perhaps for the world. Kido might have avoided war if he had advised the Emperor, who would never act on his own, to break tradition and order the government to make the concessions to the United States necessary to keep the peace. Even Tojo might then have obeyed. But the Lord Keeper didn't have the courage, nor sufficient conviction that a war could end only in disaster for Japan. At least he wouldn't permit himself to nurse this thought.

And so, at an Imperial Conference on December 1, 1941, Hirohito sat silently as Tojo declared that Japan would go to war. Characteristically, Kido now viewed the inevitable with optimism. At dawn on December 8 (Japanese time), as he rode through the streets of sleeping Tokyo toward the palace, he gazed in wonderment at the rising sun. A signal of destiny on this day of the deed. Japanese planes were even now swooping down on the "barbarians" at Pearl Harbor, finally avenging the brave Choshu samurai who had fallen at Shimonoseki. Had not his grandfather helped to create a modern Japan in anticipation of this very moment?

Kido closed his eyes and prayed that the attack would succeed. He envisaged a bright future for Japan. What could be brighter than the rising sun?

Chapter 3

THE
TRAITOR

I

While the Japanese kept their secret until Pearl Harbor was
bombed, the Allies would keep theirs until Hiroshima was
bombed. And no one guarded this secret more avidly than Klaus
Fuchs, a German-born British scientist who had escaped Nazi
terror. On the day of the bomb, he and other top scientists from
Britain were in Los Alamos, New Mexico, lending their talents to
the Manhattan Project. Working alongside American physicists,
Fuchs impressed them not only with his brilliance but also with his
concern about security. Like a jeweler protecting rare stones, he
made sure that at day's end every colleague's documents were
safely under lock and key.

And unless absolutely necessary, he himself would not share
secrets with anyone—except Stalin.

Let Szilard try to save the world with his schemes for deterring
Hitler and building ideal democracies. Fuchs had a better way:
Give Russia the know-how for the bomb.

He was not a Soviet spy for the money; in fact, he was offended
when money was offered him, though on one occasion he would

accept a nominal sum to symbolize his loyalty to the cause. Nor had he been blackmailed into treason. He was a Soviet spy because he wanted to be. And in his enthusiasm, he would sometimes infuriate even the Russians. All right, all right, he had vital information. But deliver it through channels, not to the first Russian you find.

On the eve of Hiroshima, with so much to tell, there was no Russian he could find. For he was penned up, together with thousands of other scientists, technicians, and servicemen, behind the barbed wire of Los Alamos. And though he could occasionally run into Santa Fe, the nearest town, the security rules barred him from going farther without special permission. Fuchs wasn't angry. The camp needed such precautions to make sure the enemy didn't get hold of any secrets. But why didn't the Americans realize that Russia was an *ally*, not an enemy? That it deserved to know the secrets?

Secrets he would continue to spill in another few weeks, on September 19, 1945. A Soviet courier he knew as "Raymond" would be coming to Santa Fe for their second meeting in that town. They had met there in late May—and earlier, several times, in New York, where Fuchs had been working on another phase of the project—but the situation had drastically changed. In May, Fuchs told his contact: The bomb could not be finished in time to be used against the Japanese. The project might even have to be abandoned. But on July 16, he had witnessed a test explosion of the bomb and the boiling white cloud that had risen into the sky had left him "awestricken." He had been wrong. The project was a success, and *he* had contributed to it.

Fuchs had hoped at first that the bomb might be ready for use against Germany—to assure Russia's survival. But with Germany out of the war, the weapon had suddenly become a *threat* to Russia, not a lifesaver. For who could save that country from capitalist blackmail after the war? He was therefore giving the secrets to Stalin so that the USSR would have the bomb, too.

Meanwhile, atomic bombs would destroy whole Japanese cities, and he would attempt to rejoice with his colleagues so they would never suspect his true sentiments. He enjoyed the camp parties, anyway; they made life in Los Alamos quite pleasant despite the enormous pressures of the laboratory. He would drown himself in whiskey or gin, join in the good cheer, lead the conga

line, then sit quietly in a corner, his knees crossed with one foot
twirling in rhythm with the music, chain smoking, utterly sober
and in control of himself—though once he passed out cold behind
the bar.

Yet nothing about Fuchs' appearance, except perhaps his frail,
lithe body, suggested that he might lead a conga line. His serious,
dark eyes peered through thick, horn-rimmed glasses, his huge,
veined forehead bulged beneath a receding hairline, and his weak
chin swooped down into a long tree trunk of a neck. Nor was he
very scintillating in small talk. In fact, he could be as morose as he
was merry and often seemed to cherish solitude. At lunchtime he
would sit alone by a pond outside his building and throw crumbs to
the ducks. One friend called him "Penny in the Slot" Fuchs because of his reticence. A person had to drop a sentence in to get
one out.

But however great were his social shortcomings, everybody
liked Klaus Fuchs, especially the women. As a bachelor with the
perpetually missing button, the spot on the shirt, the slightly lost
air of an innocent who needed the caring support of a female,
Fuchs appealed to the maternal instinct. And he returned the
affection. He was generous and always ready to help others,
whether to sit with the children or to fill out the dinner-guest list,
though the hostess knew she had better stock up with more than
the usual quantity of liquor—which had to be "smuggled" in, since
spirits were officially banned from the camp.

On Christmas, Fuchs would give gifts to the kids, and perhaps
books to their parents, including copies of *I Chose Freedom*, Victor
Kravchenko's anti-Soviet best seller. And anyone who wanted a lift
to town could always get a ride in Fuchs' secondhand, two-seater
Buick (except, of course, when he was meeting his contact),
though the passenger could never count on getting back on time.
If the car broke down, Fuchs, despite his scientific brilliance, seldom knew how to make it go. But no one minded. The biggest
worry was getting back at all. For Fuchs drove with the fury of a
meteor, and, with a schoolboy bravado, especially loved skids that
would test his skill at survival—just as he loved climbing mountains and skiing down dangerous slopes. Once, when a colleague's
wife died in Albuquerque, he lent the man his car to go there to
arrange for the funeral, and then called his friends: Would they
please invite the poor fellow to dinner so he wouldn't be alone for
the next few days?

Yes, good old Klaus—kind, considerate, charmingly adolescent, great with children. . . . Who could imagine that he had betrayed them all? Sometimes, apparently, not even Klaus Fuchs.

II

According to Fuchs, he used his Marxian philosophy to conceal his thoughts, "which had to be separated into two compartments. One side was the man I wanted to be. I could be free and easy and happy with other people without fear of disclosing myself because I knew the other compartment would step in if I reached a danger point. It appeared to me at the time that I had become a free man because I had succeeded in the other compartment in establishing myself completely independent of the surrounding forces of society. Looking back now, the best way is to call it controlled schizophrenia."

Whatever label he gave his mental state, Fuchs had simply done what many husbands and wives do when they cheat on their spouses—live a double life, often without too much inner friction, by dividing their minds into two compartments. Fuchs managed to make his compartments airtight; he had no qualms of conscience at all. Why should he, when he was only *obeying* his conscience? He was the monstrous product of two opposing influences, each anathema to the other, that, when combined, exploded with all the destructiveness of a chemical mixture that a madman might concoct. He had blended the absolute principles of God and communism, and emerging from the spiritual test tube was a new god—himself. He thus owed obedience to no one, just to his own conscience. The problem was that his own conscience was not really his own, but the veiled captive of communism. God was gone.

Yet Fuchs had grown up with God, feeling His guiding hand from the moment he was born in the German village of Russelsheim in 1911. His singleminded father, Emil, was a Lutheran pastor who tramped from town to town preaching that "behind all fate of individuals and peoples stands the eternal creative power. It leads everything to its goal." Emil Fuchs followed faithfully and taught his children to do the same—Klaus, his elder son Gerhardt, and his daughters Kristel and Elizabeth.

But not everybody thought Emil Fuchs knew the way. For he preached hope to the impoverished, peace to the politicians, and generosity to the people of every religion and class, whom he regularly invited to his home. The divine path, he told all, led through a garden of socialistic justice and undiluted pacifism. To the German religious establishment, Fuchs was abandoning not only its conservative traditions, but even Jesus Christ. The reverend, however, defied such criticism and in the 1920s helped to form a group of Religious Socialists, then became a Quaker and the first pastor to join the Social Democratic Party.

At home he would teach his children: Do whatever you consider right in the eyes of God regardless of the consequences. If God was alive in a person's soul, how could that person take the wrong path? But in the political and economic chaos of the 1920s, which saw the ruin of the middle classes, despairing citizens of the German Socialist Weimar Republic cared more about the contents of their stomachs than of their souls, and the students in particular were in no mood to ponder God's will. In their desperation, however, they did ponder the cries of extremist politicians on the right and left, especially the Nazis and the Communists, who promised them grandiose solutions not only to their own problems but to the problems of the world, soothing panaceas that served as rationale for interpreting any political situation anywhere, and even personal conflicts.

But if many students rebelled against the moderate if paralyzed Weimar government, Klaus Fuchs did not. True to his father's creed, he stood up to the rebels in his high-school class, refusing to tear off his Weimar badge even at the price of ostracism. And when he enrolled in the university at Leipzig, he joined the Social Democratic Party, as his father had done. But as the pressure grew and violence racked the campus, he began to use his father's logic to alter his own path. Since he had been taught to do what he believed was right in the eyes of God, he decided that God would want him to resist the Nazis. So he broke with his father's pacifism and joined the Reichsbanner, a semimilitary group that stood ready to defend the Social Democrats if they were attacked.

Soon, as Nazi brutality continued to spread, Klaus began to wonder why God did not stop it. After transferring to the university at Kiel, he felt that he must help God out. Passive defense was not enough. He would not join the Communists, who were always ready for a brawl; he still couldn't swallow their atheism, regimentation, and bitter assaults on the Social Democrats, who, they seemed to find, were more of a threat to their ambitions than were the Nazis. But he compromised. He joined, and soon led, a mixed group of dissident Social Democrats and Communists.

And now Fuchs decided to act alone, without God. How could one fight the Nazis with a God Who didn't act? He himself would judge what was right and what was wrong. And he proceeded to doublecross the Nazis—pretending that his group would cooperate with them in an illegal strike, then exposing their plan at the last minute. Was not deception justified against so brutal an enemy? The Communists commended him. That's what they had been saying all along. It was all right to deceive the enemy— whether a Nazi or any other foe of communism. That is, if he wanted to save the world. Was God, if He existed at all, even trying to save it?

Fuchs' dilemma was finally solved, it seems, during the elections of June 1932. The Social Democrats agreed to back the rightist but non-Fascist candidate for President, Paul von Hindenburg, in order not to split the anti-Nazi vote and permit Adolf Hitler to slither into power. The Communists had something else in mind. Why *not* let Hitler slither into power? He would certainly be ousted soon, and in the confusion *they* could slither into power. But they camouflaged this devious maneuver. No decent leftist would dream of backing a rightist candidate, they cried. Instead, leftists should form a united front against all rightists, Nazi or otherwise—the very united front they had been resisting with cries that the Social Democrats were weak and cowardly.

Fuchs' hatred of the Nazis apparently blinded him to the Communist tactic. Support a rightist? His conscience, which had replaced his God, rebelled. He spoke at a Communist rally and was promptly expelled from the Social Democratic Party. Fuchs now wavered precariously at the edge of a gaping moral chasm from which there would be no escape. The Nazis pushed him over the edge one day when they pushed him into the river, after mercilessly beating him up. He joined the Communist Party and started on the road that would lead to treason against the Western Allies.

III

Hitler's rise to power in 1933 shortened the road. With thousands arrested and thrown into concentration camps, the Fuchs family awaited its fate. Even before the Nazis took over, Klaus' mother apparently went insane and committed suicide. His father, refusing to renounce his socialist beliefs, lost his professorship at Kiel and languished for nine months in a concentration camp. His sister Elizabeth, like his mother, went mad, jumping to her death from a moving train after learning that her husband was being sought by the Nazis. Gerhardt, now a Communist, too, had developed tuberculosis and fled to Switzerland. And Klaus went into hiding with his mistress, also a party member, until party leaders ordered him to go abroad and prepare himself for the day when he would return to help build a Communist Germany. Fuchs would have liked to stay in Germany to continue the struggle and be near his girl friend, who was deeply unhappy about the order. And he felt that he was free to do so. But his conscience, as usual, overruled any inclination to disobey party instructions.

"Now, for the first time," Fuchs would say later, "man understands the historical forces and he is able to control them, and therefore for the first time he will be really free. I carried this idea over into the personal sphere and believed that I could understand myself and that I could make myself into what I should be."

Thus, he still considered himself to be a free man—as his father taught him to be. In fact, a freer man now. Even while worshiping at the Soviet altar, he reveled in the power he wielded as his own god.

For the next few years, Fuchs studied in England, trying to mold himself into what he should be—a valuable servant of the communism he rationalized was freedom. With financial help from charitable institutions, he received his doctorate in physics and mathematics in 1937, then a doctorate in science from Edinburgh University two years later. At home he studied Marx and read the newspapers, hoping to read one day that Britain had declared war on the Nazis. Then the time would soon come when he could go home and fulfil his destiny. And one day he did read that Britain was at war, only to find that his destiny would take a devious turn. He and other German refugees were interned in May 1940 and whisked to a camp in Quebec, Canada.

Later Fuchs would say that he understood the need for internment—the British, after all, could not risk trusting any German. He was not offended. Curiously, many British were, questioning the need for such blanket cruelty, even in wartime. But to Fuchs, the British government acted efficiently in its own interest, whatever pain it caused, acting as any Communist government would have done. In the future, he, too, would act efficiently in *his* own interest, and he hoped that his democratic friends, if they found out, would be just as understanding.

IV

Many scientists, holding Fuchs and his work in high esteem, pressed vigorously for his release, and finally, in January 1941, he was set free. He returned to his laboratory at Edinburgh University but didn't stay long. To his joyous surprise, he was offered a job at Birmingham University by nuclear physicist Rudolf Peierls, who was secretly conducting research on the atomic bomb.

Peierls, a German refugee like Fuchs, had been searching for a good assistant, but almost all qualified British scientists were working on radar or other "more urgent" wartime projects, from which foreigners like himself were banned. He thus combed the refugee ranks for the right man. Peierls found Fuchs, who, though not very experienced, had been an exceptional student; he would have to do. Fuchs did very well indeed—so well that volumes of classified information soon piled up on his desk. He had, in fact, been given top security clearance, though at first the specific purpose of his work was not revealed to him.

True, the Nazis had reported shortly after Fuchs first arrived in England that he was a Communist, but they were calling almost all German refugees Communists. Besides, Peierls and his motherly wife, who took this lonely, impoverished lad into their home, found him kind, shy, and terribly fond of children and dogs. Hardly the Communist type. Anyway, no Communist would betray secrets to the Nazis. Perhaps to the Russians, but Russia *was*, after all, an ally and its knowledge, even if potentially dangerous, wouldn't affect Britain's ability to survive the Nazi threat. And Britain at this time thought only of survival.

Fuchs thus suddenly found himself thrust into a position of enormous power. Some of the most important technical information in history would now go through his hands—and into Stalin's. He could play a major role in saving the world by helping to Sovietize it, or at least by keeping the Western Alliance from exploiting it. Nor would his conscience rebel. For Germany had invaded Russia a short time earlier, and the democracies, it seemed to Fuchs, were deliberately letting the two countries fight to the death. They were opportunists who would permit Russia to die before it could fulfil its great liberating mission.

Fuchs conceded that Russia had made mistakes. For example, the pact that Stalin had made with Hitler before the Führer betrayed him. Russia's errors, however, were those of a desperate parent trying in any way to save her children. Still, he would criticize Russia occasionally, if only to confirm that he was his own master. But whatever Russia's errors, it was his duty to help that country, and thus mankind, in any way he could. The Russians, he was sure, would not be able to build an atomic bomb in time to use it in the war, but they might be able to build one in time to keep the Western powers from threatening them with it after the war.

V

Actually, Russian scientists had been assiduously probing the atom for several years, and Moscow now was getting not only the West's atomic secrets clandestinely but its raw material for the bomb legitimately. The Russians put uranium ore low on the list of things it requested from the United States under the Lend-Lease program, hoping that the Americans would not carefully check individual items. When this ploy failed, they brazenly insisted on "prompt delivery." The Americans refused, but the Russians were undiscouraged. They bought some ore from private U.S. and Canadian firms after General Groves, counting on Russian ignorance of the importance of the ore, recommended that Washington issue an export license to them "rather than be pointing a finger at the material if the license was refused." American supplies were finally cut off, but Canadian firms sold thousands of pounds more.

Originally, Russia had launched an atomic research program not only to meet defense needs but to boost Soviet prestige. Stalin would prove to the West that the USSR was no longer a backward country of creaking oxcarts and primitive workshops. By 1930, two nuclear research centers were operating in Leningrad and one in Kharkov. And in 1939, a year before Roosevelt set up a Uranium Committee, Stalin created a similar organ, and his researchers found that a bomb could be built with only a few kilograms of U^{235}. When World War II broke out that year, Lavrenti Beria became head of the NKVD security services and took over all Soviet war production, including nuclear research, and Russia's atomic bomb project modestly began. In April 1942, at a meeting with scientists and NKVD officers at Volynskoye, near Moscow, Stalin ordered a full-fledged drive to build a bomb, and scientist Igor Kurchatov was appointed "scientific manager." Among the men he managed were important captured German scientists.

Meanwhile, geologists sifted the sands of Soviet Central Asia searching for uranium, even checking the drinking habits of camels, which, according to legend, sought wells with "life water" that might have been radioactive. Finally, in the mid-1940s, uranium deposits would be found in the Ural, Altai, and Turkestan regions—probably the greatest breakthrough in the Soviet program.

America was entirely unaware of Russia's growing nuclear program, though Russia was up to the minute on America's. Beria informed Stalin in 1942, almost before General Groves could rasp his first whipcracking command, that the U.S. Army had set up the Manhattan Project. And not surprisingly, for, as a British nuclear physicist, Klaus Fuchs knew what his American colleagues were doing.

It was in late 1941 that Fuchs, after consulting his conscience again, went to seek a Soviet contact. Through another German Communist refugee, he soon found one—Simon Kremer, secretary to the Soviet military attaché in London, a man he knew only as "Alexander." Fuchs passed on information to him the first time they met, in a private house near London's Hyde Park, but he apparently began to worry that Alexander might not be the man he claimed to be. So he strode into the Soviet Embassy and asked about him, heedlessly violating a cardinal rule of espionage. He would serve the Russians, yes, but on his own terms; his conscience was his only master. And the Russians, overwhelmed by the extraordinary nature of his service, apparently did not complain. Let Fuchs think he was a free man.

After meeting with Alexander several more times, Fuchs was given a new contact, a woman who agreed to meet him near Birmingham, where he worked. Again Fuchs served on his own terms, at his own convenience. But he served well. He gave the Russians mathematical data on, among other things, the gaseous diffusion process for separating U^{235} from U^{238}. And he did so with pride. Much of the data was based on his own calculations. In fact, he was so busy calculating that he could barely fit these meetings into his schedule.

Fuchs did, however, find time to attend naturalization hearings on August 1942 and swear "by Almighty God" that he would be faithful to his newly adopted country. Having rejected Almighty God, he didn't even have to refer to his conscience on this hallowed occasion, though he did leave himself free, in his words, to "act in accordance with my conscience should circumstances arise in the country comparable to those which existed in Germany in 1932."

Naturally, any danger to Russia, the hope of mankind, would fit into the circumstances.

VI

If Klaus Fuchs was proud of his work in the Birmingham laboratory, so was his boss, Rudolf Peierls, who had hired him. It was thus with great satisfaction that one day in late 1943 Peierls informed his protégé that the two of them, along with several other British scientists, would shortly sail to the United States to carry on their work on the gaseous diffusion process. Peierls had insisted that Fuchs go with him, and the young man was delighted. Another stroke of luck! First he was offered the job in British nuclear research, and now he would be able to learn America's atomic secrets as well. How fortunate that the two Western democracies were cooperating on the atomic bomb.

Such cooperation hadn't come easily. Each nation wanted its own bomb. While Washington set up atomic installations, London formed a scientific group, code-named the MAUD Committee, to supervise atomic energy research under G. P. Thomson, professor of physics at Imperial College, London. It was only after the British had surged to the fore in 1941 that Roosevelt wrote Churchill suggesting that the Thomson and Bush committees coordinate their activities.

Pinched for money and fearful that Hitler's missiles would destroy any nuclear plants they might build, the British agreed, even though they would have preferred going it alone so their country could assure itself a top niche in Europe's power structure after the war. But after less than a year of sharing secrets, the Americans, especially Bush and Conant, had second thoughts. With research formulas ready for conversion into bombs, the United States no longer needed anybody's help. Nor did the Americans desire a deal for full nuclear cooperation in wartime. It would spill over into peacetime and permanently entangle America's foreign policy with Britain's. Besides, why increase the risk of leaking secrets to the enemy or potential enemy, not to mention British businessmen who would compete with Americans in the industrial use of nuclear energy after the war? How could nuclear information help the British war effort anyway? Thus, on January 13, 1943, the British were politely told that henceforth they—and the Canadians—could have such information only if they could show how it would help win the war.

Churchill was rabid. Had not Roosevelt proposed cooperation in the first place? Did America want to build an atomic bomb as quickly as possible—or not? Churchill struck a delicate American nerve. For the United States knew it would lose invaluable British and Canadian scientific help with its new policy, and this loss would inevitably mean a slowup in progress, which, in turn, could mean that Germany might win the atomic race—and the war. But as American leaders reflected for the first time on the potential peacetime power of the atom, they found irresistible appeal in the prospect of a postwar monopoly on atomic energy that would keep the Russians in their place militarily and the British in theirs commercially.

However, in May 1943, Churchill stormed into Washington armed with irresistible arguments. The United States would stand to lose, he told Roosevelt, if Britain had to divert men and materials from other war projects to keep up with the American atomic program—and if Russia controlled postwar Europe because Britain didn't have the power to resist it. Roosevelt reflected on these arguments. He had followed his advisers' counsel until now, but what did they understand of the political realities that would shape the future? On the other hand, Churchill's views melded with his own crystallizing vision of that future. A united world, he now felt, might not be possible after all, however tempting the idea. How could he force Russia to withdraw from the areas it overran in Europe and perhaps parts of Asia? As the President would tell a colleague in 1944:

"We have no idea as yet what [the Russians] have in mind, but we have to remember that in their occupied territory they will do more or less what they wish. We cannot afford to get into a position of merely recording protests on our part unless there is some chance of some of the protests being heeded."

Thus, the prospect was for a divided world, not a united one, though he could not tell this to his people—or even to his advisers, who might leak the information to them. No, there could not be a close Big Three relationship after the war similar to the wartime alliance. Instead, he began to view the postwar geopolitical structure as based on spheres of influence that would cooperate in maintaining a balance of power. But for the democratic world to offset Russian power, Britain, as Churchill pointed out, would have to be strong. And to be strong after so draining a war, it would have to keep a few atomic bombs in its diplomatic attic.

Thus, on August 19, at an Anglo-American summit conference in Quebec, Roosevelt and Churchill signed a secret accord. They would share nuclear data and work together under a Combined Policy Committee.

Unknown to the two leaders, Stalin would join in the sharing plan. For in November 1943, Klaus Fuchs, his faithful servant, stepped aboard a troopship in Liverpool bound for the United States, where he would once again practice what his father preached, if without any meddling by God.

Chapter 4

THE
ENFORCER

I

Like Klaus Fuchs, Secretary of War Henry L. Stimson wanted a more nearly perfect world, but he would never betray people to get it—though he might sacrifice some. He cared about people. He was kind to his servants, subordinates, and neighbors, who every Thanksgiving were invited to Highhold, his sprawling, old-fashioned country estate in Long Island, for a glorious day of games and horse racing. Stimson even felt sympathy for the Japanese whose cities were being turned into infernos, cautioning the air force to attack only military targets where possible. And as the man in charge of the atomic bomb, he tried his best to avoid a nuclear holocaust. But as Kido accepted the inevitable when he couldn't prevent war, so did Stimson when he couldn't stop the bomb.

Yes, Hiroshima would have to be sacrificed in order to save American lives—and values. From the ashes a new, wiser world would emerge, wise enough, he hoped, never to use the bomb again.

Few people doubted the wisdom of Stimson himself. In his 78 years he had served six presidents with distinction. And though he wasn't the type to be voted into office—he flashed neither FDR's ivory smile nor Truman's folksy wit—his reserved manner and distinguished appearance made people instinctively trust him. He was square-shouldered and straight, as might be expected of an outdoor man who had spent almost every vacation for a quarter of a century exploring the wilds of the Rocky Mountains or Canada. He had short grayish hair and bangs, with a neatly cropped mustache to match. And he almost always wore a starched collar and a heavy gold watch chain across his high-buttoned vest. He was the perfect patrician gentleman, even down to his passion for fox hunting and deck tennis.

Yet it was not only Stimson's elegance that bred trust. His cool surface cloaked a crusader's soul, which was reflected in his intense blue-gray eyes and in his fiery words that echoed across the seas. He was the respected, no-nonsense schoolmaster of the world who would punish wayward nations until they learned to obey the law. But if people trusted Stimson, it was at least in part because he trusted them. As Secretary of State under President Herbert Hoover, he even stopped secret code-breaking operations that monitored messages between foreign embassies in Washington and their governments because "gentlemen do not read each other's mail."

"The chief lesson I have learned in a long life," he would tell President Truman, "is that the only way to make man trustworthy is to trust him."

Stimson often came to Highhold from Washington, especially when he was tired or depressed. Here, at the peak of a grassy hill, he would gaze down on both the ocean and the Sound and, in silent meditation, free himself for a few hours or days from the terrible burdens of his job. But on the day of the bomb, as he awaited word that the sacrifice had been made, even this misty scene of peace could not have cheered him. However justified, the killing of 100,000 people at a blow was not something to gladden the heart, certainly not that of a humanitarian like Henry Stimson. In any case, his heart was weak, and he was in no condition for even a garden stroll. After flying back from the Potsdam Conference a few days earlier, he was "nearing the limits of his strength."

Nevertheless, thoughts of Potsdam helped to revive him. He could not forget the electric moment at the conference when he opened the cable from Washington: The test explosion of the atomic bomb on July 16, 1945, was a triumph! It was the moment he knew that his country was invincible, that World War II was about to end, that Russia, in the hope of sharing atomic secrets, might now hesitate to devour Eastern Europe and chunks of Asia. But it hadn't been easy helping President Truman deal with political masters like Stalin and Churchill in deciding how to wind up the war with Japan and draw up a map of the postwar world.

If Stimson's policies and advice often seemed fickle and inconsistent, it was not surprising. Coming from a long line of soldiers, lawyers, and clergymen, the Secretary had the traits necessary to succeed in all three callings, traits that constantly struggled for predominance and gave his policies a contradictory texture. He condemned Woodrow Wilson's plan for a League of Nations, then embraced the League when it was formed; he crusaded against militarism abroad, but fought for a peacetime military draft at home; he blasted the use of force, but would use force to impose peace; he urged the dictators to free their people, but sided with colonialism as the white man's burden and duty.

And naturally, since atomic policy was a matter of life and death for the world, the struggle within Stimson was all the more intense when he debated with himself how and whether to use the bomb. In the end, he issued the order to drop it on Hiroshima with a soldier's cold-bloodedness, he justified it with a lawyer's rationale, and he lamented it with a clergyman's compassion.

But if Stimson was an intellectual chameleon, whatever his view at a particular moment he backed it with all his power—political, or military—convinced that it alone would lead to human progress, if not survival. He changed colors thoughtfully in the light of new circumstances and after examining every shred of evidence, as prescribed by his lawyer's code. And he wasn't afraid of getting into political trouble by changing his mind or trying to change a superior's, even though he craved the approval of those in authority.

Stimson had learned at an early age how to oppose someone whose approval he wanted without damaging the relationship. He had managed, for example, to finally win his father's blessing for his marriage, though the old man had vigorously opposed the match because the bride came from a more common stock than the Stimsons.

II

The Stimson stock, which helped to form the character of the man who gave the order to drop the atomic bomb, had deep military roots. The Secretary's forbears on both sides, migrants from old England to New England in the seventeenth century, fought in every American war, and Stimson himself, though already 30, enlisted in the National Guard during the Spanish-American War. At the same time, he gained a specialized knowledge of the army and the War Department from Secretary of War Elihu Root, whose law firm he joined on passing the bar. And although Stimson became Secretary of War himself under President Howard Taft, he did not hesitate, after leaving the post, to rush off to the front when America entered World War I in 1917. As a colonel, he commanded an artillery regiment and would always savor his glorious army experiences.

However, the honor and patriotism implied in army duty did not alone drive Stimson. Doing "good" for people was his prime motivation, which had its roots in his childhood—an unhappy one after the age of 9 when his mother died and he went to live with his grandparents. After being graduated from Phillips Academy at Andover and then from Yale, he even considered becoming a clergyman like his uncle, who deeply influenced him.

But Stimson's father, a wealthy surgeon in New York, recognized his son's remarkable ability to focus on a problem until it was solved, and encouraged him to be a lawyer. And the young man, constantly seeking his father's affection, entered Harvard Law School. But though, after graduation, he would develop into a first-class lawyer under Root's paternalistic tutelage and would look upon his distinguished mentor with awe, he still longed to work not simply for money but for good causes. He thus began dabbling in New York Republican reform politics and shortly found himself, with Root's help, United States Attorney for the Southern District of New York.

President Theodore Roosevelt then discovered him. One day, while riding a horse in Washington's Rock Creek Park, Stimson saw Roosevelt and Root on the other side of the creek.

"Come on over," Root called. "The President of the United States through the Secretary of War orders you to report immediately."

Stimson spurred his horse into the turbulent stream and barely managed to reach the other side. The President greeted him with a huge smile.

"I didn't think you'd be so foolish," he said. "But I'm delighted."

So delighted by such pluck and compliance that in 1910 he chose Stimson to run for governor of New York. Stimson lost and never ran for public office again, but his attempts to reform government only whetted his desire to "do good" for people. In 1927, President Calvin Coolidge sent Stimson down to Nicaragua to quell a bloody revolution there and he sat with the rebel chieftain in a jungle hut until he finally intimidated him into signing a peace accord. Soon he was down in the tropics again, this time as governor general in the Philippines, where he fought against independence. The Filipinos weren't ready for self-government, he said like a parent admonishing a wayward child. They would be easy prey for political extremists or an aggressive neighbor, and needed the United States to keep the peace in which democracy could grow. He was thinking only of *their* good.

In 1929, when President Herbert Hoover named him Secretary of State, Stimson tried again to force people to be peaceful and law-abiding. As Japanese troops marched into Manchuria in 1931, he cried: A breach of treaty! An unlawful act! Without backing from the President or the American public, he pushed the League of Nations to condemn Japan as if he were in a county courtroom demanding punishment for someone accused of trespassing on private property. Undiplomatically, he brandished an unloaded pistol, and when the League supported his view, Japan simply dug more deeply into Manchurian soil. But Stimson was impatient with lawbreakers.

And he grew ever more impatient as the 1930s unfolded, even after he went out of office with President Hoover. Stop shipping oil and scrap iron to Japan! he cried. Build up an army strong enough to meet the Nazi threat! he roared. When World War II broke out in 1939, he felt relieved.

"It seemed to mark the end of the hopeless years of concession and appeasement," he rejoiced.

And his cries grew even more shrill: Repeal the Neutrality Act! Don't let Britain go down!

Finally, someone listened. On June 19, 1940, another Roosevelt called him. Would Stimson please be his Secretary of War? Stimson was astonished. He was 73. He was a Republican.

He hated the New Deal. But he loved his country. And its destiny was to create and lead a new world, even if on the ruins of the old. Someone had to advise the President how to do it. And so he accepted, though he knew his party would brand him a "renegade."

The question now was how to get the United States into the war so that it could fulfil its destiny. Stimson pushed for Lend-Lease to Britain and urged the Cabinet to "forcibly stop the German submarines by our intervention." He pressed the President to ask Congress for a declaration of war, assuring him that Americans would favor a first strike against Japan. He sent poison gas to the Philippines so that American troops based there could, if necessary, use it against the Japanese.

Finally, Stimson got his wish, if at a high price. At about 2 P.M. on December 7, 1941, he was having lunch when President Franklin D. Roosevelt called him.

"They have attacked Hawaii!" the President cried. "They are now bombing Hawaii!"

Well, Stimson thought to himself, that was an excitement indeed.

And with remarkable calm, he returned to finish his lunch.

The Japanese had fired the first shot, as Stimson had hoped. And even though the danger to America was much greater than he might have wished, the country could finally go about the business of getting rid of the evil bandit governments and building a world ruled by law. As he began rearming America, he watched with deep satisfaction as planes, tanks, and guns rolled off jammed assembly lines. And as some of the world's greatest scientists worked on the most powerful weapon of all—the atomic bomb. . . .

III

Actually, not many top scientists were working on the bomb before Pearl Harbor. Leo Szilard and Enrico Fermi, however, were among the few, and as war neared they worked together once more at Columbia under the new government-sponsored program. Fermi finally realized that Szilard was probably right after all about graphite; it could be the catalyst that would trigger a chain reaction. But if the two men now had financing, they found themselves victimized by government bureaucracy, inefficiency, and sheer lack of enthusiasm. When Szilard complained to the Bureau of Standards that the uranium metal and graphite it supplied were not pure enough for necessary experiments, the bureau snorted that he was simply quibbling and should be satisfied with what he got.

At the same time, the government continued to discriminate against scientists who were not "Americans of long standing." Thus, a pure-blooded American scientist like Harold Urey, who was working at Columbia on the separation of U^{235}, was ordered not to reveal the results of his research to Szilard and Fermi, who were doing related work on the nuclear properties of uranium. Szilard's fury was exceeded only by his sense of irony.

"While up to this point," he said, "we had suffered from the lack of official recognition, during this period we were suffering from *having* official recognition."

As a result, foreign scientists Peierls and Frisch, barred from "important" war work in Britain but allowed to dabble in nuclear physics, were the first to find that it was possible to separate a sufficient quantity of U^{235} to make atomic bombs.

The American government, learning this from the British in the summer of 1941, finally saw a point to all the research on a chain reaction it had only halfheartedly sanctioned. The United States could really build an atomic bomb! What a shame the British had discovered this first. And it was shame, indeed, that many felt when Marcus Oliphant, a leading Australian physicist working in Britain, visited the United States and sneered at its uranium program. If the embarrassed bureaucrats had only reluctantly listened to Szilard, whom they regarded as an eccentric pest, they listened with great care to Oliphant, who, after all, was speaking from a tower of triumph.

Now driven by pride and promise, Washington expanded the chain reaction project, moving it in early 1942 from Columbia to the University of Chicago and placing it under the supervision of Arthur H. Compton, chairman of that university's physics department, a Nobel Prize winner, and an "American of long standing." But Szilard was still not satisfied. In a letter to Vannevar Bush on May 26, 1942, he complained about a new division of authority "along the wrong lines" that was slowing up work, and declared in his frustration:

"In 1939 the Government of the United States was given a

unique opportunity by Providence; this opportunity was lost. Nobody can tell now whether we shall be ready before German bombs wipe out American cities. Such scanty information as we have about work in Germany is not reassuring and all one can say with certainty is that we could move at least twice as fast if our difficulties were eliminated."

Like a relentless bee, Szilard kept stinging away until Bush agreed to see him on June 20. Szilard then echoed orally what he had written, reminding Bush that the world's survival could hinge on his decisions. Bush, a product of science himself, wanted to give the scientists a role in running the project, but he had other projects, too. He couldn't, at this uncertain stage, bless one with all his attention. What would happen if it failed?

Szilard thus returned to Chicago without any honey and continued to buzz around Compton, who, perhaps in part to placate his tormentor, had wired Vice-President Henry Wallace on June 20, the day Szilard spoke with Bush:

"Have strong evidence Germans will have this weapon ready for use in 1943. If we are not similarly ready this would mean disaster. Can see no safety from this threat short of all-out effort to develop countermeasures. Please check with Bush to ensure making such effort possible."

The "strong evidence" was apparently based on the knowledge that Hitler had banned the export of uranium ore from the mines he controlled in Czechoslovakia, and on Szilard's appraisal of German scientific ability and aggressiveness.

Compton, an impressive-looking man at 50, with his thick, dark mustache, jutting chin, and solid build that served him well when he played college football, had a crisp, authoritative manner. But mellowing it was an extraordinary patience and an almost exaggerated consideration for others, nurtured perhaps by his rural and religious upbringing. His father was both a Presbyterian minister and a professor of philosophy at Wooster College in Ohio, and his older brother Karl, who inspired him to pursue physics, was president of MIT. Viewing science as a "glimpse of God's purpose in nature," he often carried a Bible to meetings and read aloud appropriate passages from it. He felt that science should be as separate from politics as politics should be from religion. He therefore placed great trust in the politicians and was reluctant to second-guess them in matters they better understood. After all, what did a simple Middle American from Ohio, even a Nobel Prize winner, know about the intricacies of running a war or setting up a peace?

That, Compton felt, was the trouble with Szilard. He tried to mix science and politics. When he wanted money for experiments, did he go to the foundations like any American scientist would? No, he thought he was back in Europe where the government was the patron of science. First, he clamored for Washington to finance and build an atomic bomb. When he had his way, he complained about the way Washington was doing it. Compton's patience had finally worn thin. How could he manage an organization with Szilard continually carping about it, and Washington continually carping about Szilard? Compton summoned Szilard on October 26, 1942, and gave him the news:

He must leave Chicago within forty-eight hours! He would be given work elsewhere.

Szilard was unperturbed. He wasn't even surprised. Yes, he would leave, but he wouldn't work elsewhere. Here is where he could do the most good. In order to live, of course, he would need adequate royalties from the government for use of his inventions relating to the chain reaction.

Compton was silent, his eyes no longer demanding. The government, he knew, wanted the rights to these inventions, but not the obligation of paying for them. Besides, as he had already written to an official in Washington after being pressured to oust Szilard or limit his activities, Szilard "is extensively informed with regard to the details of our project. . . . If dropped . . . he would have reason to be so dissatisfied that his loyalty to the country might be shaken." Was it not better to have a potential "traitor" inside the project than outside? The project, ironically, that had sprung from the same impetuosity now seen as hindering it.

In any case, Szilard had a great mind, Compton conceded, and he could be useful despite his agitation. Szilard was removed from the payroll for a while—though he continued to work—but was soon put back, to his relief. It was much easier saving the world with his stomach full—especially full of those delicious hors d'oeuvres.

Gradually, the "Metallurgical Laboratory" at Chicago began fitting Szilard's image of what it should be, thanks in large measure to his carping. Pure uranium dribbled in and high-quality graphite blackened the hands of men bursting with new spirit. They would build history's first nuclear reactor, which they called a "pile," on an indoor squash court beneath the stands of the university's old Stagg Field football stadium, despite the danger that potentially radioactive material might possibly poison the city of Chicago. Compton assumed the responsibility without conferring with Robert M. Hutchins, president of the university, fearing he might veto the experiment on the university grounds.

Enrico Fermi would direct the project, and this was all right with Szilard, whose idea of using graphite—against Fermi's better judgment—had made this experiment possible. He had shown the way, and now, when he wasn't scampering from office to office demanding more supplies and less bureaucratic tyranny, he was, as head of the Technological Division at Chicago, planning to use the reactor for the large-scale production of plutonium, a new radioactive metallic element that emerged from fission and could replace uranium in the making of the bomb. The idea was to transmute U^{238} into plutonium by chemical means. This would be easier than isolating the rare U^{235} by physical means. Szilard also helped to clear up major problems holding up progress on the reactor, but he left the mundane details to others. And the glory, too, if glory there was in creating a monster that could devour mankind.

If a scientist was distinguished and had no axes to grind, Szilard felt, his ego should be satisfied enough. Besides, glory did not always encourage the dispassion required of a searcher for truth. Szilard joked years later that he would like to have named after him some mountain—"on the back side of the moon." And he feigned regret that he hadn't won the Nobel Prize for Peace for *failing* to make a chain reaction in the early 1930s. If he had succeeded, Hitler would probably have had the atomic bomb in time for World War II!

IV

Secretary Stimson had learned of the bomb only early in October 1941 when Roosevelt named him a member of a Top Policy Group, which also included Wallace, Bush, Conant, and General George C. Marshall, army chief of staff. They would keep the

President's ear tuned to all that was happening in the nuclear arena with the help of a new Atomic Energy Executive Committee that was attached to Bush's organization and supervised by Conant. It was apparently not until December 16, at a "particularly important meeting" with Bush and Wallace, that Stimson learned the full details of "certain experiments" that, he reports in his diary, could lead to a "diabolical" new invention.

The Secretary was elated by the possibilities of making an atomic bomb, but he was also worried. What if the enemy built one first? Then all the planes, tanks, and guns that his factories were grinding out would be worthless. He felt personally slighted, too. Since he was Secretary of War, shouldn't Roosevelt have first come to him when he learned that such a weapon might be feasible? Instead, he had been told only just before Pearl Harbor. Did the President think that stories of a possible bomb were too far-fetched to bother him with—or that they were too important to be shared with him? Too important for the man who would have to use this terrible weapon?

Stimson's spirits rose, however, when, in September 1942, with giant atomic factories and laboratories about to mushroom, the War Department was given the responsibility for building the bomb. Stimson thus blossomed into the President's senior adviser on atomic energy. But even with his new power, he was chagrined. For Bush and Conant spent more time in the Oval Office talking to Roosevelt about atomic matters than he did, since the President seemed mainly interested in the technical side of the program. Roosevelt consulted with no one about how and if the bomb should be used or about how it might be controlled after the war. So Stimson, despite his top role, was still largely frozen out of atomic policy and would not even be told about some of the President's nuclear negotiations with Prime Minister Churchill in 1943.

Not surprisingly, therefore, Stimson until late in the war confined most of his thinking on the bomb to its military use during the war. He launched the Manhattan Project, the most important construction effort ever undertaken, and ordered General Groves, its chief, to produce an atomic bomb at almost any cost. The two men understood each other. Though Roosevelt originally decided to build the bomb simply to deter Hitler from using one first, Stimson and Groves now thought of destroying enemy cities.

As Stimson would explain after the war, the bomb was a "great new instrument for shortening the war and minimizing destruction," and the United States must "be the first to produce an atomic weapon and *use* it." It was, after all, "as legitimate as any other of the deadly explosive weapons of modern war. . . . The entire purpose [of the atomic program] was the production of a military weapon; on no other ground could the wartime expenditure of so much time and money have been justified."

Groves agreed. As he would put it:

"When we first began to develop atomic energy, the United States was in no way committed to employ atomic weapons against any other power. With the activation of the Manhattan Project, however, the situation began to change. . . . As time went on, and as we poured more and more money and effort into the project, the government became increasingly committed to the ultimate use of the bomb, and while it has often been said that we undertook development of this terrible weapon so that Hitler would not get it first, the fact remains that the original decision to make the project an *all-out* effort was based upon using it to end the war."

Thus, to justify the expenditure of so much time and money, the bomb would be used. This "decision" was perhaps instinctive to two old soldiers like Stimson and Groves. To them, as to most soldiers, the purpose of a military weapon was to use it in war. Later in the war, however, the clergyman's conscience and the lawyer's logic emerged in Stimson and would compete with the soldier's instinct in the struggle to determine American atomic policy before and after the fighting ended. Meanwhile, time was running short because the German scientists were also hard at work, and money, needed to buy time, was running low because costs had soared so high.

V

Getting the money was especially difficult because of the need for secrecy. With the fate of mankind at stake, the Manhattan Project had to be the best-kept secret in history. A secret kept not only from the enemy but from an ally—Russia. At least until after the war when Stimson would share some nonmilitary atomic data with Stalin in exchange for basic reforms inside Russia's borders and civilized behavior outside. If Stalin were to learn the secrets during the war, what bargaining power would America have after the war? And of course, if he learned too much, he could build his own bomb.

But how could ever larger sums of money be wrenched from Congress without having to spill all to talkative congressmen? Some were already beginning to ask questions about the sums they had approved so far for "secret projects." Stimson grew obsessed with the problem of secrecy, especially when Congressman Albert J. Engel demanded information on how money was being spent on the gaseous diffusion plant in Oak Ridge, Tennessee.

According to General Groves, Stimson was so troubled by this demand that when William Bundy, his devoted special assistant, disagreed with the general's view about how to respond, Stimson "blew up and in quite profane language told Bundy he was not interested in his ideas . . . and that [he] should get out of the room."

And then there was the senator from Missouri, Harry S Truman. Head of the Truman Committee, which investigated military misuse of funds, the senator insisted in 1943 on looking into a "questionable" project at Hanford, Washington.

Stimson refused. "Now that's a matter," he told Truman, "which I know all about personally, and I am one of the group of two or three men in the whole world who know about it."

"I see."

"It's part of a very important secret development."

"Well, all right then. . . ."

"And I . . ."

"I herewith see the situation, Mr. Secretary, and you won't have to say another word to me. Whenever you say that to me, that's all I want to hear."

Some months later, however, Truman would make new demands for inspection. But heartened by this first response, Stimson, with Bush and Marshall, called together leaders of both Houses in separate meetings, described the Manhattan Project to them, and asked for the needed money. It soon flowed in, together with pledges of silence. Secretary of the Treasury Henry Morgenthau was less obliging. Authorize a deposit of $20 million in a Federal Reserve Bank? Not unless he was considered fit to be trusted with the "secret" of how the money would be used. Morgenthau remained in the dark.

In his obsession with secrecy, Stimson also thwarted an effort, which even the President had backed, to bring an antitrust suit against the Du Pont Company, since it was doing "important work" on the bomb. Who knew what testimony might dribble out? At the same time, he headed off attempts by labor leaders to organize some of the laboratories. Nobody was supposed to know who was working where, and a strike could be disastrous. He also fiercely protested to the British, with Roosevelt's support, when they permitted a French scientist who had been working in a Canadian branch of the Manhattan Project to return to occupied France. The man would surely report to Joliot-Curie, who was hiding out in that country, and wasn't Joliot-Curie a Communist? In any case, no Fascist or Communist must know what would happen in Chicago on December 2, 1942.

VI

This was the day the atomic "pile" at the University of Chicago would be poked and prodded to reveal whether the neutron was really the key to a bomb that could save, and perhaps ultimately destroy, humanity.

On a balcony 10 feet above the squash-court floor, which was slippery with graphite dust, Szilard gazed at the crude reactor with about forty other scientists who were working on some phase of the infant nuclear program. Fermi barked orders to subordinates as he stood near the 500-ton pile of graphite bricks, stacked in 57 layers, in which tiny cubes of uranium or uranium oxide were embedded. Two shifts of workers had labored sixteen days to build the 16-foot-high structure.

Long control rods, plated with the metallic element cadmium, were set up so they could be inserted into holes in the graphite and withdrawn. The graphite would slow down neutrons emitted by the uranium and the cadmium would absorb them. As the control rods were withdrawn, fewer of the neutrons from the uranium would be absorbed, inducing greater fission. Finally, at some point of withdrawal, fission would produce neutrons faster than the cadmium would absorb them, and a chain reaction would result. If it started going out of control, a three-man "suicide squad" standing on a platform overhead would dump buckets of cadmium solution over the pile, and someone with an ax would cut the rope holding a safety rod.

After a number of control rods were withdrawn, Fermi gave the order to an assistant to withdraw the final one: "Pull it to 13 feet, George."

And he intently watched the meters that measured the neutron emission inside the pile. Not enough. Another foot. After several hours, at 3:25 P.M., the meters went crazy.

"This is going to do it," Fermi said, his fingers working a slide rule to calculate the rate of fission, his eyes darting from dial to dial. Then his intense expression suddenly dissolved into a smile.

"The reaction is self-sustaining," he declared, calmly ushering in the nuclear age.

Eugene Wigner pulled the cork out of a bottle of Chianti, and Fermi sent for paper cups. Szilard, a strangely obscure figure amid the band of elated men, said little for once. Everyone realized at this ecstatic yet solemn moment that the world would never be the same again. But Szilard was apparently worried about the direction the change would take. Would his long, frenetic campaign result in the conservation of human life—or in its extinction?

When the party was over, Szilard and Fermi stayed behind and shook hands. "This day," Szilard said, voicing his fear, "will go down as a black day in the history of mankind."

Stimson was fearful, too. If he achieved nothing more in this stupendous effort to enforce the laws of civilization, he would keep the bomb a secret from the lawbreakers.

Chapter 5

THE

PUPPET

I

While the bombmakers began to wonder if a nuclear world would survive, Emperor Hirohito began to wonder if his dynasty would. For though the Sun Goddess had proclaimed it eternal, many of Japan's military leaders, even on the day of the bomb, were determined to fight to the last Japanese.

In fact, the reinforced concrete bunker Hirohito now inhabited under the *Obunko*, the long, one-story Imperial Library where he worked in normal times, suggested a last-stand refuge, a burial place for myths. Hidden in a hill under 45 feet of earth, the bunker protected the Emperor from the bombs that had turned most of Tokyo into rubble and did not differentiate between men and gods. He had to move through dank passages from room to room and could seldom gaze upon the gardens he had personally helped to cultivate. Or pick the wild flowers that delighted him. He could only read about them in the scientific books that lined his underground library, his only escape from the horror of watching the nation slowly die in his exalted name.

Hirohito did not know that the atomic bomb existed, but he believed the promise of the Allied leaders at Potsdam that they would destroy Japan if it didn't surrender immediately. And even if it did surrender, there was no certainty that the Allies would let the country keep its Imperial system. Yet he wanted peace now at any price, even if the price was his throne—or his life. Better that his people live without their god than their god live without his people.

But the militarists didn't agree. How could they control the people without a god? No, they would surrender only if they could retain power, and to retain power they must have their god. Better that their people die, the fanatics felt, than they live free of the military yoke. So, while Hirohito would make any sacrifice to end the war before catastrophe struck, he was, ironically, not free to do so for the nation that was zealously sacrificing itself for him. He was worshiped as a god, yet he was a powerless pawn of his keepers. Probably no godly figure ever felt as mortally helpless as Hirohito did at this moment in history.

The Emperor was an unhappy deity indeed. His solid though slightly stooped 5-foot-6-inch build had wasted from 140 to 123 pounds, making his beribboned general's uniform hang on him like a rented costume. Gray streaked his thinning black hair, aging him beyond his 44 years. His right cheek twitched more persistently than ever. His full, sensitive lips, accentuated by a weak chin and graced by a short mustache, were more pursed than usual, his high-pitched voice more shrill, his oval face puffier, and his narrow eyes pouchier as they peered hauntedly through thick round lenses that exaggerated the ravages of insomnia.

II

Yet Hirohito could persevere because he was used to being unhappy. He had even been deprived of the normal joys of Japanese childhood. Japanese parents have traditionally given their children great freedom. The mother may gently scold her child or threaten to withdraw her love from him, but she seldom punishes him so he will learn the difference between right and wrong. That will come later, she tells herself, even as the child is throwing a tantrum or poking holes through the paper walls of the house. She knows that there is a more thorough and unrelenting discipline awaiting her child—that great machine of indebtedness that will chokingly bind him to the Japanese community. So let him enjoy his early years.

But Hirohito never enjoyed his. He never knew a mother's love or the pleasure of defacing the family home—though he once gallantly took the blame for damage that his comrades had inflicted on a palace wall. Only three months after birth, the boy, a puny child, was sent to live with the family of an admiral, since tradition called for Imperial heirs to be separated from their parents in infancy—originally in order to keep ambitious uncles or concubines from doing away with the child so that their own children could become heirs. When the admiral died a few years later, the boy was brought back to the palace, where he was permitted to see his mother only once a week and his father, the Crown Prince, hardly at all.

Hirohito wasn't allowed to climb walls like his younger brother, Chichibu, or even to play strenuous games with comrades like Koichi Kido. A future Emperor, especially a frail one like Hirohito, couldn't risk injury to his body or his dignity. At the same time, his guardians and teachers taught him strict discipline, making him go hungry if he complained about the food, or refusing even to let him in the door if he returned home late. He thus learned to accept "orders" from his keepers and grew up utterly unspoiled. He would give his best toys to Chichibu and, even as Emperor, with an income of more than $1.5 million a year, would often wear old, mended clothing. In fact, he became so frugal that he would write on both sides of a sheet of paper and run pencils down to a stub. And if the lights were left on or a faucet was dripping, an Imperial flick of the finger or twist of the wrist would soon stop the meters.

But life without fun or freedom could hold little joy for a child, and Hirohito's only real pleasure as a boy was to visit his grandfather, Emperor Meiji, several times a year, and to be hoisted to his shoulder or patted on the head. The future Emperor was as mesmerized by this "god" as people would be in his own presence when *he* sat on the throne.

Young Hirohito, however, needed to love not only a god but a father. And at the age of 7, he fulfilled this need when placed under the tutelage of General Maresuke Nogi, one of the heroes of the 1905 Russo-Japanese War, whose own two sons had died in that conflict. Hirohito, in a sense, replaced them. Love flowed silently from the gentleness of the teacher's voice, which in the war had gruffly ordered thousands to their death, from the brightness of the pupil's eyes, which had been listless and sad. Nogi taught Hirohito the story of Japan's divine origin; the Constitution of 1889, which stressed this origin; and the Imperial Rescript on Education, which described the duties and obligations of the Japanese subject to the Imperial ancestors, the Emperor, the state, and society. He would ask the prince and other aristocratic children in his class:

"What is your dearest ambition?"

And the children would reply joyously:

"To die for the Emperor!"

And this was, in fact, Nogi's own dearest ambition.

Emperor Meiji died in 1912, and on the evening before the funeral, the general called Hirohito to him and, as they knelt on the *tatami* (matting) of his home, questioned the new Crown Prince about his studies and said calmly in words that, in the Japanese lexicon, subtly conveyed his emotion and affection:

"Please remember that my physical presence is not necessary for me to be with you in your work. I shall always be watching you and your welfare will always be my concern. Work hard, for your own sake and for the sake of Japan."

When Hirohito left, Nogi stabbed his wife to death and then ripped open his own stomach so that he might continue serving his god in heaven.

On learning of the tragedy, Hirohito did not weep. For Japanese do not show emotion; and he was the future Emperor. But he churned with agony, resentment, and confusion. To die for the Emperor! What a waste of life. What a squandering of love. And now he was alone again, alone to brood about his godly fate. How terrible to be a god—especially since he believed he was a mortal.

III

And it seemed he was. For would a god feel guilty about being worshiped as one? Hirohito was a decent soul, deified or not. He tried to be honest with others and with himself. The trouble was, he couldn't be. From the moment he was born, he was doomed to live a lie. A deadly lie. How many subjects had been tricked into slashing open their bellies for him? How many into blindly rushing enemy machine guns, *wanting* to die for him, to repay him *chu*, the special debt owed an Emperor for his divine goodness? And yet he could never repay his own huge debt to them. What greater plague could afflict an honest mortal (or god)?

Any other Japanese who collected on a false debt could redeem his honor by resigning his job or perhaps committing suicide. But Hirohito could not solve his terrible dilemma so easily. He was fated to live with his shame. For if an Emperor or his heir gave up his throne or took his life, he might be exposing the lie, the lie that nourished the Japanese soul. Without it, Japan would be a country with neither past nor future.

To the shock of his mentors, Hirohito, shortly after Nogi's death, began to express doubts that he was divine and that it was proper for men to die for the Emperor. Prince Kimmochi Saionji, a former Prime Minister and one of the most powerful Imperial advisers, was shocked. He had taught Hirohito to approve all government actions and thus endow them with divine infallibility. How could they be infallible if the Emperor denied he was a god? He would have to knock some superhuman sense into the boy.

Why didn't Hirohito believe he was a god?

Because it was biologically impossible.

But wasn't Amaterasu the Sun Goddess?

Horror. What was truth? What the people believed. And they all believed the legend of Japan's divine birth. It was the kernel of the Japanese religion, Shinto, the "Way of the Gods." To migrants from East Asia who settled in Japan before the 7th century, Shinto was the simple worship of the wonders of nature, such as an oddly twisted tree or a high mountain. But ultimately it would embrace the greatest wonder of all—the nation's heavenly conception. Could anyone deny that this was a tremendous political feat that gave the people a deep sense of national destiny? Hirohito could not—but that was the problem. The nation's destiny was based on a fairy tale!

Once upon a time, the god Izanagi and the goddess Izanami searched the earthly abyss below from the Floating Bridge of Heaven and poked a jeweled spear into the ocean. When they withdrew it, the brine that dripped from the point of the spear solidified to form an island. The divine couple descended the Stairway of Heaven to this island and gave birth to all the islands of Japan. Izanami was eventually burned to a cinder giving birth to fire as well, while Izanagi begot the Sun Goddess Amaterasu from his left eye, the Moon Goddess Tsuki-no-kami from his right eye, and the Sword God Susanoo from his nostril.

Susanoo, known as the Impetuous Male, violated his sister Amaterasu, and she fled in shame to a cave, plunging the whole world into darkness as only a Sun Goddess could. She was, however, lured out by her warriors who told her of a beautiful goddess who had been dancing for them. When Amaterasu asked to see her, the warriors held up a mirror to her own face. Jealous of the image, which she did not realize was her own, she emerged from the cave, apparently to confront her rival, and brought light back to the world. She then gave birth to her brother's son, whose own son, Ninigi, descended to earth after the Sun Goddess told him:

"The Luxuriant Land of Reed Plains is a country that our descendants are to inherit. Go, therefore, Our Imperial Grandson, and rule over it. And may our Imperial lineage continue unbroken and prosperous, co-eternal with Heaven and Earth. . . ."

Carrying three divine symbols of authority—a sword for justice, jewels for mercy, and the mirror into which his grandmother, Amaterasu, had gazed for truth—the young god landed on a Japanese mountain, and in 660 B.C. his great-grandson Jimmu was crowned the first Emperor of Japan. . . .

Biologically and physically impossible? Far be it from a mere man to argue with a god. But would it be wise to tell the people that? asked Saionji. Hirohito shouldn't disillusion them. They believed in his divinity and needed a faith to guide them to glory, to make life—and death—worthwhile. If Hirohito himself wasn't a believer, he should at least be an actor. It wouldn't be hard. His advisers would teach him to be the finest god this side of heaven. As fine as his illustrious ancestors.

Hirohito listened carefully. Yes, he would have to act, though he would never enjoy his role. It was, in fact, a role that few men could play well. Emperor Jimmu himself invited eighty foes to a banquet, and then gave a signal to butlers standing behind each one to slay them all. Emperor Muretsu, A.D. 499, cut off people's heads, sliced open pregnant women's bellies, plucked out fingernails and toenails, pulled hair out by the roots, and with a bow and arrow shot human targets out of trees for fun. Other Emperors, to keep their servants in heaven after death, ordered that they be buried alive with them. Some devoted themselves mainly to deflowering court virgins. Emperor Keiko, the father of eighty children, was advised by his manipulators to sit motionlessly on his throne, crown on head, several hours a day in order to avert war, fire, or famine, but he simply placed the crown on the throne and rushed off to bed. No one really cared. The longer an Emperor stayed in bed, the stronger became his ambitious nobles, who were perfectly willing to risk war, fire, and famine for power.

Not all the Emperors were cruel or corrupt. Some were as humble as their impoverished subjects. Emperor Go-Tsuchi was so poor that when he died in the late fifteenth century his body lay rotting for forty days outside the palace gates because there was no money to bury him. And for the next twenty years, his son couldn't sit on his throne because nobody could afford to pay for the coronation. One Emperor lived in a hut, another on the streets as a beggar, and more than one starved to death. In 1690, an enterprising one managed to survive by ordering the ladies and gentlemen of his court to make straw baskets for sale.

If all these Emperors, good and evil, rich and poor, acted suspiciously like human beings, why shouldn't they have? Many, including Hirohito's own father, were born of concubines from the lower echelons of Japanese society. And no Empress ever gave birth to an island. . . .

But why spend so much time on history? Saionji said to Hirohito. It was too controversial and might confuse him. Couldn't he focus on some other subject?

Well, he liked collecting butterflies and insects and he loved studying fungi. He was curious about how and why life on earth existed and wanted to keep records on all that he learned to help mankind make progress.

Natural history! Just the thing to keep the future Emperor's mind off his nation's unnatural history. And Saionji was right. Hirohito was to become, in fact, a marine biologist of world renown. After ascending the throne in 1926, he built a laboratory in his palace and spent much time at his seaside home near Tokyo sailing in search of new species of marine life. He dumped his catch of starfish, algae, and sponges in the pocket of his white smock like a schoolboy collecting frogs. Then, in his laboratory, he examined and classified each item with all the enthusiasm he was expected to show one day when, as a spirit, he would judge who should cross the Floating Bridge of Heaven. In scientific truth Hirohito had found a way to ease the pain of living an Imperial lie.

Yet the militarists would try to deprive him of even this mild sedative. They needed a full-fledged myth to justify and approve their plots of aggression, and some people might ask why a myth would dabble in Darwinian data. The Emperor must never appear as a mere mortal, for who would die happily with a mortal's name on his lips? He must have no contact with the people. No one must even look down upon him from a window as the Imperial car streaked through the city at lightning speed amid an orgy of bowing by his awestricken subjects. Actually, the militarists felt they were quite liberal. In centuries past, anyone who dared set eyes on the Emperor would be put to death.

The wall cutting him off from his people was like a prison wall to Hirohito.

Couldn't he at least smile to them as he passed?

Gods didn't smile!

Unless they went abroad. Hirohito would always recall with joy his only sojourn outside Japan. As Crown Prince, he toured Europe in 1922, when he was 21, a time when democracy began to bud in Japan and militarism, as elsewhere in the world, was out of fashion. And now he smiled—at a Western opera in Malta, at the horse races in Gibraltar, at folk dances in Glasgow, in a subway in Paris (incognito), and in Buckingham Palace in London, where he was greeted by a half-dressed King George V, who, to the dismay of the Imperial aides, slapped him on the back while offering to give him "everything you want while you are here."

But the more Hirohito smiled, the more worried were the politicians, militarists, and nationalist plotters back home. And when he returned, Prince Saionji shuddered at the prospect of an Emperor "filled with dangerous delusions of liberalism." Saionji had something to shudder about. The man who would not be god envied the freedom of his new friend, the Prince of Wales, who could go among his people, dine in restaurants, attend the theater, throw parties for anyone he wished to invite. A party! Why not? Hirohito invited his old classmates to a homecoming celebration, instructing them to forget for the evening that he was the Crown Prince. And they did. Scotch whiskey flowed, Western records pounded, raucous laughter sounded—loud enough for his mentors to shake in their Imperial boots.

If the prince wanted to have a drink or even seduce a lady-in-waiting, that was one thing. But an orgy of fun with a bunch of human beings? How could his advisers rule the nation in the name of such a god? Even worse, the prince would soon suggest that it was time to bury old myths and begin a new, closer relationship between the Emperor and his people, like, say, in Britain.

Hirohito would deny his divinity! Did he think the army and the ultranationalist Black Dragon Society, however unpopular now, would allow such blasphemy? His advisers were alarmed. He needed more than fungi to take his mind off the lie. A concubine perhaps? The prince didn't seem interested. A wife, then.

Actually, the scramble to find one had begun even before Hirohito had left for Europe. Normally, an Emperor or Imperial heir would simply accept the choice of his advisers without question. What did it matter? He would have his enjoyment with his concubines. But Hirohito was different. It would take a special woman to distract him from matters that shouldn't concern him—such as his origin. And so they would let him choose his own wife from a carefully screened list of suitable, attractive women. Hirohito thus met and vigorously approved Princess Nagako, the unassuming, highly intelligent daughter of an aristocrat from the Satsuma clan.

However, members of the rival Choshu clan, which traditionally provided the Empresses, delved deeply into her family background and came up with a flaw. Her family was plagued with colorblindness. Nevertheless, Hirohito stood firm. He became engaged to Nagako, but saw her only nine times in five years before finally marrying her in 1924. So loyal was he to her that even when she gave birth to four girls in a row, he refused his advisers' pleas to bed down with a concubine in a desperate effort to produce an heir—winning his gamble when his wife finally yielded one, and in fact another later on.

But if Nagako, for all her husband's frantic bedtime activity, could not rid him of his rebellious views, destiny would—when, in 1926, when Hirohito's father died and the prince ascended the throne as the Son of Heaven. For not even a god could scale the walls of heaven.

IV

After tasting the delights of Western freedom, Hirohito found life in his palatial prison cruelly confining. But he could accept it because he had learned from infancy that every Japanese must accept his niche in life, however agonizing—even if he was a god at the top of the social pyramid. And since the rules deprived him of any choice, it was easier for him to obey them. A Japanese had to be fatalistic to survive. Especially if he was born to sit on the throne.

In any case, if heaven was a prison, it was like no other. Behind the moat-rimmed walls in the middle of Tokyo was an exquisite little world of gardens and greenhouses, pools and pavilions—a pavilion each for the Emperor and the Empress, one for the princesses, another for ladies-in-waiting. Hirohito would swing at balls on a nine-hole golf course he had built after visiting Europe, while young kimonoed women of the court strolled the lanes, clip-clopping in their *geta* across tiny bridges that spanned winding streams.

Here in this paradise the government would have Hirohito hibernate, sealed off from the world as any good god must be, waking only to "approve" documents drawn up by those in power. He must be an obedient god, for this was Japanese tradition, and no god would violate tradition. Actually, when Hirohito came to power, people had begun to forget he was a god. He had seemed too human—traveling to Europe, smiling at the Prince of Wales when he visited Japan, sometimes even waving to his subjects on ceremonial occasions.

The military secret societies and the ultranationalist parties that supported them, however, were determined to squelch this Imperial attempt to be human. And the conflict between the civilian and uniformed leaders grew. Actually, it had been growing for decades, ever since Emperor Meiji had died in 1912. Until then, the samurai who had orchestrated the Meiji Restoration ensured that the government and the military were in harmony. In fact, both groups allowed Emperor Meiji to exert more power than tradition normally permitted, since neither greatly feared the other would try to manipulate the Imperial strings to its own advantage.

But after Meiji died and the founders of the new Japan had gone, the government and the military gradually split apart as the civilian leaders attempted to integrate Japan into an increasingly democratic world, and to use their puppet for this purpose—a task made easier because Hirohito's father had been mentally ill and incapable of governing at all. Thus, when Hirohito inherited the throne, Japan's leaders were locked in a bitter struggle to dominate the road to destiny, while time had corroded even the little power an Emperor could effectively exert.

For more than a decade after Meiji's death, the government had the upper hand, especially in the early 1920s when the military was extremely unpopular, and the civilian leaders even dared to trim the military budget. But in 1924, the military and ultranationalist fanatics found a route into the Japanese psyche—thanks, ironically, to the United States, which about two decades later would cut the route with the atomic bomb. Congress passed an immigration bill that discriminated against the Japanese in allotting national quotas, and now the militarist path was set. America hated Japan, the extremists screamed, and would soon try to destroy it. And they shouted an old slogan: What should be the dearest ambition of every Japanese? To die for the Emperor!

To die for the Emperor! Hirohito remembered the cry echoing through his classroom. He remembered General Nogi acting out the cry. What irony! Hirohito called his reign *Showa*—"Enlightened Peace"—and now, to his chagrin, some fanatics were asking people to die for him. But he wanted peace—didn't the militarists and nationalists acting in his name understand? They didn't. Gradually they hypnotized the people, and with the Mukden Incident of 1931, they set off the chain of violence and aggression that was to make a mockery of *Showa* until the atomic bomb finally made them understand.

For a while, in February 1936, it appeared that Hirohito himself might make them do so. Up to this time, he followed tradition as the militarists expected him to, blindly accepting the court's advice, pathetically objecting to aggressive acts with only vague questions about whether they were wise. But then a fanatical group of young officers bent on attacking Russia went wild with rage after extreme rightists lost ground in some elections and orders were received to transfer their division to Manchuria, where they would be less able to threaten the government.

Revolt! these officers ordered their division. Kill the Japanese leaders, including the Emperor himself if he didn't agree to their designs (though they were acting in the Emperor's name!).

While teams of killers embarked on their grisly missions, rebel troops surrounded the palace and an officer reportedly entered, found his way to the Emperor's study, and burst in.

Hirohito stood up and scowlingly faced him.

"How dare you come in here?" he cried. "Do you not know that I am your Emperor?"

The officer stared at his god resplendent in a general's uniform and dropped to his knees, bowing his head to the floor. Then he got up, backed away, and bowed out of the door. He returned to his men and, apologizing for having sullied the Emperor, fell on his sword.

The revolt gradually petered out after three days of terror, but not before the rebels had slain seven statesmen—including the Lord Keeper of the Privy Seal, the finance minister, and the military education inspector general. Nor before Hirohito, for the first time—and the last, until the atomic bomb was dropped—personally ordered the military fanatics to obey him. Enraged as never before by the cold-blooded murders, he bluntly warned the rebels:

"His Majesty the Son of Heaven now orders you to return to your barracks. If you fail to obey, you will be traitors."

The rebels surrendered. And though the army command pleaded for leniency, thirteen officers and six civilians were executed and more than eighty others were either sent to prison or cashiered from the army. Hirohito had defied the military and taken his revenge. But the military would not be defied again. Even though the revolt was crushed, it helped senior officers backing the Emperor to strengthen their hold on the Imperial strings at the expense of civilian advisers helpless to stem the military tide. And these officers wanted to attack not Russia, but China, Southeast Asia—and the United States, if necessary.

The event was actually more frightening after it happened than when it happened. Hirohito had shown great courage in defending himself and in seeking punishment for the guilty. But viewing the mutiny through the prism of history, he—and his advisers—gasped at the thought of how close it came to returning Japan to the days of the Tokugawa, when the Emperor was a faceless unknown.

There could be no more risk of such a catastrophe. Besides, Imperial advisers such as Koichi Kido had learned that appeasement was the best insurance for a long life.

And thus, five years later, Pearl Harbor.

V

It had happened. This is where the lie had led. Hirohito's country was at war with the Western nations whose liberal ways he had once tried to emulate. With those who had so warmly welcomed him during his fabulous European tour. His troops were attacking the soldiers who had saluted him, the villagers who had danced for him, the friends who had taught him how to throw a party—and to smile. And they would blame him for the bloodshed because he was the Emperor, the god of his people, not realizing that even the most powerful god on earth could be the least powerful man. Worse, they would think he was treacherous for striking without warning. And the military brass could not comfort him by blaming snarled communications with the Japanese Embassy in Washington. A Western king had given him a slap on the back and now he had repaid his *giri* with a stab in the back.

Before putting his seal to the Imperial Rescript of War, the Emperor inserted a sentence of his own:

"It has been truly unavoidable and far from Our Wishes that Our Empire has now been brought to cross swords with America and Britain."

Perhaps his old friends would now think better of him. Perhaps they would still consider him an honorable man—if they understood that the war was "truly unavoidable" because he didn't have the power to avoid it.

But while the surprise attack on Pearl Harbor jolted the Emperor's conscience, even as the great victory cheered him, Kido and most other Japanese leaders suffered no excruciating pangs of guilt. After all, did not this attack follow in the tradition of the Shimonoseki affair in which Kido's grandfather ordered his warriors to fire without warning on an American ship as it entered the straits? Had not Japan's gallant soldiers started the Russo-Japanese War with a surprise bombardment of the Russian fleet? The affluent, more powerful nations could afford to abide by the meaningless "rules of war." Japan, a small island country with scant resources, could not. Japan's history had borne out that war was not immoral, however conducted—only defeat was. And if Japan did not fully exploit every advantage, it would risk defeat.

Even Hirohito knew what the immorality of defeat could mean—destruction, perhaps even the end of the Imperial system.

He had no choice now but to place his faith in the armed forces; it was useless to question any longer the righteousness of their cause. He must now concentrate on curbing the military appetite and negotiating a reasonable peace, using conquered nations as bargaining chips.

Worried over the gamble, ignored by the military except when it used his name in trumpeting heavenly triumphs, Hirohito wandered aimlessly through his gardens, barely aware of the wildflowers and the azaleas, the dragonflies and the bees that painfully reminded him of more peaceful days. With thousands dying for him, he lived an appropriately austere life. He seldom puttered in his laboratory now, even though Kido said he could ignore military objections that such an Imperial hobby was unfitting, especially during war. And he no longer dived for specimens or indulged in such British-inspired joys as golf and a breakfast of bacon and eggs.

But news from the war fronts relieved his forebodings. Within six months, most of the Pacific and Southeast Asian islands had fallen into Japanese hands—Guam, Wake Island, Hong Kong, Malaya, Singapore, the Philippines, the Dutch East Indies, Burma. Gradually relief turned into euphoria. Hirohito had never wanted to conquer neighboring countries, but now that it was happening, victory, of course, was sweeter than the unthinkable alternative. And wasn't Japan enhancing its bargaining power with every one? On the other hand, the Emperor was proud of his armed forces. They hadn't, as most Japanese felt, achieved such glory because of his "divinity," but simply because of their military skill.

"It is my sincere belief," Hirohito told Kido after the Lord Keeper informed him of Singapore's fall, "that the excellent results which we are repeatedly favored with are the results of thoroughly thought-out plans."

Kido "could not help but weep" at the Emperor's uplifting words. But he stopped weeping after the Indies and Burma collapsed. He rushed to Hirohito with the news.

"The fruits of war," said the Emperor, "are tumbling into our mouth almost too quickly."

The Emperor, "beaming like a child," was "so pleased," Kido would write in his diary, "that I hardly knew how to give a congratulatory answer."

Nevertheless, Hirohito's joy was tainted with doubt, almost as if Amaterasu, to save herself, had miraculously extended the Emperor's vision across the Pacific into the laboratories where men had ironically begun harnessing the power of the sun to destroy the land suckled by its sacred patroness.

On February 5, 1942, as Singapore was crumbling, Kido warned the Emperor against overoptimism. Yes, the military leaders expected the war to end swiftly and decisively, but it would not. While the well of Japanese military power would gradually dry up, the American well was gradually filling up. Unfortunately, the surprise attack on Pearl Harbor had strengthened the American will to fight rather than broken it as the military had predicted. His Majesty must therefore "grasp any opportunity to bring about the earliest possible termination of the war."

The Emperor needed little persuasion. He "leaked his heart" to the Empress, who apparently encouraged him to maneuver toward peace, and a few days later, on February 10, he summoned Tojo. The Prime Minister, as he bowed low to the man he held in both awe and contempt, surely expected only Imperial accolades and prodding toward new glories. But the Emperor said:

"I presume that you have given due consideration not to lose any opportunity for ending this conflict. It would be undesirable to prolong the war without purpose, for that would only increase the suffering of the people. I want you to keep this in mind and do everything possible for peace."

Tojo departed in a sulky mood. What if the Allies *were* gaining in strength? Japan's resources were also growing as the empire gobbled up Southeast Asia. Anyway, how could he convince his subordinates, especially the young officers, that they should lay down their arms while they were enjoying such success? Yes, he would keep peace in mind—after he settled the China problem, consolidated military gains in Southeast Asia, and sank the remainder of the American fleet.

In June 1942, off Midway Island, he watched for the bubbles that would signal he had sunk it. But most of them popped over the graves of Japanese ships. In a momentous naval battle, the Imperial fleet was forced to retreat—minus four first-line aircraft carriers. Pearl Harbor had been undone in a single blow, and Japan's precious margin of naval superiority had vanished.

VI

When Kido learned of this enormous setback, he was almost afraid to tell the Emperor.

"I had supposed," he would confide to his diary, "that the news of the terrible damage would have caused him untold anxieties, yet his countenance showed not the least bit of change."

"The setback," said Hirohito, "was severe and regrettable." But the naval leaders must make certain that "the navy does not deteriorate [and that] the future policy of the navy [does not become] inactive and passive."

Kido was "very much impressed by the courage displayed . . . by His Majesty, and . . . was thankful that our country [was] blessed with such a good Sovereign."

Why did the Emperor react so mildly to the devastating news, and Kido so admiringly to his reaction? Perhaps because Tojo and his colleagues would now realize they had gone far enough and try to make peace.

But Tojo didn't. Instead, he mocked the Emperor by invoking his name more frequently than ever in a frenzied campaign to assure the people that the war was sacred and that they must fight to the last suicidal moment.

Meanwhile, Kido, who had expected a military reverse all along and was certain there would be more of them, conspired for peace with the Jushin, or council of the Elder Statesmen—former Prime Ministers who wielded on the national level the influence of elders in a family or village, exercising it as a matter of right within the Japanese social hierarchy. Most members, however, were *former* Prime Ministers precisely because they had feared to provoke the military, which had held a gun to their heads. And they were still allergic to gunsmoke. Even so, one member, Prince Konoye, pushed Kido relentlessly to take steps toward peace. If Kido didn't, Konoye warned, as he had many times, the Communists might take over Japan and destroy the Imperial system.

But Kido, the wariest survivor of all, was as ambivalent now about making peace as he had been before the war about keeping peace. Again, he felt, he must move cautiously. One top diplomat suggested that China be given back its independence as a stride toward peace, a plan that Kido favored—until he saw the scowl on Tojo's face. And when another diplomat proposed sending Konoye to Switzerland to make peace contacts, he did not even wait for the scowl.

"There is much to be considered," said Kido skeptically.

For example, the value of staying alive.

The idea was shelved.

Finally, Kido concluded that the only way to control the military and end the war was for the Imperial family to use its swaying power. After all, bullets were less likely to be fired at puppets than at puppeteers. So he pushed Prince Takamatsu, the Emperor's youngest brother, to tug on military lapels and urge peace. But the prince, it seems, simply tugged on those of "My Dear Brother," the Emperor, writing him that peace was necessary, though Hirohito already knew it. The "peacemakers," in their fear and desperation, were pleading with each other. It was safer than risking the wrath of Tojo.

Then Tojo, prodded by his new foreign minister, Mamoru Shigemitsu, agreed in mid-1942 to a "new China policy" that would treat occupied China on a "basis of equality," political and economic. This did not mean that he would replace the Japanese concept of hierarchy with true equality, though he would nevertheless make some concessions—not to win peace, heaven forbid, but to win over the conquered peoples to Japan's side. Maybe in their mistrust of Western imperialism, they would forget the atrocities that Japanese invaders committed against them. Tojo even set up a Greater East Asia Ministry that would dispense doses of the new Big Brother policy—and make sure that Little Brother understood that the price of "equality" was to back Japan in the struggle against the West. At the same time, Kido and the Emperor hoped that America would understand this new policy as a reasonable response to its demands—and agree to a "just" peace.

But neither the Asians nor the Americans understood what they were supposed to understand. And even a prayerful visit by Hirohito on December 11, 1942, to the cypress hut housing Amaterasu's sacred mirror, could not halt the American advance. Kido "did not dare to guess the depths of his feelings" as the Emperor begged his godly ancestor to exert magic powers he knew she didn't possess.

Tojo was alarmed—less over the defeats, however, than over the danger that Hirohito might use his Imperial wand to force surrender. The Emperor must be compromised, as Tojo himself was, to make sure he wouldn't do so. Knowing that Hirohito never refused a government request, Tojo thus asked him to put his seal on an Imperial Rescript commending the general's troops for their "great victory" on Guadalcanal and other islands . . . which the Americans had captured!

How could His Majesty now speak the truth about these battles or act on it?

Meanwhile, Japanese bureaucrats, industrialists, generals, and admirals fought it out on the domestic battlefield, blaming each other for supply failures. The industrialists, feeling strangled by ever-tightening government controls, began to sabotage war production. And the army and navy tried to produce their own war goods, competing so fiercely with each other that the army decided to build its own submarines and refused to accept even technical advice from the navy.

Japan's whole war effort thus started to crumble under massive external and internal pressures, and morale plummeted. Civilians, including children, worked twelve- and sixteen-hour shifts, walked the streets without shoes, and ate mainly a watery soup with shreds of eggplant. The air force had to cease training for lack of gas or oil. Shipbuilders turned out wooden ships for lack of steel. And Kido, in January 1944, drew up a peace plan that he immediately withdrew for lack of nerve.

Under the Lord Keeper's grand design, some occupied countries would be given independence and become neutral Switzerlands, and other countries would be administered by an international committee that the Big Powers—Japan, the United States, Britain, Russia, and China—would set up. But this plan, Kido decided, would be taken out of mothballs only when and if Germany was beaten. Then Russia might even press the Allies to accept such a plan. Meanwhile, Kido would keep it a secret, for what would the military think—or do—if it learned prematurely of this scheme, which, he conceded, "may at first glance appear too conciliatory and weak-kneed"? At second glance, Kido's real intention became clear: to continue the struggle against the West, if clandestinely and without war.

"Looking over the future trend of the world," he would confide to his diary, "I believe we must keep and cultivate our real power within the state for about one century. We must conclude this from experience in the Sino-Japanese conflict, from the German-

Soviet war, from the development of aircraft, from our knowledge of the true strength of the United States and Russia, and from the cost of war to us in national power."

But while American leaders were already thinking of a re-formed postwar Japan that would support American policies against Russia, Kido now thought of quietly cooperating with Russia and China against America and Britain. After all, the Russians and Chinese were "essentially Oriental in their thinking. Through them we can maintain our stand against the Anglo-Saxon powers . . . while we watch developments." At the same time, Japan would profit from the rivalry between America and Russia. This was, for Kido, the brightest ray of the new sun that would surely rise again from the black horizon of defeat.

America and Russia "will be the only nations unhurt after the present struggle," he wrote. "If so, Japan, being placed between these two powers, will suffer greatly. It is not necessary, however, to be too pessimistic, for . . . they will gradually relax and ulti-mately be corrupted. It won't be difficult for us, therefore, to come out on top if we cultivate a spirit of modesty and fortify ourselves with stern resolution."

But stern resolution did not save the 30,000 Japanese soldiers and sailors and 15,000 civilians who died on the island of Saipan on July 6, 1944, mostly in a savage orgy of suicide, after the U.S. Marines overran the island. Japan itself was now within range of the B-29 bombers, and General Groves could drop his atomic bombs on Japanese cities at his leisure.

VII

Kido was, of course, ignorant of the bomb. But he scented catastrophe, even as he searched for the new sun. Tojo must go, he—and the Jushin—decided. And even many senior army and navy officers now agreed. Kido had originally chosen Tojo as Prime Minister because he thought that only Tojo could force the army to keep the peace. Now Kido must get rid of Tojo because the general wanted to prolong the war. A new peace Cabinet must come to power. But an ugly rumor was afloat; Tojo was ready to "bathe Tokyo in blood" if he was ousted. How could Kido get rid of him and live to admire his own courage? He couldn't. But he found someone who could—Vice-Minister of Munitions Nobusuke Kishi, Japan's economic czar and a fellow Choshuite, who would become Prime Minister after the war.

Kishi realized perhaps better than anyone else that the economy was collapsing and that there was no alternative to immediate peace. And he was rare among the Japanese politicians: He was willing to risk his life for it. So let him! Kishi had already tried to bring down the Tojo government, stating at a Cabinet meeting that "this Cabinet must take full responsibility for the conduct of war." Tojo, however, refused to resign but demanded that Kishi do so.

Kishi now visited Kido at his home, arriving as the Lord Keeper was feeding his dogs—several chows and police dogs locked in cages in front of his large wooden house. Kido felt safer with the animals around and reportedly made sure that despite the critical food shortage they had enough red meat to stimulate their viciousness. He would feel safer still if Kishi agreed to take a little more heat.

Should he resign? Kishi asked, after planting himself on the *tatami*.

"Tojo hopes to prolong the Cabinet by changing some of its members," Kido replied. "But there is a strong tendency among the Jushin to favor dissolution. We cannot overlook the opinion of the Jushin or of the public."

So Kishi should refuse to resign and thus help to pressure Tojo to dissolve his whole Cabinet.

The following day, Kishi went to see Tojo. He minced no words: "The whole Cabinet is responsible for starting the war. We are all responsible for the way the war is going. So if one of us falls, we must all fall. . . . I have decided not to resign unless the whole Cabinet resigns."

"You dare defy me?" Tojo cried. "Do you realize that I can have you arrested?"

But Kishi would not yield. And finally, after more than two hours of bitter argument, Tojo gave up.

Kido was delighted, and so was the Emperor when his Lord Keeper told him. Now if Kishi would take one more step: Call on the whole Cabinet to resign at its next meeting. Two other members were also to do so, but at the meeting they reneged and said nothing. Kishi, however, got up and urged a resignation *en bloc*. When few Cabinet members protested, Tojo, his voice heavy with bitterness, asked them all to resign.

He then drove to the palace to inform the Emperor and was greeted by a gentle-voiced Kido.

"Who would you recommend to replace you?" he asked in a manner that suggested he was sorry Tojo saw fit to resign when his services were so badly needed.

The general replied sarcastically: "I don't think you need my opinion. I am sure the Jushin has someone in mind already."

Kido froze at the tone and must have been glad that he had enough red meat for his dogs.

Tojo then submitted the resignation of his entire Cabinet to the grateful Emperor. On the same day, July 18, 1944, Imperial General Headquarters belatedly revealed to the public the news that American forces had demolished the Saipan garrison, which "victoriously fought to the last man." Then Radio Tokyo calmly explained the natural consequences of this "planned" rout: "The American occupation of Saipan brings Japan within the radius of American bombers. But we are well aware of this contingency and have made the necessary preparations."

VIII

In Hiroshima, preparations were already in full swing. And Seiko Ogawa would soon be doing her part, together with her classmates, digging narrow shelters in the hills to protect people living in nearby wood-and-paper houses—just to make sure no one got hurt if the "barbarians" dropped a bomb or two.

Colonel Paul Tibbets (right), pilot of the B-29 *Enola Gay*, introduces Navy Captain William S. Parsons at a final briefing of the crew before takeoff from Tinian. Parsons, who had led the team that assembled the atomic bombs, was the weaponeer and tactical commander on the *Enola Gay*'s mission—the destruction of Hiroshima. (*Smithsonian Institution.*)

Rear Admiral W. R. E. Purnell, Brigadier General Thomas F. Farrell, Tibbets, and Parsons in Tinian awaiting the day of the bomb. Parsons persuaded Farrell, his superior, to let him arm the bomb in midair so that an accidental explosion would not kill everyone on the island. (*Defense Audio-Visual Agency.*)

Seiko Ogawa, a Hiroshima victim, as she appears at 53. Her wounds from the bomb caused her to undergo eight plastic surgery operations. (*Dan Kurzman.*)

A sleepy riverbank scene in Hiroshima before the atomic bombing. After the bombing, the rivers turned red with blood as survivors like Seiko Ogawa leaped into them to cool off their scorched bodies. (*National Archives.*)

Albert Einstein and Leo Szilard reenact their historic 1939 meeting at which Einstein agreed to write President Roosevelt urging him to build an atomic bomb before Hitler's scientists could. (*American Institute of Physics.*)

Leo Szilard and Gertrud Weiss, whom he would marry after a 17-year relationship. Szilard preferred living in a hotel rather than in a home of his own, feeling he needed his independence to stimulate new ideas for saving the world from catastrophe. (*Egon Weiss.*)

President Franklin D. Roosevelt and Prime Minister Winston Churchill·secretly agreed that the atomic bomb should be dropped on Japan only after "mature consideration." They also decided that after the war the United States would share atomic secrets with Britain but not with Russia. (*National Archives.*)

A replica of the atomic "pile" tested at the University of Chicago on December 2, 1942. Enrico Fermi, Leo Szilard, and other nuclear scientists proved that a large-scale chain reaction was possible and that an atomic bomb could thus be built. As Szilard said after the experiment, the world would never be the same again. (*American Institute of Physics.*)

Marquis Koichi Kido, Lord Keeper of the Privy Seal, was Emperor Hirohito's chief adviser. Kido tried to ward off war with the United States, feeling that Japan could not win, and plotted to end the conflict after the first few months of victorious battle. But he was hamstrung by his fear that the fanatical militarists would kill him and take the Emperor prisoner. (*National Archives.*)

Klaus Fuchs was a German physicist who became a British subject and worked on the atomic bomb in the United States—in the service of Russia. He gave Stalin almost all the atomic secrets, managing to avoid the numerous security traps laid by army intelligence. (*Los Alamos National Laboratory.*)

Soviet scientist Igor Kurchatov, who gave his country an atomic bomb in 1949; the reports from Klaus Fuchs possibly saved Russia 18 months of experimentation in different bomb-making methods. (*Sovfoto Eastfoto.*)

Secretary of War Henry L. Stimson (left) and Army Chief of Staff George C. Marshall. Stimson hoped that the atomic destruction of a Japanese city would not only shorten the war but would stimulate Russia to loosen up its police state and change its aggressive policies in return for atomic information usable for peaceful purposes. Marshall was reluctant to drop the bomb, at least without first demonstrating it to Japan. (*National Archives.*)

Emperor Hirohito (left) visits an army camp. He opposed the war but followed the Imperial tradition of agreeing to all government decisions. (*National Archives.*)

The Emperor astride his horse. The military leaders seldom conferred with him about military matters and ignored his suggestions that they seek peace. Only at the end of the war did he demand peace, issuing a direct order they could not refuse. (*National Archives.*)

General Hideki Tojo bows to the Emperor. Imperial adviser Kido chose Tojo as Prime Minister shortly before Pearl Harbor in the hope that Tojo could control the army. Instead, Tojo led Japan into war. (*National Archives.*)

General Tojo tried desperately to remain in power as the Americans captured island after island en route to Japan, but he was finally ousted in July 1944 by a peace group under Marquis Kido. (*National Archives.*)

Secretary of War Stimson pins a medal on Brigadier General Leslie R. Groves, who directed the Manhattan Project. Groves drove his scientists ruthlessly to produce the weapon before the war ended, fearing that he would be left with a useless $2-billion relic and faced with an investigation by a congressional committee. (*Defense Audio-Visual Agency.*)

Captain Parsons (left) and General Groves. Groves selected Parsons to be his chief of ordnance at Los Alamos, New Mexico, the man in charge of designing the bombs. Groves made it clear that Parsons and not Colonel Tibbets was "running the show" aboard the *Enola Gay*. (*Defense Audio-Visual Agency*.)

he gaseous diffusion plant built at Oak Ridge, Tennessee, to produce uranium 235, e atomic fuel, was the largest factory in the world. Bicycles were often used to move rough the endless miles of corridors. (*Defense Audio-Visual Agency*.)

Yoshio Nishina, Japan's leading atomic scientist, who attempted to build an atomic bomb but failed. (*Defense Audio-Visual Agency.*)

Yoshio Nishina's team of physicists, which failed to produce a bomb. Tadashi Takeuchi, Nishina's principal assistant, is at the extreme right. In March 1945, American incendiary bombs destroyed Nishina's Tokyo laboratory, ending the bomb-building operation. (*Nishina Foundation.*)

Theoretical physicist J. Robert Oppenheimer brilliantly supervised the building of the American atomic bomb. He was driven by the tremendous scientific challenge, his craving for professional recognition, and his desire for acceptance by the establishment that he had spurned in prewar days, when he moved in leftist circles. In the end, the establishment had its revenge. (*National Archives.*)

J. Robert Oppenheimer, Enrico Fermi, and Ernest O. Lawrence. (*American Institute of Physics.*)

A desolate scene at Los Alamos, New Mexico, where the atomic bomb was built. Eventually facilities mushroomed into a community of thousands of scientists, military technicians, and workers. Oppenheimer and the others savored the peaceful setting as they labored to build history's most destructive weapon. (*Los Alamos National Laboratory.*)

Japanese Prime Minister Kantaro Suzuki, a venerated old war hero, wanted to fulfill the Emperor's wish for peace, but fear of the militarists drove him to play a double game. He edged toward peace while making the militarists think he was committed to fight to the bitter end. (*National Archives.*)

Chapter 6

THE
WHIPCRACKER

I

General Groves, chief of the Manhattan Project, was also making preparations—to render all bomb shelters obsolete. Like Klaus Fuchs, he was a minister's son, but unlike Fuchs, he didn't abandon God. How could he when God had become his role model?

But if Groves looked up to the Almighty, he looked up to no mortal—except his father. The heroic image of his father was constantly before him. A highly decorated army chaplain, the elder Groves had given comfort to men in the midst of battles fought from China to Cuba, ignoring the risks, conquering attacks of yellow fever and malaria. At home he had been a martinet. He taught his son how to discipline himself and how to discipline others. He taught him how to surmount impossible obstacles. And now, on the day of the bomb, Groves could not let his father down. The bomb would not fail because he would not let it.

Ever since he had landed the most extraordinary construction job in history, the general had been confident it would succeed. By the day of the bomb, he had poured more than $2 billion into the project and built thirty-seven installations in nineteen states and Canada that employed 120,000 people, including many of the finest scientists and engineers in the world. Haste, with or without waste, was his watchword.

Huge amounts of silver were needed for the electromagnetic method of separating uranium? Get it out of the U.S. Treasury!

The new machinery to build a special filter in the gaseous diffusion process for separating uranium might not work? Tear it all out and design new machinery!

Plutonium could not be used in the gun-assembly method of triggering the bomb? Find a new method!

No problem was insoluble to Groves. There was no such thing as failure if one refused to give up. And if there was, he would not admit it even to himself. Tacked to a wall of his office in Washington was a drawing of a turtle with its neck stretched forward, illustrating a caption that read:

"Behold the turtle! He makes progress only when his neck is out." His voice, in a sense, was that of the turtle.

Groves drove his scientists and engineers as mercilessly as he drove himself, and most stuck out their necks, even while swearing under their breath. What did a mule-headed army officer know about science and engineering? many asked. But they were dragged along by the sheer momentum of his pile-driver thrust. In his fury, Groves refused to "waste time" building pilot plants, and he ignored normal safety precautions. He also terrified most of his office personnel with his gruff demands on their time and energy. On his previous job he had fired about one secretary per week, though he finally found one, Jean O'Leary, who was good enough to keep, and who would eventually become his administrative assistant on the bomb project. Everyone would work from about 8 A.M. to 7 P.M., and the general himself—when he was in town at all—would often stay until 1 A.M., rushing home for an early dinner only if his wife phoned that she was serving clam chowder, a lure almost as great as the bomb.

Yes, he took enormous risks with men's lives while thoroughly disrupting the lives of others, but how else could one make a miracle? Now he knew how God was able to create the universe in seven days! The day of the bomb was the "seventh day" for General Groves, and he rested.

Sitting stiffly behind his desk, he shuffled through some papers and waited for word from Tinian that Hiroshima lay in ruins. His aides, who gathered around him, could not detect even a glimmer of doubt in his piercing blue eyes. He was as composed as ever, a vigorous, stocky man of 49 with a neatly trimmed mustache bordering thin, unsmiling lips, and shiny dark brown hair that had earned him the nickname "Greasy" at West Point. Nor was there reason to doubt. The bomb would work, the scientists had assured him. The weather would be good and the bombing would take place as scheduled, General Farrell had informed him.

So why had no word come through yet? The plane should have taken off by 1:30 or 2 P.M. (Washington time). But 2 P.M. had come and still no word. Time dragged on, yet Groves was not upset. What could go wrong? Had he not provided for every contingency? Anyway, it was a sunny Sunday afternoon. Peaceful. The kind of day that made one happy to be alive. Tennis, anyone? Groves zipped in his car to the Army-Navy Country Club and displayed his considerable forehand skill, while an officer sat nearby, his hand on a telephone, and called the general's office every fifteen minutes to ask if any message had arrived yet.

Shortly, Groves showered, slicked back his hair, and, once more immaculately uniformed, returned to his office. An aide answered the phone. General Marshall? No news yet, but he would call General Groves to the phone.

"I don't want you to bother General Groves," Marshall replied. "He has enough to think about without answering any unnecessary queries."

But what was there to think about? The situation was beyond Groves' control now, so all the thinking in the world would not help. The general had learned to gear his temperament as well as his mind to logic, to expend emotional energy only when it could do some good. Why dally around the office? He would return to the club for dinner with his wife and daughter, who knew nothing about his job or about the impending holocaust. They would be joined by George Harrison, Secretary Stimson's special assistant and president of the New York Life Insurance Company.

When Groves met them at the club, he turned to Harrison and whispered, "No news yet." General Thomas T. Handy, Marshall's deputy, then stopped by their table and heard the same message. At 6:45 P.M., Groves was called to the phone, and as he left he could feel the eyes of Harrison and Handy "boring into [his] back."

At last, news! The plane had left on schedule. He stopped by

Handy's table to tell him, then took Harrison aside and informed him. When he returned to his table, Groves' wife and daughter did not detect any change in his manner or mood. He calmly ate his dessert, and his wife drove him back to the office.

When would he be home?

He wouldn't tonight, he replied.

Neither his wife nor daughter asked why, even though this was the first time during the war he had stayed out all night while in Washington. They had learned to live with secrecy.

Back in the office, Groves plunged into paper work. He was still confident, but he was angry and embarrassed. The wire he had received was five hours late, and the strike message still hadn't come, though it was long overdue. The army could swiftly build an atomic bomb but was late in communicating the most important message in history! To ease the tension among his aides, he took off his tie, opened his collar, and rolled up his sleeves. A collective gasp: Was this General Groves, who was always so formal, who would not even call his friends, the few he had, by their first names? What had the bomb done to him?

II

It had, for one thing, turned Groves into perhaps the most powerful man in the world, at least for the moment. Although he was only a brigadier general and led no armies, he had so hypnotized his superiors with his incredible creation that they gave him virtual carte blanche in deciding its wartime use. And this, Groves was convinced, was in the national interest.

"The military are completely dominated by the civilian people," he would later complain. "We're . . . in danger someday of a complete destruction of the country [because of] this philosophy of civilian control." The President should exert control at the top through his Cabinet officer, but "from that point on down, you don't want civilian control, you want the best control you can get, whether it is civilian or military."

Best or not, Groves controlled the bomb. He never asked if the bomb should be used, for why risk a "no"? As long as nobody said "no," the answer was "yes." As Groves would explain, "there was never any question raised by anyone as to my decision that we would drop the bomb in combat. . . . This was, of course, a complete violation of all military doctrine and if we had been unsuccessful, I would have been held up to scorn. . . . I was always surprised that General Marshall never, even once, raised a question about it."

In fact, Marshall virtually handed over his authority to Groves on all matters concerning the bomb.

General staff officers should start planning the bombing operation, Groves had suggested to Marshall.

"Is there any reason why you can't do that yourself?" Marshall replied.

Groves couldn't think of any. And Marshall would say no more about the bombing operation.

When the air force "assumed that the atomic bomb would be handled like any other new weapon, that when it was ready for combat use it would be turned over to the commander in the field," Groves did not equivocate. *He* alone would control the bomb until the moment it was dropped on Japan.

Nor did anyone raise a question about Groves' plan to drop *two* bombs on Japan, with "the second blow [coming] as soon as possible to hasten the surrender." As Groves saw it, "the first would show the Japanese what it was, and the second would show them that we had more than one." After the first bomb struck, how much time should the Japanese have to surrender? Groves would determine that, too. Would a third bomb be built? Yes, he decided.

"I consulted with General Marshall," he would explain, "as to whether if the [third] bomb was not used, the war would be over before 1946. His initial reaction was that it would be, but . . . later, he sent word to me that the considered opinion of the staff was that it would not be. It was on this basis that I went ahead on the addition. I had not asked for approval of the extension."

After the second bomb was dropped, Groves claims, he took another initiative. He asked for an order not to ship to Tinian "any more atomic material for several days." Marshall complied and sent Groves a note "to the effect that a third bomb would not be dropped without prior approval of the President." Although a third bomb would have been ready about ten days after the Hiroshima bombing, Groves didn't want to pile it on. Two bombs and 150,000 or so dead were "just enough." At least for the time being.

Which Japanese cities should be bombed? Groves again had the biggest say—though it wasn't big enough for him. His first choice was Kyoto, the old cultural capital of Japan, the home of palaces and castles of feudal lords and more temples than Buddha had curls. Only Stimson's personal intervention prevented Kyoto's destruction. Groves was furious.

"Now it goes right on down where [the civilians] are actually designating targets and things of that kind," Groves would protest.

But he added Nagasaki to his list—even after General Carl Spaatz, commander of the Strategic Air Force, cabled Marshall that captured Japanese soldiers reported that Allied prisoners of war were being held only a mile north of the city's center. Hiroshima was the only one of four target cities with no reported POW camps, Spaatz said. Would this information affect the choice of the initial target?

Groves drafted the reply after conferring with Handy: "Targets previously assigned . . . remain unchanged. . . . However if you consider your information reliable, Hiroshima should be given first priority. . . . Information available here indicates that there are prison camps in practically every major Japanese city."

If some American soldiers died in an atomic explosion, well, that was the luck of war. And apparently the luck of Tom Cartwright and his buddies, who were, unknown to the planners, locked up in Hiroshima Castle.

"Handy wanted to bring the matter to Stimson's attention for decision," Groves would explain, but "I held that this was not fair to Stimson and that I should make the decision. . . . *After the message was dispatched to Spaatz,* I took a copy into Stimson and showed it to him. He thanked me but made no objection to the action or to its having been taken without prior reference to him."

Groves was determined from the start that bombs be dropped only on Japan, even if they were available before Germany was knocked out of the war. And he did not hesitate to argue this point with President Roosevelt himself.

If the Germans managed to prolong the war, Roosevelt told him in December 1944, during the Battle of the Bulge, it might be necessary to atom-bomb Germany.

That would be a mistake, Groves replied.

Why?

If the bomb failed to explode, said Groves, the Germans, unlike the Japanese, might be able to use this model to build a bomb of their own. (He didn't explain what might stop Japan from turning over a dud to the Germans.) Besides, the bomb would flatten Japanese buildings, many of them made of paper and wood, more easily than the more solidly constructed German buildings. And in any case, the United States had no B-29 bombers in Europe to carry the bomb. Groves would deny after the war that he was motivated by racial bias.

The fighting in Europe was not prolonged, but Roosevelt was impressed by Groves' logic and apparently never again mentioned Germany as a target.

Groves had thus conquered all obstacles to success, just as his father had taught him. And the general was ruthless in carrying out this legacy, while grasping at every psychological straw he could find to justify his action. Was it worse to kill 100,000 people in a single instant with a single bomb carried by a single plane than to kill them over several hours with many bombs dropped by many planes? And why feel sorry for them anyway after Pearl Harbor and the Bataan death march? Yet other questions would seep out of another part of Groves' mind, questions that deeply reflected his moral upbringing and sought to balance his feelings toward Japan.

"It is difficult at times to determine," he would allow himself to say after the war, "just how much of a willful aggressor Japan was. We should not forget the actions of the United States under the direction of Roosevelt and [Secretary of State Cordell] Hull in an obvious effort to force Japan into war." He also "wondered if our encouragement of Russia's breaking her Neutrality Pact with Japan was entirely honorable. . . . It does not become any the less dishonorable because we did it."

But of course, such hidden thoughts would remain hidden until his bomb exploded over Japan. For Groves could not let them suppress his zeal in forcing history to record that this miracle weapon, under his supervision, had won World War II.

III

If Groves was notably aggressive, this was perhaps an inherited trait. His father, for whom he was named, was an impetuous and dynamic man. He became a successful lawyer, but a sudden feeling of mission inspired him to switch to the ministry in 1889. Unlike the son, the father was driven mainly by compassion, not ego. He wanted to work with God, giving men faith in the face of sudden death. In 1896, a few months after his youngest son, Leslie, was born, he joined the army and two years later, during the Spanish-American War, he left his wife and four children to slog through the mud of Cuba. Chaplain Groves contracted both yellow fever and malaria there, but he almost immediately volunteered to serve in the Philippines and then in China where, during the Boxer Rebellion, he knelt beside more broken bodies. He returned home this time with tuberculosis, but, when he recovered, would still not slow down his pace in the service of God.

Young Leslie was in awe of his father. The chaplain was a hero who feared nothing, a man with an uncompromising sense of right and wrong and an iron will unweakened by doubt, though the boy himself would have preferred to carry a gun rather than a Bible.

Did he want to succeed in whatever he did? asked his father. Then study. Work hard. Drive yourself. And don't give up.

The youth complied meticulously. He first tasted the delights of academia at the University of Washington and the Massachusetts Institute of Technology, then, in 1916, proudly donned the gray tunic of West Point, fulfilling his "greatest ambition." Having lived on army posts all his life, he was convinced that nowhere could he find men with stronger character and devotion to duty than in the army. "They were good solid Americans," he would say, "and, in general, far superior to men of equal education in civilian life."

But he was disturbed because his father disapproved of an army career for him. Hadn't the family squeezed enough pennies in the army? the chaplain argued.

Like his father, Groves did not judge success by the size of his bank account. Success was what his father had achieved—a reputation for doing what he thought was right and getting it done. And that was his own aim. Ironically, in opposing his father, he would prove that he was worthy of him. And his compulsion, it seems, was nurtured by a feeling of inferiority fed by his father's apparent favoritism toward his two other sons. As Groves' wife Grace, a colonel's daughter, would write before she married the young officer:

"According to my father, Dick was treated unfairly by the chaplain, who devoted his attention too greatly to the older boys. . . . Very little came Dick's way."

Groves' apparent sense of inadequacy may have nourished his aggressive attitude and would come to the fore most virulently when he would seek to convince the scientific geniuses working on the bomb under his direction that he was their intellectual equal.

He was, at any rate, bright enough to graduate from West Point in 1918 fourth in his class. And powerful enough to make second-string center on the football team. There was nothing like a tough contact sport, he felt, to give one the will to win at almost any cost. An athlete who harbored the slightest doubt about himself—and admitted that he did—would never win.

Groves apparently felt the same about romance. Though he decided he would marry Grace the moment his father introduced him to her, he found time to see her only twice while at West Point. (And a rainstorm ruined one of those meetings, soaking Groves to the skin when he refused to walk under the umbrella of his prospective bride and tarnish his macho image.) Grace would wait for him. Could he let himself think she would not?

Even after they married, Grace waited, for he was too busy making a reputation to spend much time at home. Working his way up to the rank of colonel in the army engineers, Groves had, by mid-1942, directed $10 billion worth of military construction in this country, including the Pentagon Building. He had a record that he readily admitted "flabbergasted" those who reviewed it. Finally, in September 1942, he was offered an overseas combat assignment, the dream of every regular officer—but not one that Groves was fated to realize.

IV

"About that duty overseas, you can tell them 'no.'"

Groves stared incredulously at Major General Brehon B. Somervell, head of the army services of supply and his top superior.

"Why?" Groves asked, trying to repress his shock.

"The Secretary of War has selected you for a very important assignment."

"Where?"

"Washington."

"I don't want to stay in Washington."

"If you do the job right," General Somervell said, "it will win the war."

These soothing words did not placate Groves, who had learned his fate in the corridor of the new House of Representatives office building after testifying about a construction project before the Military Affairs Committee. There would be more bureaucracy. More testimony. This meant he might never see combat.

But all he could say was, "Oh!"

Groves' feeble response reflected not only his disappointment but his realization what his new job would be.

"In my position," he would later write, "I had to learn enough about what was going on to realize that he was talking about the as-yet-unnamed Manhattan Project," an enormous gamble that no officer in his right mind would willingly risk his reputation on.

At Somervell's direction, Groves headed immediately for the Pentagon to see his boss' chief of staff, Brigadier General William D. Styer.

"Who on earth recommended me to the Secretary of War?" Groves asked.

He didn't need an answer. As he would write in his notes, he was sure that Styer himself, "not wanting the job, cast about desperately for someone who could take the job and he settled on me." Who wanted a job that seemed doomed to failure? At the same time, Somervell knew that if Groves was "placed in charge . . . the chances of a flare back on him would be greatly diminished. . . . It would be strictly in my lap and [he knew] that I would not try to duck it."

Skirting the question, Styer made Groves' new assignment seem as easy as that of Army's star quarterback in the game with Navy. "The basic research and development are done. You just have to take the rough designs, put them into final shape, build some plants and organize an operating force and your job will be finished and the war will be over."

And so would Groves' military career—if he failed.

Groves, however, was not a man to worry, especially when he had no choice. If it was humanly possible to get the job done, he would do it. But was it humanly possible? He began to wonder as he looked through some reports. Rough designs? Put them in final shape? What designs? There were none, rough or otherwise.

There had only been some primitive laboratory research by a few harebrained dreamers. The project was nowhere near the production stage. And he was to turn out an atomic bomb before the war ended!

Groves felt deep down that his chance for success was 60 percent. Yet the challenge gradually seized him, and he "almost deliberately deceived himself" into raising the figure to 100 percent. His father had prepared him for impossible challenges, and he had prepared himself. Who else could boast of so "flabbergasting" a record in military construction? General Somervell had said, no doubt with irony, that the bomb to be built would win the war. What he didn't realize was that it really would.

That afternoon, Groves went to see Vannevar Bush, who had still not given control of the project to the army. He fired questions with machine-gun velocity until Bush, clearly mistrustful of this brash stranger, virtually showed him to the door. Hardly had the door slammed shut when Bush called General Styer.

"Who is this Colonel Groves?" he demanded.

"What do you think of him?"

"He looks too aggressive."

"He is . . . but he gets things done."

"I'm afraid he'll have trouble with the scientists."

"You may be right . . . but the work will move—I can assure you of that!"

Bush, however, remained skeptical.

"Having seen Groves briefly," he wrote in a memorandum to Stimson's aide, Harvey Bundy, "I doubt whether he has sufficient tact for such a job. I fear we are in the soup."

V

At his own request, Groves did not officially take charge of the Manhattan Project until his promotion to brigadier general came through, for he wanted to impress the scientists with his rank. If he took over as colonel, they would always think of him as a colonel. Finally, on September 23, 1942, the day he became "General Groves," he met in Secretary Stimson's office with Bush, Conant,

Marshall, Somervell, Bundy, and Rear Admiral W. R. E. Purnell to form a committee that would exercise supreme control over the project. Stimson watched Groves carefully, sizing him up. Was he too aggressive, as Bush claimed? Were they all "in the soup"?

A new Military Policy Committee must replace the Top Policy Group, the Secretary explained, because he, Marshall, and Vice-President Wallace were too busy to supervise the project on a day-to-day basis. Seven to nine officers from the army, navy, and Office of Scientific Research and Development would be about right.

No, this number would not be right, protested Groves. "Three is the ideal number, I could keep three people reasonably well informed and also obtain their advice much more readily."

Groves clearly was a man who knew what he wanted. Very well, the others agreed, a three-man committee plus an alternate. Bush would head the group and Conant would be the alternate, with Purnell representing the navy and Groves the army. Groves was delighted. Even Stimson and Marshall, the top commanders, had listened to this neophyte general. They might as well learn now who would really be boss. Suddenly, Groves stood up, glanced at his watch, and said:

"I am very sorry, Mr. Secretary, but I have to catch a train. . . . If there is no reason to stay I would like to leave."

He was, after all, a busy man and had things to do.

A moment of startled silence, then Stimson excused him. What else could he do? And then the soup began to boil. Groves should *not* be on the committee, Bush insisted; Styer should represent the army. How could they control Groves if Groves himself was in the controlling group? No one argued. The general was then tossed a bone. He would be the committee's executive officer. Later Somervell would try to soothe Groves' feelings:

"That abrupt departure of yours . . . was a smart thing to do! You made me look like a million dollars—I told them that if you were put in charge, things would really start moving!"

They did. Groves burst into the office of Donald Nelson, who headed the War Production Board, and demanded AAA priority for the Manhattan Project.

"No! Absolutely no!" Nelson exclaimed. "We have too many other war projects of capital importance that are waiting desperately for higher priority ratings."

"All right, Mr. Nelson, in that case I must recommend to the President that the Manhattan Project be abandoned because the War Production Board is unwilling to cooperate with his wishes."

Groves walked out with AAA priority.

Like a whirlwind, the general swirled around the country from one branch of the project to another, usually dressed in civilian clothes so people wouldn't suspect he was on a special mission. There were as many branches as there were ways of separating U^{235} from U^{238}. And they were all being tried simultaneously to make sure that no time would be lost in finding the fastest way. Was it by the gaseous diffusion, the electromagnetic, or the centrifuge method? And what should be used to make plutonium—a heavy water reactor or a graphite one? Hitler would not permit the United States the luxury of trying each process in turn; his scientists might already have found the quickest method.

At Columbia University, Groves was intrigued by the challenge of gaseous diffusion as Harold Urey, a Nobel Prize winner and the project leader, led him through a maze of glass tubing in the laboratories. The idea was simple: Convert uranium into a corrosive, radioactive gas, uranium hexafluoride, and force it through the microscopic holes of a filter, or "barrier." Since the lighter U^{235} molecules would pass through faster than the U^{238} molecules, the gas on the far side of the barrier would contain more U^{235} isotopes than that on the near side. Filter the gas multiple times and ultimately almost all the U^{235} would be separated.

But to set up this process on an industrial scale would mean using several thousand filters, each with billions of invisible holes, all nickel-plated to prevent corrosion. A whole new industry would have to be built complete with as yet uninvented tools and equipment.

We can do it, said John Dunning, a gaseous diffusion expert.

I'm not so sure, said Urey.

And neither was Groves. But Urey dared admit his doubts. He was a great scientist but a bad administrator, disorganized and absent-minded. Worst of all, in Groves' opinion, he was a "coward." Surely not a man to do the impossible.

At the University of California, Berkeley, Groves found a man who thought he could—Ernest O. Lawrence, who had won the Nobel Prize for his cyclotron atom smasher. Yet the electromagnetic method of separation he was working on seemed even a greater gamble than gaseous diffusion. Tall, blond, and youthful, with blue eyes that gleamed with enthusiasm, Lawrence had invented a new kind of cyclotron, called the "calutron," which would separate U^{235} in an ingenious way. Atoms would be accelerated through a vacuum tube at tremendous speed and thus forced to enter a powerful magnetic field that would curve them into circular paths. The U^{235} atoms, being lighter than the others, would be bent into a separate circuit and be collected at the end of the arc in a separate container.

Groves stared with wonder at the huge cyclotron magnet suspended inside the domed building on Radiation Hill. It was being used for the calutron.

"How much [U^{235}] do you get in the baskets?" Groves asked Lawrence.

Well, hardly anything. But just wait. . . .

Wait? There was no time to wait!

Yet Lawrence was Groves' kind of man, and the general instinctively trusted in his success.

At the Westinghouse Research Laboratory in Pittsburgh, Groves was in for an even greater shock. Here, the centrifuge process was being tested. The idea was to spin at blinding speed large cylinder drums containing uranium, once more causing the lighter U^{235} atoms to separate.

"How long have you run this?" asked Groves, pointing to one of the drums.

"Well, up to about fifteen minutes."

Groves was furious. What the hell did these people do the rest of the day? No wonder they hadn't produced anything yet. He shut down the project.

VI

At the University of Chicago, Groves knew *he* would be tested even more thoroughly than the method. For working in the Metallurgical Laboratory here were some of the most brilliant scientific minds in history—Nobel Prize winners Fermi, Compton, and James Franck, as well as Wigner and Szilard. They would surely try to make a fool out of him, to question the ability of a mere army general to administer so complex a scientific and engineering project. He prepared meticulously for his meeting with them. He could easily deal with individual Nobel laureates like Urey and Lawrence, but at Chicago they would gang up on him.

Szilard, in particular, he had heard, was an arrogant trouble-maker who had given Bush and others a hard time. Besides, of the top scientists in Chicago, only Compton, the head, was a long-standing American. Fermi was an Italian, Franck a German, and Szilard and Wigner, Hungarians. And the last three were Jews, like so many other scientists in the program. He would write to a friend later:

"Something that has never been written about because of the tremendous power wielded by persons of Jewish descent in this country's mediums of public information is the fact that most treasonable breaches of security in the last war were committed by persons of Jewish blood. . . . First, the Jews in many instances never had any particular feeling of loyalty to the country in which they lived. This may well have been due to the restrictions under which they lived in many European countries for generations. It may also be due to their religion founded as it is on the Old Testament with its emphasis on their being the chosen people with no obligations to others. Second, those individuals who were dis-loyal and in every case I know of abandoned the faith of their fathers and at the same time had not become Christians. The result was that they had no moral principals on which to base their lives."

But Groves added, not wishing anyone to misunderstand him: "I don't like certain well-known characteristics of the Jews, but I'm not prejudiced. . . . This was demonstrated by the reliance I placed on Jews and the positions of authority in which I placed them during the critical period."

Groves planned to boast of his own intellectual prowess to this collection of "crackpots," prima donnas, and Jews to win their respect, but he felt this would not be enough. He thus ordered Lieutenant Colonel Kenneth D. Nichols, his deputy, and Colonel James C. Marshall, who had previously directed the atomic project, to help show how "much education we had all had in the course of our career. . . . The whole idea was to build up in their minds that we were not only engineers but also we were educated people and while our education might have been in a different field, we were just as smart academically as they were. . . . You had to move right in and see to it that they knew. . . . This was just typical public relations in advance—advertising, if you want to call it that."

Groves' advertising campaign began soon after he arrived in Chicago on October 5, 1942, when he met with the scientists of the Metallurgical Laboratory. Four possible cooling methods were being considered for the plutonium reactor they were building. Too many, Groves grunted. Don't fiddle around. Drop all but one or two. He impressed Szilard and the others with his decisiveness, and they reduced the choices to two, helium and air, dropping water and heavy water. A good start. But Groves was sure they were setting a trap for him when they moved to the conference room to discuss how much fissionable material was needed to make an atomic bomb.

"They went all through the demonstration on the board," Groves would proudly relate later, "and I think they were really quite disappointed when they looked at me and saw that all of their symbols did not bother me at all when they started to deal with integral calculus and differential equations. . . ."

Groves noticed that one scientist had scribbled a figure that seemed to be wrong. But could he challenge the mathematics of a scientific genius?

"I looked at this thing and thought to myself," the general would say, "This is one of my major decisions because so much depends on it.' I was not going to let them slip anything over. . . . Maybe they have deliberately made a mistake. . . . So I finally said, 'Between your 4th and 5th equation there, I don't follow how you got from the 4th to the 5th. . . . You had 10 to the minus 6 in the 4th and now in the 5th it is 10 to the minus 5.' The man looked at it and said, 'That is wrong,' and he took his finger and erased it."

Groves was convinced he had won his biggest battle so far. And he was not through. Before the meeting ended, he told them how smart he was:

"When I was at West Point my recitations in calculus were always perfect. Once in a while they would mark me down to 2.9 but usually a straight 3.0 across. . . . If I had not been going to West Point I would have majored in physics when I got to MIT."

"Well, that kind of shocked them," Groves would say. And he further told the scientists: "I always found it [calculus] so easy. Maybe it was because I was lazy that I liked it. . . . I took college

algebra twice and descriptive geometry twice and plain trigonome-
try twice and spherical twice."

Groves added: "There is one last thing I want to emphasize.
You may know that I don't have a Ph.D. . . . But let me tell you
that I had ten years of formal education after I entered college.
Ten years in which I just studied. I didn't have to make a living or
give time to teaching. I just studied. That would be the equivalent
of about two Ph.D.'s, wouldn't it?"

Afterwards, Groves would say, "I think that I made a good
impression." But his talk was greeted by an embarrassed silence.
And when he strutted out, Szilard told a colleague:

"You see what I told you? How can you work with people like
that?"

VII

This question signaled the beginning of a bitter struggle between Groves and Szilard over how to build the bomb in the least
possible time, then, when Germany had been knocked out of the
war, over whether to drop it on Japan. The struggle would develop
into a savage battle among the scientists themselves and between
many of them and the military, clashes that would continue to
rage into the postwar period over momentous questions that
could decide the fate of the world: Should America build the much
more powerful hydrogen bomb? Who should control nuclear
weapons—civilians or soldiers?

Szilard and Groves were as opposite as two men could be.
Szilard was a dreamer, a messiah with a mission to save humanity;
Groves was a pragmatist, a soldier with the more modest mission of
winning the war—and the respect of anyone who dared doubt that
he would succeed. Szilard was a thinker who would sit in the
bathtub for days before deciding on how to approach a problem;
Groves might, while rushing through a shave, reach a decision
based on intuition and demand that all research questions be answered within hours. Szilard solicited support for his arguments
with intricate logic; Groves barked orders with military brevity.
Szilard, after serving in the Austrian army, viewed the military
mind as narrow and biased; Groves perceived the scientific mind as

childish and egocentric, arguing after the war, "I was always right, and [the scientists would never] believe that or even forgive me for it". Szilard had no genuine roots but was a wandering Jew who lived most of his life alone in hotel rooms in many different countries; Groves was a superpatriotic American Wasp of virtual Mayflower vintage whose life after work, what there was of it, revolved around family, home, and church.

It was thus easy for the two men to despise each other. Yet their mutual antagonism was perhaps stirred more by their similarities than by their differences. Both were fanatically dedicated men who could not be discouraged by setbacks in seeking a coveted goal. Actually, until the German defeat, both had a common goal—not only to build the bomb but to use it. Groves saw his career and reputation at stake.

If the bomb was not used, the general would explain, "people would [say], 'Why did you do it?'"

Congress, he feared, might even investigate why he spent $2 billion on a bomb that could have saved lives but didn't. Hans Bethe, who was one of the top scientists in the project, says:

"Groves would have been disappointed if the war had ended before the bomb could be used."

Szilard, on the other hand, would write in a memo to himself in September 1942 that the scientists had but two choices:

"We may take the stand that the responsibility for the success of this work has been delegated [to others] . . . and we can lead a very pleasant life while we are on duty. . . . Alternately, we may take the stand that those who have originated the work on this terrible weapon and those who have materially contributed to its development have, before God and the world, the duty to see to it that it should be ready to be used at the proper time and in the proper way."

And the "proper time" to Szilard, as well as to Groves, was the earliest possible date so that the war would not end first. Szilard wrote to Bush: "This weapon will be so powerful that there can be no peace if it is simultaneously in the possession of any two powers unless these two powers are bound by an indissoluble political union. It would therefore be imperative rigidly to control all deposits [of uranium], if necessary by force, and it will hardly be possible to get political action along that line unless high efficiency atomic bombs have actually been used in this war and the fact of their destructive power has deeply penetrated the mind of the public."

The "proper way"? Drop the bomb on a German city—after warning the inhabitants to get out.

Oddly, it was because they shared a bulldog characteristic that Szilard and Groves apparently felt a hidden respect for each other. After the war, Szilard offhandedly, perhaps inadvertently, praised Groves' wartime decisiveness to the Atomic Energy Commission, while Groves reacted with obvious pride to this unexpected compliment from someone he had been calling a second-rate scientist and a near-traitor, according to a report he filed in his private archives.

Szilard's anger was nourished by a sense of betrayal. Was it not *he* who had finally persuaded the government to build a bomb? Was it not *he*, together with Fermi, who had proved that a nuclear chain reaction was possible? And now the army, under what he considered a vain brute, was trying to tell him and his colleagues how to make an atomic bomb, refusing to acknowledge that the ultimate responsibility for success or failure lay mainly with the scientists.

Szilard had complained about government priorities and administration almost from the moment Roosevelt gave the order to start the project. But now with Groves, he felt, the blunders were being institutionalized. The general planned to turn the scientists into puppet soldiers. Did he think that they could generate ideas by the numbers? Or that they could work while strapped into a military bureaucracy? Once, in summer 1943, when a group of young scientists gathered to discuss the postwar implications of the bomb, Groves even interrupted with the warning that they might end up in Guadalcanal if they didn't disband immediately. Groves' policies, Szilard was sure, would hold up production of a bomb for at least a year—and he would claim after the war that he was right. Did Groves want Hitler to control the world?

Groves didn't, but neither did he want Szilard or any other scientist to control the Manhattan Project, which the general viewed as an army enterprise.

"It was always very difficult to tell," he would say, "whether the scientists in Chicago were as much interested in the national interest as they were in continuing to work on something which was extremely interesting to them with unlimited financial backing.

. . . They wanted to participate in all decisions, and in most of these decisions they were very ill-prepared. . . . I did not realize when I first moved into the Manhattan Project the great ignorance of scientific people outside their immediate spheres. . . . They knew nothing of history, either American or other. . . . They never in their lives had to produce. . . . If they proved that something couldn't be done, that was really almost as good as proving that it could be done."

To Groves, Szilard was the most aggressive, ignorant, and obnoxious of the lot. He wanted to run the whole project personally, yet what had he ever done? Yes, "if it hadn't been for Szilard, [the bomb project] would never have reached the President. Only a man with his brass would have pushed through to the President. Take Wigner or Fermi—they're not Jewish [actually, Wigner was]—they're quiet, shy, modest, just interested in learning." But Szilard, "the chief promoter and agitator . . . was anxious for personal glory and personal enrichment. . . ." On patent matters, "he wanted every penny he could get, no matter how unjustified his claims might be. . . . He was not a great scientist himself."

Besides—and this complaint was unstated—Szilard had little respect for the general's intelligence or authority, and if there was any man who needed, craved, and demanded the respect of his peers and underlings, with or without their affection, it was General Groves.

Why, then, did Groves not fire Szilard? Because this "would have created a great deal of dissension," and also because Szilard knew too much and might betray America since "he had no moral standards of any kind." But the general did try to have him interned.

Was it possible? he asked Bundy.

Bundy conferred with Stimson and found there was no legal way to do this.

In exasperation Groves then made a proposal to Conant. Would he offer Szilard a job at Harvard? Groves would "reimburse Harvard for all of its expenditures in connection with his employment as long as I had funds which could be devoted to the maintainance [sic] of security."

Conant laughed. No, he said, he wouldn't have him at Harvard if the general endowed the university for life.

Groves then tried another tack. He would turn other scientists against Szilard. The "quiet, shy, modest" Wigner seemed like a good bet, even though the general discovered he was Jewish. But Wigner proved difficult (as he had earlier when he threatened to quit because of discrimination against foreign scientists).

"Every time that we tried to make hay with Wigner," Groves would sadly relate, "I would say, 'Well, I think Wigner is all right.' . . . [But] within 10 minutes, he would be down in Szilard's office or Szilard would be in his office, talking to him in Hungarian Yiddish, convincing Wigner that I did not like scientists, that I hated physicists above all else, and that I did not like foreigners and I disliked particularly Hungarians and I had no use for Jews. . . . And Wigner would be right back where he was before," even threatening once more to quit his own job if Szilard were fired.

Groves was not beaten yet—he would find another way. He would get rid of Szilard by forcing him to accept a less sensitive job someplace where he couldn't cause trouble. He would capitalize on Szilard's "greed." He knew that Compton had once tried to move Szilard out of Chicago but had changed his mind when Szilard refused to work elsewhere and said that in order to live he would have to demand adequate royalties from the government for the use of his inventions. The government did not think it should have to pay for the rights to the inventions of an employee even though Szilard made them *before* working on a government project, and wanted to contribute the money to a research foundation, if he could live without it.

Szilard was now given an ultimatum: Either accept $25,000 for the right to all his inventions related to the chain reaction or leave the project. If Szilard, the government argued, were to have an unsettled claim against it, he might use his access to secret information to his advantage. The perfect excuse to get rid of Szilard and perhaps switch him to a job outside the project!

As expected, Szilard was outraged. He was being asked, he felt, to virtually give away his rights. He would agree, he said, to renounce forever any claim against the government, but he would retain the rights to his inventions.

The government persisted: Accept or get out!

Szilard was in a quandary. Why was the government doing this to him?

"We may be all blown up," he would say with more sorrow than bitterness, "and then maybe the government should sue me for damages."

No, he couldn't let the Germans get the bomb first. What, after all, was more important than saving the world?

Very well, he told government officials, they could have his inventions. But he wouldn't accept the $25,000. He would agree only to be reimbursed for the $16,000 he had spent to create the inventions.

Foiled again, Groves was bitter. "It would have been very beneficial," he would say, "if [Szilard] had had a very sudden accident. . . . Compton could not handle Szilard. Nobody could handle Szilard. The only way to have handled Szilard was to have shot him. And there was no reason for shooting him."

So Groves finally had to settle for having his security men trail his nemesis with special dedication.

VIII

What conflicts stoked such animosity between the two men? One was over the pivotal role that private companies would play in the project. Szilard, backed by other research scientists, wanted engineers to be hired as needed from any firm that could provide the best. The scientists would supervise their work and design the equipment that had to be built. Szilard himself was, after all, a first-class engineer with numerous patents to his credit. But even before Groves started directing the Manhattan Project, the Boston construction firm of Stone and Webster began taking over the engineering work from the research scientists. And when it proved unqualified, Groves' deputy, Colonel Nichols, went after Du Pont.

Thomas H. Chilton, who headed Du Pont's design division, showed initial interest but then had second thoughts. How could his company possibly design reactors for chemically separating an unknown element (plutonium)?

"You took advantage of me!" he screamed at Nichols. "God, they don't even have this stuff yet! It's not in existence. . . . My company is not going to risk its neck on something we don't even know will work!"

In fact, Chilton had not yet been told that the plutonium was needed for an atomic bomb, since a final contract was still to be signed.

Du Pont's reaction came as no surprise to Szilard. What did industrial engineers know about nuclear physics? They would have to be supervised step by step. But Groves took a different view. American industry could build anything, and Du Pont was perfect for this job. Szilard and the other scientists could never handle it. Let Du Pont design and build as it saw fit; Szilard and his gang could, of course, make whatever comments they wished.

Groves stormed into Du Pont headquarters in Wilmington, Delaware, and politely confronted the president and his men: Did Du Pont want to make sure the Allies would win the war? Did it want to save American lives? Then how could it refuse?

It couldn't. The company would build a whole maze of industrial plants in Hanford, Washington, near Pasco, in a desolate region of gray sand and sagebrush. Soon other firms also fell into line. Tennessee Eastman, a subsidiary of Eastman Kodak, began laying out plans for operating electromagnetic plants in the green wilderness of Oak Ridge, Tennessee, and the Kellex Corporation, a specially formed subsidiary of M. W. Kellogg Company, would build the largest, most complex factory in the world at Oak Ridge, a gaseous diffusion plant for separating U^{235}, even before some of its vital equipment had been invented.

But how, asked Szilard, could someone put theory into practice without understanding the theory? He ridiculed Du Pont. First, it decided to design a helium cooling system for a plutonium reactor. No, it then concluded, this couldn't work. Yes, it could. No, it couldn't. Finally the company decided to build a water cooling system designed by Wigner—but without Wigner. Who needed scientists?

Meanwhile, at Hanford, the sand and the sagebrush had been swept away to make room for a plant with a helium cooling system. But there would be no helium cooling system—the water cooling system would be used instead. The plant would be sitting in the wilderness with a vast supply of electric power that it did *not* need (the helium plant would have needed it), and a short supply of manpower, which it *did* need (it would have been built in a more populous area if the helium plant had not needed the electricity). So much confusion, so much lost time. And all this could have been avoided, thought Szilard, if only the Du Pont engineers had consulted with the scientists.

In any case, if other firms found a better, more economical way of getting a job done, Szilard asked, why not let them do it? Du Pont, he charged, wanted to assure itself a postwar monopoly of atomic energy and thus tried to stop the scientists from collaborating with other companies, even when it couldn't match their methods.

Groves, however, vigorously backed Du Pont. Its engineers didn't know how to build a heavy water power unit? Never mind. Scrap the plan. Why bring in more firms than necessary? The fewer the firms, the greater the chance for secrecy.

IX

Secrecy! It could be more valuable to Hitler, in Szilard's view, than a dozen nuclear scientists. Of course, the secrets of the bomb should be kept from the enemy, or from any potential enemy. After all, when the chain reaction was only a dream, Szilard had urged other scientists to stop publishing their findings on nuclear matters. But now, he felt, secrecy was being imposed in a way that could fatally slow up production of the bomb. General Groves had issued the order: All information must be compartmentalized. One scientist couldn't even talk to himself without disobeying orders, since he directed two departments simultaneously. The idea was to minimize damage if someone was to pass information to an enemy or potential enemy, perhaps inadvertently, by saying too much on a train or in a bar. Who knew if a German—or a Russian—spy was listening?

No man on the Manhattan Project was above suspicion, Groves assumed, so no man would escape his watchful eye. He would make sure the secrets were safe. To do this, he set up his own counterintelligence corps under two lawyers, Colonel John Lansdale, Jr., and Lieutenant Colonel William A. Consodine. He kept the Federal Bureau of Investigation out of the project because he wanted to control security personally. About 500 men in mufti, some posing as bartenders, waiters, and salesmen, secretly penetrated every branch of the project, eavesdropping on conversations at work and in nearby towns, shadowing the scientists and engineers, hiding microphones in their homes, probing every security leak and suspected case of sabotage. In addition, all mail was carefully censored, telephones were tapped, and discarded papers were burned by illiterate guards, while scientists who had to travel did so under a pseudonym.

Some were forbidden to travel—at least to Russia. When Groves learned that several had been invited to Moscow for a scientific meeting, he was horrified. What if someone should talk too much? His agents learned who the invited men were and politely asked them not to go. But one, Edward Condon, insisted on going in the name of scientific freedom, even after the company Groves had borrowed him from threatened to fire him.

Condon had to be stopped! And he was. The Russian plane that was to fly him was delayed all day because of mysterious mechanical trouble, and then, after dark, was "accidentally" rammed by a truck, which damaged one wing. And before Condon could board an American plane, he was notified that his passport was not valid for travel to Russia.

Compartmentalization was, to Groves, the heart of his security program. For it would presumably bar anyone but himself and his top administrators from knowing all the secrets necessary to make an atomic bomb. As it was, foreigners like Szilard knew too much. But Szilard didn't think the scientists, especially the foreigners, knew enough. Scientists thrived on learning from each other, he argued. Each built theories and discovered facts based on what someone else might write on his blackboard. Without the cross-pollination of ideas, there could be little scientific progress. And so in the interest of saving the world, he ignored Groves' orders, as many scientists did, swapping equations with all those he thought might stimulate his own thinking. And indeed, the scientists spoke freely at meetings they held periodically.

Nevertheless, the bomb project had been slowed down, Szilard felt, because scientists at one site found it hard to communicate with those at another. Little wonder they had failed to realize it was possible to build small, efficient atomic bombs sooner than they did, or to perfect the centrifuge method of separating U^{235} before Groves decided to dump it. Perhaps most devastating of all, Szilard would write, the scientists felt "unhappy and incapable of living up to their responsibility. . . . [Their] morale has suffered to the point where it almost amounts to loss of faith. [They] shrug their shoulders and go through the motions of performing their duty."

Meanwhile, the German scientists, Szilard had heard, were forging ahead.

"Unless I completely misjudge the psychology of the Germans," he wrote Lord Cherwell, Churchill's scientific adviser, in summer 1944, "they must have gone full-scale into this work soon after Stalingrad at the latest. . . . They ought to be making now one or two bombs a month."

And here, at this critical time, Groves, in Szilard's eyes, was virtually sabotaging the American bomb.

No, it was the scientists who were sabotaging, Groves felt. Their morale was sagging not because they were compartmentalized, but because Szilard was working the others into a state of rebellion. Let no one say that General Groves wasn't doing everything humanly possible to safeguard the secrets of the bomb. He had probed into the background of every scientist connected with the project—except, of course, members of the British team of physicists that would be coming to work on the bomb. British intelligence, after all, had assured him that each one had been rigidly screened. Groves didn't like the British, whom he considered "stuffed-shirted" snobs, but their intelligence system had been tops. How else could Britain have survived the war against Hitler until now? There was no sense wasting time and money double-checking. Besides, why antagonize an ally unnecessarily?

Groves neglected to ask if the British in their determination to survive the war had given much thought to surviving after the war.

X

As Klaus Fuchs gazed down from his room in the Taft Hotel upon the throngs of New Yorkers packing the stores, carrying Christmas packages, honking their horns in rhythm with the vibrant heartbeat of the city, he was thinking of Russia's survival. There would be no merry Christmas for the Russians. The German armies were smashing deep into the hinterland, killing millions; and if the Soviet Union died, so would communism, the only real hope for saving humanity. And even if the USSR survived the German assault, could it survive one by America and Britain—

especially if they had the atomic bomb? The two nations were sharing the secret with each other but refused to share it with their beleaguered ally. What could one conclude from this?

The ship carrying Fuchs and the other members of the British delegation invited to help on the Manhattan Project had landed at Newport News, Virginia, on December 3, 1943, and the group was immediately spirited to Washington, where each scientist signed a pledge to keep all that he learned secret. Fuchs had not hesitated for a moment; again it was perfectly honest to lie for a cause larger than loyalty to any person or nation. And was there any cause larger than mankind's salvation? The next stop was New York, and here he would take a giant step toward his goal. He would be trading ideas on the atomic bomb with the Americans who were building one.

After a short stay at the Taft Hotel, Fuchs moved to the Barbizon-Plaza, then rented an apartment at 128 West 77th Street so his movements would be less conspicuous. He darted back and forth between the Kellex Corporation offices, where he gathered information, and the British Ministry of Supply Mission, where he wrote his reports. With Kellex constructing the huge gaseous diffusion plant at Oak Ridge, the British were asked to help solve the problems of plant design, though they were not told where the plant was being built. Some were aghast at Groves' order to move ahead with construction even before it was known if the key part in the plant—the billion-hole filter—worked. But Fuchs apparently remained silent. He wasn't there to criticize but to observe. If the Americans could somehow hurdle all the obstacles, they could destroy the Nazis. And how much money and time Stalin would save when he learned how they did it.

So Fuchs did his best to help the Americans, working out calculations on the control ability and separation performance of the gaseous diffusion project. He soon stored in his brain, ready for transfer to Stalin's, the size of units, the various stages involved, and the diffusion area; he knew what instruments and type of power were being used. With extraordinary diligence, he wrote report after scholarly report, such as "The Optimum Pressure and Back Pressure in the Diffusion Plant," "Cascade of Cascades in the DS Scheme," and "Fluctuations in a Diffusion Separation Plant."

Although the Americans were not impressed by many of the British ideas, they were greatly impressed by one of their scientists—Klaus Fuchs. One Kellex scientist, Hanson O. Benedict, was even "awed" in his presence, describing him as "polite, businesslike, dreamy, and abstract." Fuchs helped to solve some of the most difficult theoretical physics problems.

General Groves, however, wanted to get not only British answers but British approval. For what would happen if the visitors returned home disheartened and told Churchill that the whole program would fail? Churchill would tell Roosevelt, Roosevelt would tell Bush, and who knew what Bush might tell Groves? So on December 22, 1943, in the Woolworth Building in Manhattan, the general presided over a meeting of the British scientists and the top Americans working on gaseous diffusion, and soon the British were learning almost everything they wanted to know about the project. Groves made sure, however, that no one outside the briefing room knew the meeting was even taking place. Why take a chance that a leak would reach the wrong ears—and turn all his attempts at secrecy into a bitter mockery?

XI

With his head full of data and his suitcase full of gifts, Fuchs had every reason to be in a good mood when he left New York to spend the Christmas holidays with his younger sister Kristel, who was living with her three children in Cambridge, Massachusetts. He had not seen Kristel since 1935, when they briefly met in Paris before he went to Britain to study and work his way into the top rank of nuclear physicists. During his internment in Canada, she had kept in touch with him through a Communist acquaintance who lived there, but she had no contact with him again until he landed in the United States.

When they met in Paris, Kristel had been en route to America on a student visa under the auspices of the Quaker Friends Service Committee, which their father supported. She attended Swarthmore College, where she met Robert Heineman, a Communist Party member, and married him. Kristel would deny that she was ever a Communist, claiming that, like her father, she was too religious to ever become one, but she understood and appreciated Marxist ideas. And she was proud of her brother for having followed the dictates of his conscience.

Despite their long separation, brother and sister remained close, and Fuchs yearned to see Kristel again. He had, after all, lost touch with other members of his family. His brother, Gerhardt, a fellow Communist who had fled Germany with him, was being treated in a Swiss sanatorium for tuberculosis, and his father was still in Germany, perhaps in jail. And, of course, his mother and another sister had committed suicide years earlier. Kristel was his sole link with the past. And beneath his professorial reserve, which was occasionally diluted with calculated flings at being human, Fuchs was a sentimental man. He had always had a protective attitude toward his ill-fated family, which, through his own twisted concept of communism, he extended to mankind.

And Fuchs' protective instincts were apparently aroused when, after a joyful reunion, he learned of Kristel's unhappiness. She and her husband had separated, at least temporarily, and she had few kind words for him. Confidential records of Westboro State Hospital in Westboro, Massachusetts, where she would be confined for a while after the war as a mental patient, indicated that an old college friend of her husband, Konstantin Lafazanos, was actually the father of her three children. Lafazanos reportedly acknowledged that this was true.

Already burdened with the weight of Nazi-inflicted family tragedies, Fuchs was so distressed by his sister's suffering that he decided he would, after settling into the routine of his work, ask her and the children to live with him in New York. But he made the most of the holiday, sleeping late and going for walks with the children, for whom he developed a genuine affection. He apparently said nothing to Kristel about his job or his spy activities, not wishing to get her involved. And she asked no questions. Yet, in an emergency, he felt, he could always use her address for meetings or message drops. Unfortunately, her husband and Lafazanos were often around, but her husband, at least, was a fellow Communist. Whom but his sister could he trust in this country of strangers? Just one other person—and he hadn't met him yet.

XII

Shortly, Fuchs was back in New York and ready to gather new data for Stalin. On January 5, 1944, American and British experts on the gaseous diffusion process met once more in the Woolworth

Building to examine plans for the diffusion plant. It is unclear whether Fuchs himself spoke, but the British now, after studying the plans, questioned whether the American design was feasible at all. Did the Americans really expect to control the process through thousands of diffusion stages? Impossible!

But Groves and his men shrugged off this skepticism. Never mind, they could do it. Now what about the filter? Engineers had been working on one particular model for two years, and a whole plant had already been built for its manufacture, even though no one yet knew whether the model could work. But in the meantime, a new-type filter had been developed. Which one should be used?

The new one was promising for future use, the British said, but you don't switch filters in the middle of the game. Why not work on both simultaneously?

No, there were neither the resources nor the time. A choice must be made now!

One American engineer who favored the new process then made a bold suggestion: Rip out the present machines and replace them with new ones.

Absolutely reckless! replied a Briton. What if the new ones failed after all the millions already spent on the old? This could set back the production of U^{235} until the summer of 1946.

But another Briton disagreed: Be plucky. Push ahead with the new one.

And a few days later, General Groves did: Strip the plant for the new filter! he ordered.

XIII

Fuchs hoped Groves' gamble would pay off. Russia's life—and bomb—might depend on it. Meanwhile, in the next few weeks he gathered facts like blueberries at a summer picnic. And finally, the long-awaited Saturday came, the day when he would meet the stranger he could trust. Before he had left England, his woman contact there had given him the precise details for the meeting, and he had been calmly preparing for the encounter.

Now, as he left on his mission, Fuchs' calm dissolved in "apprehension." Was he being followed? What if he couldn't make contact? He strode into a subway station in midtown Manhattan at about 3 P.M., and as he sat down in the train his tension grew with every click of the wheels. He got off on the Lower East Side and walked to Henry Street with a tennis ball clutched in his hand. At the designated corner, he stopped, looked around, and saw a man wearing gloves and carrying an additional pair, as well as a book with a green binding. Just as his contact in Britain had indicated.

"I'm Raymond," the man said as he walked up to Fuchs. The stranger was short and round-faced with slouching shoulders.

"I'm Dr. Klaus Fuchs," said the scientist, giving his real name in defiance of the basic axiom of espionage.

The stranger stared at Fuchs with shrewd eyes that reflected dismay.

Didn't Fuchs know about security precautions?

Fuchs sharply replied that he knew all about such precautions.

He was pleased to meet Fuchs, said Raymond, hoping to warm up the relationship. He had been expecting him and was happy to have been chosen for such an important assignment.

The two men walked for a few blocks, trying to get comfortable with each other, then took a taxi to Manny Wolfe's Restaurant on Third Avenue. Over dinner they discussed Fuchs' job.

What was Fuchs doing?

Working for the British mission on the Manhattan Project. Fuchs then described the makeup and activities of the British group.

What was his main function?

Analyzing how to separate uranium isotopes for eventual use in an atomic bomb.

Raymond, it seemed evident, was acquainted with the bomb, since he didn't ask for an explanation.

The scientists worked in extremely tight compartments, Fuchs said, and one group didn't know what the others were doing. But he had heard that a large-scale installation for separating isotopes would be built somewhere, perhaps in Georgia or Alabama. The Oak Ridge site was still unknown to him.

Fuchs did not turn over any material at this first encounter with his Soviet contact. He wanted to size him up first and build up a feeling of trust. During a walk after dinner, he arranged to meet Raymond again.

Hardly had they parted when Raymond dashed off to report to "Sam," his superior, recounting everything that Fuchs had said.

Raymond, actually Harry Gold, had been working for Sam, Semion Semionov, since early 1935. Semionov was Russia's chief spy in the United States, and he had been impressed by Gold's diligence and ability to deliver, but, most of all, by his willingness to obey. And since he was a chemist, he seemed the right man for what was probably the most important courier job in espionage history.

Yet Gold was not a professional spy, but simply a good amateur one. Spying was a kind of hobby to him, a hobby gone wild. He had been thinking of quitting the spy game, but he was too committed. People depended on him. And besides, he believed in what he was doing; communism would free mankind. Of course, he lived in constant fear that he would be discovered and his family disgraced. But he could conquer such fear, for, like Fuchs, he had managed to divide his mind into two compartments, if in a different way. He lived two lives, and if they started to merge, he would simply create a third life, a fantasy life. Though a bachelor, he once imagined himself marrying, fathering children, squabbling with his wife, separating from her, all the while building up the fantasy with facts borrowed from his mother's past. Another time, he "killed" his brother and adopted a cousin he liked. Stealing atomic bomb secrets was, in a sense, like a fantasy, and he could switch from one life to another if ever his conscience felt overburdened.

Gold's political extremism apparently sprang from his impoverished roots. The son of poor Russian immigrants, who arrived in the United States in 1914, he was bundled from town to town in his father's search for work. *Something* was wrong with the system! As a young man, Gold worked in a Philadelphia sugar factory and eventually learned enough to become a chemist. When a Soviet agent visited him in 1936 seeking industrial information for the Soviet Union, Gold did not hesitate. Why not contribute to a system in which no one had to search endlessly for work? And thus began a period of industrial espionage that lasted until Sam promoted him to the "big time"—after all, the atomic bomb was simply a more spectacular product. And wasn't Russia America's ally?

Soon Gold was working for "John," who replaced Sam. Anatoli Yakovlev was apparently higher up in the intelligence hierarchy than his predecessor, a sign that Stalin was determined to make the most of this atomic windfall. In March, about three weeks after their first meeting, Fuchs and Gold met again at 59th Street and Lexington Avenue and strolled north along First Avenue. Still feeling "Raymond" out, Fuchs once more failed to bring any documents and merely offered additional details about his job.

Now he felt more at ease, and after a third meeting on a cold night later that month—on Madison Avenue in the upper seventies—they quickly turned into a dark side street, where Fuchs slipped a package of documents to Gold, who immediately walked ahead of the scientist and down Fifth Avenue toward 75th Street. There Yakovlev was waiting in the shadows to receive the precious data.

When the two spies met a fourth time in May, in front of a movie theater on the Grand Concourse in the Bronx, Gold thought a celebration was in order. He took Fuchs to dinner at Rosenhein's, and the two men, now warm, trusting friends, chatted about their common interest in chess and classical music. Music sparked an idea. It could provide a plausible explanation of how they'd met—in case anyone ever asked. Gold would look at the entertainment section of a newspaper, select a New York Philharmonic Orchestra concert at Carnegie Hall, and copy down the program for that concert. He would then inform Fuchs of the program so that they could both say they attended the concert and happened to have adjoining seats. The two spies finished off the evening at a small bar in upper Manhattan, enjoying each other's company over a few drinks.

Some weeks later, at a fifth meeting, Fuchs handed Gold another package of invaluable data in Queens, near Queensboro Plaza, and Gold swiftly strode to a nearby elevated station and took the train heading toward Jackson Heights, where Yakovlev was again waiting eagerly for the information.

Meanwhile, Fuchs was haunted by Kristel's unhappy state, and she was on his mind when, in June, he met Gold for the sixth time, in Brooklyn near Boro Hall. His sister was having great difficulty with her husband, said Fuchs, and she planned to come to New York. Would Gold please ask his superior if she and her children would be allowed to live with him. Gold met Yakovlev later that evening but did not broach the subject. He was moved by Fuchs' concern for his sister; why take the chance that the Russian would say "no"?

At their seventh meeting, Fuchs had some news. He met Gold

in early July near the Museum of Modern Art off Fifth Avenue and they strolled for an hour and a half along the twisting paths of Central Park. Later in the year, Fuchs said, he would be transferred to the "Southwest." (Gold understood him to say possibly Mexico, though Fuchs would claim he said New Mexico.) Gold didn't press for any new arrangement since his friend's departure did not seem imminent. Before they parted, he gave Fuchs some news of his own: It would be perfectly all right for his sister and her children to move in with him.

Gold had reason to feel bold and generous. Despite all the security precautions of General Groves, despite the guards and the guns, the screening and the scrutiny, the badges, bans, and barbed wire, Fuchs had already given Russia enough knowledge about the bomb to change the shape of the postwar world, at least faster than it would otherwise be changed. He had delivered handwritten copies of all thirteen reports on the gaseous diffusion process that he had prepared for Kellex, as well as additional information on tolerances, filters, working plans, the size of the plant being built, and the principles of the mathematical theory.

But Gold, pushed by Yakovlev, was greedy for still more, and hoped to get it at their eighth meeting, to take place in front of the Bell Cinema in Brooklyn in late July. Only Gold showed up, however. As for Kristel, she and her children did not move to New York.

Klaus Fuchs had vanished.

Chapter 7

THE
PATRIOT

I

In Tokyo, the whole world of Yoshio Nishina had vanished. But even on the day of the bomb he foresaw a golden era for Japan. Nishina, the leading Japanese nuclear scientist, gazed beyond the wreckage to a postwar world harnessed to the power of the atom. The vision of a new tomorrow somehow made defeat more palatable.

Look what atomic energy would do for Japan, he declaimed to his colleagues. What the Japanese scientists learned about this energy during the war could be sublimated into peacetime use for factories, ships, planes. After defeat, Japan could rise from the rubble and emerge as one of the world's top nuclear centers— thanks, ironically, to government funds that would never have flowed in peacetime.

Nishina had tried to build an atomic bomb but had failed. He was not too disappointed, however, for he knew he must fail; Japan had neither the money, the materials, nor the men to build one before the war ended. And he did not really want to build one anyway, knowing its potential for destruction. Thus, he never had to ask himself: Should the bomb be dropped on the enemy? He didn't have to struggle with his conscience as Western scientists did.

Actually, Nishina, despite the shortage of resources, had been making some progress in the search for a uranium separation process—until April 1945, when the building housing his nuclear laboratory in Tokyo's Institute for Physical and Chemical Research was suddenly decimated by an American incendiary bomb. And it was too late to start all over again. But his work, Nishina felt, had not been a waste. He and his assistants had learned much for the future, a future he now pondered as he sat in his office in a charred building that had survived the raid, behind a mountain of papers that he never bothered to file.

On the day of the bomb, most buildings of the vast institute, which sprawled haphazardly in a parklike compound in the Komagome section of Tokyo, still stood amidst the burned greenery, regally defiant despite their scars. Almost all the machinery and personnel, however, had been moved from Tokyo to be out of the range of the B-29s, and only Nishina and a few other staff members remained. But all work on nuclear energy had ceased, and the military had ordered Nishina to research more practical projects such as radar, cosmic rays, and ultrashort waves, which, it was thought, might lead to the development of a "death ray."

Nishina's main worry now was that more bombs might ruin his two cyclotrons (a third one was housed at Osaka University), which offered a constant reminder that after the war Japan would be transformed into a scientific giant. One of the Tokyo cyclotrons, weighing 200 tons, was as large as the one run by Ernest Lawrence at Berkeley, and was, in fact, built with the help of scientists there. To Nishina, the cyclotrons symbolized the postwar Japan that would reconstruct itself and fulfil its blessed destiny despite the greatest adversity.

The institute was now virtually Nishina's home, and he worked in his office and new makeshift laboratory until his mind ceased to function. For one thing, he was lonely and had little else to do. Like his nuclear department, his home outside the walls of the institute had been demolished by bombs in April, and he had sent his family away—his sickly wife to stay with her parents outside of Tokyo, and his two teen-age sons to a school in western Honshu.

Nishina had a room in a nearby dormitory, but he often slept on a cot behind his desk.

It was not only loneliness that spurred him, however; it was also patriotism. The trouble was, he was a patriot who fed on facts rather than fantasy, and, unlike most Japanese, could not ease the anguish of war with illogical morale-lifting myths. He had been outraged by the militarists' adventures from the beginning—the Mukden Incident, the invasion of Manchuria, the assassinations and attempted coups. And when Radio Tokyo enraptured the nation with the news of Pearl Harbor, he was shocked.

"What an insane war Japan has launched!" he exclaimed to a colleague. "Any fool knows the power and the might of the United States. The consequences to Japan can only be disastrous. We are all aboard a sinking ship."

Nishina dared say this though he knew such a statement, despite his lofty scientific status, could land him in jail or even the morgue if the Kempei Tai learned of it. In fact, some officers, aware of his thinking, would later plot to kill him. But characteristically, Nishina added, "We must do what we can to save the ship."

His dilemma was rooted in an agonizing conflict between his traditional values and his modern logic.

II

Nishina was an unimpressive-looking little man with a square face, flat nose, thin lips, and a large head accentuated by a deeply receding hairline. But there was drama in his melancholy eyes, which stared through round, thin-rimmed glasses, betraying his inner tension and turmoil. Born in 1890 in Okayama, west of Osaka, when Japan was flexing its muscles for a leap into great-power society, he was fiercely proud of his country's extraordinary overnight rise from feudalism and observed Japanese religious and social ritual to the letter. He was unswervingly loyal to the Emperor and apparently would even commit suicide if the facts showed that he had brought shame upon him. Yet Nishina wasn't religious and he didn't believe that the Emperor was divine. His observance and loyalty were based not on superstition but on tradition. It was simply Japanese to act that way.

At the same time, Nishina's modernism had been refined during the six years he studied physics in Copenhagen under the Danish genius, Niels Bohr, who had taught him not only the structure of the atom but the structure of the peaceful world that must evolve in the coming nuclear era. While there, Nishina had mingled with scientists of all countries and, unlike most of the Japanese militarists and politicians, he understood the Western mind well.

In some ways, his own mind, molded by logic and a sense of independence, had grown more Western than Japanese, and especially resembled Szilard's. Like Szilard, he righteously expounded on his theories with anyone who would listen, sometimes up to ten hours at a time, yielding to an argument only when confronted with irrefutable proof. He was a scientific dilettante, an engineer turned scientist, who abandoned one project for another as soon as the results became obvious. He craved tackling the impossible. He was drawn to biology because he cared about human beings. And if he had no scheme to save the world, he had one to save Japan: Make it a mecca of international science.

But Nishina could not relieve his tension with sparks of humor, as Szilard could, except when he occasionally imbibed a bit too much *sake*. Nor, since the war began, would he allow himself to unwind with a game of tennis or even a hike, activities he loved but cast aside at a time when thousands were dying on the battlefield. The only therapy left to him was to let loose his temper, and he alternated brimstone with benevolence in prodding his assistants toward scientific breakthroughs.

His assistants responded with enthusiasm, for they loved *Oyabun* (the Old Man), as they called him, regarding him as a father. He gave them freedom to let their minds wander down untrodden scientific paths, and also a chance to survive the war. He had asked for their release from military duty, they knew, not only to have them work on war projects but to safeguard them, like priceless national treasures, for the Utopian years of postwar science when they would be competing with their Western friends in the drive of man for a better life—cooperating, as in prewar days.

Since he was familiar with the Western mind, Nishina knew what Western science and industry could do. But even he underrated their capability, perhaps because he wanted to. He was sure that America, with all its resources and scientists, couldn't build an atomic bomb in time for this war, though the navy had told him in 1942 that the enemy was working on one. If he had thought it could, he would surely have broken down government doors to warn leaders: Surrender now before it's too late. . . .

Why *didn't* they surrender? It wasn't logical for Japan as a nation to commit suicide. America didn't need the atomic bomb to crush Japan; it could do so with conventional weapons. Wasn't that what the Potsdam Declaration meant when it threatened "prompt and utter destruction"? His whole people might die—and never taste the fruit of a nuclear age.

III

Nishina had been craving the fruit ever since he was graduated from Tokyo Imperial University in 1918 with honors in engineering and physics. It was four years later that he went to Copenhagen to study under Bohr, and there with a colleague he calculated a formula for scattering gamma rays that would make atomic research much easier. He returned to Tokyo in 1928 and opened his own laboratory in the Physical and Chemical Research Institute three years later, at a time of radical development in nuclear physics, especially with the neutron lured out of hiding. But with his unbounded curiosity, Nishina probed not only the atom but cosmic rays and X rays, and introduced quantum physics to Japan. And with all this, he still found time to lecture, write, and grant press interviews in a furious struggle to draw enough funds to pay for the research.

As Szilard would gradually focus on nuclear physics in the early 1930s, so did Nishina, who anticipated the day when the atom could be smashed, together with the obstacles to a modern industrialized society, which, he felt, even the Meiji Revolution had not entirely achieved. The magic of a nuclear age and not the dangerous dream of military conquest was the cure for Japan's economic anemia. What he needed was an atom smasher, and, in 1937, that's what he got. In what almost seemed like a race with the militarists invading China that year, he and his assistants built one weighing 28 tons. But it only fired Nishina's relentless ambition for Japan. It was too small for a man in a hurry.

They must build a 200-ton cyclotron, he ordered his assistants.

Gasps. That was the size of the Berkeley cyclotron! And they hadn't even started to exploit the small one yet. It didn't make sense.

But it did to Nishina. Japan had to keep pace with America. It had to find an alternative to brute force in Asia. . . . By building the small cyclotron, had they not learned how to build a big one? Get to work!

And his men did—more than one hundred of them. But Pearl Harbor exploded before Nishina's atoms had a chance to. The military had won the race. To Nishina, this was the ultimate disaster. There would be no more collaboration with American scientists. No more private funds, which would now flow to the military. The large cyclotron would probably not be ready during the war, and by the end of the war Japan would be devastated and its scientific progress would lay stagnant.

And yet, he must do what he could to save the ship.

IV

Nishina soon had the opportunity. The Japanese scientists did not press government leaders to build an atomic bomb as the American scientists did after nuclear fission was discovered. On the contrary, these leaders—the military—pressed the scientists. Nishina, for one, however nationalistic, was not eager to build a weapon that would help the military grab control of a world he felt should be dealt with in a spirit of friendship and equality. But if war was a reality, he wanted a negotiated peace, not an atomic holocaust. Atomic energy was fine—for peaceful purposes.

So it was a military man with an engineering background, Lieutenant General Takeo Yasuda, who first pushed the idea of building an atomic bomb. Yasuda, the director of the Aviation Technology Research Institute of the Imperial Japanese Army, picked up a scientific journal one day and was riveted as he read about the new phenomenon of nuclear fission—apparently Joliot-Curie's famous article. What could this lead to? In April 1940, he ordered Lieutenant Colonel Tatsuaburo Suzuki to find out. Six months later, Suzuki turned in his report to General Yasuda. Meanwhile, across the turbulent waters, leaders in Washington were perusing their own paper—the Frisch-Peierls report from Britain. Both studies reached the same conclusion: An atomic bomb could be made.

But Yasuda did not launch a massive project as the American leaders did. In fact, he sat on the idea for several months. Finally, in April 1941, he summoned Masatoshi Okochi, director of the Physical and Chemical Research Institute. Find out if an atomic bomb is feasible, he ordered. Okochi dropped the project in Nishina's lap. And Nishina called together his assistants and, with all the fervor of a man ordered to set his house on fire, gave them the news: The Imperial Japanese Army wanted an atomic bomb.

As a pragmatist, Nishina knew he had to deal in the military coin. Anyway, he began to realize, the coin had two sides. With military support he could continue his atomic research during the war. But after a few months' research, he notified the army: He couldn't build a bomb before the war ended if he tried. And he wouldn't try very hard. Understandably, the army lost patience as well as interest in the project.

But then the navy, which bitterly competed with the army for power and influence, rushed to fill the nuclear vacuum. On December 17, 1941, a little more than a week after Pearl Harbor, it called a meeting of scientists and naval technicians at the Naval Officers' Club in Tokyo, and Nishina was there. Captain Yoji Ito of the Navy Technology Research Institute addressed the gathering:

"The navy wishes to develop an atomic weapon not only for . . . defense but also for . . . attack. We know, of course, that such a project will entail enormous labors, great ingenuity, and fearsome problems. What we want to know from you gentlemen is whether the project is feasible. If it is, we want to begin it immediately, and we want you to take part in it."

Could Japan build a bomb?

"It would be very difficult, but I believe it is worth trying," said Nishina, though he had been "trying" for months.

What about uranium?

"At the institute," replied Nishina, "we have several tons of uranium-bearing ore. This represents only a small amount of actual uranium. I understand that, in Shanghai, our army has about 800 kilograms [1,760 pounds] of uranium oxide from South Africa. I don't know whether that would be available. . . . And as you know, there are no sources of uranium in Japan. Perhaps the navy, too, could get it in Africa. . . . It might be available in [the Belgian Congo]."

"Then we'll get it. If the army could get it, we can get it."

Tsunesaburo Asada, the chief physicist at Osaka University, who had also opposed the war, then spoke up: "But even if you found an unlimited supply of uranium, nobody can promise to develop an atomic weapon. We still have three essential things to learn. We don't yet know how to concentrate the uranium isotope so its energy can be released. We haven't yet developed a mechanism to create a chain reaction. And we don't yet know the critical amount of the uranium isotope needed to sustain a chain reaction. Without a chain reaction, there can be no explosion. Without knowing how to create an explosion, we can't develop a weapon."

Could these problems be solved?

"Perhaps, eventually," Nishina replied.

Could it be done quickly enough to use in the war?

"That is what we would have to find out," said Nishina. "I don't think you should count on it."

Could the Germans help?

"I doubt it," said Asada. "Most of Germany's atomic scientists happened to be Jewish, and they've been expelled from the country. Some of them have gone to the United States. In my opinion, only the United States has the potential to develop an atomic weapon."

"The United States *and* Japan!"

Nishina was asked to take charge of the project.

"The navy has the money," said Ito.

Nishina felt a twinge of conscience. Would it really be "all right to spend the money" on a wasteful atomic bomb project while soldiers were dying at the front? But his assistants reassured him. After all, he was working for Japan's future, wasn't he?

V

Almost seven months later, on July 8, 1942, the scientists and naval technicians met once more at the Naval Officers' Club. Little progress had been made. Nishina had instructed several young scientists to prepare data for both the army and the navy, but he had assigned no one to study the bomb problem exclusively. Research had to proceed in a leisurely, orderly way, according to academic custom. No need to rush just because there was a war on—when they didn't want to build a bomb anyway. Now, at this meeting, Nishina said very little, letting his colleagues speak for him.

Could Japan produce an atomic bomb before the war ended or not?

They still weren't sure. It wasn't impossible, but they couldn't say it was possible either.

One professor reported that "the American embargo on exports of uranium, thorium, and radium seems proof enough that the United States is undertaking intensive research into the production of the atomic bomb." But this news did not alarm anyone. Of course, the Americans were dabbling in the atomic field as Japan was. But they were no doubt just as confused as the Japanese scientists were.

Nevertheless, the navy decided Japan should push ahead, and it financed new research to the tune of $4,700, almost as much as the American government gave Szilard and his colleagues for *their* early experiments.

A month later, the same group met again. And this time rumors were rampant that the United States had launched an all-out effort to build a bomb. Everyone was surprised, but still not alarmed. Captain Ito, in fact, seemed almost ecstatic.

"So it *can* be done after all!" he cried. "So it can be done!"

Yes, the Americans were building an atomic bomb that could destroy Japan, but the important thing was that they were convinced they could build it. So Japan could, too!

When one professor described the difficulties and said the process would take a number of years, Ito was furious.

"You college professors," he said, "are apt to be too conservative. You tell us the problem is so difficult that success within a reasonable time is impossible to hope for. But listen to me. People who make warships have a different way of approaching problems. Even though they may feel that it is impossible to have a ship finished in time, they do their best, and in most cases, let me tell you, that ship is off the production line ahead of schedule. I ask you, then, not to tell us that you are unable to produce the bomb within the necessary time but rather to exert every effort to do so. I want you to continue your research."

Nishina and the other scientists agreed, though all felt it would take from five to ten years to build a bomb, and that it would take America perhaps just as long. Why argue with the military? Take the money and run. And they did. Meeting after meeting produced almost the same response: Not impossible, but probably not possible.

At each meeting, Nishina seemed more depressed, for Japan, after six glorious months of military triumph, had begun to lose the war. Japanese ships were being sunk. Allied forces were on the move. And Japan's economy was beginning to totter. Just as he had predicted. And yet, Nishina was Japanese, as Japanese as the boys dying on some distant island. He couldn't let them down. True, it was impossible to build a bomb quickly enough. But Captain Ito was right. He shouldn't say it even if it was. Rather, he should "exert every effort" to succeed.

"We have to do something for our country," he told a colleague.

And so, at about the time the atomic pile of Fermi and Szilard proved that the world was capable of blowing itself up, Nishina began making his own bomb. He was a good soldier, and this was, after all, what he was most qualified to do.

Chapter 8

THE

MAKER

I

J. Robert Oppenheimer was a good patriotic soldier, too. But no one would ever know it from perusing the FBI file on him, for it read like a page out of a Communist *Who's Who*. That, however, was the old Oppenheimer. There seemed little in common between the old and the new, between the politically innocent idol of a campus band of leftists and the military-managed maker of America's atomic bomb.

In late 1942, General Groves had plucked this scientific genius from Ernest Lawrence's shining citadel atop Berkeley's Radiation Hill and plopped him in the middle of a magnificent New Mexican mesa called Los Alamos with the order to build the bomb itself. And assisted by some of the world's greatest scientists and engineers, who worked indefatigably behind miles of barbed wire, he had done the job.

On the day of the bomb, in the jagged summer shadows of the Sangre de Cristo peaks that soared over the bomb factories with heavenly beauty, Oppenheimer awaited the news that his work had not been in vain. He was Krishna of Bhagavad-Gita, his favorite Indian mythology. Krishna, the shatterer and savior of worlds, who told a guilt-torn warrior that he should not worry about taking lives in war since men were but pawns in a great scheme of things and that human responsibility was thus meaningless.

"I am death, the all-devouring, and the origin of things that are yet to be," preached Krishna. "And of feminine things, I am fame, prosperity, speech, memory, intelligence, firmness, and patience."

Krishna was all these things—and so, it apparently seemed to Oppenheimer, was he. The deity's words were like poetry to a man who wanted to feel godly but not guilty. Yet Oppenheimer had shrouded himself in Krishna's mantle only after seeing the sky thunderously erupt in a test of the bomb over the New Mexican desert. He had built the weapon with little thought of becoming death; he had been too preoccupied with the challenge and the reward to dwell on the price.

Oppenheimer seldom passed up a serious challenge, however dangerous or seemingly insurmountable. As a boy he had sailed his boat into a stormy sea just to show that he could do it, barely making it back into the embrace of parents ravaged by worry. At school he shone most brightly when the problem seemed least soluble. And now, what could be more insoluble than the problem of building a bomb that could obliterate a whole city instantly?

At the same time Oppenheimer craved recognition, never having won the Nobel Prize, though many of his colleagues had won it. According to a statement Lawrence made to the FBI after the war, Oppenheimer wrote to him in 1945 that he "had always been the 'underdog' and felt bad because he had never done anything really great or at least had not been recognized for such work." The problem was that while Oppenheimer knew more than almost all his colleagues, he accomplished less than some. For, as scientist Hans Bethe would point out, he focused "so hard on making profound discoveries that he missed the more available ones." Moreover, his interests were too diversified to allow him to concentrate on any one problem. His study of the Hindu religion was especially distracting, magnifying the mystery of the universe in his mind, and thus sapping his confidence that he could find the full answer to any question in physics.

Still, few men were blessed with a mind that could grasp so much so quickly as Oppenheimer's could. And he never forgot what he learned. At any meeting, he shaped the discussion, dominated it, and kept it to the point, because he understood more than the others.

Typically, he was walking down a corridor in Los Alamos one day when he glanced into a room where a man was sitting in front of a blackboard reflecting on a complicated problem. He entered, strode to the blackboard, picked up an eraser and a piece of chalk, and changed one figure in the equation. The man gaped.

"I've been looking for that mistake for three days!" cried Enrico Fermi, who *had* won the Nobel Prize.

At least now, with his new job, the world would be aware of J. Robert Oppenheimer.

II

General Groves, for one, was convinced that this thirst for recognition was the main source of the man's zeal. In denying to the FBI in 1943 that Oppenheimer was a security risk, Groves said that his gifted administrator "would not allow anyone to leak information which might assist others in developing the project before [he did] since this would destroy his chance for world recognition." Furthermore, Oppenheimer's wife, Katherine, or Kitty, "was pressing him for fame" because she felt that "Lawrence has received all the limelight and honors" while "she thinks her own husband is more deserving."

Groves felt that patriotism played no role at all in keeping Oppenheimer loyal to the United States.

"If it was found that subversive activity was actually being carried out," the FBI quoted Groves as saying, "Oppenheimer would not regard this as disloyalty to the United States, but rather . . . as being disloyal to him alone. In other words, it is not a question of the country's safety, but rather whether a person might be working against Oppenheimer in stopping him from obtaining the reputation which will be his, with the complete development of the project."

There is, however, no evidence that Oppenheimer was any less patriotic or dedicated to the "country's safety" than other Americans. In fact, he was probably motivated even more by selfless

ideals than some after he learned firsthand how Hitler was treating
the Jews from relatives who fled Germany shortly before the war.

But if Groves, while seeking to protect Oppenheimer, slan-
dered him in the process, he was, by his own standards, being kind
to the man. His paradoxical evaluation reflected the implausibility
of their relationship, which itself appears to have been a potent
element in Oppenheimer's drive to succeed in his job. Groves and
Oppenheimer could hardly have been less alike in appearance,
taste, or character. The general at least shared certain traits with
Szilard, such as stubbornness and inflexibility. But there was almost no common ground with Oppenheimer.

Groves was explosive, gruff, blunt, stiffly military, with little
interest in art or literature, and, while scorning tobacco and alco-
hol, he constantly inflated his substantial paunch with chocolates
he hid in his office safe with other valuable secrets. Oppenheimer,
controlled and sensitive, though cuttingly contemptuous of stu-
pidity, was a chain smoker and martini addict, a man with an insatiable curiosity in both the sciences and the arts that drove him to
master even ancient Sanskrit, a slightly stooped, string-bean 6-
footer who loped instead of walked and barely jogged the scales
with his meager 135 pounds—actually 113 by the day of the bomb.
Their backgrounds, too, were a study in contrast. Groves came
from a Presbyterian chaplain's family of modest income, Oppenheimer from a nonobservant Jewish businessman's family of considerable wealth. Groves' father had been a strict disciplinarian,
Oppenheimer's a libertarian of sorts, who hesitated to even scold
the boy. And yet, Groves and Oppenheimer would be linked for
life by a strange mutual trust born of mutual need.

Groves needed Oppenheimer because the scientist could mes-
merize people with his sharp, eloquent words and fathomless blue
eyes that serenely illuminated a gaunt, ascetic face. The general
himself had been beguiled, and he instinctively knew that this was
the Pied Piper who could lure into the wilderness some of the
world's most brilliant "crackpots" and induce them to work together. True, Oppenheimer was a Jew, and an unreligious one at
that, the very kind he felt could never be loyal to any country.
Nevertheless, unlike Szilard, Oppenheimer was a "good" Jew. For
one thing, he treated Groves with respect and didn't sneer at his
impressive academic credentials. In fact, he agreed with most of
Groves' opinions, and when he didn't, he gave pungent argu-

ments, but in the manner of a subordinate addressing his superior.

Oppenheimer was even willing to put the scientists into uniform and pin a lieutenant colonel's insignia on his own, until his colleagues, horrified by the thought of saluting a strutting "egomaniac" like Groves, revolted. Only Oppenheimer could see the benefits of working under army discipline. Yes, a good Jew, however questionable his Americanism.

If Groves needed Oppenheimer in part because he yearned for the respect of so brilliant a man, Oppenheimer needed Groves because he yearned for respectability. He was proud to be chosen for his job by a man who might have been expected to denigrate him as a "bleeding heart" egghead with little understanding of true American values like patriotism, puritanism, and free enterprise. Especially considering Oppenheimer's political past. As he himself confessed to Groves with "shame" before he got the job, he had contributed to just about every fellow-traveling organization on the West Coast. His wife, brother, sister-in-law, and former fiancée had all been Communists, and his best friends were varied shades of pink. He had been living in a shabby little world within a world, and now General Groves, the very essence of the establishment, had liberated him, accepting his services despite the taint of earlier days. By switching to conventional values, Oppenheimer felt somehow more patriotic. And he was grateful to Groves, though, ironically, the general would never feel that patriotism was his administrator's strongest suit.

Actually, Groves' trust was rather cynically pragmatic; it was a calculated gamble. His goal was to build a bomb as swiftly as possible—before the war ended. He could deal with all less urgent matters later. Anyway, he didn't believe, or want to believe, Oppenheimer ever "accepted Communist dogma or theory." And besides, didn't the man already know as much about atomic energy as anyone? At least inside the project he could be easily watched, and reminded that General Groves was aware of his pinkish past and in a position to shape his future—though, shortly before Oppenheimer died in 1966, Groves would deny attempting this form of blackmail. He assured the scientist that "I never intended to gain unusual control over you. . . . As to any sword of Damocles hanging over your head, there was no special one for you."

If Oppenheimer hired Communists to work on the bomb, how would he explain it? When the FBI asked Groves this question in 1943, he replied with audacity, as only a hard-core Red-baiter could:

"Oppenheimer would say that all scientists are liberals and that it would be nothing to be alarmed about, and that no action would be prosecuted to either remove or curtail the Communist activities of the named employees."

And Groves' own view?

Even if "every one of the employees might be ascertained to be Communist . . . the project would have to go along with these particular persons, and . . . they would have to be used."

But wasn't Groves afraid of espionage?

"Concrete evidence of actual espionage laid before both [myself] and . . . Oppenheimer would be enough to convince [us] that a person was bad and in that case [we] would get rid of that particular person."

Yes, Groves hated the Communists, and Russia to him was as much the enemy as Germany. But if the Reds helped him to win the war and prevent Congress from ruining him, why interfere? Compartmentalization would keep them from learning too much. And no matter how much they learned, Russia would still lack the skills and resources needed to build a bomb for the next twenty years. Anyway, being a religious man and the son of a preacher, he believed in redemption. True Oppenheimer himself had given "considerable sums of money to Communist purposes," . . . but "this was perfectly reasonable." As Groves told the FBI, "Young people who attended a Communist meeting or two and later realized their mistakes should not be forever damned." Especially if they could be used for a blessed end.

The FBI was less pragmatic. "It looks as if Groves," one agent scrawled at the bottom of a report, "was completely naïve as to the menace of Communists."

III

Not quite as naïve, though, as Oppenheimer, who had reached for a quick ideological fix to ease the pain and problems of humanity, which he had ignored until well into manhood and then suddenly recognized in a cruel burst of revelation.

Oppenheimer was born in 1904 into a golden cocoon impervious to the tears of the outside world. How could he worry about other people's tears when they were virtually forbidden in his own home? Even as a child, Oppenheimer almost never cried. His father and mother were lenient, but he knew they expected flawless behavior from him, and the family apartment on Riverside Drive in New York City, with its plush carpets, fine furniture, and original Van Goghs that incongruously lent an orange tint to the general melancholy, itself seemed to demand proper decorum. The front windows framed the only outside world Robert—and his younger brother Frank—were really aware of. A world of ferryboats churning lazily down the Hudson River, of trains smoking furiously along the riverbanks, sleepy scenes as brightly suggestive of peace and harmony as the Van Goghs.

Oppenheimer's father, Julius, though amiable, was as proper and passionless as the environment. He stepped off a boat from Germany in 1888 and into the storeroom of a thriving clothing firm built up by his uncles, learning the business bolt by bolt until he found himself head of the company. He dressed impeccably, excelled in the social graces, and turned his home into a splendid gallery of artistic treasures. But the real custodian of these treasures was Oppenheimer's mother, Ella, herself an artist who had studied in Paris and taught painting at her own studio in New York. She was beautiful, slender, gentle, and strangely sad, perhaps because she was born without a right hand and had to wear a prosthetic device, which she hid by wearing gloves. She was endowed with a strong will.

What she willed most of all was a staid, dignified life for Robert and Frank, a life that was purposeful but unsullied by the shabby realities around them. A life like her own. She and her husband lavished their love on Robert especially, often by proxy through the butler or maid, who cared for his every need. And the boy reciprocated with model behavior, not only holding back tears, but studying hard at the School of Ethical Culture, walking and talking softly as one would in a museum, and simply living up to the "J" in his name, which stood for nothing except a parental pining for aristocratic stature. How could he hurt people who loved him so dearly? Their love thus disciplined him, in a sense playing the role of a strap. And the youth sometimes submitted, it seems, with the reluctance of a boy who had been spanked.

When his mother died years later, Oppenheimer would reply to a friend who told him she had loved him very much: "She loved me too much."

In school, under Felix Adler, the young Oppenheimer learned not only to write off evil as a human characteristic, but to form his own concept of goodness and not depend on any dogma or theology. But he seldom discussed his ideas with the other children because, as a prisoner in his cocoon, he treated them haughtily, unable to relate to them. Nor did he join in their games since both he and his schoolmates were conscious of his frailty and awkwardness. He wouldn't even walk up the stairs, preferring to wait for the elevator. Ignored or harassed by the others—being the smartest in the class didn't help—he strolled the corridors in the school miserably alone, wanting to be liked but not knowing how. In summer camp once, his schoolmates nearly killed him when they locked him naked in an icehouse for hours.

But often he enjoyed being alone, especially when he buried himself in Chekhov, Mansfield, Huxley, Eliot, Homer, or Plato. Encouraged by his parents, he devoured books, but almost none about modern society and its problems. He never read a newspaper or listened to the radio, and this pattern of apathy about the world he lived in would not change until he was in his thirties. He apparently didn't even know about the 1929 stock market crash until a friend told him long after it happened. And yet, he learned all about life in ancient India and Egypt.

About the physical world, too. He had started learning about it in his sixth year when his grandfather gave him a collection of colored mineral rocks. He was soon searching the neighborhood for new samples, studying each one, cataloguing it, polishing it. When he was 12, he delivered a paper to the New York Mineralogical Club, thus embarking on his extraordinary scientific career. A few years later, after a bout of colitis followed by a fit of depression, he was in Harvard studying chemistry, though he shortly switched to physics because "it was the study of order and regularity, of what makes matter harmonious and what makes it work." It fit the kind of structure that characterized his life, a life, ironically, from which he could finally break loose.

Still, his character had already been molded, and he would always show traces of the snobbish, arrogant cocoon mentality. When he visited one professor at his home and was told the date of a Greek temple in a picture he admired, he startled his host by correcting him. No, the date was fifty to one hundred years earlier, he insisted. In class he would bombard his professors with questions to show off his knowledge, craving recognition of his brilliance, though afterwards he often deplored these manifestations of a childhood from which he could not entirely extricate himself.

After being graduated from Harvard summa cum laude in three years, he was off to Cambridge in England, determined to accomplish something bold in physics. Instead, he found he had no talent in the laboratory, while he even stumbled in theoretical physics. He stood by the blackboard for hours at a time waiting for some momentous inspiration to strike him, but it never did. Shattered by this first taste of academic failure, he slunk off to Brittany in France, where he walked along the beach, as he would write, "on the point of bumping myself off."

But why hurry? He decided to pick himself up and try again after being accepted by the University of Göttingen in Germany, then the world capital of theoretical physics. Here he would work under such luminaries as James Franck and Max Born and compete with other gifted students, some of whom would later assist him on the bomb. His ego was soon restored as he surpassed them all, in part because his broad cultural knowledge helped him to understand how people applied science in the past and thus gave his physics an extra philosophical dimension. He now passionately embraced the new controversial quantum theory, pushing it with such vigor that colleagues, jealous of him and convinced that he was showing off, asked the professors to stop this "child prodigy" from dominating their discussions.

Offshoot resentment now rippled through the campus. He wore expensive English tweeds and carried specially bound books. His table manners were repulsively exquisite. And if anyone admired an item he owned, he had the patronizing gall to offer it as a gift. Worst of all, he chose only the most talented colleagues as his friends and would sarcastically belittle or turn his back on anyone who dared make a banal remark.

The professors were disturbed, but they nevertheless admired him—though Professor Franck could not, of course, foresee the day when he would visit Oppenheimer's class in Berkeley, ask a question, and receive the gratuitous reply: "The meaning of that question is a foolish one." In any case, Oppenheimer's aggressive attempt to seek at Göttingen the recognition he felt he deserved made him enemies once again, turning even his generosity and refinement into "shortcomings."

Adding to his unhappiness was the "miserable German mood,
. . . bitter [and] sullen," which began to depress him, and he
could hardly wait to get his doctorate so he could rush home. He
was impatient anyway to bring into the American classroom the
"new physics" he found so exciting, and turn some fortunate university into another Göttingen. Finally he left, diploma in hand,
followed by a young woman he had courted on the campus—
though she would shortly leave him because of his "immaturity"
and inability to relate to her.

Soon, in 1928, Oppenheimer was teaching at the California
Institute of Technology and a year later in Berkeley as well for part
of the year, choosing Berkeley over other schools because he was
"enchanted by the collection of 16th and 17th century French
poetry in the university library." Now, at last, he would find a
comfortable level of relationship with people—that between an
idol and his idolizers.

IV

Starting with a single graduate student at Berkeley, Oppenheimer gradually built up a following, though no one immediately
fell to his knees. In fact, some of them all but fell asleep in the
lecture hall as their new professor droned on in a "fast whisper"
about uncharted realms of physics they had barely known existed.
Gradually, he slowed the pace of delivery and his language grew
clear. Language rich and flowing, full of the wonder of a new,
intriguing physical world, of incredible vistas almost beyond the
imagination of man.

The brightest students now understood what he was saying,
and he understood what they were dreaming. He would help them
make their dreams come true. He would be a father to geniuses
and soon the world's greatest theoretical physicists would come to
Berkeley to pay homage. And they did, as Oppenheimer's theoreti-
cians, along with Lawrence's experimentalists, converted Berkeley
into a great international center of physics.

Oppenheimer had accomplished what he had set out to do.
And he had done it not in the loneliness of the ivory tower but in
the limelight of the pedestal. His talented students not only worshiped him, they emulated him, walking on the balls of their feet,
imitating his speech, rushing to light people's cigarettes in the

"Oppie" manner. They dined with him in the finest seafood houses, rode horseback with him at his ranch in New Mexico, followed him to Cal Tech when he taught there. Only his lone female student, it seems, grew disillusioned. He parked with her in the Berkeley Hills one night, got out to take some fresh air, and, suddenly preoccupied with a physics problem, walked all the way home and went to bed, leaving the furious young woman to curse all geniuses. Occasionally, other students, too, realized that a disciple could never quite know his master as a total person. Still, Oppenheimer had come a long way since that nightmarish time when his fellows locked him in the icehouse. It was nice to be loved—if only as an idol.

But even on his pedestal, Oppenheimer apparently felt a gnawing sense of emptiness. He was extremely nervous, constantly fidgeting when he sat, crossing and uncrossing his legs, biting his knuckles, stretching his neck. When teaching, he paced and stalked and punctuated almost every sentence with a violent puff on a cigarette. Some people even thought he flirted at times with insanity, perhaps suicide. One rumor abounded that he would sometimes vanish into the woods and scream as loud as he could to relieve his terrible tension.

While Oppenheimer was enormously admired by present and potential Nobel Prize winners, he realized he would probably never be one himself. It was apparently not the failure to win the prize itself that most disturbed him, despite his hunger for recognition; it was his failure to achieve what was necessary to earn one. Brilliant as he was, he was more adaptive than creative. He was not the original scientist he had hoped to be, lacking the temperament to shape grand new ideas. Like Szilard, he was a scientific dilettante, though Szilard didn't really care for fame. As one fellow scientist would say, Oppenheimer "just would not take off his coat and really get stuck in. He'd got the ability certainly, but he hadn't got the staying power."

V

If for all his success Oppenheimer felt somewhat frustrated in his career, he would in the stormy year of 1936 find a new outlet for fulfilment—Jean Tatlock. Tall and slim, with dark hair and beautiful green eyes, Jean, in her mid-twenties, opened up a new, shabbily splendid world to him. And soon they shared not only a deepening if tempestuous love, but the agony of exploited people everywhere.

This was a time when fascism began goose-stepping through Europe and threatened to devour Spain in civil war, while the democracies stood neutrally aloof, leaving it to the Communists to lead the resistance. This was a time when men searched their souls for a way to end human suffering even at the cost of more human suffering, when Stalin's purges were looked upon even by many non-Communists as a necessary evil that would clear the way to Utopia. It was in such an atmosphere that Jean Tatlock, an on-again, off-again Communist, guided her lover through the dismal underground corridors of leftist conspiracy, where shadowy figures lurked, their minds enchained, their fantasies aflame.

For a man who only recently learned about the stock market crash, these fantasies were a shock and a revelation; they finally freed him from his cocoon. He had begun to break out of it when relatives escaping from Germany arrived with tales of anti-Semitic horror under Hitler, and when his Ph.D. graduates, victims of the Depression, were unable to find jobs. Oppenheimer's naturally generous and caring attitude, which had been largely limited until now to the small circle of those he loved and those he respected professionally, suddenly found a universal outlet. He discovered, it seemed, the path leading toward a solution of all political, economic, and social problems. In its misleading logic, it was a logical path for someone who had seldom been aware of these problems before. As he himself would put it, he had "no framework of political conviction or experience to give . . . perspective in this matter."

Oppenheimer now devoured Marx, Engels, and even the Communist *People's Daily World*. The way to human redemption—it was all there. He was a theorist, and the theories that now overwhelmed him seemed sound. What happened in the process of converting them to practice did not occur to him any more than it did to many idealistic teenagers suddenly aware of the world. In his relation to society, Oppenheimer, the scientific genius, was in fact still a teenager.

Yet even Jean Tatlock could not completely capture his mind. Part of Oppenheimer's greatness as a scientist lay, after all, in his reserve of doubt about every theory until it was scientifically proven. Thus, while he viewed communism sympathetically, he could not give himself over to the system. He was in fact stunned and distressed to hear that his brother and sister-in-law had joined the party. It was enough, he felt, to back Russia's international policies, especially in its struggle with fascism. And the Communists felt it was enough, too. For Stalin's aim was not to turn every possible candidate into a card-carrying member of the Communist Party, but to use sympathizers, gathered in popular fronts, for his own ends. And who could be more useful than J. Robert Oppenheimer?

Oppenheimer was soon donating money to Communist front organizations, especially Spanish Civil War relief groups. He attended front meetings and rallies and helped to organize the Communist-dominated East Bay Teachers' Union, even addressing envelopes and licking stamps in drives to attract new members. It was during such frantic campaigns that he developed a fateful friendship with the president of the union, Haakon Chevalier, a handsome young professor of romance languages at Berkeley. He was a pro-Communist intellectual who had translated the works of André Malraux and written a book on Anatole France.

Chevalier and his wife would often visit Oppenheimer in his two-room apartment in a rambling, oak-sheltered wooden house on Tamalpais Road high in the Berkeley Hills. While sipping their host's special martinis and dining on his exotically spiced dishes, about the only food Oppenheimer would eat despite his colitis, they would listen to classical records or discuss Mozart or Marx. Chevalier grew to love his friend, who would remain grateful forever, or at least until the price of gratitude soared too high.

Oppenheimer's leftist world was exciting and meaningful. He had new friends who cared about mankind and a young woman whom he cared about—enough to propose marriage many times. But though Jean Tatlock loved him, too, she never said yes, resenting his tendency to revere her without revealing himself. Possessive, manic-depressive, she wanted neither his flowers nor his jewelry, nor even just his passion. Extreme in all her demands, political or personal, she wanted his soul and cruelly taunted him with tales of her other affairs when he held back. But his soul was the one thing he still could not share with anyone. And so they parted in 1939, symbolically at about the time that Oppenheimer began to realize, with the help of the cynical Nazi-Soviet pact, that the real world was much larger than the Teachers' Union or the lost civil war in Spain.

VI

Also symbolic of this awakening was Oppenheimer's meeting with another dark, slender woman at a garden party shortly afterwards. He immediately fell in love with Katherine Puening, who, though Nazi General Wilhelm Keitel's niece, had joined the Communist Party when she married her previous husband, a Communist who had died in the Spanish Civil War. Kitty, as she was called, had since turned against the party and married a British physician. Oppenheimer invited the couple to his ranch, but, as fortune would have it, the husband couldn't go. Kitty went alone and, amid the pines, the fates of all three were determined. Kitty abruptly divorced her husband and on the same day married Oppenheimer—to the gasps of some disciples, who were startled, and a little scandalized, at the thought of their idol turning out to be as human as anyone else.

Kitty led her new husband out of the underground corridors into the parlors of more distinguished folk, though he did not entirely give up his leftist friends—certainly not Chevalier. How could he snub or hurt people who had befriended him? Kitty loved him dearly, but, unlike Jean, did not demand what she couldn't have. Ambitious and resourceful, she knew what she *could* have: a husband whose genius would be known the world over. It was just a matter of time. And the time would be much sooner than she might have expected—thanks to General Groves.

VII

Groves first met Oppenheimer in October 1942, when the general visited Berkeley to inspect Lawrence's electromagnetic project shortly after taking over the Manhattan Project. Lawrence was escorting him around his laboratory and explaining how U^{235} was being separated when Groves asked:

"How pure will it have to be?"

Lawrence referred Groves to his top theoretician, who was drawing up plans for the bomb. Ask Oppenheimer, the real expert on that question, he suggested.

Oppenheimer was a barely familiar name to the general. A fine scientist, he had heard, but a fuzzy-minded leftist who ran off with somebody else's wife. Yet Oppenheimer had been associated with the project for about a year. It was by accident that he learned of it. In September 1941, Marcus Oliphant, the Australian scientist who had urged Washington to push ahead more swiftly with the atomic project, was lunching with Lawrence and Oppenheimer and mentioned the nuclear work that was being done in the United States and Britain. Oppenheimer was embarrassed and quietly noted that he wasn't cleared to hear this information since he was not involved in the work.

"But that's terrible," Oliphant replied. "We need you."

Lawrence immediately agreed, and soon after the two Berkeley scientists were sitting together at a meeting with their peers in Schenectady, New York. Oppenheimer's calculations proved invaluable; it was he who determined how much U^{235} would be needed for a bomb to form a critical mass, the point at which a chain reaction would start. Shortly, he would help to supervise the designing of the bomb, and, in May 1942, take sole charge of this program, though he had no prior administrative experience and little experimental background.

Oppenheimer locked himself in two rooms at the top of Berkeley's LeConte Hall behind windows covered with steel netting and a door with a special lock to which only he had the key, and began his work. He invited seven theoretical physicists to spend part of the summer with him for an exchange of ideas, and they all came, including Edward Teller, Szilard's Hungarian colleague, who had helped to persuade Einstein to push for the bomb in the first place. Teller, who in the future was to give Oppenheimer endless trouble, now made a good start.

Oppie wanted to build an atomic bomb? Why not? However, Teller would work on a "Super"—a hydrogen, or thermonuclear, bomb, which would make the atomic bomb seem like a firecracker. With enough heat, he explained, light nuclei, such as hydrogen, would fuse and release unheard amounts of energy, and an atomic bomb, used as a trigger, could provide such heat.

Yes, work on a Super should go forward, Oppenheimer agreed.

But the main focus must be on building an atomic bomb so that Hitler wouldn't make one first. The Super could never be finished before the war ended.

But Teller was adamant. He wanted to concentrate on the more ambitious project, even if it could have no effect on this war. It wasn't patriotic duty that primarily motivated him, he would admit. It was the scientific challenge. And the Super was the greater challenge.

If Oppenheimer and the others were disturbed by Teller's apparent stress on personal gratification, they were frantic when one day he stepped to the blackboard and scrawled some literally world-shaking equations on it. He had been calculating how effectively an atomic bomb explosion would detonate a fusion reaction. And, he proudly announced, he was right. The heat generated *would* cause fusion in deuterium, an isotope of hydrogen. Unfortunately, however, it might also explode unstable hydrogen nuclei and cause a reaction between deuterium and nitrogen.

The other scientists stared at the equations and were speechless. What would happen to the hydrogen in the water and the nitrogen in the atmosphere? The fission reaction of an atomic bomb could set the oceans and atmosphere on fire—ending life on the planet! A pale Oppenheimer rushed to the telephone to call Arthur Compton, his superior, then flew to Chicago to see him. Compton was thunderstruck.

"This would be the ultimate catastrophe," he cried. "Better to accept the slavery of the Nazis than to run a chance of drawing the final curtain on mankind!"

But the scientists, with an enormous sigh of relief, soon discovered that Teller had miscalculated. There was apparently only a three in a million chance of the final curtain being drawn. Odds probably not much different from those of winning the Irish Sweepstakes. A fair gamble. The bomb would be built.

VIII

And now Oppenheimer, who normally shunned the company of the "intellectually prosaic" military man, would show General Groves, the new top boss, how valuable he could be. The unique scientific challenge and the chance to save the world from Hitler and win international recognition converged to make him accommodate even to the military mind in order to stay on the project.

When Groves had seated himself behind the steel netting sealing in Oppenheimer's office, the scientist, with deference and simplicity, described to him the details of fission. Groves was impressed. Never had it been put to him so clearly. He thanked Oppenheimer, who modestly replied:

"There are no experts. The field is too new."

No experts? Of course! Now Groves could ask the questions he had always hesitated to ask for fear of looking silly to the scientists he had to dominate. If there were no experts, how could anybody expect him to be one? Oppenheimer might be a typical eastern Jew, a moral midget, and even a fellow traveler, but he could be damned helpful. He seemed to know about every facet of the atom and about the men working on it and what they were doing. What's more, he clearly respected Groves' rank and knowledge, not like most of the other "crackpots." And he didn't ask for anything, either. Yes, a good Jew—at least a useful one.

And he bombarded Oppenheimer with questions, which the scientist fielded skillfully and channeled into a bold suggestion that had been on his mind for some time. The scientists were making progress, he said, but they could be making much more.

How?

Well, it wasn't easy for scientists who worked on a single project to be separated from each other and ignorant of what was happening in another laboratory. Of course, he realized why the general insisted on compartmentalization. But there was a way to satisfy scientific needs without sacrificing security: Put the scientists to work in one large laboratory, at least for bomb design, in an isolated area where they would have little or no contact with the outside world. Things then would really move.

Groves was intrigued by the idea of a huge, isolated laboratory, if not by the thought of scientists telling their comrades everything they knew. He called Oppenheimer to Chicago as soon as he arrived there, and the two men further explored the plan as they watched the Midwest plains roll by from a train compartment en route to New York. Yes, one large laboratory, they agreed, sealed in by the army.

Would the scientists join the army, wear uniforms, and accept military discipline?

Of course. Oppenheimer himself would be glad to be an officer.

Groves beamed. He was sold on Oppenheimer.

Oppenheimer also beamed. He had sold his plan.

Now who should run what would be the most important laboratory in history? Groves pondered this question with the gravity of the Almighty choosing his Moses. A Nobel Prize–winning experimental physicist, of course.

Of course.

Lawrence would be perfect, but the electromagnetic process couldn't succeed without him. Compton was needed in Chicago and wasn't much of an administrator, anyway. Edwin McMillan was too young. Wolfgang Panofsky was even younger. Isidor Rabi was too committed to radar research. When Groves ran out of Nobel laureates and top experimentalists, he was left with— Oppenheimer. Bush, Conant, Lawrence, Compton, and other scientists protested. How could Groves choose a theorist with such little experience in administration? The FBI then put its investigative nose into Oppenheimer's file. He had too many Communist friends. And it sent Groves a thick dossier crammed with "evidence" of Oppenheimer's Communist leanings.

His Communist "Party connections and sympathies . . . are known to exist."

He "is familiar enough with Steve Nelson, a high party official, to call him by his first name."

"It is felt that [in a group including Oppenheimer] may lie an even higher governing body or strategy committee for the Communist Party than among those more openly affiliated."

He "has the background which would lend credence to the possibility that he may be rendering aid to the . . . Communist Party in the successful culmination of [its] efforts to organize the employees of the Radiation Laboratory and to place members in key places."

And, in fact, the FBI pointed out, a former student of Oppenheimer, Giovanni Rossi Lomanitz, a Communist, was already working in Lawrence's Radiation Laboratory under orders from the party.

One FBI agent even advised that Oppenheimer be considered for custodial detention "in the event of a National Emergency."

Groves put down the dossier. He was unimpressed. There was only one relevant question: Was Oppenheimer the best available man for the job of building a bomb to save the country—and General Groves? The answer was yes. And so Oppenheimer, instead of being "custodially detained," was entrusted with the job of *ending* the National Emergency—the job he had coveted all along.

If Oppenheimer had managed to subtly convince Groves that he was the ideal man, he would now subtly lead him to the ideal site. Before entering Harvard in his youth, Oppenheimer, racked by colitis and fits of depression, had been sent by his father to the mountains of Colorado and New Mexico to recover physically and mentally. For weeks the youth and his English teacher bumped their way by wagon and on horseback over dusty trails that finally ended in the Sangre de Cristo range, where the boy savored the magic beauty of the swift rivers snaking through lush pine forests and wind-blown green meadows. He even fell in love with an attractive woman who owned a guest ranch where they stayed.

Several years later, when Oppenheimer started teaching at Cal Tech, he visited his old girl friend again and they rode together into the hills where, amid the ponderosas and brightly hued button flowers, they came to a house made of adobe-covered pine trunks. When she told him he could rent it, he cried, "Hot dog!" And that was the Spanish name he would give this house—*Perro Caliente*. Oppenheimer bought some horses and eventually the house, and here he would lounge in enchanted isolation whenever he could find time.

So why not *work* in enchanted isolation? Again there was the search.

A site north of Los Angeles?

No, said Groves. The scientists would be tempted to go out on the town.

One near Reno?

The winter was too cold.

Oppenheimer then had an "idea." He knew a place far from any town, where the weather was always mild.

Groves wanted to see for himself.

Sure thing.

And shortly the two men stood at the precipice of deep, rock-walled Jemez Canyon, north of Albuquerque. Still no. Not enough room for expansion.

Well, about 30 miles to the north, said Oppenheimer, was another place Groves might like to see, since they were in the area anyway. One of the trails he had ridden years earlier had led there, and it could be suitable.

He, General Groves, would decide that.

Of course.

Their car bounced up the road to the top of a 7,000-foot-high mesa about 20 miles from Santa Fe and groaned to a halt before the timber and adobe buildings of a run-down boys' school. Only these rickety structures corrupted the breathtaking sweep of cottonwood emptiness that merged in the distance with the red cliffs of the snow-topped Sangre de Cristo, where Oppenheimer's ranch stretched hidden under a canopy of pines. The scientist looked at Groves and Groves looked at the land. Little water. No power lines. No good road to town. . . . But just the place. Oppenheimer nodded, bewitched as he always was, by the magnificent savagery of this peaceful scene.

Yes, just the peaceful atmosphere needed to build man's most murderous weapon.

IX

Toward the end of 1942, Oppenheimer, thrilled by this greatest of challenges and the opportunity to make history, set to work organizing the laboratory he would build in the wilderness. He scrawled an organizational chart. He would need about thirty men to build the bomb. His assistants were shocked. How could thirty men accomplish so enormous a task?

Well, then, maybe one hundred.

"Where are the shipping clerks?" someone asked.

"We're not going to ship anything," Oppenheimer replied.

Now who should he have on his team? He studied a list of candidates, analyzing the pros and cons of each one as if he were casting a Broadway play, their personalities, traits, quirks. Would they not have to live as one big family? There would be special quarters for childless couples so they could have quiet. . . .

His assistants shuddered. Was this the job for a poet? When they pressed for solutions to practical administrative problems, he sometimes grew furious, especially after a martini or two. Would they stop harassing him with such niggling matters?

But then he went out on the road to gather his cast and proved an impresario without match. He swept into universities, commercial laboratories, private homes.

Come with me! Oppenheimer cried with evangelistic fervor. Come explore the heart of the greatest scientific mystery that ever challenged man—though he wasn't free to say yet what the challenge was, except that the work could help win the war. Come join the people's army!

He was calling them to the colors with the terminology he best understood, which he might have used earlier to recruit volunteers for the Abraham Lincoln Brigade. But whatever his terminology, the scientists and their families—girl friends were out—followed Oppenheimer into the Los Alamos desert with the unbounded faith of the ancient Israelites who had followed Moses into the Sinai.

As dusty, dilapidated buses popped into the mesa after a long, bumpy ride from Santa Fe, creaking under the weight of sweaty passengers, bulging bags, potted plants, and kiddie kars, the new faithful scrambled out and joyously breathed the cool mountain air. Just like summer camp when they were boys—except for the barbed wire surrounding this camp and the army guards at the gate.

But fun dissolved into frustration as they moved into army prefabricated houses and thin-walled apartments with heaters that didn't work and wood-burning stoves that didn't light, where privacy was being always within earshot of a G-2 spy with a snap-brimmed hat, and where square dances and parties were not enough to replace baby making as a way to overcome the boredom of isolation—to the rage of economy-minded General Groves, who ordered his officers to "do something" about the babies before they multiplied his housing and schooling woes. Couples were simply "taking advantage" of the free hospitalization. Perhaps more social events. At a rendition of *Arsenic and Old Lace*, Oppenheimer even agreed to play a corpse, and there were moments, at least in the chaos of the first weeks, when some wished he were not acting.

Yet Oppenheimer somehow thrived on the chaos and gradually the poet became the planner; the actor, the arbiter. His "hundred-man" staff soon grew to 1,500, ultimately to more than 4,000 civilians and 2,000 military working in almost 250 buildings and living in more than 500 apartment houses, dormitories, and trailers. Even shipping clerks were found useful. There were gripes, arguments, feuds—almost all settled by the prophetic leader, whose stale, smelly pipe, floppy porkpie hat, and wrinkled suit, which hung on him as if on a hanger, became his priestly hallmark. He popped into laboratories and offices without notice, suggesting, encouraging.

People who permitted some problems to slow up their work left his makeshift office strangely content, if not altogether absolved from the sin of delaying progress toward the Promised Land. Who could ignore the blue glare of the stare, the mumbled commandment? Not a day, not an hour, not a minute must be lost! No work could await the completion of other work. A bomb would have to be built largely on the basis of theory until enough U^{235} and plutonium were available to experiment with.

But this could result in serious miscalculations, some scientists said.

Oppenheimer replied like a true prophet: *He* would shoulder the burden of blame.

So keyed up was this new batch of disciples that some even sawed open the stockroom doors after they were locked at 5 P.M. so they could work until dawn, staying awake with coffee gulped down between equations. When Fermi would eventually come from Chicago, he was stunned by the change in atmosphere. In Chicago, people worked hard on the bomb because Hitler forced them to build it. In Los Alamos, they worked hard, it seemed, because they *wanted* to build it.

Even so, not everybody wanted to. Edward Teller still preferred—in fact, demanded—to work on the Super. He was furious and hurt because Oppenheimer named Hans Bethe rather than him as chief of the Theoretical Division. After working under Bethe for a year, Teller refused to cooperate with him any longer, leaving Oppenheimer little choice but to let his wayward colleague go off in a corner and work almost exclusively on his postwar bomb. Teller could still be valuable as a consultant on the atomic bomb.

X

One man who wasn't wayward was Captain Parsons, who would one day arm the bomb en route to Hiroshima. He had the tenacity nurtured by a pioneer life and a profound respect for his father's will to survive. His father, after failing in Chicago as a professional singer, had moved the family in 1909, when Deak was a boy, to the frontier town of Fort Sumner, New Mexico, hoping for a stabler, more fulfilling life. But he failed twice more in business ventures before he finally did modestly well as a small-town lawyer.

To Deak's father, however, succeeding was less important than doing one's best. And to help his four children do their best, he gave them the finest education possible. With his encouragement, Deak kept skipping grades in his storehouse school, assisted by mother and grandmother, who tutored the children amid a library-ful of scholarly books. One brother would become a Rhodes scholar, a sister would earn a Ph.D., and Deak himself would receive an appointment to Annapolis at the age of 16. Parsons would always view his father as a gentle person, yet strong and proud. The man who, harassed one day by the town bully, dealt him a powerful blow to the jaw that Fort Sumner would long remember with glee. A man who filled him not with awe—they were too close for that—but with gratitude. For Deak, doing his job well was one way of repaying him.

It was also a way to satisfy his intense intellectual curiosity about gadgets—how they worked, how they were made. A curiosity manifested since childhood when he would sit by the railroad and watch as a train ran over pins he had placed on the tracks and turned them into wonderful tiny scissor shapes. And it was a way to express his deep-seated patriotism. He was harsh on others who, in his opinion, were not doing enough for the country.

General Groves had snatched Parsons from the navy to head Oppenheimer's Ordnance Division, one of four divisions that would work on the bomb in Los Alamos; the others were the Theoretical Division under Bethe, the Experimental Physics Division under Robert Bacher, and the Chemistry and Metallurgy Division under Joseph W. Kennedy. Groves was glad to get Parsons—because no qualified army man was available for the job. Parsons, he agreed, was probably the best technician the navy could produce, though in his view he still couldn't compare with the army's best.

Groves first met Parsons in the early 1930s while he was working on infrared for the army and Parsons on radar for the navy. And when Bush recommended the captain for the atomic ordnance job, Groves approved despite his reservation about naval aptitudes. He was amused, however, on hearing that a guard at the Los Alamos gate, who was unfamiliar with naval insignia, frantically called his sergeant when Parsons arrived.

"Sergeant!" he cried. "We've really caught a spy! A guy is down here trying to get in, and his uniform is as phony as a three-dollar bill. He's wearing the eagles of a colonel, and claims that he's a captain."

The incident apparently was symbolic to Groves. Why should anyone connected with a really important project expect to see a naval officer around? Still, Groves was impressed with Parsons' credentials and wrote Oppenheimer that he was "sure Parsons is the man we need." Oppenheimer thought so, too.

In fact, the two men and their wives, who lived comfortably in houses that were once owned by faculty members of the evacuated boys' school, became close friends, though they differed in many ways. While Oppenheimer enjoyed parties, where with martini in hand he would captivate people with his glittering stories, Parsons thought parties were a waste of time and often dragged his charming apple-cheeked wife home after his first sip of ginger ale—even though she was in charge of social affairs. He preferred to raise morale by helping the community to meet its needs, such as setting up schools. He even snatched wives away from their pots and pans and dirty diapers and planted them in the schoolroom as teachers, and pressured Groves, who saw no reason for "frills," to send enough desks and supplies.

Parsons loved tennis and did not mind losing to his hard-hitting, athletic wife; Oppenheimer would never pick up a tennis racket or engage in any other sport for fear of losing, though he was fond of horses because they could transport him into spellbinding hinterlands. He was less even-tempered than Parsons, too. When he was angry, he would still put a person down with a slashing tongue. Parsons, in his reserve, could almost never be jarred, whatever he might feel, and was reluctant even to correct people unless it was necessary for his work.

There was still a lingering shyness from the past. At Annapolis, Parsons had been too shy even to date girls, and when he invited his mother's younger cousin to the graduation ball and the less attractive elder one showed up, he gallantly spent the evening with her, if in boiling silence. Now, many years later, there were still moments of boiling silence, which frightened some subordinates, though the more perceptive ones sensed the gentleness that lay beneath.

But for all their differences, Oppenheimer and Parsons had much in common. Both had cultivated a love of literature, poetry, and classical music from childhood. And both were serious men with insatiable curiosities that delved deeply into every detail of the work they were doing. In a sense, they shared a symbiotic relationship. Parsons, who had always felt his education had been too narrow, consumed himself in Oppenheimer's broad knowledge, while Oppenheimer, who had never been close to a "true" if liberal-minded patriot before (Groves being simply a benevolent boss), savored the opportunity to associate himself more intimately with the establishment.

The other scientists also appreciated Parsons, but their zeal was restrained. Yes, he was intelligent, civil, modest. But why shouldn't he be modest? He was only a military engineer and lacked deep scientific training. He often used, they felt, inappropriate military engineering techniques and forced them to meet military schedules, while allowing them no time at all to indulge in scientific reverie. Why should he head one of the four main groups in Los Alamos, placed on a level with Nobel Prize winners and those who deserved to be? Why should he serve as chief administrator when Oppenheimer was traveling?

Yet, the scientists tolerated Parsons if only because, as a military man, he could wring materials, roads, and better working conditions from Groves, who seldom listened to them. If Parsons asked for something, Parsons got it, for Groves knew it was really needed.

Whatever people thought, Parsons soon proved himself. Dressed in open shirt, denim, and sneakers, which strangely clashed with his military bearing, he swiftly organized his Ordnance Division, setting up firing ranges, laboratories, offices, and housing, while directing much of the design and development of the varied components of the atomic bomb and drawing up plans for their manufacture. It was an especially intricate task since the bomb had to be small enough to fit into a B-29 bomber.

The way in which the bomb would work, the gun-assembly method, was simple enough: Inside the bomb's casing was a cannon barrel that fired a projectile containing a subcritical mass of U^{235} into another subcritical mass of U^{235} in front of the muzzle. Since the two subcritical masses, on contact, would become the critical mass, a nuclear explosion would occur. Parsons performed test after test and was sure the bomb would work.

The problem was U^{235}. Would he have enough to put into the bomb? With all the separation plants operated by tens of thousands of people, only microscopic quantities were dripping forth. Parsons, it seemed, might have to depend on plutonium, which, obtained chemically from U^{238}, wouldn't require separation; and he was gearing his gun-assembly equipment to operate with that new element as well as with U^{235}. But plutonium was still in the experimental stage, and no one was certain yet that it could even be used. His responsibility, however, was simply to have the bomb ready for action when any type of fissionable material arrived. And everything was pointing to a successful explosion—when some "know-it-all" scientist, as Parsons would identify the man, had to mention "*im*plosion."

The man was Seth Neddermeyer, a tall, scrawny figure with bushy hair and lips constantly curled around a cigar. At one meeting of scientists in early 1943, Neddermeyer raised his bony hand and suggested that "implosion" might be a better method of setting off the bomb than Parsons' gun-assembly method. The idea was to squeeze a subcritical mass in upon itself from all sides simultaneously, thus compressing its nuclei so tightly that they would all begin to fission at the same time and cause a huge blast, or "implosion."

The other scientists—and Parsons—scoffed. To squeeze the mass, a countless number of chemical explosions would have to be set off around it, all of them occurring simultaneously in order to produce a symmetrically converging shock wave. How could the shock wave be perfectly uniform at every point? Impossible! Besides, Parsons saw the idea as a threat to his entire program. Even if implosion ultimately worked, so much money, time, and effort would have to be devoted to experimentation that the war would be over before the bomb could be built. In a crash job like this, with men dying each minute, it would be absurd, Parsons felt, to divert resources to some new fantastic idea when, as a navy technical expert, he *knew* the gun-assembly method would work.

But if most of the scientists agreed with Parsons, Oppenheimer, who was himself highly skeptical of implosion, would not dismiss any fresh idea lightly, not with so much at stake for the world, the country, and himself. He called Neddermeyer into his office later and said, "This will have to be looked into." And he made him a group leader within Parsons' Ordnance Division, to Parsons' chagrin, telling him to "use as many men and as much equipment as you can." Then he grinned and said:

"If you can do it, I'll give you a bottle of whiskey."

Neddermeyer had an inventive mind, but he was a simple man who used simple experimental methods. He placed explosives around pieces of metal piping and detonated them, then retrieved the battered piping and inspected it, hoping to find a uniform collapse of the metal. Instead, all he found was grotesquely twisted piping. Parsons watched with an almost humorous contempt.

"With everyone grinding away in such dead earnest here," he remarked, "we need a touch of relief. I question Dr. Neddermeyer's seriousness. To my mind he is gradually working up to what I shall refer to as the Beer-Can Experiment. As soon as he gets his explosives properly organized, we will see this done. The point to watch for is whether he can blow in a beer can without splattering the beer."

Everyone laughed. But in early 1944, the laughing stopped, for tests showed that because of an impurity in plutonium, the isotope 240, any mass of the element produced too many neutrons for use in a gun. If one subcritical mass of it was fired against another, at whatever speed, they would both vaporize and predetonate before they could come together to form a critical mass. Groves, Oppenheimer, Parsons, and their colleagues were despondent. This meant that plutonium could not be used with the gun method. And there would be enough U^{235} for only a single atomic bomb by mid-1945—unless implosion, which *would* permit the use of plutonium, could be made to work.

Actually, there was a way to make the gun method operate with plutonium—separate the isotope 240 from it. But to do this, a whole new plant would have to be built, and there was not enough time or money for another enormous separation venture. Yet Parsons still resisted implosion, believing, as one colleague said, "there was something else that should be done, a kind of smoothing out of the difficulties with plutonium, minimizing them rather than really overcoming them." After all, the gun-detonated bomb was his baby. How could he coddle somebody else's? But Oppenheimer, despairing, his temper soaring, now demanded twins—an implosion as well as a gun-detonated bomb. He called in Neddermeyer again.

Find a way to make implosion work! he ordered.

And Neddermeyer, shaken and frustrated, went back to his pipes and set off more explosions. But still there was no implosion.

When Oppenheimer, himself harassed by Groves, was almost ready to settle for a one-bomb finale—with no follow-up if it failed—a young British scientist, James Tuck, arrived in Los Alamos with the timing of the angel who saved Abraham's son from slaughter. He had been working with armor-piercing explosives and found a way to direct the full force of the warheads toward the armor. He had used an "explosive lens." Maybe it would work in the bomb. Surround the spherical core with many of these lenses, he advised, detonate them all simultaneously, and the shock wave would be symmetrical. Thus, implosion.

Oppenheimer was ecstatic; Los Alamos might give birth to twin bombs after all. But he was also disturbed. At this late stage, he would have to start a new laboratory from scratch. And he did. With desperate pleas, he coaxed the country's most noted explosives expert, Harvard's George Kistiakowsky, to take charge of the new Explosives Division, though Kistiakowsky made no secret of his belief that Oppenheimer was "mad to think this thing will make a bomb." Soon, about 600 new men, mostly military technicians, were sculpturing lenses, handling explosives, measuring shock waves.

Parsons still controlled everything that related to converting both bombs into aerial weapons, but he was unhappy about the reorganization and began to wonder, as Kistiakowsky did, about the sanity of his friend Oppenheimer in so recklessly pursuing what seemed to Parsons a mirage. What's more, his own authority was diluted. Though nominally under him, Kistiakowsky was largely a free soul.

But Parsons swallowed his misgivings and his pride and, as usual, outworked almost everybody else. In early 1945, Oppenheimer would write to Groves that "it is impossible to overestimate the value which Captain Parsons has been to the project . . . , nor the loss we should have incurred without his services. He has been almost alone in this project to appreciate the actual military and engineering problems which we should encounter. He has been almost alone in insisting on facing these problems at a date early enough so that we might arrive at their solution. . . . He has steadfastly insisted that the project remain focussed on its military directives, and by doing so has provided a necessary counterpart to the exploratory enthusiasm of his scientific associates."

Parsons didn't have to read this letter to know what his dear "mad" friend thought about him. Anyway, he still had his baby, the gun-detonated bomb, all to himself, and he would stay with it to the end, until he saw how it worked. As he had watched in childhood a train run over his pins and turn them into intriguing shapes, as he had watched his proximity fuse turn an enemy plane into a smoking hulk, he would watch his bomb turn the sky into a flaming sunrise that would herald a new world. Then he would return home and rejoice with his family in the knowledge that he had performed a valuable service for his country.

XI

Meanwhile, in Tokyo, Yoshio Nishina hoped to perform a valuable service for *his* country as he tried to round up a group of scientists who would at least attempt to make an atomic bomb. But if he was in many ways a Szilard, he was by no means an Oppenheimer—at least in his talent for attracting the top experts to a scheme that few thought realistic. Yet this was not surprising. Oppenheimer believed in this scheme and relished the challenge, and so he could sell it to his colleagues. Nishina did not believe in it but pursued it simply as a patriot, and so he could not sell it.

An atomic bomb? the scientists exclaimed. Why waste valuable time? Besides, the best ones preferred to stay at their own universities and laboratories, where they would be boss. The scientific staffs of the various universities jealously competed with each other in the tradition of the old samurai clans, and the professor at the top of each, as fiercely proud as a shogun, was not at all eager to work under, or even cooperate with, a rival—especially for a lost or questionable cause. As one scientist who did assist Nishina would write: "They all wanted to do their own work."

Finally, in late December 1942, Nishina summoned Tadashi Takeuchi, a young man in his early thirties who was working on cosmic rays for the army's Aviation Technology Research Institute, and made him an extraordinary offer: He needed an experimental physicist immediately to work on the atomic bomb. Would Takeuchi like the job?

Takeuchi was overwhelmed. This was a job for a Nobel Prize winner. What did he know about nuclear fission?

Never mind. He would learn.

Takeuchi beamed like a college actor offered the role of a samurai hero in the classic Kabuki theater. What a wonderful opportunity—even if his work could be of no earthly use to the war effort.

On January 15, 1943, Nishina gathered his small staff in his laboratory to discuss which method they should use to separate U^{235} from U^{238}. The problem seemed staggering. How could they build a bomb with so little material, money, and technical know-how? Thus, they were forced to forget about the electromagnetic, centrifugal, and gaseous diffusion methods, all of which were being tried simultaneously in the United States. And the thermal diffusion method, separation by heat dispersion, would mean building elaborate, multistage plants, a less-expensive and time-consuming process than the others but still impractical. They finally decided on the simpler dialytic method, whereby they could separate the uranium isotope by passing a U^{238} solution across a semipermeable membrane.

When Nishina's scientific committee met again with navy officials on March 6, 1943, the scientist presented his plan for separation. But Captain Ito was impatient.

Plans! Plans! The navy had more plans than it knew what to do with. It wanted bombs, not plans!

The naval officials were especially worried because American naval power was growing ominously each day. What the navy needed most of all now were planes and radar to meet the immediate threat. Perhaps it was a mistake to invest in some visionary weapon.

Well, could the bomb be made? Ito demanded to know.

Not impossible, but maybe not possible.

What about uranium?

There was uranium in Korea, but Korea was undeveloped. Burma was promising, but who could say how promising?

Ito would later lament: "The more they considered and discussed the problem, the more pessimistic became the atmosphere of the meeting."

It might be a good idea to engage in more pressing work, he finally told the scientists. And he dissolved Nishina's committee.

But just as the navy had stepped in when the army had backed out, so now, in May 1943, the army stepped in again as the navy backed out, subsidizing what it called the "N-Project," after Nishina. And in a desperate move to save his Asian empire and himself, Prime Minister Tojo strongly supported it. Nishina and his four men—later joined by ten university graduates—now decided to focus on the thermal-diffusion method of separation after all. Research resumed in a building owned by the Aviation Institute, a two-story wooden structure with a total floor space of about 300 square yards— a Manhattan Project in miniature.

With Nishina overseeing their progress, two men largely did most of the work. On the first floor Takeuchi designed and began building an isotope separator, while on the second floor Kunihiko Kigoshi, a researcher in his mid-twenties, tried to make uranium hexafluoride, which would be dumped into Takeuchi's separator, converted into gas, and heated until U^{235} went its own way. Where was the uranium ore that was needed? Army commanders in Manchuria, China, Korea, Malaya, Burma, and the South Sea islands were ordered: Dig! But shovels scooped up little more than sand and dirt. Even Germany was tapped. Japan wanted 2 tons of pitchblend (which contained uranium)? Fine, replied the Nazis. It would be sent in two submarines. One, however, was apparently sunk and the other never left port.

Meanwhile, Takeuchi managed to assemble a crude separator, but had nothing to separate. If only Kigoshi could come up with a few crystals of uranium hexafluoride. But he seemed to have as much chance of finding the right formula as he had of finding the right deodorant for Godzilla.

"Do you truly believe we are capable of producing the bomb?"

Nishina, in his frustration, asked one of his men in November 1943.

"No, I don't believe we are," the young man replied bluntly.

Nishina's eyes flashed anger. Impudent pessimism! He called in other researchers and asked the same question. Same answer.

"If that's your attitude," he cried, "then . . . " He paused, and his flock expected him to say, "stop your work." But in a quiet voice, he went on: ". . . then go on with your work."

Nishina shook his head as his men left. Obviously he agreed with them. And he didn't really seem as angry as he tried to appear. After all, he was learning a lot, too—while serving his country.

Then, in January 1944, a small miracle occurred. Kigoshi and an assistant worked all night and finally—uranium hexafluoride gas! They cooled it, and there, before their very eyes, a crystal the size of a grain of rice suddenly materialized. The two men grabbed each other and danced for joy. However tiny the crystal, they had scored a breakthrough in Japanese science.

Of course, there were still myriad obstacles blocking a bomb. Since plutonium was not known yet in Japan, thousands of separators would be needed to supply enough U^{235} for a weapon. And huge sums of money, as well as one-tenth of the electricity and one-half of the copper in Japan, would be needed to build the separators. Nor had a uranium pile been put together yet to test a chain reaction.

And as if these problems were not enough, Nishina and his helpers had no General Groves to plow through the jungle of apathy and red tape. Sometimes they could get the expertise they needed on many problems only by picking the brains of specialists, who might be persuaded to see them during their lunch break. They had to beg the army for materials, even sugar for a heating experiment, which they finally obtained after pleading in a letter:

"We would like to obtain an extra ration of sugar to build an atomic bomb."

And only money passed under the workbench got them enough steel plates.

But patience had yielded a crystal of uranium hexafluoride, and a test would soon reveal whether this crystal would yield U^{235}, the key to a Japanese atomic bomb.

XII

To Soviet agents in New York, Klaus Fuchs was the key to a Russian atomic bomb. By vanishing without a trace, Fuchs had once more tried to show how independent he was of the Soviet apparatus that he voluntarily served. *He* would determine the terms and timing of his cooperation. For was he not still a free spirit answerable only to his conscience? And so, on being assigned to Los Alamos in August 1944, he simply packed his bags and departed, leaving Gold to wait in vain for him on a Brooklyn street corner.

When a week or two later Fuchs didn't show up for an alternate meeting in Manhattan, on Central Park West near 96th Street, Gold grew alarmed. There were many muggings in that area, and Fuchs, being of slight build, might have been an inviting prey. He immediately reported to "John," or Anatoli Yakovlev, his Soviet superior, and for two hours they speculated on what might have happened. Was Fuchs still in New York and for some reason unable to appear at the meetings? Had he gone off to "Mexico," as he once told Gold he might do? It wasn't easy dealing with so unreliable a spy.

Some days later, on a Sunday morning near Washington Square, the two men met once again and Yakovlev announced he had a lead. He had learned Fuchs' address.

Try to find him, the Russian ordered, handing Gold a slip of paper with the address.

Gold entered the nearest subway station and got out at an uptown stop, where he purchased a book called *Joseph the Provider* by Thomas Mann. On the inside cover, he carefully printed: "K. Fuchs, 128-West 77th Street, New York, N.Y." In case anybody asked why he was looking for Fuchs, he could claim that he wanted to return this book to him. Gold went to the apartment building where Fuchs lived and saw an old janitor carrying some rubbish out.

Did Dr. Klaus Fuchs live here? he asked. But when the janitor, looking bewildered, did not reply, Gold opened the door and, with relief, found Fuchs' nameplate on the wall with those of other residents. As he walked down the first-floor hall toward Fuchs' apartment, a door opened and an old woman peeked out, just as the janitor, apparently her husband, walked up.

He was looking for Dr. Fuchs' apartment, Gold said.

Dr. Fuchs had gone away.

How could he get in touch with him?

He couldn't. Fuchs had gone off "somewhere on a boat."

Gold rushed off to see Yakovlev, who was impatiently waiting for him on Broadway near 96th Street. As they walked along Riverside Drive, they debated what to do next. Perhaps they should send a letter to Fuchs' address in the hope that it would be forwarded to him.

No, too risky, Yakovlev decided. If Fuchs were working in some secret place, he might be asked for an explanation.

So what should they do?

"Sit tight," Yakovlev said despairingly.

At their next meeting, the Russian was in a better mood. He had learned, said Yakovlev, that Fuchs had a sister who lived near Boston.

Gold reproached himself. He had known this, but somehow had not thought of contacting her.

At the next meeting, Yakovlev was all smiles. He had the woman's name and address, which Gold had not known.

On the following Sunday, in late September 1944, Gold took a bus to Boston, and as soon as he arrived there headed for the designated address in Cambridge. The housekeeper answered the bell.

Was Kristel Heineman at home? Gold asked.

No, the Heinemans were on vacation. They wouldn't be back until sometime in October.

Gold was disappointed, but at least now there was hope of finding Fuchs. He returned to New York and, with Yakovlev, agonizingly waited a few weeks, then tried again.

This time a woman in her early thirties with probing eyes, short dark hair, and a pleasant smile opened the door—Kristel Heineman.

He was a friend of Dr. Fuchs, Gold said.

Kristel looked puzzled for a moment, then replied: "Oh yes, by any chance did you call sometime in September when we were away?"

"Yes, I am the man."

When they were seated, Kristel spoke fondly of her brother. She was very glad that he was now in the United States, since they were close and he loved her three children.

He had met "Klaus" in New York, Gold said, and they had become firm friends. He just happened to be on business in the Boston area and thought he would stop by to ask for him.

But Klaus had been transferred to somewhere in the southwest United States, she said. However, she expected him home about Christmastime, "as he usually made a great event of bringing presents for the children."

Gold hid his delight. His own plans and whereabouts, he said, were indefinite, and so he would leave a message telling Klaus how to get in touch with him.

He then gave Kristel a sealed envelope with a note instructing Fuchs to call a certain telephone number on any morning between 8 and 8:30 A.M., ask for a certain person, and say only, "I have arrived in Cambridge and will be here for X days."

Gold then left in an exhilarated mood. Klaus was a difficult person, but perhaps he would be returning with a special Christmas gift for Stalin.

XIII

Fuchs was, in fact, preparing an elaborate present for Stalin with all the nuclear trimmings he could gather. He worked under Hans Bethe, head of the Theoretical Division, and was learning as much about the atomic bomb as almost any scientist in Los Alamos. Together with Peierls, a third British scientist, and about ten American scientists, his task was to find the best way of bringing together two subcritical masses to form a critical mass. He was personally working on the means of detonating the plutonium bomb, including the lens and hydrodynamics system and implosion designs. And he was also contributing to research on the "Super" hydrogen bomb. He had access at *all* times to *all* sections of the Los Alamos laboratory and *all* documents, except some "top secret" ones, and he could even see *them* if they were needed for his work.

Bethe would say that Fuchs "made an extremely great contribution. He was one of the most valuable men in my division. One of the best theoretical physicists I had." In fact, Fuchs' theories materially helped speed up the production of the bomb. As Oppenheimer would later point out to the FBI, Fuchs "presented a paper in connection with his experiments on the atom bomb, which caused [others] to realize that they had been approaching a specific problem from the wrong angle."

Every Saturday night Fuchs discussed his work on implosion design at a meeting of his group, and every Friday afternoon he listened with tape-recorder ears as members of the top-level camp Coordinating Council described the bomb-making process in each division—meetings held despite the efforts of General Groves to compartmentalize Los Alamos. Occasionally, Fuchs himself would deliver a lecture on hydrodynamics, to the admiration of his colleagues, who marveled at his precision, logic, and knowledge.

No, there was little about the atomic bomb that Fuchs couldn't wrap up in Christmas paper to present to Stalin's agent. But there was one facet of the bomb that didn't seem to interest him at all—how to control it after the war. He never came to meetings on this question, which drew most of the other scientists. These political gatherings were not nearly as numerous or as heated as those in Chicago, where Leo Szilard presided, for at Los Alamos they were making the bomb itself and were thus less inclined to worry about its political implications. Nor, with the pressure mounting, did they have as much time for meetings.

But one thing many did demand was that, as a matter of goodwill, the Russians be told about the bomb and some aspects of atomic research before they gathered the facts themselves. Was it fair to give these facts to one ally, Britain, and not to another, Russia? What's more, there could be no effective international control of the bomb without the Russians taking part, and the alternative to such control was a deadly arms race.

But some doubted that Fuchs favored sharing the secret, since he never came to these discussions, though once, after listening to Peierls speak critically of the Russians, he vaguely replied, "Well, there is the other side to it." He just wasn't interested in political talk. He wanted to do his work and go back to his bachelors' dormitory, where he would relax over a good book—nothing political—or enjoy the company of girl friends, especially the two admiring young schoolteachers he courted. Discreetly, of course. Outraged wives had forced the military to throw eager suitors out of the single women's dormitory at midnight (fomenting an angry revolt among the unattached males), and Fuchs didn't want to damage the reputation of the scientific community.

Yes, with all the intellectual challenge, the parties, the mountain climbing, and the girls, life in Los Alamos was good. But he was looking forward to Christmas.

XIV

Life was good for most scientists in Los Alamos, but it was also hard and growing harder as the time approached for testing the plutonium bomb. Would implosion work? No one could be sure. But General Groves was sure about one thing: He had been right about Oppenheimer. Oppie had rounded up the "prima donnas" and hypnotized them. True, Groves knew that many of these scientists hated him, regarding him as a lesser mortal, primitive and simplistic. And he wasn't sure they sympathized with him even after he told them at a welcoming meeting in Los Alamos that they had better succeed or he would probably be investigated by a congressional committee after the war. They were too selfish to care what happened to him. (In fact, they interpreted his appeal as a sign that he lacked confidence in the project.) But all that really mattered was that they listened to Oppenheimer and Oppenheimer listened to him.

The problem was that Oppenheimer didn't always listen to him. To entice the top scientists to leave their gleaming laboratories and head for the New Mexican desert, he had promised, without Groves' explicit permission, to let them freely exchange ideas inside their barbed wire-rimmed working area, though the general wanted to limit such exchanges. And now Groves couldn't force Oppenheimer to renege on his promise for fear that the scientists might quit.

Some were already defiant, and one, Richard Feynman, to show his contempt for Groves' security rules, figured out the combination of safes stuffed with classified data and left notes in them saying, "Guess who?"

Only military personnel like Deak Parsons *had* to stay on, and Groves' rigid security regulations made even him uneasy sometimes. When he once visited home, which was conveniently nearby, and his sister suggested throwing a party for him and his family, he uncharacteristically panicked. Having told her where he was based if not what he was doing, he replied almost in a whisper, as if the security agents shadowing him might hear: "No parties! Do you want to see me court-martialed? Don't say anything about my being there, don't even say Los Alamos!"

But now Groves had to back Oppenheimer and decompartmentalize, and he was angry. So angry that he struck back by tightening compartmentalization among the various laboratories in the country. Not even Compton, Lawrence, or Urey were to know what was going on in Los Alamos, while Oppenheimer could only coordinate the work of the production plants through Groves. When Oppenheimer once inadvertently told Compton about a particular development in Los Alamos, Groves exploded and apparently hinted that Oppenheimer was, after all, dispensable. He refused to listen to arguments that his policy was slowing up production of the bomb.

After this heated exchange, Oppenheimer realized how far he could go in pushing his own views without endangering his job. In fact, so eager was he to make amends that he refused to defend his deputy, Edward Condon, when Groves accused him of instigating Oppenheimer to break the rules—though apparently he had not. Condon resigned in fury, feeling betrayed by his old schoolmate from Göttingen. Yes, Oppenheimer had learned his lesson, and he was suddenly hewing to the security rules as never before.

And so when the FBI came up with new reports of Oppenheimer's old politics, Groves grandly rewarded the scientist with his support. But by doing so, he also rewarded himself for his keen perception. As he would later concede to the FBI, if not to Oppenheimer himself, the scientist *was* "indispensable." He couldn't risk slowing up production of the bomb by getting rid of him. Besides, Oppenheimer had riled the FBI not because he was doing anything disloyal, but because he pointed a finger, if rather clumsily, at a man who apparently was.

XV

The man was George Eltenton, an English chemical engineer working for the Shell Oil Company. Eltenton, a Communist who had lived in Moscow for several years, met in 1942 with Peter Ivanov, vice consul of the Soviet consulate in San Francisco.

Ivanov was blunt:

Could Eltenton find out what kind of experiments the scientists were performing in Berkeley's Radiation Laboratory?

Agreeing to try, Eltenton invited Haakon Chevalier, Oppenheimer's old friend, to his home and pointed out, as Ivanov had to him, that the United States and Russia were brothers-in-arms. Why, he asked, shouldn't the two countries exchange information on important strategic research for their mutual benefit? Oppenheimer, who was then still in Berkeley, was known to be in charge of a vital war project and was sympathetic to the left. Perhaps he would agree to promote closer coordination. Would Chevalier, being a friend of his, sound him out on his willingness to collaborate? The Soviet consulate would be glad to reciprocate.

Chevalier would claim that he was shocked by the implications and that he replied with an unqualified "no." The idea struck him "as preposterous, because it was totally 'out of key' with everything relating to [Oppenheimer] and what he stood for."

What happened after this is not completely clear. Chevalier and Oppenheimer would later agree that they and their wives soon met for dinner, and when the scientist went to the kitchen to fetch the ice and mixings for a martini, Chevalier followed him.

"I reported the conversation I had had with Eltenton," Chevalier would say, "because I thought he should know of it, and . . . he agreed I was right in telling him."

In 1950, Oppenheimer appeared to confirm this account in a letter to Chevalier, writing:

"You had told me of a discussion of providing technical information to the USSR which disturbed you considerably, and which you thought I ought to know about."

In any case, Oppenheimer remained silent about the Eltenton-Chevalier conversation for several months, apparently feeling that since nothing had materialized anyway, why involve either Chevalier or himself in a meaningless investigation? But meanwhile, the FBI had uncovered what it believed to be a Communist cell in the Radiation Laboratory, and several of the suspects were former Oppenheimer students, including the young physicist Lomanitz. The army tried to draft him in order to remove him from the laboratory, but Lawrence defended him because he doubted that he was a Communist and needed him on his project.

When Oppenheimer, now based in Los Alamos, visited Berkeley in August 1943, he asked the campus security officer for permission to speak with Lomanitz so he could decide whether he should also defend the man. As he was about to leave to see Lomanitz, he offhandedly suggested that security officers should watch Eltenton—without saying why. If a "Communist cell" was operating in the laboratory, he felt, perhaps Eltenton could be dangerous after all. He might be contacting any number of people. Oppenheimer then went off to see Lomanitz and, convinced by the conversation that he *was* involved in Communist activities, decided not to protest his conscription.

Ironically, the day after he made this hard-line decision, Oppenheimer was back in the security office under interrogation himself. The interrogator was Lieutenant Colonel Boris T. Pash, who had been investigating Communist penetration of the university and had already reported to Groves' office in Washington that he believed Oppenheimer "still is or may be connected with the Communist Party in the Project." And Pash's suspicions had grown when his agents followed Oppenheimer on a previous visit to Berkeley virtually into the bedroom of his old left-wing fiancée, Jean Tatlock, who had been begging him to stop by for months. He had stayed with her all night, and Pash was doubtful that he did it only to ease the depression she was suffering—even when, some time afterwards, she would swallow pills, put her head in a bathtub of water, and, to Oppenheimer's shock and grief, die.

Now Pash wanted to know more about Eltenton, his comrades, and his activities, but Oppenheimer would say only that Eltenton had tried to get information for the Soviet consulate.

"To give more . . . than one name would be to implicate people whose attitude was one of bewilderment rather than one of cooperation."

What did Oppenheimer think about Eltenton's approach?

"To put it quite frankly," said Oppenheimer, "I would feel friendly to the idea of the Commander-in-Chief informing the Russians that we were working on this problem. At least I can see there might be some arguments for doing that, but I do not feel friendly to the idea of having it moved out the back door."

Well, whose help did Eltenton seek in opening the back door? Pash persisted. He only wanted "to see Eltenton's method of approach."

Finally, Oppenheimer, apparently feeling that a crumb or so might end the torment, dropped a few. Eltenton's contact had approached three people, two at Los Alamos and one at Berkeley.

When he refused to give more details, Pash gave up, let his quarry go, and wrote to Groves that, in his view, Oppenheimer had given the information about Eltenton because the conscription of Lomanitz made him fear for his job and he wanted to "retain the confidence of the army personnel responsible for the project." Pash followed this up with charges from his man in Los Alamos that Oppenheimer had recruited a large number of "known Communists or Communist sympathizers" and that he must either be "incredibly naïve and almost childlike in his sense of reality or extremely clever and disloyal."

Groves had become so dependent on Oppenheimer to make the bomb on time that hardly less than the discovery of a Communist Party card with the man's name engraved on it would have been enough to get him fired. The general nevertheless sent his own security officer, John Lansdale, to dig out more details about the Eltenton approach, but Lansdale hit bedrock.

Even Oppenheimer, it seems, felt sorry for him.

"Why do you look so worried?" the scientist asked.

"Because I'm not getting anywhere."

"Well . . . I think you're getting everywhere that I can get you."

"I've made up my mind that you, yourself, are O.K., or otherwise I wouldn't be talking to you like this, see?"

"I'd better be—that's all I've got to say. . . . It is a question of some past loyalties. . . . I would regard it as a low trick to involve someone where I would bet dollars to doughnuts he wasn't involved."

Lansdale left, frustrated but convinced that Oppenheimer was loyal, and his faith in the man solidified after he spoke with Kitty Oppenheimer, even though she had once belonged to the Communist Party.

"She struck me as a curious personality," he would report to Groves, "at once frail and very strong. I felt she'd go to any lengths for what she believed in." And she now believed in her husband. "Her strength of will was a powerful influence in keeping [him] away from what he would regret as dangerous associations."

Groves agreed, but, while traveling with Oppenheimer in a train one day, he casually repeated Lansdale's questions, if only because he was curious about Oppenheimer's reticence. He received the same answers, except that Oppenheimer, apparently worried about his job, admitted that he had personally been approached and agreed to name others involved if Groves ordered him to. But Groves didn't, at least for the time being. Like Oppenheimer, he did not see what all the fuss was about. Oppenheimer's angry rejection of the approach had probably frightened off Eltenton and any other Soviet contacts.

And besides, who really cared whether Russia learned about Lawrence's emergency electromagnetic process, which would be useless and irrelevant after the war? As Groves would explain several years later:

"We were never too much concerned about [espionage in Lawrence's laboratory] because I personally felt that while the electromagnetic process was . . . of extreme importance to us during the war, and we saved at least a year's time by doing it, that it was not the process we would follow after the war. That is one of the reasons why we put silver in those magnets, because we knew we could get it out."

Anyway, Groves felt that Oppenheimer had proved his loyalty by informing on Eltenton, even if he delayed doing so in order to protect someone. Groves, in any case, had been aware of Eltenton's activities even before Oppenheimer mentioned the man's name, but he felt that stopping them would tip off the Soviet agents that they were being watched. Better, he curiously reasoned, to let Russia get indigestion from useless data.

Oppenheimer would stay, and that was that!

XVI

Even so, pressured by his own security men, Groves visited Oppenheimer in December 1943 and gave the order. He wanted the names.

Oppenheimer now had no choice, it seemed, if he wanted to keep his job—and he did. Eltenton's contact was Chevalier.

And whom did Chevalier contact besides Oppenheimer himself?

Oppenheimer, having already betrayed one confidant, was clearly uncomfortable, but Groves would not be denied. To make it easier, though, he volunteered to make sure that the information "would not get to the FBI."

Oppenheimer then agreed to answer his question, Groves would later tell the FBI. He knew of only *one* man Chevalier had contacted, not three as he told Pash in a thoughtless moment of impatience and fatigue.

Himself?

No, his brother Frank.

Frank Oppenheimer, a physicist in Lawrence's laboratory, was asked by Chevalier to furnish information on his own work, said Robert. Frank, who with his wife had resigned from the Communist Party in disillusionment some time previously, rushed to seek his brother's advice.

"Tell Chevalier to go to hell!" Robert replied, according to FBI reports.

Groves was stunned. That explained why Oppenheimer had been so reluctant to talk—he was trying to protect his brother. And, in the general's view, also himself and Chevalier, whom he apparently confronted personally to add his own rejection to Frank's. Yet Groves was troubled by doubt. He was still not sure "whether Frank's involvement was invented as an excuse for the delay in reporting the [Eltenton] matter, or whether Frank was actually involved."

In any event, it wasn't important. Ruthlessness and ambition were hardly reasons to get rid of a man, especially one Groves needed so badly to help him fulfil his own ambitions.

Meanwhile, the general would keep his promise to Oppenheimer: The information would not get to the FBI. On returning to his office in Washington, however, he mentioned to Lansdale and his other security assistant, Consodine, that Oppenheimer had identified the man who had been approached.

Who was the man?

Groves could not say. But he pushed a yellow pad toward his two aides and asked them to write down three guesses. Lansdale jotted down three names and Consodine, one—Frank Oppenheimer. Groves "expressed surprise."

Well, since Consodine had guessed—yes, that was the man. But he had promised Robert not to tell the FBI. So, remember, not a word to the FBI.

But Lansdale, as Groves had perhaps calculated, felt that his greater loyalty was to his country and he was soon spilling all to the FBI. Yet, who could say that Groves had double-crossed Oppenheimer? The last thing Groves wanted at this delicate stage of the bomb was an Oppenheimer who no longer trusted him. After the war, FBI agents would interview Frank.

Chevalier? Hardly knew him. No, the man had never contacted him about giving information, nor did he, Frank, ever discuss such an approach with his brother.

Also, as indicated earlier, after the war Robert would say openly, and confirm in his letter to Chevalier, that it was he himself whom Chevalier had contacted. Which brother did Chevalier actually contact? Perhaps both? And whom was Robert really trying to protect? No one can be sure, but if the answer could tell something about Oppenheimer's character and the passion that drove him at Los Alamos, it could not show that he was disloyal to his country—no matter how hard Oppenheimer's enemies and the FBI would try after the war to turn inconsistent, sometimes irrelevant testimony into evidence of disloyalty.

And this Groves understood with the logic of a man who could not fail.

Chapter 9

THE
HERO

I

Admiral Kantaro Suzuki, who had reluctantly moved into the Prime Minister's office in Tokyo on April 6, 1945, had a security problem of his own. How long could he cheat an assassin's fatal bullet? But he resolutely fought to save his own life, and that of his nation, though his priority was not clear. Still, Suzuki was terrified as he sat at his desk on the day of the bomb puffing on a cigar and scanning a book on inner peace by a Chinese Taoist philosopher, his only escape from the torment of his dilemma.

Should Suzuki surrender or keep on fighting? The Potsdam Declaration promised the "prompt and utter destruction" of the country if the Japanese forces did not lay down their arms. But the fanatical militarists promised the same fate to anyone who ordered them to. And Suzuki wanted to live.

The irony was that Suzuki himself was a military man; in fact, at 78, he was the most venerated war hero alive. His lined face, with bushy arched eyebrows, straggly mustache, and huge cabbage-leaf ears, blended into a portrait of wisdom, dignity, and courage. And he *had* shown supreme courage in the 1894–95 war

with China and the 1905 war with Russia. He was the consummate
samurai, a proud, noble, honest, clean-living warrior respected by
almost everyone from the lowliest peasant to the Emperor as a
sterling example of Japanese manhood.

That was part of Suzuki's problem. The popular perception of
his qualities threw a luridly contrasting light on those of many
other military leaders and even awed Suzuki himself. Could he be
that remarkable a man? Thus, all Japanese had confidence in Admiral Suzuki—except Suzuki and some of his resentful military
peers. A perfect prescription for a hero's terror.

Actually, it would be hard for any man, however brave, to face
violent death after having already miraculously escaped this fate
several times. And aside from the normal hazards of battle, Suzuki
had. When he was 3, he toddled in front of a galloping horse and
barely missed being trampled. As a young boy, he fell into deep
water while fishing and just managed to paddle his way to safety,
though he had never swum before. As a junior naval officer, he fell
overboard in rough water one night and, too proud to cry for help,
almost drowned once more before grabbing a rope dangling from
the craft. (His comrades only learned—and laughed—about it
when a sailor asked in a loud voice, "Sir, what shall I do with your
wet nightshirt?")

But the closest call of all came when he survived a brutal attack
by army officers, who nearly robbed him of his manhood, not to
mention his life. Several bullets struck him, and a surgeon ex-
tracted one "leaden ball from the honorable golden one," as the
doctor would irreverently phrase it.

It was in the attempted coup of February 26, 1936, that Suzuki
almost lost the "golden one." Although the young officers who
revolted against the government revered Suzuki's image, they
hated him for his relative moderation, especially after his "treacherous" support of an international naval agreement in 1930 that
would limit Japanese shipbuilding and assure that Japan would
have fewer warships bobbing in the sea than the United States and
Britain. He had become grand chamberlain to the Emperor and,
in their eyes, betrayed the nation by advising His Majesty to rein in
the military.

Kill Admiral Suzuki! the order went out.

And an assassination team broke into his house after he had
returned from an enjoyable evening at the home of American

Ambassador Joseph C. Grew, where he had seen the musical film *Naughty Marietta*. Suzuki jumped out of bed and looked for his sword but was surrounded by the intruders before he could find it. A noncommissioned officer approached him with a pistol in hand and told him that he must die.

"Is that all you have to tell me?" Suzuki calmly replied. "Then shoot!"

Perhaps to Suzuki's surprise, two soldiers obliged, firing bullets into his chest and groin. The noncommissioned officer then bent down to feel the admiral's pulse. Still alive. He pressed the muzzle of his pistol to his victim's neck and was about to fire the coup de grace when Suzuki's wife, who was present, cried out:

"If my husband must die, for the sake of my honor and that of my family, let me be the one to give him the final blow!"

At that moment, the army captain who headed the assassination team entered and stopped the execution, and eventually Suzuki would recover from his wounds.

But the gun muzzle on his neck had left an impression that remained for a long time, and it seemed to have reappeared on the day he was sworn in as Prime Minister. Until now, he had felt that some "invisible power," perhaps emanating from Buddha or the gods, helped him survive his many flirtations with death. But now he saw the mark on his neck as a frightening omen. He was an old man, but somehow the older he got, the longer he wanted to live. When his son Hajime offered to become his private secretary, Suzuki replied:

"Don't accompany me to death. I have come a long way but you still have far to go."

If Suzuki's desire to come an even longer way made him hesitate to surrender to the Allies, however, he was philosophically as well as pragmatically disposed toward peace. As a follower of the Chinese Taoist philosophers, whose works lined the shelves of his 20,000-book library, Suzuki believed that obscurity was a virtue, and that a man could best achieve happiness by developing his mind freely, governing himself through nongovernment, and meeting problems through passivity rather than through action. After his experiences in war and its aftermath, Suzuki had become a pacifistic military man, almost as rare a bird as the Kauai Oo. A bird that completely baffled fellow militarists.

Suzuki the sailor was proud of Japan's armed forces even

though he disagreed with their aims and tactics. But ever since military fanatics had tried to kill him, he apparently felt little sense of *giri* toward the caste that had nurtured and honored him. While his attackers represented only one small segment of the military, he was nevertheless resentfully aware that even many responsible officers believed he had betrayed their cause.

On the other hand, Suzuki's debt to the Emperor was enormous, especially since he was very close to him. He had served as Hirohito's grand chamberlain from 1929 to 1936 and as president of the privy council from 1940 to 1945, positions of great influence in the palace. The privy council was an official body of distinguished aristocrats, Cabinet members, and princes of the blood, who gave the Emperor advice when he requested it.

Suzuki's debt to Hirohito, however, was as complex as his character. The admiral felt he had to obey his master and surrender, but he also felt he had to protect him. What if the militarists revolted? They would shackle the Emperor—and shoot the Prime Minister. Yet Suzuki knew he couldn't ignore the Imperial wish, especially since he agreed with it. Had not the Potsdam Declaration made clear the fate awaiting Japan? Besides, if the Allies let the Emperor keep his throne—and it appeared they would—he would probably be under a less restrictive thumb than if he were the prisoner of fanatics like the one who did not even respect an admiral's manhood.

Yes, Suzuki would make peace at the first propitious moment, whatever the risks. But when would the moment be propitious? The militarists would not listen to him now any more than they did in 1936. Trapped in a quandary, intimidated by a task he had never wanted, Suzuki squinted through the cigar smoke swirling around him and read Tao while Tokyo burned.

II

It was, in a sense, apropos that Suzuki should rule the nation as it collapsed into the ashes. For his life and that of modern Japan coincided almost exactly and seemed inextricably bound together. He was born into a samurai family in 1867, the last year of the Tokugawa feudal era that Kido's grandfather had helped to end. Like the new Japan itself, he was an angry child. In a country where children are seldom disciplined, he threw so many tantrums that he was called "Crying Kan." Even when he grew too old to cry, his anger persisted. He was angry at his uncles, who called him "the son of an Imperial dog," because his father supported the new, modern political leaders while *they* remained loyal to the ousted Tokugawa. He was angry at the boys in the new town his family of eleven moved to because they bullied him for daring to intrude into their clanlike community with its own cliquish traditions and hierarchy. But then his father told him one day:

"A man should not get angry, my son. People get angry because they lack tolerance. Just remember that the one with the short temper is the loser. Nothing done in anger can succeed."

Suzuki never forgot this paternal advice. He would follow it all his life—and he would succeed, just as the emerging Japan would.

In his new hometown, not far from Tokyo, Kantaro grew up to the sound of new machines grinding away in old workshops, of new, well-equipped armed forces marching proudly down the street, of new patriotic teachers leading the children in the cry, "To die for the Emperor." Suzuki watched with fascination as his nation burgeoned year by year from a clan society into a world power, and after school he read a book a day, mainly on Japan's glorious past, dreaming of a role in its future. He persuaded his father, who envisaged a medical career for him, to send him to a navy prep school, and from there he entered the naval academy.

Soon, Suzuki was playing his role magnificently, even though he was one of the most seasick sailors in the navy. His cruises from port to port opened his eyes to the outside world, and his naval skill helped to open the eyes of dismayed enemies who had considered Japan a still-primitive nation. As the commander of a torpedo boat in the Sino-Japanese War, he sank a Chinese warship, destroyed a breakwater, and rescued another Japanese vessel. As the commander of a cruiser in the Russo-Japanese War, he attacked ships of the Russian Baltic fleet, drawing so close that he could read by their searchlights, and sent two of those ships to their watery graves. He was ready to die then, at the peak of his glory, like the ephemeral cherry blossom suddenly vanishing in the wind.

But Suzuki lived, and was heralded as a hero by his people. He rose quickly in the ranks, despite the reluctance of the Satsuma clan—which dominated the navy as Choshu did the army—to allow nonmembers like himself to advance very far. He became commander in chief of the combined fleet, chief of staff, and war councilor to the Emperor before being named grand chamberlain and then president of the privy council, a position that automatically made him a member of the Jushin.

And then came World War II and calamity, a war Suzuki didn't want, fought in a way he didn't understand. He had fought cleanly as a young officer in earlier wars, respecting the enemy and sparing civilians. No one murdered prisoners of war, no one raped or robbed. And certainly no one tried to kill fellow officers for political reasons. Was this the proud new Japan he had grown up with?

This was, in any case, the Japan that was dying. And he must try to save it—and himself. He must succeed once more. But how? Until the day of the bomb, he had walked a tightrope between the peacemakers and the warmongers, practicing *haragei* to survive. This meant, in a sense, talking out of both sides of your mouth. Seek your goal by asking for the exact opposite of what you want. Presumably, this would deceive and gradually soften up your opposition and be understood by your supporters. Suzuki had refined this art to such a degree that even some of his supporters were deceived. He wasn't perturbed. If even your friends misunderstand you, surely you have fooled your foes!

Fight on! he would cry. And sometimes he was actually persuaded by his own words. Perhaps Japan should fight on. Occasionally, he would even fantasize a victory. After all, he would tell friends, Iyeyasu, the greatest Tokugawa samurai hero, had found a way to beat a rival army in the late sixteenth century when his forces had already been defeated. Sue for peace, his retainers had pleaded, but Iyeyasu refused. Instead, he ordered his troops to withdraw to the castle. He then threw open the castle gates and cried to the pursuing enemy, "If you want to come, *come!*" The enemy leader ordered his army to halt. A trap! Iyeyasu would not outsmart *him*. Withdraw! he commanded his men. And the castle was saved.

Perhaps such a bluff could now save Japan. Could there be a better way for a Taoist peace lover to win a war than without battle?

But if Suzuki now and then imagined a samurai miracle, he would soon realize that he had deceived even himself and privately assured Kido and other peace comrades that he was with them all the way. Whether the extreme subtlety of his brand of *haragei* could actually further his goal, of course, was as unclear as the real meaning of his statements. Even so, as the day of the bomb drew closer, Suzuki cautiously measured the "success" of his "peace effort" by the distance he was able to pull the silk over the militarists' eyes. Yes, make them think he wanted to fight on.

The trouble was, the Potsdam Declaration would not allow for much more *haragei*. The propitious moment for peace would have to come soon, before the Americans invaded Japan—or someone took another shot at him. But would such a moment come in time? Linked with modern Japan at birth, Suzuki seemed destined to be linked with it in death. This was perhaps the meaning of the mark on his neck. And even the "invisible power" that had saved him so many times might not be able to help him now.

III

In July 1944, atomic scientist Yoshio Nishina imagined that an invisible power would help him succeed in what he hoped would be a final test to determine whether he could separate U^{235} from U^{238}. His young collaborators attached a flask of uranium hexafluoride, which they were now producing in greater quantity, to the underside of the apparatus that was to separate the two isotopes. If all went well, the U^{235} would rise to the top of the separator, leaving a residue of the heavier U^{238} on the bottom. Nishina wasn't overly optimistic, especially since the separator itself had already failed in a test with argon. But maybe it would work with a uranium compound. Perhaps the mysterious power would take the hex off uranium hexafluoride. He desperately wanted to succeed. After all, a bomb couldn't be built before the war ended anyway.

Flanked by his white-clad researchers, Nishina anxiously watched the fluoride in the flask; a diminution would apparently mean that the gas was entering the separator. While several young men tinkered with gauges and meters and others sat with pencils poised to jot down the results, the experiment began.

"It is becoming noticeably less!" someone cried. "It is changing into gas!"

But the instruments showed that the U^{235} was not being separated. The mysterious power did not emerge. Nor did it during the next six months despite new adjustments, new tests. The only power that did emerge was American air power. In the frantic attempt by Nishina's men to hide the precious uranium compound in a safe place, several vials of it were lost. Then everything was lost when, after the air raid on April 13, the whole building went up in flames.

IV

It was a week earlier that Admiral Suzuki took over as Prime Minister. He had not wanted the job. The peacemakers had dragged him into office after another military Prime Minister, General Kuniaki Koiso, who succeeded Tojo, had let them down. Though Koiso was also deemed a relative moderate, he, too, cherished longevity. And the military ignored him anyway, keeping almost all strategy decisions from him. Koiso tried to win the army's confidence, but could not. In frustration he resigned on April 5, 1945.

Who would be the next Prime Minister? Kido was now adamant: The next one must make peace. The Americans had already landed in Okinawa, and this would be the last chance to surrender before they landed in Japan itself and exterminated it as a nation. Nothing mattered now except keeping the Imperial system. The military had been deceiving the Emperor about the current picture and the prospects for further fighting. It would lead the whole nation to suicide. The next Prime Minister must be a man whom the Emperor could trust completely. And he must have the stature to carry out the Emperor's will whatever the obstacles. There was only one such man—Admiral Suzuki.

Suzuki was a war hero and an antimilitarist military man, the only conceivable peace supporter who *might* be acceptable to the armed forces, if only because of his prestige. True, Suzuki knew nothing about politics, but that was a virtue, for he could more easily be manipulated. Besides, he was old and had been living on borrowed time anyway since his miraculous recovery from bullet wounds in 1936.

Yes, Suzuki was the man to stick his marked neck out and lead Japan to surrender before untold catastrophe struck.

Kido and several members of the Jushin thus conspired in advance to select Suzuki when the group met to discuss a successor to Koiso. Tojo, as an ex-Prime Minister, was a new member of the

Jushin and he would surely favor a man who would continue the war. And he did—with the apparent support of Suzuki, who attended the meeting as president of the privy council.

"Today," Suzuki told his colleagues, "we must of necessity fight out the war at any cost. I think that is the question that should have priority."

To Kido, Suzuki was speaking *haragei*. "We must form a Cabinet worthy of being trusted by the people," he countered vaguely.

Finally, after Suzuki had proposed Prince Konoye, a peace advocate, as Prime Minister, thus revealing his true thoughts, someone nominated Suzuki himself for the job. The admiral seemed surprised, even irritated. He wasn't a politician. He was a peace-loving sailor and Imperial aide who was uncomfortable in the limelight. He hated arguments. He hated controversy. And he hated the thought of a bullet finding another delicate spot in his body. Why test the mood of the "invisible power" that had kept him alive up to now?

"I have always thought," Suzuki replied with unusual frankness, "that the participation of military men in politics could contribute to the ruin of a country. This was the case with the Roman Empire. And also the case with the Kaiser and the Romanoffs. Therefore, in view of my principle, it would be difficult for me to take part in political affairs. Besides, I am hard of hearing, and I would like to be excused."

Tojo was glad to excuse him. "Admiral Suzuki's attitude is admirable," he said sarcastically. "The enemy is desperate. He will launch extraordinary operations. It is likely that he may invade some part of our homeland. . . . This problem must be centered around the army. Our choice must be a person in active military service."

But Kido would not let Tojo ruin his plan. Suzuki must accept. "I personally wish that His Excellency Suzuki would come forward," he persisted.

Tojo was furious. "If you are not careful," he warned, "there is a possibility that the army will turn its back. And if the army turns its back, the Cabinet would have to be dissolved."

"It would be a serious matter if the army turned its back at this time," replied Kido, his own fury rising. "Are there any signs it will?"

"I would say there are."

Kido now, apparently for the first time in the war, directly challenged Tojo: "An antimilitary atmosphere has also become pretty strong, and it is possible that the people will turn its back on the army!"

Other enraged speakers screwed up enough courage to support Kido, and the meeting adjourned ominously. What did Tojo mean by the army "turning its back" on the Cabinet? Would it demand control of the government? Would it launch a coup, possibly killing them all? What would happen to the Emperor? Emboldened by the backing he received, Kido was now more resolved than ever to have Suzuki form a Cabinet. He drew Suzuki aside.

"You were extremely reluctant," he said, "but in view of the present situation I implore you to form a Cabinet at any cost. I am sorry to trouble you, but will you accept?"

Suzuki was firm. "I must decline since I am not confident that I can do the job."

"The conditions at present are so critical," Kido pressed, "that I must beg you to make a great decision to save our nation."

The admiral felt trapped. Finally, he said, "If the Emperor orders me to form a new Cabinet, I will do it."

Suzuki may have felt that he was safe. As an Imperial adviser, he thought he knew how to handle the Emperor. But Kido, the Emperor's most intimate adviser, knew how, too.

V

Later that evening, April 5, the Lord Keeper conferred with the Emperor on the meeting of the Jushin and his talk with Suzuki.

His Majesty should certainly ask Suzuki to form a new Cabinet, he said.

Hirohito was glad to take Kido's advice. He had always felt a special affection for Suzuki. When the admiral had been grand chamberlain, he was even the one to burst in with the monumental news—after so many disappointments—that an Imperial heir had been born.

"It's a boy!" he had cried. "I saw the honorable signs of manhood myself!"

"To Suzuki," Hirohito had once said, "I could pour my heart out." Yet, in fact, an Emperor could not really pour his heart out to anyone; gods, even false ones, Hirohito had long since learned, had to keep their human feelings to themselves lest they betray doubts about their divine heritage. But Suzuki would understand. He would understand that destiny had appointed him to make peace.

Peace had become an obsession with Hirohito, especially as American bombs exploded with ever-growing wrath. But the military kept hounding him: Japan must win one more great battle before seeking peace, then it could win better terms. Until recently, Hirohito accepted this advice, if bitterly. Had Tojo obeyed him and sought peace in the first glorious months of the war, the nation, he lamented, would perhaps not be facing tragedy today. But no matter how irresponsible the overconfident military leaders had been, with Japan losing they might be right now—just one great victory. . . .

The bombs, however, gradually brought home the horrible truth to him—that Japan could no longer wait for the elusive victory. But how could he defy the military leaders? They would simply blame his instructions, as always, on the "bad advice" of his civilian advisers and continue the war, perhaps even take him under their "protection."

In desperation, the Emperor, in January 1945, asked Kido to arrange an Imperial Conference with the Jushin so he could seek its advice. But though members met individually with Hirohito, most feared to speak their minds, for the Imperial wall had many ears. Yes, peace, but only after the war was over. After such doubletalk, Tojo's assurance that Japan could still win the war was almost refreshing. Only Prince Konoye flatly stated that the Emperor should seek immediate peace—or possibly face a Communist revolution that might abolish the throne and even the god-given privileges of the aristocracy.

"Sad though it is," Konoye said, reading from a prepared text, "I believe that Japan has already lost the war. . . . What we have most to fear is not defeat itself but, rather, the threat inherent in the possibility that a Communist revolution may accompany defeat. . . . There is poverty in the life of the people, a rise in the voice of labor, and expansion of pro-Soviet feeling growing out of greater enmity toward America and Britain. . . . [Also,] a great number of young military men seem to think that communism is compatible with Japan's Imperial system. . . . At any rate, . . .

the elimination of the extremists is the prerequisite for saving Japan from a Communist revolution."

The Emperor had been listening carefully. Wouldn't it be difficult for the senior officers to purge the extremists, he asked, unless Japan scored a military success?

Yes, Konoye agreed, but "if it comes six months or a year from now, it will be too late."

Hirohito wondered aloud: If Japan surrendered, would the United States abolish the Imperial system, as the military warned?

On the contrary. If Japan continued the war, the Imperial system would be in even greater danger, Konoye replied.

The Emperor seemed impressed. After all, not only the enemy, but his own people, Communist or not, might in their disillusion turn against their god. He had studied the French Revolution with deep fascination. And the wild cheers of the masses each time the guillotine severed a royal head echoed in his mind. Yes, he must bring peace, but a shred of uncertainty still remained: Should he wait for one big victory?

After the meeting, Kido remarked to Konoye that he was "perplexed by the army, which always tells His Majesty false stories."

"His Majesty," replied Konoye, "is too trustful of the military. He should realize more clearly the gravity of the situation."

VI

Kido would see that the Emperor did. And he didn't have to describe how grave the situation was; the Americans would, especially on the wind-whipped night of March 9. They came unseen, humming in the dark like a swarm of locusts—more than 300 B-29s. And midnight alternated with noon as flashes of light illuminated the sky, fleetingly silhouetting the slender, winged insects, which buzzed past beyond the grasp of skeletal red fingers thrust into the heavens by antiaircraft guns. Within minutes the fatal wind had done its work, and the horizon was aflame as a runaway urban forest fire consumed wooden dwellings faster than the bombardiers could drop their loads.

Sparks dancing from roof to roof, tree to tree, spread the holocaust as houses collapsed on families hiding in the cellar, as infants burned on their fleeing mothers' backs, as people leaping into stinking canals died of asphyxiation before they could drown, as refugees packing the parks and gardens found themselves trapped by the flames, which would devour them en masse. The streets were littered with charred bodies, and human ashes filled the air like black snowflakes.

It is doubtful that the agony of the victims would have been eased if they had known that Secretary of War Stimson really cared about people and that his air force assured him that it was pinpointing military targets to the extent possible. Over 100,000 expired in three hours, more than would die in Hiroshima. Never had so many planes missed their target by so many miles and killed so many people.

The Imperial Palace was spared, but a few days later Kido made sure that the Emperor learned the truth. When His Majesty asked to visit the damaged areas, Kido immediately agreed. Yes, the Emperor must see the smoldering ruins of the Meiji Revolution, smell its remains, taste the ashes. The army objected, for Hirohito might then want to end the war; Kido insisted for the same reason. And so the great front gate of the palace yawned open and a wine-colored Mercedes, shielded by a convoy of cars and motorcycles, zoomed into the carbonized wasteland.

The Emperor, sandwiched between two aides, stared through the windows at his startled subjects, who bowed as they noted the Imperial emblem of the golden chrysanthemum on the side of the car. They couldn't imagine their god leaving his sanctuary to glimpse a world that had failed him. It was like Amaterasu emerging from her cave to bathe a darkened earth in sunshine. But there was no sunshine now as Hirohito's glimpse shook him to his Imperial roots. For the first time he gazed into the horrible face of war. Before him stretched a burned-out wilderness as far as the eye could see, a huge dump of twisted beams, ashen masonry, jagged walls, and black tree trunks.

People wearing singed rags hobbled along carrying heavy sacks of salvaged possessions on their backs. Some had fire-red legs, fleshless hands, faces hidden by bloody bandages. They poked through the ruins searching for the dead or for some treasured memento. Even the most respectable citizens were selling everything they owned—furniture, porcelain, paintings, books. They were fleeing Tokyo before the next raid, and they needed a few yen or, better, a sack of rice—if they could get it. Passengers were not allowed to carry baggage with them on the jammed trains.

And yet no one panicked. No one wept. No one revolted. This was, after all, a mere interlude. Had not the Emperor promised them victory? They simply ate pickled scallions for breakfast, since this onion was considered powerful enough to deflect bombs, and offered prayers to goldfish, which were also rumored to save lives. Hirohito must surely have envied these pitiful people. They were strong because they believed he was a god. But what could a god believe in, especially if he knew he was not *really* a god?

The Imperial car careened to a halt in front of the *tori* gate of the blackened Tomioka Hachimangu shrine, and Hirohito got out so an aide could brief him on the damage in the district. At every pause, the Emperor muttered:

"It must have been terrible. It must have been terrible."

He returned to the car and emerged once again in the middle of a bridge to survey the endless graveyard. He remembered the great earthquake and fire of 1923 that almost completely leveled the city. But this was somehow worse. The earthquake was a natural catastrophe; the bombing was an act of war, a war that might have been avoided if he had been a strong man instead of a weak god.

The Emperor stared silently for a final moment at the wreckage of the Japan his grandfather had so proudly built. Then he got back into his car and exclaimed:

"How awful! How tragic! Tokyo is in ruins!"

About ten weeks later, on May 25, the war touched Hirohito in an even more personal way. Bombers this time unintentionally set twenty-seven palace buildings on fire, though the Emperor was safely underground. Hirohito was actually glad. When the United States had informed him through neutral diplomats that the palace would not be bombed—Washington wanted a live Emperor in case he was needed to make peace—Hirohito had said he wished no special treatment. And now he received none.

"We have been bombed at last!" he cried. "At least now the people will realize that I am sharing their ordeal with no special protection from the gods."

He even joked as he visited the palace ruins after the fires had been put out.

"I wonder what this used to be," he said with a rare laugh, staring at the smoking hulk of one building.

It was good to feel like a man again, to be as vulnerable as his people were. He even refused to move to a safer bomb shelter the military had built for him under a mountain in Matsushiro, Nagano Prefecture.

But man or god, the Emperor would never be the same. After the military had flung Japan into war, he wanted to trust his commanders, to believe their promises and explanations. But now, as Kido had hoped, it was clear: They had deceived him, lied to him. And he had seen the dreadful truth.

VII

Hirohito grew ever more sullen, introspective, and even disoriented as city after city crumbled into dust. When he saluted, his arm shook. In the morning servants would find him in the bathroom staring vacantly, toothbrush in mouth. He became more careless than usual about his dress, sometimes greeting people in mixed military and civilian garb and wearing slippers. He even began talking to himself, carrying on arguments as if he were two people. And though he still enjoyed playing the Japanese card game *Utai* with the Empress and court officials, he sometimes buried himself so deeply in thought during a game that his wife called out, "Your Majesty! Your Majesty!" Nor could he always concentrate when he stole away in the evening to play chess with his chamberlains in their quarters. Once, during a game, he turned pale and murmured to himself:

"Mother doesn't understand and I am quite embarrassed."

Was the Emperor reflecting on his childhood, on the agony of being raised as a god?

When Hirohito talked to people other than himself, the subject was usually biology, whatever the visitor's interest in it. One guest seemed riveted while Hirohito described a new species of life he had just discovered, though the man had no idea whether His Majesty was talking about a plant or an animal. The Emperor would talk about the war only with the military chiefs and his closest advisers. And while he asked the chiefs for the details of each battle, sometimes surprising them with his tactical knowledge, he never asked now whether there was really any chance of winning. Why ask when they would lie anyway? And besides, he knew the answer.

The Emperor would sit at his desk meditating for hours, even after the sun had gone down, and disappear into another world. Perhaps he was thinking of the man with fleshless hands, the old woman selling her last possessions, the child rummaging in the ruins for a cherished toy. The people who silently suffered for him. Or possibly he was pondering the future, wondering how many would die for him in new holocausts. How many bombs would it take to bring peace?

Hirohito summoned Admiral Suzuki in the hope that he would stop them.

But Suzuki was still too worried about stopping bullets, it seems, to think about stopping bombs. When the Emperor asked him to form a Cabinet, he again rattled off his objections. He was politically ignorant. He was old. He was deaf in one ear. But Hirohito waved his objections aside.

"Your unfamiliarity with politics is of no concern," he said. "Nor does it matter that you are hard of hearing. At this critical moment there is no one but you for this task. I beg you, please, to accept."

Suzuki was moved. The Emperor almost never used the words "beg" or "please." Yet the admiral knew this was a command. And he instinctively knew, too, that he was being ordered to make peace, though the Emperor would not yet commit himself openly to this aim and risk stirring thoughts of revolt in the military mind. Suzuki recalled how he had saved his fleet in the middle of a typhoon about twenty years earlier. He had ordered his ships to sail straight through it without changing course. He must now sail toward peace with the same tenacity.

The next day, Suzuki walked past the cherry blossoms that floated to the burned earth, their fragrance mingling with the bitter smell of ashes, and entered No. 1 Nagatacho, the Prime Minister's official residence. He had once wanted to die like a cherry blossom, departing dramatically in a burst of glory. But there would be no more glory. Only the day before, Russia announced it would not renew its Neutrality Pact with Japan. And now, on this very day, what remained of the Japanese fleet he had once so proudly served had virtually disappeared in the depths of the Pacific after a massive Allied air attack off Okinawa.

Soon the cherry blossoms would disappear, too.

Chapter 10

THE
INHERITOR

I

The cherry blossoms had bloomed in Washington too when Harry Truman, one week after Suzuki took office, became President of the United States. But his fate, he knew four months later on the day of the bomb, would not be that of this delicate ephemeral flower. His burst of glory would not take him out of this world but would create a new one.

Truman sparkled with good humor as he sat down for lunch aboard the destroyer S.S. *Augusta*, which was gently plowing through the calm mid-Atlantic waters toward home. Chatting amiably with crew members seated at his table, he recounted moments of triumph at the Potsdam Conference, where a few days earlier he had met with "Uncle Joe" Stalin and Winston Churchill to chart the future course of history.

The President, placid though effusive, exuded confidence. World War II was gradually phasing out, with Germany already fallen and Japan reeling like a punch-drunk fighter. And after the war? No one need worry; he could handle Uncle Joe, whom he had gotten to know well at Potsdam. But the main reason for his confidence would emerge only when the expected cable arrived, perhaps the most important one ever sent. If nothing went awry, it would say that the U.S. Air Force had dropped an atomic bomb on Hiroshima.

Meanwhile, he nibbled on his navy rations, savoring this incredible day, which would signal to the people of the earth that they had been flung into the nuclear age.

II

On April 2, 1945, Harry Truman, as Vice-President, had been far less serene when he strolled into House Speaker Sam Rayburn's private office in the Capitol for a drink and called the White House, which had been trying to reach him.

"Jesus Christ and General Jackson!" he exclaimed, as he put down the receiver and darted out the door. So tense was he that he leaped down the stairs to the basement and in utter disdain of dignity ran all the way through the long passageway that led to his office in the Senate Office Building about a block away, his footsteps echoing like a countdown to catastrophe. Pale and panting, he rushed in and grabbed his hat. The world was crashing down upon him, but somehow he must have a hat to give him the touch of distinction he needed at this moment to fight his terrible sense of inadequacy. He raced to the White House in his limousine, and as soon as he entered Eleanor Roosevelt's sitting room, he knew that his intuition had been right.

"Harry," said Mrs. Roosevelt, placing her hand on his shoulder, "the President is dead."

Speechless for a moment, Truman finally sputtered, "Is there anything I can do for you?"

"Is there anything we can do for *you?*" Mrs. Roosevelt replied. "For *you* are the one in trouble now."

When in trouble, Truman always turned to his family for solace. His wife Bess, a plump, plain-looking woman whose dry wit shone through her reserve, had served as his secretary when he was a senator and thoroughly understood the background of all the issues. She was his confidante, assisting him with his speeches and unobtrusively advising him on political questions. When he was emotional, she was level-headed. When he was confused, she was clear-headed. With Bess calming and reassuring him, helping him to solve many of his problems, he seldom failed to get a full night's sleep. Now he needed her encouragement and political savvy as never before. He nervously telephoned her, but daughter Margaret answered.

"Hi, Dad."

"Let me speak to your mother."

"Are you coming to dinner?"

"Let me speak to your mother."

"I only asked you a civil question."

"Margaret, will you let me speak to your mother!"

In a moment, Bess was on the phone—and in tears. Harry was President of the United States!

And so was Harry S Truman hurled from virtual obscurity into the world's most awesome seat of power. On April 13, 1945, the day after he became President, he gingerly lowered himself into this seat, as if "trying it out." He "rolled back and forth on the rollers and he leaned back a bit and then he rolled forward with a sigh to the empty desk." It didn't remain empty long. Admiral William Leahy, who had been Roosevelt's personal chief of staff and would now be Truman's, marched into the Oval Office and laid a stack of urgent papers before him. Truman gazed at them in horror. He would have to start signing papers that could affect all mankind before he even understood their import!

"Boys," he would tell reporters that day, "if you ever pray, pray for me now. I don't know whether you fellows ever had a load of hay fall on you, but when they told me yesterday what happened, I felt like the moon, the stars, and all the planets had fallen on me."

And to his friend, Senator George Aiken, he dared admit: "I'm not big enough for this job."

Many people agreed with him. They could not imagine him as President. When he called former Secretary of Commerce Jesse H. Jones to tell him that "the President" had named John Snyder as federal loan administrator, Jones asked:

"Did he make the appointment before he died?"

"No," Truman sheepishly replied, "he made it just now."

And when he entered the East Room to attend a funeral service for Roosevelt, nobody even stood up, though everybody did when Mrs. Roosevelt arrived.

If he had not been the President of the United States, it is likely that no one would even have noticed him. For his presence was hardly mesmerizing. He had a shy air about him and an unremarkable face, with high forehead, pointed nose, thin lips, short graying hair, and rather sad eyes framed by oval-shaped glasses. A nondescript man who, as senator, understandably rode a bus without anybody imagining he was sitting next to a national leader.

Yes, who was this provincial figure who wore gaudy bow ties, spoke with an inelegant high-pitched twang, and spent his earlier years living in hobo camps as a railroad employee, castrating pigs on the family farm, and serving under the corrupt thumb of the Pendergast "gang" that ran Democratic politics in Jackson County, Missouri? Even Tom Pendergast himself had immodestly remarked when his candidate, Truman, won a Senate seat that his victory proved one thing: "Any man" he put up could be senator.

Truman knew how many people felt about him, especially those intellectuals and sophisticates who had been close to Roosevelt and were comparing the two men. But if he resented them, he did not show it. For didn't he himself believe that he was unfit to be President? He hadn't even wanted to be Vice-President. And Roosevelt had done little to build his confidence, having told him almost nothing about his presidential problems. Little wonder that Harry Truman was frightened.

Even more frightened than he had been that sweltering summer day in Oak Grove, Missouri, twenty-three years earlier. . . . After dropping campaign leaflets from a patched-up two-seater plane, he stumbled out, his face green from nausea, and agonizingly stammered out his first campaign speech—as a candidate for county judge—to local residents munching on hot dogs at a picnic. More frightened, too, than he had been in World War I when he was given command of D Battery, a collection of wild Irish and German Catholics, who, he was sure, would hang his "hide on the fence" when they found out he was a Protestant and a 32-degree Mason.

Truman's fright stemmed from a genuinely modest image of himself, an inferiority complex reflected in his self-deprecating remarks, which no man as honest as he could have spoken merely for effect. And his complex had deep roots. He had, for most of his life, been a "loser." Forbidden as a boy in Independence, Missouri, to play baseball because he might break his glasses, he was teased mercilessly by the neighborhood children for playing the piano instead. Like his father, who lost the family farm speculating on the grain market and ended up as a night watchman, he made bad investments, losing his savings in an oil venture, and, literally, his shirt in a haberdashery business that went bankrupt. Not surprisingly, his socially prominent future mother-in-law was little impressed by his prospects for success and strongly frowned upon him as a husband for her pampered daughter Bess.

Even when Truman, under the Pendergast wing, was elected county judge and then presiding judge of Jackson County, he was unsure of himself. Though he saved the county millions in road construction while barely eking out a living for himself, he was forced to make deals with crooked contractors in order to do his job.

"Am I an administrator or not?" he asked himself in a memorandum. "Or am I just a crook to compromise in order to get the job done? You judge it, I can't. . . ."

But he justified working for the "Big Boss," Tom Pendergast. Truman would say of him: He was "a man of his word," though he gave it "very seldom and usually on a sure thing. But he's not a trimmer. . . . Who is to blame for present conditions but sniveling [sic] church members who weep on Sunday, play with whores on Monday, drink on Tuesday, sell out to the Boss on Wednesday, repent about Friday and then start over on Sunday? I think maybe the Boss is nearer heaven than the snivelers. . . . He's all man."

The blessings of heaven couldn't save Pendergast from jail, but Truman still clung to him. Not only did he like the man, but he felt a deep sense of loyalty to him. Besides, how could he repudiate him without repudiating himself? In truth, nobody could get anywhere in Jackson County politics without Tom Pendergast behind him. With Tom's backing, a candidate could sometimes reap more than 90 percent of the vote—one way or another. Truman had to be practical; he had to think of his family's well-being first. Hadn't he suffered enough failure? The boss knew that he was an honest citizen who could never be bought. If Tom still wanted to help him, why refuse? And so Truman's conscience was clear. . . . Or was he "just a crook"?

III

If Truman was unsure of himself, he never stopped trying to hurdle the obstacles to success, to prove that he wasn't a failure. The obstacles frightened him, yes, but he simply closed his eyes and leaped. He owed it, first of all, to his mother, who had taught him to be a hard-working, God-fearing American, at least a Confederate-type American who understood the wickedness of the Union Army that had killed her livestock and stolen her chickens after the Civil War. He owed it also to his father, who kept fighting adversity until the day he died and taught him the meaning of tenacity.

When Harry was a boy, his father once bought him a pony, and they went riding together, with the elder Truman astride a horse. The boy fell off the pony and the father made him walk the rest of the way home. Young Truman had learned a valuable lesson: He must learn to climb into the saddle and stay there. (In his last years, Truman would claim that his father had *not* been a failure, for hadn't his son become President of the United States?) Before and after his marriage to Bess, Truman felt, too, that he must win and keep the admiration of this girl with "tanned skin, blond hair, golden as sunshine, and the most beautiful blue eyes I've ever seen or ever will see."

An avid reader, young Truman, in fact, "studied the careers of great men in the hope of proving worthy" of Bess, who so awed him that if he "succeeded in carrying her books to school or back home for her [he] had a big day." A great leader, he concluded from his study, was a man who had "the ability to get other people to do what they don't want to do." Men made history; history did not make men. He found that the first victory great men "won was over themselves and their carnal urges. Self-discipline with all of them came first. . . . Most of the really great ones never thought they were great. . . . I admired Cincinnatus, Hannibal, Cyrus the Great, Gustavus Adolphus of Sweden, Washington and Lee, Stonewall Jackson and J. E. B. Stuart."

Truman, however, was "not very fond of Alexander, Attila, Jengis [sic] Khan or Napoleon because while they were great leaders of men they fought for conquest and personal glory. The others fought for what they thought was right and for their countries. They were patriots and unselfish. I could never admire a man whose only interest is himself."

It was in the spirit of such great men that Truman volunteered to fight in World War I after being rejected by West Point because of his defective eyes. And despite his fright when he took over command of Battery D, he soon conquered his cynical men, who stampeded their horses and played all kinds of pranks in an effort to hang his "hide on the fence"—until they found that under the hide was a tough but fair man who would throw someone into the brig one day and, if he behaved, lend him money for a furlough the next.

At the front, Truman won over his men with acts of courage as well, slogging beside them in the mud, advancing into storms of lead to set up an artillery piece. During one heavy enemy barrage in the French Vosges Mountains, his men fled as if competing for an Olympic gold medal; but Truman stood his ground and in choice expletives ordered them to return to battle. And they did, finally sailing home to become his most fervent political supporters. Truman would never forget those days of blood and glory, topped off by his Galahad marriage to his beloved Bess, days when he could act out his fantasy of being a "great man." What could be more pleasing to someone who lacked confidence in himself?

IV

And now came the greatest test of all—the presidency of the United States. As soon as Truman was sworn in, he met with his Cabinet for the first time and told his anxious listeners that he would carry out Roosevelt's policies. And while he was going to be "President in his own right," he would welcome their advice. The meeting shortly ended and, weighing the fate of America and the world under this novice leader, the Cabinet members filed out.

One stayed behind—Henry Stimson. *He* had some advice to give—about a very urgent matter. But not just yet. However, he now touched on the subject, briefly describing in a "low, tense voice" a weapon of tremendous explosive power that the United States had been working on for years. Stimson did not identify the weapon as an atomic bomb. Nor did he assert, as he would in his diary, that "the problem of our satisfactory relations with Russia [was] not merely connected with but [was] virtually dominated by the problem of the atomic bomb." The thrust of the revelation, however, was clear. The weapon could change the course of human history. Truman stared at his fellow ex-artilleryman and perhaps wished he were back in the Vosges Mountains where a well-placed shell could do no more than change the course of a battle.

But if the President seemed puzzled, he apparently wasn't. For according to Truman's intimate hometown friend, Tom L. Evans, "after [Truman] became Vice-President, Roosevelt did tell him about [the bomb], but not the full details. He knew a lot about it."

It was after he was no longer President that Truman told Evans about this talk he had with Roosevelt shortly before FDR died:

"You remember when we [Roosevelt and himself] were together, and the pictures appeared in our shirtsleeves?"

"Yes."

"That's what we were talking about."

Why then did Truman write in his memoirs that he first learned of the atomic bomb in his talk with Stimson after the initial Cabinet meeting, an account apparently accepted by all historians dealing with the question up to now? Did he feel that he would be betraying a confidence if he admitted that Roosevelt had told him the secret—even though as Vice-President he was entitled to know, just as his predecessor Henry Wallace knew? Did he simply wish to enhance the drama of the "revelation" and accentuate his immediate mastery of White House business despite his lack of preparation? He would then be praised all the more if his "decision" to use the bomb proved wise, and blamed less if it proved unwise.

No one can be sure of the answer. But even before Truman had learned about the bomb from Roosevelt, as claimed by Evans, he knew from his Senate days when he investigated waste in defense spending that some kind of secret weapon was being built. And the man who refused to cooperate with him then was none other than Henry Stimson, the man who was now telling him about a new weapon of "tremendous explosive power."

After Truman had first agreed not to probe into the Manhattan Project, congressmen began complaining. Countless tons of scarce materials were cascading into secret army centers—and nothing ever came out. What the hell was going on? This could be the scandal of the century. Finally, Truman caved in and in March 1944 renewed his demand. He wrote Stimson:

"It may be necessary for the [Truman] Committee to consider the appointment of a subcommittee to investigate the project."

The Secretary once again refused to cooperate, but so insistent was Truman this time that Stimson noted in his diary that he "is a nuisance and pretty untrustworthy man. He talks smoothly but acts meanly."

Now, ironically, this "nuisance and pretty untrustworthy man" would be custodian of the atomic secrets that Stimson had tried so arduously to keep from him. The Secretary faced this startling reality with caution. The previous night, April 12, he wrote in his diary:

"The new President on the whole made a pleasant impression, but it was very clear that he knew very little of the task into which he was stepping and he showed some vacillation on minor matters . . . as if he might be lacking in force. I hope not."

Now, while riding back to the Pentagon with General Marshall, he listened with added concern as the general said, "We shall not know what he is really like until the pressure begins to be felt."

V

Nothing would make Truman feel the pressure more than knowing that he had a weapon in his hands that could devastate the earth. And Stimson realized this because, next to the President, he had felt this pressure more than any other man. It was his duty to make the new President aware of the weapon as soon as he took office. But before he burdened the man with the crushing weight of the details, he would let him deal with the immediate decisions of war. To make sure Truman understood the implications of the bomb, he must reveal them with the delicacy of a sculptor unveiling a prized statue. He would compress his knowledge of the weapon into a brief report that would describe what it could do and suggest how it should be used.

Used in a political sense—after the war. It wouldn't be helpful at this point to bring up the question of whether to use the bomb *during* the war. This was a confusing transitional period; Truman had come to power at a time when the original motive for taking so enormous a gamble was no longer valid—to beat the Germans to the bomb. But now Allied and Russian troops were closing in on Berlin and the war in Europe would end shortly. There was not even the danger that Hitler had a bomb and would use it at the last minute.

An Allied team of soldiers and scientists called "Alsos" (appropriately "Groves" in Greek) followed the troops into Germany to check all signs of atomic progress and found a batch of scientific papers in Strasbourg that showed German scientists were at least two years behind the Allies in nuclear development. They had built only a small model reactor and no factories for the separation of uranium. Hitler was interested only in weapons he could produce in a matter of weeks, so he never pushed the program. The desperate $2 billion race to beat him to the bomb had thus been an illusion. Had all the money and effort, spent only because the illusion gave America no choice, been a waste?

Not if the custodians of the bomb had anything to say about it. For the machine of inevitability, mindlessly unconcerned with motive, was running at full speed, and who would be the man to stop it as long as a single shot was still being fired in the war? The day before Roosevelt died, Stimson visited Oak Ridge and inspected the gaseous diffusion plant there. He was overwhelmed by the sight of this massive building, the largest in the world, sprawled in the middle of a new town of 80,000 people that had sprung up overnight in the Tennessee wilderness. Inside, there were hundreds of miles of piping and incredibly intricate equipment, much of it newly invented.

After all the sacrifices, the heartbreaks, the miracles, was it even thinkable to let the precious end product gather dust? Anyway, by taking many lives, the bomb would save many lives—and perhaps American diplomacy as well. Its bright glow could illuminate the rewards of good behavior to both Japan and Russia. But these were not thoughts to be openly discussed—especially with a new President who might not understand them. It was safer to let him simply be caught up in the machine and not to pry any decision from him. The logic of the machine, after all, countenanced no doubts, even if circumstances changed.

While Stimson himself had been caught up in the machine, he didn't like to admit he was so vulnerable. It was, he no doubt felt, the logic of the lawyer, not of the machine, that guided him. Nor, it seems, did he talk much to his colleagues about what might happen when the bomb exploded. Stimson the clergyman suffered enough thinking about the hundreds of thousands of Japanese civilians who had been turned into charcoal by the fire bombings of Tokyo and other cities since March 1945. He had told Truman that his commanders must pinpoint their targets to the extent possible because "the reputation of the United States in fair play and humanitarianism is the world's biggest asset for peace in the coming decades."

If Stimson reproached himself for permitting, as a matter of duty, the terrible death tolls, he reproached his people, too, for not condemning him for what he had to do. It was immoral not to protest an immoral act—even one that was necessary. As Oppenheimer would comment about Stimson:

"He didn't say that the air strikes shouldn't be carried on, but he did think there was something wrong with a country where no one questioned that."

Yet on the reverse side of the clergyman's plaint was the soldier's pragmatism.

"I was a little fearful," Stimson would tell his diary, "that . . . the air force might have Japan so thoroughly bombed out that the new weapon [the atomic bomb] would not have a fair background to show its strength."

In any case, even an impeccable reputation would be of little value to the United States, the Secretary felt, if Stalin refused to cooperate with the West. What could persuade him to cooperate? Perhaps the atomic bombing of a Japanese city. Stimson's aim was not to intimidate Stalin, but to entice him. In the atomic age, it would no longer be practical to threaten a punitive attack in dealing with an international lawbreaker. The atomic explosions that would shake the world in this war must echo through history as the last massive strike against any nation. Intimidate Stalin, Stimson feared, and he would whip his scientists into building their own bomb.

Instead, the Secretary would encourage the Soviet leader to liberalize his domestic and foreign policies. The same shock that would force Hirohito to drop his sword might induce Stalin to unshackle his own people and respect the sovereign rights of *all* peoples. For Stalin would vividly see how the atomic power that could destroy Japanese cities during the war could also rebuild Russian cities after the war. And to share in its secret—which could be disseminated through an international control agency— all he had to do was modify the character of Soviet rule. Was this plan for building the kind of peaceful, law-abiding world Stimson wanted too much to ask for so enormous a reward?

VI

What Stimson didn't know was that Stalin was already getting his enormous "reward" without having to earn it. And the most important chunk was crammed into Klaus Fuchs' high-domed head—atomic secrets accumulated over several months in Los Alamos. Fuchs never did get to his sister's for Christmas; his superiors insisted that he stay with his mathematical formulas until he finished work on still more secrets. But he finally got away in February 1945, after pushing substantially ahead of his colleagues, and arrived in midmonth at Kristel's home.

Yakovlev, the Russian spy leader in New York, immediately learned of his arrival, apparently from agents staked out near the house, and informed Harry Gold, who rushed to Cambridge for a long-awaited meeting with his informant. Fuchs knew that Gold would be waiting for him, since his sister had written him about the stranger's visit. And he wasn't happy about meeting the "stranger" in her home. He had told Kristel nothing of his activities and didn't want to get her involved. Kristel, he knew, was not a Communist herself and had pressured her husband, who was, not to attend party meetings.

But Gold came anyway, laden with gifts—candy for the children, a book, *Mrs. Palmer's Honey*, for Kristel, and a wallet for Fuchs. The scientist welcomed him with mixed feelings, and his sister, realizing they wanted to be alone, left to "pick up the children from school." The two spies then went upstairs to Fuchs' room, where the visitor eagerly listened to his host's stories about bombmaking in Los Alamos.

He was "getting along very well there," said Fuchs, but permission to travel wasn't granted easily.

The scientist, according to Gold, then gave him a packet of handwritten notes. The six pages included data on the whole problem of making an atomic bomb from fissionable material, the method of detonating the bomb, the type of core used, the principles of the lens system, a comparison of the critical masses of plutonium and U^{235}, and the approximate amount of plutonium necessary for a bomb. Fuchs would afterwards tell authorities that he actually delivered this information in Boston, not Cambridge, a couple of days later, apparently lying to protect his sister from charges of complicity.

At their next meeting, he would have more data, Fuchs promised Gold. It would have to take place in Santa Fe, since he probably could not leave the Los Alamos area again very soon. They would meet at 4 P.M. on the first Saturday in June.

Where?

Fuchs showed Gold a map of Santa Fe and drew his finger over the Castille Street bridge that crossed the Rio Santa Fe.

Right there, on Alameda Street.

Gold then gave a rather bewildered Fuchs his Christmas gift, the wallet. Did Fuchs need any money to put in it, he asked, either for himself or possibly for his sister—say $1,500?

Fuchs coldly refused. Did Gold think he was doing this for money? It was a matter of conscience!

So Gold went back to New York and returned the money to Yakovlev—together with Stalin's unearned reward. The Russian was pleased. A bought, compromised spy was always the most reliable, of course, but he would settle for an honest one. Did any spy ever deliver so rich a haul?

VII

Meanwhile, Stimson continued to formulate his idea for conditionally sharing the less vital atomic secrets with Stalin. This idea had been only a vague notion until just before Roosevelt died. The Secretary was too busy mapping war plans to seriously consider peace plans, though he had long sensed that the bomb would force men, including himself, to drastically change their thinking in the postwar world. He had thus focused on keeping the bomb secret from Fascists and Communists and let Bush, Conant, and Groves, who reported to his special assistant, Harvey Bundy, shape day-to-day policy.

Bush and Conant, however, had more in mind than making the monster. Like Stimson, they wanted to put it in chains after the war and give the key to some international body. But unlike Stimson, they pushed this view with crusading fervor.

Go to Roosevelt, they pleaded with the Secretary. Urge him to back such a plan before it was too late.

Bush was alarmed by signs that Roosevelt and Churchill had secretly reached a new accord: Their two countries would jealously keep atomic information from Russia even after the war to make sure the British lion would reign over Europe. Such a decision, Bush warned Stimson, would spur Stalin to build a bomb of his own. And that would mean a nuclear arms race that could end in catastrophe for the world. Besides, how long could one or two nations monopolize a scientific secret?

Bush's suspicions were justified. An agreement, signed by Roosevelt and Churchill on June 13, 1944, called for their two countries to seek control of all available uranium and thorium ore deposits after, as well as during, the war. And at a White House meeting with Roosevelt on September 22, the British were promised an apparently exclusive and "complete interchange" of nuclear information after the war. Though the public, the President feared, might not understand such an accord after so much talk of postwar multinational collaboration, he apparently felt that the only realistic way to deal with Russia would be to split Europe into spheres of influence. Russia would control Eastern Europe, since nothing could stop it from doing so anyway, and Britain would be dominant in Western Europe, with the two blocs cooperating for peace. Thus, Britain had to be strong if this balance of power was to work.

Meanwhile, when Niels Bohr, the great Danish scientist who had escaped from the Nazis, pleaded with Churchill in mid-May 1944 for a system of postwar multinational control, the Prime Minister, puffing furiously on his cigar, would hardly listen to him.

Multinational control? Tell the Russians about the bomb? Change his whole plan for British dominance in Europe? What naïveté! "Good day, sir!"

And a talk with Roosevelt on August 26 proved more cordial but no more fruitful for Bohr. In fact, the President and the Prime Minister signed a secret aide-mémoire on September 19, 1944, at Roosevelt's home in Hyde Park, again confirming Bush's suspicions. After the war, atomic energy would be monopolized by America and Britain. They would oppose multinational control and, apparently, would share information with the Russians only when palm trees grew in Siberia. Indeed, "enquiries" would "be made regarding the activities of Professor Bohr and steps taken to ensure" that he would not leak information to them.

If Bush was unaware of this agreement until after the war, his suspicions were enough to impress Stimson. The Secretary, who had also been kept in the dark about what the two leaders discussed, was hurt, as he always was when he felt ignored.

"Apparently the President," he would lament in his diary, "has been discussing the [atomic] problem without any conference with his own three American advisers [Bush, Conant, and himself] who have had control of the big secret ever since it has been developed."

But though he now feared that his plan for "reforming" Russia might die a premature death, he hesitated to see Roosevelt, as Bush urged him to do. For cables from Ambassador Averell Harriman in Moscow made him wonder whether the plan would work in any case.

The Russians were "trying to dominate the countries which they are 'liberating,'" Harriman cabled, and were "making [use] of secret police in the process."

Was there really much difference between the Russian secret police (OGPU) and the Gestapo? Would Stalin ever agree to reform Russia? Or was this simply a wishful dream?

"It would be inadvisable," he wrote in his diary, "to put [a scientific sharing plan] into full force yet until we had gotten all we could in Russia in the way of liberalization in exchange for [atomic information]."

But as the day of the bomb inched closer, Stimson began to change his mind again. Had he been too hasty? Bush thought so. You must see FDR! he continued to prod, and he handed the Secretary a memorandum for the President, prepared by Conant and himself. It predicted that Russia would have the bomb in three or four years after America had one, and that both nations would then build a far deadlier hydrogen bomb in a race to death. Even Stimson's special assistant, Bundy, grew frightened. The message was clear: Unless control machinery was set up immediately, Stalin could not be stopped from building a bomb of his own.

Stimson wavered. Was there time to wait until Stalin saw the ultimate proof of atomic power?

"We're up against some very big decisions," he conceded, and "the time is approaching when we can no longer avoid them."

Stalin should still be squeezed for concessions, Stimson now felt, but nothing should prevent a deal with him. Not even the troubles that had piled up after the Yalta Conference in February 1945 at which Roosevelt, Churchill, and Stalin had reached agreement on many wartime and postwar problems. Roosevelt and Stalin had exchanged eighteen messages since then, most of them angry charges that the other side was cheating on the Yalta accords: Russia was trying to set up an all-Communist regime in Poland. . . . America was trying to make a "separate peace" with Germany. . . . Russia wouldn't let U.S. planes pick up liberated American soldiers behind Soviet lines. . . .

Never mind, Stimson admonished his colleagues, no problem was more pressing than the peace of the world. "We must remember that [Russia] has not learned the amenities of diplomatic intercourse and we must expect bad language from her."

It was "time for me," he wrote in his diary, "to use all the restraint I can on these people who have been apparently getting a little more irritated."

One of "these people," it seems, was Roosevelt, whose irritation with Stalin was growing steadily, though the day before he died he wrote Churchill that all the problems plaguing their relations with the Russian leader would eventually be straightened out—presumably within a two-bloc balance of power system.

He must see the President immediately, Stimson now decided. But he would have to move cautiously. If Bush's intuition was right, Roosevelt had already ruled against Russia as a partner in keeping the postwar peace, and with the future of the world at stake, the Secretary's views must not be casually cast aside. He must first feel Roosevelt out.

On March 15, 1945, Stimson strode into the Oval Office and sat down with his usual starched dignity for a talk he felt might help determine the fate of the earth.

Would America and Britain hold on to their atomic secrets after the war, he asked, or would they put atomic energy under multinational control? This question should be answered without delay, he said gravely, before the bomb was dropped, before it was too late to prevent a calamitous nuclear arms race.

The President was genial. Yes, the matter must be settled soon, he replied, neglecting to say that it already had been. They would discuss the question again.

Stimson left the meeting encouraged. "On the whole," he would tell his diary, "the talk . . . was successful."

At their next meeting, he would press his own views.

But the next meeting never took place. For less than a month after their "successful" meeting, Roosevelt was dead. . . .

VIII

By the time Stimson was ready to carry his nuclear arguments to Harry Truman, the new President had completed a crash education on how he should react to great revelations. His modesty and self-deprecation, while winning the public sympathy, had not been winning public confidence, and Senator Alben W. Barkley bluntly told him so.

It was beneath presidential stature, he lectured Truman, to constantly tell people that he hadn't wanted the job. He must "develop and manifest a sense of confidence."

Truman almost immediately sublimated his sense of inferiority into spontaneous decisions and vigorous endorsement of the advice gushing from his inherited advisers. Since he was still almost completely ignorant of Roosevelt's policies, plans, and commitments, he had little choice but to agree anyway. So why not do so vigorously and at least appear decisive?

Most of the advice pouring into his ear concerned Russia. When he was a senator, he had given his own advice on how to deal with that country, and none was more acidly blunt than what he said after Germany invaded it:

"If we see that Germany is winning, we ought to help Russia," he told the Senate, "and if Russia is winning we ought to help Germany, and that way let them kill as many as possible."

Times had changed. Truman was no longer a senator trying to impress the folks back home, but President of the United States. He would have to get along with Russia for the sake of future peace. But what did "getting along" mean? Hardly had he stopped testing his presidential chair when he sought an answer from Secretary of State Edward R. Stettinius, Jr., one of those Stimson thought should be "restrained" in dealing with Stalin.

The Soviet Union, said the handsome, white-haired Secretary, had "taken a firm and uncompromising position on nearly every major question that has arisen in our relations." The Polish problem was especially disturbing, since it would set the pattern for Big Three relations in the other countries in Eastern Europe. At Yalta, the Big Three had agreed that "certain democratic leaders" living in Poland and abroad would join the Communist-inclined Warsaw Provisional Government, and that the expanded regime would hold free elections. But Stalin was reneging on his promise.

Stettinius, and other advisers later, made no mention of the ambiguous nature of the Yalta agreement or how the Soviet Union was interpreting it. They did not say, for example, that the accord called for a Polish regime "friendly" to Russia. There was only one true interpretation, they felt, and Stalin was ignoring it. He was guilty of bad faith. Truman now thought so, too.

Some days later, on April 20, Ambassador Harriman stepped off the plane from Moscow and marched in to see Truman. He was an imposing figure, a banker and industrialist of enormous wealth and impeccable breeding, with the authority of a man who knew Stalin well and could judge exactly what was going on in his Byzantine mind—and, therefore, where the world was heading. Truman, the dirt farmer and bankrupt haberdasher, could only feel awed before his ambassador.

Where *was* the world headed?

For more trouble, Harriman felt, unless the United States toughened its policy toward Russia. Stalin was playing a double game—helping the Allies with one hand and tightening his grip around his neighbors' throats with the other.

Russia wished to break with the United States?

No, not at all, not as long as it needed U.S. aid to help lift itself from the ashes after the war.

So what should the United States do?

Stand firm on important matters. Use economic aid as a weapon.

Harriman, who was still unaware of the atomic bomb, would use dollars to win Stalin's cooperation the way Stimson would use atomic secrets.

Truman grinned. Harriman needn't worry. He wasn't afraid of the Russians and would be firm. He would be fair, of course, and anyway Russia needed the United States more than the United States needed Russia.

In short, Harriman was pleased. Russian policy, he said,

amounted to a "barbarian invasion of Europe." But even so, if the
United States abandoned all illusions about Russia, it might be
worthwhile negotiating with it.

Just what Truman was thinking. Of course, he didn't expect to
get 100 percent of what he wanted, but "we should be able to get 85
percent."

When the meeting ended, Harriman took Truman aside and
said appreciatively: "Frankly, one of the reasons that made me
rush back to Washington was the fear that you did not understand,
as I had seen Roosevelt understand, that Stalin is breaking his
agreements. My fear was inspired by the fact that you could not
have had time to catch up with all the recent cables. But I must say
that I am greatly relieved to discover that you have read them all
and that we see eye to eye on the situation."

The President of the United States beamed. It was nice to get a
pat on the back from one's ambassador.

And now Truman was ready to take on Soviet Foreign Minister
Vyacheslav Molotov, who was on his way to witness the birth of
the United Nations in San Francisco and would stop off in Washington to evaluate the new President. At their first meeting on
April 22, Truman merely pointed out that "the Polish question had
become for our people the symbol of the future development of
our international relations." He was holding back his guns for a
second meeting two days later. But before firing, he needed ammunition from his top military and foreign policy advisers, for this
encounter with Molotov could set the tone of U.S.-Soviet relations for years to come.

What should he tell Molotov?

Be tough! most of his advisers counseled. Secretary of the Navy
James V. Forrestal even suggested a showdown.

Stimson was appalled. No, he said, backed only by Marshall,
show restraint. Stalin had always kept his word on major military
matters. Anyway, Soviet motives in Eastern Europe had to be
understood; Russia did, after all, border on that region. Be diplomatic, he cautioned Truman. Too much was riding on this
meeting.

Unfortunately for Stimson, Truman would be meeting with
Molotov before meeting with him for their talk on the bomb. Now
his whole "enticement" plan seemed in jeopardy. And it was, especially after Truman learned that Stalin had recognized a Commu-

nist government in Poland despite promises at Yalta. No one would say after the President's second meeting with Molotov that Harry Truman did not "manifest a sense of confidence." He went straight to the point "the moment his visitor stepped into his office."

The United States, Truman said, would never approve a Polish government that did not represent all the Poles. Bear in mind, he warned Molotov, that it was up to Congress to appropriate money for Russian reconstruction after the war, and Congress, of course, would be watching the Polish situation.

Russia was simply carrying out the Yalta decision, said Molotov, ignoring Truman's unvarnished threat. "It [is] a matter of honor."

An agreement had been reached, replied Truman, as if he hadn't heard Molotov, and Stalin should carry it out.

He *was* carrying it out.

Russia should keep its word.

The matter could be solved.

The matter could *not* be solved on the basis of a "one-way street."

Molotov turned a little ashy. "I have never been talked to like that in my life."

"Carry out your agreements and you won't get talked to like that."

Silence.

"That will be all, Mr. Molotov."

It was, in fact, too much, in Stimson's view. The verbal battle between Truman and Molotov infuriated the Secretary. A threat to cut off reconstruction aid over Poland? But that meant snipping the string attached to the atomic secrets, the bait he hoped to use in getting Stalin to open up Soviet society and cut out his subversion abroad. Men like Stettinius and Forrestal had led the President down a dangerous path. Stimson was "very much alarmed for fear that we were rushing into a situation where we would find ourselves breaking our relations."

Had Truman already quashed the power of the bomb to convince Stalin he should reform his country and his diplomacy? Stimson must warn Truman not to listen to his other advisers. As a meticulous lawyer, Stimson was upset that he had not had time at the meeting that preceded the Molotov encounter to "give the considered and careful answer to the President that I wanted to give." He would make up for it in the talk about the bomb.

IX

In a letter to Truman asking for an appointment, Stimson made sure that, as Elihu Root had taught him, he "set up [his] data . . . in such a way that [he] prepare(d) the mind of the judge emotionally" to decide for him.

> Dear Mr. President, I think it is very important that I should have a talk with you as soon as possible on a highly secret matter. I mentioned it to you shortly after you took office. . . . It has such a bearing on our present foreign relations and has such an important effect upon all my thinking in this field that I think you ought to know about it without further delay.

Stimson obviously didn't know that it might be too late to "prepare the mind of the judge." Not only Roosevelt but former Senator and Supreme Court Justice James F. Byrnes had already told Truman about the bomb. Byrnes, who himself had been informed by FDR so he wouldn't complain about the huge sums being spent on a "secret project," described the bomb to the new President as powerful enough to "wipe out entire cities and [kill] people on an unprecedented scale"—and to put the United States "in a position to dictate our own terms at the end of the war."

Some historians have interpreted this statement to mean that the United States could dictate peace terms to Japan. But it isn't likely this is what Byrnes meant since it was evident that the United States would be able to dictate peace terms to Japan with or without the bomb. He was most likely referring to diplomatic terms in postwar relations with Russia. He would intimidate the "duplicitous" Russians, not seek, as Stimson would, to reward them for good behavior. And whether Truman agreed with this tactic or not, he planned to name Byrnes his Secretary of State.

On April 25, about two weeks after Truman became President, Stimson called at the White House for a historic meeting that would replace the one he had hoped to have with Roosevelt. Symbolically, it coincided with the opening of the founding conference of the United Nations in San Francisco. Stimson was alone, for General Marshall, whom he had asked to accompany him, had decided that newsmen were keeping too close a news watch on the White House; they might suspect something "big" if they saw him go in. General Groves, however, would join Stimson some minutes later, furtively entering the White House through a back door.

Stimson sat down and removed from his briefcase a memorandum prepared for him by his assistants and Groves, distilled largely from the Bush-Conant report and his own thinking. He handed it to Truman and anxiously waited in the heavy silence while the President read it:

> Within four months we shall in all probability have completed the most terrible weapon ever known in human history, one bomb of which could destroy a whole city. Although we have shared its development with the U.K. [Britain], physically the U.S. is at present in the position of controlling the resources with which to construct and use it and no other nation could reach this position for years. Nevertheless, it is practically certain that we could not remain in this position indefinitely. . . .
>
> As a result, it is extremely probable that the future . . . may see a time when such a weapon may be constructed in secret and used suddenly . . . with devastating power by a wilful nation or group against an unsuspecting nation or group of much greater size and material power. With its aid even a very powerful unsuspecting nation might be conquered within a very few days by a very much smaller one, although probably the only nation which could enter into production within a few years is Russia.
>
> The world in its present state of moral advancement compared with its technical development would be eventually at the mercy of such a weapon. . . . Modern civilization might be completely destroyed. . . .
>
> The question of sharing [the weapon] with other nations and, if so shared, upon what terms, becomes a primary question of our foreign relations. Also our leadership in the war and in the development of this weapon has placed a

certain moral responsibility upon us which we cannot shirk without very serious responsibility for any disaster to civilization which it would further.

On the other hand, if the problem of the proper use of this weapon can be solved, we would have the opportunity to bring this world into a pattern in which the peace of the world and our civilization can be saved.

There was a blatant gap in Stimson's report. No direct mention was made of whether the bomb should be used in this war. Stimson simply took it for granted that it would be. And Truman himself would later write that the Secretary was "at least as much concerned with the role of the atomic bomb in the shaping of history as in its capacity to shorten the war." The question was, would the United States, through use of the bomb, seize "the opportunity to bring the world into a pattern in which . . . our civilization can be saved"? In fact, America had a "moral responsibility" to save civilization. How? The suggestion was clear: Share the bomb—after showing what it could do.

Truman apparently showed no emotion after reading Stimson's dramatic statement. He had to remember that to show emotion was not "presidential," especially in the presence of advisers, who would be looking for the smallest signs of insecurity, indecisiveness, or instability. He must be the master of the situation, cool and intrepid. Besides, Roosevelt and Byrnes had already given him a broad picture of the atomic bomb, though Truman did not act as if he was hearing old news; perhaps he didn't want to disappoint Stimson, who had summoned all his grandeur for this momentous "revelation."

Groves boldly entered the room through a private door shortly after the statement was read and sat down. Perfect timing for Stimson, since he knew the general—who had perused the statement before the meeting—felt he had overemphasized the power of the bomb. Was Stimson, he wondered, trying to frighten Truman into accepting a deal with Stalin for sharing atomic secrets? Groves, on the contrary, would portray the bomb as just another, if more effective, weapon—to make sure the President wouldn't have any qualms about using it.

Groves was not at all certain about Truman's astuteness and judgment, and was especially afraid that Truman might seek to "avenge" Stimson's refusal to let him investigate the project when he was a senator.

As Groves would write in a memorandum to himself, he remembered Truman well from the man's senatorial days. His twangy voice had echoed through the hall at Command General Staff School in Fort Leavenworth, Kansas, at a meeting of the student body there. Groves, then a student officer, listened intently. He was unimpressed. Afterwards, from 1936 to 1938, he met the senator several times when he was stationed in Kansas City, Missouri. He was still unimpressed.

Nor did Truman "enjoy a particularly good reputation in Kansas City." He was "always careful to avoid any action that would be inimical to the Pendergast machine. . . . No one [could] really understand Truman and his rise from an unsuccessful haberdasher to the presidency without knowing something about . . . the completely callous attitude of the Kansas City Pendergast machine of which Truman was the direct beneficiary."

What's more, Truman's "glorious" World War I record was hardly so glorious, according to Groves. The 35th Division, which embraced Truman's Battery D, was "not successful in its combat operations and until Truman became President it was always placed only one step ahead of the 92nd, an all-Negro division, insofar as battle efficiency was concerned." In the Meuse-Argonne offensive, the "artillery barrage consisted of two scattered shots." And while Groves had been told that Truman was a "thoroughly competent officer" when his division trained in the United States, the division "simply did not display any fighting qualities when it was put to its test . . . due to poor leadership . . . and poor discipline."

And now one of its leaders, the man across from him, was the man who must decide on whether and how to use the atomic bomb!

Groves handed a memorandum of his own to Truman, describing the work of the Manhattan Project.

No, said the President, he had read enough. He didn't like to read papers.

Groves and Stimson looked askance at Truman. It would be impossible, they said, to tell him about the project in more concise language. This was, after all, a big project.

Realizing that his reaction had not been very "presidential,"

Truman took the report, quickly scanned it, and asked a few questions. Groves then rose to leave but couldn't find the private door.

"Mr. President," he growled, "how on earth do I get out of here?"

Groves may have been embarrassed because he couldn't find the door, but he may also have been impatient to leave. How could the commander of a battery that fired only "two scattered shots" in a battle be relied upon to knock out all those "Japs"? The man didn't even want to read about the fantastic things Groves had done.

Stimson, however, thought the meeting "worked very well." The President at least recognized him as the driving force behind the bomb and did not challenge his statement. Surely he would study the question of whether to share the secret under some form of international control, and realize that this idea required restraint in dealing with Russia. Yes, the President would understand that the survival of mankind might depend on such restraint.

X

At the meeting, Stimson proposed forming a committee to investigate the problems connected with the bomb during and after the war. It would be composed of leading atomic scientists, Cabinet officials, and a personal representative of the President. Through this committee, each member could channel his own plans for using the bomb to serve American diplomacy and save the world—while diluting his personal responsibility for liquidating a Japanese city or two.

Whether the bomb should take this toll was, it seems, never discussed with Truman even after this meeting with Stimson and Groves, at least for the record. As a Truman aide, Eben A. Ayers, would write in a postwar report, official files revealed "nothing to shed light on the decision. . . . Apparently the presidential order or action approving use of the bomb was entirely verbal, probably the general agreement or understanding that had developed from the many discussions between Truman, Stimson and the others."

Groves was more pointed. "As far as I was concerned," he would write, "[Truman's] decision was one of noninterference— basically, a decision not to upset the existing plans."

Truman was expected to realize that it would be foolish for the United States to spend so much money and effort on building the bomb without using it. And the President knew he was expected to realize this. How could he not when a humanitarian like Stimson, a pragmatist like Byrnes, and a soldier like Groves didn't feel the question even worthy of discussion? And their view probably reflected Roosevelt's.

Truman didn't know that in the secret aide-mémoire signed by Roosevelt and Churchill the previous September, the two men had agreed that "when a bomb is finally available, it might perhaps, *after mature consideration*, be used against the Japanese." Nor did Truman know that Roosevelt had asked Bush if he thought the bomb should be dropped or simply used as a threat, and was told that it was too early to decide. Truman didn't know, in other words, that Roosevelt was not sure whether to use the bomb.

But even if Truman had known, he would have found it difficult giving the question "mature consideration." Roosevelt was a powerful, prestigious leader who might have survived a public rebellion. But Truman was an untried, "accidental" President with almost no standing, a little man who had hardly learned the rudiments of his job yet. Could he overrule his veteran advisers and perhaps go down in history as a cowardly, even treasonous, President, who let his soldiers die while he held in his hand the key to a quick victory? Could he turn off a machine that seemed to have no switch?

Yet Truman fantasized that he was free to decide whether he should use the bomb. It was the kind of problem he would normally discuss with Bess. Did he do so? It is not known. But after the meeting with Stimson and Groves, when he could finally remove his mask and become Harry Truman of Independence, he confided to his radio consultant, J. Leonard Reinsch, a man he didn't have to impress:

"Leonard, I have just gotten some important information. I am going to have to make a decision which no man in history has ever had to make. I'll make the decision but it is terrifying to think about what I will have to decide."

A pleasurable moment for President Truman at a baseball game. He had little time for such indulgence during his first months in office. Admiral William D. Leahy (in uniform, to Truman's right) was constantly at the President's side, whether at ball games or international conferences. (*Louise Leahy Walker.*)

Secretary of State James F. Byrnes (left) making a point to British Foreign Minister Anthony Eden. By dropping the bomb on Japan during the war, Byrnes hoped to intimidate Russia into "good behavior" after the war—but found that the Russians could not be intimidated. (*National Archives.*)

Scientist Arthur Compton directed the atomic laboratory at the University of Chicago. When Germany was knocked out of the war and Leo Szilard and other scientists at Chicago opposed dropping the bomb on Japan, Compton pretended to show sympathy for their cause, but quietly undermined their efforts to influence political leaders. (*National Archives.*)

The first atomic bomb rests in the tiny house atop this 100-foot tower at the desert test site, named Trinity. (*American Institute of Physics.*)

President Truman boards the SS *Augusta* on his way to Europe for the historic Big Three Potsdam Conference. After serving as President for only about three months, he was apprehensive about meeting the leaders of Britain and Russia. (*National Archives.*)

President Truman aboard the SS *Augusta*. Shortly after arriving in Potsdam, he visited the ruins of Berlin and flinched at the horrors of war. Nevertheless, if the bomb worked he was determined to use it. (*National Archives.*)

Secretary of War Stimson arrives in Potsdam. Stimson now had second thoughts about using the bomb, and would urge the President to issue a declaration stating that the Emperor could keep his throne after Japan surrendered. Japan, he felt, might then give up before the bomb was dropped or American troops were forced to invade Japan. But Truman, under Byrnes's influence, refused. (*National Archives.*)

Prime Minister Churchill, President Truman, and Generalissimo Stalin shake hands at Potsdam, where each engaged in a game of deception while feigning goodwill toward the others. (*National Archives.*)

Soviet Foreign Minister Molotov (left) greets Secretary of State Byrnes as the Potsdam Conference begins. Byrnes' plan was to stall off most major decisions until a future conference was held after the atomic bomb exploded over Japan, so the Russians would be more amenable to American demands. (*National Archives.*)

A scene at the Potsdam Conference. When Truman learned that the Trinity bomb test had been successful, he suddenly became aggressive. After one meeting, Truman walked up to Stalin and casually told him that the United States had a "new weapon" it would use on Japan. Stalin didn't seem surprised. He had learned all about America's atomic bomb from traitor Klaus Fuchs. (*National Archives.*)

Fleet Admiral Ernest J. King saw no need to drop the bomb. He felt that the navy, with the aid of the army air force, could blockade Japan and force it to surrender. (*National Archives.*)

Army Air Force General Arnold (right) also felt the atomic bomb was unnecessary. The air force, with the aid of the navy, could conventionally bomb Japan into submission. (*National Archives.*)

The American, British, and Russian military leaders meet at Potsdam. They discuss a Russian invasion of Japanese-held Manchuria to be followed by an American invasion of Japan. But one of the main U.S. aims now was to end the war with the atomic bomb before the Russians could thrust into Manchuria. (*National Archives.*)

Prime Minister Clement Attlee (who replaced Churchill), Truman, and Stalin are seated. Leahy, British Foreign Minister Ernest Bevin, Byrnes, and Molotov are standing. The Potsdam Conference ended with everybody waiting for Japan to reel under the atomic bomb, which silently dominated the discussions. (*National Archives*.)

Naotake Sato, the Japanese Ambassador to Moscow, pleaded with his government to surrender, with the one condition that the Emperor remain on the throne. (*Defense Audio-Visual Agency*.)

Stalin and Molotov apparently have a secret of their own. (*National Archives*.)

Japanese leaders wanted to send Prince Fumimaro Konoye to Moscow, where he could urge Stalin to mediate peace between the Allies and Japan. (*National Archives.*)

The Little Boy atomic bomb that was dropped on Hiroshima. This was a uranium bomb using all the U^{235} produced by the Manhattan Project. It was the only bomb ever to be used without testing. (*National Archives.*)

e Fat Man atomic bomb that was pped on Nagasaki. This was a tonium bomb, which could be ed at Trinity because the ele- t plutonium was made chemi- y and was therefore more plenti- han U^{235}. (*National Archives.*)

Several members of the crew of the *Enola Gay.* Colonel Tibbets is in the center. (*National Archives.*)

Hiroshima Castle before the atomic bomb destroyed it. At least ten American prisoners of war were held here and killed by the atomic bomb. The United States would be reluctant to admit after the war that American boys had been victims of the bomb. (*National Archives.*)

Hiroshima Castle, after the atomic bomb destroyed it, can be seen in the background of this scene of atomic devastation. (*National Archives.*)

The demolished city of Hiroshima after the bomb. (*National Archives.*)

An aerial view of the ruins of Hiroshima. (*National Archives.*)

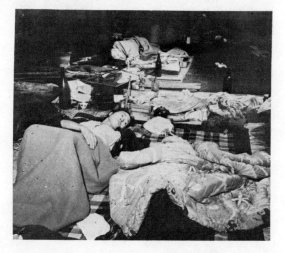

ctims of the atomic bomb lie in nakeshift hospital in Hiroshima. ational Archives.)

Japanese War Minister Korechika Anami was admired by his soldiers, especially by the young extremist officers, who viewed him as the ideal modern samurai. (*Koremasa Anami.*)

General Anami and his family. (*Koremasa Anami.*)

Admiral William D. Leahy as an Annapolis cadet. (*Louise Leahy Walker.*)

Admiral Leahy, who fiercely opposed using the bomb, is admired by his granddaughter Louise after a medal-awarding ceremony. He thought of her as a symbol of the new generation of Leahys that would follow in the proud "white knight" tradition of the family. (*Louise Leahy Walker.*)

apanese Foreign Minister Shienori Togo tried to avoid war ith the United States, then reigned shortly after Pearl Harbor. few months before the war ided, he became Foreign Minis-r again so he could press for ace once more. (*National Arives.*)

Captain Parsons is awarded the Silver Star for his role in the bombing, a lesser award than Colonel Tibbets received, though Parsons was the tactical commander of the *Enola Gay.* (*National Archives.*)

American soldiers dismantled the Japanese cyclotrons after the war, on orders issued by mistake. Japanese scientist Nishina was crushed, together with his dream of an atomic-powered postwar Japan. (*Defense Audio-Visual Agency.*)

Emperor Hirohito swallowed his Imperial pride after the war and visited General Douglas MacArthur to take full blame for the war. His humiliation was mellowed by his liberation from the lie he had been living. He announced to h people that he was not a god, but a mortal like everyone else. (*Defense Audio-Visual Agency.*)

Chapter 11

THE
WARRIOR

I

General Korechika Anami, war minister in the Suzuki Cabinet, knew that Japan had lost the war, but unlike many of his colleagues, he was not terrified. He had trained himself to remain calm in all circumstances. And archery helped him to do this. Thus, on the morning of the bomb, as every morning, he stood in the garden of his home, plucked an arrow from a quiver, and with his 7-foot-long Japanese bow let it fly at a straw target in the distance. Then several more arrows zoomed toward the target, crowding into a tight group. Anami was pleased. This showed that his emotional control was unwavering, as usual, and that he would be able to deal efficiently with the enormous problems he faced that day.

Anami's main problem was to ease Japan out of the war with its honor intact. The general and most other high officers wanted a *conditional* surrender. And the only way to get it, they felt, was to wait for an American invasion of their homeland and then throw back the enemy with all the forces Japan still had, from *kamikaze* suicide pilots and human torpedoes to old men and women armed

231

with bamboo spears. Then America, reluctant to pile up more casualties, would be forced to negotiate a peace acceptable to Japan.

Anami apparently only half-believed this was possible, but he constantly demanded one more all-out battle. The Potsdam Declaration? No—unless the enemy agreed to conditions it was unlikely to consider. Japan must be allowed to try its own war criminals, disarm its own men in the field, be free of enemy occupation, and most important, keep the Imperial system. Otherwise, let the Americans bomb Japan to bits. But Anami could barely look the Emperor in the eye when he made such statements. What agony to disquiet one's god.

Yet there was no way to reconcile his obligation to the Emperor with his obligation to the military. And he couldn't "betray" the army unless the Emperor directly ordered him to. Not because he feared for his life, as Suzuki did, but because he represented the army in the Cabinet, and thus owed it obedience. The army had given him a post even more powerful than that of Prime Minister. The two services, army and navy, nominated their own respective ministers, and could bring down a government simply by ordering these ministers to resign, and keep a new government from being formed simply by refusing to nominate a minister. Thus, they held the Prime Minister by the throat, while their ministers had the biggest say in the Cabinet.

Anami had not wanted political power. He was even less a politician than Suzuki was. And he certainly didn't want a job that would force him into betrayal whatever policy he backed. But he had the job whether he liked it or not, and his *giri* to the army was especially great since he was deeply indebted to the young junior officers, who loved him, trusted him, even worshiped him—and expected him to carry on the war.

However, it grieved Anami to ignore the Imperial wish for immediate peace, to take advantage of the Emperor's reluctance to issue a direct order. For he felt a special obligation to Hirohito, too, having served as his aide-de-camp for four years. And unlike Suzuki, Anami wasn't practicing *haragei*, calling for continued war while actually plotting peace. Suzuki was not really defying the Emperor; Anami was. In fact, he expressed not only the army's sentiment, but his own, despite a nettling suspicion that he might be wrong.

Thus, while his military colleagues regularly ignored the Emperor's wishes without qualms, Anami felt guilty for doing so. And even the precious Old Parr Scotch whiskey he stashed away in the bomb shelter he had built in his garden could not soothe his conscience. Nor could the thought that the Emperor would be in greater danger if he were obeyed than if he weren't. Anami, like Suzuki, chillingly remembered 1936 and vowed that there must be no repetition.

Unable to resolve this conflict of obligations, Anami apparently decided from the moment he became war minister that there would be only one way to alleviate his agony and protect his name—the samurai way. He would, at the proper time, commit *harakiri*, taking responsibility for the army's failure in the war, but even more important, repenting for his efforts to continue the war against the wishes of the Emperor.

After all, as chief of aviation before he became war minister, he felt he owed it to his *kamikaze* pilots, whom he sent crashing into enemy warships (though he personally opposed this means of attack), to go up in a plane himself one day and join them in death. He accepted the prospect of death, even painful death, stoically, matter-of-factly, for was not death simply an extension of life? And was not life but a means of testing the spirit to determine one's deserved niche in the heavenly hierarchy?

Death had already claimed Anami's son, who had died in China in a battle Anami himself had helped to plan. The father was shattered, but in "penitence" for the "abortive operation," he would write in his diary, apparently addressing the gods, "accept my son's death as an offering." He was "redeemed from depression" when he learned that his son had died bravely—happily, for the Emperor—refusing to accept help from overburdened medics.

Yes, death could be spiritually healing.

II

In military eyes, Anami was a far more genuine samurai than Suzuki was. True, Suzuki was revered by the whole nation for his fabled samurai battle feats. But he had "betrayed" the armed forces by advising the Emperor to keep them in tow. On the other hand, Anami never opposed military policy, and like the feudal

lord of bygone days, he carefully nurtured the loyalty of his warriors. They often visited him in his home and, over sushi and sake,
exchanged with him dreams of a never-setting sun. The general
always listened with great interest to their opinions and artfully
replied in a way that gave them the impression that he agreed with
them, whether he did or not.

Anami even lived as his sword-swinging forbears did—with
Spartan simplicity and discipline. He cared little about money.
And he mastered the martial arts, training himself to be not only
an expert archer, but a fine swordsman and *kendo* fencer who
could manipulate bamboo staves with remarkable skill. He also
held his liquor admirably and shared the samurai love of poetry,
though, unlike Suzuki, he seldom read and lacked great intellect,
even failing the entrance examination to war college four times
before finally passing it. He made quick tactical decisions, however, usually the right ones, through instinct carefully honed by
the same rigorous Zen training that had toughened the moral fiber
of Japanese warriors for centuries. And while he had little capacity
to analyze and understand long-range strategic problems, was not
sudden insight, in the Zen view, as important as serious thought in
reaching decisions?

Even physically, Anami, at 58, struck one as a mighty warrior.
He stood stiffly erect, his powerful chest thrust out. His oval,
immobile face, which rolled shinily into a broad pate, bare except
for patches of fuzz, reflected a tough if rather sad serenity. A thin
mustache bridged full lips that always seemed about to smile, and
narrow, sleepy-looking eyes under raised, barely visible brows mir-
rored both pride and resignation. He dressed immaculately; his
uniform clung to his muscular form without a wrinkle, his jack-
boots shone like glass, and his long-hilted sword, which had belonged to his slain son, gleamed at his side.

Anami was, in short, a charismatic figure among his colleagues, a man who lived up to his mother's motto that "virtue is
the best strategy of war," and who could be imagined as one of
"The Forty-seven *Ronin*," or masterless samurai, of legend. His
suppressed pain was, in fact, similar to theirs. In this famous tale of
the early eighteenth century, Naganori Asano, Lord of Ako, was
insulted by a Tokugawa shogunate official, Kozuke Kira. To repay
giri to his name, Lord Asano attacked Kira with his sword, wound-
ing him. But while getting rid of one *on*, or obligation, Asano

acquired another—from the Tokugawa rulers, whose lieutenant he had assaulted. To repay *this* debt, Lord Asano committed *hara-kiri*.

Asano's forty-seven samurai retainers, grief-stricken at the death of their lord, vowed to assassinate Kira in repayment of *their giri* to the spirit of their dead master. To finance and facilitate the plot, a daughter was sold into prostitution, a sister was given to the intended victim as a concubine, a father-in-law was killed. Finally, after two years, the vengeful samurai, posing as drunken *hinin*, or social outcasts, to avoid arousing suspicions of their plan, managed to enter Kira's house and slay him. Then, after placing his head on their lord's grave, they sliced open their bellies in final tribute to the code by which they had lived. For they, like their master, had violated *giri* to their Tokugawa shogun, and death was the only way out of the paradox.

Since Anami apparently saw death as the only way out of *his* paradox, he was more easily able to deal with his conflicting debts, knowing that in the end he would be repaying *giri* to his name while proving loyal to both the army and the Emperor. Meanwhile, he would do what he had to do.

III

In a sense, Anami felt his view was a compromise between that of the Emperor and that of the military fanatics. The junior officers who revered him wanted not simply to fight one more battle for better peace terms, but to fight a war that would end only when it was won or the whole nation committed suicide. And they had a representative who constantly had Anami's ear—Colonel Masahiko Takeshita, the general's brother-in-law, a fiery War Ministry bureaucrat. Takeshita would see to it that Anami did not stray from the divine path. A simple hint that he might be betraying his country would be enough. For a samurai's name must be as untarnished as his sword.

Anami and Takeshita, who loved and admired each other, were like twin symbols of the Japanese military tradition that had glorified the samurai before the Meiji Restoration and fathered a modern army based on samurai values afterwards. It was a tradition that, for all Japan's new industrial power, insulated them from the outside world, especially from the United States, where few officers studied or even visited. Japan was their cosmos, their absolute universe, which they perceived more as a concept than as a country. They had the courage to die with glory but not to live without it.

For Takeshita and his young colleagues, it thus seemed only logical to sacrifice the nation in its concrete form, if necessary, to preserve it as an abstract idea. Since, in their view, the Imperial system and the military were inseparable, one could not exist without the other. This view conflicted with that of the Emperor himself and the other "peacemakers," who were willing, even eager, to discard the military, especially when events made clear that it might drag the Emperor along as it sank into oblivion. What, after all, was one lost war in the context of eternity?

Fueling military fanaticism was the bitter memory of the days before the Mukden Incident, when few Japanese showed "proper respect" for the modern warriors, who had become an impoverished group retired into poverty with small pensions while businessmen and politicians lived luxurious lives complete with summer homes, geisha parties, and even audiences with the Emperor. To think that their samurai ancestors, as a ruling class, could cut down any commoner who did not know his place.

To improve their lot, these disgruntled warriors formed political organizations and secret societies—sometimes together with ultranationalist civilians—that would lobby for their rights and give them a sense of importance. They pressed for samurai virtues in government, including generous use of the sword against foes, both at home and abroad, to recapture the spirit of the clan on a national scale, with every Japanese ready to die for the Emperor as the samurai was ready to die for his lord.

Many of these new samurai, coming from poor families, fused their demand for a return to past spiritual values with a cry for modern economic and social revolution, Fascist or Communist; and a few, as in 1936, were even willing to kill the Emperor—irrationally in his own name—in order to achieve this revolution. To finance it and feed their regained pride as well, they would extract the wealth of all Asia and eventually the world, which would become one great universal hierarchy of nations under the Emperor's benevolent rule, as Amaterasu "intended."

But in this drive for power, glory, and jungle justice, the young fanatics and not their elders were usually the spearhead, and they sometimes confronted the more cautious seniors with faits accomplis, and even bullets. They carried *gekokujo*, "rule by juniors," to an extreme. Under this principle, followed in many large Japanese enterprises, even in the palace, ambitious, hard-working subordinates drew up the plans for their superiors to rubber-stamp. The young officers, their minds crammed with ideology, would become uncontrollable Frankenstein monsters who forced their teachers to rigidly follow paths that these teachers themselves had paved, often less because they believed their own teachings than because they wanted to be seen as superpatriots.

So now Colonel Takeshita would make sure that Anami hewed to the line of the gods that the general had propagated. The colonel was a bit worried, for his brother-in-law, however, admirable, didn't want to fight to the last man, woman, and child. To Anami, in fact, it didn't make sense for every Japanese to die in order to uphold Japanese honor when he alone could do so, taking full responsibility for Japan's defeat and thus cleansing everybody else of guilt. Why should forty-seven *ronin* have died when one sacrifice would have sufficed? Anami, it seems, didn't quite have a samurai's soul after all.

IV

Actually, Anami's tough exterior hid a softness that would have embarrassed a warrior of old. He was not a vengeful man and he did not cut down "commoners" or dispense speedy justice to those who disobeyed the rules. He had compassion. During an air raid one night, he ran out of his shelter to revive with artificial respiration an old woman who had suffered a concussion. And though one of his commanders left his post without permission, he could not bring himself to court-martial him as his colleagues urged. As a division commander in China when the war broke out, he treated American and British nationals trapped in his area with civility.

At the same time, Anami was a family man almost in the Western tradition. His greatest pleasure was to pile his wife and at least some of his seven children into the car and rumble off somewhere for a Sunday outing. He never dictated to his children how they should live their lives, feeling that "if parents are good to their children, they will be dutiful to their elders." This was the same philosophy that would guide him in his relations with the younger officers.

Anami, in any event, was born not into the samurai cult, but into a free-thinking, unmilitary atmosphere in a provincial town on the southern Japanese island of Kyushu, the son of a government bureaucrat. As a young boy, he was headstrong and tempestuous, and finally, when he was 13, was sent by his parents to a military academy so he would learn discipline. He learned quickly, training himself to harness his feelings completely. And the army became his life.

Anami's natural charisma showed early. A major-general grew attached to him and the youth was eventually married off to the general's daughter. It was his father-in-law, a beribboned veteran of the 1905 Russo-Japanese War, who, even more than the academy teachers, taught him the way of the samurai.

If Anami was tolerant of others' misbehavior, whether of his offspring or his officers, he was utterly ruthless with himself. And having learned, like Suzuki, the benefits of a placid temperament, he found himself rising almost effortlessly within a tautly strung military bureaucracy that needed men who could inspire with quiet charisma and cool courage.

As aide-de-camp to the Emperor, one of the most prestigious military posts, Anami cared for Hirohito as he would for his father. If other military men simply worshiped the Emperor as a god, Anami grew to love him as a man. He eventually was appointed vice-minister of war, and in 1944, after commanding units in China, became chief of army aviation.

With the war going sour, however, he pined for a new combat assignment and wanted to command the air defense of Okinawa. But the army thought he was too important to waste in battle. Both the senior and junior officers clamored for him to become war minister in the Koiso Cabinet, which preceded the Suzuki government, feeling that only he had the spirit and the strength to turn the war around. But Anami himself despaired as he contemplated the terrible trap that he would step into.

"You must live up to the expectations of the Japanese armed forces," an army representative told him in late March 1945 when Anami hesitated to take the job. He must sacrifice himself to save the nation from its crises—just as Takamori Saigo had.

Anami began to waver. Saigo was a Satsuma clan samurai leader who, in 1877, had rebelled against the new Meiji rulers when they refused to invade Korea. His troops were crushed, and he and his last 400 men committed *harakiri*. Anami knew that he was being asked to take a post that ultimately could only mean the same fate for him. What he dreaded was not death but the thought of committing a "crime" against the Emperor that would require it.

No, he decided, he still could not accept. But then Suzuki became Prime Minister, and the Emperor himself added his voice, if indirectly through others. It seemed ironic. The Emperor was forcing him to take a job in which he would have to undercut the Imperial will. Left without a choice, he finally had to give in.

V

The Emperor was delighted. Knowing Anami well, he fully trusted him. Despite army pressure, the general would obey him in the end, he was sure, just as Suzuki would. Suzuki was also thankful, since he needed a war minister who was personally indebted to His Majesty and would not resign the moment he disagreed with Suzuki's policies and thus bring down the government. If the war minister had to be a military man, Suzuki preferred Anami, who, miraculously, was embraced by both the warmongers and the peacemakers.

Most of the other militarists, who so casually welshed on their *chu* to the Emperor, didn't understand, Suzuki felt, that Anami was a man who repaid *his*. A man who would not worry about whether Suzuki was practicing *haragei*, since he would realize that the Prime Minister was himself duty-bound to obey the Emperor.

On the contrary, Anami staunchly defended Suzuki when his military colleagues questioned the Prime Minister's sincerity in calling for a continuation of the war. They distrusted him even though he had urged the nation in a dramatic radio address to "fight on."

"Now I stand at the head of a gallant nation," Suzuki said, "confident that though I fall at this, my last post of service, all you people, a hundred million strong, will march forward over my lifeless body to overcome the unprecedented crisis that confronts our fatherland."

Why would Suzuki talk about his "lifeless body"—unless he

thought he might die in the act of betrayal? Did he want the people to overcome the crisis by fighting—or by surrendering?

But Anami wouldn't listen to the doubters.

"The Prime Minister," he assured them, "is not the type of man who would deceive the people and lead them into making peace. He is not the sort who, while planning peace, shouts war."

And later, in June, when a group of young officers wanted to oust Suzuki and hoist Anami into the Prime Minister's seat, Anami cried out. "They are stupid!"

Anami believed in Suzuki because he wanted to. For if he had doubts about the admiral, he might have doubts about himself. And the general, who so valued samurai virtues, could not bear to admit that his own sincerity might be in question. It was more comforting to think that he meant what he said and that the Emperor could be persuaded to agree with his view. After all, His Majesty hadn't ordered the army to make peace—yet.

Actually, the military leaders had no intention of letting Anami, or any other candidate, join a Suzuki government if Suzuki didn't agree to certain conditions. Marshal Hajime Sugiyama, the outgoing war minister, handed him a list of these conditions. He must prosecute the war to the bitter end. He must try to unify the army and navy. And he must organize the nation to throw back an American invasion of Japan. Suzuki glanced at the list and replied without hesitation, as if in utter disdain of the Emperor's wishes:

"I am in agreement with all of these points."

And the trap closed on Anami.

Convinced that Anami would ultimately cooperate with him, Suzuki shopped around now for a peace-minded navy minister. He knew just the man—Admiral Keisuke Okada, a member of the Jushin. Like Suzuki, Okada had barely survived the revolt of 1936, when *he* had been Prime Minister. His would-be assassins killed his son-in-law, thinking he was Okada, whom the victim resembled, and when word spread that the Prime Minister was dead, the government announced that it would hold a state funeral and the Emperor himself publicly expressed his sorrow. However, Okada, dressed in a woman's kimono, managed to escape—to the gasps of the public and politicians. Hadn't the Emperor noted his death? Was Okada to make a liar out of their god? Couldn't he at least commit suicide?

But Okada wouldn't. And since then he had been trying to save the nation from committing suicide. But he couldn't be navy minister, since neither the navy nor the army trusted him. Besides, the navy, he reminded the naïve Prime Minister, nominated its own minister, who would have to be in active military service anyway. But perhaps the navy would nominate Admiral Misumasa Yonai, another Jushin member and former Prime Minister, who was also peace-minded. And for foreign minister, he suggested Shigenori Togo, who held that post at the time of Pearl Harbor and had tried to keep Japan from going to war. Oh yes, then there was Hisatsune Sakomizu, who happened to be a son-in-law of Okada. A high government bureaucrat, he knew all the political ropes and would make an ideal chief Cabinet secretary. He, too, understood the need for peace.

VI

Suzuki accepted Okada's advice and set out on his campaign to twist and turn his way to peace before the Allies struck with their full power. And he now had strong backing, with three members of the Supreme Council for the Direction of the War, or the Big Six, on the side of peace—the Prime Minister, foreign minister, and navy minister (the navy nominated Yonai). War Minister Anami and the army and navy chiefs of staff still wanted to continue the war, but they were no longer as extreme, since all six agreed that they should meet in secret without any hotheaded subordinates present to rattle their swords.

Suzuki gave Sakomizu his first assignment: Make a secret study of Japan's ability to continue the war.

Within a month, Sakomizu reported to Suzuki: Japan could *not* continue the war. There was not enough steel for ships, not enough aluminum for planes, not enough coal for munitions, not enough fuel for the transportation system, not enough food for the people, who were beginning to turn against the war as their cities were demolished by bombs.

One look at this report, Suzuki hoped, and the warmongers would clearly see there was no alternative to an early peace.

Chapter 12

THE
DISSENTER

I

Admiral Leahy, the White House chief of staff, was, on the day of the bomb, worried about the kind of peace the bomb would bring. Unlike Harry Truman, Leahy showed no sign of exuberance as he waited with the President aboard the S.S. *Augusta* for word about Hiroshima. The atomic bomb, he felt, would take the world back to the time of Genghis Khan. Dropping it on a city would be "a form of pillage and rape of a society," "a modern type of barbarism not worthy of Christian man." One day some enemy, emulating the United States, might loose this monstrous weapon on American cities. He hoped, and wishfully believed—even on this day of the bomb—that the "damned fool thing" wouldn't work.

In fact, just a few days earlier, Leahy told King George VI at a luncheon for Truman aboard a British cruiser off Plymouth, England: "I do not think [the bomb] will be as effective as is expected. It sounds like a professor's dream to me!"

"Admiral," replied the King jestingly, "would you like to lay a little bet on that?"

This was a bet that Admiral Leahy would have given anything to win. For if he lost, the world might be lost. And even if this "barbarous" weapon worked, it would not force the Japanese to wave the white flag. They were already about to surrender, having been beaten by the sea blockade and the conventional saturation bombings—bombings he had also opposed as being excessively brutal. Why was the atomic bomb being dropped?

"Because of the vast sums that had been spent on the project," Leahy would charge. "Truman knew that, and so did the other people involved."

Whether Truman "knew that" or not, he was aware that Leahy thought he knew. And yet he kept the admiral as his personal chief of staff and one of his most intimate advisers, as his representative on the Joint Chiefs of Staff and on the Anglo-American Combined Chiefs of Staff. It was Leahy who, in a dry, monotonous voice, his expression austere, his eyes penetrating under heavy knitted brows, his bald head bobbing in emphasis, relayed the President's thoughts, desires, and plans to the generals and admirals, and their own views to the President.

Why did Truman, like Roosevelt, want Leahy so near when the admiral would so frankly criticize him?

Precisely because he was so frank. He was the ideal devil's advocate, one who refused to believe he was advocating the devil. He meant every word he said, however unorthodox or even insulting. A man they could trust even as they ignored his advice. At 75, the admiral, who had won every honor that a sailor, diplomat, and presidential adviser could win, had no fear of antagonizing his boss. Once, when Roosevelt gave *him* some military advice, he got this flippant reply:

"Why the devil, Mr. President, don't you stick to your politics, of which you know so much, and leave high-level strategy to us who know something about it?"

Leahy, for his part, seasoned his military advice with political counsel, provoking Roosevelt once to turn this admonition around: "Bill, you don't know anything about politics."

Leahy was unperturbed. "Mr. President," he replied, "that's the finest compliment you ever paid me."

But the political advice continued to flow from Leahy's lips— when a cigarette, smoked at the rate of about sixty a day, wasn't dangling from them. And often the advice was: Don't use the atomic bomb! Actually, "bomb," he would later write, "is the wrong word to use for this new weapon. It is not a bomb. It is not an explosive. It is a poisonous thing that kills people by its deadly radioactive reaction, more than by explosive force. . . . I was not taught to make war in that fashion, and wars cannot be won by destroying women and children." And that included World War II. The bomb wouldn't win the war, and it might lose the peace.

Roosevelt and Truman, as well as many of Leahy's colleagues, seemed amused by such old-fashioned gallantry. Bill was a well-meaning but oversentimental Irishman. No, he didn't know anything about politics. Certainly not the politics of the bomb. He kept saying with astonishing naïveté that you shouldn't play diplomatic games when the fate of mankind was at stake.

II

The problem was that Leahy came from a more gallant generation than did most American leaders. He was still fighting the relatively "clean" battles of the past—the Spanish-American War, the Boxer Rebellion, the 1912 Nicaraguan revolt, even World War I. Those were conflicts largely fought by warriors with some sense of chivalry. Nobody tried to kill women and children; such atrocities went against the military grain. Still, he protested even in those struggles against needless brutality.

During the Spanish-American War he wrote in his diary aboard the battleship *Oregon*: "In the evening we fired four thirteen-inch shells into the town of Guantanamo, which I thought unnecessary and cruel." Ashore in one Cuban town, he even railed against the cruelty of a cockfight: "The entire exhibition of brutality was sickening and the third fight drove me out into the sunshine and fresh air." And when a captured enemy priest died from malnutrition, Leahy lamented:

"Such things make one doubt that this is the beginning of the twentieth century. What has become of the knights of our childhood stories, who delighted in battling with foeman [sic] worthy of their steel, who treated vanquished enemies as honored guests and who away from the battle were gentle souls. . . .

"Men get accustomed to the sight of suffering. They stand face to face with death so often that they lose respect for life and the training they get therefrom developes [sic] some of them into men who fear neither god [sic] nor man. . . . Resourceful, active, unfeeling, persistent, indefatigable, and with a physical courage that is unlimited, they are successful soldiers, but they are not good knights."

But if some soldiers at that time were cruel to other soldiers, today they were cruel to whole populations. Leahy, the last of the "good knights," had struggled against all kinds of mass killing. Against the conventional saturation bombings and against plans for germ warfare. Should the United States destroy Japan's rice crop with bacteriological weapons, as some of Roosevelt's advisers suggested? Leahy thundered his dissent:

"Mr. President, this [using germs and poison] would violate every Christian ethic I have ever heard of and all of the known laws of war. It would be an attack on the noncombatant population of the enemy."

And his disgust at the thought only grew when he visited the Chemical Warfare school at Edgewood Arsenal in Maryland, where his brother commanded its naval unit. As he explored the beautiful farming country in the area, he couldn't "avoid a feeling of the sharp regret that the barbarous necessities of a war had dispossessed its peaceful inhabitants in order that it might be used to produce a poison which might be employed in the destruction of other people."

And now the most destructive weapon of all—the atomic bomb.

If Leahy refused to believe the bomb would work, it was apparently because he didn't want to believe it would. He blinded himself to its power, rationalizing that as a former head of the Navy Department's Bureau of Ordnance, he knew explosives, and this bomb would "turn out to be no better than cordite, a simple smokeless powder." He spoke with Stimson, Bush, Groves, the scientists. No, they assured him, this bomb could blow up a city. But nothing they said could convince him.

Typically, he reminded Groves, the perfect modern soldier—"resourceful," "unfeeling," "indefatigable"—"that no weapon developed during a war had ever been decisive in that war," and he lamented that the general "was involved in the project as it would have been much better for [him] to have had a different and more usual assignment."

Groves was contemptuous. Leahy, he would say, was "self-serving." As a navy man, he simply wanted an admiral to "ride his white horse down the streets of Tokyo." But was Leahy thinking of a white steed—or a black stain?

When word reached Potsdam that the bomb had turned the sky over a New Mexico testing ground into a raging sea of fire and dust, Leahy was silent, morose. Not because he had been almost alone in predicting that the weapon would fail to work as expected, but because he was now certain the bomb would be used. Yet, at this turning point in history, ironically, his power to sway opinion was virtually nil. For who would listen to advice about the bomb from a prophet whose crystal ball had failed so miserably? This was the tragedy of Admiral Leahy.

III

Leahy came from a long line of "good knights," men and women who fought for causes, but always according to the rules. As Leahy would write in his diary, his family was "racially of good ancestry to whom family tradition ascribes qualities of leadership and high standing in the ancient world." His ancestors had been chiefs in Galway, Ireland, for many centuries until they were dispossessed by the British. Leahy's grandparents emigrated from Ireland in 1836 and his father fought valiantly in the Union Army during the Civil War. The elder Leahy later practiced law in Hampton, Iowa, where the admiral was born, and then in Wisconsin, where he was raised.

"Pride of ancestry," Leahy would write, "is of value to us all in that it makes repugnant any deviation from traditional ideals and gives strength with which to resist temptation to drift into a lower order of human society."

For Leahy, pride of ancestry often seemed to be a greater source of strength than love of family. He was "fond" of his family, but showed little evidence of love; he was too consumed with seeking opportunities to live up to the Leahy tradition. He seldom spent time with his parents after he entered Annapolis and did not show great affection toward his wife, Louise, who came from a "good" San Francisco family and whose brother-in-law was his superior officer. Louise married Leahy in 1904 after her brother-in-law assured her father that Leahy could look forward to an excellent career. It was a convenient marriage for Leahy, and one of mutual respect. His wife called him by his last name until they were married about five years. Nor was Leahy very close to his son, William, Jr., who would deeply disappoint him by turning down an appointment at Annapolis in favor of Princeton, though he would eventually become an officer in the navy. No son of Leahy could be a less militant knight than he himself was.

And yet, when Leahy was able to free himself occasionally from his almost stifling bond with the navy, he could show sparks of sentimentality—especially when his granddaughter Louise was on his mind. She was the daughter he never had, the symbol of future lineage he would never know. He showered her with gifts, took her on trips, helped her with her homework. Even the young girl's mother grew jealous of the admiral. How could she compete for her daughter's love with a man who sanctified the child as the guardian angel of a new generation of "good knights"?

To at least some of Leahy's subordinates, he was truly a knight, a boss who occasionally shouted and cursed, but who rewarded efficient work with kindness and a barely perceptible smile, sometimes even with flashes of dry humor. But let no one "drift into a lower order of human society." Once, he cruelly fired a servant who was accused of some minor infraction of the law even before the man had a chance to defend himself. A Leahy couldn't tolerate even the slightest indiscretion.

IV

In an often indiscreet world, Leahy chose to live the carefully structured life of the military man, a life worthy of his illustrious ancestors, and one devoted to the country he loved. Failing to enter West Point as a youth, he turned to Annapolis as a consolation prize. On graduating fifteenth in his class, Leahy began his naval career most auspiciously. Assigned to the *Oregon*, he was soon sailing around Cape Horn and into the battle of Santiago, Cuba, which the Americans won, with the *Oregon* receiving major credit for the victory. Leahy later took part in the Chinese Boxer Rebellion and the Philippine Insurrection and helped ease the misery of refugees from the 1906 San Francisco earthquake, a natural catastrophe that helped to harden his stand against launching man-made ones.

At about this time, after Japan's sensational 1905 victory over Russia, which Washington applauded, he already began to see the "rising menace to our peace [of] the little island empire. . . . The idea of a contest with the Orient for world supremacy does not seem to have entered into the minds of many people yet, but I feel sure that such a contest will come some day."

In 1912, Leahy became captain of the *Dolphin*, the navy secretary's dispatch boat, and met the man he would one day advise how to deal with the menace he had foreseen. Assistant Secretary of the Navy Franklin D. Roosevelt, who loved the sea, made several voyages with him, and after hours of exchanging naval lore they became close friends.

By the time Roosevelt moved into the White House in 1932, Leahy was a rear admiral; five years later, under his old friend, he was navy chief of operations. Still worried by the Japanese "menace," he fought a losing battle against the isolationists, who scoffed at his plea for a two-ocean navy to protect the United States against a possible simultaneous attack by Germany, Italy, and Japan.

In 1939, Leahy retired from the navy, only to begin a new career. Roosevelt appointed him governor of Puerto Rico, "because I want to have you within easy reach in case of a war, which seems to be inevitable." After giving Puerto Rico the best administration it ever had, Leahy undertook a new assignment: ambassador to Vichy France. His orders were to cultivate the friendship of Marshall Philippe Pétain, who headed the collaborationist government of occupied France, and prevent him from making further concessions to Hitler. Leahy won the trust of both Pétain, who commanded France, and Admiral Jean Darlan, who commanded his fleet. When the Allies invaded France, Darlan's ships were at their disposal.

Leahy returned home in 1942, but not in a very triumphant mood. Accompanying him was a coffin with the body of his wife, who had died in a Vichy hospital after an operation. He was pale, lined, shattered, and, as he told a friend, deprived of all initiative. A lonely man who shunned parties and had few friends, he deeply missed his wife's companionship and perhaps felt a sense of guilt for having neglected her for many years in the name of duty and ancestral pride.

But soon Leahy was at work again, driven by these same forces, devoting ten hours a day to a job that was created especially for him—chief of staff to the commander in chief. After Pearl Harbor, he also became the President's representative on the Joint Chiefs of Staff. He agreed to serve even though Roosevelt had rejected his advice on Pearl Harbor.

In 1939, when Leahy was still chief of naval operations, Admiral Joseph Richardson, commander of the Pacific fleet, pleaded with the President to let him abandon Pearl Harbor as the permanent home of the fleet, arguing that it was vulnerable there to a sneak attack.

When Richardson left, Roosevelt said to Leahy:

"What's the matter with Joe? He has got yellow."

"Joe," Leahy replied, "is not and never will be yellow. He is dead right."

"I want him fired!" the President nevertheless ordered.

Leahy obeyed with heavy heart, and shortly thereafter Japan launched its sneak attack.

Yes, his words were often ignored. But someone had to tell the President the facts, shorn of personal and political icing. Someone had to raise the moral issues of war, to recall the days of the "good knight." Someone had to cry that it was a gigantic waste of time and money to build an atomic bomb, and that it would be "barbaric" to use one—if it worked, as he doubted.

And the admiral had ample opportunity to make his case, for he was constantly at Roosevelt's side—on vacations and weekend jaunts, at the Tehran, Quebec, and Yalta conferences. If, unlike Stimson and Byrnes, Leahy did not tie the bomb to diplomacy, he nevertheless urged Roosevelt more vigorously than either of them did to resist Russian demands. When the President asked him at Yalta what he thought of the accord regarding Poland, the admiral read it and groaned: "Mr. President, this damned thing is so goddam elastic that you can stretch it from here to Washington and back again. The Russkies will make whatever they like out of it."

"I know that, Bill," Roosevelt replied. "But I am too tired to fight them."

Leahy was not. He agreed with the President that it wouldn't be possible to "exclude dominant Soviet influence from Poland," but he felt it would be possible to "give to . . . Poland an external appearance of independence." And he was ready to exert every pressure on Russia to see that it did—short of carrying the bomb in his hip pocket. Though he was "certain" that Russian dominance in Europe would greatly enhance the "prospects of another war," to threaten Russia with sudden obliteration would be neither moral nor practical. He did not understand that once Stalin saw what the bomb could do—if indeed it could do something—he might agree to almost any demands out of fear or eagerness to share in the atom's secret.

V

When Roosevelt died, Leahy was despondent and deeply worried that Truman could not fill the "need for competent leadership."

He wrote in his diary: "One cannot yet see how the complicated critical business of the war and the peace can be carried forward by a new President who is completely inexperienced in international affairs."

How unfortunate that Roosevelt had not chosen Jimmy Byrnes as his Vice-President, he lamented. Byrnes would make a fine President. Leahy was, of course, unaware at the time that Byrnes, as Truman's Secretary of State, would be one of the top leaders most enthusiastic to use the bomb, and for purposes the admiral would deem indecently cynical.

But Leahy's doubts about Truman began to melt the first day he took office. After a meeting with military leaders, the President asked Leahy to stay behind. Truman suspected that some of his advisers might not tell him the whole truth about the political and military situation, especially if things weren't going very well. But the admiral, he knew, was "direct in manner and blunt in expression." The kind of man he needed beside him.

Would Leahy continue as the President's chief of staff?

"Are you sure you want me, Mr. President?" Leahy asked. "I always say what's on my mind."

"I want the truth," Truman said, "and I want the facts at all times. I want you to stay with me and always to tell me what's on your mind. You may not always agree with my decisions, but I know you will carry them out faithfully."

"You have my pledge," the admiral said. "You can count on me."

Leahy would soon find that it was sometimes easier to carry out the decisions of a new, vigorous President who had to rely on advice than those of an old, tired one who felt little need for advice. As one of the advisers who urged Truman to "get tough" with Russia, the admiral was delighted as he watched the President virtually push an enraged Molotov out the White House door. That was the way to win Russia's respect. No bomb. No threats. Just old-fashioned firmness.

Still, Truman had begun to have doubts. He had given Molotov a "straight one-two to the jaw," but Stalin, instead of throwing in the towel, had rushed to Molotov's corner and helped him to his feet. No, Russia would not be bullied, the Soviet chief snapped defiantly.

Didn't Stalin know that the United States could cut off the aid he needed to rebuild his cities after the war? In fact, lend-lease war aid was already being slowed down now that Germany had been defeated, and the Russian dictator was crying "bully" again all the louder because an American official, misinterpreting orders, had instructed ships carrying war goods to Russia to turn back in mid-ocean. The ships were ultimately put back on course, but U.S.-Russian relations were not. Indeed, they grew worse when, in San Francisco, talks on Poland and other areas of dispute struck an impasse. The wartime alliance with Russia, so painstakingly knitted together by Roosevelt, was ripping apart only weeks after the "moon and the stars" had fallen on Truman.

The new President grew alarmed. No, he wasn't afraid of Stalin. But Stalin, it seemed, wasn't afraid of him either. Had he made a mistake with his "one-two" punch?

"So far," he cautiously wrote his mother and sister on May 8, "luck has been with me. . . . I hope when the mistake comes it won't be too great to remedy."

Had it come? Had he jeopardized the future peace of the world? Perhaps Stimson was right after all. Thrashing around for an answer, the President called in Joseph E. Davies, former ambassador to the Soviet Union, who opposed a hard line toward that country even more vigorously than Stimson did. At their first meeting on April 30, Truman described his encounter with Molotov like a troubled man recounting a bad experience to his psychiatrist. He then asked with almost pitiful uncertainty:

"Did I do right?"

True to his profession, Davies was diplomatic. Well, Truman

showed them "the quality of direct, straightforwardness of the President and the kind of square-toed dealing which could be expected from you."

But then Davies painted a portrait of the world as it looked to Stalin, one that Truman apparently never before visualized. You see, Davies explained, Russia stood silently by while America and Britain backed the Vichy leaders in Africa, the Royalists in Greece, and the right-wing Badoglio government in Italy. So why, Stalin asked, didn't the Western powers stand silently by while Russia pursued its policy in Poland, permitting it to ensure a secure western border? Nor would economic pressure on Moscow work. "It would be a desperate gamble to proceed on any such theory," for Stalin would prefer to "go it alone" rather than sacrifice vital interests for money.

"Well, what should be done?" Truman asked. "What can I do?"

"Your conference with Molotov commanded their respect," said Davies. "You must now command their confidence in our good will and fairness." What should he do? Meet with Stalin. Sit down and talk things out.

Shortly after this conversation, Davies wrote Molotov suggesting a Big Three conference. And at his next meeting with Truman on May 13, he read Molotov's reply:

"I think that personal contact of the head of our governments could play in this matter an extremely positive part."

Then Churchill also urged a meeting. And he wanted one immediately—before Russia wolfed down all of Eastern Europe and maybe more. And before American troops were transferred from Europe to the Far East, making Stalin more inflexible than ever.

"Every minute counts," the Prime Minister warned.

And some of Truman's advisers, including Admiral Leahy, agreed with Churchill, arguing that the longer the President waited, the harder Stalin's line would be.

Truman was frightened. No sooner had he unpacked his belongings in the White House than he was being pressed to help mold the future of the world. Harry Truman, ex-haberdasher, haggling with such giants as Stalin and Churchill?

"It is a terrible responsibility," he told Davies, his macho armor suddenly melting, "and I am the last man fitted to handle it and it happened to me. But I shall do my best."

And he chillingly recited a verse:

> Here lies Joe Williams, he did his best,
> Man can do no more,
> But he was too slow on the draw.

Would Harry Truman also be too slow on the draw? Perhaps not, after all. For he might have the fastest gun of all—the atomic bomb. When would it be tested? In July, Stimson had told him. Then the President would know if he had the gun.

He couldn't possibly attend a Big Three conference before the end of July, Truman thus said to Davies. "He had his budget on his hands." And there was also "another reason," too. Davies must keep it a secret, but an atomic bomb was being built and would be tested in July. Davies understood.

And so did Stimson, who, with Jimmy Byrnes, had planted the idea of atomic diplomacy in Truman's mind. Many urgent questions had to be answered:

How much pressure should Washington exert on Moscow to achieve its peace goals?

How necessary was Russian entry into the Pacific War?

Was the United States strong enough to demand a change in the provisions of the Yalta agreement favorable to Russia?

Should Russia be allowed to take part in the military occupation of Japan?

Stimson would tell several of his colleagues on May 15: "It was premature to ask [these questions as] we were not yet in a position to answer them. . . . Over any such tangled weave of problems [the bomb] secret would be dominant and yet we will not know . . . probably until after that meeting, whether this is a weapon in our hands or not. . . . It seems a terrible thing to gamble with such big stakes in diplomacy without having your master card in your hand."

Actually, Stimson wrote, the bomb together with economic aid amounted to a "royal straight flush." Once the weapon was tested and used, the United States would have the answers to the crucial questions, and that was the time for it to play its "master card."

So delay the conference, Stimson urged Truman. Meet Stalin with this card in hand.

And Truman agreed, if only to make himself feel more adequate before the prospect of bargaining with giants. In fact, as the scientists grew more confident that the bomb test would succeed in New Mexico, so did the President grow more confident that he would succeed in Potsdam, Germany, where the conference would convene.

Would Stalin agree to meet and compromise with Churchill and himself? Truman sent Roosevelt's old troubleshooter, Harry Hopkins, to Moscow to find out and, without arousing Stalin's suspicions, repair the U.S.-Soviet alliance sufficiently to keep Russia from gulping down Poland before the bomb was tested and the Big Three meeting could take place.

Stalin was willing, Hopkins reported back, happily bearing a compromise deal on Poland and a promise that Russia would support the anti-Communist Chinese leader, Chiang Kai-shek, as the leader of a united China.

To further woo Stalin, Truman sent Ambassador Davies, the Russophile, to see Churchill, an obvious hint that the United States would not join with Britain in ganging up on Russia. Davies would even ask Churchill to approve a meeting between Truman and Stalin prior to the Big Three conference in order to allay Stalin's suspicions. Churchill almost swallowed his cigar.

Never!

In any case, everything was now set—except the date. And with Stalin's appetite curbed for the time being, Truman felt he could stall off a conference until he knew the bomb worked. He pushed Stimson, Stimson pushed Bush, Bush pushed Groves, and Groves pushed Oppenheimer. Finish the bomb! When it appeared that the weapon would be tested at the beginning of July, Truman decided that the conference would take place then, too. And when the test was postponed until July 15, so was the conference. He delayed it "on purpose to give us more time," Truman told Stimson.

Churchill was furious. The meeting, he cabled Truman and Stalin, should be held "about the middle of June."

It was *Truman* who wanted the delay, replied Stalin.

Ignoring the reply, the Prime Minister thundered back: "I consider that July 15th, repeat July, the month after June, is much too late. . . . I have proposed June 15th, repeat June, the month before July, but if that is not possible, why not July 1st, July 2nd, or July 3rd?"

"I should like to tell you again," Stalin responded, "that July 15 was suggested by President Truman."

Churchill finally turned his wrath on Truman, but the President assured him—and his own impatient diplomats—that they shouldn't worry. Stalin had promised to behave, and Europe would not be drained of U.S. troops by the time of the meeting. Yes, it was all working out.

Stimson, however, was not entirely satisfied. The conference would start on July 15, the very day the bomb would explode in New Mexico. And this posed a dilemma. Stalin couldn't be told the details until one exploded over Japan, or he might attack Japanese troops in Manchuria and grab chunks of territory before the bomb could end the war without his help. But if no atomic secrets could be dangled before him, how could he be enticed to make the concessions that, hopefully, would turn the whole world into a mecca of law, peace, and freedom?

Yet Stimson realized that Truman couldn't stall off a conference any longer. Not even Churchill could be told the reason for the delay up to now, and he would never stand for another postponement. But at least Potsdam could set the stage for later meetings that would yield the kind of world Stimson wanted.

"The Polish, Rumanian, Yugoslavian, and Manchurian problems," he would say, might all be solved almost before the radioactive dust from an atomic explosion could settle over Japan. And the President was delighted. He hadn't yet indicated whether he wanted to use the bomb as an enticement or a threat, but, either way it seemed, he would have the draw on Joe Stalin. Harry Truman would not suffer the fate of the other Joe of his verse.

VI

Admiral Leahy, meanwhile, argued against using the bomb, whether to win the war or the peace, and also against invading Japan. An invasion was as unnecessary as the bomb, he insisted. Most Japanese war and merchant ships had already sunk to the bottom of the sea while most major Japanese cities lay in bombed-out ruin. A tighter sea blockade and more conventional pinpoint bombing would inevitably bring an early surrender. And surrender didn't have to be unconditional either.

But, of course, dropping the atomic bomb would be even worse than invading Japan. In fact, as chairman of the Joint Chiefs of Staff, Leahy would not bring up the bomb for discussion at any formal military meeting. Why discuss a weapon that might not even work? Nor did it seem proper for proud soldiers and sailors to talk openly about the instantaneous massacre of tens of thousands of women and children. And his military colleagues were apparently sensitive to this thought, too. As sensitive as they were to the thought that a new weapon might deny their respective services the privilege of delivering the knockout blow. Leahy thus kept the bomb out of all attack plans, as if the Manhattan Project did not exist.

Marshall, however, did talk informally about the bomb with Groves. Nine of them, dropped in three attacks to clear the invasion routes, he felt, might be useful when the Americans landed. Groves felt, according to a memoir in his personal papers, that using the bomb in a ground attack "would be difficult because the bombs were designed for an air burst. . . . I told General Marshall that I would immediately consider designing a bomb case and the interior mechanism so that we would not be limited to an air burst. . . . (But) I never permitted it to go beyond the conversation stage as I did not want to interfere with the major objective."

Military planners had begun mapping an invasion of Japan in early 1944 and finally agreed on a two-stage assault that would presumably allow the surviving attackers to return home by the summer of 1946. In Operation Olympic, troops would clamber ashore in Kyushu, the southern island of Japan, on November 1, 1945, while others in Operation Coronet would storm the beaches of the Kanto (Tokyo) Plain in March 1946 and seize the enemy-heartland. The Joint Chiefs of Staff approved the invasion plans on May 25, 1945, and submitted them to Truman for his decision.

VII

If the Joint Chiefs virtually ignored the bomb, Secretary Stimson did not. In fact, he felt more strongly than ever that he must have the weapon to end the war swiftly before an invasion could claim a "million" American lives. And before Russia could sink its claws irrevocably into Europe and Asia. As a War Department

report would say, an early "Japanese surrender would be advantageous to the United States both because of the enormous cost of
the war and because it would give us a better chance to settle the
affairs of the Western Pacific before too many of our allies are
committed there. . . ."

Russia was already pulling at the reins, and the question was,
should Stalin be encouraged to attack Japanese troops in Manchuria as he promised to do in a secret agreement on the Far East
reached at the Yalta Conference? This accord called on Russia to
declare war on Japan three months after Germany was defeated, in
return for territories and privileges it lost to Japan in the Russo-
Japanese War of 1905, including the Kurile Islands and half of
Sakhalin Island, a lease on Port Arthur, Manchuria, certain rights
in the port of Dairen, Manchuria, and at least a share in the
control of the Manchurian railroad.

Stimson was deeply concerned about this commitment. Who
knew if Soviet troops, once entrenched in Manchuria, could be
dislodged after the war? At the same time, the exhausted, starving
countries of Europe, even those liberated by Western forces, were
ripe for communism and might drop into the Soviet basket if
America didn't pour in aid and keep a large number of troops there
instead of transferring them to the Pacific.

The best answer to these dangers, it seemed to Stimson and the
President, was to shock Japan into immediate surrender by using
the atomic bomb—if it worked. And if it didn't? Then the United
States, unfortunately, must prod Russia to attack Japanese forces
in Manchuria—though few American leaders thought it needed
prodding—to split the enemy forces and ease the way for an American invasion of Japan.

In reality, the prospect of an American invasion seemed very
doubtful, whether the bomb was used or not. The Joint Chiefs of
Staff felt that the Japanese generals might well surrender if Russia
did nothing more than declare war on Japan. And once Russia
actually attacked, of course, it seemed still more likely they would
lay down their arms. In either case, Russian action would probably
erase the need to send G.I.'s into the fire . . . enough reason to
keep the Russian option open.

But Stimson and the President apparently never considered
substituting the shock of a Russian thrust for that of the bomb in
ending the Pacific war promptly, though Marshall, reluctant to use

the weapon, reminded Stimson of the Soviet card. Since Stalin planned to send his troops into Manchuria by mid-August, only a few days after the first bomb was to be dropped, why wouldn't the United States wait this short time to see if a Russian invasion would indeed trigger a Japanese surrender and thus obviate the need for either the bomb or an American invasion?

Apparently because the world would be better off if Japan could be forced to surrender by a peace-loving United States that did not covet territory than by an aggressive Russia that did. The idea, after all, was not simply to end the war rapidly, but to end it in a way that would save the world from Soviet domination. And the shock of the bomb would presumably accomplish both aims. The bomb was more than a weapon of war; it was an instrument of peace. Its secrets could entice or intimidate Stalin into a permanent grand alliance rooted in American ideals—and interests. Was not the historic sacrifice of 100,000 people or so worth such a prize?

Stimson thought so, at least until early July 1945. And so did Byrnes and most other presidential advisers. And who was Truman to disagree? It is not surprising, therefore, that Stimson would write in his diary on June 26 after meeting with Forrestal and Undersecretary of State Grew, the former ambassador to Japan, "I took up the subject of trying to get Japan to surrender by giving her a warning *after* she had been sufficiently pounded possibly with S-1 [the atomic bomb]. This is a matter about which I feel strongly."

What could be lost by warning Japan *before* rather than *after* pounding it with the bomb? Simply the future peace. As a man who cared about people and the world they lived in, Stimson apparently could not take the risk, at least at this stage, that the war might end before the bomb could be used. Leahy didn't understand at all, and even Marshall and Assistant Secretary of War John J. McCloy, Stimson's deputy, couldn't quite grasp his view. Certainly Joseph Grew didn't.

VIII

Actually, Grew was more desperately afraid of Russian gains than Stimson was and even felt that a future war with Russia might be inevitable. And he had no illusions about "reforming" Stalin after the war, with or without the bomb. What he wanted was to use a peaceful, friendly Japan as a buffer against Russia. But if he also thought a quick surrender was essential, he felt that neither the bomb nor the Russian army was needed to achieve it. On the contrary, waiting for the bomb might prolong the war.

A "shock" was needed? There already was one—the massive, devastating air raid that had set Tokyo aflame on May 25, leaving even part of the Imperial Palace in ruins. Demand surrender while the Japanese were still staggering from that blow, promise more such blows if they refused—and agree to the one condition that might yield it: Let the Imperial dynasty remain in power if the people so desired. Yet, Truman, in a speech on May 8, when Germany surrendered unconditionally, had repeated Roosevelt's pledge that Japan must do likewise. But should this pledge be carried out to the letter even at the cost of hundreds of thousands of lives? Grew knew the Japanese. They would never surrender their soul.

When Grew made this point to Truman on May 28, he was told to discuss his view with Stimson, Forrestal, Marshall, and Fleet Admiral Ernest J. King. The next day, Grew met with these men.

Grew's idea was excellent, said Stimson. In fact, it did not go far enough.

One by one, the others agreed. Then Marshall spoke. He agreed, too—in principle. But, he added, a warning sweetened with a concession to Japan *at this time* would be premature.

The meeting abruptly ended. And so did the chances of finding out whether the Japanese might have surrendered in May 1945.

Why was Grew's idea "at this time . . . premature"? Because, as some thought, it might hurt the morale of those fighting in Okinawa? Grew didn't know if this was the real reason. But Stimson did, and it is likely that he coached Marshall. Although he would later argue that a "conciliatory offer" would be taken "as an indication of weakness," he wrote in his diary that night what he really thought:

"It was an awkward meeting because there were people present in the presence of whom I could not discuss the real feature which would govern the whole situation, namely S-1. We had hesitated just before they came in whether we should go on with the meeting at all on account of that feature, but decided to let Grew, who was the one who really had gotten it up, go ahead with it."

Yes, the Japanese should be told they could keep their Emperor, Stimson agreed—but only *after* the bomb was dropped. The holocaust would then give Hirohito an excuse to surrender, hopefully before the Russians could move into Manchuria. The Tokyo fire bomb raid was simply not enough to give him this excuse. . . . Anyway, Grew's knowledge of the bomb was limited. How could he realize that it was made up not only of metals and chemicals, but of men's hearts, minds, and dreams, that out of its monstrous fury would emerge a rational, law-abiding world? . . . Of course the Tokyo raid would not be enough! . . .

Stimson inhaled the fragrance of the flowers ablaze at Highhold and fed the chickens. He would wait for the bomb. It was the quickest way to end the war.

IX

The question was, would the *Russians* wait? If the bomb didn't work, a Russian attack on Manchuria would be desirable. But if it did work, such an attack would not be desirable, for Russia would have a military foothold there and would even demand an area of control in Japan after the war, as in Germany. Yet Stalin, it was clear, would strike soon whether America wanted him to or not. Had he not canceled Russia's Neutrality Pact with Japan on April 5? Had he not assured American diplomats that his troops would storm across the border as soon as they could be transferred to the Far East? At Yalta, Roosevelt had paid a hefty price for Stalin's promise to smash into Manchuria. How could Stalin now be *stopped* from doing so—until the bomb, if it worked, exploded over Japan and ended the war?

Grew and Harriman didn't know, but they advised Truman to "rediscuss" Yalta and make new accords with Stalin. Why carry out Roosevelt's pledges if it turned out that a Russian attack in Manchuria was no longer necessary? If Stalin wanted to attack, there might be no way to stop him, but why pay him to do it?

Stimson was aghast. Break the Yalta agreements? That would destroy his plan for saving the world! Stalin would never trust the United States again.

Don't break them, he urged Truman. Just make them irrelevant. Stall in carrying out Roosevelt's commitments in the Far East.

How?

There was a built-in way. Stalin had pledged to strike in Manchuria only *after* Chinese leader Chiang Kai-shek approved the concessions Russia was to get, since Manchuria was part of China. Roosevelt had promised to urge Chiang to accept them, but if Chiang refused, Stalin would not be bound by his own promise. Even if he planned to attack anyway, he wanted those concessions approved by Chiang. So let Stalin and Chiang negotiate. Let them talk . . . and talk . . . and talk—until they were interrupted by the blast of the bomb. The war would be over, and so perhaps would Stalin's dream of a Far Eastern empire.

A perfect ploy! Truman agreed. On April 19, after only a week in the White House, he advised Chiang's foreign minister, T.V. Soong, who had come to Washington, to leave for Moscow "as soon as he could" to negotiate with Stalin. And Soong could hardly wait to go. Stalin, in return for the concessions, had promised to back Chiang in his struggle with the Chinese Communists, to let Chiang's administrators follow the Russian army into Manchuria, and to withdraw this army when the fighting ended. Chiang was more than willing to make a deal.

But ironically, by the time his representative, Soong, reached Moscow in late June, Truman was in no hurry. As Byrnes would later confirm, "Our purpose was . . . to encourage the Chinese to continue negotiations. . . . If Stalin and Chiang were still negotiating, it might delay Soviet entrance and the Japanese might surrender."

Ambassador Harriman, who was now back in Moscow, admonished Soong: Don't let Russia force you to recognize the independence of Outer Mongolia.

However, Chiang, who wanted to rule that land but wanted even more to rule whatever part of China he could get, issued a contrary order to Soong: Recognize the independence of Outer Mongolia.

Harriman countered with new instructions for Soong: Don't accept Russian demands for control and management of Dairen and the Manchurian railroads. . . . And incidentally, don't sign any agreement with Russia without consulting the United States.

Thwarted in his effort to negotiate with Stalin, Soong angrily packed his bags and flew back to China, grumbling: Let President Truman negotiate!

But Truman wouldn't—not until the bomb lit the road to Eden.

X

Meanwhile, Leo Szilard, who had conceived the bomb, now shared Leahy's view that it should not be used—lest it light the road to Armageddon. Szilard had pressed Roosevelt to make a bomb for one reason only: Germany, he was sure, was building one. And Roosevelt had agreed to spend $2 billion on the project for the same reason. Now, the great irony was that Germany was not only out of the war, but, it was clear, had not seriously tried to produce the weapon.

"I began to ask myself," Szilard would say, "'What is the purpose of continuing the development of the bomb, and how would the bomb be used if the war with Japan has not ended by the time we have the first bombs?' . . . It was not clear what we were working for."

Even before Truman took office—when Germany's defeat seemed imminent—Szilard asked Compton about the government's intentions. But Compton didn't know what they were either. Szilard's plan to drop a bomb on an evacuated German city to show the world that it must unite or die had been overtaken by events. And he opposed dropping a bomb on a Japanese city. He had changed his mind about the psychological effect an atomic bomb used in war would have on the world. It would not drive the nations together, but might drive them apart. America, leader of the free peoples, would be stigmatized forever, even if there were few casualties. Meanwhile, Russia, knowing that in a future war America might drop a bomb on it, too, would build one of its own at all costs, spurring a disastrous, uncontrollable arms race.

The best answer, Szilard now decided, was to keep the bomb a secret, at least until the end of the war when some kind of international control agreement could be worked out. Don't test it. Don't use it. If, however, secrecy proved impossible, then use the bomb in a *peacetime* demonstration after building up a huge arsenal of the weapons. The Russians would then see the power of the bomb, realize they couldn't catch up with the United States, and remember that the United States had not dropped it during the war.

Thus, feeling less threatened even while hopelessly out of the race, Stalin might be more amenable to a control plan.

Why did Szilard want to drop the bomb on an evacuated German city but then oppose dropping it on a Japanese city under any circumstances? Perhaps because his personal experiences with Nazism caused him to seek some revenge on Hitler, while his lack of personal contact with the less systematic Japanese brutality did not spark such a desire. Perhaps simple bathtub logic moved him; different bathtubs may have stimulated different logic. Whatever the reason, Szilard was again the crusader. With one threat to humanity crushed, he would now head off the next one. It would be useless, he felt, to speak with Groves, Bush, or Conant. He had gone all the way to the President to get him to build the bomb; now he would go to the President to get him *not* to use it.

Once again Szilard solicited Einstein's help. There was "trouble ahead," he told his venerable colleague. He couldn't say what kind of trouble for he was bound to secrecy, but would Einstein please write him a letter of introduction to Roosevelt so that he could personally see him. Einstein did, stating that Szilard "is greatly concerned about the lack of adequate contact between" the scientists and the Cabinet members who were formulating atomic policy.

Szilard sent the letter to Eleanor Roosevelt, asking her to arrange a meeting between the President and himself. And to his joy, he received an appointment for May 8, 1945. He immediately rushed to see Compton with a prophetic memorandum he had already prepared for Roosevelt and told him about the appointment, fully expecting him to growl his displeasure. Compton read the memorandum carefully:

The first bomb that is detonated over Japan will be spectacular enough to start a race in atomic armaments between us and other nations. . . . Six years from now Russia may have [a bomb . . . and be able] to destroy all of our major cities in a single sudden attack. . . . All that is necessary is to place a comparatively small number of bombs in each of our major cities and to detonate them at some later time. . . . Such bombs may remain hidden in cellars of private houses in our cities for any number of years or they may remain hidden below the ground buried in gardens within

our cities or buried in fields on the outskirts of our cities.
. . . It is conceivable that it will become possible to drop
atomic bombs on the cities of the United States from a very
great distance by means of rockets. . . . A [preventive] war
might be the outcome of the fear that the other country
might strike first.

The United States, Szilard wrote, would not keep its atomic
lead long and was especially vulnerable to a surprise attack. How
could nations be prevented from using atomic energy for war? One
way was to "denature" fissionable materials, adding certain isotopes that would be hard to remove. Or else simply forgo the
benefits of atomic power—unless the world was ready to accept a
control system.

> One might [therefore] consider the advisability of discontin-
> uing now the work on detonating [a bomb] and of immedi-
> ately scrapping . . . all installations for the manufacture of
> [one]. . . . [This action] coupled with an agreement with
> Russia and Great Britain, which would outlaw the building
> of such installations, might perhaps enhance the security of
> the United States in the next 25 years. . . . Conversely, it
> might be proposed that we should lose no time in develop-
> ing . . . atomic power and that we should develop within a
> few years methods for manufacturing overwhelming quan-
> tities of the active materials. . . .

In other words, the United States should scrap the bomb. But if
it refused to do so, it should build up an unchallengeable lead over
Russia as the only possible alternative for discouraging a nuclear
arms race, since it did not appear at that time that the Soviets
would be capable of making a vast number of bombs in the foreseeable future.

When Compton finished reading the memorandum, he looked
up and said: "I hope that you will get the President to read this."

Szilard was elated. An establishment man like Compton
backed his right to appeal to the President! Perhaps the President
would be impressed, too. He returned to his office, and five minutes later there was a knock on the door. Compton's assistant
entered with devastating news. He had just heard on the radio that
President Roosevelt had died.

Szilard was distraught. Had fate robbed the world of its last chance for survival? Harry Truman . . . Who was he? Would he see an "unknown" scientist like Szilard? And how could he approach him? Szilard despaired. He knew a number of people who could have reached Roosevelt, but not Truman. He then thought of his colleagues; perhaps there was a scientist from Kansas City. Albert Cahn was—and had worked for Pendergast in order to pay his way through graduate school.

Either Szilard or Cahn, apparently, telephoned the lawyer of Tom Evans, Truman's close friend in Kansas City, and asked for an appointment with Evans. The caller would be accompanied by several other men.

What did they want to see Evans about?

That was a secret, "probably the biggest secret in the history of the world." But it was extremely urgent that Evans see them.

Some days later, "five men," according to Evans, came to the office of his drug company, led by Szilard.

"I heard then," Evans would recall, "the most fantastical [sic] story that anybody could ever hear. . . . Well, it sounded like a fairy tale and . . . it just didn't make sense. . . . And they wound up saying that this [project they had been working on for Roosevelt] is so important to our country and the war effort that we have uncovered a metal whereby an airplane can take the air and never return to the ground ever; it can carry an unlimited supply of fuel. The same for ships and submarines.'"

They felt sure Truman didn't know about this project. Would Evans please arrange an appointment with his good friend in the White House?

Evans rushed to Washington and told Truman what he had heard.

"Well," said the President, "I know about it."

"And his chin sort of stuck out," says Evans, "and he said: 'It is a gigantic thing, Tom. It's the most important thing that's ever been developed in the history of the world, and I don't want you to have one single solitary thing to do with it, because it's something that would worry you sick and you're too good a friend of mine. . . . I'll tell you what to do.

" 'You get those gentlemen on the telephone, and you tell them to be here tomorrow morning at 10 o'clock, and you meet them, if you want, and bring them over to the White House . . . and then you bid them goodbye and tell them that there will be some people

[to] see them, and it won't be me, but I'll come in and shake hands with them and turn them over to some people that will handle it.'"

Evans arranged for the appointment, though he did not stay to welcome them.

Szilard rushed off to Washington with Walter Bartky, associate director of the Chicago project, and the two men were greeted in the White House by Matthew J. Connelly, Truman's appointments secretary. (The President did not appear.) Szilard handed him Einstein's letter and the memorandum, which Connelly read. He finally looked up and said:

"I see now this is a serious matter. At first I was a little suspicious, because this appointment came through Kansas City."

After all, there were many people seeking political favors from the new President.

"The President," Connelly said, "thought that your concern would be about this matter, and he has asked me to make an appointment for you with James Byrnes, if you are willing to go down to see him in Spartanburg, South Carolina."

They would be happy to go anywhere the President suggested they go, replied Szilard.

Connelly then telephoned Byrnes and made the appointment.

Szilard decided to bring along Harold Urey, since a Nobel Prize winner could impress Byrnes, and shortly after Urey arrived in Washington, the three scientists were on a train to Spartanburg.

James Byrnes? Why was the President sending them to see him? the scientists wondered. He wasn't even working for the government now. Was he to be put in charge of uranium work after the war? Would he realize how important it was not to drop the bomb on Japan?

XI

A few days later, on June 18, the military chiefs filed into the White House for a crucial meeting with Truman. How should America end the war? Present were Marshall; Leahy; King; General Ira C. Eaker, representing Air Force General Henry Arnold; and Assistant Secretary of War McCloy, replacing Stimson, who showed up at the last minute, however, after dragging himself out of a sickbed. This was not a meeting he could afford to miss.

Should there be an invasion of Japan?

Leahy dramatically made his point. The United States, with its overwhelming sea and air power, could win the war without one. Tens of thousands would die for no reason, since the Japanese would fight for every house and hill. Nor did he "agree with those who say that unless we obtain the unconditional surrender of the Japanese that we will have lost the war. I fear no menace from Japan in the foreseeable future. . . . What I do fear is that our insistence on unconditional surrender will result in making the Japanese more desperate and thereby increase our casualty lists."

Marshall and the other service chiefs argued that if sea and air power could not force the Japanese to surrender by November 1945, they would have to invade Japan.

How many casualties would America suffer in Operations Olympic and Coronet?

According to an official report prepared for the Joint Chiefs, casualties would number about 193,500, including 40,000 dead, 150,000 wounded, and 3,500 missing. Marshall now predicted that Olympic would claim not more than about 30,000 casualties in the first 30 days, when the resistance would be greatest. Leahy, who wanted to discourage an invasion, projected about 270,000 casualties in all. And Stimson, who hoped to strengthen his case for using the bomb if necessary, saw 1 million. Truman was impressed and would grab at this figure (sometimes he would mention 500,000) when, after the war, he sought to justify the atomic bombing of Japan.

He would write orders for the invasion, the President now said, "with the purpose of economizing to the maximum extent possible in the loss of American lives." He wanted to avoid "an Okinawa [where casualties were great] from one end of Japan to the other."

Should Russia be encouraged to attack Japanese troops in Manchuria as Stalin promised to do?

A Russian attack was "highly desirable" and might even be decisive, Marshall said.

Yes, King added, but it would not be "indispensable."

It was agreed: Invasion plans would proceed—though Truman would reach a final decision on the actual operation later.

The debate, in a sense, had an unreal quality about it, as if the participants were discussing some hypothetical situation in a war game. The fact was that no one really thought an invasion would be necessary. Either the atomic bomb or a Russian attack in Manchuria, or even more concentrated blockading and conventional bombing, as Leahy felt, would almost certainly end the war before an American invasion would be launched. And so all the quibbling over strategies and casualties essentially covered up a reluctance to openly consider use of the bomb or of Russian forces alone to end the war. Besides, the prospect of huge casualties, however unlikely an invasion, provided a suitable moral excuse for dropping the bomb.

Stimson backed the invasion plans, but only as a contingency. Many Japanese opposed the war, he said, but were afraid to say so. If attacked on their own ground, they would resist just as strongly as the fanatics. Why not help them to gain influence before invading? How? He didn't say, but he thought there was a "means."

Why did Stimson refer to a "means" rather than to the bomb, which he obviously had in mind? After all, everyone in the room knew it was being built. Once again, the Secretary apparently wanted to avoid a debate on the weapon. Truman had never actually stated he would use it. And who could tell if he had yet been caught in the machine, if he might have moral qualms, especially with Leahy hammering at him? And as an old soldier himself, Stimson perhaps was uneasy about openly defending the use of so murderous a weapon, especially since it could still be an embarrassing failure.

Yet, only the night before, Stimson talked with McCloy about reaching a quick peace either by dropping the bomb on Japan or by threatening to drop it, and McCloy felt he had persuaded Stimson that the threat should be made first.

Stimson's refusal to mention the bomb at this meeting startled McCloy. He had been silent up to now, for he was only an assistant secretary who happened to be there because his boss hadn't expected to be. But as the meeting ended and everyone was picking up his papers, Truman turned to him and said: "McCloy, you didn't express yourself and nobody gets out of this room without standing up and being counted. Do you think I have any reasonable alternative to the decision which has just been made?"

McCloy glanced at Stimson.

"Say what you feel about it," the Secretary said, like a man no longer able to control a bursting dike.

"Well, I do think you've got an alternative," McCloy said. "And I think . . . we ought to have our heads examined if we don't explore some other method by which we can terminate this war than just by another conventional attack and landing."

The alternative: A political solution. Don't use the expression "unconditional surrender," but spell out the terms the United States would settle for. Japan would continue to be a sovereign nation with the Emperor at its helm—if he became a constitutional monarch.

"Well, that's what I've been thinking about," said the President.

But McCloy wasn't finished. To help persuade the Japanese, why not tell them the United States had the bomb and was prepared to drop it?

The others froze. The bomb? He mentioned the bomb! It wasn't done!

But McCloy continued to do it: "I think our moral position would be better if we gave them specific warning of the bomb."

"We don't know that it will go off," someone said. "Suppose it doesn't? Our prestige will be greatly marred."

"All the scientists have told us," McCloy argued, "that the thing will go; it's just a matter of testing it out now. . . . And I think that the moral position that we would have would transcend the temporary disadvantage that might occur from our taking the risk of a dud. . . . If you don't mention the bomb, at least mention in general terms what its capacity is, something in the nature that with one blow we could wipe out a city. They'll know what we are talking about."

Truman was noncommittal: "You send your memorandum to the State Department, and we'll consider . . . this."

The military chiefs, still flustered, seemed unimpressed—not because they wanted to use the bomb without warning, but because they apparently didn't want to use the bomb at all. As McCloy would say:

"They were all anxious to employ their own forces for the conclusion of the war."

Leahy, however, was pleased by at least part of McCloy's last-minute plea; he agreed with McCloy that there should be an attempted political settlement. But he would not wave the bomb in achieving it.

The admiral was still a lonely man.

Chapter 13

THE
REALIST

I

Foreign Minister Shigenori Togo also wanted a political settlement—almost any kind he could get. On the day of the bomb, he sat in his office filled with deep foreboding as he scanned cables and awaited word from Moscow on whether Stalin was back from Potsdam. Would the Soviet leader consider mediating a peace that would at least save the throne? This could be the day that would decide Japan's fate.

Togo had been foreign minister as the sun rose over the ruins of Pearl Harbor. Now, at 62, after a long retirement, he was foreign minister again as the sun was setting over the ruins of Japan. He was hoping to atone for his role in starting the war by ending it before the nation crashed into oblivion with the thundering finality of a 400-pound sumo wrestler thrown out of the ring by an even fatter foe.

Actually, Togo had tried to ward off war—with a zeal matched only by those who sought it. Unlike Kido and others who had been wary of war, Togo did not engage in a "peace conspiracy." He openly stated what he felt. And yet, he survived—physically and politically. For the warmongers needed him. Togo, in a sense, was the Japanese counterpart of Admiral Leahy; he was the only man the military rulers could depend on to speak his mind freely, and still bow unhesitatingly to their commands. Didn't they have to know the logic of peace to be able to devise a credible logic of war?

Togo was not a man, of course, to be taken seriously. He would talk peace endlessly at conferences, in the office, in the corridor. But he was no real danger to the glorious cause. Throw him a bone or two and he would bark in harmony with the rest of them. The foreign minister was a realist. He pushed the military as far as he could, then compromised, feeling that a bone might ultimately take on flesh.

Yet it was not simply realism that made Togo accept a bone. He basically agreed with the aims of his military colleagues, though unlike them, he knew how far he could go before the danger signal flashed. Not surprisingly, Togo, who was far too frank to indulge in *haragei*, bluntly told the Diet on January 22, 1942, when the war was under way and there was no longer any reason to suppress his hunger:

"The nature of this war is for the emancipation of East Asia and for the establishment of the new world order."

Thus torn between reality and the dream, Togo constantly sought to mesh them without pulling the thread that would unravel all his peace efforts. In 1933, Togo wrote in a policy paper: By seizing Manchuria, Japan "has as much forfeited international confidence as she has enhanced her military prestige. In modern international society resort to force is a matter of the utmost gravity, especially among the Great Powers. . . . Instances are not few in history of unjustifiable resort to force resulting in disaster. . . . It is essential that . . . we avoid conflicts with other countries . . . that [might] in combination deal with Japan."

In particular, the "basic policy toward the United States should be . . . to prevent war. As the United States does not welcome the exercise by Japan of a hegemony over the entire Far East, Japan on her part should not make this her policy in the foreseeable future."

But give up Manchuria? Never!

"The urgent task for Japan," Togo wrote, "is the *development* of [Manchuria]. . . . If we succeed in this, the position in the Far East will be stabilized."

Every time Japan would grab more land, Togo said "No more!" But then the military would assure him: This is the last. And he would accept each fait accompli—not always grudgingly.

Togo's conflict with himself stemmed from both his personality and his past, which together did not jell into a typical product of the Japanese social web. He did not care what people thought of him, and they, in turn, didn't think too well of him. They found him aloof, arrogant, and taciturn—except when he was pleading for peace. An individualist. Not at all a man who could fit in a niche and submerge his views into the community consensus. He had even defied the community by marrying a white foreigner, a German woman he met while he was posted in Germany in the early 1920s. In fact, a widow with five children!

So "eccentric" had Togo become (in Japanese eyes) that he was actually faithful to his wife. No concubines, no geishas. Yet he could certainly afford them. He had no "community spirit" at all, and not even drink could yield a sign of good fellowship at the dinners he was obligated to attend. His own subordinates found him formidable and distant—when they managed to see him at all. Sometimes he would send his daughter to solicit their views on some burning matter.

Nor did a glance at Togo ease the discomfort of those forced to deal with him. He had the expressionless good looks of a waxen actor, with broad face, rather flat nose, and barely parted scowling lips under a well-trimmed mustache. His hair, which turned from gray to white in the last months of the war, was neatly slicked back, and his round glasses accentuated intimidating eyes. A well-cut suit with wing collar, dark tie, and matching pocket handkerchief added to the image of a man chiseled in ice.

II

Togo was the perfect Japanese Prussian, born into the Satsuma clan of southern Kyushu that, together with the Choshu clan, had played a large role in the Meiji Restoration. Coming from a well-off samurai family, he inherited the stubbornness and nationalist pride of his warrior ancestors though little of their devotion to an outdated moral code. And his worldliness did not encourage such devotion. At Tokyo Imperial University he majored in German literature, permitting Goethe and Schiller to balance off the myths and emotions of Japanese history.

Symbolically, Togo began his diplomatic career in 1913 as a consular officer in Mukden, Manchuria, where eighteen years later Japan would begin its drive for a "new world order." But if he dreamed then the impossible dream, he would soon realize that a dream might be not only impossible but inflammable. For an assignment in Switzerland and a prolonged stay in England due to a grave illness exposed him both to the Western character and to Western industrial power. Japan, he then decided, must never risk war with the West—whatever his samurai forefathers had vowed when they ousted the Tokugawa regime. Squeeze out what you could, but never squeeze too hard.

Thus, during World War I, when Japan was allied with the Western democracies, it had managed to squeeze out a foothold in China after attacking German bases there, and a foothold in Siberia after attacking the Bolsheviks, who had seized control of Russia. And Togo was at the Versailles peace conference when Japan was given a mandate over Germany's Far East colonies. Clearly, it was more profitable to work with the Allies than against them.

Next assignment was Berlin, where Togo viewed firsthand the devastation of war. He eventually returned to Japan with his German girl friend on his heels, and, risking his career, he married her. His career flourished anyway. What other Japanese diplomat knew as much about the Western world that Japan might eventually have to confront?

Togo was put in charge of Soviet affairs, and, though anti-Communist, struggled for good relations with the Russian Communist leaders since they were solidly in power. He urged his government to withdraw Japanese troops from Siberia and then, in 1925, won his reward—an economic and friendship treaty with Russia.

Togo then headed for Washington where, as first secretary in his embassy for four years, he found the tremendous dynamism of American society intimidating. No, it was not a country that Japan should fight. Finally, he was back in Tokyo again in charge of European and American affairs. And it was then, in 1933, with Japan surging toward the sun, that he implored the militarists to make Manchuria a model colony—and let the dream end there.

But they wouldn't. And when Togo was sent as ambassador to

Nazi Germany in 1937, he was enraged when he found that his military attaché was negotiating an alliance with Hitler behind his back. The Führer was an "upstart" in his opinion, and would draw Japan into conflict with the United States, Britain, and Russia, which one day might "in combination deal with Japan." After ten months, his relations with German leaders grew so strained that he was transferred to Moscow. Here he helped lay the cornerstone for a Japan-Soviet Neutrality (or nonaggression) Pact that was signed in 1940, and when he left for home, Molotov, toasting him at a farewell banquet, said glowingly:

"In my public life of many years, I have never known any man who insists so earnestly and so frankly as Mr. Togo on what he believes to be right. I respect Mr. Togo not only as a distinguished diplomat and statesman, but as a man."

III

The problem was that as the Japanese government moved toward war with the United States and Britain, it didn't *want* an ambassador who "so earnestly and so frankly" insisted on what he believed to be right. And so Togo found himself out of a job—until General Tojo took over as Prime Minister in October 1941 and discovered he needed someone who knew something about the countries he was going to fight. Togo fit that need and became foreign minister, though what he knew about these countries convinced him that they could crush Japan.

Togo thus felt his mission was to make a deal—without, of course, giving up too many of the gains scored by Japanese zealots, who didn't understand, as he did, where the dream must end and reality begin. Had he not warned eight years earlier that the "basic policy toward the United States should be to prevent war"?

General Tojo was tolerant. Let Foreign Minister Togo try to prevent war. What was Togo, anyway? Simply a tool. A tool, however, that was not easily manipulated. A samurai who owed his primary *giri* to common sense—even while clinging to fragments of the impossible dream.

When Japanese leaders met on November 1, 1941, to decide whether the nation should go to war, Togo steeled himself as he confronted his military colleagues.

If Japan waited any longer to attack the United States, they fervently argued, the Western economic blockade would gradually drain the country dry. There soon wouldn't be a drop of oil left in Japanese storage tanks, and Japan would be helpless. The time to go to war was now!

Wrong! cried Togo. He could solve every important problem dividing Japan and the United States.

America wanted Japanese troops to leave China? Compromise. Promise to withdraw them in five years.

America wanted Japanese troops to leave French Indo-China? Compromise. Move those in the recently occupied south to the north.

The military chiefs were aghast. They wanted to keep their troops where they were forever. But they finally relented. Very well, twenty-five years in China. And yes, they would move their forces in southern Indo-China to the north.

Togo thought he had performed a miracle. America couldn't reject such concessions. But if it did?

That would mean war, the military promised.

No, wait and see, Togo pleaded. At least until America entered the European war, which it seemed likely to do. It would be foolish, he said, to go to war on the theory that Japan could score some quick victories.

"After all, if one wins ninety-nine battles and loses the hundredth, one loses the war."

Was it logical to make the plunge with no assurance of final victory?

The military leaders couldn't answer. But neither could Prince Ito when he asked himself how Japan could possibly knock out Russia in 1905. And Japan won anyway. Togo, the military chiefs felt, had a Western mind. He understood Goethe but not the gods. America could take the concessions or leave them. And they set the deadline for the end of November 1941.

Togo thought of resigning, but his fellow peacemakers objected. Did he want a war-minded foreign minister to replace him and quash the last hope for peace? Better that he stay. Even if war did come, he could at least fight for an early peace.

Yes, Togo would stay. But this meant he had to go along with the military. What more stubborn reality was there than a stone wall? And he was a realist.

IV

But American Secretary of State Cordell Hull was, too. And, in his view, to appease aggression would be to encourage it. His reply to the Japanese negotiators in Washington was: No compromise! Japan must get out of all China and Indo-China at once.

Togo was dismayed. "I can never forget the despair which over-powered me," he would say. "I had fought and worked unflaggingly until that moment; but I could feel no enthusiasm for the fight thereafter. I tried . . . to close my eyes and swallow the Hull note whole, as the alternative to war, but it stuck in the craw."

The United States, it seemed clear to Togo, wanted war and "schemed to make Japan fire the first shot. . . . Morally, it is hypocritical, malicious and cowardly to take the position that one is free with impunity to provoke one's adversary as far as one wishes, so long only as one refrains from striking first."

But for all his despair and anger, Togo apparently felt a sense of relief. He was free now to pursue the suppressed dream of a "new world order," for it was no longer realistic to suppress it. Fate had preempted his realism. And it was too late to tinker with fate. He had vigorously argued against a surprise attack on Pearl Harbor if war came, but now he could satisfy his conscience by merely giving the United States *one hour's* notice that Japan had decided to "end negotiations," without mentioning that it would go to war instead. Let the Americans think that Japan wanted to continue serious talks to the final hour. (Ironically, Japanese diplomats botched even this warning, delivering it to the State Department after Pearl Harbor was already under attack.)

Nor did Togo now have qualms about sabotaging a last-minute peace move by President Roosevelt. Just after midnight, December 8, 1945 (Japanese time), Ambassador Grew rushed to Togo's official residence with a cable from Roosevelt to Hirohito. Mysteriously held up by Japanese telegraph authorities for ten hours, the cable, Grew told Togo, appealed for a complete Japanese withdrawal from Indo-China to pave the way for further talks.

He must see the Emperor immediately, the ambassador implored Togo.

The foreign minister was even colder than usual. Roosevelt was just echoing an old refrain. But Togo couldn't reject the request outright or Grew might guess the truth—that within hours Japan and the United States would be at war.

He would "study the document," Togo promised, and "present the matter to the throne" as soon as possible.

When Grew left, Togo went to see Tojo.

Any new concessions? Tojo asked.

No.

"Then there is nothing that can be done."

Except to draft a rejection that the Emperor could sign—and thus thwart any desire he might have to delay the war. After helping to write it, Togo seemed almost jovial. As he was about to leave for the palace, he joked:

"It's a pity to run around disturbing people in the middle of the night."

"It's a good thing the cable arrived late," Tojo replied. "If it had come a day or two earlier we would have more of a fuss."

Nothing at this point must hold up the war.

At the palace, Kido, also in an exuberant mood, greeted Togo. Roosevelt's message would not affect plans, he agreed. In fact, Japanese forces had already begun to attack British Malaya, and Kido had been listening to short-wave transmissions from the assault boats. The Emperor, too, had forgotten his fear. He "deeply moved" Togo, who saw in the Imperial countenance a "noble feeling of brotherhood with all peoples." When Togo read him the Roosevelt cable, Hirohito gave voice to this "noble feeling," but also to his "unflinching attitude." How regrettable that the cable had arrived so late. But Togo's draft reply suited him fine.

Bowing deeply, Togo departed and, gazing "up at the brightly shining stars, felt bathed in a sacred spirit." As his car sped through the palace plaza, with only the "crunching of the gravel beneath the wheels" disturbing the silence, he was sure that the course he now approved would also "find approval in the ultimate judgment of Heaven."

Togo had returned to the gods.

V

But the gods were fickle, and after Japanese forces were humiliated in the Battle of Midway, Togo was not at all sure about their ultimate judgment. The time had come for a new dose of realism. Japan must make peace with the United States while a reasonable peace was still possible. Backed by the Emperor and Kido, he

decided that China was the key. Since Japan had seized the wealth
of most of east Asia in the first months of the war, it could afford
now to withdraw its troops from China—if it could make a deal
with Chinese leader Chiang Kai-shek that would protect Japanese
interests there. This could open the route to peace.

General Tojo, however, didn't want that route—at least not
yet. He wanted not to withdraw from the conquered nations but to
cement his hold on them, and thus formalize the Greater East
Asian Co-Prosperity Sphere with Japan sitting comfortably at the
top. And a new Greater East Asian Ministry must be created, he
felt, to oversee the cementing process.

Togo bristled. Was he foreign minister or was he not? Under
Tojo's plan, Togo's ministry would be pushed aside; it would have
almost nothing to do with the countries whose future could determine whether Japan would win or lose the war. How could Togo
make a deal with Chiang Kai-shek if China was no longer within
his diplomatic bailiwick? No, he would never agree.

Then resign, Tojo demanded. And in September 1942, Togo
did. His eyes no longer reflected the sacred light of the stars, and
would shine again only in the glow of the flames that would devour
Japan.

VI

With the flames raging in April 1945, Togo was needed once
more, this time by the peacemakers. Someone had to stand up to
the military. Newly installed Prime Minister Suzuki called him
down from the mountain resort town of Karuizawa, where he had
been living with his wife and children since he resigned from the
Tojo government.

Would Togo take over as foreign minister again?

Since he had tried hard to avert the war, Togo replied, he
would "be gratified to try to end it as soon as possible." How long
did he think the war would last? he asked the Prime Minister.

"I think," Suzuki said, "that we can still carry on the war for
another two or three years."

Togo gasped. Another two or three years? Japan couldn't hold
out for another year! Sorry, but he could not accept the job. And
he stalked out into the smoky streets of Tokyo.

But the next day, the peacemakers, from Kido down, descended upon him. Togo must sacrifice himself, they urged. Suzuki needed someone to guide him. Besides, he shouldn't be taken too literally—he was just practicing *haragei*. Didn't trust anyone. But he would obey the Emperor's wishes.

Togo was doubtful about this, and anyway, how could one serve under a man who didn't trust him? But he nevertheless went back to see Suzuki. And this time, the Prime Minister all but blocked the way to the door so Togo couldn't get out.

"So far as the prospect of the war is concerned," he now conceded, "your opinion is quite satisfactory to me; and as to diplomacy, you shall have a free hand."

Togo accepted the post, and Suzuki had a visible decoy to protect him just in case the "invisible power" that had saved his life so many times wasn't around.

VII

When Germany surrendered in early May, Togo leaped at the chance to wend his way toward peace. He called in the German ambassador and accused Germany of breaking its treaty obligation by surrendering! Then he tore up all existing treaties with Japan's fallen partner, apparently feeling that such a move might impress Stalin and induce him to make a deal with Japan before he decided to join his allies in fighting Japan. Russia must be persuaded at any cost to remain neutral in the Pacific war.

The militarists now cried for such a deal. For what if the Soviets struck at Japanese forces in Manchuria while the Americans splashed ashore in Japan?

He would try, Togo assured them. But he did not have in mind keeping the Russians out of the war simply to make it easier for Japanese troops to welcome the Americans with a bloody beach party. What he wanted was to entice Russia to mediate peace between the Western powers and Japan. As a realist, Togo didn't actually think that Russia would suddenly embrace Japan as a friend. It was too late. Moscow had already announced that it would end its Neutrality Pact with Japan, though the pact still had one more year to run.

Nevertheless, Togo saw Russia as a magnet to draw the militarists toward peace. Anami and his colleagues were, after all, set on keeping Russia neutral. So maybe they would agree to go a little further—and seek Russian mediation. Togo wanted to approach the United States and Britain directly, but this would mean unconditional surrender, perhaps even an end to the Imperial system. And the militarists would never agree, especially since they might be tried as war criminals. Mediating through such neutral countries as Sweden and Switzerland would be useless because they had no influence. But Russia had a powerful hold on its allies. At least Togo could use this argument to sweeten the bitter peace pill in military eyes.

And at meetings of the Big Six from May 11 to 14, Togo tested this circuitous path to peace. Shrewdly he steered talk of persuading the Russians to stay neutral to talk of using them as a go-between. It wasn't easy. The militarists wanted to use Russia—but to help them *fight* the war, *not* to mediate peace. Keeping Russia out of the Pacific war wasn't going far enough. The navy, in particular, needed oil for the few ships it had left. Why not try to persuade Russia to sell Japan oil and other vital war goods? Was not Stalin able to defeat Germany only because Japan remained neutral in that struggle and did not come to Hitler's aid?

Togo was contemptuous. He knew the Soviet Union. "There was no longer any room for utilizing the USSR militarily or economically. . . . It was too late for Japan" to get munitions from that country. The most that Japan could expect was to keep Russia out of the Pacific war. And to do this it would have to pay a high price in territory. In fact, the only way to prevent a Russian rampage might be to use Stalin as a peace mediator.

Silence. At a formal meeting, Togo was openly suggesting surrender! The civilians stared with anxiety at the military, the military with shock at Togo. But shock amazingly dissolved into submission. Perhaps Russia *was* a way out of this miserable situation. And now the question was not whether there should be peace, but what terms Japan should accept. Togo seemed to have won his gamble. Everyone was talking peace, though *conditional* peace, to be sure. And he was still alive.

Very well, peace, agreed General Anami. But "we should remember above all that Japan still retains a large block of enemy territory. We have not lost the war so long as this is so, and we should negotiate from this basis."

Togo was appalled. He must dampen expectations of a *favor-able* peace. "Although Okinawa is the only sizable piece of our territory we have lost, it is future developments on the war front that will count and it is impossible to visualize peace conditions merely on the basis of captured or lost territory."

Russia, Anami reported, might help Japan get a decent peace. "As the USSR will be in confrontation with the U.S. after the war and therefore will not desire to see Japan too much weakened, the Soviet attitude toward us may not be severe."

Togo ridiculed this view. How could Japan be "optimistic" about Russia "when she always acted realistically and ruthlessly"?

Suzuki, though delighted by the peace talk he had been afraid to initiate, apparently grew worried as the atmosphere heated up. The military must be nursed through the trauma of peace.

Well, Stalin wasn't so bad, he asserted. In fact, the dictator reminded him somewhat of Takamori Saigo—the samurai hero whose image had helped Anami decide to accept the job of war minister. One of Saigo's feats had been to persuade the Tokugawa shogunate commander in Tokyo (then Edo) to surrender the city during the 1867 Meiji revolution.

The others could hardly imagine Stalin as the model samurai, but only through him, it now seemed, could Japan save itself. And so the Big Six agreed that Japan should:

- make "supreme efforts" to keep Russia out of the Pacific War;
- induce Russia to remain neutral and mediate peace;
- convince Russia that Japanese neutrality made its victory over Germany possible, and that in the future it is "necessary for Japan, the USSR, and China to stand hand-in-hand against Britain and the U.S."
- agree, if required to achieve these goals, to give up the territories and privileges it won in the 1905 Russo-Japanese War, grant Russia trade advantages, and stop fishing in Soviet waters.

Japan would thus offer Stalin essentially the same prizes to keep out of the Pacific war—and possibly mediate peace—that the United States had offered him at Yalta to get into it. Togo, who could only surmise what, if anything, Stalin was promised at Yalta, knew that the Soviet leader would find the prizes offered by the certain victors more enticing than those offered by the certain losers. But he had to at least approach Russia, since the only other solution was unconditional surrender.

As before Pearl Harbor, Togo, faced with impossible alternatives, could only throw Japan into the lap of the gods and hope they gave a damn.

VIII

To lay the groundwork for a deal with Russia, Togo asked Koki Hirota, a former Prime Minister who had many Soviet contacts, to feel out Soviet Ambassador Yakov Malik about closer Japanese-Russian ties. And on June 3, Hirota "casually" dropped in on Malik at a resort hotel.

Japan's fondest wish, he mused aloud, was to be a good friend of the Soviet Union.

Malik was blasé. Really? What about Japan's belligerent acts against his country, from shooting across the Manchurian-Siberian border to holding three Soviet ships in Hong Kong? And the anti-Soviet feeling in Japan?

That was all in the past, said Hirota. Now Japan longed for eternal peace with Russia.

Malik eyed him skeptically. He would think it over. Meanwhile, how about dinner the next evening?

Hirota was overjoyed, and so was Togo. Don't let go of Malik, he urged. Russia had to mediate a peace within weeks. Togo had learned that Stalin was to meet with Roosevelt and Churchill at Potsdam in mid-July, and if they got together before Japan made a deal with Russia, what chance would there be for a negotiated peace? Time was running out.

A couple of days later, Togo wondered whether it hadn't run out already. For while Anami and the other senior officers edged toward peace, fanatical junior officers like Colonel Takeshita now practiced *gekokujo* with renewed vengeance. They drew up a document called "The Fundamental Policy to Be Followed Henceforth in the Conduct of the War," and on June 6, the Big Six met to discuss it. Japan, said the document, would "prosecute the war to the bitter end in order to uphold our *kokutai* [national essence], protect the Imperial land and achieve our goals of conquest."

Anami and most of the other senior officers didn't dare resist. They feared that the juniors might not only rebel, but blacken their name by questioning their patriotism. The militarists even tried to back up their claim that Japan could fight on indefinitely by feeding civilian members of the Big Six choice cuts of the Sakomizu report on the state of the nation, taken out of context. Togo, who learned of the "Fundamental Policy" only at this meeting, was furious. His Russian initiative, it seemed, was dead.

"Going through these items," he cried, brandishing the Sakomizu report, "I can find no reason for continuing the war. As far as I can see, there is no relation between your draft proposal and the detailed items" in the report.

Anami was furious, too—at Togo. "If we cannot fulfil our responsibility as advisers to the throne," he admonished, "we should offer our sincere apologies by committing *harakiri!*"—exactly what he planned to do anyway. But part of his fury was perhaps secretly aimed at his young comrades-in-arms. "Achieve our goals of conquest?" At this stage of the war? National suicide! Carry on the struggle, yes, but not to conquer. Only to hurl back the coming invasion of the homeland in order to win better surrender terms.

But who would be unpatriotic—or daring—enough to reject the "Fundamental Policy"? Only the blunt Togo. Suzuki was his usual unblunt self. And his penchant for *haragei* drew strength from a story he had been told by a colleague before the meeting: There was a monkey trainer in ancient China whose monkey refused to perform tricks for the skimpy reward of three acorns in the morning and four in the evening. Very well, said the trainer, how about four acorns in the morning and three in the evening? The monkey, afraid that he might not get any acorns at all, agreed, and performed his tricks with the enthusiasm of a village entertainer suddenly invited to the palace to appear in a Gagaku performance for visiting royalty.

In other words, Suzuki should act like an enthusiastic monkey. Since it was useless to oppose the document now, why not practice *haragei?* Embrace it until he found a way to kill it. The Big Six approved the document, and the next day the Cabinet did, too, after Suzuki declared:

"There is only one way to win, and that is by determination.

When the whole nation possesses this will, then we shall be able to achieve victory!"

Suzuki even repeated Anami's admonition: If anyone failed to pursue victory, he should be willing to commit *harakiri*—though he retracted this statement when one Cabinet member protested. Yes, this was going a little too far. Even an insecure monkey couldn't show too much enthusiasm about performing tricks without arousing suspicion that he might be unhappy.

The "Fundamental Policy" went on June 8 to an Imperial Conference, where the Emperor would "ratify" it simply by attending.

Did anyone oppose it? Suzuki asked after a brief discussion of the contents, knowing that no one ever opposed any measure that was submitted to an Imperial Conference—though Togo once again reminded his colleagues that Japan would face extreme difficulties.

Silence.

"Well, then," Suzuki said, "I conclude that no one has any particular objection to the plan."

The ministers and their aides rose and bowed as the Emperor, stone-faced, walked out.

IX

Hirohito immediately granted an audience to Marquis Kido, who was not entitled to attend Imperial Conferences.

Why did His Majesty have such a grave look?

"They have made this decision," the Emperor replied, showing Kido a copy of the document.

Kido, who no doubt knew about the "Fundamental Policy," could understand the Emperor's despair. Was Suzuki "betraying" His Majesty by letting this plan go through, or was he simply playing *haragei*? Either way, it seemed clear that the civilians in the government could not stand up to the military.

Kido grew desperate as he saw Japan's power collapsing around him. Okinawa was about to topple, bombs were battering city after city, the nation's fighting strength was sapped—and this was Japan's "Fundamental Policy"! Did the military want to provoke the Allies into abolishing the Imperial system itself? The time had come to take unprecedented action, to actively challenge the militarists.

Kido had just read a biography of Baron Goto, a statesman of the Meiji era, who had said, "I would like to sacrifice myself once in my lifetime. . . ." The Lord Keeper wrote in his diary: "This is exactly how I feel now."

Kido, who had survived all these years by appeasing the militarists, was finally prepared to strike at them even if this meant sacrificing himself. Ironically, the military, by threatening the life of the nation, had frightened Kido and other peacemakers into conquering their fright. Deep into the night, Kido thought the unthinkable: His Majesty must *personally* order an end to the war.

After a brief, restless sleep, the Lord Keeper went to his desk and dashed off a paper he called "Tentative Plan to Cope with the Situation." At 1:30 P.M., June 9, he handed it to the Emperor, who silently read it.

Japan, the paper said, must seek peace immediately. "If we wait for a more favorable opportunity, it may be too late. Then Japan would share Germany's fate, and her minimum demands—the security of the Imperial family and retention of our national essence—might not even be met. . . . The only possible course is to ask His Majesty to intervene for the sake of the people and initiate termination of hostilities."

How? The Emperor should send a personal message to an unnamed "intermediary power," obviously Russia, stating his desire for an honorable peace and "his decision to end the war . . . on reasonable terms." Japan would withdraw its forces from all occupied areas, giving them their independence, and would disarm itself except for the minimum arms necessary for national defense.

As the Emperor looked up, Kido noted that his grave expression had mellowed. His Majesty heartily approved the idea.

Then he would start drumming up support for it in the Cabinet, Kido said with relief.

"Do it right away."

Kido met with Navy Minister Yonai, whom he knew favored peace, and Yonai was enthusiastic about the plan.

"A very good idea," he said, "but I wonder how the Prime Minister really feels about the war."

At about that time, Prime Minister Suzuki, apparently worried that the Emperor might feel betrayed by his support of the "Fundamental Policy," was about to throw aside *haragei* and hint his true feelings to His Majesty as well as to the Allies at a meeting of the Diet. He reminisced to the Diet members about a speech he made in San Francisco in 1918 while visiting there as a fleet commander. Japan, he had then told the Americans, "is not warlike. She is the most peace-loving nation in the world. There is no reason why she and the United States should come to war, but if they do, the conflict will be a long one and end disastrously. The Pacific Ocean, as the name suggests, should be the Sea of Peace with no troop transports permitted on its surface. However, if such an unhappy event should come to pass, both sides will be punished by the gods."

Suzuki seemed to delight in his old Taoist thoughts, but then he saw the angry faces in the audience. Peace? Japan as well as America should be punished by the gods? Delete such controversial phrases, some members of the Cabinet had pleaded. But this time Suzuki stood his ground. Still, he thought it necessary to appease his listeners. Of course, the nation must fight to the last man!

When he finished speaking, Suzuki had to fight his way to the door, leaving amid jeers, shaking fists, and cries of "Down with Suzuki!" But the fallen hero made his way to Kido's office down the corridor and the two men went over the Lord Keeper's plan. Suzuki liked it. And he was sure that Togo would. But he wasn't sure about Admiral Yonai, who had not said a word against the "Fundamental Policy" that Suzuki himself had dutifully praised.

"Yonai said the same thing about you," Kido replied.

Suzuki couldn't understand it. Wasn't it clear, at least to the peacemakers, that he was practicing *haragei?* They had better understand, especially with the jeers of the Diet still ringing in his ears. Hoping to regain his hero's image, or at least stay alive, he assured reporters at a press conference the following morning that "we must fight to the end, the entire population uniting as one body."

Confident now that despite such statements Suzuki was really for peace, Kido approached Togo, who, as expected, said that "if the Emperor were to say that we should work to end the war immediately . . . there could be no greater aid to my efforts."

Kido thus had the support of the Prime Minister, foreign minister, and navy minister. He now thought of Anami, whom he knew from their palace days together. When Anami had been aide-de-camp to the Emperor, Kido had been secretary to the Lord Keeper of the Privy Seal. Anami, he was sure, felt strongly indebted to the Emperor. Perhaps . . .

Anami gave him the opportunity to bring up the plan when he visited Kido about some other matter.

"I've heard that you plan to resign," Anami said, repeating a rumor born of military wishful thinking.

"No, I do not plan to resign," Kido replied, "but when you hear what I have to say, you may want me to."

"Well, what is it?"

Kido then outlined his plan to Anami and waited for a possible explosion. But it didn't come.

A good plan, Anami said with his usual calm.

Kido could hardly believe his ears.

But, Anami continued, it should be carried out only after American invasion forces have been thrust back into the sea.

The Lord Keeper gently disagreed. If Japan fought such a battle, he said, it would have no more planes or ships left for any further defense. The next invasion wave could roll all the way to Tokyo. His plan might only work *before* an invasion.

Anami listened carefully, painfully. He knew that Kido was speaking logic. But as a military man, he had been brought up to defy logic. Was it logical for Japan to become a leading world power only seventy years after emerging from feudalism? Was it logical for Japan to crush the Russian forces in 1905? Was it logical for Japan to conquer almost all of Asia in the first months of World War II? Was it even logical to believe that the Emperor was divine? Japan's spirit was not susceptible to logic. He had to believe that his country could at least win one more battle, a battle for honor. He owed it to the army, the Emperor's protector, to believe this. And yet, he knew, perhaps more clearly at this moment than ever before, that to act on this belief was to disobey the Emperor himself. Anami decided to equivocate.

No, he couldn't back Kido's plan, but if it was brought up before the Big Six, he wouldn't oppose it too strongly either.

Kido was elated. At least there was a chance to save the soul of Japan, whatever happened to its body.

X

On June 22, Hirohito summoned the Big Six to the palace. "The war," he told them, "has already been waged for three and a half years, and its havoc is becoming more severe every day. Although it has always been important for those engaged in battle to exert their utmost, I feel that we as a nation must do something to terminate the war. Do you have any plans?"

The only two present who had not been told about the Kido plan—Army Chief of Staff General Yoshijiro Umezu and Navy Chief of Staff Admiral Teijiro Toyoda—were shocked. The Emperor had, in effect, overruled the "Fundamental Policy." But this wasn't a god's job!

Yes, there were plans, Suzuki replied to the Emperor. And Togo then described the Hirota-Malik meetings, which could, it was hoped, pave the way for sending an envoy to Moscow with an Imperial message.

"What have you scheduled as the date of the diplomatic settlement?" Hirohito asked, referring to such a mission.

Someone should be in Moscow before mid-July, said Togo. Before the Potsdam Conference.

Any move, Umezu admonished, must be "treated with the utmost caution."

"Does treating the proposal 'with the utmost caution' imply acting only after having struck another blow at the enemy?" the Emperor inquired. "If we are too cautious, we will miss our opportunity."

Umezu hardly knew what to say. He alone questioned the Emperor's wish.

"Well," said Umezu, "the sooner the better then." And Toyoda, who had been silent, went along.

Anami, as he had promised Kido, did not dissent either, saying only that Japan should not appear too eager for peace lest this eagerness be misconstrued as weakness. The war minister seemed crushed. The Emperor had for the first time specifically criticized the plan for waging one more battle before seeking peace. Now, if Anami went ahead with this plan, his "crime" against the Emperor would be more heinous than ever.

The Emperor seemed greatly relieved and Togo almost managed a smile. Stalin now held the master card. How he played it could determine whether Japan would survive—at least in the Imperial form that Amaterasu had in her mythological mind.

XI

With new confidence, Togo ordered Hirota to push Malik, and two days after the meeting in the palace, Hirota was again sipping tea with the Soviet ambassador.

Wouldn't it be a good idea, Hirota suggested, for their two countries to sign a new nonaggression pact?

No need, Malik replied. The present Neutrality Pact would not be extended but was still good for a year.

Japan had rubber, lead, tungsten, tin. Russia had oil. Why not exchange these items? Hirota pressed.

Malik shrugged. Oil? Russia barely had enough for itself.

Hirota grew desperate. "If the Soviet army and the Japanese navy joined forces," he said, "Japan and the Soviet Union together would become the strongest force in the world."

The ambassador seemed bored. After all, what good was a navy that was rotting on the ocean floor? If Japan came up with a "concrete plan," he said, he would consider it. *Do svidaniya!* Good day!

A few days later, Hirota was back with a "concrete plan." Japan still wanted a new nonaggression pact and oil. In return, it would give Manchuria independence and keep Japanese fishing boats out of Soviet waters.

He would send the plan to Moscow, said Malik. *Do svidaniya!*

And he sent it—by a courier traveling the Trans-Siberian Railroad. Only *important* messages went by cable.

When no response came from Russia after several days, Togo, near panic, decided that Japan could no longer wait. Never mind the Russian ambassador in Tokyo. He would depend on the Japanese ambassador in Moscow. Ambassador Sato must go directly to Molotov and arrange for an Imperial envoy to visit the Russian capital immediately. Who should the envoy be? Fumimaro Konoye seemed the ideal man. He was a prince. He had been Prime Minister three times. He craved peace. And he was brave. He would have to be, for the young military fanatics might well try to kill him for seeking peace.

Meanwhile, the Emperor was growing impatient as reports flowed in that even middle-sized and small towns were being bombed into cinders. He summoned Suzuki on July 7.

Was there no answer from Moscow yet?

There was none.

"Then we had better dispatch an envoy with the Imperial message," the Emperor replied.

Togo, said Suzuki, was to leave that very day for Karuizawa, where Prince Konoye was staying, to ask him to undertake the mission.

The following day, Togo was there and made his plea. When Konoye agreed, the foreign minister told him:

"Try for anything short of unconditional surrender."

In other words, anything short of abolishing the Imperial system. If necessary, Hirohito would abdicate in favor of another member of the Imperial family.

XII

On July 12, Konoye was called to the palace to see Kido, who immediately sent him in to see the Emperor, though the prince had not even had time to change from his usual khakis to the formal attire normally worn at an Imperial audience. The Emperor himself, looking pale and tired, was ill-groomed. Nor did he wait for the compliments that a visitor was expected to lavish on him in greeting. He was in a hurry to get down to business and wouldn't even let an aide sit in, as protocol required, for he wanted Konoye to speak with complete frankness.

"The war seems to have reached a crucial stage," Hirohito said as soon as his guest sat down. "The longer we continue fighting, the greater will be the agony of the nation. Every minute now small towns are being attacked. I cannot sleep at night. I want to terminate the war, however regrettable that might be. What do you think?"

"The feeling prevails in the nation that Your Majesty should break the deadlock," Konoye replied, signifying that the Emperor should force the military to accept peace. "Some even lament Your Majesty's inaction. Under the circumstances, I believe it is necessary to terminate the war immediately."

"Then you, too, are of the opinion that we should negotiate as soon as possible. You may be called upon to go to the Soviet Union as my Special Envoy. Be prepared."

Recalling past mistakes he had made as Prime Minister, Konoye replied: "His Majesty graciously told me I would have to share the consequences with him, the good and the bad. With the situation as serious as it is, I shall lay down my life if it is the Imperial command."

Konoye gazed at the Emperor, nodding, as if to underscore his resolve.

And even as American scientists feverishly prepared to test a projectile that could demolish a city, Konoye zealously prepared to test a ploy that could deliver a state.

Chapter 14

THE
INTIMIDATOR

I

As the S.S. *Augusta* headed toward American shores on the day of the bomb, Jimmy Byrnes stood at the President's side—helpful, reassuring, indispensable. All the other top presidential advisers, except Admiral Leahy, had already flown home from Potsdam. But Byrnes was one adviser Truman couldn't be without. His presence on the destroyer symbolized his special relationship with the President, and now they waited together for the news that would shake and revolutionize the world.

Byrnes won over the crew with his easy Irish charm. He was a short, balding man with an angular face, thin, stubborn lips, and intense eyes, slanting sharply downward, that could either captivate a friend or cut down a foe. He now told stories of Truman's great performance in Potsdam and assured the boys that they would soon be out of uniform. Things were working out well after all. Of course, *he* should have been sitting in the President's chair in Potsdam, but Stalin, Churchill, and the others must have realized who was really conducting American policy.

Truman was, in fact, using Byrnes because he knew more about foreign affairs than did most of the people around him. But

Byrnes was also using Truman. As Secretary of State, he was in a position to deliver his own kind of peace to the world. Could Truman reject his advice when the Secretary had so intimate a knowledge of the Yalta accords, which would be the cornerstone of future American foreign policy? And with the atomic bomb about to usher in a new era, could Truman reap its full diplomatic benefits without Byrnes' political expertise? Who knew better than Jimmy Byrnes, the former Senate troubleshooter, how to wield the big stick—or the atomic bomb—to make people reasonable? Like Stimson, Byrnes viewed the bomb as the key to the postwar U.S.-Russian relationship, but he would shape the relationship in a different way. Negotiate with Russia, yes, but with the bomb itself, not Stimson's blueprint of it, in your hip pocket.

Truman and Byrnes instinctively understood each other—enough, it seems, to dispel any illusions in either's mind that their marriage of convenience could work for long. Nor would it have to, they felt, for the bomb would probably yield a prompt American-style peace. Truman's presidency would be saved, and Byrnes' reputation for being able to handle even so powerful a figure as Stalin would guarantee him a special place in history. And since the Secretary of State was next in line of succession, fate could even land Byrnes in the White House.

Both men sprang into national prominence from provincial populist roots—Truman from the shabby machine politics of Jackson County, Missouri, Byrnes from the white justice politics of Aiken, South Carolina. Both were tough, shrewd professionals with a strong feeling of independence, men who knew how to make deals—whether with the local park commissioner or with Stalin.

But which man was better qualified to be President? Byrnes was not racked by doubt. While Truman was selling underwear in Independence, he was working with President Woodrow Wilson for a world that would be "safe for democracy." Though Byrnes felt he was now in a position to finally achieve this goal, he lamented that he lacked the title he deserved. He should be President, and would be, if Roosevelt had not "betrayed" him—with the help, however unwitting, of Harry Truman. Byrnes would not forget what happened, nor would Truman, and from the moment of the "betrayal," the pair would be linked in a cruel bond of guilt, resentment, and, ultimately, hatred.

II

Byrnes first met Roosevelt in 1912 in Baltimore, where they shared a house during the Democratic convention that nominated Woodrow Wilson. Their friendship was sealed, and Byrnes would remain Roosevelt's faithful ally, campaigning for the Cox-Roosevelt national ticket in 1920, prodding FDR to run for governor of New York in 1928, helping to nominate him for President in 1932, pushing through New Deal bills in Congress for the next decade, and serving as "assistant President" during World War II almost until the day Roosevelt died. As a loyal and able disciple, Byrnes appeared destined to be Vice-President.

When Harry Truman joined Byrnes in the Senate in 1934, he brought along quite another reputation. He was tagged, however unfairly, as the "Gentleman from Pendergast," a man presumably with few scruples. And for some time he would remain with few friends. But one of the few was Byrnes, whom Truman respected as a college freshman might the graduating class valedictorian. Byrnes welcomed him warmly, helped him with Senate business, showed him the political "ropes"—at a time when the junior senator's self-esteem had plunged to near zero. Then, in 1940, when Truman no longer had a Democratic machine backing him for reelection, Byrnes raised more than his ego; he raised money for him. First, he urged Roosevelt to back Truman.

Truman? Sorry, said the President, he preferred his "untainted" opponent.

Byrnes then approached Bernard Baruch, the wealthy Democratic "elder statesman," and Truman soon had $4,000 for radio time that catapulted him back into his Senate seat.

When he returned to Washington, Truman requested more money from Byrnes, but this time, it seemed, Jimmy would be less helpful. Truman had just introduced a resolution to set up a Special Committee Investigating the National Defense Program that would look for waste in defense spending, but Byrnes, as head of the Senate Audit and Control Committee, had to approve funds for such an organ. And when it came to the budget, he was known as a penny pincher.

Why did he introduce the resolution? Byrnes asked.

Because some Missouri contractors were complaining that the big companies were getting all the defense-construction contracts, answered Truman. A little pressure on the War Department would help.

"What would you do if the resolution were reported out?" Byrnes asked.

Truman realized what Byrnes was after. A congressional foe of Roosevelt also wanted to investigate defense spending and he would surely be out to embarrass the Administration, and this worried the President. So Byrnes assured him that he "could fix that by putting an investigation into friendly hands." Now here was friendly Harry Truman.

"I know there isn't a chance in the world of your reporting it out," the junior senator replied diplomatically. "But if you did, I wouldn't conduct the investigation in a way that would hurt defense. You could count on me for that."

Byrnes smiled. How much did Truman need?

Twenty-five thousand dollars.

Ten thousand would be enough.

How could the committee operate with only $10,000?

Well, then, $15,000.

It still wasn't enough, but Truman took what he could get. Neither man could have dreamed that from this seed money would sprout a Truman presidency and a new relationship between the pair. For if Truman at first intended merely to help out his strapped constituents back home, he soon struck investigative gold as his "Truman Committee" dug up defense waste amounting to hundreds of millions of dollars and won the hearts of nearly as many taxpaying Americans.

By convention time in 1944, Truman was being considered as a possible nominee for Vice-President—together with Byrnes, who had ironically created his chief competition. Yet Byrnes wasn't concerned. For not only was Truman telling everyone that he didn't want to run for Vice-President, but from late 1943 Roosevelt was telling Byrnes that he wanted *him* to run. With FDR behind him, how could he lose?

Byrnes did not know that he was being used, that in the final weeks before the convention he was, in fact, programmed to lose. The Democrats were deeply split. Should liberal Henry Wallace be nominated as Vice-President? Roosevelt decided he shouldn't be. But who would replace him? Byrnes seemed the likely choice— except that the blacks loathed him because he came from the segregationist South and had filibustered against an antilynching bill, and labor mistrusted him because he had "stabilized" wages as wartime economic czar. He couldn't win.

Then there was Truman, a sudden hero on the civilian war front. He came from a noncontroversial border state, knew how to compromise, and had made few enemies, if only because he had been so inconspicuous until recently. The politicians didn't particularly want him, but they didn't reject him either. They didn't really know him. A man just nondescript enough to run for Vice-President! And so, a week before the convention, Roosevelt chose him.

However, with too much time to mull it over, the convention delegates might start wondering what would happen if a provincial, ill-equipped Vice-President inherited the most powerful job in the world in the middle of a war. That's where Jimmy Byrnes fit in. Let everyone think that Jimmy was still in the race. The Wallace backers would be so horrified that at the final chaotic minute they would be glad to settle for almost anyone of a slightly more liberal bent—even Harry Truman.

So, stay in the race, Roosevelt kept urging Byrnes. He would win.

Byrnes was so confident now that he telephoned Truman. "Harry," he gushed, "the President has given me the go sign and I'm calling up to ask you to nominate me."

Truman didn't hesitate for a moment. The very thought of being Vice-President, and perhaps eventually President, terrified him. Was the fate of the world to be taken so lightly? On the other hand, Byrnes, with his vast experience and strong personality, was eminently qualified for the job. Besides, had not Jimmy befriended him when others avoided him? Would Harry Truman even be a senator today if Byrnes had not helped reelect him?

Of course he would nominate Jimmy and even campaign for his nomination.

Byrnes was joyous. Who could block him now?

The President! It was time to end the charade. And when Roosevelt casually told his aides over drinks on his campaign train that Truman would be the nominee, even some of them were startled. Admiral Leahy, whose war experiences had never quite prepared him for the savagery of the political arena, groaned:

"Who the hell is Harry Truman?"

But no one was more surprised than Truman himself when

Robert E. Hannegan, chairman of the Democratic National Committee, called him to party headquarters and asked him to be a nominee for Vice-President. When he resisted, Hannegan phoned the President, and Truman heard him say:

"Bob, have you got that fellow lined up yet?"

"No, he is the contrariest Missouri mule I've ever dealt with."

"Well, you tell him, if he wants to break up the Democratic Party in the middle of a war, that's his responsibility."

And Roosevelt banged down the receiver.

Stunned, Truman finally said, "Well, if that is the situation, I'll have to say yes, but why the hell didn't he tell me in the first place?" And under his breath he grunted, "Oh, shit!"

Troubled by the pledge he had made to Byrnes, Truman immediately went to tell him about Roosevelt's decision. Would Byrnes please relieve him from his promise of support?

Byrnes' face paled into a mask. He couldn't believe it.

"I'll call the President up," he said.

But the President was conveniently unavailable.

Byrnes suddenly found himself staring in agony and humiliation at the man he had inadvertently helped to crush his dream.

Of course he would relieve Truman from his pledge.

III

But Byrnes never really did, and Truman knew it. He knew it so well that on becoming President he immediately called for him. The former "assistant President" had retired to Spartanburg, South Carolina, some days earlier after resigning his job in the Roosevelt Administration, but he now flew back to Washington in a U.S. Navy plane. Truman greeted him like a savior.

Would Jimmy become his Secretary of State?

Yes, of course. . . . At last, the next in line to be President of the United States.

The rush flight had been worthwhile after all—for Truman as well as Byrnes. The new President desperately needed a man with his qualifications. Besides, Byrnes was fit to be President while the current Secretary of State, Edward R. Stettinius, had never been an elected official and was, in Truman's view, "as dumb as they come."

But as important as the urgency of his services was the memory of the promise. As Truman himself would admit, he wanted "to help balance things up." Both Truman and Byrnes understood what this meant. How had they succeeded in politics all these years? They never expected to get everything they wanted. Whether on the county council or in the Senate, they would compromise, give and take, "balance things up." It was the only way for men with conflicting aims to move forward and get something done.

But who could "balance things up" for a man who thought he had been cheated out of the presidency of the United States? Byrnes would not be satisfied with being the conventional Secretary of State; he would, in a sense, serve as "acting President." Didn't Truman owe everything to him? Besides, Harry didn't want to be President, nor did he have the qualities of one, while *he* wanted to be and had the qualities. The nation, the world, would need a man with Jimmy Byrnes' experience and judgment to parry the dangers of the atomic age.

Byrnes, unlike Truman, had always been sure of himself, one reason why the Roosevelt "betrayal" struck him with such brutal force. How could Jimmy Byrnes, who had seldom known failure in the past, whose shrewdness and perception were legendary, fall into such a trap? Hadn't he always played the game fairly? He had never stooped to deception to get what he wanted but had earned every triumph with honest hard work. He had learned from his mother how to survive honorably.

IV

Jimmy Byrnes' mother, Elizabeth, came from a family of survivors. Stricken by the Irish potato famine of the 1840s, they had fled Ireland for the United States, where they settled in Charleston, South Carolina, never quite able to throw off the yoke of poverty. Byrnes' father died shortly before Jimmy was born, leaving his widow only $200 to support the new baby, a little daughter, an elderly mother, a widowed sister, and a young nephew. Undaunted by her fate, Elizabeth Byrnes headed for New York, studied dress designing for several months, and returned south to start a dressmaking business that would keep the household afloat for many years. Jimmy would always visualize his mother hunched

over her sewing machine working day and night, never complaining, persevering so that each of her children would grow up "to be
somebody."

To make sure they would be able to scratch out more than a
bare existence, she added a home course to their studies—shorthand. Every night, as they sat around the parlor table doing their
homework, she would suddenly stop stitching by the big lamp and
dictate a few paragraphs from a children's book for shorthand
practice. Jimmy could hardly wait until he started earning money
so that his mother would be able to put down her overused needles
and start living.

Thus, at 14, the boy, though a top student, left school to begin
his career. He was soon running errands as an office boy in the
wealthy Charleston law firm of Mordecai and Gadsden on Broad
Street, the old lawyers' row and citadel of frock-coated conserva-
tism, where great men such as Judge Benjamin H. Rutledge
pounded their gavels and their witnesses with cadenced southern
dignity. Rutledge, it happened, was a partner in Mordecai and
Gadsden and would be Byrnes' role model in the way Eliahu Root
was Henry Stimson's.

Such an intelligent boy leaving school? A shame. And Rutledge
lent him a card to the Charleston Library and personally supervised his course of reading. Jimmy devoured the classics, educating himself while performing his menial duties and supplementing
his income with stenographic side jobs. As Stimson imitated *his*
great mentor, even down to the bangs, so Byrnes emulated the
judge, cultivating the kind of courtliness that would win him many
friends in the future.

At 21, Byrnes took out his shorthand pad and started work as
court stenographer for Judge James H. Aldrich, a learned state
circuit judge based in Aiken, and was now finally able to liberate
his mother from the sewing room. He was entranced by the new
life and awed by the judge as they marched through dusty towns
behind the sheriff, who cried, "Make way for his honor," and
listened to country people air their disputes in torrid little court-
rooms. Was there any problem that could not be solved by patient
negotiation and compromise?

Byrnes immersed himself in the law books in Judge Aldrich's
library long enough to finally emerge as a lawyer himself, though
he had never even been to high school. He passed the bar and
between court sessions turned out a local newspaper that he

bought with $4,500 in borrowed money plus $500 in savings. Having learned to pinch pennies all his life, he paid off the bank in two years, showing early signs of the genius that would flower when he would direct the whole American economy during World War II. The lawyer soon turned into a fiery district attorney and earned a name for himself cleaning up sinful Barnwell County and persuading juries to regard assaults on Negroes as crimes and even to accept Negro testimony.

But Byrnes was not motivated primarily by any streak of idealism. If being a lawyer to Stimson meant staunchly defending the rules of civilized society, it meant to Byrnes matching wits with a rival lawyer, meeting the challenge, winning the game. Being a politician was even more satisfying because he could play for higher stakes—with power the prize.

In 1910, Byrnes got his prize—Congress. Ambling through its hallowed halls, he mastered the art of rolling pork barrels, twisting arms, patting backs, mixing his own personal blend of conviviality with cool logic and, when necessary, implied threat. He lost in a race for the Senate in 1924, but, typically rejecting defeat, bounced back six years later and won. Shortly he attached himself to Franklin Roosevelt and began his meteoric rise to power.

After serving for more than a decade in the Senate, Byrnes was appointed to the Supreme Court in 1941, but when Pearl Harbor exploded a few months later, he strained at his golden leash. This was a time not to *interpret* the law but to *lay down* the law. And he did—fleeing the cloistered halls of the court for a seething cubicle in the White House, so small that he had to put his teletypewriter in the men's room. From here, as Director of Economic Stabilization, he directed the wartime economy with all the gusto and authority of a coach calling the plays in the Super Bowl. He then took over the still more omnipotent job of Director of War Mobilization, wielding greater power than any American in history aside from the Presidents and in fact earning the informal title, "assistant President."

V

Roosevelt's betrayal halted Jimmy Byrnes' rise, but now, once again, Jimmy was flirting with destiny as Truman's Secretary of State—the man who would decide how to use the atomic bomb in a game played for the highest stakes in history. But he would have to wait a while, for Stettinius was still the Secretary and would lead the American delegation at the founding conference of the United Nations to take place in San Francisco in late April 1945. Byrnes, always the gentleman, the fair player, even refused the President's suggestion that he go to San Francisco as an observer. Was it right to embarrass Stettinius—as Roosevelt had embarrassed *him*? Jimmy Byrnes could wait. After all, how serious could negotiations with Russia get before mid-July, when the atomic bomb would be tested? Only then would he know whether he would ever escape the second trap that FDR had laid for him.

Byrnes had earned a reputation as a foreign affairs expert largely because of what he had learned at the Yalta Conference. He had taken shorthand notes there and had the only complete stenographic record of the talks that took place. One reason Truman had called Byrnes to Washington almost as soon as he became President was that "it's the only way I can be sure of knowing what went on at Yalta."

Before the Yalta Conference ended, Byrnes was back in Washington as its American spokesman, giving interviews, writing articles, holding press briefings. He spoke as if he knew all the secrets and was telling what could be told. The Big Three, he grandly announced, had laid the basis for postwar cooperation. America had gotten what it wanted; in particular, Eastern Europe would be free.

This is what Roosevelt wished the public to believe. He had taken Byrnes to Yalta mainly so he could influence Congress and the people to rally round the Yalta accords. The trouble was that Byrnes did not know the secrets; Roosevelt had kept them from him. He did not attend secret sessions and was unaware that Roosevelt, feeling Poland was doomed to satellite status and wishing to lure Russia into a permanent United Nations peacekeeping organization, had agreed to a Communist-dominated Polish government that would hold "free elections"—a meaningless expression in the Communist lexicon. Nor did Byrnes know that Stalin had secretly agreed to attack Japanese forces in Manchuria three months after Germany surrendered, and that he had wrested a stiff price for this promise, too.

What Byrnes didn't know, the President shrewdly calculated, wouldn't hurt Congress or the public. But it would hurt Byrnes to discover, while educating himself to be Secretary of State, that once more Roosevelt had used and misled him. From talking with knowledgeable diplomats and perusing Yalta documents he found, it was clear that Roosevelt had *not* expected to get what he wanted, that he knew Eastern Europe was fated to become a Russian preserve.

Byrnes was horrified. Not that he necessarily disagreed with Roosevelt's logic under the circumstances, but in being duped, he had himself duped the public, leading it to expect an idyllic postwar period. He had even misled Truman, who jealously guarded the only copy of Byrnes' Yalta notes in the White House safe. Would the new President have torn into Molotov had he known that Roosevelt virtually gave Russia a signal to communize Poland, asking only for some democratic window dressing? That FDR had all but settled on the idea of splitting Europe into two spheres of influence as the only realistic alternative until the world was ripe for unity?

Byrnes was thus in a quandary. He couldn't admit his blunder, certainly not when he was about to become Secretary of State. But in dealing with Russia, he would have to be guided by the facts of Yalta, not the fantasies. He would have to play realistically with Stalin and deceptively with the American public. And so would Truman, who had begun to realize that his stand against Russia was not entirely consistent with Yalta and that the United States would have to compromise.

But *would* it have to? Byrnes had just the answer to his dilemma—the atomic bomb. Whatever Yalta called for, the bomb would inevitably shape the postwar world. If it was realistic for America to recognize Russian power at Yalta, it would be realistic for Russia to recognize American power after Potsdam—when the bomb exploded over Japan. Stalin would know how far to go.

Byrnes had not always been as enthusiastic about the bomb. As director of the Office of War Mobilization under Roosevelt, he wrote Stimson a cautionary letter on September 11, 1943, warning him, without knowing the exact nature of the project, that "such huge expenditures of public funds and use of high priority material and labor will have to be justified." And as late as March 3, 1945, after Roosevelt had told him about the bomb to assuage him, he still worried about money. The cost, he noted, was now soaring to $2 billion, and no one yet knew if the thing would work. What if it didn't? Did Roosevelt want a congressional investigation after the war? Cut down on the cost, he urged, or at least let an independent team of scientists determine whether the bomb was feasible.

In short, it was foolish for a politician bred in the art of survival to spend so much money and take so great a risk. Did Roosevelt want to benefit the enemy—the Republicans?

But when Truman offered Byrnes the job of Secretary of State, Jimmy's attitude changed. He was no longer a penny pincher in charge of the wartime economy but would soon be in charge of world peace. And maybe the bomb would work after all, bestowing on him the power he needed to make Russia renounce Yalta and swallow his brand of peace.

It was at this moment of budding optimism that Leo Szilard and his two colleagues knocked on his door in Spartanburg. . . .

VI

Though Byrnes, with his warm, hospitable manner, was reputed to be the perfect southern host, Szilard was not so sure he deserved this reputation as he sat chatting with the future Secretary of State on May 28, 1945. Nor did Byrnes feel that Szilard was the ideal guest, later stating that "his general demeanor and his desire to participate in policy-making made an unfavorable impression on me."

After Szilard showed Byrnes Einstein's letter and his own memorandum, he elaborated. He and some of his associates did not know enough about the government's atomic policy. Did the United States plan to use the bomb? They wished to discuss the question with the Cabinet.

But policy was not the scientists' business.

Yes, it was, Szilard insisted. For the scientists knew many facts that policy had to be based on. Russia, he warned, might soon build a bomb of its own if the United States demonstrated the power of the weapon by using it against Japan.

"General Groves tells me there is no uranium in Russia," Byrnes replied skeptically.

Not so, Szilard countered. Russia almost certainly had low-grade uranium ores. It also had access to a small amount of rich uranium ore in Czechoslovakia. In any case, "it would be a mistake to disclose the existence of the bomb to the world before the government had made up its mind about how to handle the situation after the war." The bomb should be neither used nor tested. It should be kept a secret as long as possible to give the United States more time to stall off an arms race.

Byrnes' irritation grew.

"How would you get Congress to appropriate money for atomic energy research," he asked, "if you do not show results for the money which has been spent already?"

Szilard saw Byrnes' point. Perhaps it *would* be useless to try to keep the bomb a secret, even until the end of the war. There would be, thought Szilard, "no pressure for the government to do anything" more in the atomic field if the power of the bomb was not demonstrated.

Byrnes went on: He was "concerned about Russia's postwar behavior." Russia had moved troops into Hungary and Rumania, and it would be very difficult to persuade it to withdraw them. The USSR "might be more manageable if impressed by American military might, and . . . a demonstration of the bomb might impress" it.

The scientist stared at the politician with startled eyes, as if wondering what kind of man would doom the whole human race. He would later write:

"I shared Byrnes' concern about Russia's throwing around her weight in the postwar period, but I was completely flabbergasted by the assumption that rattling the bomb might make Russia more manageable."

And creeping suspicions that he would be unable to communicate with Byrnes matured into certainty when Byrnes said:

"Well, you come from Hungary—you would not want Russia to stay in Hungary indefinitely."

No, he would not want Russia to stay in Hungary indefinitely, Szilard replied. But that wasn't the point. He had come to see Byrnes in the hope of preventing an arms race between Russia and America.

As Szilard departed with his two colleagues, he had seldom been more depressed.

"I thought to myself," he would say, "how much better off the world might be had I been born in America and become influential in American politics, and had Byrnes been born in Hungary and studied physics. In all probability there would then have been no atomic bomb and no danger of an arms race between America and Russia."

VII

On his way back to Chicago, Szilard stopped in Washington to see Oppenheimer, who was visiting there. He had written Oppenheimer a letter some days earlier, on May 16, asking for an appointment, and now he had a chance to meet with him. In the letter, Szilard complained that "several important members of the Cabinet are not adequately informed about the postwar implications of the bomb." The United States, he wrote, was behind schedule in developing modern bomb-building methods, and without a "clear-cut policy" that would avoid an arms race "I doubt whether it is wise to show our hand by using atomic bombs against Japan."

What did Oppenheimer think? Szilard now wanted to know. "I expect that you who have been so strenuously working . . . on getting these devices ready will naturally lean toward wanting that they should be used."

Yes, he would use the atomic bomb against Japan, Oppenheimer said, but "the atomic bomb is shit."

"What do you mean by that?" Szilard asked.

"Well, this is a weapon which has no military significance. It will make a big bang—a very big bang—but it is not a weapon which is useful in war."

Then why use it?

Oppenheimer apparently did not say. After all, if those in power thought it should be used, who was he to contradict them? His rebel days were over. He would not disappoint Groves and the others who had entrusted him with so important a job despite his regrettable past. Besides, he was a scientist. His job was to build the bomb, not to worry about how it was used. Of course, he didn't want an atomic arms race either.

"Don't you think," he asked, "that if we tell the Russians what we intend to do and then use the bomb in Japan, the Russians will understand it?"

"They'll understand it only too well," Szilard replied.

Although Szilard didn't know it, they already did—thanks to Klaus Fuchs.

VIII

In early June 1945, Fuchs met with Harry Gold as planned on Alameda Street near the Castille Street bridge in Santa Fe, picking him up in his dilapidated Buick and driving across the bridge into a narrow deserted lane, where he parked the car.

What was happening? Gold asked.

He and the other scientists were working very hard, Fuchs replied. He himself was putting in from eighteen to twenty hours a day. With Germany out of the war, the scientists were desperately trying to complete the bomb in time to be able to use it against Japan, but he didn't think this could be done. Anyway, the bomb would probably be tested in July at a nearby site. He named the type of explosives to be used and indicated their likely force.

Then Fuchs turned over to Gold another packet of notes—a description of the plutonium bomb, including the core, the initiator, and the tamper, and a sketch of the bomb and its components with their dimensions. He had consulted official classified documents to ensure that all the details were accurate, he said.

The two men agreed to meet again in Santa Fe on September 19, and Gold then left, heading straight for the bus station, where he boarded the first bus to Albuquerque. He had another rendezvous there with a young military technician who was working on the implosion lens in Los Alamos. David Greenglass, at the urging of his brother-in-law, Julius Rosenberg, a top Soviet agent, would hand over to Gold sketches and a description of the lens.

Fuchs had supplied Stalin with almost all the important data on the atomic bomb, but why not give him some nuclear icing?

IX

A few days earlier, on May 31, Jimmy Byrnes saw his chance to set the United States on the right path to a bomb-imposed peace, even though he was not yet Secretary of State. Stimson had set up the atomic committee he had proposed to Truman for dealing with all wartime and peacetime atomic problems, and Byrnes was on it. Also sitting on this prosaically named Interim Committee were seven government officials and science administrators: Chairman Stimson, Bush, Conant, Harrison, Undersecretary of the Navy Ralph Bard, Assistant Secretary of State Will Clayton, and MIT President Karl Compton, Arthur's brother. They would be advised by a Scientific Panel composed of Oppenheimer, Fermi, Lawrence, and Arthur Compton, apparently a safety valve to make the scientists think they were playing a role in the solution of the problems.

To Stimson, the committee's main goal would be to guide the nation toward a system of international control that would save all mankind from the kind of holocaust that would soon wipe out a tiny segment of it. The problem was that the key member wanted one-nation control, preferably under his personal supervision. And that member was Jimmy Byrnes. Yet it was Stimson, ironically, who had chosen him after conferring with Truman. He had asked the President to pick one member who was close to him and could "keep his mouth shut," and then he himself suggested, What about Jimmy Byrnes? He would gain experience that would be useful to him when he took over the State Department.

The ideal man, Truman readily agreed. Stimson thus helped to doom his own cause.

The Secretary made this cause clear at a meeting of the committee on May 31. The atomic project, he said with grim eloquence, must be viewed not simply as a military venture but as a new relationship of man to the universe. The bomb must be controlled if possible to make it an assurance of future peace rather than a menace to civilization.

Most of those present agreed. Oppenheimer would thus say: If the United States were to offer to exchange information with other countries before the bomb was actually used, its moral position would be strengthened. Why not broach the subject to Stalin?

General Marshall, an invited guest, added that "charges and countercharges that have been typical of our relations with the Russians have proven unfounded. The seemingly uncooperative attitude of Russia in military matters stemmed from the necessity of maintaining security. [I have] accepted this reason for their attitude in [my] dealings with the Russians and [have] acted accordingly. . . . [Might it not] be desirable to invite two prominent Russian scientists to witness the [bomb] test?"

Marshall's conciliatory attitude toward Russia did not entirely surprise the others, for he was a soldier, not a politician. His goal was to win the war swiftly, and he might need Russian help to do it. But Jimmy Byrnes, who had been sitting quietly listening to one colleague after another call for sharing atomic secrets with Russia, was a politician, not a soldier, a man who knew how to exploit power. And Marshall's proposal was too much for him.

Invite the Russians to the test? Why Stalin shouldn't even be told that the bomb existed! Had not Groves assured them that Russia wouldn't have the bomb for twenty years? Bush and Conant had estimated three to five years, but Byrnes apparently chose to accept Groves' more favorable view. Let Stalin learn about the bomb when a Japanese city suddenly disappeared. Even if he were given general information, he would ask for full rights as an atomic partner with the United States and Britain. Of course Byrnes wanted to improve relations with Russia, but the United States must keep ahead in atomic production and research. That was the best way to improve relations: Make Stalin understand that he had better behave.

The talk about sharing secrets suddenly ceased. Even Stimson was silent, though he deplored the idea of using the bomb as a club and viewed sharing atomic data as indispensable to peace. Byrnes was the President's voice, and no one was ready to defy the President, confused as he might be. In any case, Byrnes was not confused. And to some, he was perhaps right: Hold a bomb in one hand and a diplomatic cocktail in the other.

With the atomic future out of the way, some dared to wonder whether and how the bomb might be used during the war. After the war Stimson would write that "the first and greatest problem [for the committee] was the decision on the use of the bomb— should it be used against the Japanese, and if so, in what manner?" But in fact this subject was not even on the agenda of this commit- tee meeting or any other. It was easier to assume that the bomb would be used than to talk—or think—about it. How could one go about planning for a brave new world while pondering on the instantaneous massacre of tens of thousands of human beings?

It was especially embarrassing for the scientists, who were less hardened than the politicians, to discuss how the bomb should be used, how many people would live, how many would die . . . as if one were counting cattle in a slaughterhouse.

"It seemed a foregone conclusion," Arthur Compton would

later write, "that the bomb would be used. It was regarding only the details of strategy and tactics that differing views were expressed."

Actually, the craggy-faced Marshall was the only one at the meeting who felt it might not be wise to drop the bomb on Japan— "from the point of view of America's postwar safety." While Marshall may have been thinking in long-range military terms, he was probably thinking in moral terms as well. Only two days earlier, on May 29, he told Stimson and his deputy McCloy, according to McCloy, that "he thought these weapons might first be used against straight military objectives such as a large naval installation, and then if no complete result was derived from the effect of that, he thought we ought to designate a number of large manufacturing areas from which people could be warned to leave— telling the Japanese that we intended to destroy such centers. There would be no individual designation so that the Japs would not know exactly where we would hit—a number should be named and the hit should follow shortly after. Every effort should be made to keep our record of warning clear."

Now, at this meeting of the Interim Committee, Marshall was going even further, arguing, as Szilard was, that it would be better not to use the bomb at all and thus "show our hand," but to keep it a secret instead. The United States would then be in a more favorable position to attack an enemy later, he said.

His listeners were shocked. But the bomb's existence, they cried, could not be kept a secret.

And Marshall, unwilling to hold out alone, seemed, according to Arthur Compton, to "accept the view that [the bomb's] use was nevertheless important."

Or did he? Marshall clearly had doubts, which may have been reinforced by a letter that Stimson had shown him a few days before this committee meeting. The Secretary wanted him to read what he called a "remarkable document" before he gave it to Truman—a 3,000-word letter from a scientist working on the bomb at Kellex in New York, where Klaus Fuchs had gathered much of his information for Stalin. In this letter, addressed to the President, O. C. Brewster wrote that if the United States set a precedent by dropping the first bomb, a "corrupt and venal demagogue" would one day try to destroy the world with the weapon for his "own insane satisfaction."

"This thing must not be permitted to exist on earth," Brewster pleaded. "We must not be the most hated and feared people on the earth, however good our intent may be." With Germany out of the war, "we must stop the project." But if the bomb was to be used against Japan, it should be demonstrated to the Japanese first. "I beg you sir not to pass this off because I happen to be an unknown without influence or name in the public eye."

Stimson, who had urged Marshall to feel "the impress of [the letter's] logic," perhaps found that Marshall felt the impress a little too strongly. Brewster wrote movingly and was obviously a man who cared about people, as Stimson himself did. And as a lawyer, the Secretary cherished logic. But the nuclear age required a more pragmatic logic. To inoculate the world against a new unspeakably brutal war, the present war might have to end with an unspeakably brutal bomb. As Brewster himself pointed out in his letter, he was not a statesman. And neither was Marshall, Stimson apparently felt, however great a soldier he was. Men like Marshall and Leahy, understandably, didn't quite comprehend the political and psychological needs of the new age.

In any case, Stimson and the others agreed with far greater zeal than Marshall did to use the bomb, though some wondered if, in fact, a demonstration announced in advance might not be enough to persuade the Japanese to surrender. Why not drop the bomb on an uninhabited area in Japan or on some small island? At lunch, Arthur Compton posed this question to Stimson, who asked the others for their views. They commented:

The Japanese would suspect trickery and might not even show up at the demonstration site.

The Japanese air force, prewarned, might shoot down the bomb-carrying plane.

The demonstration bomb might be a dud and make the United States look foolish, while at the same time falling into Japanese hands.

The fanatical Japanese military leaders would not be impressed by the mere destruction of buildings and trees.

If the demonstration failed to bring surrender, it might no longer be possible to shock Japan into giving up.

Allied prisoners of war might be sent to the target site as a dare to America.

Was there any way a demonstration might succeed? Oppenheimer was asked.

Oppenheimer was apparently uncomfortable, yet pleased. His voice would now be heard not only on technical matters but on high policy. He was not being asked how to make the bomb; he was being consulted on how to use it. And with a German bomb no longer a threat, the question was more than ever loaded with moral implications. Yet, he must be pragmatic. Seated around him were hard-headed politicians and diplomats who had to make tough decisions based on reality. American boys were dying every day. An invasion of Japan would mean hundreds of thousands more casualties. And Groves, an invited guest and the man who made sure every doubt was laid to rest, was sitting there staring at him. One could almost hear the rustle of pink-sheeted ghosts.

No, Oppenheimer said, he couldn't think of any way a demonstration might succeed. In any case, not more than 20,000, he estimated, would die in a surprise bombing.

After dessert, when the committee had filed back into Stimson's office, Oppenheimer took offense at someone who claimed that "one atomic bomb on an arsenal would not be much different from the effect caused by an Air Corps strike of present dimensions."

Of course it would be different. The visual effect of an atomic bomb would be tremendous. It would be accompanied by a brilliant luminescence that would rise to a height of 10,000 to 20,000 feet. The radioactive effect of the explosion would be dangerous to life for a radius of at least two-thirds of a mile.

No one was going to compare *his* bomb with a bunch of ordinary ones.

As the meeting ended, Stimson stated the committee's conclusions, which formed the basis for those unanimously adopted at another committee meeting the following day:

. . . We should not give the Japanese any warning.

. . . We should not concentrate on a civilian area but should seek to make a profound psychological impression on as many of the inhabitants as possible.

. . . The most desirable target would be a vital war plant employing a large number of workers and closely surrounded by workers' houses.

Would there be any inhabitants left to be psychologically impressed? No one asked.

Certainly not Jimmy Byrnes. He never spoke much when other people were speaking for him. And he never asked questions that might give these people second thoughts. He knew how to ease a bill through the Senate or a bomb through this committee. As he once explained to a reporter:

"If you haven't got the votes, talk along. If you have, keep quiet. Many a bill that might have passed in 30 minutes has been lost because somebody started to explain it."

So Byrnes kept quiet, and no one (according to the minutes) explained, or asked about, the need for dropping the bomb in the first place. How many lives would the bomb save by making an invasion unnecessary? How much chance was there for peace without an invasion *or* a bomb? These were questions for higher authority. The committee's job was to draw conclusions, not to investigate all the facts on which they were based. Anyway, why confuse matters when everybody knew that it didn't make sense to waste a hard-begotten $2 billion bomb? The experts had done their job, and the President could hardly ignore their recommendations.

And he didn't. When Byrnes told him on June 2 what the committee had advised, Truman did not question its views. "With reluctance he had to agree that he could think of no alternative and found himself in accord."

X

Meanwhile, Arthur Compton returned to Chicago, apparently troubled by the thought that he would have to face Szilard and other scientists who were fighting to keep the bomb from being used. Compton had voted to drop the bomb without warning even though he apparently had reservations himself. On May 28, only three days before the committee meeting, he wrote his superiors:

"First in point of urgency is the question of how the first nuclear bomb is to be used. This is much more a political than . . . a military question. It introduces the question of mass slaughter really for the first time in history. . . . Consideration must also be given to the political consequences on the enemy unless their complete extermination is irrevocably decided upon. . . . I merely mention [this question] as one of the urgent problems that have bothered our men because of its many ramifications and humanitarian implications."

Groves was furious. Was Compton trying to sow doubt among the policymakers? On his copy of Compton's letter, he wrote in the margin: "The air raids in Germany were not wholly unmasslike in their effect."

But Groves needn't have worried. Compton was not one to displease his superiors. And he managed to overcome his doubts—or at least make himself think he did—once he realized that the Scientific Panel was expected to endorse the Byrnes line that Groves so firmly backed. Unlike Oppenheimer, Compton did not covet the approval of the establishment, even its upper echelons. Oppenheimer had sought his job at least in part because he wanted a name. Compton had been offered *his* job because he *had* a name. As a Nobel Prize laureate, he hardly needed more recognition.

Compton backed his superiors because he was, despite his status, a humble man who felt an innate trust in them, though he would sometimes fight with Groves over nonpolitical matters such as compartmentalization, which he felt slowed up scientific progress. This *was* his business. But he had no more right to tell his superiors how to conduct a war than *they* had to tell him how to conduct an experiment. He had been asked, however, to give the government advice and so he would give it the advice he knew it wanted to hear.

Nevertheless, Compton was apparently not unhappy when he was asked to keep what happened at the committee meeting a secret from his colleagues in Chicago. At least he wouldn't have to admit that he had, in a sense, "betrayed" many of them by recommending that the bomb be dropped on Japan without warning; he had never even hinted to them that he might do this. Still, he was uncomfortable. For the scientists in Chicago trusted him, especially after he approved the memo Szilard had later shown to Byrnes. Little wonder that he mumbled as the meeting broke up:

"What shall I tell Szilard?"

Even more disturbing was his promise to James Franck. In 1942, Compton had tried to lure Franck from his work in photosynthesis at the University of Chicago into the Metallurgical Laboratory, and Franck, sensitive to the moral implications of the bomb, had agreed on one condition: that he could present his views on using the weapon to the nation's leaders before they reached a decision to use it.

Compton gave his word.

What would Franck say now if he knew that the nation's leaders had already decided to use the bomb, and that Compton himself had recommended the decision?

On arriving in Chicago, Compton found little relief from his dilemma in the uproar caused by Szilard's talk with Byrnes. Groves' security agents had followed Szilard, Bartky, and Urey to Spartanburg, and the general was crying that they committed a grave breach of security by handing a "secret document" (Szilard's memorandum) to Byrnes, who was presumed not to know how to handle secret documents. Later, the general would say:

"To be perfectly blunt about it, Szilard appeared to be interested only in revenge on Hitler. . . . The Japanese had done nothing to the Jews and Szilard was not a bit interested in the American casualties which the landing on Japan would entail."

Groves called Bartky to Washington, grilled him, and recommended that he be fired from his job. But what could he do about Szilard after failing in every attempt so far to get rid of him? He left it to Compton to discipline him for showing Byrnes the memorandum Compton himself had approved!

Compton saw only one way out of his quandary. He summoned the scientists and told them all he could about the role of the Interim Committee and the Scientific Panel. Would they want him to present their ideas about the future use of atomic energy at the next meeting of the panel? The panel would then make recommendations to the Interim Committee.

The decision to use the bomb without warning, of course, had already been made. But let the scientists think their views would be seriously considered.

Compton's listeners were delighted. At last they had a voice at the highest level of government. Yet Szilard and some others were suspicious. As Szilard would write of the Scientific Panel:

"Oppenheimer, we thought, would not oppose the using of the bomb which he had tried so hard to make. Fermi would state his opinion but would not insist that it should be heard, and would not state it a second time. Compton might be against the use of the bomb but he would not want to incur the displeasure of the powers by stressing this point of view. And of Lawrence's position we knew too little to be comforted."

But Compton now acted as if he would fight for the scientists' views with all the ferocity of a tiger protecting its cubs. He set up committees to coordinate ideas, and "kept his promise" to Franck, naming him chairman of the most important group, the Committee on Social and Political Implications, which would deal with the use of the bomb. Franck could now have his say. He began to write a report himself but, finding his knowledge of English wanting, turned his notes over to another committee member, Eugene R. Rabinowitch. But it was Szilard who actually shaped the report.

Many of the scientists were less interested in the use of the bomb during the war than in the development of atomic energy after the war. And some even wondered whether anyone would invest in a postwar program if the bomb was not first dropped on the enemy to dramatize nuclear power. Szilard himself, of course, had earlier wanted to bomb an evacuated German city, though not to promote postwar development but to demonstrate the horrors of nuclear war. Now, however, he would plead a different course, as he had to Byrnes, but toned down a bit to meet the approval of his fellow scientists. Rabinowitch would later say:

"Szilard was responsible for [the] whole emphasis on the problem of the use of the bomb which really gave the report its historical significance—the attempt to prevent the use of the bomb on Japan."

Virtually ignoring all his other work, Szilard analyzed every word of the Franck Report, much as he had the Einstein letter he drafted six years earlier. Then he had begged that the bomb be built; now, in the report, he was begging that it be banned, or at least used without taking human life. . . .

. . . The experience of Russian scientists in nuclear research is entirely sufficient to enable them to retrace our steps within a few years, even if we should make every attempt to conceal them. . . . A quantitative advantage in reserves of bottled destructive power will not make us safe from sudden attack. Just because a potential enemy will be afraid of being 'outgunned and outnumbered,' the temptation for him may be overwhelming to attempt a sudden and unprovoked blow. . . . In no other type of warfare does the advantage lie so heavily with the aggressor. . . .

About a month earlier, the President had heard essentially the same ideas from Stimson. But Szilard, Franck, and Rabinowitch had no way of knowing this. Anyway, Szilard, unlike Stimson, linked this warning to the use of the bomb *during* the war:

> It may be very difficult to persuade the world that a nation which was capable of secretly preparing and suddenly releasing a new weapon as indiscriminate as the rocket bomb and a thousand more times destructive is to be trusted in its proclaimed desire of having such weapons abolished by international agreement. . . . Thus . . . the military advantages and the saving of American lives achieved by the sudden use of atomic bombs against Japan may be outweighed by the ensuing loss of confidence and by a wave of horror and repulsion sweeping over the rest of the world and perhaps even dividing public opinion at home. . . ."

However, if a bomb had to be used,

> a demonstration of the new weapon might best be made before the eyes of the representatives of all the United Nations on the desert or a barren island. . . . After such a demonstration the weapon might be used against Japan if the sanction of the United Nations [and of public opinion at home] were obtained, perhaps a preliminary ultimatum to Japan to surrender or at least evacuate certain regions as an alternative to their total destruction. . . . If an international agreement is not concluded immediately after the first demonstration, this will mean a flying start toward an unlimited arms race. If this race is inevitable, we have every reason to delay its beginning as long as possible in order to increase our head start still further.

In conclusion,

> we believe that these considerations make the use of nuclear bombs for an early unannounced attack against Japan inadvisable.

Szilard was not satisfied with the report, for a vital element was missing—the moral question. After dealing with political leaders, especially Byrnes, he realized that only pragmatic arguments impressed them. They would not refrain from dropping the bomb because 100,000 people or a million would die, or even because all mankind might be in danger. The dangers were too great and the killing too impersonal to translate into a comprehensible image of horror. A man obsessed with winning the next election or going down in the history books as a heroic figure would listen only to politically profitable advice—how to gain more power in the world, how to keep the enemy or potential enemy from matching this power. At the same time, many of the scientists themselves demanded a pragmatic approach. And so Szilard, who wanted to save the planet, had to argue not that dropping the bomb would be morally wrong but that it would be politically ruinous.

The whole Franck committee now approved the report, though other scientists were apparently divided on the question of whether to warn the enemy. How could the report be used? Nobody on the committee wanted to wait for the Scientific Panel to meet again, especially since its views were not entirely trusted. The logical person to give it to was Secretary Stimson, whose power to use the bomb was exceeded only by the President's. Compton was going to Washington shortly; he could deliver it to him.

Would he do it?

Yes, of course. Be glad to.

But it is not sure that Compton was so glad to. He might nettle the Secretary by being a party to an opposition move against the government line that Compton himself had recommended. At the same time, he would be further deceiving the antibomb scientists by making them think he favored their view. But again Compton found a way to wriggle out of his dilemma. Yes, he would deliver the report, but attach a covering letter that would dilute its arguments. Compton would later explain:

"It was necessary for me to point out that the report, while it called attention to difficulties that might result from the use of the bomb, did not mention the probable net saving of many lives, nor that if the bomb were not used in the present war the world would have no adequate warning as to what was to be expected if war should break out again."

Yet the report did not deny that lives would be saved but stated that this saving "may be *outweighed* by the ensuing loss of confidence and by a wave of horror and repulsion sweeping over the rest of the world." On the other hand, was it logical to argue that a whole city of people should be obliterated without warning simply to show how terrible nuclear war was?

Compton's aim, it seems, was to diminish the weight of the report and at the same time demonstrate his loyalty to the powers he served.

While Szilard, Franck, and their colleagues did not realize that they had, in effect, asked the cat to guard the canary, they were suspicious enough to keep a watch of their own. Franck himself traveled to Washington with Compton. The two men went to Stimson's office in the Pentagon, where they were greeted by R. Gordon Arneson, assistant to George Harrison.

They would like to see Secretary Stimson.

Sorry, he was out of the city. (Actually, records show he was in Washington.)

Then they would see Mr. Harrison.

Sorry, he wasn't in either.

It was Saturday and neither man would be in until Monday. Compton couldn't wait, and so he handed the report, with his covering letter enclosed, to Arneson.

They needn't worry, said Arneson. He would see to it that the Secretary received it. The two men then left. On Monday, Arneson turned the report and the letter over to Harrison, who perused them, then showed the documents to Stimson, though it isn't clear whether the Secretary read them.

"Well, this report really ought to be examined and commented upon by the Scientific Panel," Harrison said. It would then be reviewed by the Interim Committee. The record would show that the government was not ignoring the scientists' views.

Stimson agreed.

So instead of Stimson taking the initiative as the scientists had intended, the report would go through channels and be studied by the two bodies that had already advised that the bomb be dropped without warning! It would, in fact, go right back to Compton. Harrison called Compton in Los Alamos, where he was visiting.

Would he please submit the Franck Report to the Scientific

Panel and then tell the Interim Committee what the panel thought about the document?

Yes, of course. Be glad to.

XI

This time Compton apparently *was* glad to. Was it his fault if Stimson couldn't see him? The scientists couldn't blame him for not trying. He had kept his promise to Franck. And now to deal with Franck's report—once and for all.

Actually, not with the report itself. When the four members of the Scientific Panel met in Los Alamos in mid-June, nobody had a copy. Compton did not bother to supply it. Oppenheimer would say after the war:

"We had nothing in writing. [The meeting] was called because Arthur Compton had been asked by the Secretary of War to discuss with us the question, 'What do the scientists think about the use of the bomb?' Certainly this request was promoted, stimulated, by the existence of the Franck Report, maybe by other things, too, but we did not have before us the Franck report when we met to talk about it."

So it was left to Compton to interpret the Franck report for the panel, which thrashed over a question it had already agreed on without seeing the painstakingly phrased written arguments it was supposed to consider. Oppenheimer would also say:

"We didn't know beans about [the military situation]. We didn't know whether [the Japanese] would be caused to surrender by other means or whether the invasion was really inevitable. But in the back of our minds was the notion that the invasion was inevitable because we had been told that."

Not surprisingly, the group concluded once again: "We can propose no technical demonstration likely to bring an end to the war; we can see no acceptable alternative to direct military use."

The Interim Committee then met on June 21 and once again approved the recommendation—also without seeing the Franck report it was judging.

The mysteriously unavailable Franck Report was dead.

XII

But Szilard and his colleagues at Chicago did not know it, and Compton could not and apparently did not wish to enlighten them. But after a while they began to suspect the truth.

"We waited and waited," Rabinowitch would say, "and we had the feeling we could as well have dropped this report into Lake Michigan."

Szilard was the most impatient of all because once again he saw the world heading toward calamity, just as he had in 1939 when the government refused to listen to his warning that it must build a bomb. And his fears grew when, in early July 1945, the scientists in Chicago were forbidden to call Los Alamos. That could mean only one thing: Los Alamos was getting ready to test the bomb and Groves didn't want Chicago to know. Would the Franck Report influence Stimson and the President now, with the machinery of doomsday in high gear?

However doubtful this seemed, Szilard felt he had to make a last desperate effort to save mankind. The Franck Report opposed use of the bomb on pragmatic grounds; he would now oppose it on moral grounds. Even if his new campaign failed, it might at least revive the Franck Report. Szilard realized that Groves would now focus all his anger on him and that some of his own colleagues would resent his "lone wolf" tactics, feeling that wartime was no time for moral preaching. But in studying for his citizenship, which he had recently been granted, he learned the Constitution well, and it clearly stated that "the right to petition shall not be abridged." Now he would exercise this right regardless of men's bloated vanities or barren values. He carefully framed a petition to the President of the United States:

"Atomic bombs are primarily a means for the ruthless annihilation of cities. Once they were introduced as an instrument of war it would be difficult to resist for long the temptation of putting them to such use. Thus a nation which sets the precedent of using these newly liberated forces of nature for the purposes of destruction may have to bear the responsibility of opening the door to an era of devastation on an unimaginable scale. . . . The last few years show a marked tendency toward increasing ruthlessness. At present our Air Forces, striking at the Japanese cities, are using the same methods of warfare which were condemned by American public opinion only a few years ago when applied by the Germans to the cities of England. Our use of atomic bombs in this war could carry the world a long way further on this path of ruthlessness. . . .

"In view of the foregoing, we, the undersigned, respectfully petition that you exercise your power as Commander in Chief to rule that the United States shall not, in the present phase of the war, resort to use of atomic bombs."

In a covering letter to each potential signer, Szilard explained: "As you will see, this petition is based on purely moral considerations. . . . However small the chance might be that our petition may influence the course of events, I personally feel that it would be a matter of importance if a large number of scientists who have worked in this field went clearly and unmistakably on record as to their opposition on moral grounds to the use of these bombs in the present phase of the war.

"Many of us are inclined to say that individual Germans share the guilt for the acts which Germany committed during this war because they did not raise their voices in protest against those acts. Their defense that their protest would have been of no avail hardly seems acceptable even though these Germans could not have protested without running risks to life and liberty. We are in a position to raise our voices without incurring any such risks even though we might incur the displeasure of some of those who are at present in charge of controlling the work on 'atomic power.' The fact that the people of the United States are unaware of the choice which faces us increases our responsibility in this matter since those who have worked on 'atomic power' represent a sample of the population and they alone are in a position to form an opinion and declare their stand."

Szilard sent a copy of the petition to every group leader in the Metallurgical Laboratory and asked him to circulate it within his group. When Groves' security officer at the laboratory, Grover C. Thompson, happened to see a copy, he immediately reported it to the general. As Szilard had expected, Groves was enraged.

Stop circulating the petition! he ordered. Didn't Szilard know that he was violating secrecy by disclosing that the bomb existed?

But Szilard refused to yield. The right to petition was anchored in the Constitution, he replied. And he would later comment, "What the army thought that we thought we were doing all the time, I cannot say."

Reluctant to be charged with countermanding the Constitution, Groves moved cautiously. Very well, let the petition circulate—but it had to go through security channels and could not be shown to scientists who had less information about the bomb than Szilard did. Since Szilard knew more than most of the scientists, this order all but killed the petition.

But in this clash of inflexible wills, Szilard was determined to breathe new life into the petition. He darted from office to office, pleading, demanding, explaining. And finally "about fifty-three scientists" signed, including almost all of the leading physicists. When the chemists refused to sign, Szilard stormed into the chemistry department.

Why? he wanted to know.

Why? Because, explained the chemists, use of the bomb should not be decided on moral grounds. The only important question was: Would more lives be saved by using the bomb or by not using it? And the government knew best.

Szilard was taken aback. He had heard this "utilitarian" argument in Germany.

"That some other issue might be involved in dropping a bomb on an inhabited city and killing men, women, and children did not occur to any of the chemists with whom I spoke," he would bitterly say.

In any event, Szilard plowed ahead. He sent copies of the petition to Wigner, who was now at Oak Ridge, asking him to distribute them there, but security officials blocked their circulation. He also sent copies to a friend in Los Alamos, physicist Edward Creutz, making the same request, and asking that one copy be given to Oppenheimer "for his information." Among the scientists there Szilard hoped to win over was his old friend Edward Teller.

Convince the scientists at Los Alamos to support the Franck Report, he had earlier urged Teller in a letter.

Teller thought the ideas in the report were "good," he would write after the war, but felt he should speak with Oppenheimer before approaching others. He showed Oppenheimer Szilard's letter.

"We should find a good way," Teller advised, "in which a demonstration could be made and life could be spared." Would Oppenheimer object if he tried to line up support for the Franck Report?

Don't do anything! Oppenheimer replied. Szilard was "using

the influence of the scientists in an improper way." Szilard, Teller, and most of those at Los Alamos were not sufficiently informed to advise the government on what to do about so important a political matter. The government knew what it was doing.

Oppenheimer apparently failed to mention that he himself had already recommended to the government that the bomb be dropped without warning.

Teller didn't argue. On July 2, he replied to Szilard:

> I have spent some time thinking about your objections to an immediate military use of the weapon. . . . I decided to do nothing. . . . First of all let me say that I have no hope of clearing my conscience. The things we are working on are so terrible that no amount of protesting or fiddling with politics will save our souls. . . . I worked [on the project] because the problems interested me and I should have felt it a great restraint not to go ahead. I cannot claim that I simply worked to do my duty. A sense of duty could keep me out of such work. . . . If you should succeed in convincing me that your moral objections are valid, I should quit working. I hardly think that I should start protesting.

And no one else at Los Alamos protested either. Oppenheimer made sure that the petition was not circulated there.

Szilard was vexed but not vanquished by his failures. For the sake of mankind's good name, even if God might be the only one around to appreciate it, he would find another way to reach more of the people who had helped him create the monster.

XIII

Groves was apparently worried that Szilard would do just that—and then manage to get to Truman. The man, after all, had gotten to Roosevelt when he wanted to build the bomb. Who knew what Truman, an old Pendergast man, might do if deftly manipulated? After all, Szilard would be backed by some weak and selfish navy men. Leahy was a danger, and so was Undersecretary of the Navy Bard, the Interim Committee member, who had changed his mind about using the bomb. Japan was beaten, Bard now said, and, anyway, it would be inhumane and unfair to drop the weapon on a city without warning. Let Allied envoys meet with Japanese representatives on the China coast and tell them of the bomb. Bard had even talked to Truman personally about this. Bard, Groves would write to himself, had been influenced by junior admirals who, like Leahy, wanted the navy to reap all the glory of victory.

Even Admiral Lewis Strauss, who was special assistant to Secretary of the Navy Forrestal and a man whom Groves respected for his toughness, was pushing for a demonstration; he would drop the bomb over a forest near Tokyo and lay out the huge cryptomeria trees like matchsticks—and Forrestal liked Strauss' idea.

It was too late for Szilard to break into the White House; Truman had left for Potsdam a few days earlier, on July 6. But he might still find some way to reach the President—and it was only days before the bomb was to be tested. Groves couldn't take a chance that Truman would switch course at the last minute. And he couldn't let history blur the greatness of his achievement. He must scrape up evidence showing that most of the scientists opposed Szilard's view. A poll would be the answer—conducted by someone he could trust. Groves hadn't especially trusted Compton up to now; the man couldn't, or wouldn't, even discipline Szilard. But the general knew that Compton was now too committed to a surprise explosion to let his superiors down.

Would Compton please supervise an "opinion poll among those who knew what was going on?"

Yes, of course. Be glad to.

Compton drew up a questionnaire with five alternatives:

1. Use [the bomb] in the manner that is from the military point of view the most effective in bringing about prompt Japanese surrender at minimum cost to our armed forces.
2. Give a military demonstration in Japan to be followed by a renewed opportunity for surrender *before full use* of the weapon is employed.
3. Give an experimental demonstration in this country with representatives of Japan present; followed by a new opportunity for surrender *before full use* of the weapon is employed.

4. Withhold military use of the weapons but make a public experimental demonstration of their effectiveness.

5. Maintain as secret as possible all developments of our new weapons and refrain from using them in this war.

The ambiguity of some of these proposals was striking—and baffling. For was not Compton a Nobel Prize winner celebrated for the precision of his scientific papers?

Number 1 appears to advocate dropping the bomb without warning, yet the "manner" of its use is not specifically spelled out.

In Number 2, what did a "military demonstration" mean? This is especially unclear because the demonstration would take place before "full use of the weapon is employed." If a "military demonstration" did not mean "full use," did it mean a demonstration on an uninhabited area or an evacuated city?

And why was there no mention of a simple *verbal* warning?

In Chicago, many scientists shown the questionnaire had never really considered the question of how to use the bomb, yet they were given only a few minutes to make their choice. While more than half of the scientists in Chicago were polled, apparently none were in Los Alamos, Berkeley, Oak Ridge, or other project centers, though, Compton would say, Oppenheimer and Lawrence sounded out "the opinions of their men." How were they sounded out, and what were the results? This was never made clear.

The results of the Chicago poll weren't very clear, either:

Number 1: 15 percent
Number 2: 46 percent
Number 3: 26 percent
Number 4: 11 percent
Number 5: 2 percent

Only the 15 percent who favored Number 1 appeared to want the bomb to be used as it ultimately was—without giving the Japanese any warning at all that it would be dropped. For no other alternative called for "full use" of the bomb without some warning. Thus, 83 percent—Numbers 2, 3, and 4—presumably wanted a warning. Compton, however, turned the figures around to find that voters who favored Numbers 1, 2, and 3, that is, 87 percent, "voted for [the bomb's] military use, at least if after other means were tried this was found necessary to bring surrender." "Other means" apparently signified a prior noncombat demonstration.

And in a letter to Groves' deputy, Colonel Nichols, Compton stressed that Number 2 was "the strongly favored procedure," and that "this coincides with my own preference and is, as nearly as I can judge, the procedure that has found most favor in all informed groups where the subject has been discussed."

But Number 2 called for a "military demonstration in Japan to be followed by a renewed opportunity for surrender *before full use* of the weapon" was employed. If this was Compton's preference, how could it be reconciled with his preference as expressed in the recommendation of the Scientific Panel—drop the bomb without any warning? Compton approved the operations that would destroy Hiroshima and Nagasaki, and their destruction reflected *full use* of the bomb. How then could Number 2 apply to those holocausts? Compton never explained.

Many of the "informed groups" referred to by Compton protested. They had voted for Number 2 because they thought it called for a demonstration on an uninhabited area *before* "full use" of the weapon was employed. But Compton wanted to feel that his colleagues supported his view, or at least the view of the powers he would not defy. And Groves wanted to be sure that if Szilard did somehow get to Truman, the President could be shown that the man was out of step with the great majority of scientists.

Everything, it seemed, was going as Groves had planned. Oppenheimer's force, working nonstop to complete the bomb before the Potsdam conference, would have it ready on time. And the bomb test would certainly succeed. When it did, *he*, General Groves, would end the war—unless, of course, Potsdam ruined it for him by causing Japan to surrender before the bomb could be dropped. And this might happen if Truman and his boys revealed its existence to Hirohito—or to Stalin, who would immediately send his troops charging into Manchuria. Still, Groves was soothed by Jimmy Byrnes' assurances.

Don't worry, Byrnes had said to him, neither the Russians nor the Japanese would be told.

And Byrnes could be trusted. He understood the need to drop the bomb on Japan before it was too late.

XIV

"Jimmy, kiss the Bible."

Byrnes kissed the Bible and then handed it to Truman, asking him to kiss it, too.

As the President put it to his lips, the sweating crowd that jammed the White House veranda overlooking the Rose Garden burst into laughter. Byrnes was being sworn in as Secretary of State on the steamy afternoon of July 3, and it was doubtful that any of his forty-seven predecessors had taken the oath in such a lighthearted atmosphere. How good to see the two most powerful men in the country so amiable with each other, as if the scent of roses had a symbolic meaning. Yet some of the laughter was uneasy. For one of the men was President, and the way they seemed to relate to each other, it was a bit difficult to tell which of them was.

Surely Byrnes wouldn't be the one to point him out. For would he not be, in a sense, the president for foreign affairs? Three days later the pair would leave for Potsdam, Germany, where the new Secretary would try to put the world in order, or at least change the kind of order that Roosevelt had agreed to at Yalta and cleverly hidden with Byrnes' unwitting help.

And Truman had full confidence in Byrnes. Understandably, since he still lacked full confidence in himself. He was not at all enthusiastic about meeting with two of the most forceful leaders in history after occupying the White House for only about three months. The day Byrnes was sworn in, Truman ruefully wrote his family:

"I am getting ready to go see Stalin and Churchill, and it is a chore. . . . Wish I didn't have to go, but I do, and it can't be stopped now."

Yet his confidence had risen sharply in recent weeks. The bomb would explode in the desert of Alamogordo at about the time he would be facing Stalin across the table in a spine-tingling game that could determine the fate of mankind. And if the weapon worked as well as Groves and the scientists expected it to, he would have the master card in his hand—and thus know exactly how to deal to Stalin. Or at least Jimmy Byrnes would.

Yes, next to the bomb, Jimmy was his greatest asset. Besides, the Secretary owed it to him to get him out of the Yalta fix. It was

Jimmy, after all, who had spread the word after Yalta that Roosevelt had squeezed concessions out of Stalin as if he were a tube of jelly. What would happen to the newly born Truman Administration if that fantasy burst and the truth became known?

Holding the card, of course, did not mean Truman would play it at Potsdam. He would wait until the bomb was dropped on a Japanese city. The thought, apparently, no longer terrorized him, for he had gradually realized that the decision to use the weapon had been made for him, that the machine could not be stopped. Did anybody ask him whether the bomb should be dropped? Truman accepted the inevitable with the help of some tortuous if soothing logic:

"The discovery of the ability to split the atom," he would later say, "is in the same category as the discovery of gunpowder as a war weapon. When artillery was first introduced into military use, whenever it was possible to capture artillerymen, they were hanged without a trial because they were considered murderers to use such a weapon."

The bomb might, in any case, make a loud enough noise to persuade Stalin that Yalta was a mistake. No, the Russian dictator could not run wild in Europe and the Far East. He would have to adjust to the realities of power—as Roosevelt had at Yalta. And it was Byrnes' job to see that he did. Truman could appreciate Stimson's view that Stalin should be enticed into cooperation and not frightened into it, but Byrnes convinced the President that the cloakroom intimidation they both understood so well would be more effective.

Stimson the moralist wanted to save man. Leahy the traditionalist wanted to save man's honor. But Byrnes the pragmatist had a more limited goal: He wanted to save the man in the White House, and thus the nation. Was this not ultimately the world's best hope, anyway? Yes, Harry Truman might be too small for the job, and he had no grand design for protecting humanity from the bomb—or even from communism. But, with Jimmy's conniving help, he would stand up to Stalin in defending American interests, even if there was no cloakroom at Potsdam.

Standing a few feet away from Truman and Byrnes in the Rose Garden was, inevitably, Admiral Leahy, dourly smiling amid the laughter. Leahy, of course, would be joining them on the presidential boat sailing to Europe. Who else could so exquisitely interpret the military view for Truman? Or tell him with such unabashed frankness what he did wrong? Or remain so loyal when his advice was so often ignored? Who else could remind him that if, as President, he *had* to make cruel decisions, he shouldn't . deceive himself into thinking they conformed to knightly tradition.

Some distance away, merged into the multitude, was Secretary Stimson, who had come late and would leave early. He apparently didn't even smile at the Rose Garden camaraderie that charmed the others. For it meant to him that the world was in danger; Truman had chosen the Byrnes' formula for using the bomb over his. As if to underscore this decision, the President had not even invited him on the trip to Potsdam, where the Americans would decide what to do with the bomb. The bomb that *he* had nurtured to maturity! He had had to ask Truman for an invitation and would know the answer only that afternoon.

Perhaps he should have resigned long ago. But when rumors spread that he might, the President wouldn't let him go.

"I want to tell you right here," he told Stimson on June 6, "that when I want you to leave the Cabinet you will hear it from me and not through the press. I have great confidence in you and I want you to stay with me if you can through the war."

Deeply moved, Stimson said he wanted to help the President out but did not wish to become "a passenger in the boat." Also, he admitted, "I was getting to a stage where I had to take short cuts now and then and where it took more time for my judgment than heretofore. [But I] still thought that my mind when it worked was working all right."

Truman laughed. *He* thought so, too, and fully trusted Stimson's judgment.

The Secretary was overjoyed. "The President's manner," he would write in his diary, "was so friendly and confident that it was a great reassurance to me as to our relations and cheered me up throughout the day."

But his joy gradually dissolved as the time for Truman's departure approached and he was still waiting for an invitation to go along. Could the President so recklessly disregard what might happen to the world?

XV

The peace of Highhold had stimulated new ideas in Stimson's mind about what to do with the bomb. The clergyman in him had suddenly taken charge, with the prodding of Grew, Forrestal, and McCloy. Stimson no longer wanted to blow up a city and *then* seek peace; he would now seek peace first, and if *that* failed, blow up a city. Yes, he would be jeopardizing his plan for shocking Stalin into more decent behavior. But could the clergyman permit the sacrifice of tens of thousands of souls, even for an overriding cause, without giving them one last chance to be saved?

Thus, Stimson, who in late May had opposed Grew's plea to warn Japan that it must surrender, now, with the bomb about to poison its skies, *was* ready to give such a warning. He carefully composed a memorandum for the President: Japan, he urged, should be warned to lay down its arms or face "utter destruction," and "given . . . ample time to permit a national reaction to set in." But the surrender would be *conditional*. As he had long felt, "we should add that we do not exclude a constitutional monarchy under her present dynasty," since "it would substantially add to the chances of acceptance."

The warning would promise the Japanese that they would not be destroyed as a race or as a nation, and that they could rebuild their economy once it was purged "of its militaristic influences." It would be issued "before the actual invasion [had] occurred and while the impending destruction . . . [had] not yet reduced her to fanatical despair."

And if Japan ignored the warning? "It was of course well forward in our minds," Stimson would later say, "that the bomb would be the best possible sanction."

On July 2, Stimson went to the White House and handed his memorandum and a draft of the warnings to Truman, remarking that the draft, which Grew and Forrestal had approved, could not be completed "until we knew what was going to be done with the S-1." The President read the documents but would not commit himself. Finally, Stimson's allotted time was up, and Truman had still not invited the Secretary to Potsdam. Well, he would bring it up himself.

Was the President afraid to ask him to go to Potsdam because he feared he "could not take the trip"?

Truman smiled. Yes, that was it. He wanted to save Stimson from overexertion.

But he was perfectly well, Stimson protested. The surgeon general had endorsed his condition. He "did not wish to push into . . . the President's . . . party at all," Stimson would write in his diary, "but thought that he ought to be able to get advice from people on the secretarial level from the War Department who were not purely military but were civilian."

Truman delayed a reply until after the swearing-in ceremony for Byrnes the following day, prolonging the agony with this seemingly brutal twist of the knife.

Finally, after the ceremony, Stimson got his answer—and would leave Truman's office with his wound only partially healed. The President, he recorded in his diary, "would like to have me to be somewhere near [him in Potsdam to] help out."

Could he bring along McCloy?

"All right."

"The whole matter was done very quickly," Stimson would report, as if emphasizing his relief that the painful encounter was over.

Stimson was not invited to sail on the presidential cruiser and, in Potsdam, would not be with the President but "somewhere near" him. Yet he had to go. After the terrible struggle to build the bomb, after all his dreams for the postwar atomic era, he must at any cost be on the spot when the most crucial decision in history was made.

Why had Truman treated him so shabbily? Did Byrnes have something to do with it? Stimson seemed to believe he did. No one was to interfere with Jimmy's plan to bludgeon Stalin into accepting U.S. demands with an atomic threat. And Stimson's last-minute scheme for a prior warning that might obviate the need for dropping the bomb could jeopardize the impact of this threat. Nor was Byrnes thrilled by the thought of telling the Japanese they could keep their Emperor. This was political dynamite. The American people would not stand for such appeasement. Anyway, he was in no hurry to end the war before the bomb was dropped.

Would Byrnes now resent him all the more for having persuaded Truman to let him attend the conference? Stimson wondered. Would he freeze him out of the talks in Potsdam? Whatever his own feelings, he must remain on good terms with Jimmy.

"I fear," Stimson would confide to his diary on July 4, "that he might think I was encroaching on his ground. So I called him up on the telephone and fortunately caught him. We had a very pleasant talk together. . . . I expressed my strong relief at having him in his post. He seemed very glad to have my help and then I told him exactly how I came to decide to go, and he seemed perfectly satisfied and glad to have me there."

If Stimson thus had to rationalize his humiliation, he would, even in his anguish, make one last attempt to avoid sacrificing Japanese cities unnecessarily and to keep Byrnes from sacrificing the world inadvertently. He must somehow guide Truman at the conference.

XVI

Jimmy Byrnes, however, was just as determined to keep the President to himself, though it wasn't always easy, especially with a coterie of Missouri comrades constantly lurking in their hometown hero's shadow. On the S.S. *Augusta* en route to Potsdam via Antwerp, Byrnes had hoped to spend almost every minute briefing his master on what to say at the conference. But Truman didn't seem in the mood. He preferred the more carefree company of his old chums, and the newsmen, too, particularly at the poker table in the evening. Was he now *that* confident? And the bomb hadn't even been tested yet!

As one of Truman's poker partners, Robert G. Nixon of the International News Service, would say:

"Byrnes wasn't getting very far with [Truman] really because he [Truman] was out on the deck walking—going from stem to stern . . . down in the engine room, in the galley, all over the place."

Finally, after one poker game, Byrnes came to Nixon "very much perturbed, not in a smiling, jocular fashion at all, and said, 'Mr. Nixon, will you boys . . . please leave the President alone?'"

"Mr. Secretary," Nixon replied, "what are you talking about?"

"I mean leave him alone in the evening. Stop occupying all of his hours. I've got to tell him what's supposed to go on at this conference."

The newsman apologized but replied: "I have no control over

this. . . . Why don't you go to the President and ask him to leave *us* alone?"

Byrnes walked away in frustration. Maybe in Potsdam, where Truman would be playing diplomatic poker with Stalin and Churchill, he would realize that he should listen more closely to Jimmy Byrnes. And he did. Almost as soon as he and Byrnes, together with Leahy and a few assistants, moved into the "Little White House" in the resort town of Babelsberg on the outskirts of Potsdam near Berlin. Here in this lakeside mansion surrounded on three sides by a magnificent garden of trees and shrubbery, Byrnes was able to corner the President and, with only Leahy around to meddle, brief him with final details on how to alter the Yalta agreements with the backing of the bomb.

The bomb test and the Potsdam conference had both been postponed twenty-four hours; so on the following day, July 16, while Potsdam could witness a great explosion when the Big Three began dividing up the world, New Mexico would witness a great explosion that could signal the ultimate *end* of the world. But now news came that Stalin had suffered a slight heart attack en route to Potsdam and would be arriving late, forcing the conference to be delayed for another day. The bomb would thus release its fury a day *before* the leaders in Potsdam would meet to release theirs, giving Truman and Byrnes advance notice on how much fury they should vent.

The tension grew as the atomic age inched toward a spectacular dawn. Within hours the two American leaders, if all went well, would have their master card. And then they could start shaping the postwar world to fit American design. As Truman would say:

"If [the bomb] explodes as I think it will, I'll certainly have a hammer on those boys."

And if it didn't? Truman—and Byrnes—could not bring themselves to imagine such a calamity. How could they ever explain away to the American public the most expensive and gigantic "white elephant" in history?

Chapter 15

THE
OUTSIDER

I

In Moscow, Japanese Ambassador Naotake Sato could not bring himself to imagine the calamity that would befall Japan if it didn't agree to virtual unconditional surrender as demanded by the Potsdam Declaration. And he had warned Foreign Minister Togo that Russia was in no mood to mediate peace. But he was nevertheless ordered to clear the way for Prince Konoye's pilgrimage on behalf of the Emperor. Molotov, however, was in Potsdam with Stalin helping to carve up the world and returned only on the morning of August 6, the day of the bomb.

Before the Soviet minister could unpack, Sato was on the phone to the Foreign Ministry pleading for an urgent interview.

Sorry, the minister could only see him two days later, on August 8.

Well, at least a date was set. Sato was relieved, even though he felt the prince's visit would fail and embarrass the Emperor. The ambassador was to find out how Potsdam shaped Soviet policy. Would Russia mediate peace between Japan and the Allies? Would it join the Allies in the war against Japan? Sato was as realistic as

Togo and even more frank, for he had the advantage of being able to speak, as he put it, "without reserve." The ambassador was far from home and didn't have to face the militarists every day as they nervously fingered their swords. Togo, on the other hand, even though outspoken, couldn't yet demand that Japan agree to surrender "unconditionally" and reasonably expect to escape a fatal swish of steel.

In fact, he was already taking an enormous risk just by keeping Sato in his job. For the military was calling the ambassador an "appeaser" and a "traitor" and pressing for his recall. But Togo resisted. To change ambassadors at this critical stage of the war would be disastrous, he argued. Not a day could be lost in seeking ties with Russia that would keep it from invading Manchuria and possibly entice it to mediate a *conditional* peace. This argument perhaps saved Togo's life, and Sato's as well. Surely no brass band would have been at the dock to welcome the ambassador back.

But as a master diplomat, Sato didn't enjoy the martial sounds of the brass band anyway. He preferred the softer sounds of reasoned debate. Few Japanese diplomats had won greater international respect than Sato, who had served as ambassador in many capitals, including Warsaw, Brussels, and Paris, and represented Japan in the League of Nations at Geneva. In a small Geneva restaurant frequented by foreign diplomats, the walls were plastered with caricatures of international celebrities, and among them was one of Sato, with his large head topping a 5-foot ramrod of a body, his lips stubbornly zipped under a thin mustache, his eyebrows knitted in righteous anger, his dark hair sleekly combed back. Underneath, the legend read:

"If Sato tells a lie, the sun will rise in the west."

Actually, this legend was not quite accurate. Sato began lying when the sun began rising in the east—the Japanese sun. He had to lie, for he was Japan's League of Nations delegate when the military plunged into Manchuria in 1931, to the dismay of the world. While Henry Stimson pressed for sanctions against Japan, Sato sweatingly tried to defend his country, spitting out each word as if he had swallowed a poisoned rice cake. What could a diplomat do when his country did something shameful? Resort to violence was uncivilized and reflected a dangerous feeling of superiority, in his view. And unlike Togo, he wasn't willing to accept an aggressive action once it became a fait accompli. Such an action was wrong, whether it succeeded or not. Not necessarily because it was immoral, but because it inevitably bred violence, which could ultimately boomerang against the initiator.

II

If Sato's approach to Japan's destiny was less opportunistic than Togo's, his attitude toward Japan's cultural code was more rigid. He felt part of the social network and more burdened with its terrible obligations. Though deeply attached to his parents, he did not hesitate as a teenage schoolboy to bid them good-bye and let another family adopt him. His father felt obligated to this family to give it a male heir, and young Naotake felt obligated to be that heir when his father wrote him a touching note proposing the switch. He was shattered by this sudden thrust into a new life with its tangle of emotional ties, but could he violate *ko* to his father?

And so the boy, whose original family name was Tanaka, became a Sato—with a ready-made wife. One of the Sato daughters, his stepsister, would marry him when they came of age so that their heirs would have real Sato blood. At the same time, to further interlink the families, another Sato daughter would wed Naotake's elder brother and become a Tanaka.

Sato's dedication to the rules of Japanese society was innate, for he came from a proud samurai family with a tradition of making any sacrifice to meet an obligation. When his second son, Kojiro, was departing for the front in 1944, Sato wrote him a letter of encouragement from Moscow reminding him of the Tanaka tradition. In the sixteenth century, he pointed out, the original ancestor of their family had sacrificed his life in a feud with a rival lord who had trampled on the name of his master, Lord Tsugaru. For generations afterwards, the family remained the loyal vassals of the powerful but small Tsugaru clan in Honshu's northernmost prefecture, Aomori. During the Meiji revolution in 1867, three Tanaka brothers, including Sato's father, fought with the clan on the Imperial side.

Sato himself was born in 1882 in Osaka, where his father had been a police chief under the Home Ministry. As a child Sato lived like a nomad, moving with his family from city to city, wherever his father was transferred. He especially enjoyed life in the primitive town of Saga City in Kyushu, where he lived in an old bat-ridden house with snakes and blue-tailed lizards crawling through the garden and foxes crying in the distance. The fox offered him his first test of diplomacy. Though he was afraid of the animal, which, it was said, bewitched people, he found a way to get back a chicken one had stolen. He left a plate of his favorite dish, boiled tofu (bean curd), for the supposedly guilty fox, and the fox (or whoever the thief was) had the decency to return the chicken.

While in Saga City, young Sato learned another lesson, too: that violence could only breed misfortune. In 1892, the bloodiest election-day riots in Japanese history exploded throughout the country, and Sato's father, as police chief, found himself in the midst of the chaos. With eight dead and almost one hundred injured, the townspeople blamed the police chief and forced him and his family to flee to another city, which in turn chased them out. Violence had made his father a virtual pariah, even though, in the boy's view, he had simply been following orders.

Sato thus began to sublimate the samurai qualities of toughness and tenacity into peaceful channels that would make many friends call him a "samurai in Western clothing." It was his mother who first encouraged this rechanneling of his heritage, for though she treasured her own family's samurai values, she began to feel that the sword was a primitive and outmoded means of asserting them. Illiterate herself, she nevertheless gave her six children a progressive education and sent them to school to learn the exploits of Amaterasu, among other prescribed subjects, dressed not in the usual kimono but, symbolically, in Western-style boots, short pants, and coats. This display of modernity cruelly made them targets of class ridicule, but the ridicule was excellent training for the lonely moments in later life when Sato would have to defy his peers in order to save the nation.

After being adopted into his new family, Sato's stepfather, a diplomat, urged him to take the Foreign Ministry examination. Sato did, and in 1905 he and only four other candidates were admitted to the ministry. The following year he was posted to St. Petersburg, capital of Tsarist Russia, as a junior diplomat. Here he lived with a Russian family and grew to admire the people whom his country had beaten in war only a year earlier. They accepted defeat as a single misfortune that would not duly change their daily lives. No, a military defeat did not have to mean the end of the world.

In 1914, Sato was transferred to Harbin, Manchuria, where as consul general he learned in a concrete way that the sword had two edges. When the Bolsheviks threatened to seize Siberia during the Russian Revolution in 1918, Sato, sensing danger for Japan, called for the Emperor's forces to join Allied troops pouring into the region. But he soon realized that all the Emperor's horses and all the Emperor's men could not put Tsarist Russia back together again.

Pull the troops out, he then counseled Tokyo, and let Japan and the Allies negotiate with the Bolsheviks. He could not have guessed that twenty-seven years later he would be pleading with the "Bolsheviks" to mediate peace between Japan and the Allies!

In 1921, Sato was sent to Paris as first secretary and remained in Europe for more than a decade. As head of the Japan Office of the League of Nations in Geneva in the late 1920s, he made a major impact on world diplomacy, working for the cause of world harmony and struggling to give Japan a leading international role as a parliamentary democracy.

But then came the Mukden Incident, and parliamentary democracy no longer had meaning in Japan. Nor did Sato's speeches, which were now dictated to the rhythms of modern day swordsmen crying "Banzai!"

"I know so well," Sato would later say, "what a sad predicament one might fall into when a country tries to carry out a policy against the majority will of the world."

Finally, in February 1933, the predicament grew worse. The League condemned Japanese aggression and Japan dropped out of the organization to become a "forlorn and crestfallen orphan."

After serving as ambassador to France, Sato, shattered by Japan's headlong drive toward "disaster," decided to retire, but in March 1937 he reluctantly accepted the post of foreign minister in the hope of patching up relations with China before it was too late. But it was already too late. After three months the Cabinet toppled, and a month later Japanese troops were flinging themselves into the boiling Chinese caldron that would shortly overflow and turn the whole Pacific into an ocean of fire.

It was in November 1941, less than a month before Pearl Harbor, that Sato returned to government—as adviser to Foreign

Minister Togo. He pressed for a compromise in the final talks with
the United States even after Secretary of State Hull demanded
complete Japanese evacuation of the Asian continent. And when
Togo said he would resign, Sato was among the peacemakers who
pleaded with him not to.

"No one could do any better," he argued.

Togo finally agreed to stay.

Fine! But staying wasn't enough. Togo, Sato urged, must not
stop negotiating. Not even if the chances for war were a thousand
to one. Compromise! Give the fox his bean curd.

But Togo was too embittered by the Hull note to listen. He was
already a captive of the gods.

III

Sato left Togo's office with a "feeling heavier than lead" and the
whine of the fox echoing faintly in a corner of his mind. But
shortly it was drowned out by the explosion at Pearl Harbor, and
he rationalized that while Japan was almost certain to lose the war,
it had to learn defeat to appreciate the rewards of peace and democracy. Meanwhile, all he could do was keep pushing the peace
button in the hope that it would set off an alarm and force his
country to come to terms with the Allies while it still had the
strength to negotiate.

Within a month, Togo asked Sato to be the ambassador to
Russia, a pivotal position for determining the kind of peace Japan
would ultimately get. Sato's first reaction was surprise.

He was "too old" to go to a "hardship post" like Russia, though
he was only 60. Besides, he felt, the burden was too great. Soviet-
Japanese relations were "hanging by a hair"—the Neutrality Pact.
Now that Japan was at war with Russia's allies, the United States
and Britain, the hair might suddenly break. True, Stalin had the
German invaders on his mind, but would he attack Japan if he
managed to push back the Germans? Could Sato persuade Stalin
to abide by the Neutrality Pact and stay out of the Pacific war? If he
couldn't, the lesson for the Empire might be fatal.

But finally, when Togo appealed to his patriotism, Sato started
savoring the vodka. In March 1942, he bade good-bye to his wife
and children, who would go to live in the country, and climbed

aboard the Trans-Siberian train bound for Kuibyshev in eastern
Russia, where the diplomatic corps had been moved the previous
fall because the Germans were threatening Moscow. Hardly had
he settled in the ramshackle building that served as both embassy
and residence, when he visited Moscow to urge Molotov to stay
neutral in the Pacific war.

Russia, replied Molotov, "regarded any promise it had made as
binding and would live up to its obligations."

But Sato felt as if he were "walking on thin ice," and after
several months he could almost feel the ice crumbling under his
feet as the Germans found themselves unable to wrest Stalingrad,
and the Japanese proved unable to rule the Pacific. Would Stalin
long resist the temptation to poke through the ice?

Stalin resisted. But finally, in November 1944, he began poking. Japan was a "habitual aggressor," he charged in a speech
commemorating the anniversary of the Russian Revolution.

Sato knocked furiously on Molotov's door. What did Stalin
mean?

His master was only referring to the past, replied Molotov. Not
to the present. Sato shouldn't worry so much.

But Sato worried. Did the statement mean that Russia would
abrogate the Neutrality Pact? It could do this in April 1945, giving
one year's notice. Stalin's charge was a bad omen.

And so was the Yalta Conference in February 1945. As soon as
Molotov returned to Moscow, Sato was again pounding on the
door. Was the Pacific war broached at Yalta?

The Pacific war? Certainly not. Soviet-Japanese relations were
a "matter exclusively between the USSR and Japan."

Sato was sure Molotov was lying. But he forced himself to think
positively. He cabled Tokyo:

> Molotov . . . was amiable and smiling, and I was con-
> scious of the warmth of his personality. . . . Judging from
> [his] manner of speaking, there is little doubt that the An-
> glo-Americans . . . have vigorously pushed their schemes
> to drag Russia into the war against Japan. . . . [But] . . . I
> do not expect any change in Russia's attitude.

About two months later, on April 5, Molotov summoned Sato
to another meeting, and this time he wasn't smiling. He stiffly

read a statement: Russia would not renew the Neutrality Pact! Conditions had changed since it was signed four years earlier. Japan was helping Russia's enemy, Germany, and was at war with Russia's allies. The pact, therefore, had become meaningless.

Shock! After all his plans, his ploys, his prayers. Sato stumbled out into the chilly Moscow spring and headed for his embassy, which, together with all diplomatic missions, had moved back to the capital as the Nazis were pushed westward. With trembling voice, he dictated a cable to Tokyo announcing the news and adding:

Nothing more regrettable could have taken place. May God grant peace to the heart of the Emperor. I certainly have disappointed the hopes of our people, and have no excuse to offer the government. . . . I feel very deeply that I cannot avoid responsibility for this development, and I therefore humbly tender my resignation.

But Sato's resignation was rejected. Suzuki and Togo had just taken office and they didn't need the problem of breaking in a new ambassador. Sato had tried his best to improve relations with Russia, and it wasn't his fault if Russia abrogated the pact. Besides, the government expected the move.

IV

In his desolation, Sato walked the streets of Moscow, sensitive even to "special glances" of passers-by who, he imagined, now viewed the Japanese as "enemies." Russia's reasons, he was sure, were simply a pretext. Yet he refused to let himself believe the worst—that Stalin was planning to attack Manchuria. No, the Russian leader probably made this crude gesture to placate America and Britain, which naturally wanted him to attack. Who knew what they offered him in return for ending the pact? Perhaps a slice of Europe. But if Stalin did not go to war against Japan, his allies would find they got very little for their concessions. And, maybe, their disappointment would aggravate the friction among the three allies.

Japan must make sure that Russia stayed out of the Pacific war. No provocations, Sato warned Togo, for Stalin was probably wait-

ing for the chance to coerce Japan into agreeing to all his demands. Tokyo must free confiscated Soviet ships in Hong Kong,
restore Russian property in Manchuria and China, and settle all
other disputes with Russia. But of course, "we must avoid making
fools of ourselves." Stalin shouldn't know that Japan was already
on its knees and licking his boots. Why should he negotiate if he
felt that Japan considered itself on the verge of collapse? Nevertheless, Japan, Sato argued, must accept the Russian decision to abrogate the pact "openly" and "with submissiveness" and do nothing
to make matters worse.

But matters were soon bad enough. Sato's warning of Soviet
coercion crystallized into a storm of complaints thundering out of
Moscow: Why were Japanese soldiers seizing Soviet-inhabited
apartments in Shanghai? What was holding up the construction of
an air-raid shelter for the Soviet embassy in Tokyo? And most
ominous of all, an average of thirty trains a day carrying troops,
tanks, guns, planes, and supplies were grinding eastward through
the Siberian wilderness.

Did this mean war? Were the Russians about to plunge into
Manchuria or let American bombers take off from Siberian air
fields on their murderous missions? Sato grew panicky, as he urged
Tokyo one day to strengthen Japanese defenses in Manchuria and
prepare for a "war of attrition," and the next to make more, more,
more concessions. Russia was "planning to seize the power of life
and death over Japan," he cabled Togo. And if it attacked? Then
"Japan would have no choice but to come to a decision quickly, fly
into her arms and, resolving to eat dirt, to put up with all the
sacrifices in order to save the national structure [Imperial sys-
tem]."

Togo was equally disconsolate. He agreed: "We must not antagonize Russia!"

But his cry was rooted not simply in fear but in subtle Oriental
logic. The military was as frightened as he was by the vision of
Russian hordes smashing through Japanese lines in Manchuria.
But that fright could be the key to peace. Now was the time to
warm up relations with Russia and persuade it to mediate an "acceptable" peace. He whipped off a cable to Sato on June 30:

Urge Molotov to accept proposals that Hirota had given Ambassador Malik.

Sato fretted. What proposals? No one had even told him about the Hirota-Malik talks until now. Anyway, it seemed "extremely unlikely," he cabled back on July 5, "that Russia would flout the Anglo-Americans and the opinion of the entire world by supporting Japan's war effort with either moral or material means."

Togo curtly retorted: "Your opinions notwithstanding, please carry out my orders." Didn't Sato realize that the military was beginning to call him treacherous and demanding his recall?

Sato "dragged" himself to Molotov's office.

Had His Excellency received the Japanese proposals from Ambassador Malik?

The detailed report had not yet arrived, said Molotov. Sato shouldn't worry. The Foreign Ministry would reply in due course.

Just as he thought! In due course, Sato feared, Japan could be dead. And his fear was fed by the long talks Chinese Foreign Minister Soong was having with Stalin. Did these talks mean they were conspiring to attack Japan?

"*Nyet,*" Molotov replied, but Sato was still suspicious. He stalked back to the embassy and cabled Togo:

> I cannot help but feel that the end result of negotiating with the Soviet government on the basis of [the Hirota] offers will be that our own uneasiness will be made glaringly apparent, the self-confidence of the Soviet government will be even further heightened, and she will thus be less inclined than ever to accept our proposals. . . . There is no alternative but to attempt to work out our own destiny by our own efforts. . . . [Let us not pin] our hopes on the utterly impossible.

V

This cable did not surprise Togo; he had already surmised Russia's reaction. He would now go a step further. In another cable to Sato on July 11, he stressed the gravity of Japan's situation. In fact, "even the termination of the war is now being considered privately." Therefore, Sato should sound out Molotov on Russia's willingness to serve as a peace mediator—but without giving "the impression that we wish to use the Soviet Union to terminate the war." If Russia wasn't interested, there was no use exposing Japan's desperation.

Togo then began to worry about the Soviet reaction. Would the Russians think Japan wanted a peace that the Anglo-Americans would never agree to? Four hours later he sent another cable telling Sato what else to tell Molotov:

> We consider the maintenance of peace in Asia as an aspect of maintaining world peace. We have no intention of annexing or taking possession of the areas which we have been occupying . . . ; we hope to terminate the war with a view to establishing and maintaining a lasting peace.

Sato was stunned by the two cables. Didn't Togo understand that Japan could not depend on Russia to make peace?

The ambassador still went for walks, but now he was oblivious of people's glances or even of the shadowy secret police agents who were constantly following him. He ate little, drank much. How could he bear to sit by while his country was being destroyed day by day. Even his own uninhabited home in Tokyo had been burned to the ground. The war had to end—now!

He cabled Togo on July 12, criticizing the foreign minister's continued use of nothing more than "pretty little phrases":

> It is an unfortunate fact that Japan is no longer in a position to be responsible for peace in East Asia. . . . Is there any sense in continuing the war no matter how many hundreds of thousands of our able-bodied men and no matter how many millions of our city people are sacrificed? . . . The government should make the great decision. Once it does, there may perhaps be some hope of getting the Soviet government to lend its good offices toward terminating the war. But there can be no doubt that the result which would face us in that event would approximate unconditional surrender. . . .

Unconditional surrender! Sato had embraced the forbidden solution, clearly and firmly. He had stepped beyond the bounds of Amaterasu's universe. Sadly, he added:

I have heard that . . . His Majesty is greatly concerned.
I find these dreadful and heartbreaking things unbearable.
. . . However, in international relations there is no mercy,
and facing reality is unavoidable. . . . I beg your understanding.

Sato didn't need to beg. Togo understood and in fact sympathized with his ambassador's views. But Sato was safe in Moscow,
while Togo could practically feel the edge of the sword. If the
foreign minister himself made such a statement, the fanatics
would probably kill him, seize the government, and take the Emperor prisoner. Then they would fight the enemy to the last Japanese. True, the Soviet Union wasn't likely to remove the boulders
on the road toward peace. But it was the only country the military
would appeal to. And if Stalin refused to mediate? Perhaps the
warmongers would then realize that the situation was hopeless,
that the Soviet leader might even join the Anglo-Americans in a
last battle against Japan, that Japan, rather than wait for the final
holocaust, should make a deal directly with the Allies, demanding
only that the Imperial system survive.

However the game turned out, playing the Russian card, in
Togo's view, would at least give War Minister Anami the chance to
edge toward peace. At a Big Six meeting on July 14, Anami was still
talking a hard line. Japan was not yet defeated, he declared, and so
it could choose terms for peace. But he would probably obey the
Emperor's wish for peace if he wasn't under such pressure from his
brother-in-law Colonel Takeshita and other young officers to remain as immovable as Mount Fuji. If he wasn't afraid that by
obeying the Emperor he might be dooming him. The Russian
initiative gave him some breathing space and might help him to
subtly persuade his "captors" to give up the dream and save the
dreamers.

VI

What did the Russians think of the Hirota proposals? Would
they agree to any of them? Togo couldn't wait for Sato to find
out. Before Stalin and Molotov left for Potsdam in a few days, they

would have to be alerted that Japan was serious about making peace. At the least, they had to give Sato a commitment that they would see Prince Konoye, if not before the conference then right after. Or else at Potsdam Stalin would almost certainly give the Anglo-Americans his pledge to join them in the Pacific war. If Stalin knew about Japan's offer, he might be wooed away from his allies or at least enticed to pressure them into a negotiated peace. Togo would have to take a chance and show Japan's despair.

On July 12, Togo thus whisked off another cable to Sato. He must now state flatly for the first time Japan's desire to end the war with Russian help:

> We think it would be appropriate [now to] inform the Russians of the Imperial will concerning the ending of the war. We should, therefore, like you to present this matter to Molotov in the following terms:
> "His Majesty the Emperor, mindful of the fact that the present war daily brings greater evil and sacrifice upon the peoples of all belligerent powers, desires from his heart that it may be quickly terminated. But so long as England and the United States insist upon unconditional surrender the Japanese Empire has no alternative but to fight on with all its strength for the honor and the existence of the Motherland. His Majesty is deeply reluctant to have any further blood lost among the people on both sides, and it is his desire for the welfare of humanity to restore peace with all possible speed. . . . It is the Emperor's private intention to send Prince Konoye to Moscow as a Special Envoy with a letter from him containing the statements given above."

Sato was disturbed by the new order. On three occasions in 1943 and 1944 he had sounded out Molotov on proposals to send a special envoy, twice in an attempt to bring about a German-Russian peace and once to improve Russo-Japanese relations and possibly move toward peace. And each time Molotov had refused, making Japan look foolish in Sato's view. Now the Emperor himself was involved in such an effort and might be humiliated. But an ambassador could not question the Imperial will.

Sato requested another interview with Molotov, but was told that the foreign minister was getting ready to leave for Potsdam and "simply could not manage it."

But the next day, July 13, Sato rushed to see Deputy Foreign Minister Alexander Lozovsky and gave him a Russian translation of the Emperor's proposal, asking him to convey it to Molotov at once.

"I should like the Soviet government to bear particularly in mind," he said, "[that] this time the envoy will be sent at the particular desire of His Majesty."

Of course the Soviet government would bear this in mind.

"The Japanese government," Sato said, "wishes to know of the Soviet government's agreement to this . . . before Molotov's departure, if that is possible."

"Some members of the government are supposed to be leaving this very night," replied Lozovsky sympathetically, "so it will be really impossible to make any reply before Molotov's departure."

Sato left the meeting drained and depressed. What must Lozovsky think after seeing him plead for Russian help in ending the war? What terrible damage had been done to His Majesty's name? He sent an urgent message to Togo:

> . . . If the proposal goes no further than we have gone in the past, if it is to be a proposal lacking in any concreteness [beyond] abstract words, then . . . we shall generate feelings of dissatisfaction at the Japanese government's lack of good faith, and thus bring evil upon the Imperial Household. . . . It is my firm conviction that . . . [the Special Envoy] can have no function except to propose an armistice and peace.

But it began to look as if Japan's good faith would never be tested, for some hours later, "in the dead of night" on July 13, Sato was awakened by a knock on the door. Handed a note by a messenger, he could almost guess what it said before he read it:

"Because of the departure of Stalin and Molotov, a reply will be delayed."

VII

When Togo learned the news on July 15, he was shaken. Had the Russian leaders really been in too much of a hurry to reply before leaving? Or did this mean the answer was "no"? He immediately asked Sato: When did Stalin and Molotov leave? Sato replied:

> It appears that [they] left Moscow . . . in the evening of the 14th. . . . In spite of the fact that they probably had at least a half-day remaining before their departure, they must have decided to put off a reply on the matter. . . .
>
> [Then he repeated:] In the long run . . . I believe that [Japan] has . . . no choice but to accept unconditional surrender or terms approximating it.

Togo also wanted Japan to surrender—but with *one* condition: retention of the Imperial system. And this, Togo knew, was what Sato meant—as he would confirm in a subsequent cable—when he referred to terms "approximating" unconditional surrender. But Togo still could not express himself so bluntly. He had to make it appear that he was asking for *conditional* surrender without specifying that he had only one condition in mind. And he had to ignore Sato's call for specific proposals. Konoye would never get out of Japan alive if the militarists knew from the cables that he was prepared to accept surrender with only the one unalterable condition. Trying to express his view through a form of *haragei* in order not to inflame the militarists, Togo cabled Sato on July 17, the day the Potsdam conference opened:

> Negotiations to strengthen Russo-Japanese amity are necessary . . . to solicit Russia's sincere good offices in bringing the war to an end and . . . in strengthening the ground for negotiations with England and America. . . . If today [those two countries] were to recognize Japan's honor and existence, they would put an end to the war. . . . But . . . we are not seeking [Russian] mediation for anything like an unconditional surrender.

But Sato did not understand what Togo was trying to say. No "concrete proposals," but more of the same "pretty phrases." He acidly replied:

The powers-that-be in Japan are out of touch with the atmosphere prevailing here. . . . [The Soviet] rejection of the plan indicates that we cannot thus accomplish the desired objective of winning over the Russians.

Nothing, it seemed to Sato, could now save the Japanese race.

Chapter 16

THE
BLUFFERS

I

Nothing might now be able to save the world. Or so it seemed to some of the scientists on the day of the bomb. For they had seen or known about the incredible explosion that had turned a portion of New Mexico into a miniature replica of the ashen graveyard the world might become as it crashed headlong into the nuclear age. . . .

Shortly after 5 A.M., on July 16, a scarecrow of a man stood in the doorway of a timbered desert dugout in southern New Mexico and clung to the post as a drowning man might to a reed. J. Robert Oppenheimer had raised from birth what could be a "white elephant," and the burden of such a beast might cripple him for life. The moment had come to find out just what kind of beast he *had* raised, and the tension was etched in the bony face, reflected in the bleary eyes.

What if the bomb didn't work? All those years of struggle, of dreams dreamt and dollars spent—all of it down the drain of history. And his only fame would come from notoriety. He will have led the nation down a false path to failure and fraud. And if the bomb did work? He will have led the world, perhaps, to its grave, where no one would recognize him anyway. In his baggy pants, sagging shirt, and floppy sombrero, Oppenheimer seemed a tragi-comic figure, a portrait of tormented man ludicrously groping, like a modern, machine-programmed Chaplin, for the power to doom man.

The countdown to a new era, possibly the last era, had begun with exquisite irony to the accompaniment of Tchaikovsky's "Sere-nade for Strings." The music was courtesy of a California radio station beaming the "Voice of America" to Latin America. It had inexplicably crossed wavelengths with the test-site frequency, thus allowing perplexed listeners to share in the wonder of the drama unfolding in the New Mexican desert, as scientists at the various stations checked last-minute details with each other.

General Groves had taken every precaution against espionage and sabotage. Scientists driving the 160 miles from Los Alamos to see the big show were told they couldn't even stop off on the way for coffee, and elaborate excuses were concocted for the press if newsmen asked any questions about an explosion. And now, as the scientists at the test site exchanged information, many ears might be tuned in.

Still, Stalin would learn little that was new. For not only Tchaikovsky but Klaus Fuchs demonstrated the fallibility of even the best-laid plans of man. Fuchs, the stubble on his pale face reflecting the hectic, sleepless pace of recent days, had come with a busful of fellow scientists from Los Alamos. He stood apart from the others on a volcanic slope of Compania Hill about 20 miles northwest of the bomb, which lay cradled in a special cabin at the top of a 100-foot-high structural steel tower. All observers had been instructed to lie face down in slit trenches with their feet toward the bomb and their eyes covered with welder-type glasses, and to get up only after the first flash of the explosion. But Fuchs had mathematically calculated that he would be safe standing from this distance, and he didn't want to miss a split second of the phenomenon.

Actually, whatever Fuchs would tell Stalin through Harry Gold, whom he would not meet again for another two months, would emerge anyway from the atomic bombing of the Japanese cities. Yet this was an important moment for Fuchs. He had helped to build the bomb and he wanted to see the results of his handiwork. Was it not Stalin's bomb as well as Truman's?

II

The results had not been achieved easily, especially after Oppenheimer decided that he must make implosion work. Trouble piled upon trouble. Oppenheimer could get neither the special new equipment he needed nor the personnel to operate it. Physicists refused to endure the primitive living conditions at Los Alamos, and engineers refused to endure the "prim" physicists already there. And many who did come soon left because of the makeshift housing and the severe water shortage. Not only was there little water, but there were few tubs to put it into. And Groves wouldn't install them even after someone claimed that hot baths made men less fertile.

Didn't the general want to lower the skyrocketing birth rate at Los Alamos?

Yes, but not if this meant spending money on needless luxuries. Oppenheimer could say nothing; he had a tub.

The unhappiest people of all were the military men recruited for Los Alamos, and their work was dragging along with their morale. They even rebelled against the tough, Irish commanding officer, who forced them to stand reveille, clean latrines, and submit to a spit-and-polish inspection. Did the *civilians* have to endure such indignities? Finally, Groves, mumbling an oath, transferred the commander and replaced him with a more gentle one after a top scientist threatened to quit because of the work snags.

But now the civilian wives rebelled against the new commander. How dare he let his cooks dish out the "dogfood" available in the post commissary? They even took to plopping bad hamburgers on his desk to make their point. The scientists invited the commander to a meeting and backed up their wives. Did he think sick men could build a bomb?

"Let's get something straight," the commander cried. "The next person who throws a hamburger on my desk—be he man, woman or child—will go straight through my screen window."

As if the myriad scientific and administrative problems holding up the bomb were not enough, Oppenheimer also had personal problems. He and his family lived in a comfortable home nestled in greenery while most colleagues barely avoided claustrophobia in ramshackle dwellings from which they emerged into the mud and dust. But Kitty was nevertheless unhappy. She had arrived with a young son and now had an infant daughter. How could she bring up children in the middle of the desert, where even feeding bottles were hard to get?

In any case, liquor bottles were not, and Kitty, to ease her frustration when she wasn't working in the biological laboratory, would often sit around the house drinking, sometimes with the few female friends she had. Or she might go away on a shopping trip to Albuquerque or California, leaving the children with a tyrannical maid and returning with a huge gift for her son to compensate for her absence. And where was Robert? she jealously demanded to know. Was there another Jean Tatlock in his life? Yet, General Groves would say, she fed Oppenheimer's ambition and seemed to find solace in the glory her husband would attain when the world knew of his genius. But in seeking this solace, did she seek to ease, or even understand, the agony of a man who was at the mercy of the machine?

Adding to the chaos of Oppenheimer's life in late 1944 was the machine itself. Might it actually grind to a halt? No, Groves would not have it. He pushed the scientists, he threatened the suppliers, and new instruments and tools began rolling off assembly lines and out of government warehouses. New men came, too; who in the end could ignore Oppenheimer's fervent pleas? For Oppie they could live with a cold shower—and the birth rate be damned.

III

Also pushing things along was Captain Parsons, who was determined to produce a bomb that would work perfectly and train an air unit that would deliver it flawlessly. However talented were the scientists, however powerful was Groves, it was Parsons who, as head of the Ordnance Division, oversaw the designing of the bombs and fitted the parts together into usable weapons. They could not be dropped without his signature on them. As Kenneth Bainbridge, a Harvard physicist who would direct the test of the plutonium bomb, would say:

"Parsons had, I guess, a unique position in the laboratory with respect to the overall control of this whole show."

Parsons' power actually stretched beyond his ordnance duties, and perhaps, ultimately, even exceeded Groves'. In an emergency, Groves would have to go through Bush, Conant, and Stimson to reach the President. Parsons had a shorter cut; when necessary, he could report directly to Admirals Purnell or King, who were especially glad to help out a navy man and had almost instant access to the President, though Parsons was careful about using this power. But he had better get the items and men he needed, especially as the day of the bomb neared.

Groves was apparently aware of Parsons' latent power, and this was possibly one reason why he called the captain in one day and gave him the news he had been yearning to hear: Deak would escort the gun-assembly bomb, his "baby," on the first atomic mission—despite the security risks of having one of the top experts on the bomb captured and possibly tortured into talking. (Groves may not have known that Parsons had no intention of being captured alive.) Yet the choice of Parsons seemed logical. Such an expert aboard the plane could reduce the risk of anything going wrong.

Parsons would now work with the man who would fly the plane that would drop the bomb. The man would be Lieutenant Colonel Paul Tibbets, a top-flight bomber pilot who had flown the first B-17 across the English Channel in World War II and tested B-29s with the cool and ease of a mechanic checking a car. Deak first met Tibbets in September 1944 at U.S. Army Second Air Force Headquarters in Colorado Springs when the pilot was given his new assignment. Parsons briefed him on the bomb, then a few days later showed him his laboratory at Los Alamos, where Oppenheimer revealed that Deak would be going on the first mission with him.

"Good," Tibbets said, "then if anything goes wrong, Captain, I can blame you."

"If anything goes wrong, Colonel," Parsons replied, "neither of us will be around to be blamed."

But Parsons was sure nothing would go wrong. It was just a matter of testing until every part worked faultlessly. When the B-29s to be flown by Tibbets' newly organized 509th Composite Group arrived at Wendover Field, Utah, the training site, Parsons complained they were in poor condition. Soon a better batch swooped in. When the company making armor for Little Boy dithered over the task, Parsons' reserve gave way again. The armor arrived promptly. When fear spread that Little Boy might explode prematurely, he designed a separation timer with nine clocks that wouldn't allow the bomb to go off until fifteen seconds after the drop. He supervised tests with dummy bombs and made sure the bomb would explode almost to the inch at a predetermined height above the target.

In short, Parsons would not rest until he made the bomb work. And he would succeed. Not because he couldn't stand failure, but because scientific laws wouldn't permit failure. No, he had no will or insurance. Who needed them? He would live because he must—to observe the final test.

IV

Oppenheimer was now less confident. True, all scientific calculations pointed to Little Boy's success, but might there be some unknown factor that had been overlooked? And, unfortunately, there was only enough U^{235} for one Little Boy, so it would be the only weapon in history that would be used without a test. On the other hand, the plutonium bomb, called "Fat Man" because of its rounded shape, *had* to be tested because it was more complicated, and fortunately enough plutonium was dribbling out of Oak Ridge to make two of these bombs—one for a test, the other for a town. And though calculations showed that Fat Man, too, should work, the chance of human error was much greater than it was with Little Boy.

Hence, the test, which the scientists would conduct at the Jornada del Muerto, the "Dead Man's Route," where in years past countless Spanish conquistadors and American pioneers pushing through the Apache Indian lands fell parched with thirst or pierced by arrows.

The region was a barren 18-by-24-mile strip of rock sand lying along the old Santa Fe Trail between El Paso, Texas, and northern New Mexico, and bordering on the Alamogordo air base in southern New Mexico. Lava peaks soared over the scorching, rattler-infested wasteland to the west and east, its dry stream beds sweeping down in mock support of the sagebrush and Joshua trees that danced in the wind to the steady hum of desert toads.

Rediscovered by test director Kenneth Bainbridge in the summer of 1945, the area seemed the ideal place to secretly usher in the nuclear age; it was desolate and far from any town, yet near enough to Los Alamos so that the scientists could easily reach it. What should the site be code-named? Bainbridge asked Oppenheimer. The evening before, Oppenheimer recalled, he had read a poem by John Donne, and a particular verse now came back to him:

> Batter my heart, three-personed God, for you
> As yet but knock, breathe, shine, and seek to mend.
> That I may rise and stand, o'erthrow me and bend
> Your force to break, blow, burn, and make me new.

"Three-personed God"—Trinity. Trinity would "break, blow, burn," and make him new, cleansing him with its unnatural violence.

The site would be called "Trinity."

V

Soon the desert was packed with measuring instruments and crisscrossed with wires as scientists got ready to record every radioactive cough and sneeze of the bomb when it blew the world into the atomic unknown. And the closer Oppenheimer came to the unknown, the less he thought he knew. Finally, his faith, it seemed, was reflected in a betting pool among the scientists— guessing the power of the blast in terms of TNT tonnage. He predicted only 300 tons, though the original projection of the scientists was 20,000 tons.

But if Oppenheimer hoped he would lose his bet, he feared he would lose his soul. Dining with Vannevar Bush some days before the test, he pensively played with his wineglass and recited a verse from *Mahabharata*, the Indian epic:

> In the forest, in battle, in the midst of arrows, javelins, fire,
> Out on the great sea, at the precipice edge in the mountains
> In sleep, delirium, in deep trouble
> The good deeds a man has done before defend him.

Silently, the two men contemplated the soothing message, perhaps grasping for good deeds they had done before.

The test was to take place on July 14, but on July 4 Oppenheimer pleaded with Groves to postpone it a few days.

Not for one day, the general replied. Truman had to be armed with the bomb at Potsdam.

Oppenheimer was shaken. How could he do it? Already everyone was working virtually from dawn to dawn. Finally, Groves relented slightly.

Very well, July 16—the day the Potsdam conference was supposed to open. But no later. Who knew what Truman, without the bomb, might hand over to Stalin?

Groves' concession would appear fortunate. For on July 14 Oppenheimer received shattering news from Los Alamos: A test of a dummy bomb had failed! The explosive assembly had not produced the symmetrical shock wave needed to trigger the weapon. Oppenheimer was devastated. How could the real bomb work if the dummy didn't? And as he desperately paced the floor of his desert headquarters, Kistiakowsky, who was blamed for the failure, suggested another wager:

"Look Oppie, I'll bet one month of my salary against $10 that this bomb will work."

Oppenheimer took the wager and walked away. He had bet that the bomb he nurtured from conception would not work!

Soon he received another message: It was all a mistake. There had been a miscalculation and the dummy bomb had *not* failed.

Oppenheimer breathed more easily now, but he didn't call off the bet. He climbed to the top of the tower to check the bomb for the last time and stood there awkwardly alone with his creation, like a tortured lover unsure of his sweetheart's fidelity, uncertain of his own love.

For all his doubts, however, Oppenheimer did not fail his boss. The bomb was ready on July 16. But at what cost to Oppie? He now weighed only 116 pounds, and his face was sunken, his neck shriveled. Only his eyes revealed the inner strength that had brought him to the brink of glory.

No one was more concerned than General Groves. Would the other scientists give a peak performance if Oppenheimer collapsed? And if they didn't, would Groves win a rightful niche in history—or face a wrathful bunch in Congress? Oppie must be calmed, nursed through the ordeal. Groves had thus asked the other scientists to keep their chief away when they assembled the bomb for its violent birth. The general had even brought brother Frank from Oak Ridge, where he had been working, and Oppie's close friend Isidor Rabi, from MIT, to help in the last-minute therapy. He had also ordered a security officer to keep an eye on Oppenheimer and had supplied a couple of psychiatrists to make sure that no one, especially Oppie, gave way under the stress. Nor did Oppenheimer himself deny the stress was great.

"Lord," he murmured to an officer, "these affairs are hard on the heart."

VI

The day before the test, Groves flew in from Washington to personally make sure that Oppie's heart would hold out. But he brought with him a new threat—rain and lightning. The general felt betrayed. Hadn't his weatherman promised good weather? He dismissed the poor fellow.

"It was necessary for me to make my own weather predictions," Groves would explain, "a field in which I had nothing more than a very general knowledge."

To be a good weatherman, he felt, one had to be more optimist than expert. But the rain and lightning continued. Would the electric circuits work? And if they did and the bomb went off, what would happen to the nearest town? The rain might inundate it with radioactive fallout. The chief radiologist and an army doctor had advised Groves to evacuate the people in nearby towns if excessive radioactivity threatened, but the general replied to the army doctor with contempt:

"What are you, a Hearst propagandist?"

Didn't they understand that any preparations to evacuate towns might tip off the public about the test and make sensational headlines? Was saving a few thousand innocent lives more important than dropping the bomb before the war ended?

But finally Groves relented—untimely radioactive deaths could, after all, create some problems with Congress—and trucks were now waiting to evacuate citizens of the smaller towns in an emergency. But there weren't enough trucks to deal with the larger cities. Postponing the test, however, might be worse than risking the fallout danger. Camp morale would plunge and the bomb might never go off. Then Congress would *really* be angry.

Oppenheimer agreed that "if we postpone, I'll never get my people up to pitch again." But several hours before the test, as he sat sullenly in the mess hall of base camp listening over bitter coffee to the rustle of rain and the rumble of revolt, he seemed confused. Dark bags hung from droopy eyes that, disdaining sleep, had focused in these frantic hours on tranquilizing Baudelaire poetry. But now it was not Baudelaire, but Enrico Fermi, a recent arrival from Chicago, who was declaiming on the frailty of life—especially at Trinity. Earlier, Fermi had drolly proposed that the scientists bet on whether the bomb would destroy only New Mexico or the whole world. But at this crucial moment, he was deadly serious. Should the wind shift, he warned, radioactive rain could flood the camp and, ironically, kill the bombmakers.

Groves, deploring the "air of excitement," walked up and loosed his fury on Fermi and other scientists present who supported him. Did they want Oppenheimer to crack? Apparently they didn't give a damn about Potsdam—or Groves' reputation. The general tried to drag Oppenheimer away, but another argument ensued. Why, the scientists asked, was Oppenheimer supposed to watch the test from the control center? It was too close to the bomb, only 5 miles away. If there were a runaway chain reaction, Oppie would be incinerated alive. But Groves wouldn't listen, and neither would Oppenheimer, who shuffled out behind his master. Could he defy him at this stage of the game? Anyway, would it be better to stay alive in failure than to burn alive in success? Whatever the answer, Groves wanted him in the control shelter, where the atmosphere was calmer.

Later, at about 1 A.M., July 16, after Groves had awakened from a sound sleep, he and his sleepless protégé drove through vast puddles to that shelter, south of the bomb, and frequently emerged from it to search the heavens for a star or two that might give them hope. Groves had already delayed the explosion from 4 A.M. to 5 A.M. and would now extend the delay for another half hour. Then it would be dawn, and since the blast could not be observed properly in daylight, it might *have* to be postponed for a day, perhaps for several, because the scientists were so worn out.

The decision would have to be governed not by the human factors involved, but, as Groves would say, largely by the "technical factors." And the technical factors were not favorable. For one thing, Captain Parsons and a scientist, Luis Alvarez of the University of California, were to fly in an instrument-packed B-29 from where they would observe the explosion at close range so they would know what to expect over Japan. However, because of the weather, they would be forced to view the phenomenon from afar.

Groves stared into the sky like a cosmic hypnotist, and finally, at about 4 A.M., the rain stopped. Even the heavens dared not defy him. The bomb would be detonated at 5:30 A.M.

VII

And now, a few minutes before that historic moment, Oppenheimer clutched the post at the doorway of the control shelter. I must remain conscious! he thought. I must remain conscious!

Groves had returned to base camp, where he would sprawl in a slit trench and observe the spectacular beside Bush, Conant, and some of the leading scientists, but a watchdog officer remained to observe Oppenheimer and make sure he wouldn't break down at the last minute and possibly ruin the show.

"It is now zero minus ten minutes."

The loudspeakers boomed into the desert like the voice of the Lord counting off the minutes to doomsday, complete with Tchaikovsky's violins.

Oppenheimer let go of the post and drifted inside to the control panels resting on tables and G.I. clothes lockers to watch over the shoulders of his men as dial needles trembled and crazy lines snaked across monitoring screens. One man twisted a knob to start the automatic timing circuits. Another gripped a switch that would stop the test if something went wrong.

Oppenheimer felt faint; all those years of agony and ambition summed up in a millionth of a second. He joined others who had gathered in the dreary yellow lamp light in front of a screen that reflected the bomb site through a periscope atop the shelter.

At base camp, Groves, as he lay in his slit trench on a tarpaulin, could think in the final seconds only "of what I would do if, when the countdown got to zero, nothing happened." Yes, what could a man who couldn't afford to fail do if he failed?

"Zero!" thundered the voice from heaven.

VIII

A tiny pellet of light suddenly streaked into the sky, then burst into a giant fireball, which dropped to earth burning with the heat of 10,000 suns. It stretched into a vast flaming dawn, bounced up, dripping molten soil, and raged into the luminous clouds with a fury suppressed for billions of years. Growing, growing, it bathed the hills in a surrealistic dazzle of colors and finally blossomed into a great, white, frothing mushroom. Almost two minutes after the first flash, the earth shook with the ear-splitting roar of the shock wave, which echoed off lavender peaks with an unearthly rumble that sounded like the last gasp of mankind.

It took a few moments for the scientists at the control panels to realize what was happening, for the explosion was so great that the red dots on the viewing scope measuring its force had scrambled off the screen. Had the bomb failed? But then as the shelter lit up in the initial ghastly silence, they knew. And when the shock wave struck with the force of a tornado, knocking some people to the ground, they knew why the dots had gone flying. Bedlam broke out in the shelters and slit trenches as scientists and engineers sprang loose years of tension in this moment of triumph. In the control center, they interrupted a snake dance to grab Oppenheimer and hug him. And Kistiakowsky bubbled hysterically:

"Oppie, Oppie, I won the bet! You owe me $10!"

Through all this, Oppenheimer, who had nearly collapsed from anxiety before the explosion, remained calm, almost aloof. He removed his wallet, glanced into it, and said quietly, with the embarrassed gravity of a tenant who didn't have enough money to pay the rent:

"It's empty, you'll have to wait."

A man who had become death, the shatterer of worlds, found it hard to joke or deal with the trivial. A new world must rise from the rubble of the old. And Krishna, in human form, had the power to renew as well as to wreck. When Bainbridge shook Oppenheimer's hand and remarked, "Now we're all sons of bitches," Oppenheimer didn't agree with him, or wouldn't admit he did. Bainbridge just didn't understand Krishna.

Overhead, the B-29 observation plane circled around the seething radioactive clouds that blanketed the desert below, and Captain Parsons rejoiced. The overcast that had hidden the bomb site from him and Alvarez had lifted just before the explosion, and the two men could easily view the boiling ball as it rose into the sky. The clear skies came too late to permit many tests, but Parsons now knew what it would be like when he dropped a bomb over Japan. How he loved to build new things and watch them work. The trouble was, of course, that this "thing" had to be used on people. But what was he in the navy for? To indulge his passion on devices that wouldn't kill people?

At base camp, bourbon spilled abundantly into paper cups as General Groves shook hands all around. When someone told him, "The war is over," he replied:

"Yes, after we drop two bombs on Japan."

Amid the jigging and the joy over the unexpected enormity of their success, which both puffed up their professional egos and promised a swift peace, few of the observers considered the corresponding enormity of human destruction that the bomb would cause if dropped on a city—whether 50,000 or 100,000 men, women, and children would die rather than the 20,000 that Oppenheimer had predicted. This wasn't a moment for troubling doubts or talk about prior demonstrations. In fact, success bred the desire for even greater success. And to some, could there be a better measure of success than the death toll in a bustling enemy city?

One man, however, did worry, for the bustling enemy city might someday be Moscow. On Compania Hill, while normally staid colleagues danced and screamed in glee, Klaus Fuchs stood watching silently and alone as the world around him settled back into the shadows of a newborn day. Partly because of his reports, Stalin well understood the danger. Russia was now at the mercy of America. Could his spiritual master hold out, Fuchs must have wondered, until the invaluable data crystallized into a Soviet bomb that would still permit communism to take God out of man's conscience?

IX

The WAC operators in the basement communications center in Babelsberg were understandably happy to read the message from the War Department addressed to Secretary Stimson. Someone apparently close to him had been very ill. The message, however, was heartening:

> Operated on this morning, diagnosis not yet complete but results seem satisfactory and already exceed expectations. Local press release necessary as interest extends great distance. Dr. Groves pleased. He returns tomorrow. I will keep you posted.

Nobody was more heartened than Stimson when this message from George Harrison was delivered to him at 7:30 on the evening of July 16 in the seedy, once-elegant summer home he inhabited. The bomb had worked! The results were still being analyzed, the coded cable indicated, but the blast was so deafening that a press release had to be issued to throw people off the track. The noise they had heard, reporters were told, was nothing more than an explosion of an ammunition depot. Stimson exulted. The bomb "as a mere probable weapon had seemed a weak reed on which to rely, but the bomb as a colossal reality was very different." Now America could buy the kind of world it wanted.

The Secretary rushed over to the Little White House and burst in to find a President drained from a long day's activities. Truman had risen early, gone for a walk, written home, conferred with Byrnes and Leahy, hosted Churchill, and toured the ruins of Berlin, where he was shaken by the terrible toll of war. He would record in his diary:

"We saw old men, old women, young women, children from tots to teens, carrying packs, pushing carts, pulling carts, evidently ejected by the conquerors and carrying what they could of their belongings to nowhere in particular."

Truman hoped for "some sort of [future] peace—but I fear that machines are ahead of morals by some centuries and when morals catch up perhaps there'll be no reason for any of it." Having borrowed the thought from Stimson, who had spoken similarly when he first told Truman of the bomb, the President would voice his fear in his diary:

"We are only termites on a planet and maybe when we bore too deeply into the planet there'll be a reckoning—who knows?"

Yet with the machine of inevitability grinding away, Truman would bore into the planet more deeply than any "termite" had ever done.

As he bounced over the rubble of Berlin, he thought of the
ancient cities that had suffered massive destruction—"Carthage,
Baalbek, Jerusalem, Rome, Atlantis, Peking, Babylon, Neneveh."
But apparently not about the city he was planning to destroy at a
single blow—until Stimson, the man who had reminded him of
man's moral delinquency, appeared before him waving the cable
of destiny.

Truman had the bomb at last! And he would not, indeed could
not, telescope centuries of moral progress into a moment of reflection. Now he had more power than Churchill and Stalin combined. And if Japan didn't surrender at once, he would use this
power just as he would use the power of any artillery shell. He now
had a "hammer" on Stalin, and he wasn't about to let him loose.

X

Truman exuberantly summoned Byrnes, Leahy, Marshall,
Arnold, and King to his office, and they "reviewed our military
strategy in the light of this revolutionary development." Although
the details of the meeting are not clear, the attitudes of the participants were no secret.

What effect would the bomb have on a Japanese city?

The military chiefs weren't sure yet, for Washington still hadn't
sent a full account of the explosion. They had virtually ignored the
bomb until now, doubting that an invasion of Japan was the only
alternative, though they agreed to continue preparing for one, just
in case. Leahy still rebelled against both the bomb and an invasion, arguing that the navy and air force could win the war without
either measure; Arnold now thought the air force with the help of
the navy could do the job; King now thought that the navy with the
help of the air force could do it; and Marshall apparently still felt
that a Russian invasion of Manchuria, or even a simple Soviet
declaration of war, could furnish the final shock. Anyway, he
didn't want to drop the bomb without a prior demonstration.

Other top military commanders who were not present also had
doubts. Even Major General Curtis LeMay, who headed the 21st
Bomber Command that embraced the 509th Composite Group,
the unit formed to drop the bomb, thought his planes could help
score a knockout blow without an atomic explosion. And the Su-

preme Allied Commander for Europe, General Dwight D. Eisenhower, who was visiting Potsdam, told Stimson on learning of the bomb that he hoped "we would never have to use such a thing against any enemy because I dislike seeing the United States take the lead in introducing into war something so horrible and destructive as this new weapon."

Truman's exuberance was perhaps tempered by the views of his military leaders. Even though Trinity had succeeded, none of them seemed to think that the bomb was needed to save a dubiously estimated half-million, or million, American lives that might be lost in an unlikely invasion of Japan—demolishing the argument that was most soothing to the conscience. But the chiefs were, after all, military men, not statesmen like Jimmy Byrnes, who realized that America should drop the bomb to save lives.

Despite his elation after reading the cable about the bomb test, Stimson was apparently impressed by the reaction of his military chiefs, which seemed to arouse the clergyman in him. Somehow, making plans for the bomb was much easier before it became a reality. The answer to his moral dilemma, Stimson now felt with growing conviction, was to win the war without battle—by inducing the Japanese to surrender with an immediate warning sweetened with a promise to let the Emperor keep his throne.

And feeding this conviction was another vital report that had just arrived from Washington, suggesting that the bomb might indeed be a dispensable option. Cables between Foreign Minister Togo and Ambassador Sato that American intelligence had intercepted showed that the Emperor and other Japanese leaders, if not the diehard militarists, were hoping to persuade Russia to mediate a peace that would at least let Hirohito stay in power. It wasn't necessary, of course, to use Russia as a mediator. Why, Stimson felt, shouldn't the United States simply toss Japan this diplomatic crumb?

XI

In Moscow, Ambassador Sato was beside himself with anguish. Tokyo simply didn't understand that the only way to save the Japanese race from liquidation was to surrender, asking the enemy to throw Japan that one crumb. On July 20, he brutally predicted the future and unmasked the past in a cable to Foreign Minister Togo:

> Just as we can assume that the enemy will one day attempt a landing [in Japan], it is also clear what Russia will do after our fighting strength has been destroyed. The enemy . . . will not only concentrate . . . on smashing our military installations and productive facilities . . . but will also attempt to deprive our people of the very means of subsistence. . . . Attempts [may] be made to destroy our crops at harvest time. . . . We will be confronted with absolute famine. . . .
>
> All our officers, soldiers, and civilians . . . cannot save the Imperial house by dying a glorious death on the field of battle. When we consider how the Emperor's mind must be disturbed because 70 million people are withering away, we must recognize that the point of view of the individual, the honor of the army, and our pride as a people must be subordinated to the wishes of the Imperial House. . . .
>
> Japan may be said to be standing literally at the crossroads of destiny and . . . our country is on the verge of ruin. While it is a good thing to be loyal to the obligations of honor, . . . it is meaningless to prove one's devotion by wrecking the State. . . . Our people will have to pant for a long time under the heavy yoke of the enemy . . . [but] after some decades we shall be able to flourish as before. . . .
>
> Immediately after the war ends, we must carry out thorough going reforms everywhere within the country. By placing our government on a more democratic basis and by destroying the despotic bureaucracy, we must try to raise up again the real unity between the Emperor and his people.

Suddenly, all the terrible agony of the past fourteen years exploded from Sato's pen as he committed the ultimate sin—crying aloud that the battles, the bloodshed, the bravery had been based on a hoax, a monstrous blunder, that it had all been a waste.

> Since the Manchurian Incident Japan has followed a policy of expediency. . . . We finally plunged into a great

world war which was beyond our strength. . . . Our foreign policy has been a complete failure . . . as a result of our having taken sides with Naziism.

Sato realized that he had broken his obligation to the government and thus to the Emperor by directly condemning official policies while serving as a representative of the government.

I am presenting these statements, [he concluded,] fully aware that they are not in accord with the treasured communication from His Majesty. I confess that my offense is tremendously great, but I have taken such a stand because I believe that this is the only way to save our country. If I am criticized as an advocate of defeatism, I will just have to put up with it, and I will gladly face any other accusations.

When Togo read Sato's dramatic message, he offered no criticism for he basically agreed with him. He only urged the ambassador to see Lozovsky again. Tell him, said Togo, that when Konoye arrives he will make "concrete" proposals for peace and better relations with Russia. He also urged Sato to try to see Molotov during a recess of the Potsdam conference "at whatever place he chooses" and convince him that a meeting with Konoye would enhance Stalin's reputation as an "advocate of world peace," and that Japan was "prepared to meet fully the Russian demands in the Far East."

Anything to get a "yes" or "no" reply.

Mixed with Togo's babble of desperation, however, was a bubble of hope. An American spokesman had announced on the radio that if Japan surrendered unconditionally, it would receive the benefits promised by the Atlantic Charter, which Roosevelt and Churchill had signed in 1941, calling for a free, idyllic postwar world. Hadn't the charter proclaimed "the right for all people to choose the form of government under which they will live?" Perhaps this meant the Allies would permit the Japanese to keep the Emperor.

The fact that the Americans alluded to the Atlantic Charter, [Togo added,] is decidedly worthy of attention. . . . It is impossible for us to accept unconditional surrender . . . but . . . there is no objection to the restoration of peace on the basis of the Atlantic Charter.

The charter would meet the one condition that Togo and Sato would attach to surrender.

XII

Whether Stimson slept well on the night of July 16 is doubtful, but he awakened early the next morning determined to make Truman understand that the United States should agree to this condition. The problem was still Byrnes; Truman listened to him. So to reach Truman he would have to persuade Byrnes. With the cable on the bomb test in hand, he headed for Byrnes' quarters in the Little White House shortly after dawn.

Jimmy . . . about the bomb. Warn the Japanese as soon as possible, and tell them they can have their Emperor, he pleaded. This might be enough to make them surrender, and then the bomb wouldn't have to be dropped.

Though Byrnes also knew of the Japanese cables, he bluntly refused—perhaps in part *because* of them. Stimson had made the point for him: An early warning to Japan, especially one letting it keep its Emperor, might stifle the voice of the bomb. Was that not reason enough to refuse? Besides, Roosevelt's old Secretary of State, Cordell Hull, had just sent Byrnes an urgent message supporting his own instincts. If such a warning and concession failed, Hull admonished, the political price at home would be staggering.

Byrnes didn't need much persuasion. Not only might the Japanese throw down their arms and defuse his bomb, but his own people might throw up their hands and demand his head. Yalta was enough of a political burden; he hardly needed another. . . . No, he would hold out for a lasting peace—on American terms. As Hull would later write:

"I received a message from Secretary Byrnes agreeing that the Potsdam Declaration should be delayed and that, when it was used, it should not contain this commitment with regard to the Emperor."

Byrnes had made up his mind. And Stimson couldn't even make a moral argument, for had he himself not rejected Grew's plea to issue an even earlier warning? He smiled. . . . Would Byrnes like to discuss other matters, such as the Open Door in Manchuria and the dismemberment of Germany?

But Stimson did not give up hope. Leahy and his Joint Chiefs of Staff had studied a new draft of the warning he had given Truman in Washington, and perhaps they would override Byrnes. They liked the draft—except for one statement: that the Japanese could have "a constitutional monarchy under the present dynasty." Actually, they were perfectly willing to let the Emperor keep his throne. In fact, "from a strictly military point of view," Leahy would write, "the Joint Chiefs of Staff consider it inadvisable to make any statement or take any action . . . that would make it difficult or impossible to utilize the authority of the Emperor to direct a surrender of the Japanese forces."

But not only the military point of view motivated Leahy. He was ready to grab at any straw of peace to stop the bomb. The nuclear sunrise at Alamogordo had still not convinced him that the bomb would work as expected, for he still didn't want to be convinced. Nevertheless, he had to find a way to end the war before the real test could be made over Japan. And if the way was to support the Emperor, he was for it.

But Leahy, backed by the other chiefs, worried that the language of the warning draft could be misinterpreted, and he expressed his fear to Truman. Some Japanese, he wrote in a memorandum to the President, might think that the Emperor would be deposed or executed and replaced by another member of the Imperial family. Others might think that Japan would be *forced* to keep its Imperial system even though a radical minority was opposed to it. Why not appeal to the whole nation by simply saying that "the Japanese people will be free to choose their own form of government"? In other words, they could have their Emperor if they wanted him.

What Leahy and his colleagues didn't realize was that this proposed transfer of sovereignty from the Emperor to the people without giving them time to digest the idea would confound them, for they could not yet imagine the godly Hirohito as their servant. Ironically, though the military leaders wanted exactly what Stimson wanted, they virtually guaranteed enough confusion in Japan to make the bomb inevitable.

Stimson the clergyman was so eager now for an advance warning that he approved this recommendation even with its ambiguous wording, and Truman accepted it as a fair compromise between the views of Byrnes and Stimson. It was broad enough to prove that the President tried his best to induce a surrender before the bomb was used, but probably not clear enough to actually induce one.

Stimson, however, did not savor his partial victory. Would the Japanese, he agonized, realize that they could retain the Emperor? Would the bomb needlessly take its ghastly toll because they misconstrued the message?

XIII

If the Potsdam Declaration would not specifically agree to the one condition Japan insisted on, neither would it specifically state the nature of the "prompt and utter destruction" that would befall Japan if it didn't surrender *unconditionally*. The atomic bomb would not be mentioned; thus, the Japanese would think that more of the same conventional bombs would cause the destruction. As the Interim Committee had dutifully advised, a huge surprise would fall from Japanese skies. And even now, as he grimly struggled to avoid using the weapon, Stimson, still seething with internal conflict, would not magnify the chances of surrender by using the words "atomic bomb" in the warning. For then, not only Japan, but Russia would know about it—and perhaps leap into the war before peace could shatter its dream of spoils.

When should Stalin be told about the bomb? What should he be told? How should he be told?

These questions had plagued Stimson for a long time. They had also disturbed the Scientific Panel, and when it met to review the missing Franck report, it recommended to the Interim Committee: Tell Russia—as well as China and France—about the bomb *before* it was used. Level with Stalin, or the chance for international control of atomic energy would be in jeopardy.

A wise recommendation, Stimson concluded, though it contradicted his earlier plan to keep all information on the bomb secret until after the first one was "laid on Japan." Now he felt that Stalin might never mend his ways to get atomic data if he suspected American motives. How could he then be stopped from making his own bomb? At his July 3rd talk with Truman in Washington, Stim-

son offered, as revealed in his diary, this advice on how to tell
Stalin at Potsdam:

". . . If Stalin was on good enough terms with him, he should
shoot off at him . . . that we were busy with this thing working like
the dickens, and that we were pretty nearly ready and we intended
to use it against . . . Japan; that if it was satisfactory we proposed
to then talk it over with Stalin afterwards, with the purpose of
having it make the world peaceful and safe rather than to destroy
civilization."

And if Stalin pressed for details?

"Simply . . . tell him that we were not yet prepared to give
them."

The President "listened attentively and . . . said that he
thought that was the best way."

In Potsdam, when Stimson visited Churchill and told him
about the successful bomb test, he gave the elated Prime Minister
the same advice. Only this time he was flatly rejected.

Tell Stalin? Utter nonsense! Drop the bomb on Japan and let it
speak for itself.

That was not the response Stimson wanted to hear, since he
was now hoping that the bomb wouldn't have to be dropped. But
Churchill's words seemed to evoke the lawyer and soldier in him,
at least temporarily. Could Churchill be right, if for the wrong
reasons? Perhaps an atomic blast over Japan *would* soften up Stalin for a deal that could make the world peaceful and safe.

Yet doubts about using the weapon persisted. And apparently
to justify them, Stimson reverted to still another earlier view that
an alliance for controlling atomic energy might be impossible until
Stalin actually started to dismantle the Soviet police state. And the
closer the day of the bomb, the more vigorously he embraced this
view. He had once taken the atom-bombing of Japan for granted,
but now he would prevent it if possible, and he was willing to
postpone his plan for saving the postwar world in order to achieve
this immediate goal.

"I have been very much impressed on this visit," he would tell
his diary in Babelsberg, "with the atmosphere of repression that
exists everywhere, and which is felt by all who come in contact
with the Russian rule in Germany. . . . I am beginning to feel that
our [Interim] Committee which . . . was so set upon opening
communications with the Russians on the [bomb] may have been
thinking in a vacuum."

And yet, the moralistic Secretary could not have been surprised that Russia was a totalitarian dictatorship. Nor should the "atmosphere of repression" in the Soviet-occupied zone of Germany have come as a total shock to him. Hitler's troops, after all, had laid waste Russia and killed 20 million people there. But the mere reminder of Soviet repression sparked his passion for enforcing the "law" as he saw it applying to all civilized lands. And Russia's guilt was especially flagrant, he felt, since its own constitution guaranteed the people freedom.

Yes, the United States must still try to lure Stalin into the law-abiding camp, but Stimson's price would be stiffer now. As he would write in a memorandum to Truman, the United States should ask itself how swiftly it should share atomic secrets with Stalin while constantly trying to change the character of the Soviet state.

This more cautious and less magnanimous approach toward Russia fit in with his growing desire to avoid using the bomb on Japan. For if the bomb wasn't used and Stalin didn't see its power, there would be little to entice him with immediately.

XIV

Meanwhile, on July 17, Truman waited with jut-jawed confidence, tinged with apprehension, for a knock on the door that would signal the start of an effort to determine how flexible Stalin might be in reshaping the earth, if not his own country. The generalissimo (he had just promoted himself from marshal) had finally arrived in Potsdam and would visit the Little White House shortly before the conference was to start. He would be greeted by a President armed with the knowledge that he had the ultimate means to impose his will on the world. Truman was no longer a failed haberdasher pitted against a giant of the times. *He* was now the giant, the most powerful in history.

Even so, his visitor would still be Stalin, the man who ruled a vast country as if it were one great slave camp, revolutionizing it, ruthlessly destroying all his enemies, a man who had not come to power by some freak accident of fate, but had taken history into his own hands and molded it to his whims. And now Harry Truman would face him.

What *should* he tell Stalin about the bomb?

Tell him nothing! Byrnes advised.

At first, Byrnes and Truman had been tempted to play their master card immediately, even though, as a member of the Interim Committee, Byrnes had demanded secrecy until the bomb was dropped on Japan. The night before the meeting with Stalin, Walter Brown, Byrnes' assistant, wrote in his diary:

"President and Byrnes want to tell Stalin about the new explosive but Churchill says delay telling him."

It was becoming clear that knowledge of the bomb might push the Russians into the Pacific war before the weapon could end it.

What, then, should Harry Truman say about the Russian promise to enter the war?

Say nothing! Byrnes counseled. Russia probably won't be needed, but one couldn't be sure until a final report confirmed that the bomb worked as expected. Meanwhile, don't encourage Stalin.

What should he discuss with Stalin?

Changing the Yalta accords.

Perhaps Byrnes' actual response wasn't quite as blunt, yet surely this is what he—and Truman—desperately wanted. Of course, at Yalta Roosevelt had secretly promised Stalin control of the port of Dairen and certain rights in Port Arthur if Stalin would send his troops into Manchuria. And the generalissimo would certainly send them now even if America no longer needed them. But the United States needed a guarantee, which Roosevelt had failed to get, that all Manchurian ports, especially Dairen, would be open to shipping from all nations.

At noon, hardly had Truman's aides escorted the squat, pompadoured dictator from his bulletproof limousine to the local "Oval Office" on the second floor, than he looked the President in the eye and said that Russian troops would thrust into Manchuria by mid-August as he had promised at Yalta. Russia always kept its word.

Silence. . . . *The bomb must then fall by early August.*

Of course, Chiang Kai-shek would first have to approve the agreement on the Far East reached at Yalta.

Smiles. . . . *Of course he wouldn't.*

The problem, said Stalin, was that the Chinese simply "don't understand horse trading." They argued over every point and couldn't see the big picture.

Yes, a difficult problem. . . . *The stall was working!* Now, about Dairen. . . .

Dairen? Stalin's rough, leathery face broke into a kindly grin. It would be a free port, open to all nations. In fact, his terms for a treaty with China would be "more liberal than the Yalta agreement, which had provided for the restoration of Russian rights."

Truman and Byrnes felt as if they had written Stalin's lines; the generalissimo had modified a Yalta accord before he had even been asked to! But they would act as if his statement was nothing more than a correct interpretation of Yalta.

Very well, said Byrnes with a righteous shrug, there would be no problem as long as the Russians acted in "strict accordance" with the Yalta agreements—though he himself was determined to change them in any way he could.

Stalin's volunteered concession called for a celebration over lunch, Truman thought. He liked Uncle Joe anyway, especially his "eyes, his face, and his expression," which showed him to be a man he could talk to "straight from the shoulder"—as he once did to Tom Pendergast.

Would Stalin please stay for lunch?

Sorry, replied the Russian, but he could not.

Truman bristled. Who was this pudgy little man who didn't seem as tough as some senators he knew, who didn't even have an atomic bomb, to turn down an invitation by the most powerful President the United States had ever had?

"You could if you wanted to!" he snapped sulkily.

And Truman now won his second victory of the nuclear era; Stalin stayed for lunch—and even praised the California wine.

Even so, the generalissimo's "Dairen strategy" soon grew clear. His proposed agenda for the conference suggested he was expecting a bagful of gifts in return. Truman would later call the items on Stalin's list "dynamite." But he wasn't afraid.

"I have some dynamite, too, which I'm not exploding now," he wrote in his diary.

And if the bomb, in the end, didn't prove feasible, well, Stalin's troops might be useful after all.

"*Fini* Japs when that comes about," he recorded.

Since Stalin plainly planned to ram into Manchuria regardless of what the United States wanted, the President might as well make a virtue out of the inevitable. But it was just possible he

would cry *"fini* Japs" *before* the "inevitable" occurred. At least
Byrnes thought so. As Walter Brown would scribble in his diary:

> JFB [Byrnes] had hoped Russian declaration of war
> against Japan would come out of this conference. Now he
> thinks United States and United Kingdom will have to issue
> joint statements giving Japs two weeks to surrender or face
> destruction (secret weapon will be ready by that time).

XV

Byrnes' more aggressive attitude sprouted from a new cable
Harrison had sent to Stimson. When the WACs in the communications center received this one, they were startled:

> Doctor has just returned most enthusiastic and confident
> that the little boy is as husky as his big brother. The light in
> his eyes discernible from here to Highhold and I could have
> heard his screams from here to my farm.

Secretary Stimson a father at his age? Wow! And Stimson himself was awed. Decoded, the message meant that the uranium
bomb was expected to be as powerful as the plutonium bomb. Fat
Man's flash could be seen for 250 miles, the thunder heard for 50
miles.

Stimson raced once more to the Little White House with his
latest cable, and the President beamed. He was so glad that the
Secretary had come to the conference. Truman would lunch with
Churchill that afternoon and convey the news to him. The two
leaders would also finally decide if and how the President would
tell Stalin about the bomb.

Truman first met Churchill two days earlier, on July 16, when
the Prime Minister visited him to size him up and offer to have his
troops share foxholes with the Americans in the Pacific war. But
Truman, he found, was not in a sharing mood. He didn't really
need British help, the President said. The Prime Minister, however, shouldn't take offense; Russian help wasn't needed either.

Churchill understood. Who needed help if he had the atomic
bomb? In fact, he would later tell an aide with admiration, mixed
perhaps with a dash of anxiety, Truman "is a man of immense

determination. He takes no notice of delicate ground, he just plants his foot firmly on it." And the Prime Minister stamped both feet on the floor to illustrate the point.

The following day, at the first plenary session of the conference, Truman himself illustrated the point. Already proud of himself after being chosen chairman by Stalin and Churchill, the President, ever more emboldened by the bomb, banged out his demands for settling the problems of new Europe. Finally, after he had ridden roughshod over the Yalta accords, it was Churchill who broke in to stop him, while Stalin sat silently savoring the moment.

"These matters couldn't be dealt with too hastily," the Prime Minister gently growled.

This subtle knock did not dispel Truman's suspicion that Churchill wanted to use him to achieve his own ends. The night before he wrote of him in his diary:

> He is a most charming and very clever person—meaning clever in the English, not the Kentucky sense. He gave me a lot of hooey about how great my country is and how he loved Roosevelt and how he intended to love me, etc., etc. . . . I am sure we can get along if he doesn't try to give me too much soft soap.

Now, at their luncheon meeting in Churchill's house, nick-named "10 Downing Street," hard debate would displace the soft soap. Should Stalin be told?

No! Churchill exclaimed. Didn't the President agree that they "no longer . . . needed [Stalin's] aid to conquer Japan"? So why frighten the Russians into the Pacific war before the bomb could terminate it?

This was Byrnes' view, too, but Truman remembered what Stimson had told him: If Stalin learned about the bomb only after it was used, he might feel that America was acting in bad faith and get his own scientists to build a bomb. Perhaps the President could drop a mere hint to the Russian—one big enough to prevent any such charge, but small enough to keep him from realizing that the weapon was an *atomic* bomb.

"I think," Truman said, "I had best just tell him after one of our meetings that we have an entirely novel form of bomb, something quite out of the ordinary, which we think will have decisive effects upon the Japanese will to continue the war."

He would tell Stalin late in the conference, perhaps too late for him to strike into Manchuria. He believed the "Japs will fold up before Russia comes in. I'm sure they will when Manhattan appears over their homeland.."

Churchill reflected for a moment. Yes, a jolly good idea. Tell Stalin so casually that he wouldn't guess what kind of weapon it was. And if Stalin wanted to know why he hadn't been told earlier, the Prime Minister said, Truman had the perfect answer: He had just learned that the bomb worked.

The two men rejoiced over their clever solution to this most sensitive problem. Now Russia could be kept from sharing in the spoils of the Japanese war. . . . Or could it?

There was something Churchill had been meaning to tell his guest. The night before, Stalin had informed him that the Japanese had sent him a peace feeler. "It stated that Japan could not accept 'unconditional surrender,' but might be prepared to compromise on other terms."

Though Truman already knew about this feeler from intercepted Japanese cables, he hadn't given it much thought because it threatened the Byrnes' drop-the-bomb-first strategy, which he had embraced. Why explore a feeler that might simply confuse the situation? There were, in fact, other peace feelers, too, that he couldn't bother to explore. Allan Dulles of the Office of Strategic Services (OSS) had come to Potsdam and reported to Stimson on one that Japanese officials in Switzerland had floated.

Now, however, Truman apparently began to fear that Stalin might try to mediate a peace in the hope of reaping the rewards he wanted without having to fight for them—as the Japanese were counting on. Neither Truman nor the Japanese apparently realized that Stalin wanted to abolish the Japanese throne, not guarantee its survival, though the generalissimo had made this clear in his talk with Harry Hopkins. What better way to promote the chaos necessary to catapult the local Communists into power?

Why didn't Stalin tell *him* about the feeler? Truman asked Churchill suspiciously.

Because, according to Stalin, he didn't want the President to think that Russia might agree to act as intermediary, Churchill replied. The generalissimo even spurned the Prime Minister's advice that he send Truman a note before the next plenary session. Let Churchill broach the matter to the President first, Stalin suggested.

With Truman's face reflecting relief, Churchill saw an opening for a plea he knew might not set right with the President. For his own part, he said, he didn't want the Americans to think that the British would not "go on with the war against Japan for as long as the United States thought fit." But he had been dwelling "upon the tremendous cost in American and, to a lesser extent, in British life if we enforced 'unconditional surrender' upon the Japanese. It was for [you] to consider whether this might not be expressed in some other way, so that we got all the essentials for future peace and security and yet left them with some show of saving their military honor and some assurance of their national existence. . . ."

First Leahy, then Stimson, now Churchill. . . . They all wanted to make the surrender conditional, to guarantee the throne. Byrnes was right. Keep the Japs fighting until the bomb knocked them out of the war, or America might get little out of its victory while the Russians would claim everything. Now, it seemed, he had to worry not only about Stalin but about Churchill.

Military honor? He didn't think, said Truman, that the Japanese "had any military honor after Pearl Harbor."

Well, they at least "had something they were willing to die for," replied Churchill, who remained hopeful that his guest would change his mind.

He perhaps wondered how Roosevelt would have reacted to his suggestion. Yes, they had secretly agreed that the bomb might be dropped on Japan, but only after "mature consideration." Franklin might have at least explored the peace feeler, to see how serious it was. But even more important, he had quietly agreed to give the bomb to Britain *after* the war so it could keep a Russian tidal wave from sweeping over Europe. Would Truman have the perception to follow through with this deal? Churchill would test him.

Britain, he said, would be in a "melancholy position" after the war. It "had spent more than half her foreign investments for the common cause when we were all alone. . . ."

"Yes," replied Truman sympathetically, "if you had gone down like France, we might be fighting the Germans on the American coast at the present time. This justifies us in regarding these matters as above the purely financial plane."

Churchill was cheered. "Until we got our wheels turning properly," he pursued, "we could be of little use to world security or any of the high purposes of [the United Nations]."

He would do his "very utmost" to help, said Truman. But, of course, any security plan would have to fit in with "the policy of the United Nations."

Churchill froze. The bomb might slip through his grasping fingers.

"That would be fine," he moaned, "so long as [military] facilities were shared between Britain and the United States. There was nothing in it if they were made common to everybody. A man might propose marriage to a young lady, but it was not much use if he were told that she would always be a sister to him."

The Prime Minister apparently deluded himself into interpreting Truman's sympathetic reaction as being "wifely." After the meeting, he would praise the President's "exceptional character and ability," as well as his "simple and direct methods of speech," and his "self-confidence and resolution."

Did Churchill understand that when Truman said he didn't need British help in the Japanese war, he was saying that, with the bomb, America could solve the problems of the world alone, in war or peace?

The meeting ended. Truman had an appointment with Stalin, and he could hardly wait to find out if the Japanese peace feeler caused new snags. He had dealt with one titan, now he would deal with another. Could the people back in Independence recognize old pig farmer Harry now? And the kids used to call him a "sissy" because he played the piano! He saw a piano on the way out, sat down and, almost defiantly, it seemed, tapped out a few notes. Then he strutted off to meet with Uncle Joe.

XVI

Less than an hour later, Truman and Stalin, with Byrnes and Molotov at their respective sides, were standing on the balcony of the generalissimo's house admiring the splendid view—the sparkling lake rimmed by trees that gently waved in the afternoon wind. A fine day for romance.

"I must tell you the news," Stalin said like an old village gossip.

And he handed Truman a copy of a message from Foreign Minister Togo that Ambassador Sato had relayed to him. As Truman would later tell Stalin about a new weapon, Stalin would now tell Truman about the peace feeler, even though he no doubt suspected that Churchill had already told him. Neither man wanted to be accused of bad faith, especially while battlefields were still aflame.

Truman scanned the message, offering no hint that he had seen it before.

Was it worth answering? Stalin asked.

Truman and Byrnes were a bit uneasy. They would now learn whether Stalin was interested in a "mediation" deal with the Japanese—at America's expense.

He had "no respect for the good faith of the Japanese," the President cautiously replied, apparently hoping to draw Stalin out.

Well, why not "lull the Japanese to sleep?" Stalin asked. "Possibly a general and unspecific answer might be returned, pointing out [that] the exact character of the proposed . . . mission was not clear."

Truman and Byrnes seemed relieved. If they didn't want the war to end until they dropped the bomb, Stalin didn't want it to end until his troops struck in Manchuria.

"Alternatives," Stalin added after a pause, "would be [to] ignore it completely and not answer, or send back a definite refusal."

The Americans shuddered. These alternatives might spur Japan to surrender *before* the bomb could be dropped! No, let Stalin, however unwittingly, help them carry out *their* plan. Let him "lull the Japanese to sleep"—until the bomb awakened them.

The first suggestion, Truman said casually, would be "satisfactory."

Molotov then cynically pointed out that such a reply would actually be "factual," for the message really *wasn't* "entirely clear."

Truman and Byrnes just as cynically agreed. Uncle Joe was certainly a shrewd politician. Not quite as shrewd as they were, but one they could identify with even if they abhorred his politics. When the bomb exploded in Japan, the message to him *would be* entirely clear. And an old pro like him would surely understand it.

XVII

The message that would ultimately reach Stalin was reflected in a dramatic report on the bomb test that Groves and Farrell would write for Stimson. The two cables that Stimson had joyously received earlier had taken a circuitous route—from Groves in Los Alamos to his assistant, Jean O'Leary, in Washington, to George Harrison in the War Department, and finally to Stimson in Potsdam. A roundabout way of transmitting coded messages, but presumably cables from Stimson's assistant would arouse less curiosity than cables from Groves in the army's communication center, and thus mean less chance of their falling into Russian hands.

Now, Groves, Farrell, O'Leary, and a fully cleared secretary worked on the historic report from early morning, July 20, to after midnight, writing, cutting, adding, polishing. At 2 A.M. a car sped it to a waiting courier plane, and Groves could finally relax. The world would soon know from this vivid document how his spectacular creation was wrought—if only the war lasted long enough.

Stimson, meanwhile, hoped that the world would not have to know for a long time, but at 11:30 A.M. on July 21, the soldier in him awakened as he read Groves' euphoric report:

> . . . For the first time in history there was a nuclear explosion. And what an explosion! . . . The test was successful beyond the most optimistic expectations of anyone. . . . I estimate the energy generated to be in excess of the equivalent of 15,000 to 20,000 tons of TNT; and this is a conservative estimate. . . .

With hard facts out of the way, Groves' pedestrian style gave way to Farrell's flare for the poetic:

> The effects could well be called unprecedented, magnificent, beautiful, stupendous and terrifying. No man-made phenomenon of such tremendous power had ever occurred before. The lighting effects beggared description. The whole country was lighted by a searing light with the intensity many times that of the midday sun. It was golden, purple, violet, gray and blue. It lighted every peak, crevice and ridge of the nearby mountain range with a clarity and beauty that cannot be described but must be seen to be imagined. It was that beauty the great poets dream about but describe most poorly and inadequately. Thirty seconds after the explosion came, first the air blast pressing hard against the people and things, to be followed almost immediately by the strong, sustained, awesome roar which

warned of doomsday and made us feel that we puny things
were blasphemous to dare tamper with the forces heretofore
reserved to The Almighty.

Stimson was transported into fantasy. He was there in the
New Mexican desert, savoring the "beauty the great poets
dream about," listening to the "awesome roar which warned of
doomsday." Was this a description of a weapons test or a spiritual
revelation? He had never thought of the bomb in poetic terms
before; it was like watching a brilliant sunrise play gaily upon the
tombstones in a cemetery. Beauty and bestiality, exaltation and
evil, light and darkness all merged into a portrait of power never
achieved by man before. And for the moment, at least, the purpose of all this power was submerged in its grandeur, as death
becomes unreal in the resplendent glow of dawn.

Stimson hurried to Marshall and read this "powerful document" to him, then rushed off to see Truman. But the President
was busy selecting gifts to send home from a list of items brought
over by a post exchange officer and couldn't be disturbed. Finally,
Truman and Byrnes called him into the sun room. Why, they
seemed to wonder, did Stimson always bother them at crucial
moments? Something important? What was it?

Stimson began reading the report aloud, stumbling over words
in his excitement like a schoolboy reciting a composition before
the class. He would record in his diary that night that the President
and Byrnes were "extremely pleased" and that Truman was "tremendously pepped up by it," and "said it gave [him] an entirely
new feeling of confidence." Again he thanked Stimson "for having
come to the conference and being present to help him in this
way."

Stimson was thrilled; he had pleased his boss. Actually, he had
done little at the conference except help Truman "in this way"—
as a messenger of good tidings. His advice was virtually ignored,
though he would claim that the President "was very cordial about
my usefulness, emphasizing it again and again." On Stimson's
request, he even agreed to see him "almost every morning" and tell
him "what happened the preceding day" at the conference. Was
this not proof that the President had great confidence in his Secretary of War?

Since Stimson was not a member of the conference and could

not attend meetings, he had learned little about what was going on before this presidential "act of faith." Each day he would wait anxiously for someone to bring him tidbits of news. To help him, he sent McCloy to get "hold of . . . one of the State Department subordinates who had been present," and McCloy "finds out from him what has happened and then brings it to me." Awkward, really. Should the Secretary of War have to scrounge for details from State Department subordinates? Finally, Stimson, conquering his pride, went to see Byrnes.

Could Byrnes at least get McCloy into the conference?

Sorry, said the Secretary of State, the seats were limited.

"My meeting with him was rather a barren one," Stimson would lament. "He gives me the impression that he is hugging matters in this conference pretty close to his bosom, and that my assistance, while generally welcome, was strictly limited in the matters in which it should be given."

The President, however, had proved more generous and, to Stimson's satisfaction, had been turned into a tiger by the report on the bomb. The bomb that *Stimson* built. When the Secretary showed this report to Churchill, the Prime Minister excitedly waved his cigar and noted its effect on Truman:

"Stimson, what was gunpowder? Trivial. What was electricity? Meaningless. This atomic bomb is the Second Coming in wrath." Now he realized what happened to the President in the last plenary session. "I couldn't understand it. When he got to the meeting after having read this report, he was a changed man. He told the Russians just where they got on and off and generally bossed the whole meeting."

Churchill himself was so overwhelmed that he now had illusions of bossing all of Europe. As the British chief of staff, Field Marshal Lord Alanbrooke, would recount:

"Churchill . . . was completely carried away. . . . We now had something in our hands which would redress the balance with the Russians. . . . Now we could say, 'If you insist on doing this or that, well . . .' And then where are the Russians! . . . [The Prime Minister] was already seeing himself capable of eliminating all the Russian centers of industry and population. . . . He . . . at once painted a wonderful picture of himself as the sole possessor of these bombs and capable of dumping them where he wished, thus all-powerful and capable of dictating to Stalin!"

XVIII

Actually, Stalin had more than held his own at the meeting Truman "bossed."

Poland, he declared, had a right to take over an eastern slice of Germany.

No, Truman protested, not until a peace conference agreed.

The generalissimo smiled. But his Polish friends had already moved into the area.

Truman and Byrnes were furious. A fait accompli! This was deception! It was too bad they couldn't tell Stalin right now that they had an atomic bomb. Byrnes even assured a colleague after Stalin gave him another "hard time" with German reparations that the "details as to the success of the atomic bomb . . . gave him confidence that the Soviets would agree as to these difficulties." Yes, in a couple of weeks . . . Meanwhile, he and Truman must ensure that Russian boots did not tread on Manchurian soil.

So far, Chinese Foreign Minister Soong, as instructed by the United States, had been stalling off an agreement with Russia based on the secret Yalta accord on the Far East. Though he perhaps didn't realize it, what he was really doing, of course, was stalling off a Soviet lunge into Manchuria. The Americans had even ordered Soong to leave Moscow so the Russians wouldn't have anyone to talk to. Chiang Kai-shek now hoped to make the most of this stall to improve his bargaining position. He thus cabled Truman in Potsdam on July 23: Would the President please try to persuade Stalin to ease up on his demands so a deal could be made?

Truman—and Byrnes—were perhaps amused. Here they had been trying to prolong the talks on China, and now Chiang was urging a swift agreement! Still, the President didn't want to continue sabotaging the talks until he heard Marshall's view once more, since the general had always favored a Russian push into Manchuria. Thus, after Truman read Chiang's message, he told Stimson at lunch that one question disturbed him: Did Marshall favor such a push? He should ask the general.

Immediately after lunch, Stimson summoned Marshall and posed the question. The general was hesitant.

He had wanted Russian troops in the war, he said cautiously, so they could tie down Japanese forces in Manchuria. However, by massing on the border, the Russians had already tied down these forces, and so perhaps an attack was not really necessary. But what difference did it make? Whatever America wanted, the Russians would probably march into Manchuria and grab what they wished.

If the Japanese could be tied down, Marshall couldn't be. Whatever he personally wanted, he knew what his commander in chief wanted. So he equivocated. And Stimson didn't press. For he himself had no desire to see the Russians entrenched in Manchuria when peace was so near, with or without the bomb. He returned to Truman with Marshall's reply, interpreting it to please his boss.

No, Marshall didn't favor getting the Russians into the war.

Truman was delighted. He knew the general would come through. The President turned to Byrnes. Send the cable to Chiang! he ordered.

And it was sent:

"If you and Generalissimo Stalin differ as to the correct interpretation of the Yalta agreement, I hope you will arrange for Soong to return to Moscow and continue your efforts to reach complete understanding."

Stalin and Chiang must haggle until the bomb was dropped. For as Walter Brown would report in his diary, Byrnes was "still hoping for time, believing after atomic bomb Japan will surrender and Russia will not get in so much on the kill, thereby [will not be] in a position to press for claims against China."

XIX

On July 24, the day after Truman cabled Chiang, Churchill and the American and British military chiefs filed into the Little White House and Truman approved a final report on plans to invade Japan. The bomb? What bomb? They acted as if it didn't exist. The Russians were then informed of the report, including a key recommendation: The Soviet Union was to be "encouraged to enter the war."

Let Stalin delude himself.

But with little other encouragement nourishing the delusion, Molotov would test American intentions. He came to Truman and Byrnes and echoed Stalin's promise to fight the Japanese. But

Russia needed an excuse to attack. Would the United States and the other Allies please formally request help from Russia?

He would think about it, Truman said. But after conferring with Byrnes, he didn't think long. Stalin, he was sure, wanted to be "coaxed" into the Pacific war so he could later claim that America couldn't have won without Soviet help, and that he therefore deserved a large share of the spoils. Absolutely not! But how could the President say this without tipping off Stalin that the Americans didn't really intend to invade Japan and thus set him to wondering why not? What's more, as Byrnes would point out, the United States shouldn't be placed in the position of asking Russia to break its Neutrality Pact with Japan. History might judge this unethical.

A legal aide found just the answer, and Truman sent it to Stalin: Russia didn't need a request from the Allies. After all, the Moscow Declaration of October 3, 1943, called on Russia and the Allies "to consult with each other . . . with a view to joint action on behalf of the community of nations." And Article 103 of the United Nations Charter obliged members to work together for peace. Never mind that these citations were quoted out of context.

While eluding Stalin's "trap," Byrnes set in motion plans for frightening the generalissimo into accepting a new Americanized version of Yalta as soon as the bomb exploded over Japan. He had deftly pushed through the conference a proposal for a Council of Foreign Ministers, which would meet periodically after the war to settle all unsettled questions—the ideal instrument for force-feeding Stalin the proper solutions. The council would constitute a mosaic of leading powers: Britain, France, and China, in addition to the United States and Russia, to give it a multinational tint. But to Byrnes, most of the stones in the mosaic were strictly for show; only the two superpowers were essential. He wanted to sit across the table from Molotov, the bulge in his hip pocket showing, and let him know exactly what the United States expected of Russia. And even Truman wouldn't be around to interfere.

On July 24, Byrnes made his pitch while there was still time. Truman was already impatient to leave, telling Stalin that morning "he was returning home . . . when there was nothing more" they could agree on. And there wasn't much more they *could* agree on before the bomb burst.

Meanwhile, at lunch with Molotov, Byrnes pointed out that the whole United Nations was to meet after the war to draw up peace treaties with the defeated states. But was such a meeting really necessary? The Council of Foreign Ministers could settle everything. The British didn't like the idea, but they would agree "when they had given more thought to the matter." Molotov listened silently. The message was clear: Who needed the British or anyone else? *America* and *Russia* could settle everything.

Molotov took the message to Stalin, and the generalissimo was willing to let the Council of Foreign Ministers deal with most questions. With Truman and Byrnes oddly stalling on final decisions, how else could he push through his own long list of demands? Stalin, it almost seemed, had flung darts at a map of Europe, the Mediterranean, and Asia and hoped to paint red all the places he hit, or at least use such claims as bargaining counters. He demanded pro-Soviet governments in Eastern Europe, huge reparations from Germany, bases in Turkey, trusteeship rights in the Italian Mediterranean colonies, and a say in Korea. As he relentlessly ticked off his demands, Truman and Byrnes diplomatically sloughed off most of them. Let the foreign ministers study them. Why compromise at Potsdam when they wouldn't have to once Stalin heard the bomb explode? At one point so many issues were reserved for the council that Stalin dryly remarked to Truman and Churchill:

"We shall have nothing to do."

XX

Did Stalin know why he had so little to do? Perhaps he did— when it came time for Truman to prove his good faith. As the President pronounced the plenary session of July 24 closed, he collected his papers, rose from his chair, and casually walked around the table to speak to Stalin, who was with his interpreter. Truman was alone, as planned, without his own interpreter, to accentuate how trivial his message was. But Churchill, Byrnes, and Leahy were watching—with a raptness they hadn't displayed at meetings that were supposed to decide the world's future. For all the thousands of words cascading into history might be meaningless as a result of this "offhand" encounter. How would Stalin react?

"I casually mentioned to Stalin," Truman would later write,

"that we had a new weapon of unusual destructive force. The Russian Premier showed no special interest. All he said [through his own interpreter] was that he was glad to hear it and he hoped we would make good use of it against the Japanese."

Truman then walked outside and as he waited beside Churchill for his car, the Prime Minister anxiously asked him:

"How did it go?"

"He never asked a question," replied Truman.

Churchill was relieved. "I was sure," he would say later, "that [Stalin] had no idea of the significance of what he was being told." Hadn't the generalissimo's "face remained gay and genial"?

Leahy would agree that Stalin "did not seem to have any conception of what Truman was talking about. It was simply another weapon."

And Byrnes also thought that the Soviet leader "did not catch the significance" of Truman's remark. But as Walter Brown would note in his diary, the Secretary "said that everything was fine tonight, but by tomorrow he thinks the importance of what Truman told Stalin will sink in and well it may."

Actually, it wouldn't take that long to "sink in." After all, how many people knew more about the atomic bomb than Klaus Fuchs—and therefore the man he was serving? When Stalin returned to his quarters after the meeting, according to Marshal G. K. Zhukov, the Soviet army chief of staff, "Stalin, in my presence, told Molotov about his conversation with Truman. The latter reacted immediately: 'Let them. We'll have to talk it over with Kurchatov [the leading Soviet nuclear physicist] and get him to speed things up.' I realized they were talking about research on the atomic bomb."

Fuchs had greatly simplified the work of Russian and captured German nuclear scientists by identifying the best uranium separation process and thus saving Russia enormous sums of money and speeding up development of the bomb by at least eighteen months. Now Stalin needed only the required amount of fissionable material to build one. And thousands of slave laborers digging into the hills of Soviet Central Asia with wooden tools and shovels had already found uranium deposits there to supplement ore being shipped in from Czechoslovakia and East Germany. In fact, a special atomic center had sprung up in the Chelyabinsk-Ziatoust region, complete with mines, plants, testing grounds, airfields, towns, and depots.

At the same time, a Soviet cyclotron had already produced tiny amounts of plutonium, while a small uranium pile was being built, apparently according to American specification, as reported by Fuchs, with graphite slowing down the atomic reaction.

Since Truman had no Klaus Fuchs of his own to signal what Stalin was doing, he seems to have been outbluffed.

XXI

Was Stalin vexed by the President's rather limited display of good faith? If so, he didn't show it. He was more amiable than ever. Thus, a few days later he pointedly informed his colleagues at another plenary session that "we, the Russian delegation, have received a new proposal from Japan. . . . We believe . . . that we should inform each other of new proposals." Weren't they all comrades and allies? He then read Sato's second request for Russian peace mediation.

"The document does not contain anything new," Stalin said. "We intend to reply to them in the same spirit as the last time."

That meant Stalin would continue to "lull the Japanese to sleep."

"We do not object," replied Truman, who had earlier learned of the new approach and still had no desire to explore Japanese intentions.

The President was encouraged. This was damn decent of Joe. But would he be so free with the news if he realized the "new weapon" Truman had told him about was an atomic bomb? Or would he perhaps try to make a deal with Japan before the bomb could end the war?

Stalin, in fact, had other plans. Let Truman and Byrnes stall. He could stall, too, perhaps for three or four years, until he had his own bomb. What could they do—drop it on Moscow? Not likely. Meanwhile, let them drop it on Japan. His troops could move into Manchuria at a moment's notice. And yet, he must have asked himself, if America could obliterate a Japanese city when Japan was already beaten, might it later obliterate a Russian city to thwart Soviet postwar plans?

Stalin, however, didn't seem vexed. No reason to be, really. This was a game, wasn't it? The stakes could hardly have been higher—perhaps even survival. But everybody played with an oddly pernicious pleasure, each coiled to collect a huge pot or call a huge bluff, as they pursued their dreams and delusions. Churchill tried to whip up quarrels between Stalin and Truman. Byrnes conspired with Molotov to squeeze Britain out of key talks. Stalin assured Truman that Churchill was an unreliable ally. And Truman and Churchill plotted to deceive Stalin about the bomb, which dominated the game as none of the players could. It was at the root of every discussion, agreement, and quarrel, "tying in," as Stimson would say, "with what we are doing in all fields."

Stalin said a lot when, after dismissing Sato's cable, he declared, "I have nothing more to add."

With everybody waiting for the master card to be dealt before playing the game for blood, what was there to add?

XXII

Back in Chicago, Leo Szilard had something to add: a final appeal to Truman not to drop the bomb. He must somehow reach the President and pierce his conscience. The petition he had circulated at the beginning of July had failed not only because of Groves' restrictions and Oppenheimer's influence, but also because of Szilard's wording. Many scientists thought he had gone too far. Don't use the bomb, period! the petition stated with moral indignation. If Szilard reworded the document to approve dropping it if Japan ignored a demonstration or a specific warning, then, said some scientists, they would sign it.

Szilard himself was now caught in a moral dilemma. He didn't think the bomb should be dropped under any circumstances. It was only a matter of time until the Japanese surrendered anyway, so why jeopardize the future survival of the world? But his moralism had a pragmatic tinge. It was better to have a slightly diluted moral statement than none at all. After all, the Franck Report he shaped argued strictly on the basis of expediency. He thus reluctantly added the necessary words in his appeal to the President:

If [a] public announcement gave assurance to the Japanese that they could look forward to a life devoted to peaceful pursuits in their homeland and if Japan still refused to surrender, our nation might then, in certain circumstances, find itself forced to resort to the use of atomic bombs. Such a step, however, ought not to be made at any time without seriously considering the moral responsibilities which are involved. . . . We, the undersigned, respectfully petition . . . that you exercise your power as Commander in Chief to rule that the United States shall not resort to the use of atomic bombs in this war unless the terms which will be imposed upon Japan have been made public in detail and Japan knowing these terms has refused to surrender.

Szilard then dashed from office to office collecting signatures like an autograph hound on Academy Awards night, but managed to get only sixty-nine in all, just sixteen more than the original petition had drawn. Though disappointed, he was not discouraged. And perhaps there was little reason to be. At Oak Ridge, sixty-seven colleagues were spurred by his petition to sign one of their own recommending that "before this weapon be used without restriction in the present conflict, its powers should be adequately described and demonstrated"; and another eighteen were also stimulated to ask for a prior warning. A counterpetition asked, "Are we to go on shedding American blood when we have available a means to a speedy victory?" and argued that the bomb was just another weapon which "future generations will come to regard with less and less regard." But it was signed by only two scientists.

Szilard was now in a desperate hurry. He had begun circulating his petition on July 15, one day before the bomb would be tested, and little time remained before one would be dropped on Japan. How could he reach Truman in Potsdam? Should he take the petition to the White House and ask one of the President's aides to send it to him? Franck and others objected. Such audacity might only antagonize the President.

Send it through channels, they urged.

Channels? Groves would kill it for sure.

But to get the signatures he needed, Szilard had to give in. With deep misgivings, he sent the petition to Compton on July 19 with a covering letter asking that "the petition be placed in an envelope addressed to the President and that the envelope be sealed before it leaves your office." Compton should then submit it to the War Department for urgent dispatch to Truman, who alone should open it. Szilard also enclosed six unsigned copies of the petition "which you may wish to communicate to others who ought in your opinion to be informed of the text."

Be glad to.

Compton got in touch with General Groves.

Send it to Colonel Nichols, the general said. Just as he had figured; Szilard would never give up.

Five days later, Compton, in no hurry, finally stuffed Szilard's petition into an envelope and sent it to Nichols. He also stuffed in the results of his poll as well as the other petitions, which Nichols had asked him to evaluate. In his own covering letter, Compton reminded Nichols that the Scientific Panel had recommended that "military use of such weapons should be made in the Japanese War." And he stressed that the other petitions, as well as his poll, supported his view—though, in fact, except for the two-man counterpetition (and letters from two scientists, one of whom had signed the petition), they appeared to support the view expressed in Szilard's revised petition, if with some reservation.

The next day, Nichols sent the whole batch of papers to Groves, recommending that they "be forwarded to the President of the United States with the proper comments. It is believed that by such actions and example it will be more nearly possible to control the individual activities of the various scientists who have ideas regarding the political and social implications concerning the use of the weapon and to confine their activities to proper channels where security for the project will not be jeopardized. Contrary to the hopes of Mr. Leo Szilard who started the original petition, thereby precipitating the other petitions, it is believed that these collective papers generally support the present plans for the use of the weapon."

It was July 25. In less than two weeks the bomb would explode over Japan and General Groves' name would be emblazoned in history. He thumbed through the papers. When would the President be leaving Potsdam for the long voyage home? It might be hard to send him any but the most important documents once he boarded the *Augusta*. The general put the papers aside and resumed preparing for his moment of triumph.

XXIII

The moment was drawing near. On July 14, a closed black truck roared out of Santa Fe, escorted by seven cars loaded with security agents. Inside the truck lay Little Boy in pieces—a large crate packed with its parts and a small metal cylinder filled with its body fluid, the major portion of U^{235}. The convoy careened into Albuquerque, where it was greeted by military men who delicately lifted the precious freight onto an air force plane heading for Hamilton Field outside San Francisco. There it was placed aboard the cruiser *Indianapolis*, which immediately raised anchor and sailed for Tinian.

Waiting for the cargo on that South Pacific island were some Los Alamos scientists and engineers who would put the pieces of Little Boy back together again. Then, as soon as the remaining portion of the U^{235} arrived by plane and the August skies were clear over Japan, the *Enola Gay* would take off with Little Boy ready to make its debut.

Bombs would be dropped on at least two cities, the second one to follow the first "as soon as possible," Groves decided. "The controlling factor on the second bomb," he explained, "was the date by which a sufficient amount of plutonium could be processed and delivered to Tinian," *not* the time that the Japanese might need to evaluate the damage caused by the first bomb and decide whether to surrender. And the politicians didn't argue. The first bomb might not be enough to end the war, but it would alert Stalin. And so the second one had to be dropped before he had time to push his troops across the Manchurian border.

Even so, Groves told Marshall, almost apologetically it seemed, that "there would have to be a gap of at least three days between successive bombs, no matter what type was used." His men "needed the time to assemble the bomb, and nothing should be hurried." He couldn't take a chance that something would go wrong. The world must never say that General Groves failed—or even that he scored only a partial success.

The question was, which cities should serve as symbols of Groves' tremendous achievement? A special Target Committee had selected four cities: Kokura, Hiroshima, Niigata, and Kyoto. And all had been "reserved"; conventional bombs could not be dropped on these targets. The atomic bomb would have an untouched city at its mercy so that the damage could be measured more accurately. Kyoto was Groves' first choice. Many war industries and workers searching for a home were moving there as other cities were ravaged, and it was large enough to contain all the bomb's rage—the better to understand the weapon's destructive power.

But even more important, Kyoto was an ideal target for psychological reasons. The Target Committee wanted the first use of the bomb to be "sufficiently spectacular for the importance of the weapon to be internationally recognized when publicity on it was released." And what could be more spectacular than the destruction of historic Kyoto, with its exquisite temples, shrines, and palaces. Since the people here, according to the committee, were "more highly intelligent" than in other Japanese cities—would stupid people live in so artistic a city?—they could better "appreciate the significance of the weapon." How many highly intelligent persons, or stupid ones, would be around to appreciate it was another question, but not one that Groves asked.

On June 12, Stimson met with Groves and casually inquired whether he had chosen the target cities yet.

Yes, he had, Groves replied. And he would ask General Marshall the next morning to approve his report on them.

He would like to see the report, Stimson said.

But this was a military operational report, Groves argued, fearful that Stimson might veto his list before Marshall had a chance to approve it.

"This is one time that I'm going to be the final deciding authority," Stimson stiffly answered. "Nobody's going to tell me what to do on this." Now would Groves please call on the phone and have the report sent right over.

Groves reluctantly obeyed, and while the two men waited for the report, Stimson asked him about the targets.

Well, there was Kyoto. . . .

"I don't want Kyoto bombed!"

Groves shrugged. The Secretary, he said, would surely change his mind when he "read the description of Kyoto and our reasons for considering it to be a desirable target."

No, Stimson replied. He most certainly would not.

But when a messenger arrived with the report, Groves began reading it aloud anyway.

Stimson refused to listen. He rose and strode briskly to Marshall's office next door. Then, on returning with the general, he said:

"General Groves has just brought me his report on the proposed targets. I don't like it."

Meanwhile, Groves sat wondering in embarrassment what Marshall must think of him for showing Stimson the report first.

Why was Stimson so immovable? For the same reason Groves was: Kyoto was the spiritual heart of Japan. The difference was that Stimson wanted to preserve that heart while Groves wanted to tear it out.

Years earlier, the Secretary had visited the city several times while on duty in the Far East and was enraptured by its matchless treasures. And if he forgot them, a young cousin who had studied Oriental history at Harvard reminded him at dinner one evening in spring 1945, rhapsodizing on the uniqueness of Japanese art and culture. Stimson was thus stimulated to read about the glories of old Kyoto, and this fabled tribute to the Sun Goddess became a symbol to him. Curiously, a symbol of American values.

What would the civilized world say if the United States, with its tradition of respect for the human spirit, reduced Kyoto to dust? Kobe, Osaka, even Tokyo it would tolerate in the name of war. But not Kyoto. Kyoto was a symbol in a more personal sense, too. For a man who agonized over the need to destroy city after city, Kyoto eased the pain—and salved the conscience. It became the world that would survive, the world he would save. And the world that would save him. For Kyoto kept alive the clergyman in him, even while the soldier blazed a fiery path through helpless multitudes. Drop the atomic bomb on Kyoto? Deprive himself of the peace that still dwelt in a corner of his restive soul? Not while *he* was Secretary of War!

Marshall scanned Groves' report and didn't challenge Stimson's objection. Groves no longer did either—for the time being. But he never quite gave up, pressing Stimson time and again to change his mind. Even when the Secretary was in Potsdam.

On July 21, Stimson was relaxing there after his usual evening massage and dinner when Kyoto again disrupted his serenity. This time through Harrison, who cabled that Little Boy was being groomed for a performance at the beginning of August, sooner than had been expected, and that Groves and his colleagues still favored dropping it on Kyoto.

Stimson sourly cabled back: ". . . no new factors for reversing myself but on the contrary, the new factors seemed to confirm it."

Apparently one new factor was that Stimson, morally disturbed, wanted to avoid dropping the bomb on *any* city. And if a city *was* to be bombed, he would certainly not compound his moral misgivings by bombing Kyoto. When the Secretary called Truman to give him Harrison's message, the President said he was "intensely pleased by the accelerated timetable" and, to Stimson's relief, "strongly confirmed" his view on Kyoto. Truman could, in this case, follow his own natural instincts without fearing that he would be attacked for being "soft" or "irresponsible." After all, he was simply backing up his Secretary of War.

On the other hand, the Secretary, having gone against his experts' advice and personally vetoed Kyoto as a target, counted on the President's backing. In fact, he needed every word of approval and encouragement the President could give him in these last momentous weeks of his career. He had to feel that he could still influence policy, however little, especially with mankind facing obliteration.

Stimson actually made more than a cultural argument for saving Kyoto. The President, according to Stimson, agreed with him that if Kyoto were bombed "the bitterness which would be caused by such a wanton act might make it impossible during the long postwar period to reconcile the Japanese to us in that area rather than to the Russians. It might thus . . . [prevent] a sympathetic Japan to the United States in case there should be any aggression by Russia in Manchuria."

Presumably if some *other* city were atomically erased, Japan might still be sympathetic. To Stimson, Kyoto was not just a city, and it was more than Japan's spiritual and cultural center. It was his moral lifeline in a sea of savagery. But could he tell this to Truman, Marshall, Groves, even to himself? To justify his decision, there had to be strategic reasons, and he found a President most receptive to them. And so Kyoto would preserve American postwar interests in the Far East. To its misfortune, Nagasaki, which would replace Kyoto on the list of four target cities, could not.

Which city would replace Kyoto as the *most favored* target? One that had been on the list from the start—Hiroshima. After all, Hiroshima, as General Spaatz reported, "was the only one of four target cities with no reported POW camps." And while Groves decided that the other three were fair game regardless, he was perfectly willing to drop the first bomb on Hiroshima. Why atom bomb a city with POW camps unless absolutely necessary? . . .

XXIV

Captive Lieutenants Cartwright and Looper, after arriving in Hiroshima, were driven to the Motomachi district in the northeast part of the city and thrown into a crowded, foul-smelling room in Hiroshima Castle, where they were finally able to remove their blindfolds. Cartwright looked around. In the dim glow of a single light overhead, he saw blurry figures sitting across from him—Westerners and Japanese. Gradually, they came into focus. Among them were six more members of his *Lonesome Lady* crew! Despite his joy, he remained silent, greeting them only with his eyes, for a guard at the wooden-barred door, rifle in hand, made sure that no one spoke a word or made a move.

Two men were missing. The tail gunner, who had been captured but sent elsewhere, and another man who had fallen to his death when his parachute failed to open. Cartwright, who did not even know he was in Hiroshima, could not have known that there were other American prisoners nearby, that two crew members of another B-24 that had been shot down, the *Taloa*, were locked up in Kempei Tai headquarters, and that at least two American naval flyers from a Helldiver fighter-bomber and perhaps other American POWs were being held elsewhere in Motomachi.

The next day, July 29, Cartwright, wobbly from lack of food and exercise, was taken to a room upstairs where a cold-eyed colonel with a swagger stick welcomed him. The prisoner tried to hide his fear as he submitted to interrogation for hours. The colonel occasionally tapped him on the knuckles with his stick, but he had little reason to use it. For Cartwright and his comrades had been instructed that in case of capture they should answer every question to the limit of their knowledge. How many troops were based in Okinawa? What were the Americans planning? Answer. What did it matter now if the Japanese knew how powerful the enemy was, how disastrous it would be for Japan to continue fighting?

Apparently because he cooperated, Cartwright, after his ordeal, was allowed to use the latrine outside, from where he glimpsed the city for the first time, its buildings, rivers, and bridges. He had been granted a rare privilege; the others had to use buckets, which one or two of them would carry each day to a cesspool and empty. This was a choice job the prisoners eagerly sought after hours and days of sitting Buddha-like until muscles grew numb and bones ached with an almost rheumatic agony, unrelieved even by the wanderings of the mind, which seethed with the irony of dying amid the final, fanatical gasps of a vanquished enemy.

Still, there was hope. If America struck hard enough, perhaps the war would end soon and they would be saved.

XXV

In Potsdam the final orders were being drawn that would seal Hiroshima's fate. If the weather was right, Little Boy would perform over Hiroshima between August 1 and 6, and Fat Man over another city by August 6. Stimson rushed to Truman with a cable from Harrison announcing these dates, and the President was "highly delighted."

That was "just what he wanted," Truman exulted. Now he had his cue for warning Japan: Surrender immediately or face "prompt and utter destruction." Not that he believed Japan would heed this warning. In fact, Truman would write in his diary that he was "sure they will not . . . [though] we will have given them the chance." And his skepticism wasn't surprising in view of what Japan was *not* being told—*how* it would be destroyed and whether it could keep its Emperor.

The warning, to be issued as the Potsdam Declaration, would be signed by the rulers of the United States, Britain, and China. What about Russia? After all, Stalin's signature would quash Japan's last hope for a Russian-mediated peace and perhaps be another way of inducing a swift surrender. But Truman and Byrnes wouldn't hear of it, despite the urging of some advisers. Let the last hope remain. Let the Japanese sleep, as Stalin himself had suggested. It made no sense to give the Russian leader a chance to claim chunks of the Far East. His signature might simply achieve what a Russian invasion would—turn a $2 billion bomb into a useless relic that could no longer shock him into renouncing his campaign to paint the map red.

As soon as Chiang Kai-shek approved the copy of the Potsdam Declaration sent to him, Truman told Stimson the ultimatum would be carried over the airwaves to Japan. Ideal timing, the

President and Byrnes felt. Japan's leaders would have only a few days to decide whether their country should be saved. Then the bomb would decide for them.

Stimson, however, was chagrined. Although the Potsdam Declaration was almost exactly like the draft he had shown Truman before they left Washington, one important line was missing— about the Emperor's status. Byrnes had substituted his own line, in the spirit of the military recommendation, saying only that there must be "established in accordance with the freely expressed will of the Japanese people a peacefully inclined and responsible government."

Stimson himself had, of course, approved such vague wording despite his misgivings in the hope of speeding up a warning to the Japanese. But as the day of horror closed in, he had to make one last stab, as Szilard did, at stopping the machine he had helped to set in motion.

Tell the Japanese that their dynasty will survive, Stimson now hammered at Truman. This point "might be just the thing that would make or mar their acceptance." Yes, the declaration had already been sent to Chiang, so it could not be changed. Nevertheless, he hoped the President "would watch carefully so that the Japanese might be reassured verbally through diplomatic channels if it was found that they were 'hanging fire' on that one point."

He had that in mind, said Truman. He would take care of it.

But like Szilard, even while desperately seeking the switch, Stimson knew that the machine could not be turned off. He could not save Hiroshima. And so he braced himself to accept the inevitable—with the zeal that his nation and history would expect of him.

He had done all he could at Potsdam, Stimson told the President. He would summon all of his waning strength for his final task—preparing the announcement that Hiroshima had been turned to ash, and thus warning the world that from this ash must spring a new civilization propelled by law and purged of war.

Stimson wished to go home? He was "perfectly agreeable," said Truman. If he wanted Stimson back, he would let him know.

He didn't want him back.

When Stimson left Potsdam on July 25, the conference had come to a virtual standstill anyway. Churchill departed the same day for Britain, where he expected to be reelected Prime Minister and then return to Potsdam a few days later. Only it was not he but docile Clement Attlee who returned as the new Prime Minister after his Labour Party won the election—making it even easier for Truman and Byrnes to brush Britain aside in dealings with Stalin.

The last thing Stimson did before leaving was approve a directive ordering General Spaatz to have the 509th Composite Group drop its first bomb as soon as there were clear skies after August 3. Other bombs would follow as they were available. This order was issued before the Potsdam Declaration was. Of course, if the Japanese unexpectedly—and in some American eyes, disastrously—accepted the declaration despite its ambiguous wording on the Emperor's status and the means of promised destruction, the order could always be rescinded. But not a day must be lost. Russian forces might bulldoze into Manchuria at any time.

Thus, the moment Truman and Byrnes received Chiang's endorsement of the declaration, they released the document—not even bothering to clear it with Stalin. Byrnes simply sent Molotov a copy saying that the press would carry it the next morning.

Nyet, the foreign minister fired back. Postpone release for two or three days so the Russians could study it.

Too late, Byrnes replied. Nothing personal. He simply had not wanted to embarrass the Russians by showing it to them. After all, Russia was not at war with Japan.

XXVI

The Potsdam Declaration thundered into Tokyo like the voice of an angry god. Yet, a merciful god, thought Foreign Minister Togo, who had been looking for an excuse to throw down the sword. Terms! The signatories used the expression "Following are our terms." There could be no "terms" attached to unconditional surrender. Besides, the Allies asked for the unconditional surrender *only* of the armed forces, not of the nation. Togo fretted, of course, about some of the provisions. He was especially concerned that no mention was made of the Emperor's status. Nevertheless, if the people could choose their own form of government, the Imperial system *seemed* safe. Perhaps the enemy would agree to clarify or revise some points.

All in all, the declaration promised Japan far greater leniency than Germany was shown. One thing seemed clear: While he would accept unconditional surrender as long as it *appeared* to be conditional, the enemy would accept conditional surrender as long as it *appeared* to be unconditional.

But if Togo was relieved, he was also restive. Was Russia silent on the special envoy proposal because it approved the Potsdam Declaration? In any case, Stalin must have known of the ultimatum in advance. Would he now hurl his troops against Japan? Was he simply waiting to see if Japan accepted the declaration? With mixed feelings, Togo rushed to the palace that morning, July 27, and Kido immediately ushered him into the underground Imperial library to see the Emperor.

Japan must not reject the declaration, Togo advised Hirohito. But it should not accept it either—until the Russians gave their answer on receiving Konoye. With Russia mediating, perhaps Japan might still be able to win better terms based on the declaration. And if the Russians refused to mediate, the military might go along with the Potsdam terms as the best that could be had. Regardless, the ultimatum must be "treated with the utmost circumspection, both domestically and internationally."

The Emperor, with Kido's approval, nodded. Yes, of course. But Japan must make peace one way or the other.

The military, however, still wanted peace only one way—with conditions that would permit it to perpetuate its dream. And at a Big Six meeting that day it found the unsettled question of the Emperor's status a convenient excuse for its intransigence. Togo's advice to the military chiefs, it seemed, came too late anyway. The junior officers had already given their own: Reject the Potsdam Declaration!

The people were bound to learn about the ultimatum, said Admiral Toyoda, and they would be demoralized. Therefore the government must immediately declare that the Allied ultimatum was "absurd" and could not be considered. Why, Japan would even lose its Imperial system!

Not true, Togo and Suzuki claimed. The Potsdam Declaration, the foreign minister argued, would permit the Emperor to keep his throne. Anyway, why not wait to see if Prince Konoye was welcome in Russia?

The military leaders finally agreed, and so did the full Cabinet later that day. A doctored text of the declaration, with no comment accompanying it, would go to the press. Togo was content with this plan to stall. In fact, he would skip the weekly joint meeting of the government and the high command that was to follow the Cabinet session. A waste of time. However, Anami and the other military leaders were willing to waste their time—and so were their fanatical aides, who did not like Togo's plan at all. With the foreign minister conveniently absent, the spider could now deal with the fly. Prime Minister Suzuki was called to another room and was told what he must do. He must unequivocally spurn the Potsdam Declaration.

Suzuki was frightened—for the Emperor and himself. He could still feel the cold muzzle of the pistol pressed against his neck. And as he looked around, he saw visible power that seemed at the moment far more real than the "invisible power" whose timely favors had permitted him to become an old man.

Well . . .

Suzuki's chief Cabinet secretary, Hisatsune Sakomizu, who was present, came to his rescue. A press conference would be held later that day. Why not have the Prime Minister answer a planted question about the Potsdam Declaration unofficially without making a formal government statement?

Good idea, all agreed. And the pressure on Suzuki's neck eased. Now what should the Prime Minister say? Pens scribbled furiously on pads. Hard lines, soft lines, ambiguous lines. Gradually, as the look in the juniors' eyes grew harder, so did the lines. Sakomizu, who wanted Japan to embrace the declaration, thought he came up with acceptable compromise wording:

"The Potsdam Declaration is only an adaptation of [previous declarations] and our government will not place much importance on it. In short, we will *mokusatsu* that for the present."

The ultimatum, in other words, was still being considered.

The militarists scoffed. They wanted some changes. The words, "for the present," certainly had to go.

Suzuki and Sakomizu finally agreed to military demands. After all, the key word was *mokusatsu*. What did *mokusatsu* mean? Many things: "no comment," "ignore," "take no notice of," "treat with silent contempt." Did it mean "reject"? No. But it didn't mean "accept" either.

At 4 P.M. that day, July 27, Suzuki met the press, and after several exchanges, someone asked: "Recently the enemy powers have been making various kinds of propaganda about terminating the war. What is your opinion about this?"

Suzuki gazed around the room. Within the hour the Allies would hear his statement and act on it. Would they understand, even if they weren't familiar with the nuances of *haragei?* Regardless, he had to protect the Emperor's life—and his own.

"I think," he said slowly and deliberately, "that the joint declaration by the three powers is nothing but a repetition of [past declarations]. The government does not see much value in it. All we have to do is *mokusatsu* it. What we should do is devote ourselves to the prosecution of the war."

After the press conference, War Minister Anami told the Information Board, which cleared all news, that Suzuki meant "reject by ignoring." And the head of the board himself went on the radio and explained this. In Tokyo, the *Mainichi* newspaper headline the next morning screamed, "Laughable Matter." In the United States, the *New York Times* headline read, "Japan Rejects Potsdam Declaration." And in Potsdam, American leaders rushed plans to end the war with the biggest headline in history.

Why quibble over the nuance of a word when there was so much at stake?

XXVII

When Togo learned about Suzuki's *mokusatsu* statement and Anami's attempt to exploit it, he was horrified. He confronted Anami: Stop saying the Potsdam Declaration was rejected! But it was too late. Now it was more urgent than ever that he find out if the Russians would agree to see Prince Konoye. Once they answered, Japan could still accept a peace based on the declaration, a mediated peace if possible, a direct surrender if necessary. But would there be time? He had to know before the Allies invaded Japan or bombed the country even more savagely than they had up to now. With the morning headlines running through his mind like a ticker tape announcing the death of Japan, Togo urgently cabled Sato:

[Interview Molotov] as quickly as possible [and find out] what the Russian position is with respect to the Potsdam

Declaration [and] whether there is not some connection between [it] and our proposal. . . . Obviously we are deeply concerned [about] whether the Russian government communicated our proposal to the English and Americans, and . . . [about the] attitude the Russians will take toward Japan in the future.

But with Molotov away, the best Sato could do was once again see Lozovsky, who was as noncommittal as ever. However, Sato used Togo's fears to bolster his own argument that Japan must surrender under the terms of the Potsdam Declaration. He replied to Togo on July 30.

[Surely the Japanese proposal] was communicated at once to the Americans and the English.[And surely they] decided to make the . . . Declaration in order to make clear [their] . . . response . . . If it is understood that Stalin was completely unable to influence their intentions . . . , [it is obvious] that he will be unable to accept . . . a Special Envoy. . . . There is no need for him now . . . to make a treaty with Japan. Your view of the situation and the actual situation are completely contradictory.

Togo was exasperated. Didn't Sato understand that Russia had to give a "yes" or "no" answer on the Konoye trip before Japan could accept the Potsdam Declaration? That with the fanatical junior officers poised to revolt, a definitive Russian reply was Togo's only chance for persuading the military leaders to agree to Allied terms?

Togo cabled Sato again on August 2, daring to reveal more of his thinking than previously:

At present, in accordance with the Imperial will, there is unanimous determination to ask the good offices of the Russians in ending the war. . . . *Under the circumstances there is a disposition to make the Potsdam . . . Declaration the basis of our study concerning terms.* . . . If we should let one day slip by, the present situation may result in a thousand years of regret.

Tokyo might accept the terms of the Potsdam Declaration! Sato had the sudden exquisite feeling of a man steaming out his tensions in a near-boiling Japanese bath. He replied on August 4:

> The [Potsdam] Declaration already provides a basis for ending the . . . war. Therefore, if Russia assumes the role of mediator, . . . the action will have to be carried out on this basis. I feel that [your] statement [on the Declaration] is an extremely auspicious one, since it shows that you are disposed at least to make the . . . Declaration the basis for study of our conditions.

XXVIII

American leaders, meanwhile, were reading the desperate Togo-Sato cables daily with the avidity of a soap-opera addict waiting in suspense for the next episode. But Togo's statement on the Potsdam Declaration was not quite so auspicious to them, even though it was a private official revelation that obviously carried far more weight than Suzuki's propagandistic press conference remark. The discrepancy between the two Japanese reactions, in any event, was clearly not worth investigating.

Yet American intelligence analysts had concluded in a report on July 21 following a study of the Japanese cable traffic that "Japan now, officially if not publicly, recognizes her defeat" and was trying to reconcile "national pride with [it]" and find "the best means of salvaging the wreckage of her ambitions." Truman and Byrnes knew from the cables that Japan might find the Potsdam Declaration the best means—even though they had refused to specifically guarantee the Emperor's status. And they knew there was a new stumbling block to surrender: Russia's silence on the Japanese proposal to send Prince Konoye to Moscow. If Japan knew it couldn't get better terms through Russian mediation, the cables strongly hinted, it would accept the terms of the Potsdam Declaration *without* Russian mediation.

And yet, Truman asked Stalin neither to mediate on the basis of the declaration, nor to flatly refuse Japan's proposal and thus pave the way for a possible direct surrender to the United States and Britain. Instead, he backed Stalin's suggestion: Lull the Japanese to sleep. Each of the two leaders would stall them off until the war ended in a way best suited to his purposes.

In fact, Truman not only worried that Stalin might attack Manchuria before the bomb could be dropped, but that he might try to mediate a peace despite his promise not to. What if Japan surrendered to the generalissimo on the basis of the Potsdam Declaration and he handed the offer to the United States and Britain? Could they refuse to accept it—and drop the bomb anyway? Meanwhile, Stalin would collect a huge commission from Japan without having to fight for the same rewards. Irony of ironies, America wouldn't even have an atom-bombed showpiece to restrain Stalin and convince him that he should behave in a civilized way.

XXIX

On August 1, the Potsdam delegates met in a final session and praised each other for their earnest efforts to build a peaceful postwar world.

"I thank you for your kind cooperation in settling all the important questions," Truman said to Stalin.

"I should personally like to thank Mr. Byrnes," Stalin said. "[He] has helped our work very much and has promoted the achievement of our decisions."

"I am deeply touched by the generalissimo's kind words," Byrnes said, "and I hope that together with my colleagues I have been of use in the work of the conference."

Stalin concluded: "The conference, I believe, can be considered a success."

XXX

So could General Groves' strategy. That same day Groves finally found the time to bring Szilard's petition and related documents to Stimson's office. It is not known whether the Secretary, who had himself tried to stop the machine, read them—before they were quietly filed away. His aide, R. Gordon Arneson, would later point out:

As the question of the bomb's use "had already been fully considered and settled by the proper authorities," and as scientists had already presented their views to the Interim Committee "through the Scientific Panel," it was felt that "no useful purpose would be served by transmitting either the petition or any of the attached documents to the White House, particularly since the President was not then in the country."

And since no one could find the switch anyway.

Chapter 17

THE
GADGET

I

"The moment has arrived," said Colonel Tibbets on the afternoon of August 4 as he began to brief the crews and scientists waiting in Tinian to launch a mission that would shake, and perhaps ultimately destroy, the world. With Captain Parsons sitting at his side, Tibbets spoke calmly, his voice echoing through the long, barnlike briefing hut with suppressed excitement. "Very recently, the weapon we are about to deliver was successfully tested in the States. We have received orders to drop it on the enemy."

Tibbets walked to a blackboard covered with enlarged reconnaissance photographs of Hiroshima and the alternate target cities of Kokura and Nagasaki, and explained the mission. Then he introduced Parsons.

"The bomb you are going to drop," said Parsons, without describing the weapon as an *atomic* bomb, "is something new in the history of warfare. It is the most destructive weapon ever produced. We think it will knock out almost everything within a three-mile area."

Amid the startled murmurs, Parsons asked a technician to switch on a movie projector that had been set up, but the film got caught in the sprockets. When the projector ground to a halt, Parsons continued, to loud laughter:

"The film you are *not* about to see was made of the only test we have performed."

And he described the enormity of the Trinity explosion. The flash was seen for more than 10 miles, even by a girl who had been blind all her life. A soldier more than 5 miles away was temporarily blinded. Another soldier 10,000 feet away was knocked off his feet.

Parsons paused to let the incredible details sink in. Then he said: Since the bomb was never dropped from the air before, no one can say exactly what will happen. But we do know there will be a flash of light much brighter than the sun, and then a cloud will rise to at least 30,000 feet, perhaps to 60,000 feet. The blast might even crack the earth's crust.

Tibbets now took over again, and Parsons faded into the background. Who had to know that he had played one of the key roles in making the bomb, that he would be the overall commander on the *Enola Gay*, as General Groves intended? He wanted not glory but the satisfaction of serving his country. And wouldn't the bomb shorten the war by six months or a year? From what the nation's leaders said, it seemed clear that the Japanese were prepared to fight to the last man. But they would change their minds when Little Boy spoke. The only recognition Parsons had ever wanted was to become an admiral. And the bomb, it seemed, would deprive him of that honor since he could hardly accumulate the required sea duty at Los Alamos.

In Tinian, Parsons was in command of the Los Alamos group, mostly scientists, who had come to put the bomb together and perfect the delivery system. He left nothing to chance, even devising a clever code for communicating the details of the blast from the *Enola Gay* to Tinian. Every possibility was listed, from an explosion that never came off to one that was greater than that at Trinity, with each one numbered so he wouldn't have to transmit the description in words.

Parsons made sure, according to Harvard scientist Norman Ramsey, who headed the scientific faction, that "he got everything we wanted, when we wanted it, if it meant he had to go down to [Pacific Fleet Commander Chester W.] Nimitz. . . . He'd pound on the table to Nimitz . . . even if it was an extra chair he wanted."

But if Parsons pounded on the navy's table, he didn't dine at it. He could have gone to the naval base nearby to have meals served on a crisp white tablecloth with napkin rings adding a touch of elegance. But he preferred to eat off a metal tray in the army air force mess together with those who would share the honor of ending the war overnight. He also slept in a tent, though he could have luxuriated in the comfortable naval quarters. When he could spare the time, he went to the outdoor "Pumpkin Playhouse" to watch a movie—sometimes sitting there dripping wet as the rain soaked his clothes—rather than drive over to the navy indoor theater. How could a man about to embark on an almost sacred mission think about personal comfort or glory?

II

The mission began shortly after midnight, August 6. Three B-29s—the *Enola Gay* and two escorting bombers, one carrying cameras and the other blast-measuring instruments—were lined up on the runways ready to go. Three other planes had already left for Hiroshima and the two alternate target cities to report on the weather, while another would soon fly to the island of Iwo Jima, almost halfway to Japan, just in case the *Enola Gay* developed engine trouble and the bomb had to be transferred to a new aircraft.

Parsons could hardly wait for takeoff. For General Groves, who wanted to be sure history would never forget this great moment, directed from afar a lavish farewell, complete with army film crew and photographers, klieg lights, and tape recorders to catch every gesture and immortal remark of the *Enola Gay* crew. Parsons was horrified as he jumped off the truck carrying the crew to the plane. Nearly blinded by the glare, he found himself in the middle of a nightmare, a carnival of ghosts: Fleeting obscure figures popped light bulbs, probed emotions, patted backs. One photographer pushed Parsons against a wheel of the plane and focused a camera on him.

"Smile!" he cried. "You're going to be famous!"

But Parsons didn't smile. Somehow it all seemed obscene. The crew was opening not a new play, but a new era. And the birth pangs, though unavoidable, would be horrendous. The captain elbowed his way to the nose ladder of the plane, pausing only to "borrow" an MP's pistol when General Farrell asked him where his gun was.

Finally, the aircraft was ready for takeoff and Tibbets, leaning out of a side window by the pilot's seat, yelled: "Okay, fellows, cut those lights!"

Fitting words from a man about to plunge a whole city into darkness. And at 2:45 A.M., the *Enola Gay* took off on its historic journey—though just barely. To gain the momentum necessary to lift the overweight load, Tibbets pulled back his wheel virtually at the water's edge. And the *Enola Gay* thundered into the magnificent moonlit night.

Fifteen minutes later, Parsons and his assistant, Jeppson, were in the bomb bay arming the atomic bomb over the Pacific. They then climbed out and sat on cushions in front of Jeppson's console so they could watch the panel on this little black box and monitor the bomb's electrical circuits. All the lights were now green, but if one turned red, it would mean something was wrong and the plane might have to return to Tinian. Everything was going well, however . . . perhaps too well for a man like Parsons. He couldn't afford to let his mind stray from his job even for a moment, to let himself dwell on his family—or the Japanese families that would soon perish.

The history-recording ghosts had not all been left behind, it seemed. When the plane reached the Japanese coast, Tibbets' voice sounded over the intercom that from now on all intercom conversation would be recorded.

"This is for history," the voice said, "so watch your language. We're carrying the first atomic bomb."

Most crew members were dismayed on learning for the first time why they would soon become celebrities. No, they would not sully their historic mission with foul language. Jeppson had guessed the nature of the weapon much earlier and together with some of his colleagues had even written General Spaatz asking that the United States demonstrate the bomb before dropping it on a city. But he now knew how to divert his mind from what was about to happen to 100,000 people: He periodically sat in the navigator's dome and indulged his passion for astronomy, counting the stars and basking in the peace of a fathomless universe.

Peace came less easily to Parsons, it seems, because he hid his feelings as arduously as he had hid the secret of the atomic bomb.

How could he have told a superior that the bomb he helped to build should be used only after warning the enemy?

At 7:25 A.M. Tibbets received a coded message from the weather plane over Hiroshima. The sky was blue over the city. He switched on the intercom and announced:

"It's Hiroshima!"

Then just after 8 A.M. Jeppson gazed at the console and, turning to Parsons, formed a circle with his thumb and forefinger. The captain got up and walked to the cockpit.

The bomb still checked out, he said.

Tibbets, staring at a crazy quilt of a city below, asked, "Do you agree that's the target?"

"Yes."

"We're about to start the bomb run," Tibbets said on the intercom. "Put on your goggles and place them up on your forehead. When you hear the tone signal, pull the goggles over your eyes and leave them there until after the flash."

The bombardier, Thomas Ferebee, peered through the bombsight at the misty circle of color—the glistening blue bay, the green stretches of land, the gray crisscrossing roads, the slender brown fingers of the muddy Ota River. And there was the Aioi Bridge, the aiming point.

"I've got it!" Ferebee cried.

Parsons grabbed the bombsight and gazed through it to make doubly sure. It was all geography, like a map, it seemed. A lifeless map.

The tone sounded in everybody's radio headset, and goggles were pulled down over anxious eyes.

"Bomb away!" Ferebee cried.

And at 8:15:17, the bomb bay doors sprang open and Little Boy plummeted toward earth. In forty-three seconds, if all went well, Hiroshima would cease to exist.

Parsons would now see how his gadget worked.

III

About 30,000 feet below, the air-raid siren in Hiroshima began to whine at almost the same moment the bomb was released. In the fire lane less than a mile from Aioi Bridge, Seiko Ogawa stopped picking up tiles and looked up into the clear summer sky and saw a silver bird she recognized as a B-29 streak overhead at a downward angle, with a white jet streamer trailing in its wake and an object flashing the sun's rays falling from "the tail." But she wasn't frightened. Since the two B-29s accompanying the *Enola Gay* were a few miles away, she saw only the single aircraft and guessed it was just another reconnaissance plane. What a beautiful bird. It was hard to believe there were people in it who would want to kill her.

Seiko was supposed to run to the shelter dug out of Hijiyama Hill nearby whenever there was an alert. And she was about to do so when suddenly a huge flash tore open the sky and a raging wind blew her off the ground. As she tumbled in midair, she heard a roar of thunder and then no sound at all.

IV

"Mother! Mother!"

Seiko was awakened by the cries of another child nearby. Then there were more cries. "Help me!" "I can't move!" "Mother! Mother!" Seiko stared into the sky. Where was the sun? Rolling black clouds seethed overhead like a shroud about to smother the earth. Sitting up, she saw dozens of her classmates sprawled on the rubble-strewn field in various twisted positions of death, most with their clothes burned off, their hair standing on end as if electrified, their skin hanging loosely from blackened fingers, arms, legs. Little Boy had exploded about 2,000 feet over Hiroshima, missing the Aioi Bridge by 800 feet. Almost every building in the city had collapsed into dust, including Hiroshima Castle, where the American POWs were being held.

At first, Seiko felt numb; nothing around her seemed real. When would she awaken from the nightmare? But then a surge of searing heat suddenly overwhelmed her, burning away all illusions. Everything was real, hideously real. Especially her own shredded, blistered skin and great black wounds that covered her arms, legs, and torso. She knew her face, too, had been damaged, though she wasn't sure how badly. Her clothes were in tatters and her bosom was exposed.

Gradually the pall of smoke lifted and the sun peeped through. But its bright rays no longer gently caressed her; they inflamed her wounds as if a match were held to them. She struggled to her feet and joined a band of other survivors, their bodies also half melted and peeling, and stumbled along with them, adding to the morbid medley of sobs and screams. The victims wandered aimlessly in circles seeking, it seemed, a god who might magically ease their suffering. Finally, they came to the river, which was already swarming with human wreckage, and leaped in to cool their wounds. Those who couldn't swim, or were too weak to, drowned. Seiko, in her feebleness, started to go under but was pulled out by a stranger just in time.

Home. She had to get home. Her pain only slightly relieved by the cold, blood-red water, she staggered up Hijiyama Hill past charred, mutilated bodies and the ashen ruins of wooden houses. Under the debris she heard voices pitifully begging for help, but how could she help them when she herself was barely alive?

Seiko was on the verge of collapse when a truck pulled up. Together with others, she climbed in the back and was driven to Tameno Hospital on the eastern outskirts of Hiroshima, about halfway to her home. Since the hospital was bursting with victims, orderlies placed Seiko on a mat in a corridor that was paved with writhing flesh, making her feel like a "fish in a market." But rest did not alleviate the pain, and soon her body swelled like a balloon. She cried for a doctor, but none was free, and when one finally came, all he had for her was some disinfectant and white ointment. What medicine could soothe such wounds?

For hours the girl lay there inhaling the stench of death and decay, enduring in semiconsciousness the ravages of atomic fire. Finally, toward midnight, she heard a voice calling out over the hubbub and hysteria: "Seiko! Seiko!"

She recognized the voice. "Father," she moaned, hardly able to move her lips.

The hospital had managed to contact her father and he had come with two neighbors to fetch her. Father and daughter could find each other only through the sound of their voices, for Seiko's face had been bandaged and her eyes were now so swollen that she couldn't open them.

"Father," she murmured again when she felt the touch of his hand on hers.

They hardly spoke, for it wasn't Japanese to express their feelings. Besides, silence conveyed what words could not. With the help of the neighbors, the father placed his daughter on a mattress in a cart he had brought, and the three men dragged the creaking vehicle 7 miles to Seiko's home, arriving about 4 A.M., August 7. The house had escaped damage because it was so far from town.

Mother, grandmother, sisters, and brothers were at the door to greet Seiko. She needn't worry. They would take care of her. They would make her well. And they treated her wounds with grated cucumbers, changed her bandages, promised to find her a husband.

They even hid all the mirrors in the house so she couldn't look at herself. Seiko, after all, dreamed of becoming a famous actress, and an actress must have an unblemished face. The girl herself was hopeful. There were ways to heal burns. If she lived, she could still realize her dream when the war was over.

But then Seiko looked through the window and saw her reflection in it. Like Amaterasu, when she gazed into the mirror of truth, the girl didn't recognize herself. One jaw was joined to the neck, the mouth was grotesquely twisted, the skin was an ugly mass of keloid scars. She stared in horror at a monster.

The machine had run its course.

V

President Truman learned of the historic explosion when he was finishing lunch with the crew of the *Augusta* as it churned through calm waters toward home. A map-room officer walked over and handed him a message, which he quickly read:

> Hiroshima was bombed visually . . . at seven fifteen PM Washington time August five. . . . Fifteen minutes after drop Captain Parsons reported "condition normal in airplane following delivery. Results clear cut successful in all respects. Visible effects greater than in any test."

Truman looked up, his face alight. In less than four months his terror had dissolved into triumph. He had won the gamble that he had had to take anyway. No, it didn't pay to fight a machine; he had learned this when he worked for Tom Pendergast. But it paid well *not* to fight it. The moon and the stars, which had so recently fallen on him, would now revolve around him. He had, after all, harnessed the power of the sun.

"Captain," he exclaimed to the officer, "this is the greatest thing in history!"

EPILOGUE

I

Although Hiroshima lay in ruins, word of its devastation did not reach military ears in Tokyo until about noon on the day of the bomb. For in the wake of the holocaust, all communication with the paralyzed metropolis was cut off. And since reports drifting in revealed that only one or two planes caused the destruction, the military leaders did not envisage an entire city reduced to rubble. In their minds, Hiroshima couldn't possibly be gutted any worse than other Japanese cities had been.

Even when President Truman announced on August 7 that it was an atomic bomb that fell on Hiroshima, Japanese leaders were incredulous. How could it be? Hadn't Professor Nishina assured them that America could not make an atomic bomb during the war?

But Marquis Kido, whose pessimism always prepared him to believe the worst, was less doubtful than most of his colleagues. He rushed to tell Hirohito of the massive destruction caused by a "new type of bomb." The Emperor was "overwhelmed with grief."

"Under the circumstances," he said, "we must bow to the inevitable. No matter what happens to me, we must put an end to this war as speedily as possible so that this tragedy will not be repeated."

Nevertheless, Hirohito still did not suggest that he personally order a surrender. He simply hoped that his men would now realize the futility of Japan's situation and agree to one. But these officers were not yet convinced. Later on the day of the bomb, the Cabinet met to analyze the impact the weapon would have on continuing the war. Togo insisted that Truman would not lie about the nature of the bomb. It "drastically changes the whole military situation and offers the military ample grounds for ending the war" without losing face, he reasoned. But Anami disagreed.

"Such a move is uncalled for," he replied. "We do not even know yet if the bomb was atomic"—whatever Truman said.

Anami promised, however, to find out the truth. He would send Professor Nishina and other nuclear experts to Hiroshima to determine just what did happen.

II

Nishina was almost certain the weapon was an atomic bomb the moment a reporter came to his laboratory and told him of Truman's announcement. The President said the bomb used at Hiroshima had the power of 20,000 tons of TNT—exactly the power one of his students had calculated an atomic bomb would have.

As his plane circled over Hiroshima on the afternoon of August 8—the aircraft had had to turn back the day before because of engine trouble—he was shocked when he saw the damage. The center of the city had been scorched, and outside the burned area houses had disintegrated. No ordinary bomb could have done this. Nishina was filled with both awe and horror. Awe at the realization that America had dragged the world into the nuclear age with this "magnificent product of pure physics." Horror at the sight of what this "magnificent product" could do.

On landing, he immediately began his investigation. He moved around the city by car and on foot, though he knew the radiation danger was great. How could a scientist think of danger at a moment of monumental discovery? How could a patriot think of it when the future of his country depended on his services? After studying the extent of damage, Nishina concluded that the bomb indeed had a force equivalent to 20,000 tons of TNT. Other evidence abounded, too. Clay roof tiles had melted because of the tremendously high temperature; Geiger counter readings indicated that soil, metal objects, the bones of corpses, and sulfur attached to insulators had become radioactive; radiation had caused photo dry plates to turn black, white corpuscle counts to decrease, and shadows to be imprinted on stones.

That evening, when Nishina completed his investigation, he rushed to a telephone and called Prime Minister's Suzuki's office. When Sakomizu answered, Nishina blurted:

"What I've seen so far is unspeakable. Tens of thousands dead. Bodies piled up everywhere. Sick, wounded, naked people wandering around in a daze. . . . Almost no buildings left standing."

"It's all true then? Hiroshima is completely wiped out?"

"Completely. . . . I'm very sorry to tell you this. . . . The so-called new-type bomb is actually an atomic bomb."

It was now about 8 P.M., August 8. It had thus taken the Japanese about sixty hours to confirm that America had a weapon that could wipe out Japan almost overnight.

Less than eight hours later, at 3:49 A.M. on August 9, a B-29 called *Bock's Car* roared into the sky from Tinian with another atomic bomb, and at 11:01 A.M. that day dropped Fat Man on Nagasaki. As General Groves had ordered, the second bomb fell as soon as possible after the first, regardless of how much time the Japanese might have needed to absorb and understand what had struck them the first time. If the Hiroshima bomb helped the peacemakers to push their case at all, the Nagasaki bomb added little to it. The peacemakers wanted peace, bomb or no bomb. And the warmongers wanted war, bomb or no bomb. The deadlock continued as if neither bomb had been dropped.

In fact, the Nagasaki bomb hit Japan only a few hours after Radio Moscow announced in a predawn broadcast that Russia had declared war on the country and was already attacking across the Manchurian border. Thus, in the wake of the Soviet attack, the Japanese were given virtually no time at all to surrender before they were struck by a third blow. How could the Nagasaki bomb be postponed or canceled, even if it wasn't needed, after so much money and heartache had gone into building it? Would an artist be content if he created two masterpieces and only one was shown?

III

Actually, Ambassador Sato had learned of Russia's intentions at 5 P.M. August 8, the day that he was finally received by Foreign Minister Molotov, though his cable to Togo informing him of these intentions never reached Tokyo. Before he could ask Molotov to reply to his desperate proposal to send Prince Konoye to Moscow, the Russian began reading a document to him:

Since Japan "rejected" the Potsdam Declaration, "the proposal made by the Japanese government to the Soviet Union for mediation in the Far East has lost all foundation. . . . The Allies approached the Soviet government with a proposal to join the war against Japanese aggression," and so "the Soviet government has joined in the [Potsdam] Declaration," and from August 9 "will consider herself in a state of war against Japan."

Strangely, Sato seemed almost relieved by this news of a Pearl Harbor in reverse. Perhaps now the military would accept peace while the Emperor still had his throne. When Molotov said that he personally regretted what had happened, Sato replied, ignoring Russia's duplicity:

"I am grateful for the goodwill and hospitality of your government. It is indeed a sad thing that we shall have to part as enemies. . . . Let us part with a handshake."

After all, Russia could be saving the Japanese race.

IV

The militarists, of course, did not see the Russians as saviors. They viewed the Soviet attack as an even greater threat to their war plans than the atomic bomb. The bomb had killed mainly civilians. How much help could women and children be to the war effort? But the Russians were attacking the Japanese *army*. The peacemakers, however, were more horrified by the bomb because they felt it could mean the almost instant destruction of all Japan, while they knew the Japanese army had been rendered almost impotent anyway.

Thus, when Suzuki learned that the "new kind of bomb" was in fact an atomic bomb, he made a historic decision. The moment had come to tear away the veil of *haragei*. Japan must accept the Potsdam Declaration without delay. He called a meeting of the Big Six for the following morning at 10:30—a half-hour before Fat Man was to annihilate Nagasaki. The peacemakers, it seems, couldn't quite keep pace with the bombmakers.

Before the meeting, at 7:30 A.M., Suzuki bowed before the Emperor and told him of his decision. Would His Majesty please give him "special help"?

Hirohito knew what Suzuki meant. He might finally be forced to give a direct command for peace. Yes, he would do it, if such help was needed. And his determination was hardened by a report that a B-29 was heading toward Tokyo with another atomic bomb, a report that sent him and the Empress scurrying to a specially reinforced room in their underground bunker, where they were locked behind a thick steel door. The report, of course, turned out to be false.

But at the Big Six meeting, the military remained adamant. Let the bombs fall, let the Russians attack. They would accept nothing less than a negotiated peace even if every Japanese had to die. In mid-conference, an aide to the Prime Minister rushed in with the news: An atomic bomb had just destroyed Nagasaki! The meeting ended but the deadlock didn't. Another atomic bomb. The horrifying novelty had worn off.

Not for the Emperor, however. Late that night he kept his promise to help Suzuki, agreeing to hold an Imperial Conference that the Prime Minister would call on false pretenses. The admiral had Sakomizu persuade the military leaders to approve such a conference in advance. It would supposedly be held sometime in the future when, as tradition dictated, the government would have already reached a unanimous decision on the policy in question. The Emperor was not to sully his dignity by listening to arguments. Their signatures were needed, Sakomizu explained to the militarists, in case an emergency meeting had to be held instantly. Of course the Prime Minister wouldn't actually call such a conference without first confirming that they wanted one.

But Suzuki did precisely this. And after many hours of violent argument, he stood up, bowed toward the Emperor, and said, to the rage of his military colleagues:

"We have no precedent . . . but with the greatest reverence I must now ask His Majesty to express his wishes." (In fact, the

Emperor had also personally demanded an end to the 1936 rebellion.)

And as everyone listened with bowed head, Hirohito, his dignity unsullied despite the bitter debate, lamented:

"I cannot bear to see my innocent people suffer any longer.
. . . The time has come when we must bear the unbearable. . . .
I swallow my own tears and give my sanction to the proposal to accept the Allied proclamation."

As the Emperor wiped the moisture from his glasses, the others, audibly sobbing, swallowed their tears, too. Suzuki stood up and wailed:

"The conference is over. We regard Your Majesty's sacred will as the conclusion of our conference."

The Emperor had finally spoken.

Anami felt that Suzuki has betrayed him by setting up the conference through trickery. And yet he apparently was relieved. He could have resigned and brought the entire government down with him. The militarists could then rattle their swords and make sure that a new Prime Minister and foreign minister sympathetic to their views would be selected. But Anami chose to remain in office, permitting Suzuki and Togo to pursue peace. The war minister seems to have realized that his own demands had been unrealistic, but how could he violate his *giri* to the young officers? However, now that the Emperor had issued a direct command, he no longer felt obligated to these officers. His duty was to calm their passions and prevent a revolt.

Anami met with his brother-in-law, Colonel Takeshita, and other young officers and conveyed His Majesty's wish.

"There is nothing that can be done," he said.

When shock turned to dissent, the war minister growled, "If anybody disobeys Anami's orders, he will have to cut Anami down!"

V

On the morning of August 10 in Washington, a Morse code message from Tokyo was picked up by American monitors. Truman, Byrnes, Stimson, Leahy, and Forrestal, all just back from Potsdam, met and discussed it: Japan agreed to the Potsdam terms, but "with the understanding that the said declaration does not compromise any demand which prejudices the prerogatives of His Majesty as a Sovereign Ruler." The single Japanese condition created an awkward situation for Truman and Byrnes. They had refused to throw this "crumb" to the Japanese before the atomic bombs were dropped, as Stimson had urged them to do in order to obviate the need for dropping them. With almost 150,000 people already killed by the bomb, would it make sense to agree to the one condition now that if agreed to before might have spared those lives?

Events had already proved that Truman and Byrnes, as well as Stimson, had miscalculated in their effort to keep Russia out of the Pacific war. They had refrained from warning Japan about the bomb—and possibly inducing it to surrender—at least partly so they could keep the weapon a secret from Stalin and thus forestall a Soviet attack. But this effort had all gone for naught—and Stalin had even mocked America by declaring to Japan that the Allies had "approached" Russia with a "proposal" to join in the fighting, when, on the contrary, the United States had *refused* to formally do this. In any case, could the conscience of the American leaders now permit them to admit they had committed an error that may have cost the lives of so many?

Stimson, who wanted to stop all kinds of bombing, still argued that the United States should agree to the Japanese condition. This concession, he felt, could save a third city from destruction. But, aware that he was dealing with pragmatic minds, he stressed simply that if Japan did not surrender even after being atom-bombed twice, "something like this use of the Emperor must be made to order to save us from a score of bloody Iwo Jimas and Okinawas all over China and the New Netherlands." And Stimson was backed by Admiral Leahy and Forrestal. Leahy, after all, had always wanted to offer this concession, though without making it seem as if the Imperial system was being "imposed" on the Japanese people.

Truman was noncommittal. How could he repudiate his pre-Hiroshima decision? On the other hand, how could he ignore Stimson's logic? Byrnes still opposed guaranteeing the Emperor his throne, but, seeing he was alone, finally agreed to compromise. He could afford to do so, for didn't Russia already know what the bomb could do? He wrote a draft stating that the authority of the

Emperor and the Japanese government to rule Japan would be subject to the Supreme Commander of the Allied Powers, and that the ultimate form of the government would be determined by the freely expressed will of the Japanese people. This was still unconditional surrender, wasn't it?

VI

When this reply was heard in Tokyo over the radio in the early hours of August 12, the Big Six met, and Suzuki and Togo immediately accepted it, even though there was no *explicit* promise to let the Emperor keep his throne. But Anami saw in the ambiguity of Byrnes' statement a reason for backing out of his commitment to the Emperor. Since all the Japanese leaders had agreed that the one unalterable condition for peace was a guarantee of the Emperor's status, was he not free to insist again on continuing the war? But *giri* to the young officers was now less a factor than fear that these fanatics would revolt if he voted to accept the Byrnes note. Colonel Takeshita had even advised his brother-in-law to commit *harakiri* if he voted so.

At the same time, with the military once again rejecting peace, Suzuki's more personalized fear returned. The mood of the young officers was clear to him, too. And in the event of a revolt, his head would probably be the first to roll since the militarists would surely try to avenge his "treachery" in using the Emperor to thwart their will. It was time to wear the veil of *haragei* again.

"If disarmament is forced upon us," he cried, "we have no alternative but to continue the war."

After this inconclusive meeting, Togo, in shock, rushed to see Kido. Now it was the peacemakers who considered Suzuki "treacherous." Kido immediately summoned Suzuki. The Lord Keeper was no longer the fearful, appeasing, conniving survivor. In the anguish of defeat, he shone with some of the grandeur of his grandfather, who had vowed that his sons would help to build a new Japan on the ashes of Shimonoseki. Now the grandson vowed that *his* sons would help to build a still newer Japan on the ashes of the modern-day Shimonosekis.

"Should we turn down the Potsdam Declaration at this stage," Kido told Suzuki, "and should the war be continued, a million innocent Japanese would die from bombings and starvation. If we bring about peace now, four or five of us may be assassinated but it would be worth it. . . . Without wavering or hesitating, let us carry out the policy to accept the Potsdam Declaration."

Clearly moved, Suzuki reflected for a moment—perhaps on the gun barrel that almost a decade earlier had pressed into his neck. But Kido's grandeur apparently reminded him of his own tarnished splendor. Was he not a national hero? Had he not sailed into the midst of enemy fleets to fearlessly wreak havoc?

"Let us do it!" he agreed.

VII

General Anami was less malleable. He went to see Prince Mikasa, Hirohito's brother, and urged him to persuade the Emperor to change his mind.

But Mikasa replied: "Since the Mukden Incident the army has at times acted not quite in accordance with the Imperial wish. It is most improper that you should still want to continue the war when things have reached this stage."

Anami was shattered by this rebuke from a member of the Imperial family, but to save the god he so affronted he continued his campaign, even asking Kido to "request the Emperor to reconsider acceptance of the [Byrnes] note."

When Kido refused, Anami meekly departed. He had done his duty—remaining loyal to the young officers while keeping the lid on the revolt they were hatching. He now knew they really planned to take over the government—and the Emperor—because Takeshita, one of the conspirators, had urged him to join the plot. They would rise up before the government could approve the Byrnes note. Anami stalled off his brother-in-law, promising to "consider" his request.

Meanwhile, Kido, sensing an uprising, advised the Emperor to break precedent once more and *personally* call an emergency Imperial Conference to approve the Byrnes note.

At this meeting on the morning of August 14, the Emperor, paler and thinner than ever, his cheek twitching frequently, stood up and did not equivocate.

"I want you all to agree with my conclusions. . . . I have come to the conclusion that we cannot continue the war any longer. . . . I find [the Byrnes note] quite acceptable."

Brushing the tears from his cheek, he continued: "I cannot let my subjects suffer any longer. I wish to save the people at the risk of my own life. If the war continues, our entire nation will be laid waste, hundreds of thousands more will die. I cannot endure this. . . . It is my desire that all of you . . . bow to my wishes and accept the Allied reply forthwith."

The Emperor paused as his ministers openly wept, with some collapsing on the floor in their grief. Turning to his war minister, he said gently:

"Anami, I understand it is particularly difficult for you, but you must bear it!"

And Anami and the others all did. For the Emperor had left no room for argument this time. Had they not been taught from youth that the Emperor was absolute? They had relied on him even as they tried to use him. Now the burden of determining the nation's destiny had irrevocably been lifted from their shoulders. And like almost all Japanese, they could accept the worst if the Emperor commanded them to.

After the meeting, Anami, with choking voice, told Takeshita and the other young officers that the Emperor's decision was final and ordered them to obey it.

"I don't want any officer in this army," he said, "to presume that he knows better than the Emperor and the government what is best for the country."

Then he urged them to live, not to die: "You officers still have a duty to perform, and you cannot absolve it through death. Your duty is to remain alive and to help your country along the path to recovery."

The officers noted that Anami had said "your duty," not "our duty." And his meaning was clear. Anami went to Togo's office and thanked the foreign minister for sending a note to the Allies asking them to limit their occupation zone and let Japanese forces disarm themselves. Then he visited Suzuki and, handing him a box of cigars, apologized for giving him so much trouble. Finally, he went to his official residence, where, with Takeshita, he sat on the tatami gulping down one cup of sake after another.

Shortly, Anami got up, wound a white cotton band around his

waist, put on a white cotton shirt given him by the Emperor when he had been his aide-de-camp, laid out a dress uniform resplendent with all his decorations, and knelt on the polished floor of the porch facing the Imperial Palace. He placed two pieces of paper beside him, each with a poem, one thanking the Emperor for his "great favors" and the other apologizing for his own "great crime." Then he drew a gleaming short sword from its sheath and plunged it into his belly. Takeshita, who had gone out, returned and saw Anami writhing in agony, unable, it seemed, to die. He took the sword and tearfully thrust it into his beloved brother-in-law's neck. The general was buried in the uniform he had laid out.

Thus, Anami, as he had long planned, finally resolved his conflict of obligations while absolving all others of responsibility for the failure of the Japanese military—which had brought down upon Japan the unprecedented terror of the atomic age. Unwittingly, he had oiled the machine of inevitability.

VIII

If Anami had at last found peace, the young officers had not. A few hours earlier, the Japan Broadcasting Corporation sent several technicians to the palace to record the Emperor making a surrender speech to the people. But even as Kido locked the recorded disk in the palace vault, thousands of rebels, disregarding Takeshita's warning that a revolt could no longer succeed, poured from their barracks and tried—unsuccessfully—to steal the disk and kill those who had advised the Emperor to make the broadcast. The anticipated coup that had for so long frozen Kido, Suzuki, and the other peacemakers, as well as Anami, was crystallizing. Crying for revenge, the rebels burned down Suzuki's home—without Suzuki in it. He managed to escape with his family in a car before the horde of assassins could find him, once more saved by the "invisible power."

Another band of rebels seized Kido's residence, but because they failed to recognize the Lord Keeper, they refused to let him enter his own home. Gratefully, he dashed back to the palace faster than the rebels could yell "Banzai," and hid himself in the underground shelter in which history had been made. The ubiquitous rebels were running around the palace, too, searching high and low for Kido, though fortunately for him, they didn't search low enough.

However, they did find the chief of the Imperial Guards and shot him for failing to join the rebellion. Others seized Radio Tokyo nearby, but when they tried to broadcast, an air-raid alarm sounded; the army, ironically, had cut all communications.

At dawn, the military police finally arrived and recaptured the building, and Radio Tokyo went on the air calmly announcing that the Emperor would speak at noon that day, August 15. Plagued by an aimless leadership, the rebel movement began to break up, and ended with five of the chiefs falling to their knees on the Imperial plaza and disemboweling themselves, as Anami, their loyal lord, had already done.

IX

One Japanese leader who didn't commit *harakiri* was Admiral Suzuki—though for months after the war extremists demanded that he tear open his belly to repent for his "betrayal." Suzuki scampered from place to place to avoid perceived assassins, but finally settled down in the village of his birth north of Tokyo and placed his destiny in the hands of the "invisible power."

At last, Suzuki was at peace, feeling that he had fulfilled the Emperor's wishes, however devious his method. He read Tao, cursed all government, and perhaps wondered why his will to live in a world that didn't understand Tao should have been so strong. He died a natural death in 1949, mumbling "Eternal peace, eternal peace."

X

In 1946, Foreign Minister Togo was placed on trial before the International Military Tribunal for the Far East for conspiracy to wage aggressive war and other crimes while he was foreign minister in the days before and after Pearl Harbor. Found guilty, he was sentenced to twenty years imprisonment, but, because of a bad heart, spent about half his remaining years in the prison hospital, where he died in 1950.

As a realist, he had expected to be punished and had no regrets. He wrote in his memoirs as he languished behind bars:

> While the future of Japan is eternal, it is a blessing beyond estimation that this most dreadful of wars has been brought to a close, ending our country's agony and saving millions of lives; with that my life's work has been done. It does not matter what befalls me.

XI

The Russians interned Ambassador Sato in Moscow from August 1945 to May 1946, when he returned to Japan feeling there was nothing left for him to do but die. However, he soon began a new life. He plunged into politics and was elected to the House of Councillors, the new upper chamber of the Diet, serving as president of that house during his first six-year term. He kept his seat until 1965. His most gratifying moment came in 1956, when he led the first Japanese delegation to the United Nations and watched, weeping, while the Rising Sun flag ascended the pole to flutter beside those of the other nations of the world. As it had when he represented Japan in the League of Nations before the rise of the military. Sato died in 1971.

XII

Marquis Kido, shrewd as he was, was not shrewd enough to convince the International Military Tribunal that he had been a lover of peace from the start. Charged with using his influence to help the militarists push for war, he was sentenced to life imprisonment—though his pain was eased when the Emperor rewarded him for his services with 20 million yen, a carton of canned food, and a barrel of the finest sake. Kido felt he deserved the reward.

"It is my sole consolation," he told the Tribunal with his usual windy eloquence, "that at the close of the war I was able to give full play to my bold activities under the august virtues of the Emperor [and] succeeded in preventing the Japanese mainland from becoming a battleground and saving the lives of hundreds of millions of people."

Released from prison in 1956, after the American Occupation, Kido went home, where he resumed feeding red meat to his watchdogs and no doubt pondered what his grandfather would have said if he knew the "barbarians" had turned Japan into a country that sneered upon samurai and spurned the sword. Kido died several years later, still certain that Japan would achieve greatness, if only it tested the international political climate before making any moves—as he had vainly urged the military to do before Pearl Harbor.

XIII

When the American Occupation forces landed in Japan, Hirohito seized an opportunity that was unprecedented for a Japanese Emperor. He would now be able to cleanse himself of shame, the shame of having caused, however unwillingly, the death of millions in his name, of "inviting" atomic holocaust. Now he could repay, at least in part, his massive debt to the people, who had made such sacrifices for him. Now, at last, he might be able to sleep, if perhaps the sleep of death.

The Emperor put on his striped trousers, cutaway, wing collar, and top hat, then stepped into his Mercedes, which took him to the American Embassy to see General Douglas MacArthur, the Allied Supreme Commander. MacArthur thought he knew why Hirohito would so humble himself: He wanted to plead for immunity from prosecution for war crimes. But though Kido had advised the Emperor to admit to no wrong, the Sovereign said, after MacArthur had lit a cigarette for him:

"I come to you, General MacArthur, to offer myself to the judgment of the powers you represent as the one to bear sole responsibility for every political and military decision made and action taken by my people in the conduct of the war."

MacArthur was overwhelmed. He knew what the Emperor said wasn't true, that at worst he had simply ratified decisions that others made.

"This courageous assumption of a responsibility implicit with death," the general would say, "moved me to the very marrow of my bones."

Though there was a strong movement in Washington to put the Emperor on trial as a war criminal, MacArthur, perhaps influenced in part by this meeting, argued that such a decision would stir unrest and possibly even guerrilla warfare in Japan. And Hirohito was not indicted. Even the enemy would not let him repay his debt. But he was no longer the same Emperor. On New Year's Day 1946, with hardly a prod from the Occupation authorities, he issued an Imperial rescript:

"The ties between us and our people have always stood upon mutual trust and affection. They do not depend upon mere legends and myths. They are not predicated on the false conception that the Emperor is divine and that the Japanese people are superior to other races, and fated to rule the world."

Hirohito had finally done what he would have done as a youth, if it had been possible. He renounced his divinity. He was not a god. He was a man. And in November, a new American-dictated constitution legalized his mortal status.

"The Emperor," it said, "shall be the symbol of the State and of the unity of the people, deriving his position from the will of the people with whom resides sovereign power."

Just like a British king—and now he could smile! He did, as he visited schools, hospitals, factories, and even gave press conferences.

Today the Emperor is seldom seen outside his palace, for his advisers feel that even a mortal Emperor shouldn't be overexposed. A little awe is still good for the people, despite Hirohito's awkward role as their "servant." But every New Year's Day, endless lines of his subjects twist their way through the magnificent gardens, past the swan-decorated ponds, and over the arched bridges of the palace grounds, where they gather in a huge grassy interior plaza to catch a glimpse of the Emperor, who greets them with languid waves—and smiles—from the balcony of a small structure especially built for the purpose.

When the Emperor appears, a great silence settles over the crowd, embarrassingly broken by scattered, hesitant applause. Someone cries out:

"That's him. He looks just like his picture, doesn't he?"

Smiling parents lift up their children so they can see the gentle little man with large eyeglasses. Photography enthusiasts stand on large rocks or boxes to snap a picture of him. Schoolboys chew on bean-paste candy. Visiting American sailors chat with pretty girls dressed in their colorful holiday kimonos.

Such a scene would never have happened in prewar days, when the Emperor's rare appearances evoked hysterical cries of *Banzai!*, set off an orgy of bowing, and produced radiant looks on the faces of people who imagined themselves touched by a magic wand. Today, the greater part of the population esteems and loves him, with an intimacy that never existed when they worshiped him as a distant spiritual image. But most Japanese, particularly the youth, feel a sense of obligation toward him hardly more binding than the *giri* due an in-law.

And the Emperor is delighted. Now he can work in his laboratory examining fungi without the cry, "To die for the Emperor!" ringing mercilessly in his ears. He is no longer a false god; he is an honest man. Now he can sleep.

XIV

Sleep, however, did not come easily to Yoshio Nishina. He had seen the holocaust. Even as he marveled at the incredible power of the atomic bomb, he agonized at the horror, at his own role in letting it happen. Yes, he knew Japan couldn't make a bomb, at least during the war, but he had never really wanted it to succeed. Worse, because he didn't want America to succeed either, he predicted it wouldn't.

How could he have failed to realize that with enough money and will American science and industry could achieve almost anything? If he had let himself admit the possibility, he would have demanded, pleaded, insisted that Japan end the war instantly— before America could harness such power. All the blackened corpses he saw, all the human shadows, all the burned and hanging flesh were due to his reluctance to see the truth. The only way to repay his debt to the dead and suffering, to the Emperor whom he deceived, was to commit suicide.

But Nishina, always the calculating scientist, soon seasoned his emotions with rationality. Could he really have persuaded the military to surrender on the basis of unsubstantiated arguments? Was it really his fault if the scope of American industry was so much greater than that of Japanese industry, if American resources were almost unlimited? No, it wasn't. So why should he not to kill himself.

But something in Nishina died nevertheless. When he returned to Tokyo, he was a changed man. He was morose, pessimistic, unable to work. How tragic that an era that would bring untold opportunity to advance the welfare and fulfilment of man should open with so great a catastrophe. His only consolation was that the war would now end.

Despite his despair, Nishina clung to a shred of hope for the future of Japan and mankind. And symbolizing this hope were the cyclotrons. On returning from Hiroshima, he immediately asked: Were they in working order? They would help him to analyze the information he had obtained in Hiroshima, to find clues to the peaceful use of the atom, in agriculture, forestry, animal husbandry, fisheries, medical therapy. Could not the deadly radioactive samples he had brought back hold the secret to new life? Japan's three cyclotrons might still be the key to a better world, though it would be founded on the graveyard of Hiroshima.

But before Nishina could gather his strength to work again, Japan surrendered and the American forces arrived. Now he could not operate his cyclotrons without their permission. So he filed a request with the American authorities, stating that he would use the machines for research in biology, medicine, chemistry, and metallurgy. A permit was immediately granted, though only for biological and medical studies.

But a few weeks later, in November 1945, Nishina received a memorandum rescinding the authorization. And then one morning an American officer arrived with several army engineers and handed him an order. The engineers were to destroy his two cyclotrons, while others demolished the one in Osaka.

Nishina was stunned.

"No, you can't do that!" he cried.

Orders were orders, the officer replied.

"But that is like dismembering my body," Nishina pleaded. "This is ten years of my life."

And as the engineers went to work, he rushed in desperation to U.S. general headquarters.

Why were the cyclotrons being destroyed? he asked.

Because the U.S. Government had ordered them destroyed, an officer replied.

Had the U.S. government consulted with American scientists before issuing the order? Nishina wanted to know.

"Yes, of course," said the officer. Dr. Karl Compton of MIT had been in Japan recently and the government decision reflected his opinion.

This was incomprehensible to Nishina. The cyclotron wasn't needed to build an atomic bomb, and the American scientists knew it. The United States might just as well burn Japanese libraries or smash Japanese printing presses. It was a heinous crime, in his view. In fact, he later learned that Compton had recommended that the cyclotrons be allowed to operate and that he wrote Secretary of War Robert Patterson, who had replaced Stimson, denouncing the destruction and demanding that the officer who gave the order be dismissed.

It was all a mistake, replied Patterson. He had not consulted with his scientific advisers.

But this admission could not console Nishina. All his dreams for Japan were shattered together with the cyclotrons. Losing his heart for personal experimentation, he started a private company to manufacture streptomycin and other drugs. If he couldn't do research on medicine to save people's lives, he could at least make medicine.

In 1951, Nishina died of cancer, believed to be caused by exposure to radiation in Hiroshima. But his funeral was an anticlimax. His body was joining a spirit long since dead.

XV

Once the curtain had fallen on World War II, America turned its spotlight on Russia. And Henry Stimson, before retiring in September 1945, once again changed his mind about how to deal with Stalin and the bomb. The bomb, after all, had already destroyed two Japanese cities and was no longer a secret. And Stalin was surely hungering for some knowledge about atomic energy that would permit him to rebuild Russian cities. Now was the time to lure him into an international arrangement for the control of this energy. Now was the time to show trust, undiluted by conditions. He went to see Truman and presented his new memorandum:

Was it practical to hope that the atomic 'secret'—so fragile and short-lived—could be used to win concessions from the Russian leaders as to their cherished, if frightful, police state? . . . Might it not . . . be better to reverse the process, to meet Russian suspicion with American candor, to discuss the bomb directly with them and try to reach an agreement on control? Might not trust beget trust; as Russian confidence was earned, might not the repressive—and aggressive—tendencies of Stalinism be abated?

Stimson now urged "immediate and direct negotiations with the Russians looking toward a 'covenant' for the control of the atom" as the only alternative to a "secret armament race of a rather desperate character. . . . If we fail to approach them now and merely continue to negotiate with them, having this weapon rather ostentatiously upon our hip, their suspicions and their distrust of our purposes and motives will increase. It will inspire them to greater efforts in an all-out effort to [build the bomb]."

The President looked up and smiled. He agreed with Stimson, he said. Why not send the old man on his way with a good feeling?

The Secretary repeated his plan in an impromptu farewell talk to the Cabinet on September 21, 1945, his seventy-eighth birthday. He then left for the airport, where he stepped into a plane headed toward Highhold, as an army band blared out "Happy Birthday." But the retiring Secretary wasn't very happy. Jimmy Byrnes was in London for a meeting of the new Council of Foreign Ministers, the body Byrnes felt would help him deal more effectively with Russia. And his "hip pocket" was bulging with an unusable bomb.

XVI

As the council met on September 11, Byrnes still thought he would be able to use this forum to intimidate Russia into making concessions. And Truman was so buried in domestic affairs that he gave Byrnes practically carte blanche in dealing with the Russians—just as Byrnes had hoped. Now he would show that the day of the bomb spelled not only peace but the right kind of peace.

The problem was, however, that Foreign Minister Molotov

spelled peace differently. To make this point, he sneeringly asked the Secretary, using a variation of Stimson's term, if he had an atomic bomb "in his side pocket." Then, at dinner, he reportedly said, "we all have to pay great attention to what Mr. Byrnes says because the United States are the only people who are making the atomic bomb." Then he boasted after downing one cocktail too many that Russia already had one!

At the same time, Molotov expressed his contempt for America's bomb at the bargaining table. When Byrnes tried to loosen Russia's stranglehold on Eastern Europe, Molotov only tightened his grasp and made new—and ominous—demands. Russia, he said, should be given a trusteeship over one of Italy's former African colonies. Why? Byrnes was sure the Russians were really eyeing the Belgian Congo with all its uranium.

Russia had *not* become more "manageable," as the Secretary had predicted to Leo Szilard. Instead of Byrnes using the bomb to dominate Molotov, Molotov had used the bomb to ridicule Byrnes, while making it clear that Russia was determined to have one of its own. All of the Secretary's carefully laid plans to build a world according to Byrnes had gone awry. And thus did much of his logic for dropping the bomb on Japan evaporate along with his bitter champagne.

On returning home empty-handed, Byrnes was pragmatic enough to recognize his monumental miscalculation, to realize that his "bomb-in-the-pocket" strategy could yield neither diplomatic fruit nor political friends. The American people, even while distrusting Russia, clearly wanted some kind of international atomic control. And so now did Byrnes, who threw down his stick and picked up Stimson's carrot, which he had once considered close to appeasement. The London meeting had chastened him. How, after all, could he get the Russians to agree to anything as long as they felt insecure? Now he wanted to share atomic information for peaceful purposes, without, of course, giving away vital secrets. A bomb wasn't really very useful—to the country or to Byrnes' future—if you couldn't drop it on anyone.

In December 1945, Byrnes flew off to Moscow to attend another meeting of the Council of Foreign Ministers. And this time, his pocket bulged not with a bomb but with a bird—a dove of peace. Stalin greeted him warmly and was, it seemed, far more reasonable than Molotov. A United Nations commission for the control of atomic energy? A fine idea, the Soviet leader agreed. All he wanted in return was a "friendly" Bulgaria and Rumania, as friendly as the Poland that Roosevelt had accepted at Yalta. In other words, Russian domination with a little democratic window dressing.

Byrnes was in a dilemma. His principal aim until now had been to *change* the Yalta accords to give Eastern Europe real freedom. But who would be free, or even alive, for long if the atom got out of hand. And with no one alive, he could never be President.

A deal!

And so Byrnes was in an exhilarated mood as he flew home, expecting this time to be welcomed as a hero for saving humanity. But at least a tiny segment of humanity was far less exhilarated, and it included Republican Senator Arthur Vandenberg and his Foreign Relations Committee. How dare Byrnes suggest exchanging atomic information with the Russians! The Secretary was soft on communism! The committee protested to Truman. And Truman suddenly realized that Byrnes hadn't bothered to consult with him about matters that could determine the fate of the world. He had even issued a conference communiqué before getting White House approval. Who did Jimmy think he was—President of the United States?

And Truman's fury was fed by Admiral Leahy, who was soft when it came to killing people but tough when it came to coddling Communists.

"It appears to me from the view of America," Leahy would write in his diary on December 28, 1945, "an appeasement document which gives to the Soviet everything they want and preserves to America nothing."

Truman agreed. Appeasement!

Hardly had Byrnes stepped off the plane when he was summoned to see the President, who was cruising on the Potomac aboard the *Williamsburg*. Byrnes would later claim that Truman said he was pleased by the progress made in Moscow. But Truman would recall in a memorandum to Byrnes shortly after this meeting, perhaps with some exaggeration:

"We went into my stateroom . . . and I closed the door behind us. I told him that I did not like the way in which I had been left in the dark about the Moscow conference. I told him that, as President, I intended to know what progress we were making and what we were doing in foreign negotiations. I said that it was shocking that a communiqué should be issued in Washington announcing a foreign policy development of major importance that I had never heard of. I said I would not tolerate a repetition of such conduct."

Nor would he permit any more "babying" of Russia.

From then on, Truman took charge of American foreign policy, and Byrnes' influence gradually waned, especially after Yalta caught up with him. Russia, in early 1946, cited the text of the secret Yalta agreement on the Far East to back its claim that Roosevelt had agreed to let the Soviet Union take over the Japanese Kurile Islands, among other prizes, in return for its entry in the Pacific war.

Byrnes, however, denied that he had known about this agreement. The trouble was that previously he had boasted that he knew about *all* agreements reached at Yalta. And had not Truman chosen him as Secretary of State partly because of his expertise on that conference? Now Byrnes' newly professed ignorance of the Far East accord made it appear as if Truman himself was appeasing Russia, and without even a clear understanding of the Yalta commitments.

And this image of softness and incompetence was hardly improved by charges in Congress that Byrnes was not backing Chiang Kai-shek enthusiastically enough in his struggle with the Chinese Communists, and that he was even harboring "Communists" in the State Department. Nor did Russian evacuation of Manchuria in 1946, under American pressure, repair the image; the Red Army left the Chinese Communists in charge of the evacuated areas. Henry Stimson himself had become disillusioned with Stalin's aggressiveness once again and was urging a tough policy.

Thus, ironically, Byrnes, who had sold Truman on a hard-line, bomb-carrying approach to communism, was now being dressed down by Truman (whether at the meeting aboard the *Williamsburg* or just in the memorandum to Byrnes) for "babying" Russia. Byrnes tried to save himself by dropping the carrot and picking up the stick again, but it was too late. He resigned in January 1947, his atomic diplomacy and his ambitions in tatters.

Elected governor of South Carolina in 1950, Byrnes would now make national headlines only when he and Truman violently attacked each other. Byrnes blasted Truman's "socialistic" policies. Truman accused Byrnes of lying when he claimed that Roosevelt had pressed him to be a candidate for Vice-President in 1944, and of virtually trying to usurp his presidency. Byrnes called Truman an ingrate for showing no appreciation for his help over the years. Each charged that the other was "soft" on communism.

The feud finally cooled off after several years but Byrnes died in 1972—the year Truman died—a bitter man, feeling betrayed by two Presidents.

XVII

Byrnes' unhappy return from Moscow marked not only the beginning of the end for the Secretary, but the end of the beginning for Truman. For Truman now had the self-confidence to be a President who could make his own decisions. And he no longer had to depend on the atomic bomb to bolster it. Reminded by the budget director shortly after Hiroshima that he had a bomb to back his policies, Truman replied:

"Yes, but I am not sure it can ever be used again."

For what had seemed to him the "greatest thing in history" on the day of the bomb no longer seemed so after the war. As he would revealingly put it to David Lilienthal, director of the Atomic Energy Commission, in discussing the "terrible thing" three years after the war:

"You have got to understand that this isn't a military weapon. It is used to wipe out women and children and unarmed people, and not for military uses."

The President thus contradicted his earlier definition of the bomb as a military weapon. Liberated from the machine, Truman was no longer forced to deceive himself, to justify approval of an action he couldn't stop anyway, and one which he had desperately needed to be able to face the two political giants at Potsdam without flinching. But even now he could listen to the echo of his conscience only in private. In public, he had to be the tough, decisive President with no regrets. Yes, he would drop the bomb on Japan if he had to do it over again. It saved a million lives, didn't it? History must never suggest that Harry Truman killed almost 150,000 people without it being absolutely necessary.

Yet Truman's conscience apparently suggested this. Why else would he privately concede after the war that the bomb "is used to wipe out women and children and unarmed people, and not for military uses"?

XVIII

Admiral Leahy clung to this same view after the war, but he didn't hide his feelings. After he returned from Potsdam with Truman, he was deeply depressed, and people close to him noted that he had "lost his verve" and that he would never fully regain it.

"We'll regret this day," he told his secretary almost as soon as he arrived. "Our country will suffer because of it."

Then he sat down and pessimistically wrote in his diary: "The lethal possibilities of such atomic action in the future is frightening, and while we are the first to have it . . . there is a certainty that it will probably be used against us."

However, Leahy felt, now that America had the bomb, it had no choice but to tightly guard its secret and built an atomic stockpile beyond the reach of any other country.

"When and if the secret of the manufacture of the atomic bomb is known to foreign governments," he wrote, "America will be in acute danger of an attack. . . . I am convinced that our safety demands effective secrecy in regard to manufacture of the A-weapon. . . . Until . . . some world organization can guarantee—and have the power to enforce that guarantee—that the world will be spared the terrors of atomic warfare, the United States must have more and better atom bombs than any potential enemy."

Leahy, in effect, called for a nuclear arms contest that would be dominated by the United States, since the "terrible mistake" in Japan had created a danger that unfortunately had to be met with overwhelming power. His logic was largely rooted in his utter distrust of the Soviet Union. And the admiral, whose imprint on policy was greater after the war than before and during the war, pressed Truman to accept this logic—and reject Byrnes' turn-around conciliatory posture in Moscow.

Leahy was thus instrumental in sparking the downfall of Byrnes, whom, ironically, he had favored over Truman as a Vice-Presidential candidate in 1944. Not surprisingly, Leahy was one of the chief architects of the Truman Doctrine—a plan to help

Greece and Turkey resist Communist aggression with military and economic aid.

But the admiral was driven after the war not only by geopolitical logic, but by a deep fear of the bomb. The fate of all mankind, not simply of armies, was at stake. Armies he could deal with, but how could he now save the women and children? Never had a good knight faced such a challenge. He would fight the enemy as his ancestors had—not with lance and steed this time, for the atomic age had ruled out that kind of war, but with war nevertheless. Cold war.

Leahy resigned when Truman left office in 1952, and died seven years later.

XIX

In 1949, a Russian atomic explosion shook the world. The American bomb was thus rendered useless either as a carrot or a stick, if it ever did serve American policy as either, and an uncontrollable arms race proved the only alternative to an international nuclear control system. Truman halfheartedly attempted to achieve such control, but he and Stalin clashed over conditions, and so atomic bombs soon gave way to hydrogen bombs, which in turn were supplanted by nuclear guided missiles.

This race would surely have escalated into the present balance of terror even if Klaus Fuchs had never existed. And in fact Fuchs and his fellow agents were not the only reason for Russia's swift atomic progress after the war. The American obsession for secrecy, ironically, offered its own contribution. In 1945, the United States gave Russia control over parts of Czechoslovakia and Germany where large uranium ore deposits were buried, though American troops arrived there first. Truman acted in accordance with a demarcation agreement reached by the Big Three; but would the Americans who helped to draw up the demarcation lines have agreed to them if they had been informed about the uranium deposits?

In any case, Fuchs clearly demonstrated the impossibility of keeping scientific progress secret for long and thus of either superpower gaining more than temporary superiority. He showed that a nuclear race could not benefit either party but could only increase their mutual power to destroy the world.

Fuchs was one of the last British scientists to leave the United States after the war, remaining behind to write reports and help in declassifying information. The leading spy in the West was thus given the task of deciding what secrets should be classified and what ones should not. The secrets he revealed so willingly to Stalin he would now jealously guard from almost everybody else!

Fuchs met Harry Gold for the last time on September 19, 1945, in Santa Fe. After picking up Gold in his car, Fuchs drove to a hilly suburb and parked. As the two men gazed down upon the lights of Santa Fe, Fuchs described the explosion at Trinity and the "tremendous wonderment that had descended upon even those who had the most intimate knowledge of the potentialities of the weapon." This wonderment was even greater, Fuchs said, after Hiroshima. He then handed over to Gold another packet of atomic information and was given instructions how to meet a contact in England when he returned there.

Fuchs left for England in June 1946, but he did not follow the instructions. A Russian atomic espionage ring had been uncovered in Ottawa, Canada, and neither the Soviets nor Fuchs thought it wise to continue spy activities until they knew how deeply Western probing would go. But in early 1947, several months after becoming head of the theoretical physics division at a new atomic energy center at Harwell in Berkshire, Fuchs renewed contact with the Russians in London. He again gave them data, mainly figures on America's bomb-producing schedule up to the time he left and on British plutonium piles. But in late 1948, Fuchs' conscience apparently began to balk.

"In the post-war period," Fuchs would later say, "I began . . . to have my doubts about the Russian policy. It is impossible to give definite incidents because now the control mechanism [in my mind] acted against me also, in keeping away from facts which I could not look in the face; but they did penetrate and eventually I came to the point where I knew I disapproved of many actions of the Russian government and of the Communist Party, but I still believed that they would build a new world and that one day I would take part in it, and that on that day I would also have to stand up and say to them that there are things which they are doing wrongly.

"It became more and more evident that the time when Russia would expand her influence over Europe was far away and that therefore I had to decide for myself whether I could go on for many years to continue handing over information without being sure in my own mind whether I was doing right. I decided that I could not do so. I did not go to one rendezvous because I was ill at the time. I decided not to go to the following one."

Thus, Fuchs still considered himself a free man whose only god was his conscience. His conscience would decide whether he should continue giving information to Russia, and how much for how long. And when the time came, he would tell Russia what it was doing right and what it was doing wrong. For was not Stalin more dependent on him than he was on Stalin? Meanwhile, he would loosen his ties with Russia and open the compartment of his mind that allowed him to work in perfect harmony with his friends and not exploit their friendship.

Yes, Fuchs was committed to saving the world, but what a pleasure to confine his task, at least temporarily, to being kind to individuals, to performing his duties loyally and well. His sudden sense of being human was like an elixir for his tensions and over-burdened conscience.

But in summer 1949, the elixir would turn sour. For the FBI discovered evidence that Fuchs might have passed atomic infor-mation to Russia, and it so informed British authorities. His name had been found in an address book picked up by Canadian police while it was investigating the Ottawa spy case.

At the same time, Fuchs himself injected the security question into the minds of his Harwell superiors. His father, who was now living in American-occupied West Germany, would soon be going to Soviet-occupied East Germany to teach theology. In view of his sensitive work on atomic energy, Fuchs asked, would he be re-quired to resign his job at Harwell? In effect, would Harwell lighten the load on his conscience and decide for him whether he should remain on a job that gave him the opportunity to pass on secrets to Russia? Would Harwell please intervene to protect itself from his ideological compulsion to betray it?

But it was too late to ease his conscience with this subtle effort to force his own resignation. For a British intelligence agent came to Harwell and questioned Fuchs, using his inquiry about his fa-ther as an excuse for interrogating him. Soon Fuchs was revealing his life story—except for his treasonous activities.

"Were you not in touch with a Soviet official or a Soviet representative while you were in New York?" the interrogator suddenly asked. "And did you not pass on information to that person about your work?"

Fuchs was stunned. "I don't think so," he blurted, apparently without thinking.

With this ambiguous reply pointing to Fuchs' guilt, the interrogator pressed on: "I am in possession of precise information which shows that you have been guilty of espionage on behalf of the Soviet Union."

Fuchs now denied the charge, but he had already done the damage. And after further skillful probing, Fuchs broke down. Yes, he had engaged in espionage. As he would later explain his decision to confess:

"I was . . . confronted with the fact that there was evidence that I had given away information in New York. I was given the chance of admitting it and staying at Harwell or clearing out. I was not sure enough of myself to stay at Harwell and therefore I denied the allegation and decided that I would have to leave Harwell.

"However, it became clear to me that in leaving Harwell in these circumstances I would . . . deal a grave blow to Harwell, to all the work which I have loved; and furthermore that I would leave suspicions against people whom I had loved, who were my friends, and who believed that I was their friend.

"I had to face the fact that it had been possible for me in one half of my mind to be friends with people, to be close friends, and at the same time to deceive them and to endanger them. I had to realize that the control mechanism had warned me of danger to myself, but that it had also prevented me from realizing what I was doing to people close to me.

"I then realized that . . . there are certain standards of moral behavior which are in you and that you cannot disregard. That in your actions you must be clear in your own mind whether they are right or wrong. . . . And I found that at least I myself was made by circumstances."

Fuchs' conscience had let him down, disregarding "certain standards of moral behavior." Thus, when he was placed under arrest, he cried out, incredibly:

"You realize what this will mean at Harwell?"

But "circumstances" would still make Klaus Fuchs. At his trial for espionage in London in 1950, he confessed all and was sentenced to fourteen years' imprisonment. He was, however, released after nine years, emerging from prison with a magnanimous attitude toward the Western powers he had betrayed.

"I bear no resentment whatever against Britain or any of the Western countries for what has happened." Fuchs announced.

He felt he got what he deserved. After all, Russia sent spies to jail, too. But that didn't necessarily mean that he thought he had done wrong. Yes, he regretted having hurt people he loved, but had his aim not been to create a more just world, one that even the Western countries would enjoy?

And Klaus Fuchs flew off for a reunion with his father in East Germany, where he would soon be appointed deputy director of the country's Institute of Nuclear Physics—a job that would again place him in a key position to serve Russia.

There was, however, one difference: Now he would learn who was boss.

XX

General Groves was never quite convinced that *he* wasn't his own boss. In fact, he kept America's postwar nuclear strength a secret even from his superiors. At a Cabinet meeting in December 1945, Secretary of Commerce Wallace was shocked to discover that neither Truman nor Secretary of War Patterson knew how many atomic bombs the United States had. And the President even stated that he didn't want to know.

"I thought it utterly incredible," Wallace would say, "that Patterson and the President should be willing to trust full information and responsibility on this to a man like Groves and his underlings without knowing what was going on themselves."

At the same time, Groves continued his personal government-backed effort to corner the market on the world's atomic raw materials for several months after the war. This effort to identify and purchase uranium ore from every friendly country that could supply it had begun in 1944.

The general remained head of the Manhattan Project until early 1947, when Congress finally set up an Atomic Energy Commission. The delay was largely caused by a struggle between

Groves and the atomic scientists, led by Leo Szilard, to determine who should be in charge of domestic atomic control. Groves favored the May-Johnson bill, which would set up a commission that could be dominated by active military officers. Szilard, still the general's nemesis, organized support for a competing McMahon bill, which called for a completely civilian commission. The military must never again control atomic energy, Szilard felt.

After thousands of pages of testimony by experts at Senate committee hearings, the McMahon bill was passed. Szilard had finally conquered the man who would have interned him as a dangerous alien during the war.

Adding to Groves' pain was the Russian atomic explosion, which occurred about the time Szilard had predicted there would be one. Groves himself had prophesied in 1945 that it might take another twenty years for the Russians to make a bomb. The general continued to give advice to the government on national and international atomic policy, but his influence gradually diminished. After retiring from the army, he accepted an executive position with Remington Rand. He died in 1973, feeling the drive to build the bomb proved that "when man is willing to make the effort, he is capable of accomplishing virtually anything."

Even Hiroshima.

XXI

Immediately after the war, Leo Szilard sought to make public the arguments of the scientists who had opposed dropping the bomb on Japan without warning; he hoped to alert the world to the danger of a nuclear arms race. But Groves, reluctant to let the controversy mar his miraculous achievement, made sure it remained secret—on grounds of national security.

Szilard, however, would not stop trying to save the world. He would personally educate the Russians and Americans, especially their leaders, by every means possible. He wrote an open letter to Stalin in 1947, met with Soviet leader Nikita Khrushchev in 1960, initiated a series of meetings between American and Russian scientists, flooded intellectual publications with desperate pleas, and boomed out these pleas on college campuses. He even wrote a whimsical book, *The Voice of the Dolphins* (1961), which portrayed a wonderful world of peace governed by benevolent dolphins, whose advice presumably was that of farsighted men like Leo Szilard.

In his frantic campaign, Szilard called for Cold War detente, an exchange of broadcasts between the Russian and American leaders, and ultimately a world government. He even came up with an imaginative way to settle superpower conflicts: Destroy property, not people. The country that planned to seize another country's territory would agree to have part of its own territory atomically razed to pay for its international crime! If Russia wanted to take over Afghanistan, for example, it would permit American nuclear missiles to wipe out, say, Kiev; and if the United States wanted to control Cuba, Miami might be an acceptable target for Russian missiles. Of course, the agreed-upon target cities would be evacuated beforehand. Let the leaders play with their missiles if they simply had to. Who cared about mere property?

In 1962, Szilard finally set up a Council for a Livable World, a peace lobby in Washington that many members supported by donating a percentage of their income. Even today it contributes to the election campaigns of senators and congressmen who actively support nuclear control.

Szilard's fear of a nuclear holocaust was real, as real as it was in 1933 when he visualized a chain reaction while standing on a London street corner and wondering if Hitler's scientists had thought of it, too. And adding to his torment, apparently, was a touch of almost Freudian guilt. Was the child he had conceived destined to destroy him, not to mention the world he had pledged to save? He personally felt so threatened by his creation that during the Cuban missile crisis of 1962 he abruptly checked out of Washington's Dupont Plaza Hotel, where he had worked and held court in the lobby, and dashed off to Switzerland with his two suitcases before the capital could be turned into a pile of rubble. Why should he die unnecessarily when he would be needed to save the remnants of humanity after his child's anger had subsided?

In trying to preserve the world and improve conditions in it, Szilard did more than campaign for nuclear arms control. He abandoned research in nuclear energy, which could lead to an end of life, and turned to biophysics, which could lead to longer life. As a professor of biophysics at the University of Chicago and later at the University of California at San Diego, he helped to invent a machine for controlling the growth of microorganisms and developed theories on the aging process and on memory. He also came up with an ingenious way to check the population explosion in impoverished countries: Feed the people inexpensive antifertility rice. And to end the agony of terminal patients, he worked on concoctions that would permit a quick, painless suicide, keeping a sample for himself in case he were so stricken.

To avoid getting "stale," Szilard also occupied himself with less vital inventions. He built a gadget that would make instant tea, found a way to speed up customer service at supermarket checkout counters, and worked on an improved injector razor. He needed such diversions to ease the agony of gradual realization that he was, after all, powerless to save the world. In his last years he grew so pessimistic that he even tried, unsuccessfully, to dissolve his own peace council, seeing it as a waste of contributors' money. Who, he gloomily asked friends, could stop some madman from encasing a half-dozen nuclear bombs in cobalt one day and exploding them in the atmosphere. The world, he calculated, would be wiped out—and all because he had lingered so long in the bathtub!

Nevertheless, Szilard continued with his schemes to improve the human mind and body, and to facilitate his work he accepted a position in 1963 at the University of California at San Diego, where he finally settled down, no doubt fitfully, with his long-neglected wife. Gertrud had some time before resigned her teaching post at the University of Colorado Medical School to share his hotel room in Washington and nurse him back to health when he fell ill with cancer. But in 1964, after only a few months of home living, Szilard died of a heart attack—apparently without regret. As he once said:

"Death is part of life. If it didn't exist, one would have to invent it. There is nothing alarming in thinking that after your death you'll be in the same state as you were before birth."

XXII

On the day of the bomb, J. Robert Oppenheimer was no longer the nervous, exhausted, dazed man he had been at Trinity. Now, like Krishna, he was strong and confident, a man under control and in control. When news of the successful bombing arrived, he jubilantly called all his scientists together in the camp auditorium. He clasped his hands over his head like a victorious prizefighter and, when the cheering died down, read aloud Captain Parsons' message from the *Enola Gay*. More cheers and cries of glee. Their work, the miracle they had performed, had won the war!

After Trinity, there had been a gay party at Oppenheimer's house. People danced, sang, got drunk. They had seen the new dawn. Why not another party to celebrate Hiroshima? someone suggested. Everybody to the men's dormitory! But strangely, few people came, and many of those who did left early. No dancing, no singing. Drunks? Well, a few. Oppenheimer found one young group leader vomiting in the bushes. The reaction, he knew, had begun. And when photos of the carnage arrived, there were hardly enough bushes to go around.

Oppenheimer tried to remain strong. He had to. He was, after all, the genius who had made Los Alamos work. If not for him, Hiroshima might still be a vital, bustling city. He could not let the gleaming image of Los Alamos—*his* image—suddenly dissolve in horror. Surely, in no other scientific undertaking in history had there been such a spirit of oneness, or "quite the feeling this was really the great time of their lives," as one scientist would put it. Yes, under his leadership they had done the impossible—but to what end? Oppenheimer did not evade the question. The scientists, he would agree, "had known sin." But how could one understand virtue without knowing sin?

So why feel guilty? Why search for a bush?

Leo Szilard felt that killing people with the bomb in this war would make it infinitely easier to kill people with it in future wars. But Oppenheimer did not, could not, agree, for he had committed himself to killing people with the bomb in this war. Doing it now, *he* argued, would make it all the more difficult to do it in future wars.

Oppenheimer's colleagues were cheered.

"Oppie says," they exulted, "that the atomic bomb is so terrible a weapon that war is now impossible."

And Oppenheimer had to believe this because it was the only way to wipe those photos of disfigured women and children from his conscience. Yes, by destroying Hiroshima he had saved the world! Like Krishna, he had become death, but he had also become hope. For he had finally won the international recognition he had pined for, and the government basked in pride as it solicited this great American hero's advice on how to deal with the atomic future. Now he could pursue hope and show that Hiroshima was worthwhile.

Oppenheimer poured this hope into a struggle for international control of atomic energy, anonymously writing the Acheson-Lilienthal Report, which was tailored to appeal to the Soviet Union without calling for the revelation of vital secrets by either side. But the report was rewritten by members of the American delegation to the new United Nations Atomic Energy Commission led by Bernard Baruch. And the new version stressed conditions that Oppenheimer knew would foil his plan and that were apparently intended to do so: There could be an atomic attack on violators of the plan. . . . There must be total disarmament, not just nuclear arms control. . . . The veto power in the United Nations Security Council must be abolished. . . .

Stalin, who might have turned down any plan, took one sneering look at Baruch's and said "Nyet!" Oppenheimer was crushed, "sabotaged" by his own people. Didn't they understand what Hiroshima was all about?

But Oppenheimer continued to give advice, refusing to abandon hope that future Hiroshimas could be avoided. He served as chairman of the General Advisory Committee of the Atomic Energy Commission and consulted with the Department of Defense on atomic weapons and on general defense policy. Let's not build so many big atomic bombs, he pleaded. Small tactical weapons that would not wipe out whole cities would do. And so would conventional arms. But after Russia exploded its own atomic bomb in 1949, the United States suddenly needed bigger, not smaller, bombs. At least in Edward Teller's view. He had been doing research on a hydrogen bomb for years, and he couldn't bear to see his work go to waste. Now, he cried, was the time to build one.

Oppenheimer disagreed. Not only were the technical difficulties too great, he argued, but such a bomb would escalate the nuclear arms race. Perhaps the United States could sign a pact with Russia agreeing *not* to develop hydrogen weapons. When he was overruled by President Truman, Oppenheimer tried to resign as chairman of the AEC committee, but his resignation was refused. The government needed him!

However, there were others who saw little need of him: the air force, which resented him for opposing strategic atomic bombing. Edward Teller, who felt he was trying to slow up plans for a hydrogen bomb. The FBI, which had never trusted him because of his leftist background. Admiral Lewis Strauss, head of the AEC, who had nominated him director of the Institute for Advanced Study at Princeton and felt he was an ingrate for making a fool of him before a congressional committee on a disputed point; and a young man named William Borden, a former director of a congressional atomic committee, who was convinced that he was a Soviet spy.

In 1953, Borden sent a letter to the FBI making this accusation—based on the FBI's own files, which the Bureau had already analyzed exhaustively—and FBI Director J. Edgar Hoover, Strauss, Attorney General Herbert Brownell, and President Eisenhower suddenly "realized" that a possible Russian agent was giving atomic advice to the U.S. government. And just at a time when Senator Joseph McCarthy was screaming that the government was riddled with Reds!

Place a "blank wall" between Oppenheimer and all secret data, the President ordered.

Fearful that a public hearing would embarrass the FBI if the charges were thrown out, Hoover pointed out to the government that Oppenheimer's contract would expire in six months and urged that it simply not be renewed. Strauss and the politicians, however, disagreed, fearing that McCarthy might preempt the case. So Oppenheimer, after refusing to resign under fire, was called before Strauss' committee and a second one dealing with security, and he again recounted his peccadillos.

Had he backed left-wing causes in the 1930s?

Yes, he had.

Had he lied to security officers about the Chevalier incident?

Yes, he had.

Had he opposed the hydrogen bomb?

Yes, he had.

Groves, who had had a hard time explaining how Klaus Fuchs had managed to slip through his security net, defended Oppenheimer—and thus himself as well. Most scientists defended their colleague, too. And even Teller conceded that the man was loyal to his country.

Then should Oppenheimer receive a security clearance?

Oh, no, Teller said. Oppie gave the government bad advice,

especially about the hydrogen bomb. He had even urged other scientists not to work on it (though no one could find a scientist whom Oppenheimer had given this advice to).

The two committees weighed the facts. Oppenheimer was an ex-fellow traveler. He was a liar. He gave bad advice to the government. . . . And Joe McCarthy was sharpening his knife, just waiting for his chance to carve up Oppenheimer—and President Eisenhower, whom he had already termed a coddler of Communists.

Clearly Oppenheimer was a security risk, at least by the standards of the McCarthy era. And the two groups voted to deny Oppenheimer a security clearance.

The whole world gasped. The man who had made the atomic bomb—a security risk? And Oppenheimer slouched back to Princeton, where he pondered the price of recognition and grew old quickly.

In 1963, President Lyndon B. Johnson, in a sense, tried to make amends, giving him the highest honor granted by the AEC, the $50,000 Fermi Award for scientific achievement. The once immodest Oppenheimer, now a sickly skeleton, was humble.

"I think it is just possible, Mr. President," he said, "that it has taken some charity and some courage for you to make this award today."

Three years later Oppenheimer died of throat cancer, a broken man, half-forgotten, remembered mainly for the day of the bomb.

XXIII

At about 3 P.M. on that day, Deak Parsons and the rest of the *Enola Gay* crew landed in Tinian to a hero's welcome. But Colonel Tibbets was viewed, at least by the air force, as a bit more heroic than Parsons.

Hundreds of officers and men jamming the taxiways burst into cheers as cameras clicked, tape recorders rolled, and beer flowed, until finally they edged back and the crew was able to line up in front of the plane. General Spaatz strutted up to Tibbets and pinned a Distinguished Service Cross on his coveralls. Parsons?

He received a Silver Star, a notch below. Spaatz, after all, was an army air force general, and Parsons was a naval officer.

Many people thought that Parsons deserved at least as important a medal as Tibbets. Was he not the man who was to "render final judgment in the event that an emergency requires deviation from the tactical plan"?

As Groves—who normally held naval aptitudes in low esteem—would later privately say:

"There was never any question on the part of anybody that Parsons was running that show. . . . The only person who didn't get that right was apparently General Spaatz."

But if Parsons felt cheated, he didn't show it, though Spaatz's action would give the world—and history—the impression that Parsons' role was of secondary importance. When one of his friends expressed outrage, Parsons replied:

"Always remember this, there is no limit to the good a man can do if he doesn't care who gets the credit; I don't care who gets the credit."

Especially for wiping out a city in a single blow. He had done "good," he was sure, because he firmly believed the bomb would end the war promptly, saving perhaps a million lives. But he did not crave credit for taking 100,000. In fact, he had wanted a prior demonstration of the bomb in the hope of averting such horror. Couldn't his gadget have exploded without killing people? One colleague, Merle Tuve of the Carnegie Institute, would say of Parsons' feelings:

"There aren't many people that measure up the way Deak did all the way through, but of course I know it hurt him too that he was on [the *Enola Gay*]. He never got over that. . . . He had some feelings that, you know—orders can be wrong, too. You kind of wish it hadn't gone that way. . . . He triggered [the bomb] and that hurt him. I don't know anybody less fitted to that assignment—by his whole personality. But it was a technical operation and he gave them that help."

When Tuve asked Parsons about the mission, the captain simply replied: "I was under orders. I had no choice, I was under orders."

And he hardly said another word to anyone about his feelings, even to his wife Martha. However, when he was driving home with his wife and two children from the airport on his return from

Tinian, he remarked that this was the "happiest day of his life" because it was no longer necessary to invade Japan. But then he mused:

"Look at all those nice houses. They would all disappear in an atomic war."

Just as they had in Hiroshima.

No, he didn't want credit. And he didn't get much, though a high school teacher revealed on the local radio that "Willie was always a bright boy," and *The New York Times* mentioned him— while featuring a photo of the wrong William S. Parsons! In any case, Deak felt his naval career was all but over. Ironically, by dropping the bomb he himself had ended it, for he had ended the war. Now it was too late to accumulate the sea duty he needed to become an admiral.

But General Groves came to the rescue. He went to see Admiral Nimitz and asked that the navy not penalize Parsons for working on the bomb. He would even release Parsons "so he could command a ship every weekend, since that seemed to be required."

Shortly Parsons was promoted to commodore and then, in 1948, to rear admiral. He was so grateful that he turned down an offer of a high-paying job in private industry.

"I owe everything to the navy," he told his wife when she suggested he accept it. "Look what the navy has done for me."

And Parsons would continue doing a great deal for the navy, especially in the nuclear field. He helped to stage the Bikini tests of the atomic bomb in 1946, and to develop the first nuclear missiles and small tactical atomic weapons. And yet Parsons foresaw the day when all such arms could be junked.

In late 1953, his sister asked him with concern his view of future American-Soviet relations.

There was no iron curtain that could keep ideas from getting through to the Russian people, Parsons replied. When they learned about "our country's ideals and aspirations, our two countries would be friends."

"What ideals and aspirations?" his sister asked.

Parsons then revealed his dream "for the near future," as reflected in his support of an Atoms for Peace program for an international stockpile of fissionable material to be used for peaceful purposes: "De-salting sea water for arid countries so farming could be done and starving people fed, a sharing of medical knowledge in the battle against such diseases as malaria; educational and cultural exchanges between all countries, and other ways to live peacefully in the world. If these things came about, there would be no more wars. But until such a time came, the United States must keep defensively as strong as possible. It would be dangerous to have it any other way."

But if Parsons saw promise, he also saw despair. For his close friend, Robert Oppenheimer, with whom he had so often discussed such matters, was being called a security risk. Oppie? There was no greater patriot. Was this an example of the American ideals he so cherished? When Parsons heard, on December 4, 1953, that Oppenheimer's security clearance was suspended, he was shattered.

"This is the biggest mistake that the United States could make," he said to Martha. "Tomorrow I am going to the Secretary of the Navy, and I'm going to ask the Secretary to take me to the President."

Parsons woke up that night feeling a pain in his chest and thought he had a cold. When his wife went to the kitchen to make hot lemonade, he characteristically took an encyclopedia and read about heart attacks. He decided he didn't have one for he had no pain in his left arm. But in the morning, his wife took him to the hospital, recalling for a dreadful moment the time they had rushed little Hannah there.

"Don't worry," he said to her as he entered the examining room. "Go to the hospital store and buy some toys for the children for Christmas."

During the examination, Deak Parsons' heart stopped. He died at 52.

"I think," Martha would later say, "[the Oppenheimer case] really had quite a lot to do with Deak's death. I think he got so tense over this thing."

Deak had done a lot for his country. And his country had let him down.

XXIV

Lieutenant Thomas Cartwright, who had been held prisoner in Hiroshima Castle, was not in Hiroshima on the day of the bomb. He had been taken on August 2 to a military camp near Tokyo, where he would be further interrogated by Japanese seeking to find out what fate was awaiting them. When they found out four days later, they were desperate.

What was this "new kind of bomb"? an interrogator demanded.

He didn't know, Cartwright replied quite honestly.

A huge soldier then wobbled into the interrogation room carrying a samurai sword, and marched him outside blindfolded.

"Kneel!" the interrogator ordered, pulling off the blindfold.

The swordsman stood before Cartwright, his hand gripping the hilt.

"This is your last chance to keep your head," the interrogator warned.

Cartwright was thankful in his terror that he didn't know anything about the "new type of bomb." And he finally convinced his tormentor that he didn't. He was taken back to his cell, unaware that this bomb had wiped out Hiroshima. He wondered what was happening to his buddies. Later, when he was liberated, he would learn.

Six were apparently killed outright when the atomic bomb exploded, together with another four or five American prisoners who had either been brought to the castle after Cartwright left or were kept elsewhere in Hiroshima. One member of his crew, Staff Sergeant Ralph J. Neal, and a navy flier, Norman R. Brissette, had the prized job of emptying the waste buckets into the cesspool, and when the bomb went off they leaped into the filth, which protected them from the force of the blast. (The two men told this to prisoners who were brought to Hiroshima after the bomb.) But they developed radiation symptoms and shortly afterward died a horrible, lingering death.

Another American apparently survived the explosion, too. A Japanese witness saw an old woman throwing chunks of concrete at a young man wearing only trunks as he stood tied to a pole near Hiroshima Castle. Later his battered body was found dead.

Japanese authorities would identify twenty American prisoners who they claimed died in the holocaust, about double the number known to be in Hiroshima. But according to the testimony of two former Japanese army officers, eight of those listed had been used in medical experiments at Kyushu University and were added to the nuclear death toll to conceal these atrocities.

About six months after the war, on February 5, 1946, the army adjutant general responded to an inquiry from Mrs. Ralph J. Neal disclosing the cause of her husband's death. Staff Sergeant Neal

> was wounded by the atomic bomb dropped on Hiroshima, Japan, on 6 August 1945, and died on 19 August as a result of these wounds. Sergeant Neal and other airmen were being held in an infantry building as prisoners of the Japanese Government. Several prisoners were instantly killed.

Three years later, on May 27, 1949, the father of Lieutenant Raymond Porter, a naval flyer, received a letter from the navy surgeon general:

> Investigation revealed that your son . . . and his crewmate, Aviation Radioman Norman R. Brissette, had parachuted safely when their plane was shot down on July 28, 1945, and that they had been captured by the Japanese and imprisoned at the Chugoku Military Police Headquarters at Hiroshima. Imprisoned with them were crew members of two army planes which had been shot down on the same day. Your son and all the prisoners but two lost their lives on August 6, 1945, as the result of the atomic bombing of Hiroshima.

However, a curtain of secrecy then dropped, and the government would not admit that any American servicemen were killed by the bomb in Hiroshima. When Cartwright and the families of the ill-fated crewmen asked about the cause of death during the next twenty years, they were told it was unknown. And when they more recently pressed for an answer, they were told that relevant files had been destroyed in a 1973 fire that razed an army records center in St. Louis.

Actually, aside from the letters to Neal's wife and Porter's father, several documents survived, including army messages dated September 23, 1945, and October 9, 1945, that indicated Americans had been killed and wounded by the bomb. And in 1949 the army buried a casket containing the mingled ashes of several of those killed in Hiroshima at Jefferson Barracks Army Cemetery in St. Louis. On the tombstone it marked under the names of eight men, including five crewmen of the *Lonesome Lady*, the date they all died—August 6, 1945. The place? It is not mentioned.

The atomic bomb, after all, was not supposed to kill American boys, and officially it did not. It was hard enough getting some people to understand that killing *enemy* civilians with the bomb was not immoral. And that it was necessary to build bigger and better nuclear missiles.

Cartwright today is a professor at Texas A & M, specializing in animal genetics.

XXV

Seiko Ogawa, after seeing her reflection in the window, wanted to die. But her family's love gradually gave her renewed hope; perhaps life might be worth living after all. In 1948, doctors tried to restore at least some of her beauty. When the burned skin on her face softened, they operated on her and grafted skin from her knees onto her face. But when the bandages were removed, Seiko received a new shock. The transplanted skin had rotted and turned black. The operation had failed, and later a second one did as well.

Seiko fell into a deep depression, and for some time she refused to go school. People in the street stared at her, while children taunted her with cries of "red goblin." But once again her family's love gave her courage. Even a handsome young cousin who had been attracted to her in the days before the bomb comforted her. He had known Seiko when she was beautiful and her new grotesque face somehow hadn't erased that image. She returned to school and, to "fight back," starred in a play she herself wrote, called *Surviving the A-bomb.* In this play, she explored the tortures of her soul, the agony of living with her deformities, the need to go on living despite them. Her audience, in tears, was stunned by the performance. Here was a great actress. But Seiko wasn't acting. And now that she had revealed her innermost feelings as a Hiroshima victim, her dream died. She knew her disfigured face would not permit her to play another role.

In 1950, when Seiko was 18, her cousin proposed marriage to her. Not directly. Being shy, he asked his mother to speak with Seiko's parents. The youth's mother was reluctant to give her blessing. She had been seriously ill since the day of the bomb, when she had searched for her missing brother-in-law and found him in his school, a skeleton identifiable only by the belt buckle and lunch box nearby. Now more than ever she wanted her son to live a normal happy life. How could he, married to a monster?

But she finally gave her consent, and so did Seiko when word of the proposal drifted down to her, though she hoped the boy wasn't motivated by pity. The wedding took place, but it was not a very happy occasion—at least for Seiko, who, at the reception, overheard a relative remark on her ugliness. She ran in shock to her father.

"My dear daughter," he sobbed when she told him, "if it weren't for the atomic bomb you would be beautiful."

Relatives tried to break up the marriage and Seiko herself was still haunted by the thought that her husband simply pitied her. But she "decided to believe" in her husband's love, and they eventually had three children. Though her husband became a well-to-do business executive, Seiko, to keep busy, taught dressmaking for fifteen years and then decided once more to seek plastic surgery. She had to stamp out her lingering suspicion that her marriage was based on pity. From 1979 to 1982, she was operated on eight times and finally emerged as an attractive woman almost free of scars.

Life suddenly changed for Seiko. She no longer hesitated to leave the house and she could look people in the face without having to see the familiar stare of revulsion in their eyes. Now she could enjoy gazing into the mirror. Now, at last, she knew her husband didn't pity her. She even studied social dancing and became a dancing teacher, volunteering her services without pay. Why not help poor people get some pleasure from life? Why not make others happy?

And yet Seiko is still apprehensive. Several of her friends have recently died of cancer believed to have been caused by radiation from the bomb, and she fears that she, too, may eventually be a victim. She fears even more that her children, or their children, might be affected by the dread disease. And she worries, too, about children around the world. She has become an active member of the Japanese antinuclear peace movement, lecturing to students, describing through her personal story the indescribable horrors of nuclear war.

Seiko has never quite forgiven the United States for dropping the bomb.

"The Allies had already won the war, hadn't they?" she says. "The bomb was unnecessary. Why should I have suffered so?"

She has tried to forgive. But then suddenly a beautiful silver bird gleams in the sunshine, and Amaterasu crawls back into her cave, enveloping the world in darkness. Sooner or later, Seiko fears, she will remain there forever.

NOTES

Full bibliographical information on all books, magazines, and documents can be found in the Bibliography. Full identities of all interviewees appear in the Acknowledgments.

PROLOGUE

I

The bomb-arming activities in the *Enola Gay* were described to the author by Morris R. Jeppson and Paul Tibbets. William S. Parsons' role on the plane is indicated in Leslie R. Groves' personal papers and in his oral history for the Naval Historical Center, as well as in the oral histories by Frederick L. Ashworth and Norman Ramsey. The safety system on the plane is described by Ashworth. The Parsons-Farrell discussion about arming the bomb in midair appears in *No High Ground* by Charles W. Bailey and Fletcher Knebel. Material on Parsons' personality and background comes from an interview with his widow, Martha Burroughs, and from her personal files, especially from a memoir by Parsons' sister Clarissa. The oral histories by many of his friends, relatives, and associates were also highly useful. Parsons' attitude toward dropping the bomb is discussed in an oral history by Merle Tuve, a scientist at Carnegie Institute. The quote concerning a warning to Japan about the bomb comes from a letter that Parsons wrote to Livingston Hartley on Dec. 7, 1948, available in the Parsons papers in the Library of Congress.

II

The story of Seiko Ogawa was told to the author by Miss Ogawa (now Mrs. Ikeda) and by her schoolmate, Miyoko Matsubara. Seiko's doctor, surgeon Tomin Harada, provided information on Seiko's multiple operations.

III

Thomas C. Cartwright described his mission and his capture to the author.

CHAPTER 1

I

A portrait of Szilard was drawn from conversations with many of his friends, enemies, and associates, including Hans Bethe, William Doering, Bernard Feld, Allan Forbes, Ralph E. Lapp, Matthew Meselson, Isidor I. Rabi, Robert Serber, Cyrus and Alice Kimball Smith, Edward Teller, Victor Weisskopf, and Eugene P. Wigner. Family members also contributed to the portrait. Szilard's comment on "Homo sapiens" is quoted in Theodore Irwin's "The Legend of Dr. Szilard," *Pageant*, Dec. 1961.

II

Szilard describes his background in his memoirs, *Leo Szilard: His Version of the Facts*, ed. by Gertrud Weiss Szilard and Spencer R. Weart. Teller and Wigner, fellow Hungarians, contributed *their* version of the facts. Alice Kimball Smith added some touches in her incisive profile, "The Elusive Dr. Szilard," *Harper's*, July 1960, as did Eugene Rabinowitch in a eulogy to Szilard, *Bulletin of the Atomic Scientists*, Oct. 1964. The quotation involving Szilard and the thoroughbred horse was stated by Allan Forbes in an interview. Wigner told the author of Szilard's poverty and need of financial help in London.

III

Szilard tells of his sudden realization that an atomic chain reaction might be possible in his memoirs, pp. 16–17. A reading of H. G. Wells' *The World Set Free* helped to set the background for this scene. Lapp told the author that scientist Frederic Houtermans stated to him after the war that he had suggested the possibility of an atomic explosion in a lecture he delivered in Berlin in 1932, a year before Szilard had the same idea. Szilard's view on "exercise" is quoted in Irwin's article, *Pageant*, Dec. 1961. His efforts to obtain aid for chain reaction research are outlined in his memoirs, pp. 18–21, and were described by his friends and associates. His relationship with Gertrud Weiss was revealed by members of her family.

IV

Wigner told the author about Szilard's visit to Princeton and Bohr's revelation that an atomic chain reaction was found to be possible. Szilard deals with this revelation, as well as with his Columbia University experiment, in his memoirs, pp. 53, 55. The story of Bohr's bomb bay seat is related in Robert Jungk's *Brighter than a Thousand Suns*, pp. 120–21. Szilard describes in his memoirs, pp. 53–54, his frustrating meeting with Enrico Fermi. Rabi offered further details in the author's interview with him. Szilard's thoughts on "sleep" are aired in Irwin's article, *Pageant*, Dec. 1961.

V

Herbert L. Anderson explains both the Szilard and Fermi experiments on a chain reaction in "The Legacy of Fermi and Szilard," *Bulletin of the Atomic Scientists*, Sept. 1974. Szilard's memoirs relate how Fermi went to Washington to seek financing of further experiments, p. 56. Wigner added details in his talk with the author. See also *The New World* by Richard G. Hewlett and Oscar E. Anderson, p. 15.

VI

Szilard's efforts to keep information on atomic developments secret are described in his memoirs, pp. 54–57; in Michael Amrine's *The Great Decision*, pp. 96–97; in Jungk (*Suns*), pp. 72–78; and in James W. Kunetka's *City of Fire*, p. 23. Rabi, Teller, and Wigner offered additional facts. The argument over graphite is covered in Szilard's memoirs, pp. 81–82.

VII

The meeting of Szilard and Wigner with Albert Einstein is detailed in Szilard's memoirs, pp. 82–83. Wigner supplemented this information in the interview.

VIII

Szilard's meeting with Alexander Sachs is described in Szilard's memoirs, p. 84. Sachs' background is illuminated in a statement issued by the Special Senate Committee on Atomic Energy on Nov. 27, 1945. See Geoffrey T. Hellman's "The Contemporary Memoranda of Dr. Sachs," *The New Yorker*, Dec. 1, 1945. An account of Szilard visiting Einstein with Teller can be found in Szilard's memoirs, p. 84. Teller added to this account, saying, contrary to Szilard, that Einstein signed the letter to the President on the spot. Sachs claimed in letters to Admiral Lewis L. Strauss dated Jan. 11 and 12, 1961, that *he* and not Szilard drafted the letter, though it is written in Szilard's style and not in Sachs', Lapp files and Sachs papers. Szilard discussed using Colonel Charles Lindbergh to take the letter to the President in letters to Einstein dated Aug. 2, 1939, and Sept. 27, 1939, Szilard papers. Szilard tells of his meeting with Union Carbide officials in his memoirs, pp. 85–86.

IX

Sachs described his Oct. 12, 1939, meeting with Roosevelt to the Special Senate Committee on Atomic Energy on Nov. 27, 1945, hearing transcript. A good description also appears in Jungk, pp. 109–11.

X

Details of the meeting between scientists and the Briggs committee are reported in Szilard's memoirs, pp. 84–85. Teller and Wigner also provided information.

XI

Washington's apathy about the bomb is reflected in Szilard's memoirs, p. 115. Teller and Wigner also commented on it. The Szilard-Einstein "blackmail" threat is dealt with in Szilard's memoirs, pp. 115–116. Szilard wrote John T. Tate, editor of the *Physical Review*, on Feb. 14 and Apr. 5, 1940, concerning publication of the "blackmail" article, Szilard papers. The following letters can be found in the Roosevelt Library: The Einstein letter to Sachs meant for Roosevelt's eyes, Mar. 7, 1940; Sachs' letter to Roosevelt with Einstein's letter enclosed, Mar. 15, 1940; and Roosevelt's letter to Sachs, Apr. 5, 1940, proposing a Uranium Committee meeting. Szilard reports on the $6,000 government contribution to research in his memoirs, p. 116. A description of the scientific advisory group meeting appears in his memoirs, p. 117. Wigner recounted the episode to the author.

XII

Sachs wrote Roosevelt on May 11 and 15, 1940, asking him to set up a defense committee and the President agreed, as indicated in the hearing transcript of the Special Senate Committee on Atomic Energy, Nov. 27, 1945, p. 552. Sachs elaborated on his achievement in a letter to Lapp on July 21, 1964, Lapp's files. A profile of Vannevar Bush appeared in *Newsweek*, Jan 10, 1944. Szilard discusses his salary at Columbia University in his memoirs, p. 117.

CHAPTER 2

I

Koichi Kido's personality and duties emerged from talks with Kido himself (in 1958), his son Takahiko, and many of his political associates, as well as from his diaries and other writings.

II

The author grew familiar with the Japanese moral code and web of obligations while serving for several years as Bureau Chief for McGraw-Hill World News in

Japan. Ruth Benedict's *The Chrysanthemum and the Sword* offers much detail on this subject.

III

Kido's remark on "Japan's intention" in Asia can be found in the interrogation report on Kido in Records of Allied Operational and Occupation Headquarters, World War II, IPS File #5, Vol V, p. 723, Kido, Marquis Koichi. Kido discussed his family background with the author. This background is also described in David Bergamini's *Japan's Imperial Conspiracy*, pp. 242, 247, 256; John Toland's *The Rising Sun*, p. 99; and the author's *Kishi and Japan*, pp. 39–40, which deals with the Choshu clan. Among the Japanese histories consulted were Lafcadio Hearn's *Japan*, Edwin Reischauer's *Japan, Past and Present*, and Chitoshi Yanaga's *Japan Since Perry*.

IV

See Section 3.

V

Kido's government career is best covered in Tatsuo Shoda's *Jyushin Tachi no Shoan Shi*. The Records of Allied Operational and Occupation Headquarters, World War II, also contain valuable material. (See IPS File #5, Vols. II, V, and VI.) Kido's diaries and interrogations by the International Military Tribunal for the Far East were also of great help. Kido and his son Takahiko filled in many details.

VI

Kido describes his visit to the shrine of the Sun Goddess in his diary, June 10, 1940. He explained his views on joining the Axis powers at his trial in Tokyo on Oct. 22, 1947, and in his diary, July 31, 1941. Kido and his son contributed information on this subject to the author. The Imperial Conference of Sept. 6, 1941, is described in Leonard Mosley's *Hirohito*, pp. 216–20, and dealt with in Kido's diary on that date. Bergamini presents an anti-Hirohito version of the meeting in *Japan's Imperial Conspiracy*. Kido's suggestion to Konoye that Japan delay a thrust into southeast Asia for ten years and concentrate on beating China appears in his diary, Oct. 9, 1941, and is explained in his interrogation, IPS File #5, Vol. V, pp. 721–22. A profile of Prince Fumimaro Konoye can be found in Sir Robert Craigie's *Behind the Japanese Mask*. See also Konoye's memoirs in *Asahi Shimbun*, Tokyo, Dec. 20–30, 1945. Kido's selection of Hideki Tojo as Prime Minister is covered in IPS File #5, Vol. V, pp. 762–73, and Kido's diary, Oct. 17, 1941. His talk with Tojo on Oct. 16, 1941, is transcribed in the same file, pp. 764–65. The Lord Keeper's cautioning of Tojo and Admiral Shigetaro Shimada in regard to the Sept. 6, 1941, war resolution and the Imperial reaction to it are described in Kido's diary, Oct. 17, 1941. See also Mosley, pp. 228–29. The reliance of Kido on the navy to save Japan from war and the Emperor's meeting with naval leaders are discussed in Kido's diary, Nov. 30, 1941. Impressions of the Lord Keeper on the morning of Pearl Harbor come from his diary, Dec. 8, 1941.

CHAPTER 3

I

Klaus Fuchs' reluctance to accept money for his spying activities was revealed by Harry Gold, FBI Fuchs file. Fuchs and Gold described their meeting on Sept. 19, 1945, FBI Fuchs file. Fuchs' life in Los Alamos emerges from the FBI files on him and from Alan Moorehead's *The Traitors*, pp. 97–98, Laura Fermi's *Atoms in the Family*, pp. 209–11, and an interview with Hans Bethe. The United Press reported from Abingdon, England, on Feb. 10, 1950, that Fuchs' landlady said the scientist couldn't make his car run smoothly.

II

Fuchs described his mental state at his trial, Fuchs trial transcript. Max Lerner provides excellent insights into Fuchs' mind in three columns in the *New York Post*, Feb. 13, 14, 15, 1950. Material on Fuchs' background can be found in the FBI Fuchs file; Moorehead, pp. 59–80; Rebecca West's *The New Meaning of Treason*, pp. 175–80; and Oliver Pilat's *The Atom Spies*, pp. 84–89.

III

Fuchs' quote about man understanding and controlling "the historical forces" comes from his trial transcript. For background sources, see Section 1.

IV

Rudolf Peierls' relationship with Fuchs is described in the FBI Fuchs file and was discussed in the interview with Bethe.

V

Russian atomic progress is reported in David J. Dallin's *Soviet Espionage*, pp. 453–60, Arnold Kramish's *Atomic Energy in the Soviet Union*, and *How Russia Became a Nuclear Power: The Untold Story of the Soviet Atomic Bomb*, an American intelligence report. Fuchs' meetings with "Alexander" are reported in the FBI Fuchs file; Moorehead, pp. 85–88; and the Fuchs trial transcript.

VI

The best accounts of the British atomic bomb program are Margaret Gowing's *Britain and Atomic Energy, 1939–1945* and Ronald W. Clark's *The Birth of the Bomb* and *The Greatest Power on Earth*. Churchill-Roosevelt relations regarding atomic energy are analyzed in Martin J. Sherwin's *A World Destroyed*, pp. 36–39,

68–91; Hewlett and Anderson, pp. 255–88; and William D. Leahy's *I Was There*, pp. 265–66. Material is also available in the Roosevelt Library, Hyde Park, N.Y., and the Public Records Office, London. Roosevelt's comment that the Russians "could do more or less what they wish" in their occupied territory was made in a memorandum to Secretary of State Cordell Hull on Sept. 29, 1944, Germany Treatment, World War II Conferences, Freeman Matthews Files, Record Group 59, U.S. Department of State Files, National Archives.

CHAPTER 4

I

Stimson's background, personality, and physical appearance are best described in Elting E. Morison's *Turmoil and Tradition*. See also Amrine, pp. 91–94, and Richard N. Current's *Secretary Stimson*, especially Chapter I ("The Shape of His Greatness"). The following articles were helpful, too: "Secretary of War Stimson" by William Costello and Edward T. Folliard in *American Mercury*, Sept. 1944; "Secretary of War" by George Creel in *Collier's*, Aug. 7, 1943; Claude M. Fuess' "Henry L. Stimson" in the *Atlantic Monthly*, Sept. 1941; and Henry F. Pringle's "Henry L. Stimson: A Portrait" in *Outlook and Independent*, Mar. 13, 1929. Stimson's own memoirs, *On Active Service in Peace and War*, written with McGeorge Bundy, delves into his political background. And his article, "Artillery in a Quiet Sector," in *Scribner's Magazine*, June 1919, describes his military experiences in World War I. Stimson's plea to Truman regarding the need for trust is quoted from a memorandum he sent to the President on Sept. 11, 1945.

II

See background sources in Section 1. Stimson's meeting with President Theodore Roosevelt is described in Pringle's article. Armin Rappaport's *Henry L. Stimson and Japan, 1931–1933* analyzes Stimson's role in forcing Japan out of the League of Nations, pp. 199–204. Stimson's quote about "the end of the hopeless years" comes from his memoirs, p. 316. Stimson's diary notes Roosevelt's phone call about Pearl Harbor, Nov. 7, 1941.

III

Szilard's complaints about government efficiency are covered in his memoirs, pp. 143–44. The quote about the scientists suffering from having "official recognition" appears in these memoirs, p. 144, as does the information about British findings that an atomic bomb was feasible. Details of these findings and America's sudden enthusiasm for the bomb are described in Arthur H. Compton's memoirs, *Atomic Quest*, pp. 60–64. Szilard's complaints to Bush in his talk with him on June 20, 1942, are reflected in a memorandum he wrote on September 21, 1942, entitled, "What is Wrong With Us?", Szilard papers. Bush's positive attitude toward getting advice from the scientists is indicated in Bush's book, *Modern Arms and Free Men*, p. 6. Arthur Compton's personality emerges from his mem-

oirs. See also Nuel Pharr Davis' *Lawrence and Oppenheimer,* pp. 92, 134–35;
Laura Fermi, pp. 185–86; and Leona Marshall Libby's *The Uranium People,*
pp. 90–92. A number of scientists helped to delineate Arthur Compton's portrait
in interviews. Szilard's talk with Compton on Oct. 26, 1942, was reported by Szilard
in an unpublished aide-mémoire dated Oct. 30, 1942, Szilard papers. Compton
wrote to James B. Conant on May 16, 1942, about the danger that Szilard's
"loyalty to the country might be shaken" if he were dismissed, Office of Scientific
Research and Development files, National Archives. Compton explains in his
memoirs his decision to perform the chain reaction experiment in Chicago,
pp. 136–39. See also Anderson's "The Legacy of Fermi and Szilard," *Bulletin of
the Atomic Scientists,* Sept. 1974, and Albert Wattenberg's "The Building of the
First Chain Reaction Pile" in the same magazine, June 1974. Szilard's joke about
his desire that a mountain be named after him appears in Hans Zeisel's "On
Szilard," also in the same magazine, Sept. 1970. His joke about the Nobel Prize
for Peace was told to the author by several of Szilard's associates.

IV

Stimson tells of his "particularly important meeting" with Bush and Wallace
in his diary, Dec. 16, 1941. Stimson's "nominal" role as Roosevelt's senior atomic
energy adviser is discussed in Sherwin, pp. 67–68. As late in the war as Sept. 25,
1944, Stimson complained in his diary that Roosevelt wasn't consulting his own
advisers on the bomb. Stimson explained why the bomb was used in "The Decision to Use the Atomic Bomb," *Harper's,* Feb. 1947, reproduced in his memoirs.
General Leslie R. Groves' explanation appears in his memoirs, *Now It Can Be
Told,* p. 265.

V

In alluding to his plan for dangling the carrot of peaceful atomic secrets before
Russia, Stimson confided in his diary on May 14, 1945: "They can't get along
without our help and industries and we have coming into action a weapon which
will be unique." See also E. Morison, p. 637. Groves describes the incident
involving Congressman Engel with Bundy in his personal unpublished papers.
Other papers dealing with the Engel problem can be found in the Harrison-
Bundy Collection, National Archives. The transcript of the Truman-Stimson
telephone conversation appears in E. Morison, p. 616. Stimson describes his
effort to obtain money for the Manhattan Project and to halt antitrust action
against Du Pont in his memoirs, pp. 614–15. E. Morison discusses the financing
issue, the problem of preventing laboratory strikes, and the Morgenthau attitude,
pp. 614–15. Papers on the case of Hans von Halban, the French scientist who had
been working in Canada, are included in the Harrison-Bundy Collection.

VI

The atomic chain reaction test in Chicago is described in Compton's memoirs, pp. 136–45; Anderson's "The Legacy of Fermi and Szilard" in the
Bulletin of the Atomic Scientists, Sept. 1974; Wattenberg's "The Building of the

First Chain Reaction Pile" in the same magazine, June 1974; and "After 20 Years: More Hopes Than Fears" in *Time*, Dec. 7, 1962. Szilard's ominous remark to Fermi appears in Szilard's memoirs, p. 146.

CHAPTER 5

I

A description of the Emperor's underground quarters can be found in Bergamini, p. 67; Mosley, *Hirohito*, pp. 293, 314; and Toland, pp. 919–20. A good physical portrayal of the Emperor late in the war appears in Hideaki Kase's *Tennoh-ke no Tatakai*.

II

The Emperor's childhood is covered in Osanaga Kanroji's *Hirohito*, pp. 3–50; in Mosley, pp. 1–20; and in Bergamini, pp. 273–89. Mosley tells how the boy took the blame for others' misbehavior, p. 5. Hirohito's relationship with General Nogi and Nogi's death are dealt with in greatest detail by Kanroji, an Imperial attendant for seventy years, pp. 47–50.

III

Saionji's talk with Hirohito on the Emperor's "divinity" is described in Mosley, pp. 32–34. A history of Emperors appears in Willard Price's *Japan and the Son of Heaven*, pp. 106–10, and Lester Brooks' *Behind Japan's Surrender*, pp. 90–91. Hirohito's interest in biology is discussed by Kanroji, pp. 58–78, and by Price, pp. 34–35. His trip abroad is reported in Kanroji, pp. 79–98; Mosley, pp. 52–75 (including the aftermath); and Bergamini, pp. 314–22. Hirohito's marriage can be found in Kanroji, pp. 104–108; Mosley, pp. 38–51, 74–75, 87–90; and Bergamini, pp. 308–12, 339–40.

IV

For the struggle between the government and the military after Emperor Meiji died, see Hideaki Kase. The 1936 revolt is analyzed in Nobuyuki Tateno's "Ni-ni-Roku Jiken no Nazo" appearing in *Tenno to Hanran Gun*. Among English-language sources are Mosley (including Hirohito's reported confrontation with his would-be assassin), pp. 134–54, and Bergamini, pp. 621–59.

V

The Emperor's regret about the lack of warning on Pearl Harbor and his inserted statement in the Imperial Rescript of War are explained by Kido in his interrogation, Records of Allied Operational and Occupation Headquarters, World War II, IPS Case File #5, Vol. 1 and V. See also Mosley, pp. 269–70. Kido advises the Emperor not to give up his biological study, Kido diary, June 8, 1944. Hirohito's comment to Kido regarding Japan's "thoroughly thought-out plans" and Kido's emotional reaction are noted in Kido's diary, Feb. 16, 1942. The Emperor's statement to Kido about the "fruits of war" and Kido's reaction are recorded in Kido's diary, Mar. 9, 1942. Kido's warning to Hirohito not to exult can be found in the diary, Feb. 5, 1942. Hirohito's statement to Tojo about not prolonging the war appears in the diary, Feb. 10, 1942. Gordon William Prange's *Miracle at Midway* is a fine account of the sea battle there.

VI

Hirohito's comment on the Midway setback and Kido's reaction to his master's "courage" are reported in Kido's diary, June 8, 1942. The Konoye-Kido talk about the Communist danger is detailed in the records of the International Military Tribunal for the Far East: Kido, p. 31068, Feb. 4, 1943. See also Robert Butow's *Japan's Decision to Surrender*, pp. 17–18. The diplomat suggesting peace terms with China was Mamoru Shigemitsu. See his *Japan and Her Destiny*, pp. 287–90. It was Shigeru Yoshida who proposed sending Konoye to Switzerland, as explained in the records of the International Military Tribunal for the Far East: Kido, pp. 31065–66. The appeal to Prince Takamatsu is in the same volume, pp. 31069–70. Brooks discusses the Konoye plan, p. 122. See Shigenori Togo's *The Cause of Japan* regarding the controversy over a Greater East Asia Ministry, pp. 248–55. Hirohito's visit to the sacred hut is recounted in Kido's diary, Dec. 11, 1942. For a picture of Japan's deteriorating economy during the war, see the author's *Kishi and Japan*, pp. 186–87. Kido's peace plan is detailed in his diary, Jan. 6, 1944 (annex).

VII

The role of Nobusuke Kishi in ousting Tojo from office is told in the author's *Kishi and Japan*, pp. 185–202. The story is based on interviews with Kishi and Kido.

CHAPTER 6

I

Groves' personality came through in interviews with his son Richard, and with Luis Alvarez, Bethe, Martha Burroughs, Kenneth D. Nichols, Rabi, Serber, Cyril and Alice Kimball Smith, Teller, Weisskopf, and Wigner. Also extremely valuable were Groves' personal papers, including memoirs by his wife Grace and his daughter Gwenn. Groves' published memoirs reveal much about the Manhattan Project but little about himself, though his dynamism is reflected on every page. Stephane Groueff's *Manhattan Project* and Lansing Lamont's *Day of Trinity* offer favorable portraits. Hewlett and Anderson as well as Jungk were very useful. The diaries of Chaplain Leslie R. Groves, the general's father, were helpful in showing the father's influence on the son. Robert De Vore's "The Man Who Made Manhattan" in *Collier's*, Oct. 13, 1945, presents additional details about the man and his career (including his love of clam chowder). The long wait for news about the atomic explosion over Hiroshima is described in Groves' memoirs, pp. 319–22.

II

Groves' remark, "The military are completely dominated by the civilian people," can be found in his statement to George Tressel, Argonne National Laboratory, pp. 34–35, personal papers. His remark that "there was never any question . . . as to my decision that we would drop the bomb in combat" is in his comment on *The New World*, personal papers. Marshall's designation of Groves to plan the bombing operation is reported in Groves' memoirs, pp. 266–67. Groves' refusal to let the air force control the bomb is mentioned in a note, his personal papers. The general's plan to drop two bombs is discussed in his statement to Tressel, pp. 25–26, and his Herbert Feis file, p. 16, Groves' personal papers. See also Groves' memoirs, p. 308. Comment on his consultation with Marshall over a third bomb comes from Groves' statement to Tressel, pp. 27–28, and comment on *The New World*, personal papers. Groves' protest that civilians were designating targets is registered in his statement to Tressel, p. 35, personal papers. The POW question is covered in his comment on *The New World*, personal papers, and his memoirs, pp. 312–13. Comment on the possibility of atom-bombing Germany is made in Groves' evaluation of an article by Hanson Baldwin in *The New York Times*, personal papers. See also Associated Press writer Andre Marton's interview with Groves appearing in the *Washington Star*, Oct. 7, 1965. Groves' doubts about Japanese aggression and America's role in the war are reflected in his comments, Feis file, p. 14, the general's personal papers.

III

Background material on Chaplain Groves comes from his diaries and from an interview with his grandson, Richard. General Groves' background is detailed in his unpublished account of his early life, among his personal papers. His wife Grace contributes her own memories of that period. Groves' comment on his "flabbergasting" record is in his Hailey file, p. B/4, personal papers.

IV

Groves tells in his memoirs of learning he is to head the Manhattan Project, pp. 3–5. See also De Vore's "The Man Who Made Manhattan." Groves' talk with Styer and thoughts about him are revealed in Groves' memoirs, pp. 4–5, but more frankly in his personal papers, Hailey interviews, pp. B/2–B/3. Groves' statement that the chance for the project's success is 60 percent can be found in his files for Ed Ronne, p. 8, and files for J. J. Ermene, p. 84, personal papers. The Groves-Bush meeting is described in Groves' memoirs, pp. 20–21, and Groueff, pp. 8–9.

V

Groves' meeting on Sept. 23, 1942, with Stimson and others is recorded in the general's personal papers, Hailey interviews, pp. C/1–C/4, and in Groves' memoirs, pp. 23–25. The Groves-Nelson meeting is described in Groves' memoirs, pp. 22–23, and in Groueff, p. 14. See Groueff for Groves' visits to Columbia, pp. 19–20; Berkeley, pp. 35–39; and Pittsburgh, pp. 17–18.

VI

For the most complete account of Groves' Chicago visit, see his personal papers, Hailey interviews, pp. D/1–E/12. See also Groueff, pp. 32–34. Groves' comment on "Jewish power" and lack of "moral principles" can be found in his letter to Kenneth L. Moll, personal papers. See also a memo from Frances Henderson to Don Bermingham concerning an interview with Groves, Mar. 8, 1946, p. 8, Szilard papers.

VII

Groves' remark that people would ask, "Why did you do it?", if he didn't use the bomb appears in his statement to Tressel, p. 29, personal papers. Bethe's statement about Groves was made to the author. Groves' warning to scientists that they might end up in Guadalcanal is reported in Alice Kimball Smith, p. 16. The general's doubts that the Chicago scientists were "interested in the national interest" are expressed in his statement to Tressel, p. 23; and in his comment on *The New World*, personal papers. The statement "Only a man with [Szilard's] brass would have pushed through to the President" appears in the memo from Henderson to Bermingham, p. 2. The assertion that Szilard was "anxious for personal glory" is from Groves' remark on Szilard's obituary, *Bulletin of the Atomic Scientists*, Feis file, personal papers. Why Groves didn't fire Szilard is explained in the general's comment on *The New World*, p. 69, personal papers. Groves voices his "suspicion" of Szilard in a memo dated Nov. 29, 1965, his personal papers. Groves' attempt to turn Wigner against Szilard is recounted in Hailey interviews, p. E/15, Groves' personal papers. The general tries to have Szilard interned, letter to Moll, personal papers. His plea to Conant to give Szilard a job at Harvard appears in the personal papers, comments on Szilard's obituary in the *Bulletin of the Atomic Scientists*. The patent ultimatum to Szilard is explained in a memorandum from Szilard to the U.S. Atomic Energy Commission, with a covering letter to Lewis S. Strauss, chairman, Oct. 7, 1955. For additional information on patent question, see the letter from Bush to Arthur Compton, Jan. 29, 1943; from Compton to Conant, Jan. 7, 1943; from Szilard to Compton, Dec. 4, 1942, S-1 Bush-Conant File, Records of the Office of Scientific Research and Development, National Archives. Szilard's comment about the government suing him for damages is quoted in Irwin's "The Legend That Is Dr. Szilard," *Pageant*, Dec. 1961. His concern about his future security is reflected in a memorandum he wrote to L. T. Coggeshall on Jan. 28, 1950, headed "Salary of Szilard," Szilard papers. Groves' comment that it would be "beneficial" if Szilard had an accident can be found in the Hailey interviews, p. E/13–E/14, personal papers.

VIII

Du Pont's Thomas H. Chilton is quoted by Groueff, p. 55. For Du Pont's recruitment in the Manhattan Project, see Groueff, pp. 54–62; Groves' memoirs, pp. 42–52; Szilard's memoirs, pp. 148–49. Szilard criticizes Du Pont in "Proposed Conversation with Bush," Feb. 28, 1944, Parts 1 & 2, Szilard papers. Wigner and Lapp offered additional information to the author.

IX

Groves' attempts at secrecy are covered in his memoirs, pp. 138–48. See also Arthur Compton, pp. 181–84. Szilard blasts "compartmentalization" in "Proposed Conversation With Bush," Parts III & IV. How Condon was prevented from going to Russia is told in Groves' Kenneth B. Nichols file, personal papers. Groves' anti-British attitude is reflected in his Margaret Gowing file, pp. 9–10, personal papers. Talks with Feld, Rabi, Bethe, Lapp, Wigner, and Richard Groves were helpful in clarifying the effects of compartmentalization.

X

Fuchs' arrival in New York and his work at Kellex are detailed in the FBI Fuchs file. Groves' meeting with the British scientists is described in Groueff, pp. 268–71, as well as in the FBI Fuchs file.

XI

Fuchs' visit with his sister is described in the FBI Fuchs file.

XII

Groves' second meeting with the British scientists can be found in Groueff, pp. 268–71 and in the FBI Fuchs file.

XIII

Fuchs' meetings with Harry Gold are detailed by both men in interrogation reports found in the FBI Fuchs file. See also Fuchs trial testimony and Moorehead, pp. 95–104. Profiles of Gold appear in the FBI Fuchs file and in Pilat, pp. 26–30.

CHAPTER 7

I

Yoshio Nishina's role in the development of Japanese atomic energy emerged from talks with his son Yuichiro and the scientist's assistant, Eizo Tajima, as well as from several books and articles: *Showashi no Tenno*, edited by Yomiuri Shimbunsha; the Pacific War Research Society's *The Day Man Lost*; Thomas M. Coffey's *Imperial Tragedy*; Tetu Hirosige's "Social Conditions for the Researches of Nuclear Physics in Prewar Japan" in *Science and Society in Modern Japan*, edited by Shigeru Nakayama, David L. Swain and Eri Yagi; *Nihon Kagaku Gijutsushi Taikei*, edited by Nihon Kagakushi Gakkai; J. W. Dower's "Science, Society, and the Japanese Atomic-Bomb Project During World War Two" in the *Bulletin of Concerned Asian Scholars*, Apr.-June 1978; and the script of the Japanese Broadcasting Company's "The Love of Science: The story of Yoshio Nishina." Nishina's quotes about an "insane war" and saving the ship come from *The Day Man Lost*, p. 23. The plot to kill Nishina was revealed to the author by the scientist's son.

II

For background on Nishina, see sources listed in Section 1.

III

The material on the cyclotron comes largely from *Showashi no Tenno* and interviews with Yuichiro Nishina and Tajima.

IV

The military initiative in the researching of an atomic bomb is explored by Dower's article and *The Day Man Lost*. The meeting between scientists and naval officials is reported by the sources listed in Section 1. Much of the dialogue is from Coffey, pp. 244–46, apparently obtained from scientist Tsunesaburo Asada.

V

The quote on the American embargo at the second meeting is from *The Day Man Lost*, p. 27. The third meeting held a month later is described especially well in the same book, which contains the quotes presented here, pp. 29–30. The chief naval representative, Yoji Ito, summarized the committee's conclusions, which appear in *Showashi no Tenno*. They convinced the navy, at least temporarily, that it should end the atomic project.

CHAPTER 8

I

The stormy sea incident is described in Peter Michelmore's *The Swift Years*, pp. 8–9. The effect of Hindu studies on Oppenheimer is discussed in *Oppenheimer* by Rabi, one of the five authors, pp. 7–8. Paul Tibbets, who was present, told the author the story about Fermi and the erroneous equation.

II

Groves' statements to the FBI about Oppenheimer are in the FBI Oppenheimer file. The general's love of chocolates is revealed in his daughter Gwenn's account of life with father in Groves' personal papers. Groves writes about the refusal of the scientists to be "militarized" in the working draft of his memoirs, p. 3, Groves' personal papers. Groves told the FBI that Oppenheimer did not accept "Communist dogma or theory," as revealed in the FBI Oppenheimer file. Richard Groves told the author that his father felt Oppenheimer could be more easily watched inside than outside the atomic project. A letter from Groves to Oppenheimer denying rumors that he had tried to control the scientist can be found in Oppenheimer's papers. Groves' comments on Oppenheimer and Communist employees were taken from the FBI Oppenheimer files, as was the note that Groves was "naïve" about the Communists.

III

Oppenheimer's background is covered in Davis; Michelmore; Jungk (Suns); Peter Goodchild's J. Robert Oppenheimer, Shatterer of Worlds; Robert Oppenheimer: Letters and Recollections, edited by Alice Kimball Smith and Charles Weiner; and in FBI reports. Insights into Oppenheimer's thinking and personality were offered to the author by Rabi and other scientists.

IV

See sources in Section 3. Alvarez discussed Oppenheimer's role at Berkeley. See Haakon Chevalier's Oppenheimer: The Story of a Friendship. The quote that Oppenheimer "hadn't got the staying power" is by David Bohm, one of his graduate students, appearing in Goodchild, p. 33.

V

The episode with Jean Tatlock is explored in Davis, pp. 81–83, 149–50; Goodchild, pp. 33–35; and Michelmore, pp. 47–50, 89. Also in reports in the FBI Oppenheimer file. Oppenheimer's relations with Chevalier are described in the FBI file and in Chevalier's book.

VI

Background on Kitty Oppenheimer and her relationship with Oppenheimer can be found in the FBI file, including her autobiography and Groves' appraisal of her as an influence on her husband. See also Davis, 104–107; Goodchild, pp. 39–44; and Michelmore, pp. 60–64. An interview with Captain Parsons' widow, Martha Burroughs, who was a good friend of Kitty's, was rewarding.

VII

The meeting of Groves and Oppenheimer and Oppenheimer's appointment as Los Alamos director are described in Davis, pp. 143–47. Interviews with Rabi, Serber, and Richard Groves shed additional light on the relationship between the two men. The September 1941 lunch attended by Oppenheimer, Lawrence, and Oliphant is detailed in Michelmore, p. 66. Teller's prediction of catastrophe is covered in Pearl Buck's "End of the World? One Nobel Prize Winner Interviews Another," *The American Weekly*, Mar. 8, 1959. See also Davis, pp. 127–32.

VIII

The Oppenheimer-Groves talk is described in Davis, pp. 144–45. The selection of a leader for the Los Alamos laboratory is discussed in Groves' memoirs, pp. 61–63, and in reports in the FBI Oppenheimer file. Serber and Richard Groves offered further information. See also Davis, pp. 146–47. The reports on Oppenheimer's leftist activities can be found in the FBI Oppenheimer file. Choosing a site for the laboratory: FBI Oppenheimer file; Groves memoirs, pp. 63–67; Davis, pp. 159–60; Jungk, pp. 128–31; Goodchild, pp. 69–70. Groves mentions in his memoirs the protests against his choice of Oppenheimer as Los Alamos director, pp. 61–62. Further details appear in an early draft of the general's memoirs, among his personal papers.

IX

Recruiting the scientists for Los Alamos: FBI Oppenheimer file; Goodchild, pp. 74–76; Davis, pp. 161–64 (including the quotes used here). Life in Los Alamos is described in Goodchild, pp. 77–82, and Kunetka, pp. 43–47. See also *Reminiscences of Los Alamos 1943–1945* and Bernice Brode's "Tales of Los Alamos," *LASL Community News*, June 2–Sept. 22, 1960. Bethe, Serber, and Teller helped to fill out the picture. Teller's "fury and hurt" is brought out by Groves in a note in his personal papers and in a statement to the FBI, Oppenheimer file. Bethe also discussed the subject. See Kunetka, pp. 120–21.

X

Parsons' background is recorded in his sister Clarissa's memoir and in the oral histories of family members, colleagues, childhood friends, and neighbors. Groves describes his relations with Parsons in one of the oral histories. An interview with Martha Burroughs yielded additional information that helped to mirror Parsons' character and personality. Alvarez, Bethe, and Teller commented on him. The Parsons-Neddermeyer dispute over implosion is discussed in the oral history given by George Kistiakowsky and also in Davis, pp. 216–17 (including Parsons' "beer can" remark), and Hewlett and Anderson, pp. 245–50. The interviews with Bethe and Serber were helpful. The letter from Oppenheimer to Groves praising Parsons can be found in Oppenheimer's papers.

XI

Japanese scientists wanted to do "their own work," according to J. W. Dower's article in the *Bulletin of Concerned Asian Scholars*. The subject of trying to organize a Japanese atomic project is also discussed in the Hirosige chapter in *Science and Society in Modern Japan*, pp. 25–26. Takeuchi's role is described in *Showashi no Tenno*, pp. 86–88. The meeting on Mar. 6, 1943 of the scientific committee is covered in *The Day Man Lost*, pp. 34–36. The roles of Takeuchi and

Kigoshi in producing a "small miracle" are explained in Dower's article and *The Day Man Lost*, pp. 37–41. Yuichiro Nishina and Tajima gave the author further details.

XII

Efforts by Harry Gold and Anatoli Yakovlev to find Klaus Fuchs are detailed in Gold's statements to the FBI, Fuchs file.

XIII

Fuchs' job at Los Alamos is described in the FBI Fuchs file. Bethe's statement is also in the file. He gave a similar appraisal to the author. Oppenheimer's statement about Fuchs can be found in the same FBI file. Information on the Coordination Council meetings and meetings on postwar control of the bomb was obtained from this file and from Bethe. Material on Fuchs' dating habits can be found in the FBI file on him as well.

XIV

Groves' welcoming meeting at Los Alamos was described to the author by several scientists. See also Goodchild, p. 83. The general mentions his compartmentalization plan in his published memoirs, p. 140, but deals with it in far greater detail in an earlier draft of his book, among his personal papers. See this draft for details on other security matters as well. Groves' talks with the FBI offer further insights into his thinking on the security question, FBI Oppenheimer file. See also Kunetka, pp. 97–100. Feynman's "guess who?" joke appears in Jungk (*Suns*), p. 122. Parsons' fear of parties at home is described by his sister in her memoir. Groves' tightening of compartmentalization to vent his anger is dealt with by Goodchild, pp. 87–88. The general's defense of Oppenheimer and his description of him as "indispensable" can be found in the FBI Oppenheimer file.

XV

Eltenton's background is detailed in the FBI Oppenheimer file and in Chevalier's *Oppenheimer: The Story of a Friendship*, pp. 52–53. Eltenton's meeting with Chevalier and Chevalier's meeting with Oppenheimer are described in the same Chevalier book, pp. 52–55. Oppenheimer wrote Chevalier a letter on Feb. 24, 1950, confirming Chevalier's account of the meeting, Oppenheimer papers. Oppenheimer's visit with Lomanitz and his interrogations by Pash and Lansdale are covered by reports in the FBI Oppenheimer file and in less detail by Jungk, pp. 142–47, 150–53; Davis, pp. 203–206; Michelmore, pp. 91–93; and Goodchild, pp. 95–99. See also the U.S. Atomic Energy Commission's *In the Matter of J. Robert Oppenheimer*. Pash's charges against Oppenheimer appear in the FBI Oppenheimer file. Lansdale's talk with Kitty Oppenheimer is described in a report to Groves in this file. See also Goodchild, p. 91. Groves' statement to the FBI that he was *not* concerned about espionage in Lawrence's laboratory and that he was willing to let Russia get indigestion from useless data is from the FBI Oppenheimer file.

XVI

Oppenheimer's admission to Groves that Chevalier had contacted his brother Frank can be found in the FBI Oppenheimer file. Groves' reaction to the revelation, his guessing game with his security aides, and the FBI's interview with Frank Oppenheimer also come from the FBI Oppenheimer file.

CHAPTER 9

I

Kantaro Suzuki's narrow escapes from death in his early years are recorded in his autobiography. The attempt to assassinate him in 1936 is also described in his autobiography. See Bergamini, p. 634; Mosley, p. 138; and Toland, pp. 19–20. The story of the "leaden ball" is from Hiroshi Agawa's *Yamamoto Isoroku*, p. 88. In an interview, Suzuki's son Hajime contributed to the account of the attack, and also described other incidents in his father's career. Suzuki's fear that his neck wound was a bad omen emerges in his autobiography and is referred to in Toshikazu Kase's *Journey to the Missouri*, p. 116. Suzuki's plea to his son not to accompany him to death is quoted in Toland, p. 863. See Brooks for an outline of Suzuki's career, pp. 29–30. There are believed to be less than a dozen Kauai Oos in existence—in Hawaii.

II

Suzuki's childhood and youth are recounted in the admiral's autobiography. Butow (*Surrender*) tells of Suzuki's reference to Iyeyasu, pp. 67–68.

III

Nishina's July 1944 experiment is described in *The Day Man Lost*, pp. 48–49; Takeuchi's memoir in *Nihon Kagaku Gijutsushi Taikei*, pp. 444–64, and *Showashi no Tenno*, pp. 101–37.

IV

The verbatim discussion of Kido and the Jushin on July 18, 1944, that resulted in Koiso coming to power can be found in the Records of Allied Operational and Occupation Headquarters, World War II, IPS Case #4, Vol. III, Kido, Marquis Koichi. The verbatim discussion of Suzuki, Kido, and the Jushin on Apr. 5, 1945, to choose a successor to Koiso appears in the same case, Vol IV. For other accounts of this meeting and Kido's plea to Suzuki to accept the premiership, see Brooks, pp. 25–26; Butow, pp. 63–64; and Toland, pp. 850–54.

V

Suzuki's message that "It's a boy!" appears in Kumao Harada's *Saionji-ko to Seikyoku*, from which the English-language *Saionji-Harada Memoirs* was excerpted, Vol. III, p. 208. See also Bergamini, p. 572. The quote, "To Suzuki I could pour out my heart," can be found in Brooks, p. 26. The Emperor's meetings with Jushin members are detailed in Butow, pp. 44–51, Hideaki Kase, and Tatsuo Shoda's *Jyushin Tachi no Shoan Shi*, Vol. II.

VI

The fire-bombing of Tokyo on Mar. 9, 1945, is described by Bergamini, pp. 1037–39, and in Robert Guillain's *I Saw Tokyo Burning*, pp. 181–88. Several survivors also told the author of the horrors. The Emperor's tour of the ruins is depicted by Hideaki Kase. Kido contributed some details in his diary, Mar. 18, and added more in his talk with the author. The bombing of the Imperial Palace is described in *The Day Man Lost*, pp. 148–49, and Mosley, pp. 283–84.

VII

Hirohito's agony in the last months of the war is reflected in the portrait of him in Hideaki Kase. Kase added to the picture in the author's interview with him. Kido also described the Emperor's misery. Suzuki's reluctant acceptance of the Emperor's "order" to take power is shown in Suzuki's autobiography; Keiichiro Kabor's *Suzuki Kantaro*; and Toland, p. 854. How Suzuki saved his fleet twenty years earlier is told in his autobiography.

CHAPTER 10

I

President Truman's voyage home aboard the S.S. *Augusta* is covered in William M. Rigdon's *White House Sailor*, p. 206.

II

Truman's sudden thrust into the presidency is described in his *Memoirs: Year of Decisions* (Vol. I), pp. 4–8; Robert J. Donovan's *Conflict and Crisis*, pp. 3–9; and Margaret Truman's *Harry S. Truman*, pp. 207–12. Truman's statements to newsmen ("Boys, if you ever pray . . ."), to Senator Aiken ("I'm not big enough . . ."), and to Secretary of Commerce Jones (appointing Snyder) appear in Donovan, pp. 15, 17. Pendergast's remark is reported in Alfred Steinberg's *The Man From Missouri*, p. 12. Truman's first campaign appearance is described in Robert Underhill's *The Truman Persuasions*, pp. 3–4. Truman expresses fear of his battery men in a note dated May 14, 1934, President's Secretary's files, Truman Library. He discusses his deal with crooked contractors and asks himself whether he himself is a "crook" in an undated note written in Kansas City, apparently in the mid-1930s, President's Secretary's files. He praises Tom Pendergast in the same note.

III

Truman writes about his childhood and family in the memoir he typed out in Kansas City, May 14, 1934. The reference to Truman's mother and the Union Army is in Steinberg, p. 21. Truman tells of falling off his pony as a boy in handwritten memoirs scrawled in the White House, President's Secretary's files. He describes his childhood sweetheart Bess in the undated memoir written in Kansas City. He writes of the great men he admired and his entry into the army in the Kansas City memoir of May 14, 1934. His battle experience overseas is recorded in Jonathan Daniels' *The Man of Independence*, pp. 89–101, and *This Man Truman* by Frank McNaughton and Walter Hehmeyer, pp. 42–57.

IV

Truman's first Cabinet meeting and Stimson's revelation about the atomic bomb are described in Truman's *Memoirs* (Vol. I): pp. 9–10, and in Margaret Truman, pp. 213–14. Tom L. Evans says in his oral history that Truman told him that Roosevelt had spoken about the bomb at a meeting of the two men shortly before FDR died. Senator Truman renewed his demand to Stimson that the Truman committee be allowed to investigate the atomic project in a letter, Mar. 10, 1944, Harrison-Bundy files, Folder #62. Stimson called Truman a "nuisance" in his diary, Mar. 13, 1944. Marshall's remark that "We shall not know what he is really like . . ." is recorded in Stimson's diary, Apr. 13, 1945.

V

Samuel A. Goudsmit describes the Alsos mission in *ALSOS*. After visiting the Oak Ridge gaseous diffusion plant on Apr. 10, 1945, Stimson wrote in his diary on that day that the project was the "most wonderful and unique operation that probably has ever existed in the world." Stimson calls for pinpoint bombing, his diary, June 1, 1945. He notes that he told Truman the air force must pinpoint targets because "the reputation of the United States" was at stake, his diary, May 16, 1945. Oppenheimer's comment about Stimson and the morality of bombing appears in *The Decision to Drop the Bomb* by Len Giovanitti and Fred Freed, p. 36.

VI

The meeting of Fuchs and Gold in Cambridge in February 1945 is detailed in statements by the two spies and Kristel Heineman, FBI Fuchs file.

VII

Bush writes that Roosevelt should be urged to support international control of atomic energy in a memorandum to Conant, Sept. 23, 1944, AEC doc. #297,

Office of Scientific Research and Development, S-1, Industrial and Social Branch, National Archives. Bohr's meetings with Churchill and Roosevelt are described in Gowing, p. 355, and Sherwin, pp. 105–14. Stimson's lament that the President was ignoring his American advisers is made in his diary, Sept. 25, 1944. Harriman's cable to Stimson and the Secretary's reaction are reported in Stimson's diary, May 10, 1945. His remark "We're up against some very big decisions" appears in his diary, Mar. 5, 1945. His quote calling for "restraint" in regard to Russia is from his diary, Apr. 3, 1945. His talk with Roosevelt on Mar. 15, 1945, is reported in his diary on that day.

VIII

Senator Alben W. Barkley's advice to Truman to "develop and manifest a sense of confidence" is quoted from his *That Reminds Me*, p. 197. Truman's statement that Russia and Germany should kill each other off appeared in *The New York Times*, June 24, 1941. His talk with Stettinius is recorded in his *Memoirs* (Vol. I), p. 38–39. Harriman's meeting with Truman is detailed by Charles E. Bohlen in *Foreign Relations of the United States (FRUS): The Conference of Berlin, 1945*, Vol. II, pp. 231–34, and Truman's *Memoirs* (Vol. I), which include Harriman's praise of him, pp. 70–72. Molotov's meetings with Truman are described in Bohlen's report in *FRUS: The Conference of Berlin*, pp. 235–36, 79–82, and Truman's *Memoirs* (Vol. I), which include his strategy meeting with his advisers prior to the second meeting with Molotov, pp. 75–82. See also Bohlen's *Witness to History*, p. 213. Stimson's plea for restraint before the second Molotov meeting comes from his diary, Apr. 23, 1945. Stimson expresses his alarm over the tenor of the second meeting in his diary, Apr. 24, 1945. Sherwin incisively analyzes Truman's meetings with his advisers and Molotov, pp. 155–61.

IX

Stimson's effort to prepare "the mind of the judge" is noted in E. Morison, p. 169. His letter to Truman appears in Truman's *Memoirs* (Vol. I), p. 85. Byrnes' discussion of the bomb with Truman is reported in Truman's *Memoirs* (Vol. I), p. 87. Stimson's "Memo Discussed With the President" can be found in the Harrison-Bundy files, Folder #60, Box 151. Truman's statement about Stimson's concern with the postwar role of the atomic bomb comes from Truman's *Memoirs* (Vol. I), p. 87. Groves' fear that Truman might seek to avenge Stimson's earlier refusal to let him investigate the atomic project is expressed in the general's comments on *The New World*, his personal papers. Groves states his views on Truman in "My Impressions of President Truman," personal papers. A letter from Groves to Truman reminding him of the "private door" incident together with other details of the meeting is among Groves' personal papers. Stimson's satisfaction with this meeting is reflected in his diary, Apr. 25, 1945.

X

The report of Eben A. Ayers that no written record of a Truman order to drop the bomb could be found is in the Ayers file in the Truman Library. Groves' statement on "[Truman's] decision" appears in the general's memoirs, p. 265. The Roosevelt-Churchill aide-mémoire is published in Sherwin, Appendix C. Truman's remark to J. Leonard Reinsch is quoted in Reinsch's oral history, Truman Library.

CHAPTER 11

I

General Korechika Anami's agony over his conflict of loyalties emerges from his diaries; Masazo Sakonji's "Mitsumasa Yonai and Korechika Anami" in *Maru* magazine, Sept. 1949; and memoirs of Yasui Fujiharu, a friend of Anami from youth; Hisanobu Hakusui, who was general secretary of the Suzuki Cabinet; former General Sadao Araki; former General Masao Toshizumi; Tadaichi Wakamatsu; and former Air Force General Torajiro Kawabe. These memoirs and other material about Anami have been gathered into a book, *Anami Korechika Den*. Brooks and Coffey also deal with Anami, mainly with his role rather than his character. Also extremely helpful were interviews with Anami's son Koremasa; his aide, Saburo Hayashi; and staff officer Uchigi Sugita.

II

See sources in Section 1.

III

The relationship between Anami and his brother-in-law, Takeshita, is dealt with by Brooks, pp. 269–71, and Coffey, p. 134. Koremasa Anami and Hayashi were especially helpful on this question. Hideaki Kase's *Tennoh-ke no Tatakai* offers valuable insights into the Japanese military mind. Sugita explained the Japanese military education. See Hillis Lory's *Japan's Military Masters*.

IV

Torajiro Kawabe relates in his diary how Anami saved an old woman during an air raid. Hayashi told the author of Anami's reluctance to court-martial an officer. Coffey writes about Anami's treatment of Western nationals when the war broke out, pp. 134–35. Koremasa Anami described to the author his father's family life and philosophy as well as his early career. Anami's close relationship with the Emperor is analyzed in *Anami Korechika Den*. See also Brooks for background, pp. 44–46. The army's effort to persuade Anami to become war minister is depicted in *Anami Korechika Den*.

V

Anami's defense of Suzuki is dealt with by Brooks, pp. 28–29. Admiral Okada's dramatic escape from would-be assassins in 1936 is described in Mosley, pp. 140–41, 146–48.

VI

For material on the Sakomizu report, see Brooks, pp. 140–41; Toland, pp. 921–22.

CHAPTER 12

I

Admiral Leahy's strong feelings against dropping the bomb are expressed in his memoirs, *I Was There*, especially on pp. 441–42. The following helped to provide a portrait of the man: Admiral William Benson; Leahy's secretary, Dorothy Rindquist; Leahy's son, William H. Leahy; and his granddaughter, Louise Walker. The quote "Why the devil, Mr. President . . ." is from Constantine Brown's column in the Washington *Evening Star*, July 21, 1959. The exchange between Roosevelt and Leahy over Leahy's knowledge of politics appeared in an article by George Kennedy in the Washington *Evening Star*, June 22, 1954. The quote "bomb is the wrong word . . ." appears in Leahy's memoirs, p. 441.

II

The quote "In the evening we fired . . ." is from Leahy's diary, p. 34. His observation about a cockfight is also in Leahy's diary, p. 71. Leahy's lament about the death of a captured enemy priest is in his diary, pp. 94–95. The admiral's plea to Roosevelt to avoid germ warfare and his visit to a chemical warfare school are found in his memoirs, pp. 439–40. Groves' talk with Leahy about the bomb is described in a note by Groves in his personal papers.

III

Leahy discusses his family history and expresses his "pride of ancestry" in the first handwritten pages of his diary. Leahy's granddaughter, Louise Walker, described to the author her close relationship with the admiral. Dorothy Rindquist spoke of Leahy as a boss.

IV

Leahy's career can be traced through his diaries and his memoirs. Noel F. Busch's "Admiral Leahy," in *Life*, Sept. 28, 1942, contains much material on his background. Leahy's pre-Pearl Harbor conflict with Roosevelt over the competence of the commander of the Pacific fleet is recounted in Constantine Brown's column, the Washington *Evening Star*, July 21, 1959. Leahy's exchange with Roosevelt on the Yalta accord on Poland is also quoted in Brown's column.

V

Leahy expressed doubts about Truman in his diary, Apr. 12, 1945. Truman's request that Leahy continue in his job is related in Leahy's memoirs, pp. 347–48, and in Truman's *Memoirs* (Vol. I), p. 18. Truman discusses the abrupt cut-off of lend-lease aid to Russia in his *Memoirs* (Vol. I), pp. 227–28. See also Joseph E. Davies' journal, Sept. 13, 1943, for background to such action. The Truman-Davies discussion of Russian policy can be found in Davies' journal, Apr. 30, 1945. Davies' second meeting with Truman is reported in his journal, May 13, 1945. Churchill's eagerness for a Three-Power conference is expressed in Churchill's *Triumph and Tragedy* and in FRUS, *Conference of Berlin*, pp. 1, 3, 10–11. See Sherwin for an excellent account of the Truman-Davies meetings and American-Russian relations, pp. 172–84. The urgent questions facing Stimson were posed by Joseph C. Grew, Stimson diary, May 13, 1945, and Grew's memoirs, *Turbulent Era*, Vol. II, pp. 1455–56. Stimson's statement that "it was premature to ask [these questions] . . ." appears in his diary, May 15, 1945. Stimson referred in his diary to the bomb and economic aid as a "royal straight flush" in the game with Russia, May 14, 1945. For Hopkins' and Davies' missions, see Herbert Feis' *Churchill, Roosevelt, Stalin*, pp. 599–600; Feis' *Japan Subdued*, p. 14; and John Ehrman's *Grand Strategy*, p. 294. Reference to a solution of the "Polish, Rumanian, Yugoslavian, and Manchurian problems" is made in Stimson's diary, June 6, 1945.

VI

Groves reports on his talk with Marshall about using atomic bombs to clear the way for an American invasion of Japan, Feis file in Groves' personal papers. For details of plans to invade Japan, see Records of the War Department General and Special Staffs, ABC 384 Japan (3 May 1944) Sec. 1-B, National Archives. Also, Joint Chiefs of Staff's "Details of the Campaign Against Japan," Reference: J.C.S. 1388 Series, July 1945.

VII

For War Department report on the advantages of an early Japanese surrender, see Ray S. Cline's *Washington Command Post*, p. 345.

VIII

Grew's plan for peace is discussed in his *Turbulent Era*, Vol. II, pp. 1406–42, and in a letter from Grew to Stimson, Feb. 12, 1947, Grew file, Stimson papers. See also Sherwin, p. 225, Giovannitti and Freed, pp. 91–96.

IX

For the "Soong strategy" for stalling off a Russian attack in Manchuria, see Gar Alperovitz's *Atomic Diplomacy*, pp. 120–25, and Giovannitti and Freed, pp. 188–90. For Byrnes' attitude toward the Soong talks, see Giovannitti and Freed, pp. 189–90; Robert L. Messer's *The End of an Alliance*, p. 105; and Walter Brown's diary, July 20, 1945.

X

Szilard's doubts about using the bomb after Germany's defeat, his meeting with Compton, and his efforts to reach Roosevelt and then Truman are reported in his memoirs, pp. 181–82. Tom L. Evans describes in his oral history his role in contacting Truman for Szilard, Truman Library. The meeting of Szilard and his colleagues with Matthew J. Connelly is covered by Szilard in his memoirs, pp. 182–83.

XI

The meeting of the military chiefs and Truman on June 18, 1945, is reported in Giovannitti and Freed, pp. 134–39, and Toland, pp. 943–46. For casualty prospects in an invasion of Japan, see "Pacific Strategy: Report by the Joint Staff Planners," Records of the War Department General and Special Staffs, ABC 384 Pacific (1-17-43)(Sect. 9), National Archives. See John McCloy's *The Challenge to American Foreign Policy* for an understanding of McCloy's views. See also McCloy's comments in the transcript of NBC's White Paper, "The Decision to Drop the Bomb," televised Jan. 5, 1965.

CHAPTER 13

I

Shigenori Togo's speech to the Diet on Jan. 22, 1942, can be found in the Records of Allied Operational and Occupation Headquarters, World War II, IPS Case File #1, Vol. I., National Archives. Togo's 1933 policy paper about Japan forfeiting "international confidence" appears in the Translator's Introduction to Togo's memoirs, *The Cause of Japan*, pp. 20–21. Togo's personality was illuminated in talks with his grandson Shigehiko and his daughter Ise, as well as with Hideaki Kase, Motojiro Mori, and Haruhiko Nishi. Also helpful was Toshikazu Kase's *Journey to the Missouri*, p. 123, and an article by Mori, "Higeki no Hito Togo" in *Kaizo* (Tokyo), Feb. 1951.

II

Togo's career is outlined in his memoirs. His translator deals with his early years and his background. Shigehiko and Ise Togo also offered many details. Molotov's toast to Togo is quoted by Togo's translator, p. 35.

III

Togo's role in the meeting of Japanese leaders on Nov. 1, 1945, and his thoughts about resigning are detailed in his memoirs, pp. 138–46. See also Bergamini, pp. 803–804, and Toland, pp. 158–63.

IV

Togo's statement that he could "never forget" his despair over the Hull note appears in his memoirs, p. 188. His condemnation of the United States for its "hypocritical, malicious and cowardly" scheme can be found on p. 208. His agreement to give the United States one hour's warning of an attack is on p. 209. The story of Roosevelt's last-minute message to Hirohito is told in Bergamini, pp. 836–42; Toland, pp. 244–46, 251–52; and Coffey, pp. 3–8, 15–17, 26–27, 30–33. Kido contributed in an interview (1958). Togo expresses in his memoirs his sacred feeling after seeing the Emperor, p. 223.

V

Togo's dispute with Tojo and Togo's resignation are described in the foreign minister's memoirs, pp. 248–55.

VI

Suzuki's appeal to Togo to become foreign minister again is detailed in Togo's memoirs, pp. 268–71. See also Toshikazu Kase, pp. 121–22.

VII

For Togo's reaction to Germany's surrender, see Brooks, p. 137, and Toshikazu Kase, pp. 127–28. Togo's pessimism about making a "deal" with Russia and the militarists' desire to keep Russia out of the Pacific war are discussed in Togo's memoirs, pp. 279–81, 284–87. See also Toshikazu Kase, pp. 185–86; Brooks, pp. 137–39; and Butow, pp. 81–85. Shigehiko Togo helped to clarify his grandfather's view on how to deal with Russia.

VIII

The Hirota-Malik talks are detailed in Togo's memoirs, pp. 287–89; Butow (*Surrender*), pp. 90–92; and Toshikazu Kase, pp. 169–71. Works dealing with the "Fundamental Policy" include Togo's memoirs, pp. 291–93; Toshikazu Kase, pp. 171–72; Toland, pp. 924–26; and Butow, pp. 93–102 (including the story of the monkey and its trainer).

IX

Kido's peace plan and the reactions to it are discussed in Togo's memoirs, pp. 294–95; Toshikazu Kase, pp. 179–82; Toland, pp. 926–32; Butow, pp. 112–15; Brooks, pp. 143–50; and Kido's diary, June 8, 1945.

X

Hirohito's meeting with the Big Six on June 22, 1945, is covered in Togo's memoirs, pp. 297–98; Toshikazu Kase, pp. 185–86; Butow, pp. 118–21; Brooks, pp. 151–53; and Kido's diary, June 22, 1945.

XI

Hirota's effort to win over Malik is described in Togo's memoirs, pp. 298–301; Butow, pp. 121–23; Toland, p. 932; and Brooks, pp. 153–54. Togo's meeting with Konoye is reported in Brooks, p. 155. Japan's apparent willingness to have Hirohito resign in favor of another member of the Imperial family if necessary is mentioned in *The Day Man Lost*, p. 200.

XII

The Emperor's talk with Konoye is recorded in Hideaki Kase. Kido offered additional details in the 1958 interview.

CHAPTER 14

I

Byrnes' relationship with Truman is deftly described in Messer. Walter Brown, Clark Clifford, Donald Russell, and John W. Snyder helped to define this relationship.

II

Byrnes details his background in his two memoirs, *Speaking Frankly* and *All in One Lifetime*. Other writings on the subject are Messer, George Curry's *James F. Byrnes*; "Sly and Able: The Real Leader in the Senate, Jimmy Byrnes," by Joseph Alsop and Robert Kintner, *Saturday Evening Post*, July 20, 1940; James L. Gormly's "Secretary of State Byrnes: An Initial British Evaluation," *South Carolina Historical Magazine*, July 1978; "Man of the Year," *Time*, Jan. 6, 1947; Beverly Smith's "Byrnes Grows Up to His Job," *Saturday Evening Post*, Jan. 4, 1947; "South Carolina Primary," *Time*, Aug. 24, 1936; B. Stolberg's "James F. Byrnes," *American Mercury*, Mar. 1946. Byrnes' assistants, Brown and Russell, filled in many details, as did newspaper articles and papers in the James F. Byrnes papers at Clemson University, South Carolina. See Truman's *Memoirs* (Vol. I), pp. 90–93; Byrnes' *All in One Lifetime*, pp. 219–31; Daniels' *The Man of Independence*, pp. 232–33; and John Partin's "Roosevelt, Byrnes, and the 1944 Vice-Presidential Nomination," *Historian*, Nov. 1979, for details of Truman's nomination as Vice-President. See Truman's *Memoirs* (Vol. I), p. 166, and Messer, pp. 13–14, for Truman's negotiations with Byrnes for money to finance the Senate Truman Committee.

III

Truman's offer to make Byrnes his Secretary of State is recorded in Truman's *Memoirs* (Vol. I), pp. 22–23; Byrnes' *Speaking Frankly*, pp. 48–49; and Donovan, pp. 17–18. Truman's description of Stettinius as "dumb as they come" is from Messer, p. 77.

IV

For details of Byrnes' childhood and pre–World War II youth and career, see Byrnes' *All in One Lifetime* and "Sly and Able" by Alsop and Kintner.

V

The story of Byrnes and the Yalta Conference can be gleaned from Messer, pp. 31–64; Athan G. Theoharis' *The Yalta Myths*; Ernest K. Lindley's "Byrnes, the Persuasive Reporter," *Newsweek*, Mar. 12, 1945; Theoharis' "James F. Byrnes: Unwitting Yalta Myth-Maker," *Political Science Quarterly*, Dec. 1966; "Roosevelt and Truman on Yalta: The Origins of the Cold War," *Political Science Quarterly*, May 1972; and "Yalta Legman," *Newsweek*, Mar. 19, 1945. See also Diane Shaver Clemens' *Yalta*; Joseph P. Morray's *From Yalta to Disarmament*; Lisle A. Rose's *After Yalta*; and *The Meaning of Yalta*, ed. by John L. Snell. Interviews with Brown and Russell were helpful. Byrnes' letter to Stimson on Sept. 11, 1943, can be found in the Harrison-Bundy files, Box 147, Folder #8, S-1 Manhattan Project, Entry 20. A copy of Byrnes' letter to Roosevelt on Mar. 3, 1945, asking the President to cut down on Manhattan Project costs is among the Byrnes papers.

VI

The Byrnes-Szilard meeting is described in Szilard's memoirs, pp. 182–85, and in Byrnes' *All in One Lifetime*, pp. 284–85.

VII

Szilard tells in his memoirs of his meeting with Oppenheimer, p. 185. His letter of May 16, 1945, to Oppenheimer can be found in the Szilard papers.

VIII

The Fuchs-Gold meeting in June 1945 is reported in the FBI Fuchs file, which includes the versions of both spies.

IX

Minutes of the May 31, 1945, meeting of the Interim Committee are available in the Harrison-Bundy files. See also Arthur Compton's memoirs, pp. 219, 236–40, and Byrnes' *Once in a Lifetime*, p. 285. R. Gordon Arneson, who was secretary of the Interim Committee, provided many details of the meeting. O. C. Brewster's letter to Truman is in the Harrison-Bundy files. The quote by Byrnes "If you haven't got the votes . . ." comes from "Sly and Able," the *Saturday Evening Post* article by Alsop and Kintner. Truman's reluctant support of the Interim Committee recommendation is reported in Byrnes' *Once in a Lifetime*, p. 286.

X

Arthur Compton's note of May 28, 1945 to his superiors and Groves' notation on it can be found in the Harrison-Bundy files. For the story of Compton's promise to Franck, see Alice Kimball Smith's *A Peril and a Hope*, pp. 30–34. Groves' statement that Szilard wasn't interested in American casualties is from the general's comments on Michael Rouze's *Robert Oppenheimer: The Man and His Theories*, written on Jan. 7, 1966, Groves' personal papers. In a signed memorandum apparently intended for his superiors, Groves, after speaking with Bartky about his trip with Szilard to see Byrnes, concluded that Bartky "should not be entrusted with any direction of the Metallurgical Laboratory," Harrison-Bundy files. Szilard analyzes the views of the Scientific Panel members in his memoirs, p. 186. Material on the Franck Report is included in Szilard's memoirs, p. 186; Smith, pp. 41–46; Compton's memoirs, pp. 233–36; Amrine, pp. 102–107; Jungk, pp. 183–86; Sherwin, pp. 210–12; and Brian Loring Villa's "A Confusion of Signals," *Bulletin of the Atomic Scientists*, Dec. 1975. Arneson filled out details of the visit of Compton and Franck to Stimson's office with the Franck Report and the aftermath.

XI

Oppenheimer's statement "We had nothing in writing . . ." is quoted in Giovannitti and Freed. See also Smith, p. 50. Oppenheimer's remark "We didn't know beans . . ." is quoted in Jungk (*Suns*), p. 186; Feis' *Japan Subdued*, pp. 44–45; and Smith's "Behind the Decision to Use the Atomic Bomb," *Bulletin of the Atomic Scientists*, Oct. 1958.

XII

Rabinowitch's statement "We waited and waited" is quoted in Giovannitti and Freed. The story of Szilard's petition is told in his memoirs, pp. 187–88; Compton's memoirs, pp. 241–42; Amrine, pp. 142–45; and Smith, pp. 54–56. Teller told the author what he said to Oppenheimer after receiving a plea from Szilard to support the Franck Report. See *The Legacy of Hiroshima* by Teller and Allen Brown, pp. 13–14. Teller's letter to Szilard of July 2, 1945, is in the Oppenheimer papers, Box 71, Teller folder.

XIII

For Bard's point of view, see his "Memorandum on Use of S-1 Bomb," June 27, 1945, Harrison-Bundy files. See also Smith, pp. 52–53. In Groves' comments on *The New World*, personal papers, he condemns Bard as "weak." Compton's poll is covered in Groves' Levitas file, personal papers; Compton's memoirs, pp. 242–44; Smith, pp. 57–59; Amrine, pp. 145–49; and "A Poll of Scientists at Chicago, July 1945" by Compton and Farrington Daniels, *Bulletin of the Atomic Scientists*, Feb. 1948. Groves reports in his analysis of *The New World* in his personal papers that Byrnes had told him he would not tell Stalin about the bomb, "though some slight notice should be given to him." And Groves comments: "I was certain that Byrnes would do all in his power to keep Truman from talking too freely to Stalin." In another notation in the same analysis, Groves says Byrnes agreed that in any ultimatum to Japan, "we should not go into details" (about how it would be destroyed).

XIV

Byrnes' swearing-in is covered in *The New York Times*, July 4, 1945; Stimson's diary, July 3, 1945; and Messer, p. 3. Stimson writes in his diary, June 6, 1945, how Truman rejected his resignation.

XV

Stimson's memorandum to Truman, June 2, 1945, is discussed in Stimson's diary for that date, as is his plea that he be allowed to go to Potsdam with the President.

XVI

Robert G. Nixon's encounter with Byrnes aboard the S.S. *Augusta* is described in Nixon's oral history, Truman Library. See the Log of the President's Trip to the Berlin Conference for Truman's activities aboard the ship, Truman Library. Truman's remark that he would have "a hammer on those boys" is quoted in Daniels, p. 266.

CHAPTER 15

I

The portrait of Naotake Sato grew out of talks with his son, Kojiro; Takeso Shimoda, a diplomat in Moscow during the war; Jiro Sakata, a journalist in Moscow during the war; Motojiro Mori; and Haruhiko Nishi. And also out of Sato's memoirs, *Kaiko Hachiju-nen*; Goro Morishima's *Kuno Suru Chu So Taishikan*; Sakata's *Suzume no Bannin*; *Kokusai Jihyo*, Tokyo, Nov. 1970; and the authors of articles on Sato listed in the Bibliography: Shinnosuke Abe, Kiichi Aiichi, Hitoshi Ashida, Akira Baba, Naka Funada, Shirokuro Hidaka, Kensuke Horinouchi, Mitsujiro Ishii, Suemitsu Kadowaki, Morinosuke Kajima, Zentaro Kosaka, Shunichi Matsumoto, Tadaharu Mukai, and Shigeto Yuhashi. Also valuable was Greg Gubler's doctoral dissertation, *The Diplomatic Career of Sato Naotake (1882–1971): A Samurai in Western Clothing*.

II

Sato's early years and career are covered in his memoirs and in Gubler. Sato's quote "I know so well what a sad predicament . . ." is from his article, "Peace Treaty and Japan's Future," *Contemporary Japan*, Apr.–June 1951. In his memoirs, p. 286, Sato refers to Japan as a "forlorn and crestfallen orphan," and calls

Japan's withdrawal from the League of Nations a great loss for Japan and the League. In his postwar article, "The League and the U.N.," *Japan Quarterly*, Tokyo, Jan.–Mar. 1958, Sato blames Japan's "excess of nationalism" for its forced exit from the League. For Sato's plea to Togo not to resign after the Hull note, see Togo's memoirs, pp. 188–89, and the International Military Tribunal for the Far East, Exhibit 3629.

III

Sato's reluctant acceptance of the ambassadorship to Russia is described in his memoirs, pp. 446–48, 469. Molotov's statement to Sato that Russia would "live up to its obligations" is from George Alexander Lensen's *The Strange Neutrality*, pp. 40–41. Sato's feeling that he was walking on "thin ice" is expressed in his memoirs, pp. 465–66. Stalin's charge that Japan was a "habitual aggressor" is discussed in Morishima, p. 98. Sato's talk with Molotov about this remark can be found in Sato's "*Niso Kaisen Made*" in *Soren Kakumei no Yonju-nen*, p. 300. For Sato's meeting with Molotov on the Yalta Conference, see "Sato's testimony on Soviet entry," June 3, 1947, International Military Tribunal for the Far East, Transcript of the Proceedings, p. 33, 579, and Sato's *Futatsu no Roshia*, p. 333. Sato's cable, "Molotov . . . was amiable and smiling . . . ," was sent to Foreign Minister Mamoru Shigemitsu, Feb. 24, 1945, Records of the National Security Agency, Magic Diplomatic Summary #1069, Feb. 27, 1945. Molotov's statement to Sato ending the Neutrality Pact is discussed in Sato's diary, p. 476; "Sato's testimony on Soviet entry," June 3, 1947, transcript pp. 23, 580; and Lensen, p. 128. Sato's cable, Apr. 5, 1945, "Nothing more regretable . . . ," Magic, #1108, Apr. 1945.

IV

Sato's sensitivity to "special glances" of passers-by is reflected in Sato's cable, Apr. 9, 1945, Magic, #1111, Apr. 10, 1945. Sato's belief that Russia simply wanted to placate America and Britain is stated in his cable, Apr. 6, 1945, Magic, #1110, Apr. 9, 1945. Sato's plea to Tokyo to avoid provoking Russia but not to make "fools of ourselves" is included in the same cable. His cry for a "war of attrition" was cabled on May 9, 1945, Pacific Strategic Intelligence Section (PSIS), Commander-in-Chief, United States Fleet and Chief of Naval Operations, Russo-Japanese Relations, June 18, 1945. Sato's warning that Russia was "planning to seize the power of life and death over Japan" is made in his cable, Magic, #1143, May 12, 1945. Sato's remark that Japan might have to "eat dirt" was cabled on June 3, 1945, Magic, #1173, June 11, 1945. Togo's wish to avoid antagonizing Russia is asserted in his cable, June 1, 1945, Magic, #1166, June 4, 1945. Sato's reply, cabled the same day, is in the same Magic summary. Sato states he "dragged" himself to Molotov's office, Sato's memoirs, pp. 489–90. His talk with Molotov about the Hirota proposals was cabled on July 11, 1945, Magic, #1203, July 13, 1945. Sato's report of the talk and his plea against seeking the "utterly impossible" was cabled on July 12, 1945, PSIS naval intelligence report, July 13–20, 1945.

V

Togo's cables of July 11 stating that "even the termination of the war is now being considered privately," that Russian mediation should be sought, and that Japan did not intend to annex any territories is quoted in PSIS naval intelligence report, July 14, 1945. Sato's plea on July 12, 1945, for a peace that would "approximate unconditional surrender" is reported in Magic, #1206, July 14, 1945.

VI

Togo's cable of July 12, 1945, telling Russia of Japan's desire to end the war with Russian help and to dispatch a Special Envoy to Moscow is quoted in Magic, same summary. Sato's efforts to see Molotov and his meeting with Lozovsky on July 13, 1945, are described in PSIS naval intelligence report, July 13–20, 1945. Sato's warning that Japan's proposal must be concrete was cabled on July 13, 1945, Magic, #1207, July 15, 1945. His report that Russia's reply would be delayed was cabled on July 14, 1045, Magic, #1208, July 16, 1945.

VII

Togo's query about the time Stalin and Molotov left for Potsdam and Sato's reply were cabled on July 15, 1945, Magic, same summary. Sato clarifies what he means by "approximate unconditional surrender" in a cable sent on July 18, 1945, Magic #1212, July 20, 1945. Togo's statement that "negotiations to strengthen Russo-Japanese amity are necessary . . ." was cabled on July 17, 1945, PSIS naval intelligence report, July 21, 1945. Sato's reply "The powers-that-be . . ." was cabled on July 19, 1945, Magic, #1212, July 20, 1945.

CHAPTER 16

I

Those who contributed information on the Trinity bomb test include Bethe, Nichols, Rabi, Serber, and Teller. Among the most helpful books were Lansing Lamont's *Day of Trinity*, Groueff, Davis, and Hewlett and Anderson.

II

For a picture of living conditions in Los Alamos, especially in 1944–45, see Brode, Laura Fermi, Lamont, Goodchild, Michelmore, and *Reminiscences of Los Alamos*. Kitty Oppenheimer's unhappiness and her drinking problem are discussed by Oppenheimer's sister-in-law in Goodchild, pp. 128–31. Friends also contributed information.

III

Bainbridge's comment on Parsons is in the Parsons' oral history collection. Parsons' short-cut to the President is reported by Bainbridge in his oral history.

Tibbets described his meeting with Parsons to the author. See also *Enola Gay* by Gordon Thomas and Morgan Witts, pp. 11–13, 38–39.

IV

How Trinity got its name is described in Goodchild, p. 133, and Lamont, p. 70.

V

Oppenheimer and Bush contemplate Bhartrihari in Michelmore, pp. 107–108. The "failure" of the dummy bomb and Kistiakowsky's bet with Oppenheimer are reported in Goodchild, pp. 157–58, and Lamont, pp. 177–78. Oppenheimer's comment "Lord, these affairs are hard on the heart" is from Lamont, p. 226.

VI

Groves' statement that he had to make his own weather predictions is from a note in his personal papers. His reluctance to prepare troops and trucks for possible evacuation of nearby towns is reported in Lamont, pp. 126–27. Groves describes his role at Trinity in his memoirs, pp. 288–98 and in his Earl Zimmerman file, personal papers.

VII

Oppenheimer's determination to remain conscious during the bomb test is expressed in Lamont, p. 230. Groves' anxiety about what he would do "if nothing happened" is reflected in his memoirs, p. 296.

VIII

The Oppenheimer-Kistiakowsy exchange over their bet is reported in Lamont, p. 237. Bainbridge's remark, "Now we're all sons of bitches," appears in Michelmore, p. 111. Groves' reaction that the war would end "after we drop two bombs on Japan" is from his memoirs, p. 298.

IX

Stimson's receipt of news that the bomb test had succeeded is reported in his diary, July 16, 1945; Messer, p. 93; and Hewlett and Anderson, pp. 383–84. Truman's description of the misery in Berlin, his philosophizing on machines and morals, and his thoughts on ravaged cities in history are from a diary he kept, made up of miscellaneous scraps of paper, during the Potsdam Conference, Truman Library.

X

Truman mentions his meeting of July 17 with his military chiefs in his *Memoirs* (Vol. I), p. 415. See Charles L. Mee, Jr.'s *Meeting at Potsdam*, p. 85;

Ernest J. King and Walter M. Whitehill's *Fleet Admiral King*, p. 621. Mee quotes LeMay as saying that the bomb shortened the war by only two weeks, p. 192. Regarding Eisenhower's attitude toward dropping the bomb, see his *White House Years: Mandate for Change, 1953–1956*, pp. 312–13.

XI

Sato's brutal views of Japan's past and future, cabled to Togo on July 20, 1945, are reported in Magic, #1213, July 21, 1945. Togo's promise of "concrete" proposals, cabled July 21, appears in PSIS naval intelligence report, July 21–27, 1945. His instructions to Sato that he try to see Molotov during a recess of the Potsdam conference and his reference to the enhancement of Stalin's reputation were in a cable of July 25, 1945, and can be found in the same PSIS naval intelligence report. For background to Togo's remark about the Americans alluding to the Atlantic Charter in a radio broadcast, see Ellis Zacharias' *Secret Missions*, pp. 359–60.

XII

Stimson's talk with Byrnes on July 17 about a warning to the Japanese is reported in Stimson's diary on that day; see also Mee, p. 70, and Hewlett and Anderson, p. 384. Cordell Hull's quote about Byrnes and the delay of a warning to Japan appears in Hull's *Memoirs*, Vol. II. Leahy's memorandum to Truman regarding the Emperor's status is available in the Leahy files, Modern Military Branch, National Archives.

XIII

Stimson's talk with Truman on how to tell Stalin about the bomb is taken from Stimson's diary, July 3, 1945. Stimson's statement on Soviet repression in Germany comes from his diary, July 19, 1945. Stimson expressed his new thoughts on Russia in a memorandum he sent to the President on July 21, 1945. The President approved his analysis at a meeting the following day. See Stimson papers.

XIV

For details of Truman's meeting with Stalin on July 17, 1945, see Byrnes' *Speaking Frankly*, pp. 68–69; Mee, pp. 71–75; Hewlett and Anderson, pp. 385–86; Charles Bohlen's *Witness to History*, and his notes on the meeting, No. 1418 in *Foreign Relations of the United States (FRUS): The Conference of Berlin, 1945*. See also Truman's Potsdam diary, July 17, 1945, which includes statements, "I have some dynamite too" and "*Fini* Japs . . ." Byrnes' change of mind about Russia entering the war is recorded in Walter Brown's diary, July 17, 1945.

XV

Stimson's receipt of the cable of July 18, 1945, confirming the success of the bomb test and the reactions of Stimson and Truman were recorded in Stimson's diary on that date. See also Hewlett and Anderson, p. 386. Churchill's statement that Truman "is a man of immense determination . . ." is from Lord Moran's *Churchill: Taken from the Diaries of Lord Moran*, p. 293. The meeting of Truman and Churchill on July 16, 1945, is described in Truman's Potsdam diary for that day, and in Mee, p. 59. The meeting between the two leaders on July 18 is reported by Churchill in his memoirs, Vol. VI, pp. 631–34. See Moran's diary notation for that day; a note from Churchill to his Cabinet, July 18, 1945, Public Records Office; Mee, pp. 86–90; Toland, p. 950. Churchill's gentle rebuke of Truman about his dealing too hastily with matters was made at the July 17 session of the conference. For details of the conference, see FRUS: *The Conference of Berlin, 1945*, and Mee. Truman's remark about Churchill's "soft soap" was recorded in the President's Potsdam diary, July 16, 1945.

XVI

Truman's meeting of July 18 with Stalin is described in Bohlen's notes in FRUS: *The Conference of Berlin, 1945*, No. 1419. See also Mee, pp. 91–92.

XVII

The Groves-Farrell description of the bomb test and its preparation is reported in Groves' memoirs, p. 303–304, and in further detail in a report entitled "Comments by Ambassador Charles E. Bohlen on My Report to Secretary Stimson on the Alamogordo Test," Groves' personal papers. Groves writes in this report that he is grateful that it "had profound effect on the events in Potsdam." Stimson's reaction and his meetings with Marshall and with Truman and Byrnes are reported in Stimson's diary, July 21, 1945. See also Feis' *Japan Subdued*, pp. 84–85; Hewlett and Anderson, p. 389; and Mee, pp. 123–25. Truman's agreement to report to Stimson on what was happening at the conference is revealed in Stimson's diary, July 23, 1945. Stimson reports his difficulty in getting news and Byrnes' reluctance to help in the diary, July 18, 1945. Stimson's meeting with Churchill on the bomb test details is described in the dairy, July 22, 1945, and in the minutes of the Stimson-Churchill talk, FRUS: *The Conference of Berlin, 1945*, July 22, 1945. Lord Alanbrooke's remark on Churchill and the bomb appears in Arthur Bryant's *Triumph in the West*, p. 478.

XVIII

Stalin's fait accompli in moving Poles into East Germany and Truman's fury are described in Mee, pp. 125–28, quoting Russian transcript. Feis states that American leaders presumably wanted to moderate Russia's demands in order to facilitate a "quick closing of an accord" with Chiang, pp. 82–83. Alperovitz states that, on the contrary, these leaders wanted to stall off an agreement until the bomb had exploded over Japan and ended the war before Russia could get into it, p. 186. Byrnes apparently agreed with Alperovitz, according to a diary notation of Byrnes' assistant, Walter Brown, on July 24, 1945, quoted in this section. Stimson's questioning of Marshall about the need for a Russian attack in Manchuria is reported in Stimson's diary, July 23, 1945. See also Hewlett and Anderson, pp. 391–92.

XIX

For details of the July 24th meeting of the American and British military chiefs, see Feis' *Japan Subdued*, pp. 91–95. The refusal of Truman and Byrnes to formally request Russia to enter the Pacific war is covered in Feis, p. 108, and Mee, pp. 195–96. Byrnes' proposal for a Council of Foreign Ministers is discussed in Messer, pp. 110–11; Mee, pp. 168–69; Truman's *Memoirs* (Vol. I), pp. 344–45; and Byrnes' *Speaking Frankly*, pp. 69–72. See also FRUS: *The Conference of Berlin, 1945.*

XX

Truman's mention of a "new weapon" to Stalin is reported in Truman's *Memoirs* (Vol. I), p. 416; Byrnes' *Speaking Frankly*, p. 263; Leahy, p. 429; Churchill's memoirs, Vol. VI, pp. 669–70; Bohlen, p. 237. See also Marshal Zhukov's *The Memoirs of Marshal Zhukov*, pp. 674–75, Mee, pp. 177–78; and Brown's diary, July 24, 1945. For Russian progress on an atomic bomb, see Notes, Chapter 3, Section 5.

XXI

Stimson's statement about the bomb "tying in with what we are doing in all fields" is noted in his diary, July 23, 1945.

XXII

The story of Szilard's revised petition is told in his memoirs, pp. 187–88; Compton, pp. 241–42; and Smith, pp. 53–57. Teller, Wigner, Feld, Nichols, Arneson, and Lapp were also helpful. The Szilard petition and others, as well as Compton's covering letter to Nichols and Nichols' letter to Groves, are in the Harrison-Bundy files, Box 153, Folder 71, Entry 20.

XXIII

The transport of bomb parts to Tinian is detailed in Groves' memoirs, pp. 305–307. Groves' plan for dropping two bombs and determining when to drop the second is discussed in his memoirs, p. 308. Groves elaborates in his Tressel and Joseph J. Thorndike files, personal papers. Groves' report to Marshall that there would be a gap of at least three days between bombings can be found in Groves' personal papers. The debate over Kyoto as a target city can be found in Groves' memoirs, pp. 273–75; Groves' testimony, NBC White Paper, "The Decision to Drop the Bomb," Jan. 5, 1965 (quoted in Giovannitti and Freed, p. 202); "Top Secret-Special Interest to General Groves" file (including quote on Kyoto's "more highly intelligent" people), Box 3, Proposed Targets, Folders 5D.1 and 5D.2; Otis Cary's *Mr. Stimson's "Pet City": The Sparing of Kyoto, 1945* (excerpted in the *Japan Quarterly*, Oct.–Dec. 1975). Harrison's cable to Stimson on July 21, 1945, is in the Harrison-Bundy files, Box 151, Folder 64. Stimson's reply is in his diary, same date. Truman's approval of Stimson's stand on Kyoto is indicated in the diary, July 22 and 24, 1945. See Stimson's diary for June 1 and July 21 for further comment on Kyoto.

XXIV

The story of Cartwright and the other Hiroshima POWs was told to the author by Cartwright.

XXV

Truman's "delight" when shown the accelerated schedule for the bomb is expressed in Stimson's diary, July 24, 1945. The President's statement that he was "sure" Japan would not accept the ultimatum was made in his Potsdam diary, July 25, 1945. Stimson's advice that Stalin should be asked to sign the ultimatum is reported in Mee, p. 195. Stimson's plea to Truman to reassure Japan it could keep its dynasty and his request to leave for home are in Stimson's diary, July 24, 1945. Release of the Potsdam Declaration, Molotov's protest, and Byrnes' response are detailed in Mee, pp. 195–96.

XXVI

Togo's reaction to the Potsdam Declaration is reflected in his memoirs, pp. 311–12. Japanese concern about Russia's attitude is expressed in Toshikazu Kase, p. 207. Togo's meeting with the Emperor on July 27, 1945, is recorded in his memoirs, p. 312. The Big Six and Cabinet meetings that day are reported in Togo's memoirs, p. 312–14. The "*mokusatsu*" incident is described in Suzuki's autobiography; Brooks, pp. 160–64; Hisatsune Sakomizu's *Secret History of the End of the War*; William J. Coughlin's "The Great 'Mokusatsu' Mistake," *Harper's*, Mar. 1953; and Kazuo Kawai's "Mokusatsu: Japan's Response to the Potsdam Declaration," *Pacific Historical Review*, Nov. 1950. Interviews with Koichi Kido, Hajime Suzuki, and Nishi contributed to the picture.

XXVII

Togo's cable instructing Sato to see Molotov "as quickly as possible" was sent on July 28, 1945, Magic, #1221, July 29, 1945. Sato's cable of July 30, 1945, predicting that Stalin would not see a Special Envoy is quoted in PSIS naval intelligence report, Aug. 7, 1945. Togo's cable of Aug. 2, 1945, stating that the Potsdam Declaration was being considered as a basis for peace is included in PSIS naval intelligence report, Aug. 7, 1945. Sato's reply on Aug. 4, 1945, is carried in the same report.

XXVIII

Truman and Byrnes were fully aware of the Japanese cable intercepts, as indicated in Byrnes' *All in One Lifetime*, p. 297; James V. Forrestal's *Diaries*, pp. 20, 74–76; Lewis L. Strauss's *Men and Decisions*, p. 188; Stimson's memoirs, p. 617; and FRUS: *The Conference of Berlin, 1945*, Vol. II, p. 1266. The intelligence analysts concluded that Japan "recognizes her defeat" in a PSIS intelligence report.

XXIX

For farewells at the final session of the Potsdam conference, see FRUS: *The Conference of Berlin, 1945*, Vol. II, and Mee, pp. 226–27.

XXX

Arneson's statement that "no useful purpose would be served by transmitting" Szilard's petition and related papers to the White House is quoted in "The Fight over the A-Bomb," by Charles W. Bailey and Fletcher Knebel, *Look*, Aug. 13, 1963.

CHAPTER 17

I

Tibbets' introduction of Parsons and Parsons' talk to the crews and scientists are described in Thomas and Witts, pp. 227–29. Alvarez, Tibbets, and Jeppson contributed details to the author. Parsons' activities on Tinian are recorded in the oral histories of Harold Agnew, Norman Ramsey, and Frederic L. Ashworth.

II

The atmosphere before takeoff and the details of the *Enola Gay*'s flight are covered in Thomas and Witts, pp. 239–42, and *No High Ground* by Bailey and Knebel, pp. 156–57. Alvarez, Tibbets, and Jeppson offered additional details. Ashworth says in his oral history that Parsons personally peered through the bombsight.

III

Seiko Ogawa told her story to the author. Miyoko Matsubara, who was in Seiko's group at school, provided further information.

IV

See Section 3.

V

For Parsons' log, see Groves' memoirs, p. 318. Truman describes his elation on learning of Hiroshima in his *Memoirs* (Vol. I), quoting himself: "This is the greatest thing in history!", pp. 421–22. See also Byrnes' *Strictly Speaking*, p. 264; Leahy, p. 430; Rigdon, p. 206; Log of the President's Trip to the Berlin Conference, Truman Library; Rosenman papers, "Material Relating to Potsdam," Truman Library.

EPILOGUE

I

Kido's meeting with Hirohito to tell him of the bomb is reported in Kido's diary, Aug. 6, 1945. The Cabinet meeting on the same day is reported in Brooks, pp. 170–71.

II

Nishina's account of his trip to Hiroshima is detailed in a report called "The Atomic Bomb," Entry 41, Pacific war—Office of the Chairman, 3c (6), Records of the U.S. Strategic Bombing Survey, Modern Military Branch, National Archives. See also *Showa-shi no Tennoh* and Coffey, pp. 284–85, 290–91, 300–302, 318–20.

III

For Molotov's announcement to Sato that Russia was declaring war on Japan, see Sato's memoirs, pp. 498–99; Lenson, pp. 152–53; Brooks, p. 172; Gubler, pp. 290–92.

IV

Suzuki's decision to accept the Potsdam Declaration and his request to the Emperor for his "special help" are discussed in Coffey, pp. 320–24; Toland, p. 998; and Butow, p. 159. Rumor that Tokyo would be atom-bombed and preparations to protect Hirohito are reported in Hideaki Kase. Meeting of the Big Six on Aug. 9, including the interruption with news of the Nagasaki bomb, is covered in Butow, pp. 160–64; Toland, pp. 998–99; and Toshikazu Kase, pp. 231–35. The Imperial Conference called the same night is described in Butow, pp. 167–77; Feis, pp. 130–32; Toland, pp. 1002–1007; and William Craig's *The Fall of Japan*, pp. 114–20. Anami's admonition to his officers to obey the Emperor is in Brooks, pp. 177–78; Toland, p. 1008; and Craig, pp. 131–32.

V

Stimson's argument that use should be made of the Emperor to end the war is stated in his diary, Aug. 10, 1945. Byrnes' draft of peace conditions is dealt with in Truman's *Memoirs*, pp. 428–29.

VI

Anami's dilemma is reflected in Toland, pp. 1018–25. Suzuki's renewed "*haragei*" is discussed in Toshikazu Kase, pp. 243–44; Kido's diary, Aug. 12, 1945; Butow, pp. 194–96; Brooks, pp. 225–31.

VII

The Anami-Mikasa exchange appears in Brooks, pp. 231–32, and Toland, pp. 1019–20. Anami's plea to Kido against Byrnes' note is in Butow, pp. 199–200. Takeshita's urging of Anami to join a revolt was described by Hayashi to the author. The Imperial Conference of Aug. 14, 1945, is covered in Butow, pp. 207–208; Toland, pp. 1028–29, 1031; and Brooks, pp. 262–68. Anami's farewells and suicide were described to the author by Hayashi. See Toland, pp. 1046–49; Brooks, pp. 332–36; Craig, pp. 184–87; 194–95, 200–201; and Coffey, pp. 478–80, 487–92, 495–96, 512–14.

VIII

Suzuki's escape from the rebels is described in Brooks, pp. 329–31; Bergamini, p. 111; and Craig, pp. 196–97. Hajime Suzuki offered further details to the author. Kido's escape is noted in the author's *Kishi and Japan*, p. 218. The young officers' revolt is discussed at length by Craig, Brooks, Toland, Bergamini, Butow, and Coffey.

IX

Suzuki's last years were described in his autobiography and by his son Hajime at his meeting with the author. See also Brooks, pp. 386–87.

X

Togo's grandson Shigehiko and his daughter Ise emphasized Togo's stoic attitude during his years in prison. "While the future of Japan is eternal . . ." is from Togo's memoirs, p. 339.

XI

Sato's last years are described in his memoirs, the memoirs of his friends (listed in the Bibliography), and in Gubler.

XII

Kido's statement to the International Military Tribune, "It is my sole consolation . . . ," is quoted in Brooks, p. 398. Kido expressed his hopes for Japan in his talk with the author shortly after he was released from prison.

XIII

For details of General Douglas MacArthur's meeting with the Emperor, see MacArthur's *Reminiscences*, pp. 287–88, and William Manchester's *American Caesar*, pp. 576–77. See debate among military leaders whether to indict Hirohito, Modern Military Branch, National Archives. The postwar attitude of the Japanese toward the Imperial Family is described in the author's *Kishi and Japan*, pp. 20–21.

XIV

Yoshio Nishina's son Yuichiro told the author how his father contemplated suicide but decided against it. Shortly after the war, Nishina mentioned his possible suicide in a letter to Hidehiko Tamaki, a professor at the University of Tokyo and a member of the Executive Board of the Nishina Memorial Foundation. *Showashi no Tenno* describes Nishina's hopes for using his cyclotrons upon his return to Tokyo from Hiroshima. See Nishina's "A Japanese Scientist Describes the Destruction of His Cyclotrons," *Bulletin of the Atomic Scientists,* June 1947.

XV

The memorandum and covering letter Stimson handed to Truman on Sept. 11, 1945 calling for greater trust of Russia can be found in the Harrison-Bundy files, Box 148, Entry 20, S-1 Russia #20. These documents also appear in Stimson's memoirs, pp. 642–46. Stimson's role at the farewell Cabinet meeting of Sept. 21, 1945, and his departure from Washington are described in E. Morison, pp. 641–43.

XVI

Molotov's sneering remarks about Byrnes' reliance on the bomb to make diplomatic points are quoted in Messer, pp. 128–30, and Gregg Herken's *The Winning Weapon,* pp. 47–49. See also Brown diary, Sept. 17, 1945, and Joseph E. Davies' memorandum to Truman regarding Molotov's dinner party remark, Sept. 29, 1945, Davies papers. Byrnes' *Strictly Speaking* describes the London Conference from Byrnes' point of view. Molotov's wish for a trusteeship over an Italian colony in Africa is referred to in Messer, p. 140. The Moscow Conference is covered in Byrnes' *Strictly Speaking,* Messer, and Herken. In interviews, Brown and Russell contributed valuable insights into Byrnes' thinking in this period. The conflict of authority between Truman and Byrnes is described in Truman's *Memoirs* (Vol. I), pp. 546–53, and Byrnes' *All in One Lifetime,* pp. 398–403. See also *Mr. President,* edited by William Hillman. In an interview, Clark Clifford offered some thoughts on this relationship. How Yalta caught up with Byrnes is shown by Messer, pp. 169–71. See also Byrnes' "Byrnes Answers Truman," *Collier's,* Apr. 26, 1952; "Byrnes-Truman Friendship Turned Sour," *U.S. News and World Report,* Feb. 1950; Arthur Krock's "Byrnes Formally Joins the Opposition," *The New York Times,* Nov. 22, 1949; Ralph McGill's "What is Jimmy Byrnes Up to Now?", *Saturday Evening Post,* Oct. 14, 1950; "You're No Caesar," *Newsweek,* Nov. 14, 1955.

XVII

Truman remarked to his budget director, Harold D. Smith, that he could not be sure the bomb could ever be used again, Oct. 5, 1945, Smith diary. His remark to Lilienthal is recorded in Lilienthal's *The Atomic Energy Years, 1945–1950,* Vol. II, p. 391. Lilienthal also quotes Truman as saying, in response to a British author's contention that the atomic bomb was just another weapon, that this was "a very serious mistake. This isn't just another bomb," Feb. 14, 1949. See Richard F. Haynes' *The Awesome Power*, pp. 60–61.

XVIII

Leahy's mood after his return from Potsdam was described to the author by his secretary, Dorothy Rindquist. Leahy's statement about the "lethal possibilities of such atomic action" appears in his diary, Aug. 8, 1945. His warning about the danger to America was given in his diary, Oct. 17, 1945, and his related statement that the United States "must have more and better atom bombs" appears in his memoirs, p. 442. For Leahy's dispute with Byrnes, see "Elder-Statesman Role of Admiral Leahy in Challenging Russians," *United States News*, Apr. 11, 1947.

XIX

How Russia won control of uranium deposits in Czechoslovakia and Germany is told by Eugene Rabinowitch's "Atomic Spy Trials: Heretical Afterthoughts," *Bulletin of the Atomic Scientists*, May 1951. Fuchs' activities after the war are detailed in reports in the FBI Fuchs file. Included in this file is his declassification task, his meeting with Harry Gold on Sept. 19, 1945, and his activities in England. His statements on his "doubts" about Russian policy after the war and his dilemma about whether to leave Harwell can be found in the transcript of his trial, and in Moorehead, Pilat, and Montgomery Hyde.

XX

For Wallace's shock that Groves knew more about American nuclear strength than the President or Secretary of War, see Herken, p. 123. The struggle between the military and the scientists, between Groves and Szilard, over the complexion of the Atomic Energy Commission is described in Szilard's memoirs, pp. 224–29. Groves states his views in his Tressel file, pp. 34–35, personal papers. See also Herken. Groves' remark that the drive to build the bomb proved man could accomplish "virtually anything" is in his memoirs, p. 415.

XXI

Szilard wrote White House aide Connelly on Aug. 17, 1945, asking for permission to make public the Szilard petition signed by sixty-seven scientists, Miscellaneous Historical Document file, Truman Library. On Aug. 28, Szilard received a reply from Captain James S. Murray, an army engineer intelligence officer, that he was forbidden to make the petition public and that he could be fired from his job if he did so, Harrison-Bundy files, Box 153, Folder #71, Entry 20, Interim Committee–British Committee. Szilard's "Letter to Stalin" appears in the *Bulletin of the Atomic Scientists*, Dec. 1957. Szilard wrote a summary of his talk with Khrushchev entitled "Conversation with K on Oct. 5 (1960)," Oct. 9, 1960, Szilard papers. On Sept. 20, 1961, he wrote Khrushchev saying they were both wrong in believing that "there will be a serious attempt to improve Soviet-American relations . . . whether Nixon or Kennedy gets elected." In a letter to Szilard dated Aug. 30, 1960, Khrushchev "welcomed" Szilard's effort to hold a joint meeting of Soviet and American scientists in Moscow. Szilard's plan for an agreement between the superpowers to bomb each other's cities if either committed aggressions is explained in Eugene Rabinowitch's "1882–1964, 1898–1964," *Bulletin of the Atomic Scientists*, Oct. 1964. An article in the Soviet humor magazine, *Krokodil*, on Apr. 20, 1960, ridiculed the plan, Szilard papers. Information on the Council for a Livable World was given the author by President Jerome Grossman, Doering, Feld, Forbes, and Meselson. Doering and Arnold Kramish described to the author Szilard's hurried departure from Washington during the Cuban missile crisis in 1962. Szilard's work on an antifertility rice and a suicide pill and his fear of a cobalt bomb attack were reported to the author by Doering. Szilard's desire to dissolve his peace council was revealed to the author by Forbes. His view of death comes from Irwin's "The Legend That is Dr. Szilard," *Pageant*, Dec. 1961.

XXII

Oppenheimer's elated announcement of the Hiroshima explosion is described in Kunetka, p. 186. The party fiasco and the vomiting are mentioned in Smith, p. 77. The "spirit of oneness" at Los Alamos is expressed in a eulogy to Oppenheimer by Hans Bethe, "J. Robert Oppenheimer, 1904–1967," *Bulletin of the Atomic Scientists*, Oct. 1967, a transcript of Bethe's speech at the memorial services for Oppenheimer at Princeton. The quote, "Oppie says that the atomic bomb is so terrible a weapon . . ." is from Smith, p. 77. For details of the Acheson-Lilienthal and Baruch commission reports, see Herken, pp. 151–52, 158–167. The Oppenheimer-Teller conflict over the hydrogen bomb is described in Goodchild; Michelmore; a report on Teller's interrogation in the FBI Oppenheimer file; and Roland Sawyer's "The H-bomb Chronology," *Bulletin of the Atomic Scientists*, Sept. 1954. Teller gave his version of the conflict to the author. Borden's accusations against Oppenheimer and the reactions of the FBI, President Eisenhower, and other political figures are covered in detail in the FBI Oppenheimer file. Complete testimony at the Oppenheimer hearings can be found in *In the Matter of J. Robert Oppenheimer*. See also a special report on the hearings in the *Bulletin of the Atomic Scientists*, June 1954. Oppenheimer's acceptance statement on receiving the Fermi Award is quoted in Davis, p. 354.

XXIII

The triumphant return of the *Enola Gay* to Tinian was described to the author by Tibbets and Jeppson. See Thomas and Witts, p. 269. Groves' statement that Parsons was "running the show" appears in a note among the general's personal papers. Parsons' statement "Always remember this, there is no limit . . ." is from Merle Tuve's oral history on Parsons, as are the subsequent quotes from Tuve. Parsons' remark to his wife, "Look at all those nice houses," was quoted to the author by Parsons' wife Martha Burroughs. The remark by Parsons' high school teacher and the account of the photo of the wrong William S.

Parsons come from Martha Burroughs' oral history regarding Parsons. Groves tells how he spoke to Nimitz about getting Parsons a promotion in a note in the general's personal papers. Parsons' rejection of a job in private industry and his feeling of obligation to the navy are indicated in Martha Burroughs' oral history. His discussion with his sister about future American-Soviet relations appears in her memoir. Parsons' reaction to Oppenheimer's loss of his security clearance and the naval officer's sudden death were recounted to the author by Martha Burroughs. The quote, "I think [the Oppenheimer case] really had quite a lot to do with Deak's death," is from her oral history.

XXIV

Cartwright's story was told to the author by Cartwright. He revealed the facts he managed to find out from official sources about how his comrades died. Also, files on nine of the Hiroshima victims were obtained from the Agent Orange Task Force, Office of the Adjutant General, Department of the Army, including the letters to Porter's father and Neal's wife. Helpful too were Barton J. Bernstein's "Hiroshima's Hidden Victims," *Inquiry*, Aug. 6, 20, 1979 (includes a report on the medical experiments on POWs), and his "American POWs Killed at Hiroshima," *Foreign Service Journal*, Oct. 1979; Robert Karl Manoff's "American Victims of Hiroshima," *New York Times Magazine*, Dec. 2, 1984; and Repps B. Hudson's "Did B-24 Crew Die in A-Blast?" *Kansas City Times*, Nov. 20, 1975.

XXV

Seiko Ogawa's story was related to the author by Seiko. Tomin Harada, Shinichiro Kurose, Miyoko Matsubara, and Akihiro Takahashi contributed to this section.

BIBLIOGRAPHY

BOOKS

Abels, Jules. *The Truman Scandals*. Chicago: Regnery, 1956.

Acheson, Dean G. *Present at the Creation: My Years in the State Department*. New York: Norton, 1969.

——. *Sketches from Life*. New York: Harper, 1959.

Agawa, Hiroshi. *Yamamoto Isoroku*. Tokyo: Shincho Shahan, 1965.

Allen, James S. *Atomic Imperialism*. New York: International, 1952.

Alperovitz, Gar. *Atomic Diplomacy*. New York: Simon & Schuster, 1965.

Alsop, Joseph and Stewart. *We Accuse*. New York: Simon & Schuster, 1954.

Amrine, Michael. *The Great Decision*. New York: Putnam, 1959.

Anami Korechika Den, (including excerpts from Anami's diaries) Tokyo.

Aptheker, Herbert. *American Foreign Policy and the Cold War*. New York: New Century, 1962.

Arnold, H. H. *Global Mission*. New York: Harper, 1949.

Asbell, Bernard. *When F.D.R. Died*. New York: Holt, Rinehart & Winston, 1961.

Attlee, Clement. *As It Happened*. London: Heinemann, 1954.

Bailey, Charles W., and Knebel, Fletcher. *No High Ground*. New York: Harper, 1960.

Baldwin, Hanson. *Great Mistakes of the War*. New York: Harper, 1950.

Barkley, Alben W. *That Reminds Me*. Garden City, N.Y.: Doubleday, 1954.

Baruch, Bernard, *The Public Years*. New York: Holt, Rinehart & Winston, 1962.

Batchelder, Robert C. *The Irreversible Decision, 1939–1950*. Boston: Houghton Mifflin, 1961.

Baxter, James Phinney III. *Scientists Against Time*. Boston: Little, Brown, 1946.

Beard, C. A. *President Roosevelt and the Coming of the War, 1941*. New Haven, Conn.: Yale University Press, 1948.

Beasley, William G. *The Modern History of Japan*. New York: Praeger, 1963.

Beloff, Max. *Soviet Policy in the Far East*. London: Oxford University Press, 1953.

Benedict, Ruth. *The Chrysanthemum and the Sword*. Boston: Houghton Mifflin, 1946.

Bergamini, David. *Japan's Imperial Conspiracy*. New York: Morrow, 1971.

Bernstein, Barton J., ed. *The Atomic Bomb*. Boston: Little, Brown, 1976.

———. *Politics and Policies of the Truman Administration*. Chicago: Quadrangle, 1972.

Bernstein, Barton J., and Matusow, Allen J., eds. *The Truman Administration*. New York: Harper, 1966.

Birge, Raymond T. *History of the Physics Department*. Berkeley, Calif.: University of California Press, n.d.

Blackett, P. M. S. *Fear, War, and the Bomb*. New York: McGraw-Hill, 1948.

Blow, Michael. *The History of the Atomic Bomb*. New York: American Heritage, 1968.

Blumberg, Stanley A., and Owens, Gwinn. *Energy and Conflict: The Life and Times of Edward Teller*. New York: Putnam, 1976.

Bohlen, Charles. *Witness to History, 1929–1969*. New York: Norton, 1973.

Borton, Hugh. *Japan's Modern Century*. New York: Ronald, 1955.

Brooks, Lester. *Behind Japan's Surrender*. New York: McGraw-Hill, 1968.

Brown, Anthony Cave, and MacDonald, Charles B., eds. *The Secret History of the Atomic Bomb*. New York: Dial, 1977.

Brown, John Mason. *Through These Men*. London: Hamish Hamilton, 1956.

Bryant, Arthur. *Triumph in the West*. Garden City, N.Y.: Doubleday, 1959.

———. *The Turn of the Tide*. Garden City, N.Y.: Doubleday, 1957.

Burns, James MacGregor. *Roosevelt: The Soldier of Freedom*. New York: Harcourt, Brace, 1970.

Bush, Vannevar. *Modern Arms and Free Men*. New York: Simon & Schuster, 1949.

———. *Pieces of the Action*. New York: Morrow, 1970.

Butow, Robert. *Japan's Decision to Surrender*. Stanford, Calif.: Stanford University Press, 1954.

———. *Tojo and the Coming of War*. Princeton, N.J.: Princeton University Press, 1961.

Byas, Hugh. *Government by Assassination.* New York: Knopf, 1942.

Byrnes, James F. *All in One Lifetime.* New York: Harper, 1958.

——. *Speaking Frankly.* New York: Harper, 1947.

Campbell, Thomas M., and Herring, George C., eds. *The Diaries of Edward R. Stettinius, Jr., 1943–1946.* New York: New Viewpoints, 1975.

Carr, Albert H. A. *Truman, Stalin and Peace.* Garden City, N.Y.: Doubleday, 1950.

Cary, Otis. *Mr. Stimson's "Pet City": The Sparing of Kyoto, 1945.* Self-published, December 1975.

Cate, James L., and Craven, Wesley F., eds. *The Army Air Forces in World War II* (Vol. V): *The Pacific: Matterhorn to Nagasaki, June 1944 to August 1945.* Chicago: University of Chicago Press, 1953.

Chevalier, Haakon. *Oppenheimer: The Story of a Friendship.* New York: Braziller, 1965.

Christopher, Robert C. *The Japanese Mind.* New York: Simon & Schuster, 1983.

Chujo, Kazuo. *The Nuclear Holocaust.* Tokyo: Asahi Shimbun, 1983.

Church, Peggy Pond. *The House at Otowi Bridge.* Albuquerque: University of New Mexico Press, 1959.

Churchill, Winston S. *The Second World War* (Vol. VI): *Triumph and Tragedy.* Boston: Houghton Mifflin, 1953.

Clark, Ronald W. *The Birth of the Bomb.* New York: Horizon, 1960.

——. *Einstein.* New York: World, 1971.

——. *The Greatest Power on Earth.* London: Sidgwick & Jackson, 1980.

Clemens, Cyril. *The Man from Missouri.* Webster Groves, Miss.: Mark Twain Society, 1945.

Clemens, Diane Shaver. *Yalta.* New York: Oxford University Press, 1970.

Cline, Ray S. *Washington Command Post: The Operations Division.* Washington, D.C.: Office of the Chief of Military History, Department of the Army, 1951.

Cochran, Bert. *Harry Truman and the Crisis Presidency.* New York: Funk & Wagnalls, 1973.

Coffey, Thomas M. *Imperial Tragedy.* New York and Cleveland: World, 1970.

Coffin, Tris. *The Missouri Compromise.* Boston: Little, Brown, 1947.

Cohen, Jerome B. *Japan's Economy in War and Reconstruction.* Minneapolis: University of Minnesota Press, 1949.

Colegrove, Kenneth W. *Militarism in Japan.* Boston: World Peace Foundation, 1936.

The Committee for the Compilation of Materials on Damage Caused by the Atomic Bombs in Hiroshima and Nagasaki. *Hiroshima and Nagasaki.* New York: Basic Books, 1981.

Compton, Arthur Holly. *Atomic Quest.* New York: Oxford University Press, 1956.

Conant, James Bryant. *Modern Science and Modern War*. New York: Columbia University Press, 1952.

———. *My Several Lives*. New York: Harper, 1970.

Criag, William. *The Fall of Japan*. New York: Dial, 1967.

Craigie, Sir Robert. *Behind the Japanese Mask*. London: Hutchinson, 1945.

Current, Richard N. *Secretary Stimson*. New Brunswick, N.J.: Rutgers University Press, 1954.

Curry, George. *James F. Byrnes*. New York: Cooper Square, 1965.

Dallin, David J. *Soviet Espionage*. New Haven, Conn.: Yale University Press, 1955.

Daniels, Jonathan. *The Man of Independence*. New York: Lippincott, 1950.

Davies, Joseph. *Mission to Moscow*. New York: Simon & Schuster, 1941.

Davis, Lynn E. *The Cold War Begins*. Princeton, N.J.: Princeton University Press, 1974.

Davis, Nuel Pharr. *Lawrence and Oppenheimer*. New York: Simon & Schuster, 1968.

Deane, John R. *The Strange Alliance*. New York: Viking, 1947.

Delbars, Yves. *The Real Stalin*. London: Allen and Unwin, 1953.

Donovan, Robert J. *Conflict and Crisis*. New York: Norton, 1977.

Druks, Herbert. *Harry S. Truman and the Russians, 1945–1953*. New York: Robert Speller, 1966.

Ehrman, John. *Grand Strategy*. London: HMSO, 1956.

Eisenhower, Dwight D. *Crusade in Europe*. Garden City, N.Y.: Doubleday, 1948.

———. *The White House Years: Mandate for Change, 1953–1956*. Garden City, N.Y.: Doubleday, 1963.

Evans, Medford. *The Secret War for the A-Bomb*. Chicago: Regnery, 1953.

Falk, Edwin Albert. *From Perry to Pearl Harbor*. Garden City, N.Y.: Doubleday, Doran, 1943.

Feis, Herbert. *Between War and Peace: The Potsdam Conference*. Princeton, N.J.: Princeton University Press, 1960.

———. *Churchill, Roosevelt, Stalin*. Princeton, N.J.: Princeton University Press, 1957.

———. *Contest over Japan*. New York: Norton, 1967.

———. *Japan Subdued: The Atom Bomb and the End of the War in the Pacific*. Princeton, N.J.: Princeton University Press, 1961.

———. *The Road to Pearl Harbor*. Princeton, N.J.: Princeton University Press, 1950.

Fermi, Laura. *Atoms in the Family*. Chicago: University of Chicago Press, 1954.

Ferrell, Robert H. *American Diplomacy in the Great Depression: Hoover-Stimson Foreign Policy, 1929–1933*. New Haven, Conn.: Yale University Press, 1957.

———. *The Far Eastern Crisis: Recollections and Observations*. New York: Harper, 1936.

——. *George C. Marshall.* New York: Cooper Square, 1966.

Ferrell, Robert H., ed. *The Autobiography of Harry S. Truman.* Boulder, Col.: Colorado Associated University Press, 1980.

——. *Dear Bess.* New York: Norton, 1983.

——. *Off the Record.* New York: Harper, 1980.

Ferrell, Robert, and Bemis, Samuel F., eds. *The American Secretaries of State and Their Diplomacy* (James F. Byrnes—Vol. XIV). New York: Cooper Square, 1945.

Fleisher, Wilfrid. *Our Enemy Japan.* Washington, D.C.: The Infantry Journal, 1942.

——. *Volcanic Isle.* Garden City, N.Y.: Doubleday, Doran, 1941.

——. *What to Do with Japan.* Garden City, N.Y.: Doubleday, 1945.

Fleming, Denna Frank. *The Cold War and Its Origins* (Vols. I, II). Garden City, N.Y.: Doubleday, 1961.

Flynn, Edward. *You're the Boss.* Westport, Conn.: Greenwood, 1947.

Fogelman, Edwin, ed. *Hiroshima: The Decision to Use the A-Bomb.* New York: Scribner's, 1964.

Frisch, Otto. *What Little I Remember.* Cambridge, England: Cambridge University Press, 1979.

Gaddis, John L. *The United States and the Origins of the Cold War, 1941–1947.* New York: Columbia University Press, 1972.

Gaimusho. *Shusen Shiroku* (*The Historical Record of the Termination of the War*). Tokyo: Shimbun Gekkansha, 1952.

Gardner, Lloyd C. *Architects of Illusion.* Chicago: Quadrangle, 1970.

Gardner, Lloyd C., Morgenthau, Hans J., and Schlesinger, Arthur Jr. *The Origins of the Cold War.* Waltham, Mass.: Ginn, 1970.

Gibney, Frank. *Five Gentlemen of Japan.* New York: Farrar, Straus, and Young, 1953.

Gigon, Fernand. *Formula for Death.* London: Wingate, 1958.

Gilpin, Robert. *American Scientists and Nuclear Weapons Policy.* Princeton, N.J.: Princeton University Press, 1962.

Giovannitti, Len, and Freed, Fred. *The Decision to Drop the Bomb.* New York: Coward-McCann, 1965.

Goodchild, Peter. *J. Robert Oppenheimer, Shatterer of Worlds.* Boston: Houghton Mifflin, 1981.

Gosnell, Harold. *Truman's Crises.* Westport, Conn.: Greenwood Press, 1980.

Goudsmit, Samuel A. *ALSOS.* New York: Henry Schuman, 1947.

Gowing, Margaret M. *Independence and Deterrence: Britain and Atomic Energy, 1945–1952.* New York: St. Martin's, 1974.

Graebner, Norman, ed. *In an Uncertain Tradition: American Secretaries of State in the 20th Century* ("James F. Byrnes" by Richard D. Burns). New York: McGraw-Hill, 1961.

Grew, Joseph C. *Ten Years in Japan.* New York: Simon and Schuster, 1944.

————. *Turbulent Era.* 2 vols, Boston: Houghton Mifflin, 1952.

Groueff, Stephane. *Manhattan Project.* Boston: Little, Brown, 1967.

Groves, Leslie R. *Now It Can Be Told.* New York: Harper, 1962.

Guillain, Robert. *I Saw Tokyo Burning.* New York: Doubleday, 1981.

Haberer, Joseph. *Politics and the Community of Science*, New York: Litton, 1969.

Hachiya, Michihiko. *Hiroshima Diary.* Chapel Hill: University of North Carolina Press, 1955.

Hammond, Thomas T. "Did the United States Use Atomic Diplomacy Against Russia in 1945?" in *From Cold War to Detente*, edited by Peter J. Potichny and Jane P. Shapiro. New York: Praeger, 1976.

Hanayama, Shinso. *The Way of Deliverance: Three Years with the Condemned War Criminals.* New York: Scribner's, 1950.

Harada, Kumao. *Saionji-ko to Seikyoku (Prince Saionji and the Political Situation)* (8 vols.). Tokyo: Iwanami Shoten, 1950–1956.

Harada, Tomin. *Hiroshima Surgeon.* Newton, Kansas: Faith and Life, 1983.

Harriman, W. Averell, and Abel, Elie. *Special Envoy to Churchill and Stalin, 1941–1946.* New York: Random House, 1975.

Hattori, Takushiro. *A Complete History of the Greater East Asian War.* Tokyo: Masu Shobo, 1953.

Hawkins, David. *Manhattan District History, Project Y.* The Los Alamos Project (Vol. I). Los Alamos, N.M.: University of California and U.S. Atomic Energy Commission, 1945.

Hayashi, Masayoshi, ed. *Himerareta Showa-shi (Hidden History of Hirohito's Reign).* Tokyo: Mainichi Shimbun, 1965.

Hayashi, Saburo. *Kogun: The Japanese Army in the Pacific War.* Quantico, Va.: Marine Corps Association, 1959.

Haynes, Richard F. *The Awesome Power.* Baton Rouge: Louisiana State University Press, 1973.

Hearn, Lafcadio. *Japan.* New York: Macmillan, 1917.

Hedley, John Hollister. *Harry S. Truman: The "Little" Man from Missouri.* Woodbury, N.Y.: Barron's, 1979.

Heinrichs, Waldo. *American Ambassador: Joseph E. Grew and the Development of the U.S. Diplomatic Tradition.* Boston: Little, Brown, 1966.

Helm, William Pickett. *Harry Truman.* New York: Duell, Sloan and Pierce, 1947.

Herken, Gregg. *The Winning Weapon.* New York: Knopf, 1981.

Hersey, John. *Hiroshima.* New York: Knopf, 1946.

Hewlett, Richard G., and Anderson, Oscar E. *A History of the United States Atomic Energy Commission: The New World, 1939–1946.* University Park, Pa.: Pennsylvania State University Press, 1962.

Hillman, William, ed. *Mr. President.* New York: Farrar, Straus and Young, 1952.

Hindus, Maurice G. *Foreign Relations of Russia and Japan.* Garden City, N.Y.: Doubleday, 1942.

Hiroshima Jogakuin High School, ed. *Summer Cloud*. Tokyo: Sanyusha Shuppan, n.d.

Hiroshima Plus 20. New York: Delacorte, 1965.

Hirosige, Tetu. "Social Conditions for the Researches of Nuclear Physics," in *Japanese Studies in the History of Science*. Tokyo: 1963.

History of United States Naval Operations in World War II (Vol. XIV). Washington, D.C.: U.S. Government Printing Office, 1950.

Holloway, David. *The Soviet Union and the Arms Race*. New Haven, Conn.: Yale University Press, 1983.

Hull, Cordell. *Memoirs* (Vol. II). New York: Macmillan, 1948.

Hyde, H. Montgomery. *The Atom Bomb Spies*. New York: Atheneum, 1980.

Irving, David. *The German Atomic Bomb*. New York: Simon & Schuster, 1967.

Ismay, Lord. *Memoirs*. New York: Viking, 1960.

Japanese Broadcasting Corporation, ed. *Unforgettable Fire*. New York: Pantheon, 1977.

Jette, Eleanor. *Inside Box 1663*. Los Alamos, N.M.: Los Alamos Historical Society, 1967.

Jones, F. C. *Japan's New Order in East Asia: Its Rise and Fall, 1937–1945*. London: Oxford University Press, 1954.

Jungk, Robert. *Brighter than a Thousand Suns*. New York: Harcourt, Brace, Jovanovich, 1958.

———. *Children of the Ashes*. New York: Harcourt, Brace & World, 1959.

Kabor, Keiichiro. *Suzuki Kantaro*. Tokyo: Bungei Shunju,.

Kanroji, Osanaga. *Hirohito*. Los Angeles: Gateway, 1975.

Kase, Hideaki. *Tenno-ke no Tatakai*. Tokyo: Shincho-sha, 1982.

Kase, Toshikazu. *Journey to the Missouri*. New Haven, Conn.: Yale University Press, 1950.

Kato, Masuo. *The Lost War*. New York: Knopf, 1946.

Kecskemeti, Paul. *Strategic Surrender*. Stanford, Calif.: Stanford University Press, 1958.

Kido, Koichi. *Kido Koichi Nikki (Koichi Kido's Diaries)* (2 vols.). Tokyo: Tokyo University Press, 1966.

———. *Kankei Bunsho (Additional Writings)*. Tokyo: Tokyo University Press, 1966.

Kihensan Jinkai. *Biography of Kantaro Suzuki*. Tokyo: Totsuban. 1959.

King, Ernest J., and Whitehill, Walter Muir. *Fleet Admiral King*. New York: Norton, 1952.

Kirby, Stanley Woodburn, with C. T. Addis and others. *The War Against Japan*. 5 vols., London: HMSO, 1969.

Kodama, Yoshio. *I Was Defeated*. Tokyo: Booth & Fukuda, 1951.

Kolko, Gabriel, *The Politics of War: The World and United States Foreign Policy, 1943–1945*. New York: Random House, 1968.

Konoye, Prince Fumimaro. *Lost Politics.* Tokyo: Asahi Shimbun, 1946.

Kramish, Arnold. *Atomic Energy in the Soviet Union.* Stanford, Calif.: Stanford University Press, 1959.

Krylov, Ivan Nikititch. *Soviet Staff Officer.* London: Falcon, 1951.

Kunetka, James W. *City of Fire.* Englewood Cliffs, N.J.: Prentice-Hall, 1978.

Kurzman, Dan. *Kishi and Japan.* New York: Obolensky, 1960.

———. *Subversion of the Innocents.* New York: Random House, 1963.

Lafeber, Walter. *America, Russia, and the Cold War 1945–1971.* New York: John Wiley, 1967.

Lamont, Lansing. *Day of Trinity.* New York: Atheneum, 1965.

Lang, Daniel. *Early Tales of the Atomic Age.* Garden City, N.Y.: Doubleday, 1948.

———. *From Hiroshima to the Moon.* New York: Simon & Schuster, 1959.

Lapp, Ralph E. *Atoms and People.* New York: Harper, 1956.

Laurence, William L. *Dawn over Zero,* New York: Knopf, 1946.

———. *Men and Atoms.* New York: Simon & Schuster, 1959.

———. "The Atom Gives Up," in *The Saturday Evening Post Treasury.* New York: Simon & Schuster, 1954.

Leahy, William D. *I Was There.* New York: Whittlesey House, 1950.

Leighton, Alexander H. *Human Relations in a Changing World.* New York: Dutton, 1949.

Lensen, George Alexander. *The Strange Neutrality: Soviet-Japanese Relations During the Second World War, 1941–1945.* Tallahassee, Fla.: Diplomatic Press, 1972.

Lewis, Richard D., and Wilson, Jane, eds. *Alamogordo Plus Twenty-Five Years.* New York: Viking, 1971.

Libby, Leona Marshall. *Uranium People.* New York: Crane Russak & Scribner's, 1979.

Lieberman, Joseph. *The Scorpion and the Tarantula.* Boston: Houghton Mifflin, 1970.

Lifton, Robert Jay. *Death in Life.* New York: Basic Books, 1967.

Lilienthal, David E. *Change, Hope and the Bomb.* Princeton, N.J.: Princeton University Press, 1963.

———. *The Journals of David E. Lilienthal: The Atomic Energy Years 1945–1950* (Vol. II). New York: Harper & Row, 1964.

Lory, Hillis. *Japan's Military Masters.* New York: Viking, 1943.

MacArthur, Douglas. *Reminiscences.* New York: McGraw-Hill, 1964.

Major, John. *The Oppenheimer Hearing.* New York: Stein & Day, 1971.

Manchester, William. *American Caesar.* Boston: Little, Brown, 1978.

Marshak, Robert E. *Our Atomic World.* Albuquerque: University of New Mexico Press, 1946.

Marshall, Katherine. *Together, Annals of an Army Wife.* New York: Tupper and Love, 1946.

Marx, Joseph Laurance. *Nagasaki*. New York: Macmillan, 1971.

Marzani, Carl. *We Can Be Friends: The Origins of the Cold War*. New York: Topical Books, 1952.

Mason, Frank. *Truman and the Pendergasts*. Evanston, Ill.: Regency, 1963.

Maxson, Yale C. *Control of Japanese Foreign Policy: A Study of Civil-Military Rivalry, 1930–1945*. Berkeley: University of California Press, 1957.

May, Ernest R., ed. *The Ultimate Decision: The President as Commander-in-Chief*. New York: Braziller, 1960.

Mayer-Oakes, Thomas F., ed. *Saionji-Harada Memoirs: Fragile Victory*. Detroit: Wayne State University Press, 1968.

McCloy, John. *The Challenge to American Foreign Policy*. Cambridge, Mass.: Harvard University Press, 1953.

McNaughton, Frank. *This Man Truman*. New York: Whittlesey, 1945.

McNaughton, Frank, and Hehmeyer, Walter. *Harry Truman, President*. New York: Whittlesey, 1948.

Mee, Charles L., Jr. *Meeting at Potsdam*. New York: Evans, 1975.

Melton, David. *Harry S. Truman: The Man Who Walked With Giants*. Independence, Mo.: Independence Press, n.d.

Messer, Robert L. *The End of an Alliance*. Chapel Hill: University of North Carolina Press, 1982.

Michelmore, Peter. *The Swift Years*. New York: Dodd, Mead, 1969.

Miller, Merle. *Plain Speaking*. New York: Berkley, 1973.

Millis, Walter, and Duffield, Edward, eds. *The Forrestal Diaries*. New York: Viking, 1951.

Mooney, Booth. *The Politicians 1945–1960*. New York: Lippincott, 1970.

Moore, Ruth. *Niels Bohr*. New York: Knopf, 1966.

Moorehead, Alan. *The Traitors*. London: Hamish Hamilton, 1952.

Moran, Lord (Sir Charles Wilson). *Churchill: Taken from the Diaries of Lord Moran*. Boston: Houghton Mifflin, 1960.

Morishima, Goro. *Kuno Suru chu So Taishikan (The Japanese Embassy in the Soviet Union in Agony)*. Tokyo: Minato Shuppan, 1953.

Morison, Elting E. *Turmoil and Tradition*. Boston: Houghton Mifflin, 1960.

Morison, Samuel Eliot. *Victory in the Pacific, 1945*. Boston: Little, Brown, 1961.

Morland, Howard. *The Secret that Exploded*. New York: Random House, 1981.

Morray, Joseph P. *From Yalta to Disarmament*. New York: Monthly Review Press, 1961.

Mosley, Leonard. *Hirohito*. Englewood Cliffs, N.J.: Prentice-Hall, 1966.

———. *Marshall*. New York: Hearst Books, 1983.

Nakayama, Shigeru, Swain, David L., and Yagi, Eri, eds. *Science and Society in Modern Japan: Selected Historical Sources*. Cambridge, Mass.: MIT Press, 1974.

National Academy of Sciences. *Biographical Memoirs: Leo Szilard* (Vol. XL). New York: Columbia University Press, 1969.

New York Times. *Hiroshima Plus Twenty*. New York: Delacorte, 1965.

Nihon Kagakushi Gakkai, ed. *Nihon Kagaku Gijutsushi Taikei* (Vol. XIII). Tokyo: Daiichi Hogen, 1970.

Nishida, Kazuo. *Storied Cities of Japan*. Tokyo: John Weatherhill, 1963.

Nishitunoi, Masayoshi. *Nenchu-gyoji Jiten* (Dictionary of Annual Events). Tokyo: Tokyo-do, 1960.

Nitobe, Inazo. *Bushido: The Soul of Japan*. New York: Putnam, 1965.

Noel-Baker, Francis. *The Spy Web*. London: Batchworth, 1954.

Office of the Chief of Military History, Department of the Army. *Command Decisions*. New York: Harcourt, Brace, 1959.

Ogata, Sadako N. *Defiance in Manchuria: The Making of Japanese Foreign Policy, 1931–1932*. Berkeley: University of California Press, 1964.

Ohtani, Keijiro. *Rakujitsu no Josho: Showa Rikugun-shi* (*The Beginning of Sunset: History of the Japanese Army in the Reign of Hirohito*). Tokyo: Yakumo Shoten, 1959.

Oppenheimer, J. Robert. *The Open Mind*. New York: Simon & Schuster, 1955.

———. *Science and the Common Understanding*. New York: Simon & Schuster, 1954.

Osada, Arata, ed. *Children of Hiroshima*. Cambridge, Mass.: Oelgeschlager, Gunn & Hain, 1982.

The Pacific War Research Society. *The Day Man Lost*. Tokyo: Kodansha, 1972.

———. *Japan's Longest Day*. Tokyo: Kodansha, 1968.

Pais, Abraham, Rabi, I. I., Seaborg, Glenn T., Serber, Robert, and Weisskopf, Victor F. *Oppenheimer*. New York: Scribner's, 1969.

Phillips, Cabell. *The Truman Presidency*. New York: Macmillan, 1966.

Pilat, Oliver. *The Atom Spies*. New York: Putnam, 1952.

Potter, John Deane. *The Life and Death of a Japanese General*. New York: NAL, 1962.

Powell, Eugene James. *Tom's Boy Harry*. Jefferson City, Mo.: Hawthorn, 1948.

Prange, Gordon William. *At Dawn We Slept*. New York: McGraw-Hill, 1981.

———. *Miracle at Midway*. New York: McGraw-Hill, 1982.

Price, Willard. *Japan and the Son of Heaven*. New York: Duell, Sloan and Pearce, 1945.

———. *Key to Japan*. New York: John Day, 1946.

Pringle, Peter, and Spigelman, James. *The Nuclear Barons*. New York: Holt, Rinehart & Winston, 1981.

Purcell, John. *The Best-Kept Secret*. New York: Vanguard, 1963.

Rabinowitch, Eugene, and Grodzins, Morton, eds. *The Atomic Age*. New York: Basic Books, 1963.

Rappaport, Armin. *Henry L. Stimson and Japan, 1931–33*. Chicago: University of Chicago Press, 1963.

Reischauer, Edwin O. *Japan, Past and Present*. New York: Knopf, 1964.

————. *The United States and Japan*. Cambridge, Mass.: Harvard University Press, 1957.

Reuben, William A. *The Atom Spy Hoax*. New York: Action, 1945.

Riddle, Donald H. *The Truman Committee*. New Brunswick, N.J.: Rutgers University Press, 1964.

Rigdon, William M. *White House Sailor*. Garden City, N.Y.: Doubleday, 1962.

Robbins, Jhan. *Bess and Harry: An American Love Story*. New York: Putnam, 1980.

Roosevelt, Elliott. *As He Saw It*. New York: Duell, Sloan and Pearce, 1946.

Rose, Lisle A. *After Yalta*. New York: Scribner's, 1973.

————. *Dubious Victory: The United States and the End of World War II*. Kent, Ohio: Kent University Press, 1973.

Rosenman, Samuel I. *Working with Roosevelt*. New York: Harper, 1952.

Roth, Andrew. *Dilemma in Japan*. Boston: Little, Brown, 1945.

Rothermel, John E. *Hiroshima and Nagasaki from God's Point of View*. New York: Carlton, 1971.

Russell, Lord. *The Knights of Bushido*. London: Cassell, 1958.

Sakomizu, Hisatsune. *Secret History of the End of the War*. Tokyo: Jikyoku Geppo, 1946.

Sansom, Sir George. *Japan: A Short Cultural History*. New York: Appleton-Century-Crofts, 1962.

————. *The Western World and Japan*. New York: Knopf, 1950.

Sato, Naotake. *Kaiko Hachiju-nen (Recollections of Eighty Years)*. Tokyo: Jiji Tsushinsha, 1963.

————. *Futatsu no Roshia (The Two Russias)*. Tokyo: Sekai no Nihonsha, 1948.

————. *Taiso Gaiko Tokuhon (A Reader on Soviet Diplomacy)*. Tokyo: Jiyu Ajiasha, 1955.

Sato, Naotake, ed. *Kokusai Renmei ni Okeru Nihon (Japan in the League of Nations)*, Vol. XIV of *Nihon Gaiko-shi (Diplomatic History of Japan)*. Tokyo: Kajima Heiwa Kenkyujo, 1972.

————. "Niso Kaisen Made" ("Japan and the USSR to the Soviet Entry"), in *Soren Kakumei no Yonju-nen (Forty Years of the Soviet Revolution)*. Tokyo: Jiyu Ajiasha, 1957.

Schell, Jonathan. *The Fate of the Earth*. New York: Knopf, 1982.

Schoenberger, Walter Smith. *Decision of Destiny*. Athens: Ohio University Press, 1970.

Segre, Emilio. *Enrico Fermi: Physicist*. Chicago: University of Chicago Press, 1970.

Sherwin, Martin J. *A World Destroyed*. New York: Vintage, 1977.

Sherwood, Robert E. *Roosevelt and Hopkins*. New York: Harper, 1948.

Shigemitsu, Mamoru. *Japan and Her Destiny*. New York: Dutton, 1958.

Shimomura, Hiroshi (Kainan). *A Secret History of the War's End*. Tokyo: Kodansha, 1950.

Shoda, Tatsuo. *Jyushin Tachi no Shoan Shi* (Vol. II). Tokyo:

Smith, Alice Kimball. *A Peril and a Hope*. Chicago: University of Chicago Press, 1965.

Smith, Alice Kimball, and Weiner, Charles, eds. *Robert Oppenheimer: Letters and Recollections*. Cambridge, Mass.: Harvard University Press, 1980.

Smyth, Henry DeWolf. *Atomic Energy for Military Purposes*. Princeton, N.J.: Princeton University Press, 1945.

Snell, John L., ed. *The Meaning of Yalta*. Baton Rouge: Louisiana State University Press, 1956.

Steinberg, Alfred. *The Man from Missouri*. New York: Putnam, 1962.

Stern, Philip M. *The Oppenheimer Case*. New York: Harper, 1969.

Stettinius, Edward R., Jr. *Roosevelt and the Russians*. Garden City, N.Y.: Doubleday, 1949.

Stillman, Edmund, and Pfaff, William. *The New Politics: America and the End of the Postwar World*. New York: 1961.

Stimson, Henry L., and Bundy, McGeorge. *On Active Service in Peace and War*. New York: Harper, 1947.

Strauss, Lewis L. *Men and Decisions*. Garden City, N.Y.: Doubleday, 1962.

Strout, Cushing. *Conscience, Science and Security: The Case of J. Robert Oppenheimer*. Chicago: Rand McNally, 1963.

Sugiyama Hajime. *Sugiyama Memo (Sugiyama's Memoranda)* (2 vols.). Tokyo: Hara Shobo, 1967.

Suzuki, Kantaro. *Kantaro Suzuki Jiden (Autobiography of Kantaro Suzuki)*. Tokyo: Hei Bon-sha, 1981.

——. *Konjo Tenno Gonichijo no Ittan (One Aspect of the Present Emperor's Everyday Life)*. Tokyo: Imperial Household Ministry, Oct. 30, 1940.

——. "Arashi ni Jijucho Hachinen" ("Eight Years as Grand Chamberlain in the Storm") in *Tenno Hakusho (White Paper on the Emperor)*. Tokyo: Bungei Shunju, 1956.

Swing, Raymond. *In the Name of Sanity*. New York: Harper, 1945.

Szilard, Gertrud Weiss, and Feld, Bernard T., eds. *The Collected Works of Leo Szilard*. Boston: MIT Press, 1972.

Szilard, Gertrud Weiss, and Weart, Spencer R. *Leo Szilard: His Version of the Facts*. Cambridge, Mass.: MIT Press, 1978.

Szilard, Gertrud Weiss, and Windsor, Kathleen R., eds. "Reminiscences" by Leo Szilard in *Perspectives in American History* (Vol. II). Cambridge, Mass.: Harvard University Press, 1968.

Szilard, Leo. *The Voice of the Dolphins*. New York: Simon & Schuster, 1961.

Tanaka, Takayoshi. *Sabakareru Rekishi: Haisen Hiwa (History of Being Judged: The Secret Story of Defeat)*. Tokyo: Shimpu-sha, 1948.

Tateno, Nobuyuki. "Ni-ni-Roku Jiken no Nazo" ("Riddle of the February 26 Incident") in *Tenno to Hanran Gun (The Emperor and the Rebel Troops)*. Nihon Shuho, 1957.

Teller, Edward, and Brown, Allen. *The Legacy of Hiroshima*. Garden City, N.Y.: Doubleday, 1962.

Theoharis, Athan G. *The Yalta Myths*. Columbia: University of Missouri Press, 1970.

Thomas, Gordon, and Witts, Morgan. *Enola Gay*. New York: Stein and Day, 1977.

Togo, Shigenori. *The Cause of Japan*. New York: Simon & Schuster, 1956.

Toland, John. *The Rising Sun*. New York: Random House, 1970.

Tolischus, Otto D. *Through Japanese Eyes*. Cornwall, N.Y.: Reynal & Hitchcock, 1945.

Tomomatsu, Entai. *Tokyo Record*. New York: Reynal & Hitchcock, 1943.

Tomonaga, Shinichiro. *Hirakareta Kenkyujo to Shidosha Tacki (The Research Institute and Its Leaders)*. Tokyo: Misuzu Shobu, 1982.

Truman, Harry S. *Memoirs: Year of Decisions* (Vol. I). Garden City, N.Y.: Doubleday, 1955.

———. *Mr. Citizen*. New York: Random House & Geis Associates, 1960.

Truman, Margaret. *Harry S. Truman*. New York: Morrow, 1973.

———. *Souvenir: Margaret Truman's Own Story*. New York: McGraw-Hill, 1956.

Truman, Margaret, ed. *Letters from Father: The Truman Family's Personal Correspondence*. New York: Arbor House, 1981.

Truman Speaks. (Lectures and discussions held at Columbia University on April 27, 28, and 29, 1959). New York: Columbia University Press, 1960.

Trumbull, Robert. *Nine Who Survived Hiroshima and Nagasaki*. New York: Dutton, 1957.

Ulam, Adam. *Stalin: The Man and His Era*. New York: Viking, 1973.

Underhill, Robert. *The Truman Persuasions*. Ames: Iowa State University Press, 1981.

U.S. Atomic Energy Commission. *In the Matter of J. Robert Oppenheimer*. Washington, D.C.: U.S. Government Printing Office, 1954.

Ward, Patricia Dawson. *Threat of Peace: James F. Byrnes and the Council of Foreign Ministers, 1945–1946*. Kent, Ohio: Kent University Press, 1970.

Welles, Sumner. *Seven Decisions That Shaped History*. New York: Harper, 1950.

Wells, H. G. *The World Set Free*. London: Macmillan, 1914.

Werth, Alexander. *Russia at War 1941–1945*. New York: Dutton, 1964.

West, Rebecca. *The New Meaning of Treason*. New York: Viking, 1964.

Whitehead, Don. *The FBI Story*. New York: Random House, 1956.

Williams, William Appleman. *The Tragedy of American Diplomacy*. New York and Cleveland: World, 1959.

Wilson, Jane, ed. *All in Our Time*. Chicago: Bulletin of the Atomic Scientists, 1974.

Yanaga, Chitoshi. *Japan Since Perry*. New York: McGraw-Hill, 1949.

Yomiuri Shimbunsha. *Showashi no Tenno* (*The Emperor of Peace*) (Vol. IV). Tokyo: Yomiuri Shimbunsha, 1982.

York, Herbert F. *The Advisors*. San Francisco: Freeman, 1976.

Yoshida, Shigeru. *The Yoshida Memoirs*. London: Heinemann, 1961.

Young, A. Morgan. *Imperial Japan, 1926–1938*. London: George Allen & Unwin, 1938.

Zacharias, Ellis. *Secret Missions*. New York: Putnam, 1946.

Zhukov, G. K. *The Memoirs of Marshal Zhukov*. New York: Delacorte, 1971.

PERIODICALS, RADIO, TELEVISION

Abe, Shinnosuke, "Sato Gaiso-ron" ("On Foreign Minister Sato"), *Chuo Koron*, Tokyo, Apr. 1937.

"After 20 Years: More Hopes Than Fears," *Time*, Dec. 7, 1962.

Aiichi, Kiichi, "Gaiko-kai no Choro Sato Naotake Sensei" ("Mr. Sato Naotake, Doyen of Diplomats"), *Kokusai Jihyo*, Tokyo, Nov. 1970.

Alexandrov, A. P., article on Igor Kurchatov, *Bulletin of the Atomic Scientists*, Dec. 1967.

Alperovitz, Gar, "The Trump Card," *New York Review of Books*, June 15, 1967.

Alsop, Joseph, and Kintner, Robert, "Sly and Able: The Real Leader in the Senate, Jimmy Byrnes," *Saturday Evening Post*, July 20, 1940.

Alvarez, Luis W., "Berkeley: A Lab Like No Other," *Science and Public Affairs*, Apr. 1974.

"American Scientist Declared Security Risk," *Bulletin of the Atomic Scientists* (special section), June 1954.

Amrine, Michael, "The Day the Sun Rose Twice," *Washington Post Book Week*, July 18, 1965.

———, "The Real Problem Is in the Hearts of Men," *New York Times Magazine*, June 23, 1946.

———, "A Tale of the Steps to Hiroshima—and Beyond," *The Reporter*, Jan. 5, 1954.

Anderson, Clinton P., "Things Were Never the Same," *New York Times Book Review*, July 18, 1965.

Anderson, Herbert L., "The Legacy of Fermi and Szilard," *Bulletin of the Atomic Scientists*, Sept. 1974.

Ando, Yoshio, "Senso to Kazoku" ("The War and the Imperial Family"), 3 parts, *Ekonomisuto*, Tokyo, Aug. 31, 1965, Feb. 22, 1966, Mar. 1, 1966.

"Another Legacy of Hiroshima: The Partially Scientific Mind," *Bulletin of the Atomic Scientists*, June 1962.

Araki, Sadao, "The Emperor Stood Forth during a Disturbance of His Reign," *Bungei Shunju*, Tokyo, Oct. 1956.

Ashida, Hitoshi, "Sato Gaiso-ron" ("On Foreign Minister Sato"), *Kaizo*, Spring, 1937.

Attlee, Clement, "The Hiroshima Choice," *The Observer*, Sept. 6, 1959.

"The Atom," *Time*, Dec. 7, 1962.

"The Atomic Bomb Secret—Fifteen Years Later," *Bulletin of the Atomic Scientists*, Dec. 1966.

Baba, Akira, "Shohyo: Kaiko Hachiju-nen" ("Book Review: 'Recollections of Eighty Years'"), *Kokusai Jihyo*, Tokyo, Nov. 1970.

Badesh, Lawrence, Hirschfelder, Joseph O., and Broida, Herbert P., eds., *Reminiscences of Los Alamos 1943–1945*. Boston: Reidel, Dordrecht, Holland, 1980.

Bailey, Charles W., and Knebel, Fletcher, "The Fight over the A-Bomb," *Look*, Aug. 13, 1963.

Bainbridge, Kenneth T., "A Foul and Awesome Display," *Bulletin of the Atomic Scientists*, May 1975.

Baldwin, Hanson W., "This is the Army We Have to Defeat," *New York Times Magazine*, July 29, 1945.

Barnaby, Frank, "The Continuing Body Count at Hiroshima and Nagasaki," *Bulletin of the Atomic Scientists*, Dec. 1977.

Barnett, Lincoln, "Oppenheimer," *Life*, Oct. 10, 1949.

"Before Hiroshima," *Bulletin of the Atomic Scientists*, May 1, 1946.

"Behind the First Atomic Bomb," *Saturday Evening Post*, July 16, 1960.

Benfey, O. T., "The Scientist's Conscience: Historical Considerations," *Bulletin of the Atomic Scientists*, May 1956.

Bernstein, Barton J., "Doomsday II," *New York Times Magazine*, July 27, 1975.

———, "The Final Bombing of Japan," *Washington Post*, Aug. 24, 1975.

———, "Hiroshima Reconsidered—Thirty Years Later," *Foreign Service Journal*, Aug. 1975.

———, "Hiroshima's Hidden Victims," *Inquiry*, Aug. 6 & 20, 1979.

———, "The Perils and Politics of Surrender: Ending the War with Japan and Avoiding the Third Atomic Bomb," *Pacific Historical Review*, Feb. 1977.

———, "The Quest for Security: American Foreign Policy and International Control of Atomic Energy, 1942–1946," *Journal of American History*, Mar. 1974.

———, "Roosevelt, Truman and the Atomic Bomb," *Political Science Quarterly*, Spring, 1975.

———, "Unraveling a Mystery: American POWs Killed at Hiroshima," *Foreign Service Journal*, Oct. 1979.

Bernstein, Jeremy, "O Crucified Jove," *The New Yorker*, May 10, 1969.

Bethe, Hans, "J. Robert Oppenheimer, 1904—1967," *Bulletin of the Atomic Scientists*, Oct. 1967.

Blakeslee, Howard W., "Germans Lost Race to Develop Atom Bomb Under Nazi System," *The Evening Star*, Washington, D.C., Aug. 24, 1945.

Bohr, Niels, "For an Open World," *Bulletin of the Atomic Scientists*, July 1950.

"The Bomb," *Politics*, Sept. 1945.

Brode, Bernice, "Tales of Los Alamos," *LASL Community News* (Los Alamos, N.M.), June 2–Sept. 22, 1960.

Brown, Constantine, "Leahy: Grand Old American," *The Evening Star*, Washington, D.C., July 21, 1959.

Bruckner, D. J. R., "The Day the Nuclear Age Was Born," *New York Times*, Nov. 30, 1982.

Brues, Austin M., "With the Atomic Bomb Casualty Commission in Japan," *Bulletin of the Atomic Scientists*, June 1947.

Bryan, John, "Take My Name Off the End of the World, Says Molly Lawrence, Widow of A-Bomb 'Father'", *Daily Californian*, Berkeley, Dec. 9, 1983.

Buck, Pearl, "End of the World? One Nobel Prize Winner Interviews Another," *The American Weekly*, Mar. 8, 1959.

Bundy, Harvey H., "Remembered Words," *Atlantic Monthly*, Mar. 1957.

Busch, Noel F., "Admiral Leahy," *Life*, Sept. 28, 1942.

Byrnes, James F., "Byrnes Answers Truman," *Collier's*, Apr. 26, 1952.

———, "Preserve People's Rights," *Vital Speeches*, Dec. 1949.

"Byrnes-Truman Friendship Turned Sour," *U.S. News and World Report*, Feb. 1950.

Cahn, Robert, "Behind the First Atomic Bomb," *Saturday Evening Post*, July 16, 1960.

"The Case of the World's Greatest Secret," *Life*, Apr. 16, 1951.

Catledge, Turner, "Portrait of a Realist," *New York Times Magazine*, July 8, 1945.

Columbia Broadcasting System, J. Robert Oppenheimer interview, CBS Evening News, Aug. 6, 1965.

Compton, Arthur H., and Daniels, Farrington, "A Poll of Scientists at Chicago, July 1945," *Bulletin of the Atomic Scientists*, 1948.

Compton, Karl T., "The Atomic Bomb and the Surrender of Japan," *Atlantic Monthly*, Jan. 1947.

———, "If the Atomic Bomb Had Not Been Used," *Atlantic Monthly*, Dec. 1946.

"Conversion of Our Three Bargainers to a Tough Attitude," *United States News*, May 3, 1946.

Costello, William, and Folliard, Edward T., "Secretary of War Stimson," *American Mercury*, Sept. 1944.

Coughlin, William J., "The Great 'Mokusatsu' Mistake: Was This the Deadliest Error of Our Time?" *Harper's*, Mar. 1953.

Cousins, Norman, and Finletter, Thomas K., "A Beginning for Sanity," *Saturday Review of Literature*, June 15, 1946.

Creel, George, "Secretary of War," *Collier's*, Aug. 7, 1943.

Crowley, James Buckley, "A Reconsideration of the Marco Polo Bridge Incident," *Journal of Asian Studies*, May 1963.

De Hoffmann, Frederic, "Pure Science in the Service of Wartime Technology," *Bulletin of the Atomic Scientists*, Jan. 1975.

Dean, Vera Micheles, "The U.S.S.R. and Japan," *Foreign Policy Reports*, July 15, 1942.

Deutsch, Albert, "The Atomic Anniversary and the Unmailed Letter to Stalin," *PM*, Dec. 2, 1947.

DeVore, Robert, "The Man Who Made Manhattan," *Collier's*, Oct. 13, 1945.

———, "What the Atomic Bomb Really Did," *Collier's*, Mar. 2, 1946.

"Did I Do Right? Atom Scientist Asks," *New York Herald-Tribune*, Apr. 5, 1960.

"Did the Soviet Bomb Come Sooner than Expected?" *Bulletin of the Atomic Scientists*, Oct. 1949.

Dower, J. W., "Science, Society, and the Japanese Atomic-Bomb Project During World War Two," *Bulletin of Concerned Asian Scholars*, Apr.-June 1978.

Einstein, Albert, "Atomic War or Peace," *Atlantic Monthly*, Nov. 1945.

———, "On the Moral Obligation of the Scientist," *Bulletin of the Atomic Scientists*, Feb. 1942.

"Elder-Statesman Role of Admiral Leahy in Challenging Russians," *United States News*, Apr. 11, 1947.

"Enrico Fermi," *Bulletin of the Atomic Scientists*, Jan. 1955.

Feis, Herbert, "The Secret that Traveled to Potsdam," *Foreign Affairs*, Jan. 1960.

Fellers, Bonner, "Hirohito's Struggle to Surrender," *Foreign Service*, July 1947.

Finney, Nat S., "How FDR Planned to Use the A-Bomb," *Look*, Mar. 14, 1950.

"First Big Test," *Time*, Sept. 17, 1945.

Fitch, Val L., "The View from the Bottom," *Bulletin of the Atomic Scientists*, Feb. 1975.

Frisch, Otto R., and Wheeler, John A., "The Discovery of Fission," *Physics Today*, Nov. 1967.

Fuess, Claude M., "Henry L. Stimson," *Atlantic Monthly*, Sept. 1941.

Funada, Naka, "Sato Sensei ni Tsuite no Omoide" ("My Memories of Mr. Sato"), *Kokusai Jihyo*, Tokyo, Nov. 1970.

Gervasi, Frank, "New Statesmen–New World," *Collier's*, Oct. 20, 1945.

Gilbert, Clinton, "Painless Statesman," *Collier's*, Mar. 25, 1933.

Gillis, J. M., "Mr. Byrnes Explains," *Catholic World*, Feb. 1946.

Glazier, Kenneth M., Jr., "The Decision to Use Atomic Weapons Against Hiroshima and Nagasaki," *Public Policy*, 1969.

Golovin, Igor, "Father of the Soviet Bomb," *Bulletin of the Atomic Scientists*, Dec. 1967.

Gormly, James L., "Secretary of State Byrnes: An Initial British Evaluation," *South Carolina Historical Magazine*, July 1978.

Goudsmit, S. A., "How Germany Lost the Race," *Bulletin of Atomic Scientists*, Mar. 15, 1946.

Gouzenko, Igor, "Stalin Sent Me to Spy School," *Coronet*, Mar. 1953.

Green, Harold P., "The Oppenheimer Case: A Study in the Abuse of Law," *Bulletin of the Atomic Scientists*, Sept. 1977.

Groves, Leslie R., "Some Recollections of July 16, 1945," *Bulletin of the Atomic Scientists*," June 1970.

———, "The Atom General Answers His Critics," *Saturday Evening Post*, June 19, 1948.

Gwertzman, Bernard, "The World Has Six Years to Live," *Washington Star*, Mar. 24, 1963.

"H-Mystery Man: He Hurried the H-Bomb," *Newsweek*, Aug. 2, 1954.

Hasegawa, Saiji, "Review of *Japan's Decision to Surrender* by Robert Butow," *Japan Quarterly*, Jan.–Mar. 1956.

Hayashi, Saburo, "General Anami at the End of the War," *Sekai*, Tokyo, Aug. 1951.

Haybittle, John, "Ethics for the Scientist," *Bulletin of the Atomic Scientists*, May 1964.

Heisenberg, Werner, "The Third Reich and the Atomic Bomb," *Bulletin of the Atomic Scientists*, June 1968.

Hellman, Geoffrey T., "The Contemporary Memoranda of Dr. Sachs," *The New Yorker*, Dec. 1, 1945.

Herken, Gregg, "'A Most Deadly Illusion': The Atomic Secret and American Nuclear Weapons Policy, 1945–1950," *Pacific Historical Review*, Spring, 1980.

———, "Mad about the Bomb," *Harper's*, Dec. 1983.

Hidaka, Shirokuro, "Sato-san to Watakushi" ("Mr. Sato and I"), *Kokusai Jihyo*, Tokyo, Nov. 1970.

"Hiroshima, with Anguish," *Bulletin of the Atomic Scientists*, Feb. 1962.

Hirosige, Tetu, article on Japanese nuclear physics, *Shizen*, Tokyo, Mar. 1972.

Horinouchi, Kensuke, "Sato Sensei no Heiwa no Tatakai" ("Mr. Sato's Struggle for Peace"), *Kokusai Jihyo*, Tokyo, Nov. 1970.

Hudson, Repps B., "Did B-24 Crew Die in A-Blast?" *Kansas City Times*, Nov. 20, 1975.

Hutchins, Robert M., "Peace or War with Russia?" *Bulletin of the Atomic Scientists*, Mar. 1946.

———, "Szilard and the Dolphins," *Bulletin of the Atomic Scientists*, Sept. 1961.

"Igor Kurchatov, 1903–1960," *Bulletin of the Atomic Scientists*, Dec. 1967.

Imai, Sei-ichi, "Confusion in the Secret Chamber—Imperial Headquarters," *Asahi*, Nov. 28, 1965.

Irwin, Theodore, "The Legend That Is Dr. Szilard," *Pageant*, Dec. 1961.

Ishii, Mitsujiro, "Sato-san o Homeru" ("Tribute to Mr. Sato"), *Kokusai Jihyo*, Tokyo, Nov. 1970.

"J. Robert Oppenheimer, 1904–1967," *Bulletin of the Atomic Scientists*, Oct. 1967.

"James F. Byrnes: Hardening of a Bargainer," *United States News*, Sept. 13, 1946.

Japanese Broadcasting System (NHK), "The Love of Science: The Story of Yoshio Nishina," transcript of television documentary, Tokyo.

Kadowaki, Suemitsu, "Soren no Tai-Nichi Sensen Zengo no Sato Taishi" ("Ambassador Sato Around the Time of the Declaration of War Against Japan"), *Kokusai Jihyo*, Tokyo, Nov. 1970.

Kajima, Morinosuke, "Sato Gaiso-ron" ("On Foreign Minister Sato"), *Bungei Shunju*, Tokyo, Mar. 1937.

Kawai, Kazuo, "Militarist Activity between Japan's Two Surrender Decisions," *Pacific Historical Review*, Nov. 1953.

———, "Mokusatsu: Japan's Response to the Potsdam Declaration," *Pacific Historical Review*, Nov. 1950.

Kennedy, George, "The Rambler," *Washington Star*, Mar. 11, 1960.

Konoye, Fumimaro, "The Memoirs of Prince Fumimaro Konoye," *Asahi Shimbun*, Tokyo, Dec. 20–30, 1945. (Translated by Okayama Service.)

Kosaka, Zentaro, "Mono Shizuka no Naka ni Danzentaru Nihonjin" ("A Quiet and Resolute Japanese") *Kokusai Jihyo*, Tokyo, Nov. 1970.

Krock, Arthur, "Byrnes Formally Joins the Opposition," *New York Times*, Nov. 22, 1949.

Lawrence, William L., "Would You Make the Bomb Again?," *New York Times*, Aug. 1, 1965.

Leighton, Alexander H., "That Day at Hiroshima," *Atlantic Monthly*, Oct. 1946.

Lerner, Max, "Jekyll-Hyde Klaus Fuchs" (three columns), *New York Post*, Feb. 13, 14, 15, 1950.

———, "Life of a Man," *New York Post*, Feb. 29, 1960.

Lieberman, Henry R. "America's No. 1 Inflation Stopper," *PM*, Oct. 25, 1942.

Lifton, Robert Jay, "Psychological Effects of the Atomic Bomb in Hiroshima—The Theme of Death," *Daedalus*, Summer, 1963.

Lindley, Ernest K., "Byrnes, the Persuasive Reporter," *Newsweek*, Mar. 12, 1945.

Lonsdale, Kathleen, "The Ethical Problems of Scientists," *Bulletin of the Atomic Scientists*, Aug. 1951.

Lubell, Samuel, "What You Don't Know about Truman," *Saturday Evening Post*, Mar. 15, 1952.

Macdonald, Dwight, "The Bomb," *Politics II*, Aug., Sept. 1945.

Machida, Shiro, "The New Foreign Minister," *Contemporary Japan*, Tokyo, June 1937.

Maddox, Robert J., "Atomic Diplomacy: A Study in Creative Writing," *Journal of American History*, Mar. 1973.

Mahony, James, "Atom Age 25 Years Old," *Boston Herald Traveler* (special section), Apr. 29, 1970.

"Man of the Year (Byrnes)," *Time*, Jan. 6, 1947.

Manoff, Robert Karl, "American Victims of Hiroshima," *New York Times Magazine*, Dec. 2, 1984.

Matsumoto, Shunichi, "Sato-san no Omoide" ("Recollections of Mr. Sato"), *Kokusai Jihyo*, Tokyo, Nov. 1970.

McClaughry, John, "The Voice of the Dolphins," *The Progressive*, Apr. 1965.

McDaniel, Boyce, "A Physicist at Los Alamos," *Bulletin of the Atomic Scientists*, Dec. 1974.

McGill, Ralph, "What is Jimmy Byrnes Up to Now?" *Saturday Evening Post*, Oct. 14, 1950.

Meitner, Lise, "Looking Back," *Bulletin of the Atomic Scientists*, Nov. 1964.

Miscamble, Wilson, "Anthony Eden and the Truman-Molotov Conversations, Apr. 1945," *Diplomatic History* 2, Spring, 1978.

Moorehead, Alan, "Traitor Klaus Fuchs: He Gave Stalin the A-Bomb," *Saturday Evening Post*, May 24, 31; June 7, 14, 1952.

Mori, Motojiro, "Higeki no Hito Togo" ("Togo, Shigenori: A Tragic Character"), *Kaizo*, Tokyo, Feb. 1951.

Morrison, Samuel E., "Why Japan Surrendered," *Atlantic Monthly*, Oct. 1960.

Morton, Louis, "Decision to Use the Atomic Bomb," *Foreign Affairs*, Jan. 1957.

———, "The Road that Led to Surrender," *New York Times Magazine*, Apr. 30, 1961.

———, "Soviet Intervention in the War with Japan," *Foreign Affairs*, July 1962.

Mukai, Tadaharu, "Sato Naotake Kun to no Koyu" ("My Friendship with Mr. Sato Naotake"), *Kokusai Jihyo*, Tokyo, Nov. 1970.

National Broadcasting Co., "The Decision to Drop the Bomb," NBC White Paper, televised Jan. 5, 1965.

———, "The Surrender of Japan," NBC White Paper, Sept. 19, 1965.

Nishina, Yoshio, "A Japanese Scientist Describes the Destruction of His Cyclotrons," *Bulletin of the Atomic Scientists*, June 1947.

Olds, C. Burnell, "Japanese Liberal Potentialities," *Foreign Affairs*, Apr. 1944.

Oppenheimer, Robert J., "Atomic Weapons and American Policy," *Bulletin of the Atomic Scientists*, July 1953.

———, "Niels Bohr and Atomic Weapons," *New York Review of Books*, Dec. 17, 1964.

Osamu, Kataoka, "A Survivor's Story: 'Friends, Please Forgive Us,'" *Bulletin of the Atomic Scientists*, Dec. 1977.

Parsons, William S., "The Navy's Contribution to the Building of the A-Bomb," *The Quarterdeck*, May 1952.

Partin, John, "Roosevelt, Byrnes, and the 1944 Vice-Presidential Nomination," *Historian*, Nov. 1979.

Patterson, Thomas G., "Potsdam, the Atomic Bomb, and the Cold War: A Discussion with James F. Byrnes," *Pacific Historical Review*, May 1972.

"Patient but Firm," *Newsweek*, Oct. 28, 1946.

Peierls, Rudolf E., "Britain in the Atomic Age," *Bulletin of the Atomic Scientists*, June 1970.

Petersen, Aage, "The Philosophy of Niels Bohr," *Bulletin of the Atomic Scientists*, Sept. 1983.

Phillips, Cabell, "The Inner Circle at the White House," *New York Times Magazine*, Feb. 24, 1946.

Pilat, Oliver, "Let's Share Atomic Energy," *New York Post*, Nov. 24, 1945.

Pringle, Henry F., "Henry L. Stimson: A Portrait," *Outlook and Independent*, Mar. 13, 1929.

Rabinowitch, Eugene, "Atomic Spy Trials: Heretical Afterthoughts," *Bulletin of the Atomic Scientists*, May 1951.

——, "Now It Can Be Told," *Bulletin of the Atomic Scientists*, Oct. 1962.

——, "Responsibilities of Scientists in the Atomic Age," *Bulletin of the Atomic Scientists*, Jan. 1959.

——, "1882–1964, 1898–1964," *Bulletin of the Atomic Scientists*, Oct. 1964.

Rosenfeld, Albert, "Remembrance of a Genius," *Life*, June 12, 1964.

Rosenthal, A. M., "Life in Hiroshima Now," *New York Times Magazine*, Aug. 1, 1965.

Sakata, Jiro, "Suzume no Bannin" ("A Keeper of Sparrows"), *Kokusai Jihyo*, Tokyo, Nov. 1970.

Sakonji, Masazo, "Misumasa Yonai and Korechika Anami," *Maru*, Tokyo, Sept. 1949.

Sato, Naotake, "Japan Among the United Nations," *Contemporary Japan*, Tokyo, Sept. 1957.

——, "The League and the U.N.," *Japan Quarterly*, Tokyo, Jan.–Mar. 1958.

——, "Nenimi ni Mizu no Jusho" ("The Award Bestowed Unexpectedly"), *Kokusai Jihyo*, Tokyo, Nov. 1970.

——, "Peace Treaty and Japan's Future," *Contemporary Japan*, Tokyo, Apr.–June 1951.

Sawyer, Roland, "The H-Bomb Chronology," *Bulletin of the Atomic Scientists*, Sept. 1954.

"Scientific Cyclone," *Newsweek*, Jan. 10, 1944.

"A Scientist-Traitor," *New York Times*, June 24, 1959.

Segre, Emilio, "Enrico Fermi: Physicist," *Bulletin of the Atomic Scientists*, Nov. 1970.

"Setting Back the Clock," *The New Yorker*, June 13, 1964.

Siemes, Father S. J., "Hiroshima—August 6, 1945," *Bulletin of the Atomic Scientists*, May 15, 1946.

Smith, Alice Kimball, "Behind the Decision to Use the Atomic Bomb: Chicago 1944–45," *Bulletin of the Atomic Scientists*, Oct. 1958.

——, "Los Alamos: Focus of an Age," *Bulletin of the Atomic Scientists*, June 1970.

——, "The Elusive Dr. Szilard," *Harper's*, July 1960.

Smith, Beverly, "Byrnes Grows Up to His Job," *Saturday Evening Post*, Jan. 4, 1947.

Smoular, Alfred, "Japan Should Take the Offensive," *Asahi Evening News*, Tokyo, Aug. 11, 13, 1956.

Snow, C. P., "The Age of Rutherford," *Atlantic Monthly*, Nov. 1958.

"South Carolina Primary," *Time*, Aug. 24, 1936.

"'Soviet Atomic Espionage,'" *Bulletin of the Atomic Scientists*, May 1951.

"Soviet Intervention in the War with Japan," *Foreign Affairs*, July 1962.

Special Report on the Oppenheimer Case, *Bulletin of the Atomic Scientists*, Sept. 1954.

"Spies in U.S. Told Russia All," *U.S. News & World Report*, Apr. 6, 1951.

Station JOTX-TV, Tokyo, "The Emperor's Recording," 1965.

Steel, Ronald, "Doomsday," *New York Review of Books*, Nov. 25, 1965.

Steiner, Arthur, "Baptism of the Atomic Scientists," *Bulletin of the Atomic Scientists*, Feb. 1975.

Steiner, Jesse F., "Can Japan's Millions Take It Till the End?," *New York Times Magazine*, July 15, 1945.

———, "Shall We Bomb Hirohito's Palace?" *New York Times Magazine*, Mar. 11, 1945.

Stimson, Henry L., "Artillery in a Quiet Sector," *Scribner's Magazine*, June 1919.

———, "The Challenge to Americans," *Foreign Affairs*, Oct. 1947.

———, "The Decision to Use the Atomic Bomb," *Harper's*, Feb. 1947.

Stolberg, B., "James F. Byrnes," *American Mercury*, Mar. 1946.

Stone, I. F., "Facts for Mr. Stimson," *The Nation*, Jan. 29, 1944.

Sutherland, John P., "The Story General Marshall Told Me," *U.S. News & World Report*, Nov. 2, 1959.

———, "Using the A-Bomb: How the Decision Was Made," *U.S. News & World Report*, Nov. 2, 1959.

Szilard, Leo, "Are We on the Road to War?" *Bulletin of the Atomic Scientists*, Apr. 1962.

———, "How to Live with the Bomb and Survive," *Bulletin of the Atomic Scientists*, Feb. 1960.

———, "Letter to Stalin," *Bulletin of the Atomic Scientists*, Dec. 1947.

———, "Minimal Deterrent vs. Saturation Parity," *Bulletin of the Atomic Scientists*, Mar. 1964.

———, "One World or None," *Life*, June 12, 1964.

———, "A Personal History of the Atomic Bomb," *University of Chicago Roundtable*, Sept. 25, 1949.

———, "We Turned the Switch," *The Nation*, Dec. 22, 1945.

Tanaka, Takayoshi, "Kakute Tenno wa Muzai to Natta" ("Thus It Turned Out that the Emperor Was Innocent"), *Bungei Shunju*, Tokyo, Aug. 1965.

Teller, Edward, "Atomic Scientists Have Two Responsibilities," *Bulletin of the Atomic Scientists*, Dec. 1947.

Theoharis, Athan, "Atomic Diplomacy," *New University Thought*, May–June 1967.

———, "James F. Byrnes: Unwitting Yalta Myth-Maker," *Political Science Quarterly*, Dec. 1966.

———, "Roosevelt and Truman on Yalta: The Origins of the Cold War," *Political Science Quarterly*, May 1972.

Tomomatsu, Entai, "Japanese Fatalism and Self-immolation," *Contemporary Affairs*, Tokyo, Dec. 1940.

Trilling, Diana, "The Oppenheimer Case: A Reading of the Testimony," *Partisan Review*, Nov.–Dec. 1954.

Van Deusen, Charles, "Russia Gets a Billion-Dollar Traitor," *New York Journal-American*, June 23, 1959.

Villa, Brian Loring, "A Confusion of Signals: James Franck, the Chicago Scientists and Early Efforts to Stop the Bomb," *Bulletin of the Atomic Scientists*, Dec. 1975.

"Was A-Bomb on Japan a Mistake?" *U.S. News & World Report*, Aug. 15, 1960.

"Washington's Dog Eat Dog," *Newsweek*, Jan. 14, 1946.

Wattenberg, Albert, "The Building of the First Chain Reaction Pile," *Bulletin of the Atomic Scientists*," June 1974.

West, Rebecca, "Rebecca West's Story of A-Spy," *New York Journal-American*, Mar. 1, 1950.

Whitman, Alan, "A Manager of Men," *New York Times*, Apr. 10, 1972.

Wilson, R. R., "The Conscience of a Physicist," *Bulletin of the Atomic Scientists*, Jan. 1970.

Winnacker, Rudolph, "The Debate About Hiroshima," *Military Affairs*, Spring, 1947.

"Yalta Legman," *Newsweek*, Mar. 19, 1945.

Yavenditti, Michael, "The American People and the Use of Atomic Bombs on Japan: 1940s," *Historian*, Feb. 1974.

York, Herbert F., "Sounders of the Alarm," *Bulletin of the Atomic Scientists*, Dec. 1975.

"You're No Caesar," *Newsweek*, Nov. 14, 1955.

Yuhashi, Shigeto, "Tai Ni-Soren Sensen no Hi no Sato Taishi" ("Ambassador Sato on the Day the USSR Declared War Against Japan"), *Kokusai Jihyo*, Tokyo, Nov. 1970.

Zeisel, Hans, "On Szilard," *Bulletin of the Atomic Scientists*, Sept. 1970.

Zinn, Howard, "A Mess of Death and Documents," *Columbia University Forum*, Winter, 1962.

DOCUMENTS AND UNPUBLISHED MATERIAL

British and Foreign State Papers, 1945–1947 (Vols. 145–147). London: HMSO, 1953.

The Brocade Banner, the Story of Japanese Nationalism—U.S. Army, GHQ, SCAP, Counter-Intelligence Sector, Modern Military Branch, National Archives, Washington, D.C.

Correspondence Between the Chairman of the Council of Ministers of the U.S.S.R. and the Presidents of the U.S.A. and the Prime Ministers of Great Britain During the Great Patriotic War of 1941–1945 (2 vols)—Moscow, 1957.

Crowley, James Buckley. *Japan's China Policy, 1931–1938: A Study of the Role of the Military in the Determination of Foreign Policy*—Doctoral dissertation, University of Michigan, 1959.

Debate among military leaders whether to indict Emperor Hirohito for war crimes—Modern Military Branch, National Archives.

Diaries of Chaplain Leslie R. Groves—Modern Military Branch, National Archives.

Diaries of Harold D. Smith—Harry S. Truman Library.

Diaries of Henry L. Stimson—Yale University Library.

Diaries of Walter Brown (excerpts)—Clemson University Library.

Diaries of William D. Leahy—Library of Congress.

Dull, Paul S., and Umemura, Michael Takaaki. *The Tokyo Trials: A Functional Index to the Proceedings of the International Military Tribunal, Far East.* Ann Arbor: University of Michigan Press, 1957.

Files of the Council for a Livable World, Boston.

Files of Eben A. Ayers—Harry S. Truman Library.

Files of the Federation of American Scientists and related organizations—Special Collections, Harper Memorial Library, University of Chicago.

Files of Leslie R. Groves, personal papers, including family history and comments on personalities, books, and articles (restricted until now)—Modern Military Branch, National Archives.

Files of Manhattan Engineering District, including general records of the Manhattan Project, material of "Top Secret-Special Interest to General Groves," and the Harrison-Bundy Collection, the files of Secretary of War Stimson—Modern Military Branch, National Archives.

Files of National Committee on Atomic Information—Library of Congress.

Files of Office of Scientific Research and Development, S-1—Industrial and Social Branch, National Archives.

Files of U.S. Department of State—National Archives.

Files on American prisoners of war killed in atomic bombing of Hiroshima—Army Agent Orange Task Force, Office of the Adjutant General, Department of the Army, and Modern Military Branch, National Archives.

Files on J. Robert Oppenheimer—Federal Bureau of Investigation archives.

Files on Klaus Fuchs—Federal Bureau of Investigation archives.

Files on William D. Leahy—Modern Military Branch, National Archives.

Files on William S. Parsons—Martha Burroughs (formerly Parsons), Manchester, N.H.

Flanagan, Scott C. *Crises in the Political Development of Modern Japan, 1880–1945; A Study of Coalition Behavior and Political Change*—Doctoral dissertation, Stanford University, 1972.

Foreign Ministry, Japan. *Shusen Shiroku (Records of the End of the War)* (2 vols.). Tokyo: Shimbun Nenkan, 1952.

Gen. *Douglas MacArthur's Historical Report on Allied Operations in the Southwest Pacific Area, 8 Dec. 1941–2 Sept. 1945*, Vol. II, General Headquarters, Supreme Commander for the Allied Powers—Office of War History, Department of the Army, Washington, D.C.

Gormly, James L. *In Search of a Postwar Settlement: The London and Moscow Foreign Ministers' Conferences*—Doctoral dissertation, University of Connecticut, 1977.

Great Britain, Ministry of Information. *Economic Developments in Japan and Japanese-controlled Territory from September 1944 to the Time of Her Collapse*, 2 Parts—London, 1945.

Gubler, Greg. *The Diplomatic Career of Sato Naotake (1882–1971); A Samurai in Western Clothing*—Doctoral dissertation, Florida State University, June 1975.

Herken, Gregg F., *American Diplomacy and the Atomic Bomb*—Doctoral dissertation, Princeton University, 1973.

———, *Stubborn, Obstinate, and They Don't Scare: The Russians, the Bomb, and James F. Byrnes*—Paper delivered to the conference on James F. Byrnes and the Origins of the Cold War, Columbia, S.C., Nov. 9, 1979.

Holloway, David. *Entering the Nuclear Arms Race: The Soviet Decision to Build the Atomic Bomb, 1939–1945*—Working paper presented at International Security Studies Program colloquium at the Woodrow Wilson International Center for Scholars, Washington, D.C., July 25, 1979.

How Russia Became a Nuclear Power: the Untold Story of the Soviet Atomic Bomb—Report by American intelligence agencies and scientific organizations.

International Control of Atomic Energy: Growth of a Policy. Washington, D.C.: U.S. Government Printing Office, 1946.

Interrogations of top Japanese officials, including Koichi Kido and Shigenori Togo, International Military Tribunal for the Far East—Modern Military Branch, National Archives.

Karl, John F. *Compromise and Confrontation: James F. Byrnes and United States Policy Toward the Soviet Union, 1945–1946*—Doctoral dissertation, University of Toronto, 1976.

Log of the President's Trip to the Berlin Conference—Harry S. Truman Library.

"Magic" files, summaries of intercepted Japanese cables, including messages sent between Foreign Minister Togo and Ambassador to Moscow Sato—Modern Military Branch, National Archives.

Messer, Robert L. *The Making of a Cold Warrior: James F. Byrnes and American-Soviet Relations, 1945–1946*—Doctoral dissertation, University of California, Berkeley, 1975.

———. *"Et Tu Brute": Byrnes, Truman, and the Origins of the Cold War*—Paper delivered to the conference on James F. Byrnes and the Origins of the Cold War, Columbia, S.C., Nov. 9, 1979.

Military plans for invading Japan—Modern Military Branch, National Archives.

Minutes, Interim Committee meetings—Modern Military Branch, National Archives.

Moore, Winfred B., Jr. *New South Statesmen: The Political Career of James F. Byrnes, 1911–1941*—Doctoral dissertation, Duke University, 1975.

Nikki, The Diaries of Koichi Kido—Modern Military Branch, National Archives.

Official papers of the British Cabinet, Foreign Office, and Prime Minister, including the Prime Minister's Operational File, which contains the record of atomic energy discussions between Churchill and Roosevelt—Public Records Office, London.

Oral Histories detailing the life of William S. Parsons—Naval Historical Center, Washington, D.C., and Naval Weapons Center, China Lake, California. Interviews by Albert B. Christman.

Oral Histories of Kenneth Bainbridge, Harvey Bundy, Norman Ramsey, and others involved in the building of the atomic bomb—Butler Library, Columbia University.

Oral Histories of President Truman's friends and associates, including Eben A. Ayers, Tom C. Clark, William K. Divers, Tom C. Evans, Milton S. Kronheim, James I. Loeb, H. Freeman Matthews, Robert G. Nixon, and J. Leonard Reinsch—Harry S. Truman Library.

Pacific Strategic Intelligence Section (PSIS) files, summaries of intercepted Japanese cables with interpretation—Modern Military Branch, National Archives.

Papers of Albert Einstein—Princeton University Library.

Papers on Alexander Sachs, including *Early History Atomic Project in Relation to President Roosevelt, 1939–1940*—Franklin D. Roosevelt Library and Mrs. Alexander Sachs.

Papers of Arthur H. Compton—Washington University, St. Louis, Missouri.

Papers of Carl Spaatz—Library of Congress.

Papers of Charles Bohlen—Library of Congress.

Papers of Charles G. Ross—Harry S. Truman Library.

Papers of Clark Clifford—Harry S. Truman Library.

Papers of Franklin D. Roosevelt—Franklin D. Roosevelt Library.

Papers of Harry S. Truman—Harry S. Truman Library.

Papers of Henry H. Arnold—Library of Congress.

Papers of Henry L. Stimson—Yale University Library.

Papers of Herbert Feis—Library of Congress.

Papers of J. Robert Oppenheimer—Library of Congress.

Papers of James F. Byrnes—Clemson University Library.

Papers of James V. Forrestal—Princeton University Library.

Papers of Joint Chiefs of Staff—Modern Military Branch, National Archives, Washington, D.C.

Papers of Joseph C. Grew—Houghton Library, Harvard University.

Papers of Joseph E. Davies—Library of Congress.

Papers of Joseph and Stewart Alsop—Library of Congress.

Papers of Leo Szilard—University of California at San Diego Library.

Papers of Marshall MacDuffie; folders on Leo Szilard—Columbia University Library.

Papers of Robert P. Patterson—Library of Congress.

Papers of Samuel I. Rosenman—Harry S. Truman Library.

Papers of Tom Connally—Library of Congress.

Papers of Vannevar Bush—Library of Congress.

Papers of William L. Clayton—Harry S. Truman Library.

Papers of William S. Parsons—Library of Congress.

Partin, John W. *"Assistant President" for the Home Front: James F. Byrnes and World War II*—Doctoral dissertation, University of Florida, 1977.

Public Papers of the Presidents: Harry S. Truman, 1945–1947. Washington, D.C.: U.S. Government Printing Office, 1961–1963.

Record of the affidavits, charges, evidence and cross-examination of the accused at the International Military Tribunal, Far East—Modern Military Branch, National Archives, Washington, D.C.

Record of meetings of Japanese Supreme War Council and Elder Statesmen during the war—Modern Military Branch, National Archives, Washington, D.C.

Records of Allied Operational and Occupation Headquarters, World War II—Modern Military Branch, National Archives.

The Report of the Royal Commission to Investigate the Facts Relating to and the Circumstances Surrounding the Communication, by Public Officials and Other Persons in Positions of Trust of Secret and Confidential Information to Agents of a Foreign Power—Edmond Cloutier, Controller of Stationery, Ottawa, 1946.

Rigdon, William M. *Log of the President's Trip to the Berlin (Potsdam) Conference*—Harry S. Truman Library.

Smith, Jean Edward. *The Resignation of James F. Byrnes: A Milestone in the History of the Cold War*—Paper delivered to the annual meeting of the American Historical Association, Dallas, Texas, Dec. 1977.

Supreme War Council records—National Defense College, Tokyo.

U.S.S.R. Ministry of Foreign Affairs. *Stalin's Correspondence with Churchill, Attlee, Roosevelt and Truman, 1941–45*, Vols. I & II. New York: Dutton, 1958.

U.S. Army Air Force. *Mission Accomplished: Interrogations of Japanese Military, Industrial and Civil Leaders of World War Two.* Washington, D.C.: U.S. Government Printing Office.

U.S. Army, Army Forces Pacific, Psychological Warfare Branch.
Special Report No. 4, "The Emperor of Japan," July 22, 1945—Modern Military Branch, National Archives.

Special Report No. 5, "Inside Japan—Youth Pawn of Militarists," July 23, 1945—Modern Military Branch, National Archives.

U.S. Congress, House, Committee on Military Affairs. *Hearings on an Act for the Development and Control of Atomic Energy*, 79th Congress, First Session, Washington, D.C., 1945.

U.S. Congress, House, Committee on Un-American Activities.
Hearings Regarding Communist Infiltration of Radiation Laboratory and Atomic Bomb Project at the University of California, Berkeley, Calif., 81st Congress, First Session, Washington, D.C., 1949, 1950, 1951.
Hearings Regarding Shipments of Atomic Material to the Soviet Union During World War II, 81st Congress, First and Second Sessions, Washington, D.C., 1950.
Report on Soviet Espionage Activities in Connection with the Atomic Bomb, 80th Congress, Second Session, Washington, D.C., 1948.

U.S. Congress, Senate, Special Committee on Atomic Energy. *Hearings* (Alexander Sachs, Nov. 27, 1945; Leo Szilard, Dec. 10, 1945), 79th Congress, First Session, Washington, D.C., 1945, 1946.

U.S. Department of the Army, The Manhattan Engineer District. *The Atomic Bombings of Hiroshima and Nagasaki*—Modern Military Branch, National Archives, Washington, D.C.

U.S. Department of Defense. *The Entry of the Soviet Union into the War Against Japan: Military Plans, 1941–45*—Washington, D.C., 1955.

U.S. Department of State. *Foreign Relations of the United States. Annual Volumes, 1945–1946.* Washington, D.C.: Government Printing Office, 1960–1970.
————. *Foreign Relations of the United States: The Conference of Berlin (The Potsdam Conference), 1945*, 2 vols. Washington, D.C.: U.S. Government Printing Office, 1960.
————. *Foreign Relations of the United States: The Conferences at Malta and Yalta, 1945.* Washington, D.C.: U.S. Government Printing Office, 1955.
————. *Foreign Relations of the United States: 1946, Council of Foreign Ministers.* Washington, D.C.: U.S. Government Printing Office, 1970.

U.S. Office of Strategic Services.
Biographical Notes on the Japanese Cabinet, 1945—Modern Military Branch, National Archives, Washington, D.C.
Crisis in Japan, Apr. 20, 1945—Library of Congress.
Developments in Japanese Reactions to Surrender, Aug. 31, 1945—Library of Congress.
Japan-Conflicting Political Views, July 23, 1945—Library of Congress.
The Japanese Emperor and the War, Sept. 8, 1944—Library of Congress.
Japan: Winter 1944–1945, May 18, 1945—Library of Congress.

U.S. Senate. *Senate Miscellaneous Documents. 79th Congress, Second Session*, Washington, D.C., 1947.

U.S. Strategic Bombing Survey. *The Effects of Atomic Bombs on Hiroshima and Nagasaki.* Washington, D.C.: U.S. Government Printing Office, 1946.
————. *Japan's Struggle to End the War.* Washington, D.C.: U.S. Government Printing Office, 1946.

The United States and the United Nations: United States Atomic Energy Proposals. Washington, D.C.: U.S. Government Printing Office, 1962.

Verbatim reports of the trial of Klaus Fuchs in March, 1950, London.

INDEX

U

ABOUT THE AUTHOR

Dan Kurzman, former foreign correspondent for the *Washington Post,* has authored eight previous books and received five major awards for his writings. He won the National Jewish Book Award for his 1983 book, *Ben-Gurion: Prophet of Fire. Miracle of November: Madrid's Epic Stand 1936,* earned him the Overseas Press Club's Cornelius Ryan Award for the best book on foreign affairs in 1980. *Subversion of the Innocents* won for him the same award in 1963. And another book, *Santo Domingo: Revolt of the Damned,* was based on articles that gained for him Long Island University's George Polk Memorial Award in 1965. His dispatches from Cuba yielded the Front Page Award in 1964.

Genesis 1948: The First Arab-Israeli War (1970) was described in the *Washington Post* as "the best thing on the 1948 (Arab-Israeli) war that this reviewer has ever read—or is likely to read," and by James Michener as "brilliant." *Kishi and Japan* (1960) was viewed by the *New York Times Book Review* as "one of the most important biographies of the year," and by the *San Francisco Chronicle* as "the best book on the Japanese point of view yet written in English." *The Bravest Battle: The 28 Days of the Warsaw Ghetto Uprising* (1976) was hailed by Meyer Levin as "monumental and

awe-inspiring . . . the definitive story of the Warsaw Ghetto uprising." *The Race for Rome* (1975) was seen by the *Christian Science
Monitor* as a "monumental work, equally valuable and enjoyable
as history, as information, as pleasure."

Kurzman has written or broadcast from almost every country
in Europe, Asia, Africa and Latin America. Before joining the
Post, he served as Paris correspondent for the International News
Service, as Jerusalem correspondent for the National Broadcasting
Company, and as Tokyo bureau chief of the McGraw-Hill World
News Service.